THE PASSIONATE ECONOMIST

How Brian Abel–Smith shaped global
health and social welfare

SALLY SHEARD

First published in Great Britain in 2014 by

Policy Press
University of Bristol
6th Floor
Howard House
Queen's Avenue
Clifton
Bristol BS8 1SD
UK
Tel +44 (0)117 331 5020
Fax +44 (0)117 331 5367
e-mail pp-info@bristol.ac.uk
www.policypress.co.uk

North American office:
Policy Press
c/o The University of Chicago Press
1427 East 60th Street
Chicago, IL 60637, USA
t: +1 773 702 7700
f: +1 773-702-9756
e:sales@press.uchicago.edu
www.press.uchicago.edu

British Library Cataloguing in Publication Data
A catalogue record for this book is available from the British Library

Library of Congress Cataloging-in-Publication Data
A catalog record for this book has been requested

ISBN 978 1 44731 484 4 hardcover

Cover design by Policy Press
Front and back cover photos: John Sarbutt Papers
Author photograph (back flap): Sarah Sheard
Printed and bound in Great Britain by TJ International, Padstow

MIX
Paper from
responsible sources
FSC FSC® C013056

Contents

List of illustrations and sources   vii

Acknowledgements   ix

Sources and abbreviations   xii

Prologue   1

Part 1: Inheritances and duties, 1926–51

1   Inheritances: 1926–46   11
    Smiths and Abel-Smiths   11
    An English education   16
    After Haileybury   24

2   A wider world: 1946–51   29
    National Service   30
    Austria: Brian's cold war   34
    Cambridge   38
    A political education   46
    Postgraduate   48
    The British Council universities debating tour   51

Part 2: The politics of policies, 1951–79

3   Beveridge's Britain: 1951–55   61
    The new British welfare state   62
    Useful academics: the London School of Economics   64
    Social science and social policy   66
    Richard Titmuss   68
    Peter Townsend   72
    The Fabians   75
    Tony Crosland and *The Future of Socialism*   77
    The Reform of Social Security   80
    Costing the National Health Service   83
    Too political for research?   88

4   Political ambitions and private passions: 1955–59   91
    An independent life   92
    New Pensions for the Old   93
    Dalton's heir   102

	Whose Welfare State?	107
	National Insurance	110
	National Assistance	113
	Reconceptualising poverty	114
5	Health and happiness: 1956–64	119
	Judgements and predictions: health and medicine in Britain	120
	Funding health service research: collaborations and conflicts	124
	Bedpans and balance sheets: managing the NHS	127
	Friendships and partnerships	134
	A natural historian: *The Hospitals 1800–1948*	138
	In the public's eye	142
6	*Lingua franca*: 1956–67	147
	Health economics	148
	Mauritius: three is the magic number	157
	Paying for Health Services	181
7	Distractions and diversions: 1964–68	187
	The disappearance of national superannuation	190
	The professors of poverty	196
	Child Poverty Action Group	200
	The new Supplementary Benefits Scheme	204
	Managing the Poverty Survey	207
	A legal interest	210
	(Only) Just Men	214
8	Values: 1968–70	219
	Policy from the inside: advising Richard Crossman	220
	Health enquiries	229
	AEGIS and the Ely scandal	233
	Restructuring the National Health Service	239
	The LSE, 1967–69	248
	The end of the Titmice	251
	'The Poor Get Poorer Under Labour'	255
9	Patriarchy and authority: 1970–74	261
	Health and social policy: theory and practice	261
	Enquiries: abuse of social security, NHS management, Thalidomide	267
	'Quite like old times': pensions	270
	International interests: health economics	273

Development, poverty and population control 276
Losses 279

10   'Such marvellous fun': 1974–76 283
Chocolate soldiers: the rise of the special adviser 284
Private concerns 286
'One of us': advising Barbara Castle 288
Labour's policy machine 293
National Health Service: 'The ark of our covenant' 303
Pay beds 305
Resource Allocation Working Party 310
Mental illness, mental handicap and disability benefits 314
Pensions: third time lucky 318

11   Disillusionment: 1976–79 323
Ennals, 'Deep Throat' and the Cabinet papers leak 325
The Castle Diaries 329
The Royal Commission on the National Health Service 334
The 30th anniversary of the National Health Service 340
Inequalities: the Supplementary Benefits Review and the Black 344
Report
Peter Shore and the Department of the Environment 348
Labour in 1979: assessments and strategies 352

12   International commuting: 1975–79 357
Value for Money in Health Services: A Comparative Study 358
Return to Mauritius 365
The European Economic Community 371
A new European advisory role 377

Part 3: Shifting the balance of power, 1979–96

13   In and outers: 1979–91 389
Health for All by the Year 2000 393
HFA2000: health, wealth and health economics 398
Making a Financial Master Plan 402
Special adviser to Mahler 407
Health promotion 411
HFA2000: targets and assessments 412
The rise of The World Bank 417
The Commission on Health Research for Development 419
Kenya 424

14 The end of the party: 1979–90   431
       Labour in opposition   433
       Reform or dissolution? The National Health Service in   439
       Conservative Britain
       London's health services   441
       The new academia: a business of knowledge   446

15 On the move: 1990–96   451
       Reform: the progressive rise of health insurance   451
       LSE 'retirement'   455
       Cost Containment and New Priorities in Health Care   459
       Tanzania, Indonesia and Thailand: personal and professional   461
       interests
       The new language of health and social welfare   474
       Health: political and personal   477

Epilogue: Stories, histories and biographies   483

Bibliography of Brian Abel-Smith's publications   495

Endnotes   507

Index   567

List of illustrations and sources

1. Brian Abel-Smith's father, Lionel Abel-Smith (1870–1946) (*Lionel Abel-Smith Papers*)
2. Brian Abel-Smith's mother, Geneviève (Vivée) Abel-Smith (1898–1988) (*Lionel Abel-Smith Papers*)
3. Brian Abel-Smith with Lionel and their mother Vivée (early 1940s) (*LSE archives*)
4. Brian Abel-Smith in his early teens (*John Sarbutt Papers*)
5. Brian Abel-Smith as Haileybury School head boy in 1945 (*John Sarbutt Papers*)
6. Haileybury School's Elysium club, Spring 1945 (*John Sarbutt Papers*)
7. Brian Abel-Smith with fellow recruits of the Nonne Boschen Platoon, Oxfordshire and Buckinghamshire Light Infantry at the Gujarat Barracks in Colchester, Essex, December 1945 (*LSE archives*)
8. Brian Abel-Smith at his desk in the Schönbrunn Palace, Vienna, 1947 (*John Sarbutt Papers*)
9. Brian Abel-Smith in Positano, Italy, 1949 (*LSE archives*)
10. Brian Abel-Smith in Wengen, Switzerland, with Susan Hamilton and Tony Bambridge, 1949 (*LSE archives*)
11. Brian Abel-Smith on Middle East holiday, 1951 (*LSE archives*)
12. Cambridge Labour Foot Beagles Ball, November 1950. (*John Sarbutt Papers*)
13. Cambridge Union Society, 5 June 1951 (*LSE archives*)
14. Brian Abel-Smith speaking at a debate on the British Council universities debating tour of India, Pakistan and Ceylon, 1952 (*LSE archives*)
15. Brian Abel-Smith, 1950s (*John Sarbutt Papers*)
16. Brian Abel-Smith and Richard Titmuss, 1950s (*John Sarbutt Papers*)
17. Brian Abel-Smith and Peter Townsend at the LSE, 1956 (*John Sarbutt Papers*)
18. Brian Abel-Smith with Sue Holman and Shirley Worthington, *House Beautiful* article, September 1956 (*LSE archives*)
19. Brian Abel-Smith with Edith Summerskill, Labour Party annual conference, Brighton, October 1957 (*LSE archives*)
20. Brian Abel-Smith and Hugh Dalton on holiday in Italy, August 1957 (*John Sarbutt Papers*)
21. The WHO/ILO working party on the costs of medical care, Geneva, 1958 (*John Sarbutt Papers*)

22. Brian Abel-Smith with Richard Titmuss, Tony Lynes and Edwin de Robillard of the Compagnons Batisseurs in Mauritius, shortly after Cyclone Alix, March 1960 (*John Sarbutt Papers*)
23. Brian Abel-Smith visiting a hospital in Kiev, Ukraine, in 1961, as a member of Milton Roemer's working party visit to the USSR (*John Sarbutt Papers*)
24. LSE Department of Social Science and Administration, 1971 (*LSE archives*)
25. Brian Abel-Smith and John Sarbutt on holiday in Malta, 1972 (*David Blewett and Arthur Sheps*)
26. John Sarbutt, 1980s (*John Sarbutt Papers*)
27. Brian Abel-Smith with Alf Morris, Minister of State, DHSS, and Sir John Donne, Chairman of South-East Thames Regional Hospital Authority at the 30th anniversary of the NHS, July 1978 (*John Sarbutt Papers*)
28. Brian Abel-Smith with his brother Lionel and mother Vivée at a Christmas lunch, 1970s (*Lionel Abel-Smith Papers*)
29. RHDAC meeting at WHO EURO Copenhagen, 24–26 April 1984 (*John Sarbutt Papers*)
30. First Health Economics short course, LSHTM, 1986 (*John Sarbutt Papers*)
31. Meeting of the Academic Advisory Committee of the Center for Public Health Research [forerunner of the National Institute of Public Health of Mexico], Mexico City, circa 1987 (*LSE archives*)
32. Brian Abel-Smith at the Euro-Pharma meeting, 1993 (*LSE archives*)
33. Brian Abel-Smith accepting his LSE award of Honorary Fellow, 14 July 1995 at the Savoy Theatre (*John Sarbutt Papers*)
34. At Beatrice Webb's desk, LSE, 1995 (*John Sarbutt Papers*)
35. Brian with his Battersea rescue dog, Nicky (*John Sarbutt Papers*)
36. The house and garden at Tanglewood, Westwell, Kent (*John Sarbutt Papers*)
37. Mauritius stamp (*John Sarbutt Papers*)

Acknowledgements

This biography originated in discussions with Elias Mossialos and Walter Holland at the London School of Economics and Political Science's (LSE) Health and Social Care Centre in 2006. I am grateful to them, and to the LSE, for financial and practical support for the research. Most writers can pinpoint why and when a project becomes attractive, or is rejected. I was hooked by an item I found on my first visit to look at the papers that Brian Abel-Smith had deposited at the LSE (some when he retired, others added after his death). My sampling of the 140+ archive boxes spanned from the 1940s to the 1990s. The sheer quantity was daunting: all Brian's copy correspondence, sometimes dozens of letters a day. I deliberately selected what I thought would be dry, uninspiring materials: drafts of Labour Party manifestos, for example. Yet in one of the first boxes I opened there was a copy of *House Beautiful* magazine from September 1956. Flicking through, I found the explanation for its inclusion: an article entitled 'Entertaining in a small flat'. There was Brian, 29 years old, photographed in the act of preparing supper for his friends 'Shirley and Sue', discussing how he had styled the rooms, and where he had bought the wallpaper and furniture.

The *House Beautiful* article provided a wonderful entrée to discussions with Brian's family, friends and colleagues over the next five years. I took it when I went to meet his partner John Sarbutt, and also to meet his brother, Lionel Abel-Smith. Both of them were welcoming and enthusiastic about a biography of Brian, and have been a source of advice and encouragement. I could not have written this book without the help of John, and his partner Nigel Cox. They have tolerated and corrected my misinterpretations and provided guidance for the periods and themes not covered by archive material. I know how fortunate biographers are to have the involvement of their subject's families, but I am also especially grateful for their friendship and hospitality. Lionel died in 2011. He was enormously helpful in providing family history, and in commenting on the early chapter drafts. His sharp barrister's mind cut through some of my waffle and I enjoyed hearing his life story as much as I did Brian's.

When I began the research in 2006 I was given a copy of Brian's contacts list and his last (1995) Christmas card list, and from there I selected an initial group of friends and colleagues to interview. There have been many moments of serendipity, when apparent dead ends have stimulated new lines of enquiry. I would like to express my thanks to the following individuals for their support, which has ranged from interviews to providing information, reading draft chapters or more practical sustenance: Ralph Abel-Smith, Eva Alberman, Ralph Andreano, the late Jack Ashley, the late Joe Asvall, Alec Atkinson, Richard Baker, Diana Bambridge, Tony Benn, Geoffrey Bindman, Tessa Blackstone, David Blewett, Helen Bolderson, Nick Bosanquet, Emma Burns, John Carrier, Popsie Chadwick, Paul Chapman, Michael Cichon, John T.C. Collins, Jean Corston, Tony Culyer, David Cowling, the late Percy Cradock, Jimmy Davis, Göran Dahlgren, Tam Dalyell, David de Ferranti, Frank Dobson, David Donnison, Nick Edwardson, Bryan Ellis, Jane Falkingham, Shirley Fanshawe, Michael Fairbairn, Frank Field, Josep Figueras, the late Denzil Freeth, Julio Frenk, Deme Nicolaou Frini, Lucy Gilson, Geoff Harcourt, Walter Holland, Howard and Ann Glennerster, Edward Greenfield, Milton Grundy, Julian Tudor Hart, Mike Hartley-Brewer, Dianne Hayter, Geoffrey and Elspeth Howe, Edward Hunter, Stephen Hunter, Panos Kanavos, Michael Kaser, Gerry Kearns, David Kynaston, Hilary Land, Julian Le Grand, David Lipsey, Roger Lockyer, Tony Lynes, Annabelle Mark, Alan Maynard, Ted Marmor, Anne Mills, Janet Morgan, the late Jerry Morris, Patrick Nairne, Vicente Navarro, Ann Oakley, David Ogilvy, David Owen, Michael Partridge, David Piachaud, Bob Pinker, Nick and Sarah Potter, Anne Power, Alex Preker, the late Mike Reddin, Geoffrey Rivett, Jenny Roberts, Bill Rodgers, Pat Rosenfield, the late Sally Sainsbury, Nina Schuller, Arthur Sheps, Liz Shore, Adrian Sinfield, Robert Stevens, Jack Straw, Dick Taverne, the late Peter Townsend, Jill Turner, Marina Vaizey, Patrick Vaughan, John Veit-Wilson, Rosemary Villars, Catriona Waddington, Gill Walt, Ronald Waterhouse, Robin Wendt, Shirley Williams, Michael Zander.

The main archive source for the biography is the Brian Abel-Smith papers held at the LSE. Sue Donnelly and her team, especially Nick White, who catalogued Brian's papers, have been tremendously helpful. I have regularly drawn on their expertise in 20th-century British political history and its sources. I acknowledge with gratitude the other archives that I have consulted for this biography, and the expert assistance of their archivists: Clare College, University of Cambridge; the Rare Books and Manuscripts collection at the University of Cambridge Library; the Barbara Castle archive at the Bodleian Library, University of Oxford; Haileybury College, Hertfordshire; The National Archives, Kew; and the World Health Organization archives, Geneva. I am particularly grateful to Michael Fairbairn, who allowed me access to personal papers of Lionel Abel-Smith; to David Blewett and Arthur Sheps for permission to use Brian's correspondence with them and a rare photograph of Brian and John together; and to Michael Kaser, for sending me his diary account of the 1961 study tour to the former Soviet Union. I was fortunate to have assistance for two parts of the archive research from Nat Ishino and Andrew Platt, both of whom brought their own excellent research skills to the project. My thanks also go to Alison Shaw, Susannah Emery, Kathryn King, Jo Morton, Dave Worth and the rest of the team at Policy Press.

Throughout the research and writing I have benefited from discussions with colleagues, and from their feedback on seminar and conference papers. Their academic generosity has included suggesting sources and book structures, and reading chapter drafts. I would like to thank in particular Virginia Berridge, Sanjoy Bhattacharya, Anne-Emanuelle Birn, Ted Brown, Dan Fox, Martin Gorsky, Susan Howson, Rudolf Klein, Socrates Litsios, Pat Starkey, John Stewart, Simon Szreter, Andrea Tanner, Pat Thane, Nick Timmins, Charles Webster and John Welshman.

The process of writing tests not only one's personal capabilities but also relationships. Four good friends have kept me motivated with tales of their own research, and sustained me with conversation on the more important things in life: thank you Laurinda Abreu, Lucy Borland, Helen Bynum and Anna Marie Roos. Thank you most of all to Jon, Tom and Sarah Sheard for your unfailing love and support and for letting Brian intrude into our life.

Sources and abbreviations

Sources

BA-S	Brian Abel-Smith
BA-SP	Brian Abel-Smith Papers, London School of Economics
BBK	Beaverbrook Papers, House of Lords Records Office
CCA	Clare College Archives, University of Cambridge
CUA	Cambridge University Archives, Cambridge Library manuscripts room
GP	Gaitskell Papers, University College London
HA-S	Harold Abel-Smith [Brian's uncle]
HSA	Haileybury School Archives
KCLMA	Liddell Hart Military Archives, Kings College London
LA-S	Lionel Abel-Smith [Brian's brother]
LPA	Labour Party Archives, Manchester
RMTP	Richard Titmuss Papers, London School of Economics
TBP	Tony Benn Papers
TNA	The National Archives, Kew, London
VA-S	Vivée [Genevieve, Brian Abel-Smith's mother]

Private sources

DBASP	David Blewett and Arthur Sheps Papers
JSP	John Sarbutt Papers
LA-SP	Lionel Abel-Smith Papers, held by Michael Fairbairn
MKP	Michael Kaser Papers
RWP	Robin Wendt Papers

Abbreviations

ABPI	Association of the British Pharmaceutical Industry
ADB	Asian Development Bank
AEGIS	Aid to the Elderly in Government Institutions
ARP	Air Raid Precautions
ATC	Air Training Corps
BEUC	Bureau Européen des Union de Consommateurs
BMA	British Medical Association
BUPA	British United Provident Association
CAB	Citizens' Advice Bureau

CBI	Confederation of British Industry
CEC	Commission of the European Communities
CHP	Country Health Planning
CIOMS	Council for International Organisations of the Medical Sciences
COHRED	Council on Health Research for Development
COS	Charity Organisation Society
CPAG	Child Poverty Action Group
CREDES	Centre de Recherche, d'Études et de Documentation en Economic de la Santé
CUF	Community Unemployment Fund
CUI	Community Unemployment Insurance
DALY	disability-adjusted life year
DEA	Department of Economic Affairs
DFID	Department for International Development
DG	Directorates General
DHSS	Department of Health and Social Security
DoE	Department of the Environment
DRG	diagnosis-related groups
EACMR	European Advisory Committee for Medical Research
ECAFE	Economic Commission for Asia and the Far East
EEC	European Economic Community
ERAP	European Research Action Plan
FAO	Food and Agriculture Organization
FCO	Foreign and Commonwealth Office
FIS	family income supplement
FSU	Family Service Unit
GDP	gross domestic product
GLC	Greater London Council
GNP	gross national product
HAS	Health Advisory Service
HIF	Health Information Foundation
HMC	Hospital Management Committee
HMO	health maintenance organisation
HPSS	Health and Personal Social Services
ILO	International Labour Organization
IPPF	International Planned Parenthood Federation
ISSA	International Social Security Association
JCC	Joint Consultants Committee
JRMT	Joseph Rowntree Memorial Trust
LHPC	London Health Planning Consortium
LPEC	London Project Executive Committee

LSE	London School of Economics and Political Science
LSHTM	London School of Hygiene and Tropical Medicine
MARU	Medical Architecture Research Unit
MOH	Medical Officers of Health
MP	Member of Parliament
MPNI	Ministry of Pensions and National Insurance
MPU	Medical Practitioners' Union
NAB	National Assistance Board
NALGO	National Association of Local Government Officers
NCIP	non-contributory invalidity pension
NCRC	National Communities Resource Centre
NEC	National Executive Committee
NGO	non-governmental organisation
NHA	national health accounting
NIESR	National Institute of Economic and Social Research
OCPU	Outer Circle Policy Unit
OCTU	Officer Corps Training Unit
ODA	Overseas Development Administration
OECD	Organisation for Economic Co-operation and Development
OHE	Office of Health Economics
OPCS	Office of Population Censuses and Surveys
PAHO	Pan-American Health Organisation
PAYE	pay-as-you-earn
PAYG	pay-as-you-go
PEP	Political and Economic Planning
QALY	quality-adjusted life year
RAWP	Resource Allocation Working Party
RHB	Regional Hospital Board
RHDAC	Regional Health Development Advisory Council [WHO-EURO]
SBC	Supplementary Benefits Commission
SERPS	state earnings-related pension scheme
SIDA	Swedish International Development Agency
SRS	state reserve scheme
SSRC	Social Science Research Council
TUC	Trades Union Congress
UN	United Nations
UNCHR	United Nations Commission on Human Rights
UNDP	United Nations Development Programme
USAID	United States Agency for International Development
USPHS	United States Public Health Service

VAD	voluntary aid detachment
VPRS	voluntary price regulation scheme
WEA	Workers' Educational Association
WHO	World Health Organization

Prologue

Shortly before midnight on Christmas Eve in 1965 Brian Abel-Smith left BBC Broadcasting House and folded his lanky six foot three inch frame into his silver-grey Sunbeam Alpine sports car. His route home to Belgravia took him under the Christmas lights of Regent Street, past the darkened windows of Fortnum & Mason's on Piccadilly, skirting the edge of Green Park – the trees now sparkling with a hard winter frost. Most British people would have either seen or heard him earlier that evening. He had been to the ITV studios for a live interview on the 9.00pm news (sandwiched between 'Ready Steady Go' and 'Peyton Place') before going to take part in the 'Ten O'Clock' radio programme on the BBC's Home Service. It was the culmination of a media onslaught on childhood poverty that he had initiated the previous day through a meeting with Harold Wilson at 10 Downing Street.

This newly promoted Professor of Social Administration at the London School of Economics and Political Science (LSE) – still only 39 – was already well known to the British public. On documentaries and discussion panels his cut-glass English accent and elegant disposition embellished an innate talent to communicate. He spoke with authority and compassion about what was wrong with British society. On Christmas Eve in 1965 his message was intended to disturb the comfortable families in their warm homes with well-stocked larders and presents wrapped under their Christmas trees. He spoke about the rising levels of poverty in a country that had had 20 years of Beveridge's welfare state. There were nearly a million children living in hardship. A pre-recorded documentary shown on BBC One that evening, which had filmed some of these children in their homes, demonstrated that these were not the 'feckless poor' but honest families whose earnings could not provide nourishing food and adequate clothing. For these children there would be no presents on Christmas Day. Brian, along with other members of the newly formed Child Poverty Action Group (CPAG), wished to bring these contemporary Tiny Tims into the public's gaze. He trusted that, when presented with new evidence, people would react, as Dickens' Ebenezer Scrooge eventually did. That evidence was to be found in the book he had just published with Peter Townsend, *The Poor and the Poorest*. It was to be one of the major turning points in British post-war social policy.

There are few academics who have affected change on a global scale, but those who fall into that elite group have usually been acclaimed during their lifetimes. Despite regular media appearances, Brian Abel-Smith remained an essentially private person throughout his life. His achievements were accompanied by genuine modesty. His value to Britain, and to many countries around the world, requires careful unpicking from the intricate tapestry of social, economic and cultural change that occurred in the second half of the 20th century. He was, to quote Julian Le Grand's obituary tribute, a 20th-century Tom Paine: 'My country is the world, and my religion is to do good.' He was a political academic, or an academic politician manqué – whichever way would most effectively achieve his chosen objectives. His expertise in economics and health and social welfare policy was from the outset coloured by his unwavering self-declaration as a socialist.

Economists usually work in an abstract, unpopulated world, in which all decisions are grounded in a desire for financial gain or efficiency. Pushed to its theoretical limits, it champions the inequality that is evident in extremes of wealth and poverty, and that underpins social class. But people are not perfect economic actors. Choices and decisions are determined by many more factors than monetary gain. Brian Abel-Smith was determined to use his skills to push for a society that placed a greater moral value on equality – levelling out abhorrent extremes of income and opportunity – in which everyone participated to the full extent of their abilities.

Brian returned from his Christmas Eve television and radio appearances to a home that was in stark contrast to those occupied by the million British children living near or below the poverty line. The solid front door on his Victorian townhouse was a physical, social and emotional boundary between his public and private lives. He had bought 34a Elizabeth Street using a substantial inheritance from an uncle – money carefully passed through several generations of the Smith banking family. It was a perfect visual mnemonic of his upper-class heritage – family portraits and silver trinkets, a long mahogany dining table that seated up to a dozen. At the heart of Christmas is the family. One of his cousins would be spending Christmas at Windsor Castle with the Queen, as a married-in member of the extended royal family. Brian would be spending the day with his widowed mother and his brother.

John Sarbutt, his partner of five years, had already left their shared home to be with his family in Norfolk. Their relationship – illegal until 1967 – was acceptable behind closed doors, but British society was not yet comfortable with the intrusion of this unconventional family unit into traditional festive celebrations.

Academic economist, political adviser, 'champagne socialist', Brian Abel-Smith was one of the most influential figures of the 20th century in shaping health and social welfare, commanding the attention and respect of governments worldwide. Between 1953 and his death in 1996 he helped to steer policy development in more than 50 countries. His personal and professional papers, which he deposited in the LSE archives, offer a superb insight into his world: an early acute awareness of his social privilege through his public school education, yet living a frugal childhood in a Kensington flat, left relatively poor due to classic English inheritance traditions. The true extent of inequality dawned on Brian in his teens, cycling through the blitzed north London streets, where the deprivation he witnessed made a lasting impression. When he reached the age of 18 in 1944 he joined the Labour Party, and attended the rallies of its leaders before the 1945 post-war election, in which it won an unexpected victory – with one of only two substantial majorities it achieved in the 23 general elections held between 1918 and 1997.

After National Service, which he spent in newly partitioned Austria, as Aide de Campe (ADC) to the British Commanding General, he returned to take up a place at the University of Cambridge to read economics. His active involvement in the Labour Party and the Fabian Society, alongside other mature undergraduates such as Jack Ashley, marked him out as a potential future Member of Parliament (MP). Hugh Dalton, then Labour Chancellor of the Exchequer, saw him on one of his talent-spotting visits, and over the next six years helped Brian to work up a political CV – campaigning during his holidays and writing political pieces. His decision to stay up at Cambridge to do a PhD was partly motivated by a need to kill time until a political career became possible, but also by a genuine belief in the power of evidence to change society. In 1953, soon after writing his first political publication for the Fabian Society – a pamphlet called *The Reform of Social Security* – he was invited to become the research assistant for the new enquiry into the cost of the National Health Service (NHS), led by the economist Claude Guillebaud.

Brian's work for the Guillebaud Committee was co-supervised by Richard Titmuss, who was to become his academic godfather and inspiration for the next 20 years, until Titmuss's early death in

1973. Titmuss, who had recently taken up a professorship in the Department of Social Administration at LSE, was the intellectual successor to R.H. Tawney and T.H. Marshall. He challenged the current concepts of rights, values and choices, and forged from social administration's core concern for human disadvantage a new discipline of Social Policy. This was also reflected in a new morality, later articulated by David Donnison: 'We should not explore and record human suffering unless we are trying to do something about it.'[1] Through Brian's appointment as Junior Lecturer in the LSE's Department of Social Administration, along with another young Titmuss disciple, Peter Townsend, the intellectual basis of social administration was brought into active policy formation within the Labour Party.

The Titmice, as they were known, stimulated wider discussions about the nature of left-wing thought and policy. Their research forced analyses of the deficiencies of Beveridge's welfare state, and its underlying principles of universality and risk sharing. Working as a close-knit team through the 1950s and 1960s, they conducted mammoth surveys of the extent of poverty in Britain, and the relationship between social welfare, health and inequality. Through their contacts with Labour politicians they were able to permeate the policy-making arena, and to suggest more efficient ways to achieve social justice. Although Titmuss was seen as the senior member of the team, it is clear from this biography that Brian Abel-Smith deserves equal billing. He was the architect of key policy innovations on benefits, pensions and health service reforms. He enhanced Titmuss's philosophical texts with his exceptional ability to shape academic research into politically charged rhetoric, always underpinned by solid economic authority.

Brian Abel-Smith recognised that academic research *per se* would not change existing social and economic inequalities. To translate ideas into action he needed to be a politician, or to have a close relationship with politicians. The first route, which had been his preferred option, he decided to close in 1957, when he rejected the offer of taking Hugh Dalton's parliamentary seat. In an era when homosexual acts were illegal it was an unacceptable risk, particularly for the potential impact his outing would have on his establishment family. Instead he forged a reputation as an expert adviser, to whom politicians could turn for policy advice. By the 1960s there were only a handful of academics who had served in this unofficial capacity to British governments. Harold Wilson's 1964–70 governments formalised the relationship, and Brian became one of the first 'special advisers', when he was recruited (part time) to support Richard Crossman, the new Secretary of State for Social Services in 1968. When Labour were defeated in 1970, and Brian returned to his full-time post at the LSE, Crossman described him as 'my closest personal friend and without whom I could have done very little in the past two years'. Labour returned to government in 1974, and Brian was immediately re-appointed by Barbara Castle, for his 'high brilliance' to balance the 'guile and low cunning' of her political adviser (and later Justice Secretary) Jack Straw. After Castle was sacked in 1976, Brian was kept on as a special adviser by her replacement at the Department of Health and Social Security (DHSS), David Ennals. In December 1978, Brian moved to work with Peter Shore at the Department of the Environment (DoE). This partnership lasted only five months, before Labour lost the 1979 election, and were to remain in opposition for the rest of Brian's life.

Brian Abel-Smith's vision for British social welfare came closest to fruition in the mid-1970s. His ingenious policy developments helped to create a fairer system for distributing funds to the NHS, a new pensions scheme that eased the poverty of old age and removed discrimination against women, and new benefits for people with disabilities and families. In addition to his core academic interest in social policy, he extended his campaign for social justice to include other aspects of British society. He co-authored three provocative books on the British legal system that helped to stimulate the biggest reform to the judiciary ever seen and a greater sense of justice for the 'man in the street'. He was involved with the development of Citizens' Advice Bureaux, and served on several influential committees, investigating compensation for victims of the thalidomide disaster and rights for people with disabilities.

This was more than enough work to keep an average person satisfied. Yet Brian continually looked for new projects, some of which were linked with his research interests, and others he took on for personal reasons. In 1965, the same year that he helped to launch CPAG, he had opened the first of a successful chain of men's clothes shops, with the provocative name of 'Just Men'. This began as a business venture to give employment to one of his former partners, but it became an integral part of London's fashion world in the swinging sixties. His King's Road and Beauchamp Place shops competed with Biba, John Michael and other iconic brands. He took an active role, regularly travelling to Italy to buy stock, and visiting the shops on Saturday mornings to meet his celebrity customers who included Mick Jagger, Warren Beatty and Julie Christie.

Brian Abel-Smith's family and education were suffused with colonial heritage, which understood Britain as an integral (and sometimes superior) part of the wider world. He had first been abroad during his

National Service in 1947. It was the start of a love affair with travel and foreign cultures that lasted throughout his life. His natural inclination, therefore, when analysing the British NHS in 1953, was to look for international comparisons. How did other countries, particularly in the developed world, finance and organise their healthcare and social services? What were the benefits of insurance-based schemes such as Germany's compared to Beveridge's taxation-funded system? This triggered a more fundamental set of research questions, on how nations planned and accounted for health. In 1956 he was invited, on the strength of his recent successful completion of the joint report with Titmuss on the cost of the NHS, to work for the World Health Organization (WHO) as a freelance consultant. He pioneered the creation of national health accounts (NHAs) and international comparative analysis of healthcare services, beginning with establishing shared definitions, and later developing detailed critiques of how efficiency and equity in health and social welfare systems could be achieved.

Brian's international work always fitted into his main duties at the LSE. Every year, from 1957 onwards, he undertook at least one overseas project, either for WHO or for one of the other international organisations. In 1959 he took on a project for the British government's Colonial Office to visit and advise the newly independent Mauritius on how to introduce a comprehensive health and welfare system. This was an opportunity to express his social welfare philosophy on a 'clean slate'. Working with Titmuss, he spent two years integrating fieldwork and enquiries into a detailed blueprint. This was the first of many similar projects, and helped to establish a *modus operandi* for dialogue between expert advisers from the developed world with the governments of the developing world.

Fundamental ideological differences and practical problems caused an irrevocable split in the Titmice in 1968. The death of Titmuss in 1973 also permitted Brian to refine his own social welfare philosophy. This was increasingly influenced by his international work, which was encountering new sets of problems as governments struggled to cope with global economic recession. Value for money emerged as a key research theme, alongside inequalities. His ongoing involvement with WHO, the International Labour Organization (ILO) and other organisations made him a natural choice for further studies on cost containment in healthcare. He engaged with the latest research from other leading health economists such as Alain Enthoven and John D. Thompson in developing his own theories on health and social welfare systems. Despite an unwavering commitment to socialism, and practical support for Britain's Labour Party, Brian Abel-Smith was a pragmatist, not a purist. His original discipline of Economics permitted a more nuanced appraisal of alternative models of social welfare. He was willing to explore the possibilities offered by markets, user fees and choice of service providers at a time of escalating public sector expenditure.

After the WHO Alma Ata Declaration in 1978, which promised a re-balancing of health systems in developed and developing countries away from expensive secondary care, Brian Abel-Smith worked closely with senior WHO staff to develop and implement the 'Health for All by the Year 2000' (HFA2000) strategy. It forced an acknowledgement of the paucity of health economics expertise at global and national levels, which he helped to address through writing practical manuals, devising the 'Financial Master Plan' approach, and establishing new academic and training courses. Many of the students who attended his lectures on the joint LSE/London School of Hygiene and Tropical Medicine (LSHTM) MSc in Health Policy, Planning and Financing went on to significant careers in the governments of developing countries, taking with them and implementing his social welfare principles. By the 1980s Brian was an internationally respected authority on health and social welfare. He was invited into developing countries such as Kenya, Costa Rica, Thailand and Indonesia to maximise the benefits from their scarce resources. Through this direct, practical involvement in policy design and implementation he began to challenge the dominant World Bank model of social welfare, proving the unhelpfulness of its 'one size fits all' strategy.

Brian Abel-Smith had an intellectual authority and influence on the world stage comparable to figures such as William Beveridge. He occupied parallel worlds: from upper-class Belgravia, where he was renowned for his stylish hospitality, to the appalling poverty of developing countries, in which he spent many months each year helping to understand the root causes of their problems. He moved easily between academia and politics, imbuing each with the essence of the other: precise research skills delivered with a sometimes cutting wit, pared to the bone of the political message. In his carefully managed private life he was a social chameleon, at home in networks of the great and the good alongside closer gay friendships and partnerships. He was a consummate compartmentaliser.

For more than 40 years Brian Abel-Smith was at the epicentre of the transformation of British and global culture: from 1950s British domestic politics to the explosion of the business of expert consultancy in the 1990s through organisations such as the WHO and The World Bank. His life is a perfect example of that fascinating territory where history, politics and economics collide. Policy formation has become increasingly complex, and the object of vast amounts of theorising and modelling. What is often forgotten is that these processes have distinct temporal dimensions and involve real people. Brian Abel-Smith was a curious man, in both senses of the term. His colourful life was played out at dizzying speed: a ceaseless traveller looking for intellectual and social stimulation. This book shows the impact of personal authority and connections on policy formation and the power of an individual to affect change on a worldwide scale.

Note

[1] D. Donnison (2000) 'The academic contribution to social reform', *Social Policy & Administration*, vol 34, no 1, p 42.

Part 1

INHERITANCES AND DUTIES, 1926–51

1

Inheritances: 1926–46

Smiths and Abel-Smiths
An English education
After Haileybury

Smiths and Abel-Smiths

The Times announced the birth of Brian Abel-Smith on 6 November 1926, at 24 Kensington Court Gardens 'to the wife of BRIG-GEN Lionel Abel-Smith, late Royal Artillery'. As with most of the 21 births announced in *The Times* on the same day, his first name was not given – 'a son' or 'a daughter' was the most information these establishment families chose to disclose for a guinea. The newspaper had provided his mother with dismal home news for the final weeks of her pregnancy: unemployment was up to 1,516,200, and there was a rush for coal rationing permits, required because of the worsening coal strike. On 1 November *The Times* warned of the 'Socialist Menace' posed by Labour candidates at that day's municipal elections: 'this year a "record" poll is essential. The great danger is the apathy of the "silent voter" who, forgetting the experiences of the General Strike, when Labour Councils failed to co-operate with the Government, may not think it worthwhile to go to the poll.'[1] On the day of Brian's birth it reported a Labour gain of 146 seats.

The Times gave almost as much coverage to Imperial News as it did to Home News, reporting favourably on the Viceroy of India's inspection of the new North West Frontier outposts, designed 'towards making the tribesmen a guard instead of a menace to India'.[2] The Foreign News section commented on the Soviet celebrations of the ninth anniversary of the Bolshevik Revolution, and in Italy the suppression of all newspapers opposed to *Fascisme* and the abolition of all societies and institutions with anti-Fascist aims after an assassination attempt on Mussolini. The Abel-Smiths might have been interested to learn that the new three-propeller de Havilland Hercules, which would operate an air route from Egypt to India, had carried out demonstration flights. Test telephone calls between England and the US had reached the level of 50 to 60 transmissions per day, and it was hoped to begin a commercial service in early 1927. Mr Anthony Asquith, son of Lord Oxford, was fined 20 shillings at Bow Street on 4 November for causing an obstruction with his motorcar in St Martin's Place, London, on 24 September. At the Hereford Assizes Mr Justice Swift passed sentence of death on Charles Houghton, 45, butler, for the murder of Miss Elinor Drinkwater Woodhouse at Burghill Court, Hereford, on 7 September. Jerome K. Jerome was to be made a freeman of Walsall, where he was born. The Court Circular provided the Abel-Smiths with the minutiae of their social class's existence, from the daily presentations and receptions at Buckingham Palace, to the movements of Marquesses, Earls, Honourables and army officers.

In Brian's first week of life Parliament reassembled on 9 November, where Prime Minister Stanley Baldwin's Conservative government got down to business with stabilising the economy and raising funds (£3,250,000) to relieve unemployment. Armistice Day was observed on the 11th, with the King attending the service at the Cenotaph, 30 million 'Flanders poppies' made by disabled ex-servicemen having been sold to raise money for Lord Haig's British Legion Appeal Fund.

The Abel-Smiths had settled in their Kensington Court Gardens flat soon after the General, as he was known, retired from the Royal Artillery. Situated just off Kensington High Street, this block of red-brick flats provided a convenient base from which the General could go to his Piccadilly club – the Naval and Military – each day. Brigadier General Lionel Abel-Smith was a member of one of England's longest established banking families. Smith's Bank had been founded in Nottingham in 1653, pre-dating the Bank of England by some 35 years. Thomas Smith (1631–99) was the founder, a mercer with a suitably secure set of cellars in which his business contacts could store their money and valuables. By dint of some careful speculation, he quickly increased his own fortune, and his sons established several financial projects. The next two generations proved significantly more ambitious, and Abel Smith II (1717–98) formed the Smith Payne and Smith's banking house in London in 1758, and local banks in Lincoln and Hull, where they entered into business with William Wilberforce, grandfather of the Member of Parliament (MP) and antislavery campaigner. The Smiths developed a reputation as trustworthy and reliable bankers. Robert Smith I (1752–1838) acted as a financial adviser to the Prime Minister William Pitt, and was rewarded by being created Baron Carrington in 1797. One particularly useful connection was made when a rather scruffy Nathan Rothschild turned up at the bank with a wheelbarrow full of money, having being rejected as a potential investor by other banks. Smith accepted his money, and the two families retained a close connection. John Abel Smith was one of two supporters for Lionel Rothschild's successful entry into the House of Commons in 1858 – only possible after the required oath with its declaration 'upon the true faith of a Christian' had been relaxed to allow Jewish participation.

By the end of the 19th century the provincial Smith banks were looking for merger and expansion opportunities. After a number of abortive negotiations, all the banks and property (except 1–6 Lombard Street) were sold to the Union Bank in 1902 for £1,156,543, the equivalent of around £100 million in today's money. The Smiths maintained their close involvement with the city, with several of them holding influential posts in other banks and financial institutions. In 1959 *The Economist* calculated that 17 descendants of the Smith family collectively held 87 directorships in 75 companies. At least 26 members of the family pursued political careers, including most recently Sir John Smith (1923–2007), the Conservative MP, and the present Lord Carrington (1919–), the sixth Baron, who served as Foreign Secretary in Margaret Thatcher's Conservative government. Another significant number have provided service to the Royal Household, acting variously as Gentleman Usher, Equerry, Lady of the Bedchamber and Mistress of the Robes. From the 18th century the family wealth supported the acquisition of several fine country residences. Brian's branch of the family descended from Samuel Smith MP (1754–1834) of Woodhall Park in Hertfordshire. He handsomely provided for his sons by investing in further estates at Sacombe Park, Wilford House, Goldings and Wendover.

Brian's grandfather, Albert Smith (1841–1914), was the fourth in a family of 10 children. The three elder sons followed the traditional establishment career allocations – politics, family business, the military – and convention lined up Albert for a life in the church. He served as the incumbent at Wendover, Buckinghamshire, but the estate (with its village and extensive farmland) was initially the property of his elder, unmarried brother Philip, who had had a distinguished career, becoming a general in the Grenadier Guards (although his service had been rewarded with a CB rather than a KCB because Queen Victoria apparently disapproved of his lifestyle that entailed several mistresses.) In 1834 Philip had inherited £20,000 (about £2 million in today's values), and the Wendover estate, which produced an income of about £3,000 pa (£300,000 pa now). According to a family history written in 1930, he 'ran through his money pretty quick and had to mortgage Wendover pretty heavily…'.[3] When Philip died in 1894, he left his share of the Smith wealth in a will which made Albert and then Albert's second son Lionel (Brian's father) the heirs to Wendover, and completely cut out Albert's eldest son Edwin, who had been seen as Philip's natural successor.

A 'Deed of Settlement' was created in an attempt to put things right, as the surviving family saw it. After Albert's death the property was to pass to Edwin for his life, and failing male issue, then to Edwin's younger brothers in turn and their respective male issue. To compensate Lionel for possibly losing part of his inheritance, financial provision was made for him out of Albert's personal estate and the property itself. This was not the end of the matter as the youngest brother Sam (who had gone to farm in New Zealand in 1902) felt that he had lost a large part of what might have come to him on his father's (Albert's) death, and Edwin considered that his three daughters had not been provided for. The result was bitterness and legal battles between the brothers, and Lionel came back to England from India where he was serving to try and sort matters out. This went on for many years, with no contact between Edwin and Lionel between 1923 and 1927. Since Lionel and Sam each had two sons, Edwin realised that it was unlikely that his daughters could ever receive any benefit from the property, and things settled down.

Albert Abel Smith had the benefit of the living of the Parish where he was vicar for 46 years following his education at Harrow and Christ Church, Oxford. He put a huge effort into his parish and the estate at Wendover – restoring the church, building schools, a library and a clock tower for the village.[4] This English system of inheritance, while usually appearing relatively brutal to all but the first-born son, prevented unnecessary dilution of family fortunes, and preserved estates for subsequent generations. Such careful manoeuvring could not, however, outwit the tougher legislation introduced in 1894 which extended Estate Duty to cover all of a deceased person's possessions. Colloquially known as Death Duty, further increases were introduced in 1909–10, to a maximum of 15 per cent of an estate's value, up to a ceiling of £3,500,000. This undoubtedly affected inheritances in several branches of the Smith family in the early 20th century. In Brian's immediate family, a significant amount of the property on the Wendover estate had already been mortgaged during Philip's lifetime (possibly to pay for his project to build the Guards chapels at the Wellington and Caterham barracks). The estate had to withstand three charges for death duties between 1914 and 1946 on the deaths of Albert, Edwin and Lionel, each time taking several years to pay off.

Brian's father, Lionel Abel Smith, was born on 8 November 1870 at Wendover, the second son of the Revd Albert Smith. A bachelor until he was 53 (as was common for many army officers of the time) he was educated at Haileybury College, which had been co-founded by one of the Abel Smiths in 1862. He was commissioned into the Royal Artillery in 1890 and was initially posted with the 80th Foot Brigade in Ireland at Athlone. He later served for many years in India and was awarded the Distinguished Service Order (DSO) in January 1918 for his service in Mesopotamia. Owing to injuries sustained during the First World War, he was put on 'half pay', and only occasionally recalled to serve with his regiment. When not serving, he lived with his two spinster sisters, Helen and Maud. In 1922 Lionel's branch of the Smith family added a hyphen by Deed Poll to change their surname to Abel-Smith. This subtle 'social insurance policy' attracted mild ribbing from other branches of the family. It had been felt necessary to secure their proper social status after Lionel's sisters had found that their undistinguished names of Miss Smith had failed to gain them invitations to the right tea parties in Paris where they served as voluntary aid detachments (VADs) during the war.

Brian's mother, Geneviève Matilda Lilac, known as Vivée, was born on 9 May 1898, the youngest surviving of six children of Robert Walsh, a wine merchant of Armagh, and his wife Jeanie (Elizabeth Jane Carson, 1870–1927) of Warrenpoint in County Down, Ireland. While working as a travelling companion to an English lady, she met the newly hyphenated Lionel Abel-Smith at Menton in the South of France, who was holidaying there with his sisters. Following a short courtship, they married on 22 August 1923 at Rostrevor, County Down, on the border of the recently proclaimed Irish Free State.[5] The bride, according to the announcement in *The Times*, wore a gown of ivory and silver broché trimmed with silver leaves and flowers and orange blossoms, and a white hat trimmed with osprey feathers. A reception followed at the Great Northern Hotel.[6] The marriage, by all accounts, was not greeted with unrestrained delight: Lionel's apparent disadvantages were his age (28 years older than Vivée), and his English establishment background. Although one of her brothers gave her away (her father had already died), some members of her Irish family subsequently refused to have any contact with her. Vivée's primary disadvantage, from the Abel-Smith point of view (most visibly reflected in the face of Lionel's sister Maud on the wedding party photograph) was her relatively low social status.

At the time of their marriage Lionel was stationed in England, where Vivée joined him. In 1924, in anticipation of Lionel's imminent retirement from the army, they took the lease on a London flat, 56 Weatherby Mansions, in Earls Court. It was there, while Lionel was away on duty, that their first child, also named Lionel, was born on 1 September 1924. They subsequently moved into another flat at 24 Kensington Court Gardens, where Brian was born two years later. It appears to have been a happy marriage, if one in which Vivée ensured that her husband's well-established bachelor routines were never compromised or disturbed by the children. Even allowing for the ages at which they became parents (Lionel was 54, Vivée was 26), she seemed to find it easier than he to display her affection for the boys. Perhaps this reflected both her Irish, and more relaxed family upbringing and Lionel's traditional upper-class English reserve, entrenched through early boarding school and then a military life. It was Vivée who wrote the weekly letter to the boys when they went to school, usually beginning 'Hello Love!', and recounting their father's activities.

Summer holidays provided an opportunity for Vivée to take her boys home to Ireland. They spent several Augusts in the 1930s in Portrush, meeting up with her sister Cherrie to whom she remained close. Other August holidays were spent in Bognor, Littlehampton and Broadstairs. As the boys grew up, the summer trips lengthened. In 1935 Vivée took them for six weeks to stay with an old friend of hers who was living in County Wicklow, and the following year they stayed for three weeks at the Marine Hotel in Blackpool, shortly after Brian had spent nearly two months recovering from whooping cough. After Edwin died in 1936, Brian's father was able to have use of the family property at Wendover, which had now passed to him as his Uncle Philip had wished. The family spent a month there during the summer of 1937, as well as a short seaside stay at Bexhill. In 1938 and 1939 the family combined time at Wendover with a month at the Greengates Hotel at Worthing.

An English education

The selection of schools for Brian's education followed a conventional English upper-class, and specifically Abel-Smith, tradition. In September 1932 Brian joined his brother Lionel at the kindergarten at Kensington

High School for Girls, which their third floor flat in Kensington Court Gardens overlooked at the back. One of his closest friends from this time was Susan Hamilton, two years younger than Brian, whose family lived opposite. Popsie, Susan's younger sister, remembers the high jinks that Brian, Susan and occasionally Lionel would get up to. They had a makeshift 'telephone' strung across the street between their upper windows, with cans on each end. Much fun came from using water pistols on visitors waiting below to be let into the blocks of flats. Kensington Gardens provided an escape from the confines of life in the flat, and Lionel and Brian regularly went to tea at the Hamiltons', where food seemed to be more lavish than at home. Brian and Susan got into trouble there for raiding the huge boxes of chocolates Mrs Hamilton kept in a cupboard – artfully re-tying the ribbons so that they would not be found out (although their subsequent sickness gave the game away). Even at the age of seven Brian appeared acutely conscious of social class, asking Susan what her father did and what his income was. When she told him that he was the managing director of a small firm making polish he replied, 'Oh – trade!'[7] Vivée seemed to the Hamilton children to be wonderfully flamboyant, with a mass of shockingly (for that era) untamed black hair, a deep, resonant contralto voice and an infectious laugh. In a room full of people, she was always a natural focal point.

At the age of nine Brian began as a boarder at Hordle House Preparatory School in the village of Milford-on-Sea in Hampshire. The Abel-Smiths chose this school through Harold Abel-Smith, Brian's uncle, who had settled in Milford after a failed attempt at ostrich farming in South Africa (an ostrich removed one of his eyes) and a period as a land agent in Essex. Hordle House was a relatively new school, founded in 1926 by the Revd E. Whately-Smith. Patrick Nairne, with whom Brian later worked at the Department of Health and Social Security (DHSS), was also a boarder there, and recalls a happy environment, with much time spent walking down the cliffs for early morning swims, or spotting the important liners making their way in and out of Southampton. The older boys ate with the headmaster and his wife, and were encouraged to help with *The Times* crossword.[8] Brian became a prefect and second head boy at Hordle, and developed hobbies such as photography.

During the 'phoney war' autumn of 1939 Brian followed in the footsteps of his father and other male Smiths and took the entrance exam for Haileybury, beginning there in January 1940. He was 13 years old, and fitted easily into Edmonstone House alongside Lionel, although he did not enter as a junior scholar, as his brother had done. Admissions were made in every term of the school year, flexibility that no longer exists within the British educational system. Placement and progress through the school was then tailored to suit the individual boy. Brian's uncle, Edwin Smith, had stayed in the 'Removes' – the basic year – for four years, and had also been placed in Hailey House, then intended for the more delicate boys. Brian entered Haileybury into the 'Middles' and was the second youngest of that term's intake of 21 boys. His first term's report assessed him to be 'immature ... writing slovenly as is his thinking ... knows quite a lot and is anxious to learn'.[9]

The school must have looked much as it had when their father was there in the 1880s. The original buildings, designed by William Wilkins for the previous occupants, the East India College, were arranged around the largest academic quadrangle in Europe. Wilkins was a Cambridge graduate, and the great quad of Trinity College had been his model. He later went on to design the National Gallery in London, and the King's Parade Screen at Cambridge. The East India Company had founded its college to ensure a ready supply of administrators for its businesses. Prominent members of teaching staff included the Revd Thomas Malthus, who taught history and political economy there from its foundation in 1806 until 1835. East India College closed in 1858, the victim of falling roll numbers after the appointments system for the company was made more open. In January 1862 negotiations began to re-develop the buildings for a school 'with a firm Christian basis'. Abel-Smith MP agreed to be one of the patrons, providing an initial loan of £500, and Robert Smith of Goldings was one of the three trustees.

The Haileybury architecture provides a visual mnemonic for all that encapsulates the British public school establishment: domed chapel, library, dining hall, the grubber (tuck shop), cricket pitches, Latin inscriptions over entrance arches: 'Ostium mihi apertum est magnum' which translates as 'A great opportunity is open to me', and the school motto: 'Sursum corda', 'Lift up your hearts'. Arcane rules determined which button of a boy's jacket could be undone, who could wear particular caps and colours, and who might possess an umbrella.[10] The entries in the Beatings Book suggest that Edmonstone (under the mastership of W.A. Tregenza, known as Trigger) was a less authoritarian environment than some of the other houses. Societies and clubs were the mainstay of the boys' non-curricular activities. The Elysium was the province of the four top prefects of the school who, with three others of their choice from the sixth form, ate in their own dining room. Members were identifiable by their brightly coloured waistcoats. A more exotic and unconventional society was the Guild of Pallas. Seen as a parallel elite to the formal school system of prefects, membership of this 'secret' society was by invitation only, and the meetings were reputed frequently to be drunken affairs. Other more erudite societies, in which Brian participated, included the prestigious Senior School Debating Society, the Gramophone Society and the Antiquarian Society.

The master at Haileybury during Brian's time was Canon E.F. Bonhote, known affectionately by both staff and boys as 'The Boot'. He had been a natural sciences scholar at Clare College Cambridge, before teaching posts at Rugby and at St John's College, Agra. He was a reforming master, abolishing the complicated system of house caps, and individual prizes in singing and athletics. He was also noted for reconfiguring the seating in the chapel so that all the boys faced the front, and the older boys could not 'eye up' the younger ones. Although as a bachelor his regime lacked some of the softening influence of previous masters' wives, Bonhote was devoted to the school. He used his influence with Haileyburian Clement Attlee (1883–1967) at the outbreak of the Second World War, when he was Lord Privy Seal, to cancel plans to turn the school into an emergency hospital.

Haileybury had always encouraged its pupils to develop a sense of social responsibility. Attlee, who had left Haileybury in 1901, made a long-overdue visit to see one of the school's philanthropic schemes in the East End of London in 1905. This led to his decision to work as manager of Haileybury House, a military-style venture providing social and educational pursuits for working-class boys in Stepney. Attlee lived in the house from 1906 to 1909, and claimed that the poverty and strong working-class community support he witnessed there converted him to socialism.[11] The Haileybury Guild Boys Club, which was run from Haileybury House in Ben Johnson Street, was assisted by prefects from the school on Tuesday evenings. The boys were affiliated to the 1st Cadet Battalion of the Queen's (Royal West Surrey) Regiment, which provided them with uniforms and boots, and a sense of unity and purpose. Attlee continued to retain close connections with Haileybury, finding time to be Guest of Honour at Speech Day in 1946 despite his new position as Prime Minister. As with other walks of life, political old Haileyburians sought each other out, and Attlee promoted three in his government: Lynn Ungoed Thomas (1904–72), Geoffrey de Freitas (1913–82) and Christopher Mayhew (1915–97).

Despite falling numbers, Haileybury remained open throughout the war, with the boys ordered to take shelter under their beds during air raids as there was not enough space for all of them in the hastily constructed dug-out shelters. All 3,000 of the college windows had to be blacked out and the boys and staff joined Air Raid Precautions

(ARP) and fire-watching groups and the Home Guard. The houses also competed in competitions to grow potatoes (which were stored in the racquets court) and helped with local agricultural work and month-long harvest camps during the summer holidays. The school faced the same rationing and shortages as the rest of Britain – there was often no hot water for weeks at a time – and suffered chronic problems with the supply of books, paper and food. Railings and saucepans were donated to help the scrap metal collection for munitions. Although the number of boys fell below 400, the school maintained what it could of normal activities. Visiting speakers included Attlee and the new MP Tom Driberg. Sporting teams continued (when petrol rations allowed) to travel to away matches, and plays were produced. To cope with the financial and staffing pressures, in 1942 Haileybury agreed to merge with the Imperial Service College, based in Windsor, which was in an even more precarious position.

After a shaky first year, when Brian's school reports seemed to focus more on his handwriting than his academic performance, subsequent pithy statements from his masters revolved around 'good work ... industrious and alert ... satisfactory term'. In his School Certificate, taken in July 1941, he gained a distinction for English Literature, and credits for Additional Maths, Latin, Greek, English Language, History and Scripture, and a pass for French. These exams were taken against the backdrop of some of the heaviest bombing of the Second World War. By the summer of 1941 over two million homes had been damaged or destroyed in Britain (60 per cent of them in London), with the loss of around 43,000 civilian lives.[12] As Richard Titmuss, later to be a colleague of Brian's, pointed out in his volume of the official history of the war: 'not until over three years had passed was it possible to say that the enemy had killed more soldiers than women and children'.[13] The Abel-Smiths' flat in Kensington Court Gardens had been blasted out on 26 April 1941 and his parents looked for somewhere to live outside central London. They moved to 33 Lancaster Avenue, Hadley Wood, in August 1941, from where they sent weekly letters to Lionel and Brian at Haileybury with tales of rationing, gardening and bomb scares. They were now close enough to the school for the boys to be able to cycle the 15 miles to visit on permitted weekends, when Brian was not occupied with running the school swimming club.

In the summer holidays of 1943 Brian made his first visit to the Houses of Parliament with a school friend Derek Canter, where they met George Muff, Labour MP for Hull (later Lord Calverley). This was to be the first of Brian's political contacts, and it resulted in intermittent meetings and exchanges of letters. Brian clearly made a lasting impression on Muff, who later wrote in 1946: 'I wish you had told me about the "incident". I would not have hurt your feelings for worlds. I have, I know a funny way of saying things, well let me know and we will put things right. You see Brian when I was 16/17 I was very sensitive and reserved & you are a little bit like I was. That is why I am drawn to you. Well you know where to find me when you have time.'[14] That summer he also visited Maud and Harold (his father's brother and sister) whom old age and finances had forced to live together at Milford-on-Sea in Hampshire. Brian then cycled 40 miles from their home to spend four weeks at a Varsity and Public Schools (VPS) camp at Clayesmore School at Iwerne Minster in Dorset.[15]

Brian returned to a busy term at Haileybury in September 1943, becoming a school prefect, secretary of the Antiquarian Society and the Edmonstone Reading Society, and president of the Gramophone Society. The winter term ended with a spirited performance of Gilbert and Sullivan's *Gondoliers*. The following spring he conducted the house singing competition and acted in the play *Men in Shadows*, culminating with his selection as Head of House in May. One of his new duties was to write up the House records. At the age of 17, these first 'public' words display the nascent Abel-Smith sense of civic responsibility:

> One of the main effects of a war on a public school is that it makes all boys leave much earlier than they would have done in peace time. Consequently all the prefects are younger and less experienced, and less able to wield that amount of authority which could be safely placed in the hands of their older predecessors. This perhaps is the root cause of the irresponsibility in high places which has been felt in the school for the last year or two. Prefects have been confusing licence with liberty and unconsciously consulting their own interests rather than those of the school. Edmonstone has had its share of such prefects and an excellent example of irresponsibility is the uncompleted state of the records for last term. By the end of last term the bad example of older boys in house had affected the whole house and its position in the school. The discipline had been slack and the reputation of Edmonstone was very poor. We had a bad name for inefficiency and general slackness.... Edmonstone has always been run on liberal principles; but when the privileges of democracy are abused a firm hand must be used until the privileges are respected once more, when philanthropic emancipation may gradually be exercised.[16]

Brian's lack of prowess at field sports was compensated for by other non-academic achievements: he had a fine singing voice and was a proficient pianist, playing Mozart's Fantasia in D Minor in house competitions and serving as one of the school's organists. He completed his pilot and navigator qualifications in the Air Training Corps (ATC) and gained the rank of sergeant, with responsibility for training a class of 20 junior boys in navigation skills. He was seen by his contemporaries as a confident, skilled, witty debater, participating in regular inter-house debates on such erudite subjects as allowing female serving staff into the school dining room and the abolition of the House of Lords (Brian defended its retention). By his mid-teens he was tall and skinny, already exhibiting the self-conscious poise that characterised his adult years. At six feet three inches tall he was just shorter than Lionel and although he had a handsome face, it was badly scarred with teenage acne. John Collins, who shared a study with him in 1942–43, remembers him as 'a clever boy ... young for his age, and slightly histrionic (in a nice sense!). He would leap about the study in his enthusiasms for this and that ... I think of him sitting at his school desk, waving his pencil in the air searching the ceiling for inspiration, and then writing rapidly. We talked endlessly, about English literature, about Christianity (we were both searching at that time) and we both loved classical music.'[17]

The summer of 1944 was disrupted by the bombing of his parents' house on the night of 23 August by a V1 bomb, often known as a 'doodle bug'. Brian was away at another VPS camp, but his father had a narrow escape, and would have been killed if he had not chosen to move to a different bedroom at the rear of the house a few nights before. His parents moved locally to 53 Crescent West in Hadley Wood (also later damaged by a doodle bug), but the experience convinced them that they might as well be back in central London, and they found a flat in Durward House, only a few hundred yards from their original home in Kensington Court Gardens. Brian's mother wrote frequently to him, sending cakes and oranges when rations allowed. News of Lionel, now posted to the Mediterranean with the Royal Navy, was relayed, along with updates on the domestic help crises, and how the garden was doing.

Brian's senior position at Haileybury was consolidated in September 1944, when he became Head of School. This brought responsibilities additional to those he held as Head of Edmonstone House, for which Tregenza had praised him in his school report. Other teachers were not so happy, noting his weak Greek and Latin translations, and the difficulties he would be likely to have in getting a university scholarship, but he benefited from having R.L. Ashcroft as his Classics tutor, one of the outstanding Haileybury masters at the time. The minutes of the prefects' meetings show Brian as a commanding leader, allocating such unpalatable responsibilities to prefects as bicycle monitoring and organising appointments for haircuts.[18] He made light work of reforming school rules, where boys were permitted to walk, punishments for being late into prep, and so on. At the January 1945 prefects' meeting he proposed to 'try and abolish the two words – the President [Brian] refused to utter them – which were considered not fit for innocent and unsuspecting parents to have bellowed in their ears while quietly partaking of a cup of tea in their son's study....' Bonhote had asked Brian to do a full revision of all the school rules, and he produced this in the spring of 1945, just before he left. Writing later with news of their publication, Bonhote added: 'I am thinking of including a dedication page "To BA-S but for whose continual prodding of the Master these rules could not have been produced. He broke none and enforced all."'[19] Brian also set up a House 'advisory committee' to brief him on various issues, and a card system to record each boy's daily exercise, 'so that none may slip into inactivity.'

Whether these initiatives gained the respect of his contemporaries is not known, but he appears to have successfully maintained discipline during his time as Head of School. All these duties, along with running the school squash club, acting as vice president of the Senior Literary and Debating Society, treasurer of the Edmonstone Reading Society, putting on a production of the *Mikado* and renovating the house library could have left little spare time, but he still managed to produce erudite, if precocious, comments on the development of his fellow pupils:

> There is no doubt that the most difficult time for all boys is that spent in the houserooms. In the DC [dormitory classroom] boys are kept busy with fagging, are still rather awed by the novelty of a public school, and are still satisfied with the freedom given them as opposed to that at their prep schools. When a boy gets into studies, he has developed some interests in the school work or games or both and possibly is taking some part in the running of the school. The community life of the houserooms however is the really difficult time, apart from other reasons because it is the time of puberty when boys are at a stage of mental and physical change. Between the ages of fourteen and sixteen the personality of a boy is decided. At this stage it is easy to go off the rails one way or another. This is the turning point in a boy's career. As the houserooms are segregated from the rest of the house it is

easy to neglect them. Therefore it is all the more important that the houserooms should be closely but unobtrusively watched.[20]

Tregenza made the final entry in his school file: 'excellent H of H [Head of House], departure leaves gap diff. to fill. Devoted so much time to duties that failure in Schol. not surprising. Wish all success in future.'

After Haileybury

Brian left Haileybury in April 1945. His scholarship exam for Clare College Cambridge in March had not gone well enough, and he failed to secure a place for the forthcoming academic year. As an alternative plan, he was accepted into the Royal Air Force (RAF) to do his National Service. However, owing to problems with recruitment, he was told that his expected April call-up had been delayed by at least six months. He returned to live with his parents in their Durward House flat in Kensington, occasionally inviting Haileyburian friends to stay to relieve the boredom. His father – the General – now 74, had a comfortable daily routine of going to his club or matinee films, returning for dinner, which was always served at 7.30pm prompt. When John Collins had visited their home in Hadley Wood in 1942 he and Brian were delayed in getting from the station, and arrived just after 8.00pm: 'As we crept into the hall, the dining room door opened and a tall figure emerged – bristly iron grey hair, a deep red face – it was General Abel-Smith. He looked us up and down, and said in a splendidly resonant growl "Bri-i-i-an you are in disgrace". He then turned around, went back into the dining room and closed the door. The next moment Mrs Abel-Smith descended upon us. She hugged us both – said it didn't matter in the least, and whisked us away to have supper – but not in the dining room! The next morning she sang to us and danced about the drawing room.'[21]

Correspondence with Lionel, who was now posted on HMS Croome in the Mediterranean, helped to keep up his morale, and diffuse some of the tensions of living permanently with his parents. Lionel sent Brian Russian cigarettes, with enquiries as to whether their mother was 'still under the spell of theosophy, fatalism and religion'.[22] Brian also made his first appearance at the annual Smith family luncheon, held each summer at the Fishmongers Hall in the City of London. These were all-male affairs, steeped in traditions. 'Did you smoke a cigar?' Lionel enquired of him. 'I was frightened when I went.' Through the brothers' correspondence their emerging political tendencies are evident. Lionel ribbed Brian: 'So you are a bloody socialist. I am a Tory…. If we had socialism you couldn't go to Hurlingham; you'd be sorting sewage.'[23]

VE (Victory in Europe) Day – 8 May 1945 – witnessed some of the biggest, most exuberant crowds that London has ever seen. Churchill made several speeches, and appeared on the balcony of Buckingham Palace alongside the King and Queen and the young princesses Elizabeth and Margaret. Brian provided a first-hand account to Lionel, who was on Navy duty in Tunisia, in what must surely be one of the most eloquent VE Day histories. As he sat on a number nine bus travelling towards Piccadilly Circus in the late afternoon of 7 May he saw shopkeepers beginning to unfurl flags. Getting off, he walked among the gathering crowds and bunting down Whitehall to Parliament Square. On hearing that Churchill had been prevented by Stalin from making the official announcement that evening, Brian took the Underground home to the Kensington flat to enjoy a celebration dinner given by a neighbour. The following day he was back at Westminster with two friends in a vast crowd to hear Churchill's broadcast. In a human point-to-point, they raced up the Mall, arriving outside the Palace to join in the chants of 'We want Georg-y' and 'We want Lizzie', led on by an Australian soldier who had climbed up the palace gates. Brian saw the royal family on their third balcony appearance at 5.30pm.

After a brief rest back at the flat, they set out again for Buckingham Palace at 8.30pm and pushed their way through up to the gates: 'once again the patriotism of the crowd was manifested in its silence. So we heard Big Ben and the King's speech and then the National Anthem while all were still. As the National Anthem ended the hundred thousand cheered loudly.' Afterwards they walked through the park, 'across the few remaining squares of grass – like stepping stones over the sea of sprawling, necking, kissing, cuddling, humanity' and into Westminster Abbey, where a service was beginning at 10.00pm. Afterwards they were in time to see 'Winny' yet again, on the balcony of the Ministry of Health building in Whitehall. The Guards band struck up *Land of Hope and Glory* before he spoke, and ended by playing *For He's a Jolly Good Fellow*, the searchlights picking out the tears in his eyes. Brian asked Lionel to:

> … imagine an area bounded by Westminster Abbey, Charing Cross Road, the river on one side Hyde Park Corner and Victoria on the other just one mass of merrymaking people so tightly packed that no one can move in anything other than single file and that only very slowly. Imagine here and there groups of people dancing round bonfires, imagine rockets continually flying into the air,

imagine occasional flashes and explosions as thunderflashes were let off in the streets. And more important of all imagine every building of note floodlit and all the searchlights mounted so as to pour lights over the streets moving to and fro among the crowd, now catching a couple kissing, now illuminating a salvation army band. Imagine several million people all either singing or shouting, each pair or groups of pairs a different tune – everything from the modern jazz tunes & last war marching songs to traditional English folk tunes....[24]

The late evening's descent from British respectability was increasingly evident as they walked up to Trafalgar Square, where a 'rather drunken party of soldiers were bathing in the fountain pools in their underpants and nothing else', then on to Piccadilly Circus where a group were taking down the war-time protective boards from around Eros. This newly uncovered vision of love provided Brian with 'one of the most sordid sights I have ever seen, for on top [of the Piccadilly Underground station] a girl was displaying her private parts and inviting all and sundry to look at them. Of course she was very drunk....' Ambulances were beginning to ferry the casualties away from the partying, and the Underground stations were packed with suffocating people trying to get on the last train home. Foot-sore and exhausted, Brian and his friends walked back to the flat in Kensington, finally going to bed at 3.30am after a restorative meal of scrambled eggs and spam.

After the hysteria of VE Day came the shock Labour victory at the general election. Brian had attended rallies by the Labour leadership, and also the meetings held by Harold Laski at the London School of Economics and Political Science (LSE) – another inspirational figure on the political left.[25] After the partial return to post-war normality, Brian needed to find some worthwhile occupation to fill the interval before his RAF call-up, so he offered to help out at the Haileybury Guild Boys Club in Stepney, where he had worked as a volunteer during his last two years at school. Like Attlee before him, Brian was deeply impressed by this exposure to another side of London life, a step nearer abject poverty than the scenes that had already moved him of the relatively poor housing in some parts of Kensington. During the spring and summer of 1945 he worked at the club on an almost full-time basis, cycling there from Kensington through blitz-damaged London. The historian Eric Hobsbawm was also alive to the radicalising potential of this form of transport: 'If physical mobility is an essential condition of freedom, the bicycle has probably been the greatest single device for achieving what Marx called the full realisation of the possibilities of being human invented since Gutenburg ... cyclists travel at the speed of human reactions and are not insulated behind glass from nature's light, air, sound and smells. ...'[26] The club had been re-located in a Territorial Army drill hall on the Mile End Road after a V2 rocket had destroyed the original building in 1944, and Brian assisted a retired Haileybury master, W.F.L. Newcombe. Activities arranged for the boys included table tennis and boxing, and trips were also made to Haileybury to use the school's swimming pool and shooting range.

The Boys Club provided Brian with a reason to maintain contact with Haileybury, but he seems to have wished to continue this anyway, especially with the master, E.F. Bonhote, with whom he regularly corresponded. Brian received an invitation from 'The Boot' in April 1945 who was on holiday at the Osborne Hotel in Torquay to join him there for dinner, and in June he wrote again to Brian to make arrangements for him to visit Haileybury. On these trips Brian used Bonhote as a sounding board for ideas on what he should do next, and on 14 July, after learning that his RAF call-up could still be six months off, Bonhote invited Brian to return to Haileybury in the autumn term to teach Mathematics, to fill in for one of the masters who had not yet returned from military service. Brian declined this offer, but Bonhote continued to look for suitable activities for him. In August 1945 he wrote on Brian's behalf to the chairman of the Air Ministry's Inter-Services Languages Committee to see if Brian could transfer his RAF application to be trained in oriental languages, in the hope that this would generate an earlier call-up. Bonhote's unsubtle references to Brian's Brigadier-General father and Brian's ATC service gained him an interview at the Air Ministry on 10 September, but failed to secure a transfer. Sir Theodore Adams sent Brian a handwritten reply from the Offices of the War Cabinet on 29 September explaining that they had enough recruits from the services without having to call on schools.[27] Brian filled his days instead with Japanese and secretarial lessons, and also learned to drive.

Even if Brian's emotions of the summer of 1945 were those of frustrated adolescent boredom, he could not have failed to notice the sea change in the British mood. This was due not only to the ending of the Second World War, but also to the massive victory for the Labour Party at the general election, which ended Churchill's Coalition government. When Brian's fellow Haileyburian Clement Attlee went to Buckingham Palace on 16 July to ask the King's permission to form a government, it sealed a result that, as Peter Hennessy puts it, 'had startled virtually everybody', although for those who looked carefully, evidence of the turning philosophical and political tide had been there from the summer of 1940.[28] Most of Brian's working life would revolve around the radical output of this new Labour government, a British welfare state that became the yardstick for all subsequent attempts to emulate it across the globe.

2

A wider world: 1946–51

National Service

Austria: Brian's cold war

Cambridge

A political education

Postgraduate

The British Council universities debating tour

This is the greatest advance in our history. There can be no turning back. From now on Beveridge is not the name of a man; it is the name of a way of life, and not only for Britain, but for the whole of the civilised world. (William Beveridge to Harold Wilson, 1942)

After leaving school Brian completed the mandatory National Service including an army posting to Vienna. He returned in 1948 aged 21 and went up to Cambridge to read Economics. This provided him with a perfect environment in which to develop his political ambitions. He was active in the Cambridge Union and the University's Labour Club, and began campaigning for the Labour Party. Hugh Dalton marked him out as a potential future MP. Brian's love of foreign travel began in 1948, and during the long undergraduate vacations he toured Europe and the Middle East, keeping detailed diaries that show his interest in the social and economic issues of the places he visited, including the new state of Israel. In 1951 he decided to register for a PhD at Cambridge, and spent two months of his first postgraduate year on a British Council debating tour to India, Pakistan and Ceylon. It was this exposure to the culture, and especially the poverty, of developing countries that strengthened his socialist convictions and interest in the economics of health and social welfare.

National Service

Finally, after months of kicking about in London, Brian was called up to begin his National Service on 17 October 1945. His plans to enter the RAF came to nothing, and he was enlisted into the General Service Corps within the Territorial Army, with his initial posting to the Nonne Boschen Platoon at the Gujarat Barracks in Colchester, Essex, on 6 December. In January he was transferred to the Oxfordshire and Buckinghamshire Light Infantry and he spent a bleak winter, rising at 6 am to a cold water wash and shave, then instruction in lorry driving. He posted his socks home to Durward House each week for washing, where his mother (or rather, their housekeeper, Mrs Webster) duly obliged and returned them by next post. He filled his spare time making pithy assessments of his fellow recruits and superiors, noting for example: 'Sgt Chapman – 20, Scotch, dark, good looking, tough but not sure of his staff.... Sgt Billings – 22, fair, well built, good footballer, tough, scrounger.... Private Fred Taylor – slow and dumb, warm hearted, jazz music, printing, sentimental on girls.' He compiled profiles for all 26 privates in his platoon, using descriptors such as 'married and unfaithful ... typical cockney ... born gambler ... bit snobbish ... never writes home ... drinks ... oily ... communist ... well-liked... ruddy ... good boxer ... above average intelligence.'[1]

In May he was transferred to Wrotham in Kent, having passed the War Office Selection Board in March for officer training. This proved to be a dismal place with little to stimulate him intellectually. At every opportunity he went up to London, where his social life remained centred on events such as the Grafton Hunt Ball, and taking Susan Hamilton, his childhood friend, to dances at the Hammersmith Palais and the Trocadero. He spent some weekends at the Hamiltons' new home in Watford, where he engaged in fierce after-dinner political debates with Susan's father, or at the Old School House in Rudgwick, Sussex, home of Ivor, Ros and Audrey Cooper. Brian, like his mother, was loved and valued for his *joie de vivre* – his name was always at the top of the list when the Hamiltons planned their parties, as Brian's presence was guaranteed to get them off to a good start. He could be outrageously (but safely) flirty with women, and a witty raconteur with men. His brother Lionel, meanwhile, was posted as the Flag Lieutenant to Vice-Admiral Crutchley VC, the Flag Officer for Gibraltar and the Mediterranean Approaches. Here he assisted with as many social as military events, escorting ashore passing dignitaries returning home from the Far East such as Hugh Fitzroy, Earl of Euston (later Duke of Grafton), who was to marry their cousin, Ann Fortune Smith.

In July 1946 Brian was transferred to Trentham Park in Staffordshire. His expectations were high, for he could imagine nothing worse than Wrotham. The transfer from the train station to the barracks took them past Trentham Hall – reminiscent in scale and style of some of the Smith family country residences – and Brian's hopes were raised for sheets to sleep in, regimental silver to feed from, and batmen to do all the work. At last he had found a military establishment that appreciated his abilities, and he revelled in team-building activities, so redolent of Haileybury. He took on the editorship of *Choin*, the 'C' Company magazine. Not content with the 'conventional form for Company magazines' he determined to re-style it with the ambition 'to make some lasting souvenir of our seventeen weeks here which will bring back pleasant memories of it'. From Brian's pen we thus learn that he had been president of the Entertainment Committee, which (naturally) had arranged some of the best dances and smokers (a mixture of stand-up and sketches) ever held by the Officer Corps Training Unit (OCTU). The smoker sketches were heavily imbued with army stereotypes, and Brian collaborated in producing musical numbers such as the 23rd Psalm as an ode to a car. At the Passing-Out dinner at Trentham on 22 October Brian acted as toast master.[2]

Brian gained his commission as 2nd Lieutenant on 26 October 1946, and joined the 43rd Regiment of Foot of the Oxfordshire and Buckinghamshire Light Infantry. This must have pleased his father, who was increasingly ill, suffering with bouts of asthma and phlebitis. Brian spent his extended leave in November back at the flat, before moving to the Cowley barracks at Oxford in mid-December. The General died on 20 December 1946, at the age of 76. On the first anniversary of his death, Brian wrote a long, somewhat self-indulgent reminiscence to his mother:'I have been thinking of him a lot and of you and of that bleak December day. The only thing I liked George Rach [Commanding Officer of Ox and Bucks] for was the way he broke the news and let me go off so promptly ... sadly gazing at the towers and spires of Oxford ... no memory of the train journey or taxi back ... running up the stairs to find you breathless and shaken – grief beyond tears ... then came the removal ... the next few days were spent in breaking associations – the last pipe, the ring, the clocks, the glasses. Then the funeral arrangements in which we both inwardly disbelieved – submitting only to convention when we knew we must....'[3] The funeral was held at Wendover two days before Christmas. Lionel found it impossible to return from Gibraltar to the UK, and so Brian and his mother were supported by the senior Abel-Smiths. Harold was especially diligent, sending money to make sure that Vivée had enough until the family finances were sorted out, and making regular trips to stay with her at the flat.

Brian returned to the Cowley barracks in Oxford in January 1947 and threw himself into learning Russian (probably because he had advance notice that he would be posted to Austria later in the year, where the Russians were one of the occupying powers). His political tendencies were becoming more apparent, and he engaged in debates with Uncle Harold by letter, the latter admitting that 'On consideration I think a Socialist govt of educated young men similar to yourself would be excellent as you would have regard to upholding the dignity of the Empire, no class hatred, inconsideration for minorities etc as shown by the present Soc. Party.'[4] Harold was writing during one of the bleakest winters of the 20th century, when arctic winds and snow swept down from Scandinavia bringing a bone-freezing chill that lasted for weeks. The Kew Observatory recorded no sunshine at all from 2 to 22 February, and the temperature did not rise above freezing between 11 and 23 February. It was as if the weather empathised with the state of the British psyche – millions unemployed and breakdowns in newly nationalised power supplies forcing the re-introduction of restrictions on using electricity and coal for domestic heating and cooking. The RAF dropped food supplies to cut-off rural areas, and even Big Ben's mechanisms froze solid, removing the distant comfort of the 'Nine O'Clock News' 'bongs' on the BBC's Home Service.[5]

When Lionel returned from Gibraltar in February 1947 he made appointments to see the family lawyer and agent to clarify his financial position.[6] He had inherited the Wendover estate on the death of his father, but this brought with it a significant Death Duty liability. Although only 22 (two years older than Brian), he was acutely aware of the responsibilities that came with this new status. He had already had some difficult correspondence with Brian, prompting a letter before he returned: 'Dear brother, put thine arsenic away; I long to see you but not through mists of hate and jealousy. Yours sorry Lionel.'[7] Later, after he had made his first visit to Wendover as the new Lord of the Manor (an honorary title that he had also inherited, but which came with some traditional duties), he wrote to Brian: 'I feel as proud as a Spaniard at writing to you from my ancestral seat (would that the Reform Act of 1832 had not been passed and I should be able to return two members for my pocket borough – Tories of course, not blithering idiots).'[8]

Their mother Vivée had decided she could raise some extra income by sub-letting rooms in the Durward House flat – 'sharing', as the family delicately put it – for seven guineas per week. The first 'sharers' only stayed a short time, but it proved a successful arrangement, and not too intrusive as the flat was large enough to provide separate sitting rooms and bathroom facilities. This was one immediate way of easing the family's financial affairs. Vivée had to live on the interest from her late husband's personal estate, now invested in a trust fund, and she estimated that she would have about £450 a year. She was 49 years old. Once the immediate post-funeral sorting out was done she went to Derry for an extended stay with her sister Cherrie. Her accent now reflected her long absence from her homeland: 'my voice is not enjoyed here in the shops or buses – everyone looks round.'[9] When she returned to London in July she slowly and with some difficulty began to build a new life, based on her love of music and theatre.

In May 1947 Brian took his first foreign holiday in Paris with one of his fellow cadets in the Oxfordshire and Buckinghamshire Light Infantry. They checked in with Air France in central London and were then taken by bus to Northolt to board the 26-seater plane for the short flight across the channel. Brian described his first flight in great detail in a letter to his mother – the attitude of the hostesses, lounges with coffee and newspapers, and the cardboard box distributed during the flight which contained '12 different items each wrapped in cellophane paper ranging from a bar of chocolate to a bully beef and cucumber sandwich'. This was the beginning of his life-long love affair with international travel.

How his mother must have felt, still in the depths of post-war austerity and rationing, reading a 17-page letter on the delights of Paris, is unrecorded.[10] Brian recounted how he and his friend made their base at the British Officers Club 'in a lavish Park Lane mansion standing in its own grounds opposite the British Embassy'. Here they dined, paying £3 for a four-course lunch or a five-course dinner, 'and by paying a little extra have in addition omelettes, ham, steak, asparagus, etc which I confess we often did – gourmets!' They spent their days seeing sights such as the Louvre and Versailles 'violently' and the evenings at the club, where there was dancing in the ballroom. He shopped for cosmetics for his mother and bought 'good pre-war elastic braces' for Lionel and himself, marvelling that 'on entering French shops just one's looks & clothes would bring an assistant up to one saying with a Mayfair accent "and what can I show you?"'.

On his return Brian resumed training the cadets at Cowley barracks, and also undertook some further training of his own, attending a weekend residential course at Ashridge, a 'vast' country house in Hertfordshire, acquired by the Bonar Law Trust in 1921. It had been a 'College of Citizenship' since 1929, primarily intended to help the

Conservative Party strengthen its intellectual forces against the Fabian Society. Brian participated in lectures and group discussions, spending the evenings socialising with its Director Lord Paget and his wife: 'a charming though gushing hostess in spite of her empty head'. Brian seemed more impressed by the surroundings and the social networking than the intellectual programme, but he wrote to his mother that he hoped to go again soon. He also discussed his political ambitions with Richard Baker, a friend from Haileybury with whom he regularly corresponded. Baker commented: 'If you do go into politics I shall be satisfied with nothing less than Prime Minister for you – and I don't expect you will either!'[11]

Yet while Brian was camping with the Ox and Bucks battalion at Lepe in Hampshire in the glorious summer of 1947, politicians were in an unenviable position, engaged daily in 'behind the scenes' bargaining with the Americans to provide the financial bailout that Britain so urgently needed. Despite the successful delivery of 'Marshall Aid' (the European Recovery Programme), Attlee was finally forced to agree to suspend sterling's convertibility on 20 August to prevent more dollars haemorrhaging from Britain's meagre reserves. It was a declaration of huge symbolism, a message to the world that Britain could no longer maintain the façade of economic superpower. For the Chancellor Hugh Dalton it was a very personal defeat. He retreated to the home of his friend Nicholas Davenport: 'I had noticed that Hugh was emotionally exhausted. After a few drinks he was holding my wife's hand and tears were running down his face.'[12]

Austria: Brian's cold war

In October 1947 Brian was promoted to Lieutenant and posted as aide-de-camp (ADC) to General John Winterton in Vienna, where he was immediately appointed Temporary Captain.[13] Winterton was a powerful individual as head of the British occupying forces, which together with the French, Americans and Russians had divided Austria into four zones at the end of the war. Vienna was located within the Russian zone, but was home to representatives from all the four powers, a geographical hotspot in the increasingly icy relations that preceded the 'Cold War'. This was a time of irrational fears based on scanty intelligence and played out with the very recent memory of European disintegration. Within eight months of Brian's arrival in Vienna, Prague would witness Soviet aggression and Berlin would require an 'airlift' to survive its isolation.

Vienna had lost nearly 20 per cent of its housing during the war, and conditions were little improved, with severe rationing and frequent currency crises.[14] A black market flourished, as recounted in Graham Greene's novel (and later film), *The Third Man*. The British Commander-in-Chief, General Alexander Galloway, and the British Foreign Minister, Sir Henry Mack, spent their days in futile negotiations to produce an agreement to acknowledge the new Austrian government, which had to have all its decisions ratified by the Allied Council. Karl Renner, the new communist Chancellor of Austria, likened the situation to 'four elephants in a boat'.[15] Brian joined a small team supporting Winterton, and was given an impressive office in the Tapestry Room of the Schönbrunn Palace, whose state rooms had hosted Mozart, Napoleon and Marie Antoinette. After the rugged training and barrack life, this was the ideal type of military duty for him: a large amount of his time was taken up with organising and attending parties, and looking after Mrs Winterton. His English public school education and family background made it a relatively easy job, given his intuitive appreciation of social etiquette and the nuances of such matters as the seating order at formal dinners.

Brian wrote frequently to his mother, Lionel, Uncle Harold and Aunt Maud with news of his duties and pleasures: 'I have access to all the Top Secret Foreign Office and War Office information.... The General seems quite foreboding until one knows him. Cols and Brigs describe our office where they wait to go before the great man as a dentist's waiting room & they come in with their tails between their legs.'[16] The atmosphere in the Officers' Mess was convivial: 'besides Paul [Hyde-Thomson] and myself there are four others. Two of them very huntin shootin & fishin – these are Lord [David] Ogilvy (from the Earl of Airlie) age 21 who is ADC to the C in C, & John Bell Irving MA to Sir Henry Mack the British Minister. The other two are Major Charles Boycott – military and dull, and Miss Mary Fisher – 35 & panel PA to the C in C....We are planning to give a party in the mess. Our villa is very very Viennese & you would think it extraordinarily ugly and depressing ... panelled walls, gilt plaster angels, vast glass chandeliers. The furniture is clad with baroque gilt and red inlay and embossment.... Last Friday I went and had dinner at the Hotel De France – a dozen oysters, jugged hare, French gateau and champagne.... We went on to a party given by some stray Austrian persons in their private palace. There were a lot of charming American people there. They are so friendly.' Lionel replied approvingly: 'the families you associate with are good, particularly, the Thurn und Taxis.' Back at home Lionel was proud to point out to his friends while watching the wedding of Princess Elizabeth on 20 November 1947 that his 'cousin Henry's breastplate sparkles finely next to the King's carriage in the procession to the Abbey'.[17]

Vivée sent out a suit and sheepskin coat for Brian for the impending winter, using up her clothing coupons. By return he acknowledged her poor quality of life in London:'I can imagine you staggering about trying to get food. And here am I with good food & waiters on hand and foot, cars, parties and hundreds of contemporary friends. It should be the other way round. I should marry you and bring you out here as my family. All love Brian. PS please send this on to Lionel.' When not at Oxford, Lionel lived at the flat with Vivée, using his letters to Brian gently to vent his frustration about the claustrophobia of life at home after his previous freedom: 'She can never be unorthodox. When she thinks she is being "crazy" it is all formal. It is announced to us and we are told we are enjoying being "mad". It seems all planned. No day can drift along without the incessant "Oo-ah" "Luncheon" "Oo-ah" "Te-ah". You have always said it before, and now I agree that it is a little nerve-wracking.... Don't think that I am dissatisfied at home. I am not, but one has to concentrate on keeping the peace.'[18]

Vivée's widow's income was small, and she continued to let out rooms in the Durward House flat, which also provided some company when Lionel was away. Maybe Brian thought it would ease his mother's loneliness to hear that he at least was enjoying life, 'dancing till 4 in the morning beneath liquid-looking chandeliers to my favourite waltzes'. He went to a Beethoven concert conducted by Furtwangler, who was slowly being rehabilitated after his Nazi-sympathising war years. Outside the concert hall there were demonstrations, while inside Furtwangler 'took 10 calls – a thing unknown in London'. Vivée sent ski boots for his Christmas present, in preparation for his first lessons. Brian had hoped to spend his Christmas leave in Prague with Paul Hyde-Thomson, but their plans collapsed as they couldn't convince General Winterton that they could get their currency legally. Instead they went to Kitzbühel, after securing travel permits from their French ADC counterparts, and taking their rations of tinned stew to supplement any meals they might be able to get in restaurants. It turned out to be a more luxurious trip than they expected, as they got rooms at the Grand Hotel, which they used as a base for skiing lessons. After Christmas they travelled to Salzburg in the American zone. They went to a performance of *La Traviata* at the opera house and took a trip over the border into Germany to visit Berchesgaden and Hitler's eyrie at Oversalzburg, where they were shown round by one of his former bodyguards. With their prudent use of various exchange rates and vouchers, they had managed to have a good five-day holiday for only £5.

On 4 March 1948, in a letter to his mother to let her know of his safe return to Vienna after a period of leave with her in London, Brian expressed his concern for her well-being: 'you have been much in my thoughts. I am worried that you have not enough friends to play with. I quite see that it must be hard for you to start making friends now, but I hate to think of you working at Durward and being lonely or bored with the monotony.'[19] Later that month Brian wrote to her again, expressing relief that she had sought medical help, was feeling better, and had resumed her singing.

Although Vivée did have friends close by, her life had revolved around her husband, fitting in with his routines and habits. The wider Abel-Smith family provided a source of support and comfort for her and the boys after his death. Maud and Harold in particular were very fond of Brian and Lionel. They exchanged letters (often weekly), and sent money for birthdays and Christmas. Harold offered to pay for Brian's university education – an offer Brian refused as he felt that his cousins were in more need of the money. Vivée, Brian and Lionel made regular trips to visit Harold and Maud in Milford-on-Sea, where they moved into a hotel when they could no longer care for themselves in Harold's house. Harold also often stayed with Vivée at the flat to indulge his love of classical music and London life.

Brian's eagerness to keep in touch with his mother and Lionel generated letters with vivid descriptions of his trips. The Christmas trip to Kitzbühel had produced an eight-page typed account that was duplicated for Harold and Maud's entertainment. At Easter 1948 he skied in the Austrian mountains above Klagenfurt, experiencing 'four blissful days ... the weather was phenomenal – deep, really deep blue sky from horizon to horizon & bright shining snow & fir trees on the ground ... the air was exhilaratingly fresh & the sun radiating a pleasant moist heat rich in ultra-violet ray & vitamin D – incredibly healthy for one.... I have come back with a healthier tan on my face than ever before and not a blemish', a reference to his problems with acne. He also reported that he was learning German frantically: 'I have just finished Victor Hugo's "German in 3 Months" in 3 weeks.' Such travel around Austria into the zones controlled by other powers was only possible with written permission. There were ongoing tensions with the Russians in particular, who demanded that the British show their identity papers on entering and leaving Vienna. General Winterton refused to agree to this and in April 1948 there was a deadlock until the Russians gave in. Brian meanwhile wrote home to his 'Dear Mama' with news of yet another holiday, this time to escort the General's son on a week-long skiing trip, visiting precipitous, Disney-inspiring Austrian castles to call on princes and princesses (some with Nazi pasts), and enjoying the hospitality of the zone commanders. By May Brian was writing with tales of weeks spent playing tennis and swimming in the General's pool in Vienna, followed by weekends at the General's country residence in the British zone where they fished for trout. He later confessed that 'I do not really enjoy this fishing business. It is not the sport for me. However, I would rather do it than not do it if you see what I mean.' In June he was 'extra busy' planning a party for 350, including the whole of the Hallé orchestra, John Barbirolli and William Walton. In one week alone he attended or gave 10 parties between Monday and Friday.

The end of Brian's Vienna tour was scheduled for the beginning of August 1948, but before that he planned to take his summer holiday in Italy. When not fully occupied running errands for the General, Brian indulged in some entrepreneurial activities. He bought material to go with lining fabric that he had brought from home, and arranged to get an Austrian tailor to make up a sports jacket for a third of what a London tailor would have charged. He also bought a Swiss watch for £6 10s which 'I hope to sell in Italy or London for a profit – the Smith business instinct'. He took lessons in pastry making with a Viennese lady cook. In July Lionel visited Brian in Vienna, enjoying the relative luxury of life in the ADCs' villa where they were waited on by batmen. They went to the opera, walked by the Danube, visited all the usual tourist sites, and partied. Lionel left for Rome, and Brian travelled down a few days later through Trieste, Venice and Florence before meeting up with his brother in Positano on the Amalfi coast. Brian then returned to Vienna on 6 August, before travelling home to London on the 12th. He was discharged from the Army with the honorary rank of captain.[20]

Cambridge

> People from the big cities who go to Cambridge realise what it
> is like to live in the country. Each Cambridge winter day began
> with the river smell, mixed with the scent of damp leaves and,
> often as not, bonfire smoke, hanging in the tall bedrooms, windows
> ritually open. Then a quick run outside to the lavatory.... The
> atmosphere of a broken-down country house was made more
> powerful by the survival of college servants with East Anglian
> accents; old women who made the bed and shifted the dirt

around a bit; mice; and extraordinarily bad food – it was rationed for fourteen years – served in surroundings of some grandeur by waiters, amateur and elderly, but still clearly servants.[21]

Brian had been unsuccessful in obtaining an open university scholarship in the spring of 1945, partly because of his devotion to his Head of School duties at Haileybury. Bonhote judged him to have had a narrow miss, and to have been 'somewhat near scholarship standard'.[22] Brian pursued Henry Thirkhill, Master of Clare College, through regular letters asking if there was likely to be space for him. He was eventually called for interview on 24 August, and secured a place to begin in October 1948, reading Economics. Thirkhill had a reputation for selecting men for Clare whom he thought would be rather nice to have around, but if they were academically gifted or showed sporting prowess, so much the better. Clare was head of the river at that time, and supplied large numbers of Blues for various sports, but was also seen as a reasonably intellectual establishment.[23] Brian's financial concerns were eased by the award of a further education grant (state scholarship) of £262 per annum, and he arrived in Cambridge on 6 October, along with a bicycle on indefinite loan from Uncle Harold. He took great interest in Brian's affairs: 'So glad your financial arrangements worked out without undue anxiety…. You have been very clever scheming out all your needs. I am so glad you turned down the idea of the Stock Exchange.'[24]

The first few weeks at university are usually unsettling times for new undergraduates; for many it is the first time they have been away from home and they are forced rapidly to find their niche among strangers. Brian had none of these troubles, having been on the move and socially accomplished for the past three years with the army, and before that schooled in the art of conviviality at Haileybury. He was not alone – many of the freshmen in October 1948 were coming to Cambridge from military service – men (and a few women) in their early to mid-twenties, who had experience of life after school. There were some old faces: John Collins was also at Clare, Richard Baker had been at Jesus for a year already. Those Haileyburians who were not immediately recognisable by face could be identified by the school tie – although Richard Baker discovered an imposter who had purchased one in a second-hand shop.

In his first fortnight Brian had an interview with his college tutor, the maritime historian John Parry (1914–82), who had arrived at Clare as a tutor and university lecturer in History in 1945. He left in 1949 after Brian's first year to take up a chair in Modern History at the new University College of the West Indies. Brian attended introductory lectures by Kenneth Berrill (economic history), Brian Reddaway (statistics), Maurice Dobb (social problems) and Claude Guillebaud (economic statistics). Kenneth Berrill (1920–2009) had been appointed as a lecturer in 1949, and combined teaching at Cambridge with a range of external consultancies, especially for The World Bank and the Organisation for Economic Co-operation and Development (OECD). He later became Chief Economic Adviser to the Treasury. Brian Reddaway (1913–2002) had published his magnum opus *Measurements of Production Movement* in 1948. He became the Director of the Department of Applied Economics in 1955 and Professor of Political Economy in 1969. His reputation was as a practical economist, who later worked extensively in developing countries. Maurice Dobb (1900–76) was one of Cambridge's rare communist academics, and the founder of Marxian economics in Britain. Claude Guillebaud (1890–1971) was a nephew of the economist Alfred Marshall, and Brian was to work for him later on the Guillebaud inquiry into the costs of the NHS, appointed in April 1953.

Jack Ashley was a year ahead of Brian, but also reading Economics, and recalled another three of the academics who taught them and their personalities: Denis Robertson (1890–1963), 'sardonic and witty', was known for his work with Keynes in the 1930s. Joan Robinson (1903–83), 'authoritative and clear' according to Ashley, had been appointed Assistant Lecturer in Economics at Cambridge in 1934 and worked with Keynes on his General Theory. She published *Economics of Imperfect Competition* in 1933. Her major work was *The Accumulation of Capital*, published in 1956. She spent considerable time researching Marxian economics, especially in socialist countries such as China and the former Soviet Union. Stanley Dennison (1912–92) was considered by Ashley to be 'intellectual and informative'. He had been appointed Lecturer in Economics in 1945 and was valued by the students for his deep practical knowledge of the structure of industry, gained on secondment to the government during the Second World War. As an anti-Keynesian, he found Cambridge intellectual life difficult.[25]

John Vaizey was less enthralled with the quality of the teaching at Cambridge: 'My chosen subject was Economics. It was taught, not by some magical don, but by a carpet-bagger who came down once a week from London, while the lectures were dull, with no revelation of the mysteries I had longed to penetrate.' He was more impressed by Joan Robinson: 'in battle-dress dyed navy blue, brilliant and ferocious'.[26] Eric Hobsbawm gives a don's impression of Cambridge's Economics

Tripos in the early 1950s, when he marked economic history papers: 'it was even more difficult *not* to get a degree at *all* … we decided, not entirely with tongue in cheek, that anyone who knew the difference between production and consumption should pass the line'.[27]

Brian quickly established a group of squash partners and went to the usual round of freshmen's tea invitations (including one for the Conservative Society). One of the flyers sent to him in his college rooms (L4 Memorial) was from the University Labour Club, and headed *The Intelligent Freshman's Guide to Political Cambridge*. After denigrating the other political clubs, including the Socialist Club, it listed the expected speakers for the term, including Kingsley Martin, Philip Noel-Baker, Douglas Jay and Bessie Braddock. The Prime Minister, Attlee, had also promised to attend the annual dinner on 12 November. The very real sense of tangibility with politics through such visiting speakers dazzled undergraduates such as Vaizey and Brian: 'At Cambridge, you could not only see them close to, but by a kind of mass propulsion, you could sit with them in the bar after the meeting…. The process from total anonymity to dining with a Cabinet minister took fifteen weeks.'[28] Subjects for discussion included the NHS, then just 12 weeks old, the Berlin airlift and the escalating Israeli–Palestinian conflict. In addition to the regular Friday night and Sunday afternoon talks, the Labour Club also met on Sunday evenings in members' rooms. Jack Ashley was Chair when Brian joined, later followed by Edward Greenfield.[29]

The other big attraction for Brian was the Cambridge Union. This private members' club mimicked London establishments such as the Athenaeum and Carlton, and of course, the House of Commons. Its premises centred on the debating chamber, supported by a library, dining room and other facilities. For a relatively modest annual subscription gentlemen members indulged in a lifestyle to which they hoped to become accustomed, able to summon uniformed staff at the ring of a bell. The main attraction of the Union was the weekly debate, held on Tuesday evenings at 8.15pm prompt. Formal motions for debates covered a wide range of topics, from the trivial and political to the philosophical; all enabled the speakers to demonstrate their rhetorical powers and intellectual nimbleness, knowing that this would undoubtedly assist their post-Cambridge careers.

Brian settled into a routine of lectures, essays and supervisions, with games of squash several times a week, and attending the Union on Tuesday evenings for the debates, which were opened by the white-tied, tail-coated president. Morning coffee at one of the town's coffee shops (often at the Whim in Trinity Street), and afternoon tea in rooms with friends were almost daily rituals.[30] As they got to know one another the friendship and rivalries deepened and political persuasions became more explicit. Although the Whim coffee mornings were 'very chummy and very very funny', he was in the minority as a Labour Club member (along with Peter Mansfield and Edward Greenfield). They enjoyed the banter with people like Norman St John Stevas and Hugh Thomas, the latter having the somewhat exhausting reputation of being the wittiest man in Cambridge.[31] Visitors in Brian's first term included Susan Hamilton, whom he entertained for a Saturday afternoon, showing her round the Union and other Cambridge sights.[32] Susan partnered him to several of the big Cambridge social events, and they were photographed together for *The Tatler and Bystander* magazine in November 1951 at a ball at the Dorothy Café.[33] They were good friends, and Susan had hopes that Brian might propose marriage.[34]

Christmas 1948 was spent at Pelsham, a country house hotel, near Rye in Sussex – a solution proposed by Lionel who had concerns about their mother: 'better to be away from Wendover and Bar Trouble'.[35] However, Brian was wracked with toothache, to such an extent that Lionel drove him back to London on Christmas Eve to see his dentist, before going back to the hotel. On Christmas Day his toothache was worse, and he returned to London again to have the tooth removed, returning late to the hotel to resume the ping pong tournament with their fellow guests (and Durward House neighbours), the Fisher family.[36] Early in 1949 Lionel was facing the tricky issue of settling their father's death duties. He calculated that he could sell property at Wendover to raise £17,500, but that would still leave him £10,000 short.[37] Lionel took his Lord of the Manor duties seriously and travelled from Oxford to Wendover whenever he was required.[38] Despite the pressure to raise the Death Duty he managed to continue to send Brian small Wendover 'windfalls' to help with the cost of his forthcoming French holiday and his tailor's bills. In the summer of 1949 Brian received a legacy from Aunt Helen, one of his father's spinster sisters, which also helped to ease his Cambridge costs.

During the long summer vacation of 1949, both Brian and Lionel went abroad: Lionel travelled in Scandinavia, spending time with a Finnish family, where he sunbathed and sailed; Brian embarked on a marathon tour of Europe, the first of many ambitious summer trips. In July he left England with his Cambridge friend Tony Bambridge, driving Lionel's car 'Lady Mildred'. Their three-month route took them from the Netherlands down to southern Europe, passing through Geneva, Wengen (where they met up briefly with Susan Hamilton) and into Italy. They re-visited some of the places Brian had seen the previous summer and got as far south as Positano, before retracing their tracks up to France, and along the Mediterranean coast. In Monte Carlo they spent an hour in the casino without laying a bet, watching elderly Americans losing their money. The journey across the south of France was plagued by punctures, but they managed to visit Avignon and Carcassonne, before heading to Biarritz on the west coast. From here they took a bus into Spain to see a bullfight in San Sebastian, where Brian saw General Franco with his family in the Royal Box. Lady Mildred's mileometer now recorded nearly 3,500 miles from leaving London. They were bearded, dirty and running out of money. Brian was forced to sell his gold cufflinks, but they found enough cash to buy some Courvoisier to take back to Cambridge.

Brian had spent his first year at Cambridge in rooms in college, but for his second and third years he went into digs at 'Braeside', a college-owned house on the Chesterton Road, with Jimmy Davis, Simon Everard and Geoff Weston. Like Brian, they had done their military service before going up to Cambridge. Weston had had a particularly eventful service, having been on HMS Amethyst when it was trapped during the Chinese civil war on the Yangtze River, and helping to plan its daring escape. Their housekeeper, Mrs Laurie, frequently reminded them that she had had far more interesting student lodgers in previous years, including Lord Burghley, who had won the gold medal in the 400m hurdles at the 1929 Olympics. Davis, at least, was impressed by sharing digs with an Abel-Smith – the name was widely known since the Queen's niece Lady Mary Cambridge had recently married Henry Abel-Smith. To his housemates Brian appeared to cultivate a dilettante façade – breezing through his academic work and gaining a reputation for his brittle humour. He stood out from the crowd at social events in his white tie evening dress against the more conventional dinner jackets. He was seen as good fun, but on his own terms – not part of the established drinking groups such as that at the renowned Eagle pub – clearly at home in the political hothouse of the Union.[39]

Lionel visited Brian in Cambridge early in the autumn term to collect 'Lady Mildred'. Having left Oxford in the summer, he had joined Lincoln's Inn. As in the previous year, Brian, Lionel and Vivée went to the hotel at Pelsham for Christmas. By January 1950 Brian was beginning to consider his options after graduation. He was interested in the possibility of staying up another year, or going to Harvard in the US to continue his studies there. A more immediate concern was where to go for a spring break. He and Lionel, now settled in his legal life, attending court and awaiting his first brief, decided to go to Paris for five days in April.

One of the fixed points of Brian's Cambridge life was the Union, and his first big scheduled participation in a debate happened on 2 May. Speaking first in favour of the motion 'This House prefers Madame du Barry to Mrs Pankhurst', his debut was an outstanding success. The *Cambridge Review* reported that:

> The theatrical Mr Abel-Smith rose to make his first paper speech confidently in a red bow tie and matching cummerbund, which latter was dramatically revealed late in his speech and turned out to the surprise of the House, to be a Debating Point. He alternated two tones of voice. One was of soft, star-gazing, romanticism, of hushed intensity, as when he whispered, "Madame du Barry was a woman of exquisite beauty", "she loved to oblige", or "she was a woman". On these occasions Mr Abel-Smith appeared as a rather polished and desiccated swain adoring his nymph with soulful eyes. His other tone of voice was more harsh, grating and scornful and was chiefly reserved for Mrs Pankhurst.[40]

His performances were not restricted to the Cambridge Union debating chamber and later in May he took part in a televised debate from Alexandra Palace.

In early July 1950 Brian joined fellow members of the Cambridge University Labour Club, including Greville Janner, Ted Greenfield and Jim Storey, in the Clarion election campaign. They were seconded to the Spelthorne constituency, centred on Staines in Surrey, which had experienced one of the closest votes in the February general election, at which Labour had secured a narrow win. The Labour candidate in Spelthorne, however, had not been so fortunate, and lost the seat to the Conservatives. The junior Labour Party Clarion Groups were a response to this defeat, and their work involved a week of doorstep campaigning. They canvassed over 3,000 homes, mainly in the 'posher' bits near the river, as the local Labour Party thought that their public and grammar school demeanour might be more appealing. Greenfield remembers leaving one block of flats when a woman leaned out of a top floor window and shouted down 'you are traitors to your class!' Laughing, they ran off, pleased to have riled, if not converted, this voter.[41] They also participated in a public meeting, at which Brian made a speech, denouncing the Conservatives as 'dogs' whose bark was worse than their bite, and urging the audience to join the Labour League of Youth.[42] While campaigning they were billeted with local Labour Party families – usually working class. Brian kept in touch with his host family for many years.

In between revising for his second year exams, Brian found time to plan his summer 1950 trip. After the success of the previous year's tour of southern Europe, he wished to venture further afield. Lionel was not keen on lending him 'Lady Mildred' again, fearing that the car would not stay the course for the punishing itinerary which included Yugoslavia and Greece. So, after the dutiful visit to Uncle Harold and Aunt Maud, and a weekend yachting off the Essex coast, Brian set off for a two-month tour, which Lionel subsequently suggested had exceeded the hedonism of previous summer trips in a novel way: 'Glad you have lost yr virginity in some union consummated in verbiage and Latin luxury.'[43]

Before the summer vacation, Brian had asked Jack Ashley if he could help him to arrange a tour of factories. Ashley had worked in a metal factory, and served as a Widnes Borough councillor and on the Executive of the Chemical Workers Union before going up to Cambridge to read Economics in 1948. He provided details of a number of places where Brian could see the working conditions and also offered to arrange for him to attend a meeting of the TUC in Widnes. The visit, made in September 1950, appears to have stimulated Brian's interest in industrial psychology, as well as strengthening his political convictions. His reputation within Cambridge debating and political circles was also rising. In November Peter Cropper from Gonville & Caius College invited him to do a Politics and Economics Club (PEC) paper between 'the stolid John Vaizey and the mercurial heroine-worshipping Anthony Haynes'.[44]

Brian's small branch of the Abel-Smith family shrank further on 22 January 1951, when Uncle Harold died in his nursing home in Milford-on-Sea. He left Brian his signet ring and the bulk of his estate of £11,404 – equivalent to around £250,000 in current values – a considerable inheritance for the 24-year-old. Brian was now in his final year of undergraduate studies at Cambridge, and Harold would have been pleased to know that he continued to live life to the full. Brian was one of the organisers (along with Jonathan Charkham of Jesus College and Greville Janner of Trinity Hall) of the Peace Breakers Ball, which was held at 'Cellar Dotzki' on 26 February under the auspices of the Labour Foot Beagles. Their mock-officious printed posters stated that 'All loyal Democrats will attend. Ideologically sound music will be provided by Derekzki Tozerovitch and his Revolutionary Rhythm. There will be a Cossack Cabaret ranging from the Volga to the Don. Admission will be free. Entrance visas may be obtained at a price of 6s for men and 4s for women (special concession for the mothers of six children).' Greenfield, Chair of the Labour Club, was deeply embarrassed – not only by the establishment tone of Brian's planned fundraiser, but also by his insistence that Ted appear in drag. He reluctantly agreed (but wore his trousers under the long evening dress).[45] At the Cambridge Footlights smokers Brian collaborated with Geoffrey Beaumont and Alistair Sampson to produce and perform such songs as *A New Technique* (on how to seduce girls) and *We must keep up the Standards of our Dress*. Their output was more often politically inspired: *The Red Flag*, *Two Mayfair Socialists*, and *The Beagle Song* (sung to the tune of *John Peel*), whose humour was at the expense of the Pitt Club, where Cambridge Conservatives socialised.

A political education

Hugh Dalton, an elder statesman of the Labour Party, recognised the potential of 1950s Cambridge as a political recruiting ground. He had graduated in the new discipline of Economics from Kings College Cambridge in 1910, and took great pleasure in regularly returning to 'scout' for emerging talent. As historians and biographers have subsequently made clear, such trips also fulfilled other needs for Dalton. Hennessy portrayed him as a man who 'oscillated between great exuberance and genuine depression (he had a rotten private life and his sexual appetites were decidedly ambivalent). His most consistent features were the conspiratorial gossip in which he constantly indulged and the booming voice in which he conducted it.'[46]

In March 1951 Dalton was introduced to Brian after speaking for democratic socialism at the Union. He recorded in his diary: 'Found one very promising young man – Brian Abel-Smith of Clare – Haileybury, ADC to General Winterton in Vienna, military-cum-City background, but good socialist, intelligent, good presence and personality, doing economics. I saw a good deal of him, and other less outstanding men.'[47] Dalton wrote to Brian afterwards: 'I should like to thank you for the very efficient and pleasant way in which you acted as *my* ADC last weekend! I much enjoyed hearing and seeing something of you and other members of the Labour Club. Please take me at my word when I said that I should like you to keep in touch with me and let me know occasionally how you are getting on.'[48] Brian promptly replied (keeping a copy of his typed letter), and accepted an invitation to supper in London on 16 April (after going to the National Association of Local Government Officers [NALGO] conference), enclosing an essay on higher education which Dalton had requested he prepare, and risking a familiarity that undoubtedly endeared him: 'I hope that you as one of the strongest members of the cabinet are not also worn out by the strain of too many late nights. Or possibly your philosophical "soirees" at Cambridge have proved such a good training that you are not affected by that sort of thing.'[49] Over supper they had a wide-ranging discussion on imperfect competition in British industry, with Dalton drawing up an impromptu reading list and advising on Brian's career choices. Dalton noted afterwards: 'I am glad you now think public finance will give you a better research subject than industrial psychology.' Brian refused the invitation to join him for the annual Durham Miners' Gala, and Dalton jested 'your political education will be very incomplete until you have seen this particular show'.[50]

The following month, in May 1951, Brian hosted another political guest at Cambridge: this time Donald Chapman, the young Labour MP for Birmingham and General Secretary of the Fabian Society. Chapman was pleased to have made contact with members of the Cambridge Labour Club, especially those who came from London and 'who might help with aspects of our work'.[51] As Geoffrey Howe, a Cambridge contemporary and friend of Brian's has noted, this was 'a time when inter-university politics were starting to come to life.' Howe had converted from liberalism to conservatism during his second year at Trinity Hall and joined the Cambridge Tory 'mafia'. A number went on to have Westminster careers, including Denzil Freeth, Douglas Hurd, Patrick Jenkin and Norman St John Stevas.[52]

Having devoted considerable time and energy to the Cambridge Union since his arrival at Cambridge in October 1948, Brian thought he stood a good chance at being elected as its secretary – a prestigious post. The Union was running into financial difficulties in late 1950, and Brian was the driving force behind a review of all its income and expenditure. He proposed a number of novel fund-raising solutions, including installing a dance floor for weekly dances, admitting females as full members, having a late bar and other new social events. To reduce expenditure he proposed cutting subscriptions for periodicals, charging for gallery tickets for the debates, and making committee members pay for their own beer and cigarettes which were consumed in the president's room after debates. He manipulated the Dance and the Economics Sub-committees into successfully proposing other reforms, including raising the membership fee to 25 shillings per term.[53]

As he was the senior committee member of the Standing Committee in the Lent term of 1951, he was 'next in line for promotion', so to speak. However, because Jack Ashley vacated the presidency early to take part in a debating tour to the US, there was an unexpected re-shuffle, and the presidency went to Gautam Mathur, with Donald

Macmillan remaining as vice president, and Greville Janner as secretary. In the next round of elections in June, to determine the officers for the Michaelmas term, Brian lost the secretaryship to Douglas Hurd. Hurd wrote afterwards 'You must stay and fight another day.… I do feel ashamed of having robbed you of a reward which you have done so much more than I to deserve. Which is pompous but very much meant.'[54] Brian had lost by one vote, memorialised by the subsequent rhyme that did the rounds of the Union and colleges:

> This is the tale of Abel–Smith
> Beloved by all his kin and kith
> Who forgot to speak a friendly word
> And lost his seat to Douglas Hurd.

Percy Cradock, who had been president of the Union in 1950 (later to become British Ambassador to China), suggests that Brian had snubbed someone at a party immediately before the election, and that person had then failed to vote for him.[55]

Dalton also sent his condolences on missing the secretary-ship of the Cambridge Union, but with congratulations on his 2:1 degree 'and that qualifies you to be Chancellor of the Exchequer thirty-five years hence. If you haven't already started for Ankara ring me up and come & have a meal!'[56] But Brian was already on his way, keen to move on, and possibly also to forget that there were only two firsts in Economics that year: Potts of Emmanuel and Vaizey of Queens. In late June 1951 he was in Venice with friends, from where they travelled by jeep down to Positano, then to the Dalmatian coast before moving on to Beirut and Haifa in August, keen to see for themselves how this region of the Middle East was faring without British imperialism.

Postgraduate

In May 1951 Brian had begun the process of registering to stay up at Cambridge as a research student, to study public finance in the Economics Faculty. (He had also given serious thought to applying to the Harvard Graduate School of Business Administration, now having the necessary finance from Uncle Harold's estate.) Contrary to the usual postgraduate registration for a named degree, Brian chose to apply for one year in the first instance.[57] Joan Robinson wrote to the Board of Research Studies in support of his application: 'I have been taking Abel-Smith at Clare this term in Mr Reddaway's absence. He is an excellent man + very well qualified to profit by another year here. I know Mr Reddaway had a good opinion of him and would have said the same.'[58] Michael Stoker, Brian's tutor at Clare, also wrote in support, adding a further explanation for his unconventional application: 'it's mainly because of his chance of Presidency of the Union. He admits this.'[59] Brian was duly accepted as a research student for October 1951 under the supervision of Joan Robinson.

Joan Robinson was a key member of the community of 20th-century academic economists, engaging in some of the most intellectually stimulating debates of the inter-war period. She was John Maynard Keynes' primary discussant during his transition from writing *A Treatise on Money* in 1930 to *The General Theory* of 1936.[60] Her academic interest in economics was derived from an objection to inequalities in income and wealth and the increasingly visible social injustice of poverty in Britain. Her biographer Geoffrey Harcourt suggests that 'more than any other economist of the twentieth century [she] became a model for progressive radicals, fearlessly following arguments to conclusions no matter how incompatible they proved to be'.[61]

By the time that Brian encountered Robinson as one of his undergraduate tutors at Cambridge (where she had been promoted from lecturer to reader in 1949), she had already acquired a wide range of contacts outside the academic world. She had worked in the early 1930s for the New Fabian Research Bureau, where her recognition that the economy was increasingly being influenced by monopolistic industrial practices informed her study, *The Economics of Imperfect Competition* published in 1933. Her research assisted the development of the Labour Party's focus on two broad dimensions of the economy: its allocative efficiency and its aggregative performance. Along with other socialists within the Labour Party, such as her husband Austin Robinson, Hugh Dalton and James Meade, she contributed to a critique of capitalism that in the post-war period really opened up the attack on weaknesses of the market structure and the associated problems with demand and employment.[62] Although she was not a Marxist, she appreciated the usefulness of some Marxian theories, which had been adopted by the Fabians in their promotion of state control for key sectors such as fuel, finance, foreign trade and travel. She saw that nationalisation of these areas would assist with reducing inequalities and would also address the problem of insufficient investment demand. Harcourt and others have tempered this vision of Robinson as a 'rebel with a cause' with the recognition that she was at times an uncritical, idealistic champion of Soviet planning. Brian would have seen her as one of the more vivacious and inspiring teachers, bringing her experiences of China and other overseas economies direct to the lecture theatre and tutorial room. He would have been aware that, like other economists such as Keynes, and Austin Robinson, she could move between the worlds of academia and politics, and beyond theoretical economics into developing specific policy recommendations. Brian's nascent political allegiances were in tune with hers. She was a role model for his later career.[63]

Cambridge in the autumn of 1951 epitomised the re-balancing of post-war Britain, with the fall of the Labour government, and return to a Conservative administration under Churchill. John Vaizey wryly observed: 'The young men changed. In place of the fatherly ex-servicemen who had packed the halls where the Labour Club met, flat caps and checked suits clambered out of little red MGs. The chinless wonder from the peace-time army was there again with the evening dress. May balls, backless gowns – a conscious revival of a mythicised 1920s. They read English and voted Tory.'[64]

After going in September to help the Spelthorne Divisional Labour Party with campaigning for the forthcoming general election, Brian returned to pick up his old Cambridge routines from new lodgings in Barnabas Road.[65] He was on fine form at his first Union appearance of the new academic year. The *Cambridge Review* noted approvingly: 'Mr Abel-Smith has a suave soigné style admirably suited to his material, but he has acquired the art of roughening the smooth edges here and there to prevent his listeners from being soothed into quiescence. Much of his humour is risqué, but rarely offensive and always sufficiently subtle for those who might be offended not to understand.'[66]

He also wrote a series of eight weekly articles for the *Varsity* newspaper – ostensibly giving advice for freshmen, but providing an eloquent display of his faintly sardonic upper-class wit.[67] 'Interior Decoration' provided a guide on gaining the maximum social kudos from one's rooms: 'Debrett with just a little doctoring, will always open at the right page.... Team photographs are modestly hung in the bedroom – just visible when the door is left open. A wad of invitation cards stands on the mantle-piece (chimney piece if you read Nancy Mitford). The top one at least is current. But never leave a friend alone in your room. The card on your door has the word captain before your name crossed out neatly but not erased.' He addressed the topic of fashion a few weeks later in 'The Cambridge costume': 'If you want to be smart, the part that clothes play is largely verbal. This has the great advantage of being so inexpensive. Here are a few OK futile phrases to start you off: "When I was in Locke's [sic] the other day a feller came in and asked for a Bowler Hat". "You can't buy anything at Scott's, it's got branches." "A feller asked me the other day what sort of a hat one wears with a dinner jacket. I told him that the problem couldn't arise as a dinner jacket was for dining at home".'[68] The Labour Foot Beagles' 'Coming Out Ball' held at the Dorothy House Hotel on 14 November epitomised so much of what Brian had been bluntly hinting at with his 'social' reportage. The theme was release from prison, and Brian contributed a cabaret piece, which he performed in white tie and tails. The following evening he appeared at the Cambridge Footlights Dramatic Club Smoking Concert, performing *Mayfair Socialists* for which he wrote the lyrics with his good friend Alistair Sampson.

One of Brian's main reasons for wishing to stay on at Cambridge after his graduation was to have another crack at getting an officership of the Union. His opportunity came in November 1951. Clare College Falcon Club held a dinner in hall to support him and Lionel wrote encouragingly: 'good luck for your fight tomorrow & hope you unseat the fellow. You deserve to get it this time.' He was yet again beaten, but determinedly remained as a senior committee member. This persistence had a novel pay-back. The Union was invited by the British Council to nominate a Cambridge participant for a British universities debating tour the following spring. This was just the confidence boost Brian needed, as Dalton had observed:

> Brian Abel-Smith to tea. I like him a lot, but he stayed 2½ hours and then I had to push him out. Just missed office again at the Union by a narrow vote (against Young Hurd for Vice President). He won't stand again. He's doing economic research under Joan Robinson, who is more interested in politics than economics now, and is a Bevanite. Abel-Smith is inclined to do something on inherited wealth, and propose something very drastic.... I ask if he's badly bitten by the political bug. He says Yes. But should one go straight into Parliament from being a Don? I said Tony Crosland (already mentioned by him in another connection) did.... Abel-Smith is not so good looking, or so intellectually able, or so dashing, but he's the best young man for politics I've found at a university since Tony [Crosland]. Ruth, who stays part of the time, says he's very governing class. And why not – we want some more of that in a national party.[69]

The British Council universities debating tour

Brian's selection for the British Council universities debating tour to India, Pakistan and Ceylon was a welcome opportunity to extend his foreign experiences. He had taken annual European holidays since his army posting in Vienna in 1947–48. This was a chance to go further afield and in an official capacity.[70] Aunt Maud, who had spent several years in various outposts of the British Empire, got vicarious pleasure from this news, sending him money to buy a new camera, and displaying a surprisingly modern attitude for her 84 years:

> I am really glad and greatly relieved at the last sentence in your letter that the British have woken up at last & that you wish to treat the natives as EQUALS or at least in a human way & not with that horrible swank as if you were little tin gods on earth. We have brought all this unrest and hatred abroad of ourselves entirely through our own fault in the past. I was horrified to see how the quite small children were allowed to behave to their devoted ayahs and bearers. It is probably the same in Egypt. The so called "worm" has turned. I marvel that they stood it as long as they did. They had not had the advantage & education we have had. Blessings on you and I shall be wondering how the present India will strike you.[71]

There were two other members of the debating team: Alistair MacDonald from Glasgow University and Roy Manley, a Liverpudlian studying at Reading University. Brian and MacDonald travelled out together and arrived from the gloom of an English winter into the glare, heat and dust of Delhi. From the first moment Brian was enthralled by India. It was part of his family's heritage, having heard his late father talk of his army postings there, and his mother's adoption of Indian colonial culture, which lived on at the Kensington flat in the form of curries and quaint terminology: 'Shabash!' was one of her favourite exclamations.

The schedule for the tour was hectic. During the first three weeks in India there were debates at 11 universities along with other meetings organised by the British Council and cultural events. His temporary permit to 'consume and possess for personal consumption bottled foreign liquor or Indian-made foreign spirits' proved invaluable. Brian remarked on the familiarity of the lifestyle, no doubt aided by attending events such as garden parties and the Caledonian Ball at the British club in Madras. Despite having been a republic since January 1950, the sense of British rule still lingered in India. Their British style of debating was not, however, fully appreciated by their audiences. A.B. Gerrard, the British Council's officer in Agra, was not happy with the reports he received in the wake of their debates, and he sent a letter to await Brian's arrival in Lahore: 'the practice which you and Macdonald have been adopting of piling facetious abuse on each other's heads is not going down very well and certainly is not being understood. . . . I imagine both of you are pretty sick of the same old gags and would rather welcome an opportunity to drop them so I suggest that in everybody's interest it would be a good idea to do so.'[72]

Motions debated included 'A degree is the only benefit obtainable from a university education', and 'That a fully socialised state must eventually become a tyranny.' In Calcutta they made radio broadcasts and took part in 'Brains Trusts' where they gamely took on all questions, including whether English girls expected to be kissed on first dates. In Bombay Brian was entertained to lunch at the home of Sir Navroji Wadia, Vice-Chancellor of the University of Bombay. They walked in stocking-clad feet on the cool marble floors of the Taj Mahal by moonlight, and examined the appalling working conditions in mines for their mainly female labour.

The next leg of the tour was to the other section of the former British India: Pakistan – its acronymic name reflecting its disparate culture and geography (P for Punjab, A for Afghanistan, K for Kashmir, S for Sind and TAN for Baluchistan). During this four-week mini-tour Brian ventured to the furthest outpost of the Khyber Pass, re-tracing his father's footsteps and finding his name in the visitors book from 1916. The border with Afghanistan had no no-man's land – just a chain across the road, guarded by gruff and unsmiling Afghans in German-style uniforms. He found Karachi as a small municipal town, in the process of being transformed into a capital, but with little regard for the thousands of refugees who squatted on its margins. But the rural people of Pakistan gained his admiration: 'Everyone in the market seemed to be armed … there was a glow of mutual respect as I spoke to them. They were tough and brave and I loved them for it. And I was English and of good status and they had learnt at least to respect my race. Never before have I felt pride at being a MAN.'[73]

The Karachi Civil and Military Gazette, before their arrival, had published 'thumb sketches' of the British debaters, noting that 'Mr Abel-Smith (24) who has been engaged in research work on the economy of under-developed areas, had the reputation of being a very witty speaker'.[74] Another newspaper found him 'more sober and less witty' than MacDonald: 'he minces no words when it comes to defending British policy in Malaya and Egypt. Eveready [sic] to enter into any discussion he is keen on knowing as much about this country as he can within their short stay in Pakistan. He starts his speech with both hands in his trouser and the rest of the time he keeps putting them in and out. His speech in the Mock Parliament of Law College defending why Pakistan should stay within the Commonwealth of Nations was a lucid piece of objective thinking, and clear cut arguments.'[75] In Lahore MacDonald caught dysentery, and with Manley left behind recovering from sickness in Delhi, Brian did the debate on his own, arguing both for and against the motion in front of an audience of over 2,000.

Another visitor on a whirlwind tour of the Indian sub-continent in February 1952 was Eleanor Roosevelt (then President of the United Nations Commission on Human Rights [UNCHR]), who had accepted an invitation from the Indian Prime Minister Jawaharlal Nehru to try to improve American understanding of this complex country. Brian, MacDonald and Manley's itinerary followed much the same route as hers, but they were usually a couple of days in advance. Finally their paths crossed at the University of the Punjab. Brian was unimpressed by her speech to the students. The articles he wrote on his return provided a critical rejoinder to the American upbeat publicity campaign that surrounded Roosevelt's fact-finding tour. His (rejected) article for the *New Statesman* focused on the evils of communism in the context of American blitzkrieg aid: 'Only a few indoctrinated workers will be required to organise the peasants and draw the Iron Curtain down to the Indian Ocean. America is hastening rather than retarding this grim prospect.... America is frankly unpopular: she is feared for her strength and despised for her cultural inferiority ... her anti-communist propaganda is a joke amongst Marxists and non-marxists alike.... Young India is turning towards Britain.'[76] Their tour had brought them into contact with 'real' Indians, Pakistanis and Ceylonese. Mrs Roosevelt is unlikely to have had the opportunity to get merry on arak in Kandy and return from picnics on the beach singing songs in the car. (Brian's party piece was *The Foggy, Foggy Dew*.)

Generally, however, the perpetual emotion expressed in his diary and in letters home was one of intense happiness and satisfaction: 'I am loving this tour. Wandering around universities wearing a charming smile and making spontaneous appreciative comments by numbers. I sign about 30 autographs after each debate and sit in the car waving to the cheering multitudes as we drive off. It is like being the Royal family.'[77] The royal family indirectly interrupted the debating tour, when the King's death was announced on 6 February. Another death, closer to home, was conveyed to Brian by airmail letter – Aunt Maud had died on 5 March, having outlived her brother Harold by just over a year. Vivée had been there with her in the nursing home in Milford-on-Sea. It was the end of an Abel-Smith generation.

By the end of their two-month tour, they had travelled 11,500 miles, visited 16 universities and their associated colleges, spoken at 56 events attended by over 50,000 people, and attended 100 social engagements. After they returned to the UK they were required to submit a report to the British Council. This took some time to pull together, with each of them drafting sections and then circulating. They judged that the value of their tour had been to improve the image of the British Council among the young, offer a more genuine non-establishment source of information on Britain, and it had brought them into contact with 'those young men who are likely to become the political leaders of the future'. They thought that having a female member of future tours would be a good thing, but that the qualities she would require, 'apart from the ability to speak … are femininity, poise, resilience and physical attractiveness. We feel that the composition of our team – a politician, a rake and an oddity – was ideal for the purpose of the tour.' A further sign of the times: 'we suggest cigarettes should be accountable. They are essential in a goodwill tour.'[78] They wrote articles for *Overseas*, the monthly journal of the Overseas League, in which Brian suggested 'Superficially one might say that the legacies of British rule were irrigation, cricket and Gothic architecture. But there is also admiration for efficiency, integrity and justice … our failure was in social relations.'[79] Brian also exploited the tour for material for a BBC radio programme called *Meet the Commonwealth*, and he gave a talk to the Majlis Club on his return to Cambridge.

Brian resumed his political journalism on his return, submitting an article for *Tribune* through Donald Chapman, who sent it to Michael Foot for comment.[80] After a meeting with Chapman at the House of Commons in May, he began to re-work the article for the Fabian Society, who sent it to Brinley Thomas and D.N. Chester for review. These academics were still considering it in September, before finally agreeing that it could be published in the Fabian Research Series (it appeared a year later in September 1953 as *The Reform of Social Security*). He was also considering returning abroad, after Austin Robinson enquired if he was seriously interested in a post in Bangkok with the Economic Commission for Asia and the Far East (ECAFE). The Commission were looking for 'an Englishman' who was capable of collating contributions from various ECAFE countries into a readable and coherent first draft report. Robinson thought that this might be an opening into UN posts, and that Brian could use Bangkok as a stepping-stone to the UN New York headquarters.[81] The Cambridge authorities took a less indulgent view of his overseas interests. Shortly after his return from the two-month debating tour he received a stern letter admonishing him for not applying for permission for going out of residence. He was required to make a formal application for retrospective leave to intermit his course of research for the Lent term, accompanied by his supervisor's written report. This required tracking down the elusive Joan Robinson, who was looking to offload Brian's supervision from the Easter term anyway. She wrote to Brian at the end of April: 'Hope your tour was a success. I am still feeling completely dizzy after returning from Moscow. I have arranged for Mr Reddaway to take you on so would you get in touch with him?'[82]

By July 1952, Brian had made up his mind to stay up at Cambridge, and he requested registration for a PhD, which was duly granted on Brian Reddaway's recommendation.[83] While Brian was pursuing his academic career, Lionel was successfully installed as a barrister at Lincoln's Inn. Having inherited the family estate at Wendover, he was able to indulge his brother in some welcome financial support. He sent £75 to Brian along with news of the situation at the flat, where another set of lodgers had left, unhappy at Vivée's somewhat overbearing friendliness: 'We need lodgers … your mother is never satisfied to live her own life.'[84] Vivée was also trying to direct their lives, in a naturally motherly way, drawing their attention to how many of their friends were 'settling down' with girlfriends. Aunt Maud had left them each £100 and a brooch. Brian and Lionel persuaded her to sell these, and she forwarded them the proceeds, directing hopefully that it: 'be put in savings to accumulate to buy one for your wife-to-be'.[85] She was, however, acknowledging that her sons (now 26 and 24) would not always be so intimately bound to her, and perhaps even beginning to question their sexuality. Writing to Brian when he was still up at Cambridge she conceded:

> I quite see that for your creative work you are better on your own, in your own surroundings & I shall not mind you living somewhere else in London, without home restrictions as to meals etc. I appreciate how you feel, so I do hope you will get the job you want when you come down. You can work I hope, with little interference from me (let me know when to expect you?) As individuals let us live our lives without unhappiness....[86]

In August 1952 Brian took his usual long summer holiday in Europe, and then went on behalf of the British Council to Scandinavia. Vivée went to Ireland, leaving a peaceful Lionel at the flat. He relayed Brian's post and messages, adding 'Hope you are enjoying yourself.

I hope you are doing everything I wouldn't have the courage to do.'
One item of interest in Brian's post was a letter from the Harwich
Constituency Labour Party's General Secretary, asking if he would
accept a nomination as their prospective parliamentary candidate, as his
name had been put forward.[87] This was the first of several invitations
offering a political career.

Part 2

THE POLITICS OF POLICIES, 1951–79

3

Beveridge's Britain: 1951–55

The new British welfare state

Useful academics: The London School of Economics

Social science and social policy

Richard Titmuss

Peter Townsend

The Fabians

Tony Crosland and *The Future of Socialism*

The Reform of Social Security

Costing the National Health Service

Too political for research?

There is a case for claiming that the Fifties actually began in May 1951, with the opening of the Festival of Britain and the start of the Goon Show. The Festival laid out the future pattern for architecture, town planning and design, while the Goons set about reducing to rubble the redundant edifice of British Imperial smugness. (Dave Gelly, 1991)[1]

While studying for his PhD, Brian was offered work as a research assistant on the 1953 inquiry into the cost of the NHS (the Guillebaud Inquiry). One of his supervisors was Richard Titmuss, a new Professor of Social Administration at the LSE, and Brian joined his Department as Assistant Lecturer in 1955. In the early 1950s Brian had become closely involved with the Fabian Society and in 1953 published his first academic/political pamphlet, The Reform of Social Security, *which exposed the inequity in Beveridge's welfare state.*

In 1956 the Guillebaud Report was published, which helped to establish Brian's reputation as an economist working on health issues. He had also begun to collaborate with the sociologist Peter Townsend, who joined him as one of Titmuss's disciples at the LSE. Together they developed research-for-policy projects, especially into health and social welfare services. During these years Brian was also actively developing a political presence through lectures and campaigning for the Labour Party.

The new British welfare state

In October 1951 Britain rejected her six-year-old Labour government, which had clung on to power after the 1950 general election with a majority of six. MPs then had been brought from hospital beds in ambulances to Westminster to vote.[2] The turnout of 83 per cent in 1951 demonstrated the public's interest, but perhaps more the contemporary sense of political duty. The Conservatives' victory was narrow: 321 parliamentary seats against Labour's 295 (the Liberals' six seats were inconsequential). But the Conservatives actually took 48 per cent of the votes compared with 49 per cent for Labour (and 3 per cent for the Liberals). Their victory was set against Labour obtaining the highest vote ever recorded for a political party in Britain. It was an affirmation of what had gone right in the past six years.

In 1946, when it was decided to give Beveridge's audacious social services plans a run for their money, there actually wasn't much money in Britain. The Second World War had cost far more than the First, wiping out overseas investments and increasing the national debt to an unsustainable level. Britain suffered an economic setback far more severe than some of the other countries that had been involved, yet there was a sense of duty in honouring the pledges that had boosted morale during the darkest days of the war. Peter Hennessy, one of the most eloquent chroniclers of 20th-century Britain, adopts the title *Never Again* for his volume devoted to the period 1945–51: 'for me the phrase captures the motivating impulse of the first half-dozen years after the war – never again would there be war; never again would the British people be housed in slums, living off a meagre diet thanks to low wages or no wages at all; never again would mass unemployment blight the lives of millions....'[3] He could have extrapolated from these core demands to include never again unnecessary morbidity and premature mortality. There was no need to spell this out – it went without saying that poor housing, income and diet caused both chronic and acute ill health. This was a well-known association, and had been quantified by such people as Edwin Chadwick and Frederick Engels more than 100 years earlier. This is not the place to enter into detailed analyses of why the British state accommodated such a lag in evidence-based policy, or why the British public tolerated it. It is sufficient here, in addition to pointing readers in the direction of scholars such as Derek Fraser and Rodney Lowe, to say that it had much to do with George Orwell's personification of Britain as:

> ... a family with the wrong members in control ... a rather stuffy Victorian family ... with not many black sheep in it but with all its cupboards bursting with skeletons. It has rich relations who have to be kowtowed to and poor relations who are horribly sat upon, and there is a deep conspiracy of silence about the source of the family income. It is a family in which the young are generally thwarted and most of the power is in the hands of irresponsible uncles and bedridden aunts. Still it is a family. It has its private language and its common memories, and at the approach of an enemy it closes its ranks.[4]

Fraser, Lowe and many others have charted the emergence of what has become familiarly known as the 'British welfare state'.[5] Significant parts of this bundle of services pre-date Beveridge's 1942 report, *Social Insurance and Allied Services*. The embryonic welfare state can be seen as far back as the 'new' Poor Law of 1834; Beatrice Webb first suggested a 'state medical service' in the Minority Report of the Royal Commission on the Poor Laws in 1909; and the adoption of a Bismarckian Health Insurance system in 1911, although limited in its coverage, also extended the boundaries of what the state saw as its natural responsibilities. By the 1930s the Labour Party had adopted a manifesto commitment to a national health service, but it is fair to say that Beveridge's report, while loathed by some in the Treasury, inspired wider cross-party support for its broad philosophy. It was Churchill's wartime Coalition government that passed Butler's 1944 Education Act and the Family Allowances Act in 1945. All political parties could therefore bask in the reflected glory of Britain's new welfare state.

How long did this nirvana last? That has been a matter for intense academic and political debate ever since. For some, such as Corelli Barnett, Labour's 1945 commitment to implement the Beveridge plan in full within three years of its election (by 5 July 1948) was at the root of all of Britain's subsequent woes: '... the illusions and dreams of 1945 would fade one by one – the Imperial and Commonwealth role, the world-power role, the British industrial genius, and, at the last,

New Jerusalem itself, a dream turned to a dank reality of a segregated, subliterate, unskilled, unhealthy and institutionalised proletariat hanging on the nipple of state maternalism.'[6] Less hysterical assessments have demonstrated that Britain actually invested less per person in its post-war social services than its European neighbours.[7] There were also viable welfare state models offered by Sweden and New Zealand that gave Labour confidence that their plans were not so far-fetched. Beveridge's choice of a contributory insurance system to fund the new services had an initial logic, and as José Harris has shown, it 'fitted in with current evaluations of fiscal reality and with current evaluations of virtue, gender, citizenship, personal freedom and the nature of the state. It was a package that was to prove extraordinarily tenacious.'[8]

Useful academics: the London School of Economics

The philosophy underpinning Attlee's political administration was based on socialism, with the core principle of engineering a better, more egalitarian society. This was to be achieved not only through implementing Beveridge's 'welfare state' but also through nationalising key industries such as transport, coal, electricity, gas and iron and steel.[9] While in opposition during the inter-war period the Labour Party had exploited a number of academics to inform the development of specific policy initiatives, many of whom had come through contacts with the Fabian Society. The Fabian Society had been formed in London in 1884 as an intellectual movement that favoured advancing the principles of social democracy through gradualist and reformist rather than revolutionary means. By the early 20th century prominent members included George Bernard Shaw, H.G. Wells, Virginia Woolf, Ramsay MacDonald and Emmeline Pankhurst. The key academic force came from Sidney and Beatrice Webb, who, along with Graham Wallas and Shaw, founded the London School of Economics in 1895. The Fabians published their blueprints for social justice in pamphlets, and from 1913 through the weekly publication the *New Statesman*. They were also influential in the formation of the Labour Party in 1900, and their members played significant roles in parliamentary enquiries, such as that on the Poor Law, which reported in 1909. They campaigned for a minimum wage, socialised healthcare, the nationalisation of land and the abolition of heredity peerages. During the inter-war period a new generation of influential Fabians included R.H. Tawney, G.D.H. Cole and Harold Laski.

Undoubtedly, the inter-war intellectual strengthening of Labour Party ideology also drew heavily on other universities such as Cambridge, where academics such as John Maynard Keynes and Brian's tutor Joan Robinson willingly moulded theory into potential government policy, but it was at the LSE that the political–academic relationship became closest. By the mid-20th century it had amassed a collection of academics that rivalled Oxford and Cambridge, and attracted internationally acclaimed scholars such as Friedrich von Hayek, Karl Popper and Harold Laski. In the inter-war period the free marketers appeared to have the upper hand, and the School was the natural home for characters such as Lionel Robbins, who reigned in the Economics Department between 1929 and 1968, with a brief interregnum when he served as a Whitehall adviser during the Second World War. In addition to its strongholds of economics and political theory, the LSE's reputation was further enhanced through the work of other social scientists, such as A.H. Halsey and Karl Mannheim.

The LSE, probably more so than Oxford and Cambridge, thrived on networks. Take, for example, William Beveridge, who was its Director between 1919 and 1937. He had been introduced to Churchill through Sidney and Beatrice Webb. Other key contacts included John Maynard Keynes and Joseph Rowntree, from whom he extracted the economic and social theories to construct his vision of a 'social service state'. Two of the lecturers on his staff at the LSE were Clement Attlee and Hugh Dalton, who later, as Prime Minister and Chancellor of the Exchequer respectively, were to implement his 1942 *Social Insurance and Allied Services* report. Despite subsequent assessments of Beveridge as 'vain, humourless and tactless', or autocratic and arrogant, he knew the value of networking.[10] There may have been a more deliberate political strategy to the LSE networks than the Oxbridge ones, but they shared the same male exclusivity (with a few stellar exceptions such as Brian's Cambridge tutor Joan Robinson). Women were slightly more visible in some LSE departments such as Social Administration, but they were in the lower ranks of social workers and university teachers – critically distinct from lecturers by their different university pay scale.

The LSE's formation in 1895 had been made possible by a bequest from the Fabian Henry Hunt Hutchinson to forward the Society's objectives. Sidney Webb hoped that this socialist philosophy would prevail at the LSE, but was alive to the value of alternatives, as long as they were based on his fundamental principles of 'knowledge, science and truth'. Despite its dominant socialist founding fathers (and mother), it cannot accurately be described as a wholeheartedly left-wing institution. In fact, for significant periods, it can be seen as an overtly conservative institution, as Robert McKenzie puts it, 'in almost every sense of the term'.[11] The School joined the federal University of London in 1900, initially serving as its Faculty of Economics. Its location at Aldwych, neatly placed between London's commercial, media, legal and political powerhouses of the City, Fleet Street, Holborn and Westminster, made it a natural epicentre for the study and research of social sciences. It expanded rapidly, gaining purpose-built accommodation in Clare Market and Houghton Street, and filling a niche in Britain's academic structure through its tuition of a diverse range of mainly mature students. For staff and students alike, it was a life-changing atmosphere: the LSE 'pulsed with the pulse of the capital'.[12] The LSE was people, not the physical fabric, demeaned by Chaim Bermant as 'a charmless pile, like the head-office of a minor insurance company, hidden away in a back street'.[13]

Social science and social policy

As the LSE was a new academic institution in 1895, so too was the academic discipline of social science. This term encompassed longer-established disciplines such as economics, law and history, drawing intellectual strength from its adoption of 'scientific' principles developed in the natural sciences to explain social phenomena. Its genesis needs to be seen in the context of the 'curious strength of positivism in English social thought' as represented by intellectual clans such as the Booths, Bosanquets, Rowntrees and, of course, the Webbs.[14] It was an acceptable 'leisure-time' activity that initially offered few professional prospects. Its institutionalisation was aided by the foundation of a Department of Social Science and Administration, when the LSE absorbed the old School of Sociology and the Charity Organisation Society (COS) in 1912. This was initially funded by the Indian philanthropist Ratan Tata until the School took over its funding in 1919.

In the inter-war years, the Department catered for students on a variety of vocational courses, including mental healthcare, childcare and social work (and much of the teaching until the 1950s took place in the evening).[15] In his history of the LSE, its former Director, Ralf Dahrendorf, suggested that for the first 40 years of its life, the Department of Social Administration was 'at the margin of the real School' precisely because it catered for these unconventional students (he also noted that 70 per cent of them were female). T.H. Marshall claimed that from the 1920s it had been 'popularly regarded as a convenient place for wealthy mothers to send their daughters to when disturbed by the dawning of a social conscience'.[16] This marginality brought strengths and weaknesses. By slipping under the School's administrative radar, the social administrators spent less time in school committees or seconded to governing bodies of prestigious but academically irrelevant institutions such as the Tate Gallery. They were also not as likely to be seen as potential candidates for peerages. Without such distractions, they had more time for getting on with their work.[17]

Much has been written about the differences between natural and social sciences, and their respective strengths and weaknesses. Natural sciences are commonly viewed as more 'scientific' (a term that implies objectivity and neutrality). Social sciences, faced with this impressively robust definition, have had to find their authority in complementary adjectives: Arthur Pigou, in his 1920 book *The Economics of Welfare*, made the case for the 'usefulness' of the social sciences.[18] More recently social scientists such as Martin Bulmer, Jane Lewis and David Piachaud have stressed the strength of 'applied' as opposed to 'basic' social science.[19] From this marriage of theoretical insights with empirical enquiry has emerged a specific concern with 'social policy', a chameleon term that is almost easier to define by what it leaves out than by what it includes. At its core is a concern with inequalities and divisions in society, or more precisely, with the problems that seem to arise from such inequalities and divisions. Since its conception academics have been variously dismissive and welcoming, appreciating its useful vagueness, but deeming it a 'field of study' rather than a 'discipline'. This view hinges on the relative paucity of theories compared to disciplines such as Economics, and the apparent 'implicit' theory and range of assumptions about the nature of social welfare.[20] In Britain social science failed to generate a more science (that is, evidence)-based social policy, as had happened in the US. Bulmer attributes this to the dominance in Britain of social surveys, and the greater permeability of the boundary between social scientists and policy makers.[21]

Social policy research is essentially question and value-driven, in direct contrast to the way that the natural sciences strive to be value-free. It is often motivated by a deep desire to effect change in the real world, selecting facts as 'ammunition' with which to support the disadvantaged in society – the social services users who, as Howard Glennerster puts it, cannot exercise the 'power of exit' of classic economic theory.[22] Its practitioners operate within a cultural and political milieu that respects (indeed fosters) their overt moral commitment to specific social policy agendas. The close networks that have developed within and between institutions such as the LSE and Whitehall facilitate their work. The Fabian concept of 'permeation' is useful here in understanding how social scientists effectively operate in this environment. Yet their academic positions ensure that their research (and subsequent policy advice) retains a vital independence and authority. Their work is usually problem-centred and often critically 'research for policy'.[23] As this study of Brian's life shows, the relationship between academics and politicians has become increasingly nuanced since the establishment of the discipline of social policy in the early 20th century. There is a wide spectrum of experience: from researchers lined up like 'cabs in a taxi rank' to take the next government instruction, to passionate individuals determined to choose and pursue their own research agendas.[24] It is to one of the best exemplars of this last type that we now turn.

Richard Titmuss

Richard Titmuss's name is synonymous with the development of 20th-century social policy and the academic discipline of social administration. He was born into a lower middle class family in 1907, and following the death of his father when he was 19, he trained at a commercial college before finding employment as an insurance office clerk. An 'indefatigable autodidact', he spent his leisure researching vital statistics (typed up from 1937 by his new social worker wife Kay) which were in the tradition of R.H. Tawney's humanistic social accounting, and which brought him into contact with intellectual politicians such as Eleanor Rathbone and Harold Macmillan. His first book, published in 1938, was *Poverty and Population: A Factual Study of Contemporary Social Waste*. He was subsequently invited to write a volume for the official history of the Second World War, which was published as *Problems of Social Policy* in 1950.[25] He was known in Whitehall for his 'really creative insight into human problems' and 'most unusual gift for asking the right questions'.[26] Although there has subsequently been discussion about the accuracy of Titmuss's portrayal of inter-war poverty, at the time it was received enthusiastically and opened up a new career path in academia. He was already in a semi-academic post, working as Deputy Director of the new Social Medicine Research Unit, funded by the Medical Research Council and directed by one of his writing partners, Jerry Morris.[27] With the publication of *Problems of Social Policy* he was now in the fortunate position of being offered two new chairs in social administration. Titmuss chose the LSE over Birmingham and was appointed in 1950, despite having no university qualification.[28]

Titmuss was the natural intellectual successor to the sociologist T.H. Marshall, who had developed the concept of civil rights to encompass social rights. Titmuss did not profess to be a sociologist, but claimed for his own an academic discipline he called social policy. Although his chair was initially located in the Department of Sociology, he disliked the sociologists' ferocious internal wars, which their leader, David Glass, appeared unable to control. The explicit naming of Titmuss's chair as 'Social Administration' reflected his ambition to fully engage with the development *and delivery* of social policy. Titmuss had the necessary charisma, impressive assurance and ambition to develop this new discipline. He continually pushed for more resources, and he recruited young gifted academics to the LSE. They shared his enthusiasm and commitment to assess the nature and causes of social waste. In ideology, Titmuss's department was closer to Michael Young's Institute of Community Studies than to some of the traditional departments at the LSE such as Economics, Philosophy, Anthropology and Political Science. Indeed, there were academics who made no secret of their view that social administration had no place in a university. Titmuss's personal philosophy was almost Benthamite in its scope: 'just as man by his actions creates ill-health and misery, so can man by his work create health and happiness'.[9] His values resonated in his new home, which acquired nicknames such as the 'Department of Applied Virtue'.[30] In Keith Banting's assessment:

> Titmuss was not only a careful investigator of social life; his work was also a moral statement, and he became a philosophical leader not only of an academic generation but also of parts of the Labour Party. This group of intellectuals was convinced that myths about the generosity of the welfare state were blinding Britons to the persistence of hardship and inequalities in their midst. They therefore set out in the 1950s to map the contours of British society, and to generate ideas and evidence that would legitimate social reform. Their research was explicitly political; its aim was to reshape policy-makers' interpretations of their environment.[31]

Titmuss's 'boldness in rejecting value-free social science was a considerable achievement'.[32] His focus on latent function rather than pure service provision enabled a much wider scope for investigation and policy intervention than had previously been achieved. All of this precocious ability was contained within a surprisingly frail human frame, displaying an 'El Greco quality with "his great eyes, emaciated face, long body and that indefinable air of what one could only call saintliness"'.[33] Junior staff referred to themselves as 'disciples' and to Titmuss as 'God'. Although his team included some gifted women (such as Eileen Younghusband, Kay McDougall, Clare Winnicott, Kit Russell and Christine Cockburn), they were never part of the inner circle, which essentially was young white men, mainly democratic socialists.

How, then, did Brian come within the orbit of the Titmuss star? In 1952 he was already recognising his natural research affinity with economic and social policy issues as he began his postgraduate studies at Cambridge. He was also beginning to draft articles for the political press, unsuccessfully submitting them to *Tribune* and the *New Statesman* before gaining an acceptance from the Fabian Society Research Series for an audaciously broad draft on the reform of social security. This was a marked departure from the potential research interests, such as industrial psychology, he had been discussing with Dalton in 1951. What caused this change in direction was his introduction to the work of Richard Titmuss by John Vaizey.

Vaizey was one of Brian's enduring contacts from his undergraduate days, later to become the academic-turned-politician who gained notoriety for his late-in-life conversion from socialism to Thatcherite conservatism. They had both graduated in Economics in 1951, and were both involved with the Union and the Labour Club. In his autobiographical writings, published posthumously in 1986, Vaizey professed his shyness and lack of confidence at Cambridge. As a Lewisham grammar school boy, from a lower middle-class family, he was acutely aware of his social position relative to the majority of his fellow undergraduates. In 1943 he had contracted osteomyelitis of the spine, which required lengthy hospital treatment and left him with a visible weakness and chronic pain. He felt that his friendship was sought mainly because of his academic talent, and his known association with the dons. This 'chip' manifested itself throughout his life – Frank Field claimed Vaizey possessed one of the most fertile wits of his generation, but that primarily his humour 'was a weapon raised against the pompous of this world'.[34] Yet in his private correspondence with Brian, Vaizey comes across as an exuberant personality. There is a sense that theirs was an intense, true, friendship, albeit coloured by a degree of mutual envy at academic and social success: Vaizey writing to Brian, 'Fletcher obviously adores you, you winning creature you. I too am in the grip of a hopeless passion – Pembroke this time (now becoming quite an OK college).'[35] Vaizey had gone to Geneva in 1951 after taking his first class degree, where he worked for a year as a research officer at the UN Economic Commission in Europe. He returned to a research fellowship at St Catherine's College Cambridge, before moving in 1956 to Oxford as Lecturer in Economics and Economic History.

Vaizey had found the Cambridge undergraduate Economics course unsatisfactory. Despite the plethora of world-class economists who taught it, he bemoaned the 'almost complete absence from the syllabus of any serious concern with social policy'.[36] Having read Titmuss's book, *Problems of Social Policy*, he wrote to him asking for a meeting. Duly impressed, Vaizey wrote to Brian on 14 August 1952: 'I saw Titmuss for ages the other day and told him all about you. He is a tall man, very professorial with dark hair & tired, wise, kind eyes and spectacles he takes off. He is magnificent and you are going to meet him.[37] Vaizey's letter is also interesting for the admission it contained:

> Darling, I have decided my feelings towards you are decidedly ambivalent. I have an enlarged photo of you & the prof. beside my bed, which I positively interrogate. Sometimes I positively loathe you for all sorts of reasons & at times I envy, & at other times admire. What ought I to think? Is your charm, your wit, your adultness innate, acquired or admirable?... I do look forward to seeing you again – even though you are one of those ghastly people who make others feel dessicated [sic] and dull. Love to Norway. Yours to the revolution, J.[38]

In another letter later that summer:

> I really must write again to let you know that Titmuss is a genius & the more we see of him the better. He is utterly charming about my work and writes most enthusiastically sending me copies of his inaugural lecture and of a lecture at Bedford College. On women he has your marvellous idea of age-prosperity charts, assoc. with the rdn. of the death rate & the fall in birth rate, plus earlier & more marriage creating privileged groups of young workers and middle-aged couples. The problem of the old he shows to be a problem of old women. It really is blissikins.[39]

Brian declined Vaizey's offer to go and live with him at Madingley Hall, then an adult education centre on the outskirts of Cambridge where Vaizey taught part time under the auspices of the Workers' Educational Association (WEA), but he did follow up on the introduction to Richard Titmuss.

Brian, like Vaizey before him, was captivated by this charming man. Titmuss's authority was overwhelming, particularly as they were also welcomed into his family as well as his intellectual circle. Titmuss and his wife Kay were genial hosts, and the initial invitations to their home in Acton for coffee gradually developed into suppers with their daughter, Ann.[40] Vaizey and Brian would visit on a regular basis, at least once a month. 'Richard sat characteristically on a low chair, smoking heavily, the floor covered with piles of papers he was annotating and of students' work (including one's own) that he was correcting and criticising, his shoulders hunched, his long legs curled under him, his eyes behind their glasses, deep-brown, almost hypnotic, and his carefully enunciating voice.'[41]

Yet Vaizey, although initially enthralled, never became a full Titmuss acolyte. After establishing his own academic credentials at Oxford he queried the intellectual basis of Titmuss's social administration, published in a series of sharp profiles of some leading 20th-century thinkers, *In Breach of Promise*.[42] Vaizey felt no discomfort in retrospectively coupling his former hero with the fortunes of the socialist movement he himself had abandoned: 'Titmuss's story, in its own way, is the story of the intellectual decline of the Labour Party, of collective ideas, and in its myths and totems'.[43] He chose not to acknowledge and explore Titmuss's very real and substantial contributions to the development of social policy and administration.

Peter Townsend

Peter Townsend was another willing Titmuss disciple, but this time it was Brian who made the introduction. Townsend came from a working-class background and had also been at Cambridge from 1948 to 1951, where he read Social Anthropology at St John's College. Although he and Brian had met there occasionally, their friendship did not develop until Townsend took a research position at Political and Economic Planning (PEP) (a forerunner of the Policy Studies Institute) in 1952, after a visiting scholarship in Berlin. Their common research interest in poverty brought them into regular contact. Townsend's pamphlet, *Poverty: Ten Years After Beveridge*, was published by PEP in 1952, as a response to Seebohm Rowntree's study of poverty published in 1951.[44] Rowntree's first study, published in 1901, had provoked widespread debate with its extrapolation from York (where his family's chocolate factory was located) that approximately one third of the British people were living below a 'poverty line'.[45] Townsend's pamphlet boldly suggested that Rowntree's new research 'gave an exaggerated picture of change and improvement and was not really worth the paper it was written on'.[46] Townsend left PEP in 1954 for a two-year research post with Michael Young at the new Institute of Community Studies (which Titmuss had helped to raise funds for, and chaired the Advisory Committee), but increasingly collaborated with Brian and Titmuss on joint research projects in his spare time.[47] He officially joined the LSE in 1957, as a researcher, then lecturer, on funding he had obtained from the Nuffield Foundation for a study of old people's homes.[48]

His interview with LSE Director Sir Alexander Carr-Saunders was a formality only: Titmuss wanted him on his team.

Titmuss and the Titmice – as they were later to be known – complemented each other perfectly. Titmuss had his insurance industry background that provided valuable commercial experience, Townsend contributed the discipline of sociology, and Brian brought economics. Both Townsend and Brian felt very much like apprentices to Titmuss throughout their time at the LSE.[49] Observers have likened it more to a father–son relationship, with Titmuss filling a vacuum in both their lives (Townsend had been brought up by his single mother; Brian's father had died in 1946). There was certainly a direction from Titmuss that went beyond the normal guidance of a senior colleague. Townsend was impressed by his deliberate style of speech and authoritative personality, seeing him as 'an adviser for me about what to make of my life'. They both benefited from Titmuss's ability to analyse a question, to see it from a variety of perspectives. The relationship was powerfully symbiotic: 'the process of inspiration was cumulative when we were together.'[50] Yet despite the respect that Titmuss engendered in his disciples, and his impression of always being in charge, Townsend later felt that he also was uncertain about some of his ideas, evident in his habit of seeking extensive feedback on his drafts. Townsend further provoked debate by claiming that 'the more authoritative mind, was in fact Brian. And Brian has always played a very humble role, well humble isn't the right word in relation to him, but a very modest role in relation to the joint work they produced, and all three of us produced. He held things together in a way which carried immense authority. He was an economist. He had a terrific grasp of briefs.'[51]

Other new arrivals in Titmuss's Department of Social Administration at LSE included David Donnison, who joined in 1956 as a reader from a three-year research post in the Department of Government at the University of Manchester. He had been recruited by Titmuss after meeting at a seminar and was attracted to his LSE Department by its academic broadness and its practical attention to questions such as 'how can we create a fairer and more caring society?'[52] Donnison was to stay at the LSE for 13 years, eventually taking over as Head of Department from Titmuss.

Within the widening world of social policy, the LSE Department of Social Administration was by the 1950s an exemplar of the best way of combining research, teaching and policy development. The three elements fed off each other, with teaching being seen as equally valuable. Part of this orientation was due to the presence in the Department of Eileen Younghusband (1902–81), the 'unusual, flamboyant, yet deeply committed social work teacher', who had been a student at the LSE (perhaps one of Marshall's disturbed daughters with a social conscience, and another with an academic post but without a degree). Between 1944 and 1958 she advocated a generic training for social workers, provoking bitter disputes with her colleagues, and forcing Titmuss to articulate his vision for social work training more clearly. In 1955 she chaired a Ministry of Health working group that led to the establishment of a Council for Training in Social Work and a Certificate in Social Work qualification, before resigning from her position at the LSE in 1957.[53]

The fieldwork components were ably handled by Kit Russell, who joined the Department in 1949 as the new fieldwork tutor for the Diploma in Social Administration. Over the next 25 years she found placements for some 2,500 students, drawing on her earlier career in community development in a Victorian settlement in Bermondsey, and her extensive knowledge of community projects and voluntary associations. Russell was an extraordinary individual, ensuring the whole programme worked smoothly but also bringing her own counselling skills into the Department. She and her husband Sheridan (a cellist before the war and after it a hospital almoner and one of the first male social workers in the UK) were seen as true English eccentrics, renowned for the musical soirées held in the large flat they occupied in Chelsea's fashionable Cheyne Walk. Brian and Peter Townsend were frequent guests at performances of Mozart and Bach by invited quartets – Sheridan also playing until his deafness prevented this, despite a Victorian-style trumpet hearing aid.

Townsend in particular relished the intensive contact with mature students, and the freedom to infuse his teaching with fresh, immediate ideas drawn from current research. The LSE teaching style resembled the Oxbridge system of individual tutoring, and meant that academic staff had a very close involvement with student research. Townsend took students to interview the residents of tower block flats in the East End of London, witnessing at first hand the difficulties of even simple acts, such as monitoring from the 14th floor their children playing below, and the domestic drudge of carrying shopping up and laundry down in the (frequently out of action) lifts.

Despite the enthusiasm of staff, for much of Titmuss's period at the LSE the Department suffered from an unrelenting workload and little internal recognition and support. The university seemed disinterested in the teaching side of its activities (paperwork was titled 'The Burden of Teaching', with references to 'The Student Load').[54] When Titmuss had taken over the Department in 1950 there were only 13 staff, mainly social workers, who were ineligible for university-scale salaries (or status). By the time of the Department's 50th birthday in 1962 it was the largest of its kind in Europe, equal to its North American counterparts. The appointment of senior staff had given it a flexibility to engage in a wider range of external projects than Titmuss had initially been able to support.

The Fabians

Britain, somewhat to her surprise, managed to implement Beveridge's grand vision for a comprehensive set of social welfare services by 1948. Yet, even by the early 1950s it was increasingly clear that this was not a 'once and for all' system – the new services were not meeting the intended welfare needs of the British people, especially the poorest sections of society. It is important to acknowledge the very real challenges that such a radical expansion of state responsibility for welfare had entailed. There had been no conscious reassessment of whether 'Whitehall' – the geographical epicentre of the British civil service – had in place an administrative machine capable of managing the new, complex welfare state.[55] Instead there was the perpetuation of an inter-war 'care and maintenance' ethos. Civil servants supported government ministers in implementing their policies, with the best civil servants in this period valued for their generalism rather than their expertise in specific policy areas. This was not the only available model – the French had developed a much more sophisticated approach, a 'can do' attitude, supported by the dedicated training system provided by the Ecole nationale d'administration.

In Britain the process of policy formation remained firmly with the politicians, which required continual collaboration with experts. We have already seen how Beveridge brought his academic research interests in social welfare to Churchill's wartime Coalition government. He is a very public example of a growing trend towards the engagement of academic experts by politicians. Likewise, Harold Laski straddled the worlds of academia and politics, between 1937 and 1949, serving on the Labour Party's National Executive while Professor of Political Science at the LSE. In the post-war period, the links between academics and politicians became increasingly strong.

Titmuss was not a natural Labour Party man – his early allegiance was to the Liberal Party. It was the process of researching and writing his classic book, *Problems of Social Policy* that pushed him towards the Labour Party.[56] Yet, as his fellow academic A.H. Halsey noted, Titmuss's socialism was as English as his patriotism – ethical and non-Marxist. Titmuss wanted to show 'what a compassionate society can achieve when a philosophy of social justice and public accountability is translated into a hundred and one detailed acts of imagination and tolerance'.[57] This meant direct collaboration with policy makers: 'The fundamental purpose of social security research and the ideas that may flow from research is not to tell other people how to do things differently but, much more modestly, to offer policymakers a wider range of culturally adaptable possibilities and to help them make better informed choices.'[58]

The Fabian Society aimed to 'help the reconstruction of society in accordance with the highest moral possibilities.'[59] Fabians were not populist. George Bernard Shaw in 1892 had bemoaned the fact that the Society needed members to spread the cost of its activities, rather than their individual intellectual contributions. If he had had his way, 'we should be tempted to propose the limitation of our society in London to a hundred picked members'.[60] It saw 'manual workers and the mass of people more as objects of reform than as active subjects who made history'.[61] Although the Society was not as selective as Shaw might have wanted, it did remain relatively small, working on the principle of 'permeation' of institutions, through its publications and through education. Summer schools were held from 1907, modelled on German examples, where members could spend a week at a rented country house, engaging in daily lectures, walks, sports and sightseeing. Local Fabian Societies offered evening lecture series, arranged from the Society's London home at 11 Dartmouth Street.

The Fabian Society supported the Labour Party through its formal affiliation, but more specifically through the contribution of its members to Labour's intellectual development. Publications such as the *New Statesman* offered an effective way to disseminate new ideas, and stimulate discussion on policy developments. By the time of the general election in 1945, there were 230 Fabians in the parliamentary Labour Party, 37 of whom were in the new Labour government.[62] The success of Labour at the election stimulated interest in the Society, and membership increased to around 4,000, with nearly 3,000 in the local societies.[63] Townsend became a Fabian at the age of 17 in 1945, impressed by Michael Young's drafting of Labour's manifesto, *Let Us Face the Future*.[64] It is not clear exactly when Brian's relationship with the Fabian Society began – possibly during his enforced year at home in 1946 before he was called up to do his National Service.

Despite its close involvement with drafting the 1945 manifesto, the Society appeared to relax during the first years of the Labour government. It wasn't until 1948 that it recognised and drew attention to the absence of a Labour policy for the period after 1950. Ian Mikardo stimulated this process by reviewing the targets that had been set in *Let Us Face the Future*, and identifying those that might be achieved before the next general election.[65] One of the society's most loyal and significant patrons, Gavin Faringdon, made his country home, Buscot Park in Oxfordshire, available for a series of conferences with the overarching title 'Problems Ahead' from 1949. Fabians used these events to discuss the new interpretations of socialism that were beginning to emerge from Labour's first post-war experience of government. An immediate outcome of the Buscot conferences was the decision to produce a second volume of Fabian essays. Even if this could not secure a further Labour term of office after its very narrow majority at the 1950 general election, it might at least to try to ensure that socialism remained a viable political force in Britain. The first volume, *Fabian Essays in Socialism*, had been edited by George Bernard Shaw in 1889 from a series of lectures given that year by prominent Fabians such as Annie Besant and Sidney Webb.[66] This second volume did not appear as planned in time to support Labour at the October election, when Attlee lost to Churchill. *New Fabian Essays* was finally published in 1952 and sold over 5,000 copies, but proved less radical than its 1889 predecessor.[67] The focus was now 'practical socialism', a re-assessment wrought from the hard lessons of Labour's post-war government. The essayists represented the diversity of socialism that existed both within the Fabian Society and the Labour Party – a deceptively united augur of the forthcoming political fractions.

Tony Crosland and *The Future of Socialism*

At the second Buscot Park conference in January 1950 one of the most provocative discussion papers was provided by Tony Crosland, 'Happiness in the Welfare State', later to form part of his seminal work, *The Future of Socialism* (1956).[68] Crosland, born in 1918, was the son of a civil servant and a university lecturer. After attending Highgate, a north London public school, he gained a scholarship at Trinity College Oxford in 1937 to read Modern Greats, as Philosophy, Politics and Economics were then known. He was conscripted in 1940, an example of E.P. Thompson's contention that the war was formative for the political consciousness of that generation:

> I recall a resolute and ingenious civilian army, increasingly
> hostile to the conventional military virtues which became – far
> more than any of my younger friends will begin to credit – an

anti-fascist and consciously anti-imperialist army. Its members voted Labour in 1945: knowing why, as did the civilian workers at home. Many were infused with socialist ideas and expectations wildly in advance of the tepid rhetoric of today's Labour leaders.[69]

Crosland returned to Oxford in 1946 where he became active in the University Socialist Club and was elected as president of the Union, before taking a first-class degree and remaining as a lecturer in Economics until his election as MP for South Gloucestershire in 1950. For the new post-war generation of Fabians such as Bill Rodgers, Crosland was:

> ... a figure of conspicuous glamour. His capacity to reject with contempt a flawed argument presented with bogus authority, or to strip away the sentiment from a conventional political assumption, was greatly admired. So too – although with awe rather than approval – was his ability to be stunningly rude to women when he was simply bored by them. The combination of high intelligence, a wartime record in the paratroops, matinee-idol good looks and a hint of sexual ambivalence made him immensely attractive to those of us ten or more years younger.[70]

The Future of Socialism provided a salient discussion of equality that ensured it quickly became the bible of the revisionists.[71] Crosland argued that the dramatic changes that Britain had experienced since the Second World War were part of longer-term economic trends, seen through the transfer of power in industry from owners to managers and workers.[72] Yet at the same time he identified increasing social inequalities and a gradual change in the pattern of need, acknowledging that poverty was not an absolute but a social and cultural concept.[73] The ultimate socialist aim for Crosland was a multi-faceted equality, of opportunity, status, income and wealth. For him, '"Keynes-plus-modified-capitalism" wholly fails to provide an adequate answer to the social problems which persisted even in the face of the post-war economic prosperity.'[74] His solution was by 'levelling up' – the poor would be helped to improve their situation without affecting the position of the rich, especially through education and tax reforms. Although he attracted strong criticism from both the left and right wings of the Labour movement, *The Future of Socialism* proved to be a 'slow burner', its influence steadily increasing.[75] His political philosophy has endured since his early death in 1977.

After the defeat in October 1951 few people expected Labour to be out of office for the next 13 years. Once the initial despondency had passed, the Fabians re-grouped and focused on supporting Labour in opposition. Donald Chapman, who served as General Secretary between 1949 and 1953, was succeeded by Bill Rodgers, who held the post until 1960 (supported by Gerald Kaufman and then Dick Leonard as Assistant Secretaries). Together they stimulated a recruitment drive and looked to align commissioned research projects with contemporary political issues. The 'Bureaux' through which the Fabian Society managed its domestic and international interests were re-defined, partly to reduce expenditure. By the early 1950s membership, lecture attendances and book sales were falling. Perhaps this was a reflection in part of the success of Labour's 1945–51 government – that the immediate stimuli to popular political activity had been smoothed by the new welfare services and nationalisation of key utilities. The 'Never Again' generation was being replaced by the complacency of the 'Having It So Good' crowd. Yet although the average age of the Fabian member remained in the forties, there were signs of rejuvenation. The Executive now contained a younger cohort including Tony Crosland, Richard Crossman, Hugh Gaitskell, Roy Jenkins, Ian Mikardo and Harold Wilson. Young members of the Colonial Bureau were stimulating debate on international issues – Julius Nyerere, Hastings Banda, Jomo Kenyatta, J.B. Danquah, Nnamdi Azikiwe, Kenneth Kaunda and Tom Mboya, to name only the most active.[76]

A further forum for serious political debate was created in February 1954, when Bill Rodgers and Dick Taverne set up a regular discussion group independent of the Fabian Society. Known as 'The Group' it was intended as a forum to maintain the 'High Attlee' political associations formed at Oxford. Members included David Donnison, Tony Benn and Ronald Waterhouse. Non-Oxford members invited to join included Brian and Peter Shore. Shirley Williams would very much have liked to participate, but Rodgers and Taverne decided at the outset that it would be purely male, 'wishing to maintain the quality and seriousness of the political discussion and not making it a social occasion' (which presumably they expected the presence of females – de facto, wives – would do). Williams saw it as a response to the political threat she posed at a time when many of this cohort were actively seeking parliamentary seats.[77]

The Group met in each others' homes and discussed current issues, often with a heavy legal bent, as 10 of the 26 were lawyers. Rodgers saw Brian as the most original thinker in the group, using it as a forum to propose radical reforms to the Beveridge scheme long before others adopted that view. But he was surprised that Brian chose to participate in a group that did not match his intellectual level. On a social level too, his 'courtier style' could make people feel clumsy and his body language clearly showed a dislike for some of the gossip that went on at the meetings. To some of the group he appeared fastidious and a bit of a loner, protected by his intellectual carapace.[78] For the next six years The Group met regularly – dining afterwards at local restaurants such as the Salamis after meeting at Brian's flat in 1958. 'The boys', as Sylvia Rodgers called them, used their last meetings to discuss Labour's draft manifestos in early 1960. After that individual members of The Group made their own political fortunes over issues such as the Gaitskell split and the Campaign for Democratic Socialism.

The Reform of Social Security

Brian had first drafted a 'political publication' in the summer of 1952, after he returned from the British Council's debating tour to India, Pakistan and Ceylon. It was rejected by *Tribune*, but Donald Chapman felt that it might work as a Fabian Society pamphlet. The working title was *Taxation: a Social Service.* The reviewers were initially lukewarm, with D.N. Chester, the Oxford public administration expert, responding: 'I thought that the general approach was rather naïve and theoretical.…Actually I find myself somewhat allergic to the kind of approach made by Mr Abel-Smith. He seems to be obsessed with the idea that socialism means as many people as possible receiving cash benefits from the state.' Brian subsequently met Chester, who revised his opinion: 'He struck me as being a very good person and one who should be encouraged.'[79] Brinley Thomas, the second referee, was already in correspondence with John Vaizey about their research, and keen to meet both him and Brian.[80] He liked Brian's idea of a Ministry of Social Welfare, and dropping the insurance principle, but found his style difficult – 'not enough statistics to satisfy the academic mind and is too theoretical and classificatory to appeal to the politicians'.[81] Brian also showed the draft to his new mentor, Titmuss, who provided valuable criticism on its context and structure, and the title and focus underwent a subtle but significant shift to *The Reform of Social Security.* Brian timed his article to discuss the impending first quinquennial review of the new post-Beveridge social security system, and the suggestions for radical change that were already beginning to emerge. The Conservatives Iain Macleod and Enoch Powell claimed the rising costs of social security meant that Britain had 'reached a crisis in the social services' which required overturning the Beveridgean principle that services should be provided without means tests.[82] Brinley Thomas urged Brian not to shy away from acknowledging that there were problems with the current system: 'One must not hide behind phrases like "the rationalisation of the rent structure". Already some Local Authorities in their rent rebate schemes are trying to discriminate against people receiving assistance: they exclude them from rebate and expect the NAB [National Assistance Board] to pay the increased rent. There are several variations of this dodge and Labour councils are as partial to it as Tories.'[83]

Brian produced an accomplished analysis, finally published in September 1953, underpinned by an enduring political rhetoric: 'Britain in adversity is still two nations', becoming Titmuss's 'two nations in old age'.[84] He attacked the means test favoured by Macleod and Powell as 'a hangover from the old Poor Law' which perpetuated the class divide and offered no real efficiencies. Yet he was also critical of Labour's refusal to meet this intellectual challenge head on with radical solutions, preferring instead to argue for better benefits within the existing failing system: 'Private superannuation schemes for the salaried and the upper crust of workers are growing so fast that the provision for old age through the state system is gradually becoming a sump for those excluded from other superannuation arrangements, be it by grade or occupation.'[85] He drew on recent research by the think tank PEP that showed that in Lancashire there was reluctance by unemployed people in real need to go to NAB for help because of the indignity of its means test.[86]

Following Titmuss, Brian's analysis proposed that all 'social transfers' should be considered together: 'we should deal not only with Insurance and Assistance but also with family allowances, war pensions and even possibly food subsidies and interest on the National Debt'.[87] He touched on the most fundamental issues of post-war society:

> The crisis in social security is not an economic crisis as usually understood, it is a political crisis – a conflict in social values. How far are those with safer jobs prepared to help the weak? How far are the fortunate prepared to help those overcome by misfortune? How much taxation of all kinds will we accept to achieve these objectives? But has distress to be absolute – the absence of a basic minimum standard of living – or is the state to make some contribution to those whose distress is only relative to their previous standard of living, and who have some means of their own to help them in their misfortune? The problems of

social security raise the whole question of the rationale of the social services.[88]

Inspired partly by the Swiss model, Brian proposed a system that allowed for variable contributions and variable benefits. There would be a minimum and maximum pension (worth only twice the minimum) and paid regardless of an individual's contributions. He thought that the phrase 'superannuation benefit', as used in New Zealand, might carry less stigma than 'old age pension'. His proposals cut through some of the faults in the existing system. Why not delay paying sickness benefit until someone had been ill for two weeks? This would not only 'discourage shirking' but also remove the burden on the over-worked general practitioners (GPs) whose 'certificates are testimonials not so much to their diagnosis as to the eloquence of their patients'.[89] Those bills that caused real anxiety during periods of adversity, such as the mortgage, could be met by 'loans' from a social security agency. Rents needed special consideration, given the wide regional differentials; Beveridge's schemes were based on 'the highly unrealistic behaviour of what might be called a "subsistence housewife".' Brian highlighted how little was really known about family survival. A good start would be by 'having a look at the way people spend their money in real life'.[90]

At the heart of *The Reform of Social Security* was the core socialist principle of equity − a challenge to the 'anomalies which arise from allowing the cold logic of an outmoded insurance principle to cast its inflexibilities over a social service'. His conclusion paraphrased Barbara Wootton: 'The strongest argument for showering gifts upon rich and poor alike is that nobody need then know who is poor and who is not. That however, is an argument from equalitarian premises; and as such it has an academic ring if the rich prefer to continue to look after themselves and are also left free to do so. Real equality is only achieved when all classes not only can, but do, use the same services.'[91]

This first political publication, produced when he was embarking on postgraduate studies in Cambridge, finishes with a classic politician's call to arms: 'In spite of all the plans, hopes and dreams of the past ten years we have failed to abolish *all* want, to meet *all* need. This bleak truth is a challenge to every Socialist.'[92] It was well received within Fabian circles, but also triggered public criticism, especially for implying that tax reliefs benefited the rich more than the poor. Douglas Houghton responded via the *Socialist Commentary*: 'There is such a strong case on social and economic grounds for considering universal superannuation through a National scheme that there is really no need to start a witch-hunt to gain support.'[93]

The Reform of Social Security did not immediately change the course of Labour Party policy. However, it is a good example of Brian acting as what Keith Banting has termed an 'ideas advocate':

> The Individual who analyses problems in a new way or who recombines existing elements so as to introduce a novel pattern, takes the first indispensable step towards innovation. Those who contribute to such conceptual shifts are major agents of innovation, however insignificant they may appear otherwise in politics.[94]

But he did not yet fulfil Hugh Heclo's definition of an 'agent of change', the requirement for effective policy formation of being one of the 'middlemen at the interfaces of various groups'.[95] Brian in 1953 was further still from having Anthony Seldon's four factors necessary for producing policy change: ideas, individuals, interests and circumstances.[96] He had the ideas and interests but was not yet an individual capable of, or in the right position to, effect change.

The publication of *The Reform of Social Security* was significant in marking Brian's arrival on the national political scene. He had previously campaigned for the Labour Party through the Clarion groups within constituencies and involved himself in Cambridge Labour politics. By publishing a pamphlet, he was effectively announcing his participation in intellectual political life. At the age of 26, this made him one of the more junior members of the Fabian Society, and a valued contributor of fresh ideas. The large numbers of Fabians involved with the Labour Party had not guaranteed the generation of new policies. Many of the achievements of that Labour administration could be traced back to Fabian proposals from the 1920s, or to Liberal intellectual debates from the 1930s.[97] Brian offered a new perspective on the achievements of post-war socialism.

Costing the National Health Service

Alongside cultivating his academic relationship with Titmuss, Brian also recognised the value of maintaining his political friendship with Hugh Dalton. In November 1952 Dalton went to speak at the University of Cambridge Labour Club: 'Brian Abel-Smith, who remains rather shyly young and a little twisty-faced and spotty complexioned, but whom I still definitely like, and who liked having a day and a night, on my initiative, at Newton Hall, and was treated nicely this time by Catherine [Walston], again on my initiative – tells me that my only "black" was when I praised Queensland over coffee, as a White Man's Country in the tropics. All these young men are very much against racial and colour prejudice – all for mixed marriages and miscegenation and a grey race emerging.'[98]

In March 1953 Brian was again invited by Catherine Walston to Newton Hall near Cambridge, where other guests for lunch included Dalton, Gunnar Myrdal and Nicky Kaldor. Dalton had arranged for Brian to stay the night so he could use him as a chauffeur for the return to London. Brian arrived with news: he had been offered a two-year research post at the National Institute of Economic and Social Research (NIESR) on the recommendation of Austin Robinson, who chaired its Executive Committee. The NIESR was a relatively new independent research organisation, founded in 1938 and housed at 2 Dean Trench Street, Smith Square, Westminster.[99]

It was agreed that Brian would retain his registration as a Cambridge PhD student, and have full access to the libraries of the LSE and the Royal Statistical Society while working in London.[100] Dalton judged that Brian's move to the NIESR was timely: 'he has been long enough in Cambridge and should do this work well, and make a reputation as an authority before coming into Parliament'.[101] Brian's relocation to London also served Dalton well personally, providing him with another young and eager assistant who appreciated that favours were likely to be returned. In the summer of 1954 Dalton noted in his diary 'Brian Abel-Smith will join me in catching misprints in *Public Finance* [Dalton's book]. He lunched with me last week, after an interval, and I am commending him to Attlee, as an old Haileyburyer and on other grounds, and suggesting he be seen....'[102]

Although Brian had applied to be registered as PhD student in July 1952, he did not provide a research topic until prompted to by the Board of Research Studies in spring 1953. He submitted the title as 'A study of the history, theory and philosophy of horizontal transfer of real income, with particular reference to the problems of the larger family'.[103] Yet his research interests were increasingly stimulated by the energetic inquiries of mentors such as Richard Titmuss and contemporaries like John Vaizey and Peter Townsend. The offer of a post at the NIESR signalled a marked refinement, tied as it was to providing research assistance to Claude Guillebaud, and with Titmuss appointed as his joint supervisor (along with the NIESR Director, W.A.B. Hopkin). His post had been created to support the parliamentary committee appointed in April 1953 to enquire into the cost of the National Health Service. After the formation of the NHS in July 1948 costs appeared to be significantly higher than the predictions that had been produced for Beveridge when he was planning his state-of-the-art 'welfare state'. One of the supposed advantages of moving to a state-funded health service was to be the economic efficiency that would follow. This had been promoted as early as 1911 by the Fabian Lawson Dodd:

> The economy of organisation, the greatly lessened cost of illness due to the increase in sanitary control, and the immense amount saved in the reduced number of working days lost through illness, would make the health tax seem light, and it would be regarded as a profitable form of insurance.[104]

The original estimate had been for an annual recurrent expenditure of £179 million. However, in 1949/50, the actual cost had been £305 million, and it increased year on year thereafter. Enoch Powell, writing with the hindsight of 1961, referred to this as a miscalculation of sublime dimensions.[105] What must also be factored into the immediate assessment of the relative cost of the NHS are the other demands that were pressing on the UK budget, especially the escalating cost of developing a nuclear 'deterrent' and the Korean War re-armament which began in 1950. Against the fundamental Beveridgean ethos of a NHS that provided universal healthcare free at the point of delivery, charges were introduced for dentures and glasses in 1951. Aneurin Bevan resigned his post as Minister of Health in protest. After the fall of the Labour government in October 1951, there was increasing pressure on the Conservative administration to staunch this financial haemorrhage. Prescription charges were introduced in 1952, but a more radical solution was required, and the Treasury proposed a small independent inquiry.

Claude Guillebaud was the nephew of the Cambridge economist Alfred Marshall. He also had studied economics at Cambridge, and made his academic career there. It has been suggested that he was chosen to head the inquiry into the cost of the NHS precisely because 'of his unexceptional middle-of-the-road record. His reputation as a "professional just man" was arguably more valuable for disarming Labour critics than for determining that the committee should be economy-minded.'[106] Guillebaud's committee of four took their time on the inquiry, not publishing their report until January 1956.[107]

Guillebaud could not have accomplished such a wide-ranging and intellectually innovative review of the NHS without research assistance. Brian analysed the cost of the NHS (in England and Wales) for the period 5 July 1948 to 31 March 1953 in social accounting terms. He adapted statistics from the Ministry of Health to measure the cost of the service in terms of current productive resources. He analysed the capital expenditure, and assessed the rate of hospital building by comparison with pre-war construction and contemporary US data. He calculated the expenditure required to maintain the present hospital infrastructure (it was estimated that 45 per cent of hospitals predated 1891, and 21 per cent 1861).

The political usefulness of Brian's thesis really came in his final chapter. His analysis showed that whereas the factor cost of the services expressed in current prices increased from £375.9 million in 1949–50 to £435.9 million in 1952–53, the cost expressed in constant (1948–49) prices increased only from £374.9 million to £388.6 million. This relative increase in costs was due to additional services and inflation, not, as the Treasury wished to believe, to inefficiency and extravagance. Expressed as a percentage of the gross national product (GNP) the cost of the NHS had actually declined from 3.82 per cent in 1949–50 to 3.52 per cent in 1952–53. Brian also modelled the effects on the NHS of changing prices, charges and population changes, and boldly extrapolated future changes in costs. He called in favours with Ian Stewart in the Department of Applied Economics at Cambridge to supply him with detailed breakdowns of agricultural prices, and in return sent him a copy of his working paper on the cost of the NHS for 1948.[108]

Brian's research thus provided the backbone for the somewhat unexpected Guillebaud Committee's conclusion: that the NHS was actually very good value for money, and that it demanded a greater share of GNP rather than the current retrenchment, as some politicians were suggesting. With his usual enthusiasm, Brian also elaborated in his thesis on a number of related questions – the role of trading activities, the costs of part-time and whole-time specialists, the comparative costs of domiciliary and hospital confinement and the use of capital expenditure to save annual recurrent expenditure.

Brian had to make an eleventh-hour formal application to Harvey, Secretary of the Board of Research Studies at Cambridge on 2 November 1954 to align his registered topic with the real focus of his research.[109] He submitted his thesis, 'The cost of the National Health Service (an application of social accounting)' on 25 January 1955 and the oral exam took place at the LSE on 9 March 1955, with Claude Guillebaud travelling from Cambridge to act as examiner, along with Alan Peacock, Reader in Public Finance at the University of London.[110] Guillebaud's examiner's report commended Brian for displaying 'much ingenuity', but did not find his additional research, presented in the appendices, very satisfactory. Brian had resorted to using data supplied to him by the Treasurer of the South West Metropolitan Regional Hospital Board (RHB), and Guillebaud found this unrepresentative of other RHBs. Despite this relatively minor technical gripe, there were no difficulties with passing the oral exam. Guillebaud reported that 'he seems to me to possess, in addition to good academic ability and remarkable industry, qualities of insight into the nature of the material he is studying which make his investigation a constructive piece of work and not a mere assemblage of facts and figures'.[111] His PhD was given unanimous approval by the Faculty of Economics and Politics Degree Committee on 3 May. The members of the Committee read almost like a first XI of 20th-century economics: Guillebaud, Robertson, Robinson, Brogan, Kaldor, Prest, Cohen, Stone, Dobb, Reddaway, Sraffa and Youngson.[112]

Brian's PhD research had not been a solitary affair, as with so many postgraduate projects, but conducted in collaboration with, and under the supervision of, Titmuss. The output was threefold and with varying levels of impact: Brian's Cambridge thesis (three copies), the eventual Guillebaud report published in January 1956 by HMSO and, more significantly, his first book, co-authored with Titmuss, *The Cost of the National Health Service in England and Wales*, published by Cambridge University Press in March 1956.[113] Guillebaud was initially uncomfortable with the provocatively broad sweep of the Abel-Smith/Titmuss research when they submitted their memorandum to him in January 1955.[114] Yet it was entirely in sympathy with their academic raison d'être: to investigate the wider context of social services provision in post-war Britain. Brian had already effectively politicised these academic interests through his Fabian pamphlet, *The Reform of Social Security* (1953).

Guillebaud accepted the Abel-Smith/Titmuss evidence, and the government was forced to accept that dismantling the NHS could never be a politically feasible option. But the Guillebaud enquiry did admit that there were problems with the system. Sir John Maude, one of the Committee members (who had been Permanent Secretary at the Ministry of Health during the initial planning for the NHS), used the report to register what has become a chronic complaint, that the original tripartite structure for the NHS (hospital services, GPs and local authority services) was its major flaw, and that no amount of additional funding would correct this. The official government press release on 25 January 1956, 'No fundamental changes recommended. Service needs time to settle down', belied the more nuanced Abel-Smith/Titmuss research findings, which were duly picked up by publications such as *The Times* and *The Lancet*. After the initial news had sunk in, there was growing dissatisfaction that actually Guillebaud had taken three years to tell us little new. It was in keeping with the personality of this mild-mannered Cambridge don not to champion radical reform. When Iain Macleod, the Minister of Health, presented the 500-page report with its 50-page conclusion to the Prime Minister, Anthony Eden confessed: 'I'm afraid it has very few useful proposals'.[115] The Treasury naturally found it 'pretty awful' and 'highly disappointing and indeed unsatisfactory'.[116]

Too political for research?

While working at the NIESR Brian had also become heavily involved with the Workers' Educational Association (WEA), which provided evening courses and residential schools aimed at working-class people, some of whom were able to participate for free or at reduced rates. It stressed in its adverts: 'No formalities, no qualifications are required, the atmosphere is friendly and informal'. Between January and April 1954 Brian travelled weekly to Kings Langley, a few miles north of London in Hertfordshire, where his course 'Economic and Social Problems' included lectures on 'The Dollar Problem', 'The British Population Problem', 'Agriculture' and 'The Housing Problem'. In July he spoke at the WEA Eastern District weekend course held at Sidney Sussex College Cambridge, and also at the National Summer School at Broadstairs in Kent. In November he was one of a panel of lecturers (including Asa Briggs, T.E. Chester of the Acton Society Trust and Brian Keith-Lucas) for the Oxford University Extension Lectures on the theme of 'The Social Services'. Also during the winter he gave WEA lectures for the Bishops Stortford branch.

In July 1955 he was a guest lecturer at the National Assistance Board's (NAB) Cambridge Summer School at Sidney Sussex College, where he lectured on 'The Economics of Social Security' and led a study group on 'The Meaning of Subsistence and Problems of Inflation'. The following week he was in Broadstairs for the WEA's fortnight-long summer school as a member of the resident teaching staff, and in the autumn he returned to give a series of six weekend tutorial classes with the theme 'Ten Years After', advertised as a focus on 'salient problems in British social and economic affair that have emerged since 1945'. During the autumn and winter he also gave lectures to the Yiewsley and West Drayton WEA branch on 'The Citizen and the Community' and spoke at weekend schools in Oxford and Rochester on 'The Welfare State and Local Government', 'The NHS', and 'Population Changes: Some Consequences for Social Work'. Nearly every autumn weekend was taken up with some form of public lecture. In April 1956 he spent three of the four weekends travelling to give talks: to Broadstairs, this time to speak at the NALGO and South East District Committee's weekend school, to Torquay to speak at the Institute of Hospital Almoners South West Region annual conference (on the cost of the NHS), and to the Institute of Hospital Administrators' Sheffield Region's weekend school at Skegness Convalescent Homes ('The Financial aspects of the Report of the Guillebaud Committee'). These were all done *gratis* (apart from travelling costs). Brian also had the occasional paid public speaking engagement, for example, a six-minute piece for the BBC's *At Home and Abroad* radio show, when he spoke on compensation for redundant workers in July 1956, for the fee of 10 guineas.

There was a hiatus between Brian successfully completing the NHS research and his PhD in the spring of 1955, and the eventual publication of the Guillebaud report in 1956. As his fixed-term post at NIESR drew to a close he began to explore with Richard Titmuss potential follow-on research projects. One of the most logical would be to conduct a detailed study on pensions and the conditions of old age, an issue he had flagged in his Fabian pamphlet in 1953, *The Reform of Social Security*. Under Titmuss's guidance Brian drafted a three-page project outline, 'Social Provision for the Old in Great Britain 1900–1950', to incorporate the history of British pensions, comparative analysis with other countries and projections for future pension needs. It was planned as a three-year project, and costed at around £5,000 for Brian's salary and research costs. Titmuss made a preliminary proposal to W.A. Sanderson at the Nuffield Foundation in February 1955, following up with a telephone call to explain that while their work for the Guillebaud Committee on the cost of the NHS remained confidential, he could say that they had proved the demand for a similar study of pensions, and that Brian was well-equipped to do this research.[117] Sanderson wrote on 25 March with the news that the trustees did not think that a full application would be successful. Titmuss pressed for some explanation, and was told, 'off the record', that they were not impressed by the political partiality of Brian's new Fabian pamphlet *New Pensions for the Old*.

Brian took this rejection very personally, berating the Nuffield Foundation not only for failing to take up a reference on his work from Hopkin at the NIESR, but also seeing it as a slight on Titmuss's own academic reputation. 'The effect of all this on me is to make me all the more determined to go on with the job at any price. As you know, I have some private means and like Beatrice Webb I shall use them to do the work if all else fails.'[118] He suggested to Titmuss that he write to Sanderson and offer the trustees a face-saving way to reconsider the proposal, by suggesting that he had rushed them into a decision before they could solicit independent referees. This was unsuccessful and provoked a further response from Sanderson that Titmuss would be better to let matters rest rather than risk damaging his own reputation with the Foundation.[119] Titmuss now sought another way to keep Brian in employment once his NIESR fellowship finished at the end of May. He created a post for his protégé at the LSE. Brian was duly interviewed in June 1955 and appointed as Assistant Lecturer in Social Science from 1 October 1955 at a salary of £650 pa. He was to remain at the LSE in varying capacities for the rest of his life.

4

Political ambitions and private passions, 1955–59

An independent life

New Pensions for the Old

Dalton's heir

Whose Welfare State?

National Insurance

National Assistance

Reconceptualising poverty

The history of the island in the twentieth century divides sharply into two halves – to put it in a phrase, before and after the simultaneous shocks of Suez and Rock and Roll. (Eric Hobsbawm, 2002)[1]

In his late twenties, and before the legalisation of homosexual acts (1967), Brian managed to develop a comfortable, independent private life that he could share with his partners. However, this strained the relationship with his widowed mother who relied heavily on support from her two sons. His public life continued to be centred on his academic work at the LSE, where research was explicitly policy-orientated to assist the Labour Party, who continued to be out of government. His work, especially on poverty, National Insurance and National Assistance with Peter Townsend, made them invaluable to politicians such as Richard Crossman. In parallel to his British work, Brian was also beginning to take on international consultancies for organisations such as the World Health Organization (WHO) (discussed in later chapters). In 1957

Hugh Dalton announced his retirement from politics and offered Brian his safe MP's seat. It provoked one of the major decisions of Brian's life.

An independent life

Having secured his new, permanent, academic position at the LSE Brian was able to make some domestic decisions. After he gained the NIESR post he returned from Cambridge to live at the Durward House flat with Lionel and his mother Vivée, then leased a flat at 16 Vincent Square Mansions in Walcott Street as soon as he was able to in 1953. He initially shared this with J.J. Davies, a Cambridge friend, and then with John Vaizey. It was a small two-bedroom flat, on the fourth floor of a Victorian apartment block in the Pimlico area of London. Brian, through Uncle Harold's bequest, now had the funds to indulge in interior design on a much more ambitious scale than he had accomplished in his Haileybury study or Cambridge rooms. He also saw – in true Abel-Smith entrepreneurial style – the potential to profit from his expenditure: he sold a feature article on his newly refurbished flat to *House Beautiful* magazine.[2]

Two friends were invited to be photographed having supper with him. Introduced in the feature as Shirley and Sue, Brian had no doubt also chosen them because they provided the elegant human factor to complement his design taste. They were, however, real friends: Shirley Worthington was a well-known model, whose family had been flat sharers at Durward House. Sue Holman was the only child of Vivien Leigh, who hoped that Brian would be suitable marriage material for her 'rather plain' daughter. (Brian exploited this contact: when he wished to move out of Vincent Square Mansions, he offered it first to Laurence Olivier after he heard he was looking for a flat.) The glorious technicolour *House Beautiful* photographs are accompanied by a description of how Brian subdivided the kitchen and constructed a false harlequin ceiling from fibreboard – suspended to allow for suitcase storage above. In the sitting room egg boxes were stuck to the ceiling to enhance the acoustics and in his bedroom a 'wine cellar' filled the gap between bookshelves and cornice. The flat was a riot of colour: yellow and maroon walls in his bedroom, olive green and lilac for the guest bedroom, and curtains made from black and white towelling in the bathroom. A list of stockists was provided for those magazine readers who wished to emulate the Brian Abel-Smith look.

16 Vincent Square Mansions was the epitome of Brian's life: stylish yet discreetly monied. It was designed to impress, from the portrait of

his distant ancestor, Baron Carington, to the beaded kitchen curtain brought back from one of his foreign trips. He had been in Italy again in September 1955 with his brother Lionel for a late summer holiday. In 1956 he acted as chauffeur and seasoned guide for the Titmuss family, when they squashed into his sports car to drive to Munich for an academic conference. They drove across France, having put the car on the Bristol Freighter plane for the short crossing from Southend airport to Calais. He charmed 12–year-old Ann by ordering for them in French in restaurants, and teaching her to dive in Alpine lakes. While he and Richard attended the conference, Kay and Ann, with Geraldine Aves, were sent off to buy him a goatskin.[3]

New Pensions for the Old

Labour's welfare policy formation had been surprisingly stale since the inter-war years. The Fabian Society had continued to reiterate its primary proposals developed in the 1920s: economic planning and nationalisation of major industries and public utilities. Six months before Labour's 1945 victory, the Party had no agreed policy programme, and many of the subsequent initiatives were actually re-packaged Liberal ideals that had inspired Beveridge in 1942.[4] Bill Rodgers, General Secretary of the Fabian Society, summed up the optimistic naivety in which they met to develop new policy initiatives in the 1950s: 'Our generation – or so we thought – would help make socialism once again relevant to the people. We did not know that we were exploring a future that we would fail to bring about and that Labour would be in office for only eleven of the next forty years.'[5] Labour were pitted against 'the skilful economic management of R.A. Butler and the emergence of a new generation of clever and mainly liberal Tory ministers in Iain Macleod, Reginald Maudling, Enoch Powell and Ted Heath'.[6] Yet the Conservatives did not have an easy ride during their governments. The mid-1950s was a time of international crises – some unfortunately homemade such as Suez in 1956. Others, such as the Soviet's violent crushing of the Hungarian uprising in the same year, threatened a new world order.

Beveridge's 'five giants' had not been slain overnight with the development of social welfare policies after the Second World War. Although the NHS had brought immediate and free attention to ill health, the underlying cause for many was a level of poverty that appeared immune to the new social security system. At the root of this was a failure to fully elaborate the concept of egalitarianism. While the war had 'contributed to a solidaristic environment', this did not automatically mean treating all members of society equally.[7] Beveridge was not proposing to make his social welfare programme into a redistributive mechanism. Although such ideas had been raised by think tanks such as PEP, Beveridge rejected what he saw as 'the epitome of the Santa Claus state'.[8]

Brian and Peter Townsend had both been researching and publishing on social welfare since the early 1950s (Townsend's pamphlet, *Poverty: Ten Years After Beveridge*, was published by PEP in 1952; Brian's Fabian pamphlet, *The Reform of Social Security*, appeared in 1953). Although Townsend had not yet made the official move into the LSE, he was already de facto one of Titmuss's men. They also discovered that they shared the same neighbourhood: for a year in 1952–53 Townsend and his wife Ruth lived in a single-room flat at 21 Maunsel Street, only 100 yards around the corner from Brian in Vincent Square Mansions. Their first son Matthew had been born in February 1952, and Townsend spent many hours round at Brian's flat discussing their joint political and research interests.[9]

In 1955 Brian and Townsend jointly published a pamphlet that opened up a radically different discussion on the welfare of the retired. It had been commissioned by the PEP think tank, but then rejected, as Brian later recalled, 'on the argument that flat rate pensions were the British way of doing things'. Brian and Townsend took it instead to the Fabian Society, who published it within three weeks.[10] *New Pensions for the Old* developed Brian's idea of a system that was based on earnings-related contributions and benefits, rather than the flat-rate Beveridge model.[11] They proposed addressing the problem of old-age poverty through a new scheme of 'national superannuation'. This was to have a redistributive element so that income inequalities from working years would not be carried into retirement, but pensioners would be guaranteed a minimum standard of living. In part it was a response to the *Report of the Committee on the Economic and Financial Problems of the Provision for Old Age* – the Conservative-appointed Phillips Committee – that advocated restraining costs by the expansion of private pensions and means-tested supplementation for those who were not adequately covered.[12] The Abel-Smith/Townsend scheme was a provocative yet attainable proposal. Through sections with headings such as 'Beveridge Repudiated', 'The Subsistence Principle', and 'Two Nations in Old Age' they sought to produce a vision that the general public could understand. Brian sent a copy to his mother, inscribed 'To Ma to explain why her son has been so busy love Brian'.[13] Brian had also been busy writing for the *Socialist Commentary*, highlighting how the government currently subsidised private pensions, in a provocative article entitled '£500 million for the Rich'.[14] But despite the close association between the Fabian Society and the Labour Party and these public statements, it was not easy to introduce such innovation into policy development. It took the interest of Richard Crossman to lift Titmuss and the Titmice from the ranks of keen Fabian Society supporters into useful policy collaborators.

Richard Crossman, known as Dick by his friends (and by his opponents as 'Double-Crossman'), was of Titmuss's generation, but from a different background. After attending Winchester and Oxford he pursued intermittently academic and journalistic careers, with a wartime spell in 'black' propaganda. His election as Labour MP for Coventry East in 1945 began a political career that never really reached the heights that he hoped for. To many he was seen as the perennial dilettante, not quite a serious player either in political theory or practical politics. Liverpool MP Bessie Braddock described him as 'a man of many opinions, most of them of short duration'.[15] Crossman described himself as possessing a 'bump of irreverence', a reaction to his right-wing establishment family (his father was a High Court judge), albeit expressed in a casual manner.[16] He did, however, give serious consideration to the major split in the post-war Labour Party, coming down firmly on the side of the *Keep Left* camp who called for a purer and more radical socialism than the compromise that Herbert Morrison and others had proposed.

As the factions consolidated around Bevan and Gaitskell in the 1950s, Crossman steered a centrist course, switching allegiances as his personal socialist ideology developed, but he contributed little to the refinement of social democratic doctrine.[17] During the 1950s he made a name for himself as a provocative essayist, journalist and commentator: 'the prime function of the Labour Party, as of the Liberal Party before it, is to provide an ideology for nonconformist critics of the Establishment. A Labour Party of this kind is likely to be out of office for much longer periods than the Tories.'[18] This quotation fits well with his colleague Roy Jenkins' assessment: 'his style was the antithesis of the austerely academic. His central desire was to grip the attention of his audience, almost to seize them intellectually by the throat, and to this end he would always prefer a slightly shocking generalisation, whether or not well founded in the facts, to platitudinous verities.'[19]

The history of how Crossman came into contact with the ideas of the Titmice on pensions contributes to the mythology of this somewhat maverick politician. In one account, he claimed to have been given a copy of the *New Pensions for the Old* pamphlet the night before he had to make a major speech on pension demands at the 1955 Labour Party annual conference in Margate:

> I took it [the pamphlet] to bed. Now there come times in the life of an intellectual when illumination happens. I read that pamphlet. I understood it. I'm not very good usually at economics but I understood it. With a blinding flash I understood national superannuation.[20]

The eleventh-hour invitation to Crossman to give the speech had come from Edith Summerskill, then chair of the Party. As shadow Minister of National Insurance (the position she had held in Attlee's government in 1950) she would normally have made the response on this issue herself, but her chair's position prevented her from speaking. By asking Crossman (then a rival Bevanite) to do it, she hoped to cause some humiliation to this section of the Party. To the surprise of most, Crossman 'delivered one of those bravura displays of sheer expository power that no figure in the Labour Party has ever been able to match. He spoke with barely more than a note for nearly an hour and did not lose the rapt attention of his audience for a moment.'[21] His speech kick-started a more radical reform of Labour's pensions policy than its National Executive could have anticipated.

The pamphlet had been given to Crossman by Peter Shore, then Head of the Labour Party's Research Department, who was in contact with Brian and Townsend. In a later, more measured account, Crossman acknowledged that he had been aware of the Titmuss group's research on social welfare for some time before the conference. Crossman had been a member of the National Executive's Social Services Sub-committee since December 1953, and in December 1954 had used his article 'The end of Beveridge' in the *New Statesman* to declare that 'the Beveridge method has run into a dead-end'.[22] After the conference, in 1956, Brian, Titmuss and Townsend were invited to join the Study Group on Security and Old Age – a sub-committee of the Labour Party's National Executive Home Policy Committee. Under Crossman's chairmanship they worked to provide the technical detail required for a new pensions policy.[23]

Titmuss was not a natural Labour Party man. Before the war he had been an enthusiastic member of the Liberal Party. The state's refusal to support families to his exacting standards slowly drove him towards socialism, not initially to the Labour Party, but to the short-lived Commonwealth Party that had been formed in 1942. This chimed with his 'simple utopianism', especially his insistence on family life founded on traditional British cultural values. In 1955 he delivered a provocatively revisionist lecture, 'The Social Division of Welfare', in which he highlighted the damaging narrowness of the government's current definition of social services.[24] He advocated a reassessment that saw welfare not just in terms of cash welfare payments but also included the benefits in kind such as tax allowances and the occupational welfare that results from employment. Some credit for this remarkable lecture must go to Brian, who had been informally tutoring Titmuss in economics while they worked together on the costs of the NHS report for the Guillebaud Committee. Titmuss was now armed with social accounting analytical skills to demonstrate the weaknesses of the hallowed Beveridgean 'welfare state', and to do this at the epicentre of Labour Party policy formation.

Townsend's initial impression of working with Crossman was overwhelming: impressed by his 'intellectual versatility and tenacity and sheer dexterity', one of 'the three best minds I've ever met, undoubtedly fast … he had a kind of Socratic ability to cross-examine and to knock the bottom out of arguments'.[25] To others 'his reputation was that of an intellectually-arrogant bully or steam-roller (but himself thin-skinned and insecure); someone who could or would not listen to others, who was inconsistent and unreliable in his views and judgements (Double-Crossman); who approached politics in a Machiavellian and conspiratorial way but at the same time was his own worst enemy and amazingly gaffe-prone.'[26]

The Study Group met once a week in the late afternoons at the House of Commons. Heclo, informed by his discussions with Brian and Titmuss, says that they were 'chaotic affairs'.[27] Other members of the Study Group (which Crossman called his 'working party') included the former Ministers for Pensions and National Insurance Hilary Marquand, Edith Summerskill and Jim Griffiths; Peggy Herbison, the Scottish MP who was to later steer the pensions issue in the 1960s; Harold Wilson, Hugh Gaitskell, G.I. Brinham and R.J. Gunter from the Labour Party's National Executive Committee (NEC), and Douglas Jay, an economist turned MP and former adviser to Dalton. There were three possible solutions to what has since been termed 'Beveridge's straitjacket': more generous benefits given through a means test; increasing Exchequer contributions to the pensions scheme to raise all benefits; and combining the flat-rate benefit with graduated contributions. The Titmice considered the third option the most feasible.[28] This was not a novel solution – a similar scheme was operating in the US and was also being considered in Germany and Sweden.[29] They also wanted to link it to prices and average earnings, with more generous provision for women and transferable benefits for those who changed jobs.

The trade union representatives such as Dick Dale held firm to their insistence on flat-rate contributory insurance, but slowly acknowledged that contributions under this scheme would never be enough to ensure subsistence for the poorest.[30] It was not until September 1956 that the Study Group finally recommended establishing a national superannuation scheme 'as a supplement to the present National Insurance Scheme'.[31] Titmuss continued to take the lead in refining the scheme through the autumn and winter, producing another report for the Committee in December 1956.[32] This was also informed by Brian's attendance at an international seminar in Copenhagen in October that discussed European pensions. Brian played a further key role, meeting with the Woolwich Transport & General Workers' Union branch at members' homes in south London and helping to draft their own report.[33] Getting trade union approval was only part of the journey from Crossman's 'blinding flash' in Margate. The tension between academic and political timescales became clear when Titmuss suggested that 'it would be desirable for another group of people to study the more technical aspects of the matter for perhaps two or three years.'[34] Crossman could not afford that luxury.

Crossman relied heavily on the Titmice during the spring of 1957, taking them along to meetings with the trade unions, exploring solutions to financing problems over dinners:

> ... by now I have got to know them very well. Abel-Smith is said to be thirty-eighth in succession to the throne, while Peter Townsend tells me that he spent his youth going round each summer to the seaside piers, where his mother was a pierette. Peter has done three years studying old age and poverty in Bethnal Green, while Abel-Smith is the intellectual who works out all the mathematical formulae. The relationship between them and my three Transport House men is fascinating because it is the same relationship as that between the public school intellectuals and the secondary school intellectuals in the Parliamentary Party. Each is intensely suspicious of the other.[35]

At every stage Crossman went back to Gaitskell and Harold Wilson (shadow Chancellor) at the Home Policy Committee to approve the draft plan. As the time of publication drew near in March 1957, Wilson suggested a crafty division of ownership: why not have the first three chapters as a Party statement, with an Appendix signed by Titmuss,

Abel-Smith and Townsend: 'We shall get all the kudos for their research and they will have to be responsible for all the detailed figures.'[36] Titmuss was then in the US on a research visit with his family, and reliant on Brian and Townsend to handle the negotiations.[37] Through a series of transatlantic letters and cables he approved of signing the Appendix, and of the final adjustments to the plan.[38] Titmuss was able to show the galley proofs at a meeting of 'all the top level boys and girls from Washington' including Bob Ball, Alvin David and Ida Merriam. Frustratingly they spotted a number of 'critical problems', but too late in the day to amend the final draft.[39]

Brian worked closely with Crossman on the final draft, clearly revelling in his new role:

> I read your latest edition last night. I was not expecting to enjoy it. I was quite frankly rather bored at the prospect of having to read through the stale old arguments again. I was however, completely fascinated by it. I really think it is a masterpiece. In fact I am already trying to copy your short sentence style! It reads so swiftly and carries the reader, as Beatrice Webb said, "inexorably to the intended conclusion".... I suppose it is the job of a technical adviser to point out any little slips.... I hope you will forgive me for adopting the royal warning style, but that is, I suppose, the job of the unpaid civil servant.[40]

Brian was prepared to go the extra mile in this role, taking advantage of a research trip to Geneva the following week to gain more support for Crossman's model from discussions at the International Actuaries conference. Townsend kept up the transatlantic dialogue with the Titmuss family, his letters full of political gossip and Townsend family holiday plans, signing off, as was now usual for both Brian and Townsend when writing to their professor and mentor, 'lots of love'.

The Committee's agreed plan finally appeared in May 1957 as *National Superannuation: Labour's Policy for Security in Old Age*.[41] Brian sent advance copies to individuals who had been instrumental in its development, including Red Somers at the Department of Political Science at the University of California, Berkeley: 'The appendix owes an awful lot to the many talks we had together.'[42] His Cambridge friend Jack Ashley, now Industrial Talks Producer at the BBC, gave a dinner to bring Brian together with Michael Stephens, producer for the Third Programme, so that *National Superannuation* could be given publicity on the day of its launch. The economist Alan Peacock and the

Conservative politician Sir Keith Joseph were selected as commentators, and Brian sent them embargoed copies of the report.[43]

The work on pensions did not stop after the press launch. Titmuss began drafting the outlines for a substantial research project and book: *Pensions in Britain (or the Social Endowment of Old Age: A study in the Ethics of Redistribution).*[44] In June, through an Abel Smith relative, Brian arranged for Townsend and himself to have lunch with W.J. Foster, one of the partners at the city stockbroking firm of de Zoete & Gorton, to discuss long-term share price trends, a critical issue if national superannuation funds were to be invested in equities.[45] He also accepted an invitation from Geoffrey Hutchinson of the NAB to give another talk at its July Cambridge Summer School. He used this opportunity to highlight the insidious stigmatisation that the NAB perpetuated, citing its Bedford office where claimants were forced to use a separate entrance from those on other business.[46] Hutchinson later responded – no money to re-structure the entrance to the offices, but he hoped Brian would lunch with him soon at his club.

In July 1957 Brian took a busman's holiday, driving Peter Townsend in his silver-grey sports car down to the Fourth International Conference of Gerontology at Merano, Italy. They took it in turns to drive, so the other could sunbathe on the back seat, with stops to cool off in the glacial north Italian lakes.[47] Brian's paper was on the subject of 'The Cost of Support of the Aged' and reflected the work he and the Study Group had been engaged with over the past two years. On his return, Brian began to help Crossman gain the TUC's blessing at their annual conference in Blackpool, a necessary step before progressing to the Labour Party conference in Brighton in October, where it was formally accepted. Crossman's speech at Brighton disingenuously credited the Woolwich Transport & General Workers Union for the origins of the plan – a history designed to appeal to the rank and file of the Party and to show that ordinary members of the Labour Party could influence policy. To have credited Titmuss and his team would not have produced the same morale boost.[48]

National Superannuation proposed a redistributive scheme that favoured blue- rather than white-collar workers, but was not so egalitarian as to rile Gaitskell. As a political concession to the seven million people in occupational schemes it proffered a system of partial contracting out for approved existing schemes, and full transferability of pension rights. Strong statutory controls were proposed to address concerns about potentially large capital accumulation funds by private insurance companies. This fitted well with Labour's new preference for 'back door nationalisation' through the purchase of equity shares rather than direct purchase of industries. Brian was concerned, however, that this element of the plan would lead to criticism that the Labour Party intended to gamble with pensioners' savings.[49] He tried to dispel this rumour by building his autumn programme of public talks around national superannuation. Nearly every weekend between the middle of September and the end of November he spent at regional meetings, speaking at the Labour constituency parties at Deal and Dulwich, the WEA weekend school at Birmingham, giving talks for Fabian Society groups in Norwood, Grimsby and Hull, and addressing the University of Oxford Labour Club.

It is interesting that the conceptualisation of poverty in *National Superannuation* predates the more recognised revisions of the early 1960s. It demonstrated that the existing state pensions system resulted in workers losing their quality of life:

> This is poverty. No arbitrary and sophisticated attempt to draw lines of minimum subsistence could supply a better definition. We believe that an adequate pension can best be defined as a pension which prevents this catastrophic fall in living standards as a result of retirement or declining earning power. It means the right to go on living in the same neighbourhood, to enjoy the same hobbies and to be able to afford to mix with the same circle of friends.[50]

Seven years later Brian and Townsend would flesh out this concept into their classic work, *The Poor and the Poorest*.[51] For now, it provided Crossman with a populist image on which to pin his vision of a fairer welfare state.

The Conservative government's reaction was to immediately denounce the plan – the work of 'the skiffle group of London School of Economics professors' – as unworkable. John Boyd-Carpenter was particularly aggressive in his attack on the calculations that lay behind Crossman's scheme. Crossman, Brian, Titmuss and Townsend responded with letters to *The Times*, but there was some substance to Boyd-Carpenter's claims.[52] As *The Spectator* put it, 'It cannot be pleasant to be told that you are a little matter of £2,750 million out in one of your most important calculations (the estimated surplus after ten years); but what must have hurt most was the fact that several of the miscalculations were not matters of abstruse mathematics but matters of common sense, such as taking into account the cost of administering the scheme or noticing that the revenue from Northern Ireland might possibly entail expenditure there.'[53]

Given Labour's promised level of immediate pensions ('retirement on half pay, etc'), this Crossman scheme was effectively moving Britain from paying pensions out of the National Insurance Fund into a 'pay-as-you-go' (PAYG) system. This issue had troubled the Titmice for some time, and had been fudged by the creation of a seemingly larger fund than required to give the assurance of 'actuarial rectitude'.[54] Brian conceded its necessity: 'If we openly condemn the actuarial approach, then the Life Offices would probably manage to convince the country that we were asking the community to commit its savings to a scheme which was far from safe – to a scheme, in short, which Mr Crossman has thought up in his bath.'[55] For Brian, Titmuss and Townsend this was their first taste of being on the inside of policy formation, with all its hard-fought compromises. As Crossman noted in his diary:

> The striking fact, looking back, is how un-ready-made Titmuss's ideas were when he was challenged to cook up a scheme. Suddenly he and Abel-Smith discovered that they hadn't the answers to half a dozen major problems.... So for them this has been a tremendous education, to see the relationship between real politics and their academic study of social services. Right up to the last moment I was catching Abel-Smith out with unsolved problems in their own working model at the end of our report. And still the scheme is only three-quarters baked – but then it can't get baked any more without public discussion.[56]

Dalton's heir

In June 1957 Dalton told Gaitskell that he intended to retire after the annual October Labour Party conference. It was to be a 'planned sunset', and Dalton was insistent on having a hand in choosing his successor as MP for Bishop Auckland. The right person had to be 'somebody of whom he was fond, whom he could trust, and who could be expected to rise far and fast within the Party'.[57] Brian fitted the bill perfectly. In August he faced the final test, when he accompanied Dalton on his annual month-long summer holiday. They travelled together through Italy, with transport provided by the Italian government, making a series of unofficial inspections of re-forestation schemes, and visiting Mussolini's Second World War hide-out. Dalton relished Brian's company: 'one of the best of my young friends, not only young, but charming and handsome, energetic, quick at every uptake, easily amused and amusing, a perfect companion on such a holiday.'[58]

On their return Dalton wrote to Gaitskell: 'I want to fix a lunch with you and Brian Abel-Smith, my favourite so far, as my successor ... if you like him, we must commend him to Sam Watson, & arrange a meeting.'[59] This he did in October, following his official retirement announcement. Brian travelled to Dalton's Bishop Auckland constituency to meet Watson and to address a miners' meeting. All seemed to be going well, until Brian got a bad case of cold feet. Ben Pimlott, who interviewed Brian for his biography of Dalton, provides a wonderfully vivid account of how this played out: 'Abel-Smith, who had gone along with Dalton's plans up to now, suddenly changed his mind. He decided that he did not wish to be a politician after all.... Dalton refused to believe it, then flew into a rage. Finally he tried flattery and bribery: he would extract from Gaitskell a firm promise that once in Parliament, Abel-Smith would not stay on the backbenches for long. None of this worked. Ruth [Dalton's wife] showed the young man out after his ordeal. "I can guess what that was all about," she said. "You've turned him down". "Yes", said Abel-Smith. "Thank God," she replied. "I remember another enthusiastic young socialist years ago in the same situation. He's a very different man today. I'm referring to Hugh Gaitskell".'[60]

Pimlott is generous in this assessment of Brian. He might have been 'young' at 31 relative to Dalton's 70 years, but he was a mature, confident character. He had spent the best part of 10 years establishing a reputation as an academic socialist, and forging alliances in political circles. He counted Tony Crosland and Dick Crossman as personal friends, and was increasingly active and influential after his election to the Fabian Society Executive in 1956. He was closely associated with other political groups, including The Group organised by Bill Rodgers and Dick Taverne, which met monthly from 1954 for wide-ranging political discussions.[61] He also accepted an invitation to join the secretive XYZ club, which brought together politicians, economists and city financiers at monthly meetings at the House of Commons. Many of his contemporaries were already beginning parliamentary careers – Shirley Williams fought the Harwich seat that Brian had rejected in 1952.

Brian's political flirtation with Dalton had begun in 1951, and he had invested heavily in earning the elder statesman's respect. He was acutely aware that he was being groomed by Dalton to be his successor, so why the very late withdrawal? Brian did not doubt his own political abilities, but fears outweighed self-belief. Townsend recalls a late night discussion in which Brian talked candidly about the risks involved in accepting Dalton's proposal. These centred on the very real risk of prosecution if his sexuality were to be publically exposed.[62] As a homosexual he would be seen as unfit to hold the office of MP. Yet other gay politicians had been prepared to take this risk. Perhaps the most flagrant example was Tom Driberg, whose sexuality was an open secret in Westminster, despite his marriage. Other homosexual and bisexual MPs had also overcome these dilemmas in pursuit of political careers. Some had taken the route of a sham marriage, and Brian discussed this option with Ruth Townsend, whom he was very close to. He loved 'Ruthie', as he called her, and respected her opinion. She would have put the moral position to him very clearly.[63]

Perhaps the fact that Dalton immediately forgave Brian for his last-minute change of heart should be seen as genuine empathy based on shared experience? He sent him (another) copy of *The Fateful Years* inscribed 'Storm is over. Hugh'.[64] The following summer he arranged for Brian to accompany him to a weekend house party at Cherkley Court, the home of the press baron Max Aitken, Lord Beaverbrook.[65] When in March 1959 he suffered a stroke, Brian was one of only three people who were told the real diagnosis (the others being Gaitskell and Crosland), and he remained a faithful friend until Dalton's death on 13 February 1962.

By his early thirties, despite his last-minute rejection of the political career offered by 'Daddy' Dalton, Brian exuded self-assurance. To his friends, family and increasingly the public (through his appearances on the BBC and in press) he was the modern intellectual, with his Pimlico flat, annual skiing holidays and man-about-town sports car. He was seen as one of London's eligible bachelors, with royal family connections. His aristocratic demeanour only helped to strengthen the widely held myth (which was still in circulation when Townsend wrote Brian's obituary) that he was 27th in line to the throne. How Townsend had arrived at this conclusion is unclear, but Brian did not actively seek to disabuse it, and Crossman also remarked on it in his diary.[66] Brian seemed content for friends and colleagues to read him as they wished. His friendship with one of the daughters of the Weston family (the biscuit manufacturing magnates) provided a useful foil to the inquisitiveness of both his mother Vivée and his colleagues at the LSE. It took some time before David Donnison finally realised why Brian did not really want to be set up with dates.[67]

Homosexual acts were illegal in Britain until 1967. Brian was acutely aware of the risks of being outed, witnessing high-profile court cases such as that of the 28-year-old socialite Lord Montagu of Beaulieu, the youngest peer in the House of Lords, who was prosecuted, along with the *Daily Mail* journalist Peter Wildeblood and the Dorset landowner Michael Pitt-Rivers, in 1954.[68] This case is often seen as the catalyst for the Wolfenden Report published in 1957, which initiated the Sexual Offences Act of 1967. Despite the legal reforms, the attitudes of the British public remained illiberal on this and other contemporary issues such as abolishing the death penalty and legalising drug use. A 1973 survey found that only 12 per cent expressed a 'tolerant' attitude towards homosexuality in contrast to 24 per cent who felt 'revulsion' and 22 per cent 'pity'.[69]

Understandably, as for many other gay men, the 1967 Act did not diminish Brian's personal anxieties. He remained an essentially private man throughout his life, with very few of his straight friends and family permitted to share this other part of his life. He developed a necessary discretion that became an invaluable skill in his professional life too. Heterosexuals are often blind to the methods of communication that the illegality of gay life then required, and which public attitudes have perpetuated into the 21st century. Such was Tom Driberg's concern about his autobiography, *Ruling Passions*, that he instructed it be published after his death.[70] Its detailed accounts of casual gay sex encounters shocked most but not all of his fellow peers. Matt Houlbrook's excellent study *Queer London* describes the development of an intricate gay culture, with its own social hierarchies, geography and traditions.[71] Ironically, the requirement to be one step ahead of the police and their agents provocateurs meant there was actually very accurate knowledge within the gay community of how to find other gay men in the metropolis.

From Lionel's epigrammatic reply to one of Brian's letters in the summer of 1950, it seems that Brian lost his virginity in the heat of southern Europe, where he was holidaying with his Cambridge friends. Yet his good friend Tony Bambridge, who travelled extensively with him, claimed not to have known that Brian was gay until he read the obituaries. Other Cambridge friends, such as Ronald Waterhouse and Percy Cradock, also suggested they were unaware of Brian's sexuality.[72] Cambridge, like London, had its own façades: while invited female guests chatted at formal dinners and balls, gay men knew that they could arrange post-party contacts through subtle sign language at the bar. Yet openly gay men at Cambridge at this time offer a different perspective. Roger Lockyer remembers it as a time when he felt a great deal of personal freedom and openness in his life, even a degree of envy from some straight friends who thought they were missing out on a glamorous gay world.[73] Their community was not exclusive: people such as the editor and social commentator Mark Boxer also felt at ease in gay Cambridge society. From Brian's correspondence with John Vaizey, it seems that at least between themselves they were open about their sexuality at Cambridge. Their close friendship continued, with Vaizey sharing Brian's Vincent Square flat after another Cambridge friend, J.J. Davis, moved out.

Vaizey was both enthralled by Brian's background and irritated at the apparent social assurance that the Abel-Smith family name gave him. He found Brian unconsciously patronising, perhaps because he continued to be acutely aware of his own lower middle-class origins. Yet his position as Brian's lodger gave him a wider social circle, including Brian's 'good-looking' barrister-brother Lionel, who had set up home in South Eaton Place in Belgravia. Brian, like Roger Lockyer, refused to be ashamed of his sexuality. He was convinced that the laws were wrong, and he aimed to live as open and honest a life as he could without putting himself into risky situations. The frequent parties held at his flat encompassed a wide group of friends, including Colin Rutter, a policeman whose beat covered Vincent Square.[74] Domestic parties and dinners offered a safer way of seeing gay friends such as Denzil Freeth, the Conservative politician, some of whom were more cautious than others in their social activities.[75] Brian was also a member of the exclusive gay club, The Rockingham, near Piccadilly Circus, which catered to upper-class English establishment tastes. He attended on a regular basis, using it as another way to see gay friends.

Brian and Vaizey remained close, despite Brian's relationships with his two subsequent flat sharers, Charles Schuller, a South African who was then a dancer with the Royal Ballet, and then from 1958, with Laci Tomazi, a Hungarian boxer. After Brian bought his house in Elizabeth Street, Vaizey paid the 'key money' to take over the lease of 16 Vincent Square from him. It came as a shock to Brian when Vaizey announced that he was getting married. His fiancée was an American postgraduate arts student, Marina Stansky.[76] Brian threw a party for them after their marriage, but his friendship with Vaizey lost its intimacy.

Vincent Square Mansions provided Brian with a comfortable home for seven years. Perhaps he chose it already aware of the area's increasingly vibrant gay community, facilitated by the anonymous apartment blocks, and gay clubs such as The Spartan in Tachbrook Street. He would have known that it was also favoured by politicians – Crossman was at 9 Vincent Square – conveniently within calling distance of the Westminster division bell. By the late 1950s Brian's flat had become a convivial nexus for like-minded intellectuals. His reputation as a fine cook and generous host turned political meetings into social events. Along with the Crossmans, he entertained the Benns, the Shores, the Croslands, and a wider circle from the Fabian Society. This increasing familiarity helped to break down popular preconceptions about him. Shirley Williams, who got to know him well through their collaboration on the Fabian Executive, recognised a shyness and self-protection that others could choose to interpret as arrogance. Brian, unlike some male colleagues, was supportive of her work and senior position in the society: 'he never patronised me, he never tried to reduce the complexity of his thought because I was a woman'.[77] He was ever eager to take on new responsibilities: in April 1955 he had accepted a three-year appointment to the Management Committee of the Lambeth Group of Hospitals.[78] In 1956 he was appointed to its parent body, the South West Metropolitan RHB. A year later in 1957 he was appointed as a governor of St Thomas' Hospital.[79]

Whose Welfare State?

All these duties took up a significant amount of Brian's time, especially the associated committee meetings. Yet he continued to write, and his reputation was now international. Henry Kissinger, then Director of the Harvard International Seminar Programme, wrote to Brian in October 1957 (at the suggestion of Denis Healey), offering US$100 for a 3,000–5,000-word article for his magazine *Confluence*. He proposed the topic of 'Possible Goals of the British Labour Party'.[80] In 1958 he contributed an essay 'Whose Welfare State?' to *Conviction*, a book edited by Norman Mackenzie. It sat alongside provocative essays from Peter Shore, Raymond Williams, Paul Johnson, Iris Murdoch and Peter Townsend.[81] Brian's essay, which went through several drafts and detailed sets of comments from both Townsend and Titmuss, opened with:

> Why are the British middle classes such hypocrites in their attitude to the Welfare State? Why do they want to emasculate the social services, from which they derive so much benefit, in order to punish the better-off sections of the working classes? Why do they pretend to others – and to themselves – that they get no advantage from the social services? They seem convinced that they are giving social services to the working classes who receive and do not pay. They are quite prepared to help the very poor. But they resent giving to people who seem as well off as they are, and they object to providing standards of services which

are in line with their own standard of life – nourishing cottage pie but not roast chicken.[82]

Brian argued in his essay in *Conviction* that it was the middle classes who had benefited most from the creation of Beveridge's welfare state. He saw his mission as an academic to expose such issues: 'I try to be a continuous but fair critic of the "Establishment view".'[83] Using personal anecdotes drawn from his acquaintances, he sought to show how 'his' class milked the system: 'I live in Westminster and friends of mine who are actors or who have recently been barristers call in on their way to draw unemployment benefit. Some have quite large unearned incomes but they have paid their insurance like everybody else and they are not ashamed of taking advantage of what they have paid for.' Given that his brother Lionel was a barrister, perhaps this was a little close to the bone. The tone of Brian's piece, using supposedly overheard bus conversations by the wealthy on how they intended to exploit the system, especially family allowances and child tax allowances, struck Townsend as a bit 'shrill', but his accounts of his first visit to a mental hospital had a powerful and memorable honesty:

> I found a dormitory with eighty beds in four rows with about nine inches between the beds and eighteen inches between the rows – no lockers, no wardrobes, no chests of drawers, no bed lights – no furniture at all except eighty beds with stained white cotton bed covers in a room which hadn't been painted for thirty years … what about the four lavatories … so ingrained with faeces that no disinfectant could hide the smell…. And four out of five old people in LCC welfare accommodation are living in the old workhouses. Go and see them sitting in those long bare rooms, staring at the radiator, waiting to die.[84]

Brian contrasted the new Shell skyscraper and the luxury banking houses of London with the low state funding for new hospitals, the shortage of doctors and nurses, and lack of operational research. He condemned the 'petty meanness' of the system and the absence of basic privacy for welfare clients discussing their personal circumstances in public offices:

> Can't we make public services serve the public? Let me make it quite clear I don't want to drag anyone down. Rather I want to raise the standards of welfare for working people and for the minority groups in every social class – the mentally ill, the disabled,

the infirm, and the aged and the mental deficients and the millions who live in the mean streets of our industrial cities. I want to see working people being treated in the same way as the middle classes treat themselves. More money must be spent on welfare.[85]

Brian's proposed solution was to overturn the principle of the subsistence minimum, and to increase taxation – an unfashionable idea in Macmillan's 'Never Had It So Good' 1958. He finished with his vision for what would be possible with better funding – rebuilding hospitals, providing *full* home care services, family allowance at £1 per week for *all* children. This long breathless narrative exudes Brian's passionate personal conviction: 'Here is the outline of a programme for fifty years.... I wouldn't be human if I didn't wonder how the reviewers will treat this essay, or for that matter what my academic colleagues will say when I am not there (why shouldn't I bring my bias out into the open?).'[86] He concluded with a cynical mock review of his essay, in which he rehearsed the establishment's excuses for not adopting his proposals – lack of funding and policy inertia. This essay reads like a manifesto for his abortive political career.

The reaction to *Conviction*, and to Brian's essay, was mixed. Peter Shore wrote to say that it was 'a thrilling and intellectual experience', while Dame Margaret Cole, the veteran socialist reformer, was less enamoured: 'it distresses me to see you leave your flank wide open by wild statements'. She took particular exception to Brian's 'spiteful post-mortem insult' to Beatrice Webb: 'I do not like to see people trying to make their names by spitting at those who went before them'.[87] Brian had also sent a copy to Uncle Bill and Aunt Phyllis, perhaps hoping to disturb their Kensington establishment cocoon. Their response epitomised precisely that which Brian had attacked in his essay, with Phyllis replying: 'All the "yapping" about "equality" is absurd. Firstly it leads to regimentation and secondly the Labour Party's chief backbone being the (so-called) "working man" who shows day in day out that what they want is "differentials" of all kinds, wages, position, etc etc. There is far more snobbishness among them than among the so-called upper classes.'[88]

Conviction received some good press reviews, with John Strachey in the *Observer* finding Brian's essay 'extremely enlightening'.[89] Tony Crosland's review for *The Spectator* valued it for its redefinition of the welfare objective, but judged that the collection as a whole did not make a major contribution to socialist thought, nor provide 'the much-sought-after "new dynamic" (whatever that may mean)'.[90] Kenneth

Tynan chose it as one of his books of the year in the *Observer*.[91] *The Guardian* leader writer proclaimed:

> Here is the material for a stirring campaign – and one which, except in modest financial terms, need not threaten the prosperity that so many people have found since 1950 and rightly do not want to lose. A fair number of those who have been christened 'semi-detached Tories' still have consciences, even if they also have mortgages and television sets. Social welfare may not be strictly socialism, but it is humanity and good sense.[92]

National Insurance

The late 1950s was the critical period in pensions policy development: 'the last practical moment at which a state earnings related pension could have wiped out the bulk of demand for private provision'.[93] The Conservatives' supplementary 'graduated' state pension scheme, prompted by Crossman's plan, emerged in 1958. Their main concerns were to cut the growing National Insurance deficit and to protect and encourage private occupational pension schemes. Contracting out from the state system was actively encouraged.[94] As Macmillan had noted, 'In the long run we shall all be dead and before some of these calculations mature we may well be a Communist society or destroyed by a bomb. So do not let us bother too much as long as we do not spend too much for the next two or three years'.[95] After the publication of Labour's national superannuation plan, Brian continued to assist Crossman, and to tour regional Fabian groups giving talks about the new plan.

The Study Group also now benefited from the unofficial input of another of Richard Titmuss's protégés – Tony Lynes. He had joined the LSE Department after working as a chartered accountant, and completed the two-year non-graduate Social Science Certificate in 1958. Brian had been his tutor in the second year of the course, and afterwards he was employed to assist Titmuss's pensions research, and was based in Skepper House in Endsleigh Street, along with other Social Administration researchers such as Sheila Benson and Mike Reddin. Lynes was devoted, as the whole Department of Social Administration was, to supporting Titmuss, in awe of his intellectual authority. Titmuss was one of those people whose views on a topic could not be predicted, but as soon as he had uttered them, they seemed so naturally right to his disciples.

Lynes brought excellent analytical skills to Labour's somewhat sketchy blueprints for social security. His ability to assess the political climate was equally valuable, prompting him to conduct a mini-poll of 50 members of the public which demonstrated that less than a third of them had heard of Labour's new pensions plan, and fewer still understood its details.[96] Crossman viewed Brian as his main adviser, with Lynes at this stage more a back-room number cruncher. Yet they both attended the discussions with representatives from the life insurance industry. Lynes, who put in long hours on the minutiae of the proposals, and probably had a better understanding of related issues such as taxation of benefits, at times felt exploited: 'I was appalled to find myself holding the fort singled-handed on Tuesday against Duval and 3 MPs, having assumed you would be there. I am afraid I made a fool of myself. Duval is formidable and I am sure his influence will on the whole be salutary' (emphasis in original).[97]

Crossman continued to listen to proposals from the skiffle group. A key one emerged at a 'really magnificent dinner' that Brian cooked for the Titmusses, Townsends and Crossmans in March 1958. Why not extend the principle of graded benefits from pensions to sickness and unemployment benefit as well? Crossman approved: 'It is one of those extremely simple plans which are also extremely brilliant.'[98]

Through the 'Abel-Smith/Townsend brains trust' Crossman was given substantial amendments to propose for the Conservatives' National Insurance Bill in spring 1959.[99] The Conservatives appeared to have little enthusiasm for their own legislation. John Boyd-Carpenter was reluctant to put his name to what the insurance world dubbed a 'political gimmick, not a pension scheme', and which Iain Macleod dismissed as 'a little mouse of a scheme'.[100] The resultant Act did, however, appease the Treasury, in successfully reducing the Exchequer cost of existing pensions.[101] Labour pinned its hopes on national superannuation as a vote winner at that year's general election. At Gaitskell's request, Crossman brought Brian together with Tony Crosland over dinner so that Crosland could give the necessary approval to the financial mechanics of the scheme. In Brian's typed-up account (the Titmice usually sent such memos to each other after significant meetings) he noted that Crosland had rung him in advance, concerned that Gaitskell's request to 'look over their shoulders' would be difficult to do without months of work. 'The dinner at first was not a success. After a few minutes I mentioned to Tony that the social security contribution was a tax. Dick Crossman took this up, arguing that it was not a tax and making his usual point about the moral importance of people being made to save. Crosland then said that the whole argument was semantic. Dick would not have this and the argument became quite bitter and lasted for about an hour until Dick had to go and Divide.'

Crosland suggested that one of the main problems was the sidelining of the so-called Economists Group from the strategy:'all these measures of policy needed to be put together and some decisions taken. This Harold Wilson did not do'. This surprised Crossman who had 'imagined that there was an inner group of economists which controlled the Labour Party and from which he was excluded. He now learned that the economists felt themselves completely isolated from their leader on the economic side – Harold Wilson.'[102]

Through the summer of 1959 the Study Group on Security and Old Age continued to fine-tune Labour's pension plans. Brian and Lynes produced a paper for the working party on tax avoidance and evasion, showing how private pension schemes were currently being exploited for such purposes. Gaitskell's casual suggestion to remove the earnings cap on widowed mothers was taken up as a potentially free vote winner, allowing some 250,000 women to take a job without losing their late husband's pension benefits. This had already been petitioned for by the National Council for Women, championed by the MP, Lena Jeger.[103] Crossman used his column in the *Daily Mirror* to plug the broad features of the plan. In the event national superannuation was not the vote winner that Labour needed. The public either did not understand or did not like the scheme. Probably the former, Crossman conceded.

Although national superannuation was a failure for Labour at the general election on 8 October 1959, it proved enduringly useful to both Brian and Crossman. Part of the success of their partnership was undoubtedly their common background:

> The secret of Winchester – and, indeed, of the classical tradition
> in our leading public schools – is that it imposes on a boy's mind
> a complex structure of rules, a rigid hierarchy of values and a
> system of taboos, privileges and obligations utterly remote from
> his home life or from the world outside.[104]

Both Crossman and Brian excelled in debating, a product of the public school system – Crossman exhibiting the classic Wykehamist 'brutal' and 'intellectual arrogance' in comparison to Brian's more genteel Haileyburyian technique. Tam Dalyell, Crossman's friend, Parliamentary Private Secretary and biographer, sees education as fundamental to understanding Crossman's character: that his 'bump of irreverence' was contained within an overall respect for the establishment and a secure sense of his own position in the elite of the nation.[105] It was a social background that Brian shared and it facilitated their genuine friendship, as did their common academic careers. In many ways

Crossman had remained the university don despite his subsequent media, journalistic and political roles. This intellectual capability was not enough to win over some of his fellow socialists. For Denis Healey, Crossman 'had a heavyweight intellect with lightweight judgement. He was an exciting teacher, and would have been a magnificent successor to Laski at the London School of Economics. As a politician, and even more as a minister, he left much to be desired.... Like a Greek sophist, Dick was always more interested in the process of argument rather than its conclusion.'[106] Jack Jones, leader of the Transport & General Workers' Union, put it more bluntly: Crossman 'typified for me the academic, who, in working class parlance, "didn't know his arse from his elbow".'[107]

National Assistance

Crossman had been lucky. He had 'caught the Labour Party at a time when its social policy was in flux'.[108] He pushed through the Titmice's innovative scheme of national superannuation onto Labour's policy agenda despite historical constraints and opposing interests. Yet he achieved less than his efforts and his intellect warranted. He 'continued to produce sudden flashes of illumination – but in the manner of a revolving lighthouse whose rays dazzle for a moment, and then leave the darkness even blacker than it was before'.[109] Crossman remained as chair of the Study Group on Security and Old Age, but after the 1959 general election, at which Macmillan consolidated the Conservative Party's government, Labour appeared to give little thought to social policy. Although one of the key determinants of Labour's adoption of national superannuation was its promise of reducing old people's dependence on National Assistance, it did not generate policy discussions on the same scale as assistance measures had in the past.

The roots of National Assistance lie in the 19th-century Poor Law. Edwin Chadwick's audacious 1834 scheme to cut the cost of poverty had produced a system both admired and hated for its cold-hearted efficiency. State assistance for people in need was now conducted under the glare of Poor Law union officials in the gloom of workhouses. The principle of 'less eligibility' deterred all but the most genuinely in need.[110] The philosophy of minimum state support pervaded all subsequent reviews, including the Royal Commission on the Poor Laws (1905–09) in which the Fabians, through Sidney and Beatrice Webb, played an influential role.

In 1908 the poverty of old age had been partly alleviated by new legislation, administered by Customs and Excise and paid through post offices, which provided a meagre, means-tested, non-contributory pension for those aged 70 and over. Provision was expanded in 1925 through a contributory scheme, which reduced the age of entitlement to 65.[111] Benefits for the unemployed had been centralised in 1934 under the new Assistance Board. The outbreak of the Second World War re-focused attention on the poverty of the elderly and in 1940 it was re-titled as the Public Assistance Board and authorised to grant means-tested 'supplementary pensions'.[112] Within two years almost 50 per cent of the 500,000 non-contributory pensioners were receiving cash assistance from this new Board.[113]

When Beveridge produced his review of social insurance and allied services he was confident that his views represented the status quo: 'The State, in organising security should not stifle incentive, opportunity, responsibility…. In establishing a national minimum, it should leave room and encouragement for voluntary action by each individual to provide more than that minimum for himself and his family.'[114] For some in the government (and indeed also for the International Labour Organization, ILO), Beveridge's report was too radical, leading to a postponement in its publication. But when it finally emerged on 1 December 1942, the wartime public seized on it as a vision of what would be possible when peace returned.

Beveridge proposed a single system of universal social security from 'cradle to grave'. It would integrate the former piecemeal insurance and health service provisions and be funded (in part) by National Insurance contributions. With the introduction of a universal contributory pension in 1948, Beveridge anticipated that the numbers of claimants for supplementary National Assistance would wither away. Yet inflation quickly eroded the value of the planned pension, even before the Appointed Day, and the numbers of people requiring support through means-tested National Assistance began to increase. The Public Assistance Board was also once again re-titled in 1948 to become the National Assistance Board. It is perhaps surprising that Beveridge, the radical reformer, opted to perpetuate the principle of flat-rate benefits that had been in place since 1908. In the heat of post-war promises and the immediate introduction of the full state pension, Beveridge's national minimum got heavily squeezed.

Reconceptualising poverty

The discussions on both national superannuation and National Assistance that Brian, Townsend and Titmuss had been engaged in since the early 1950s were the first signs of a re-conceptualisation of poverty. In January 1952 Brian wrote a draft manuscript, 'The Definitions of Poverty', in which he proposed a survey which would include the collection of data on family nutrition levels.[115] Townsend's 1952 pamphlet, *Poverty: Ten Years After Beveridge*, published while he was still at the Institute of Community Studies, took issue with the classic Rowntree definition, which saw poverty as an absolute condition.[116] Townsend, supported by Brian and Titmuss, argued that a relative definition provided a more realistic and useful approach.

Brian's research was well known within the NAB, and he participated in its Cambridge summer school in 1955, in a working group focused on the meaning of subsistence and the problem of 'inflation'.[117] He had also been collaborating with John Utting at Cambridge and Miss Shaw at the University of Bristol to use their data sets for household types to test his ideas on minimum subsistence.[118] Through placing parliamentary questions via Hilary Marquand, he was also able to extract from the government official statistics to inform Labour's draft policy. His radio broadcasts on the issue of pensions, poverty and National Assistance also drew letters from the public, sending him details of their personal circumstances. He sometimes personally tried to mediate for them with the NAB. When Miss Margaret Allen of Highbury Hill, London, wrote to him about her cut in benefits, he asked a NAB official he had met at the summer school to investigate her case.[119] He also stimulated discussions on provision for the elderly through a presentation to the XYZ club, the invitation-only discussion group that brought MPs into contact with economists and city analysts.[120]

By the late 1950s Brian, Titmuss and Townsend were well placed to direct academic research into issues of poverty that supported Labour policy development, and Titmuss produced a position paper on future research issues in November 1958, suggesting they concentrate on allowances for children and the development of a comprehensive graded Social Service Contribution.[121] For several years Titmuss had been close to Philip Rowntree, Chair of the Rowntree Trust. When a prolonged period of sick leave in 1958 left Titmuss out of action, it was Brian who took the initiative. He gave a dinner for Philip Rowntree to meet one of his junior researchers, Bob Pinker. Rowntree subsequently proposed a 'link up' between the LSE and the Rowntree Studentship Fund, and that Titmuss, when fully recovered, might wish to be considered for a position as trustee. This would give the Titmice unrivalled contact and leverage on research funds for poverty studies.[122]

From the autumn of 1957 the meetings of the Labour Party's Study Group on Security and Old Age began to discuss the broader agenda of unemployment and sickness benefits. Titmuss saw this as a logical development from their work on national superannuation, but that politically it might be difficult to address issues that ultimately could split the systems providing support to the working and middle classes.[123] When Brian or Titmuss was absent from the Study Group Townsend took copious notes and his informal memos lay bare the underlying issues:

> The most extraordinary thing about the whole meeting was the time we devoted to the question of abuse. Edith Summerskill raised this and she and Douglas Jay showed the most anti-socialist principles imaginable. Plainly they did not trust the workers to respect white collar systems of social security.... At one point after both Titmuss and I had made various emotionally charged references to the evidence of the *Lancet* and the National Assistance Board and others, that there was no abuse of any significance, she turned to Titmuss and said, "I happen to have lived in this world and I know all about it," going on to argue that as soon as there was even a reasonable incentive to stop work, many British people would do so.... Crossman and Marquand, Marquand as one would expect but Crossman perhaps unpredictably, both followed rather lamely in the Jay-Skill footsteps. Neither showed the resolution to oppose reactionary arguments.[124]

During 1958 Brian liaised with the Acton Society Trust on their questionnaires on redundancy, and with a contact of Richard Crossman's in the Coventry office of the Ministry of Labour on their research on the benefit claims made by the unemployed.[125] He also engaged one of the Study Group members, W.H. Clough, who worked at the Actuaries firm Bacon and Woodrow, to obtain confidential information on the calculation of pensions for company directors.[126] Meanwhile Townsend and Audrey Harvey used their interviews with people living in poverty to write some of the most moving accounts of this seemingly invisible section of society. They exposed the very personal life stories of widows sinking deeper into debt to feed and clothe their children, and of families who could no longer afford to pay rent being separated by London County Council, whose 'Family Units' only admitted women and children under 16 into residential care (and only during the hours of 9 to 5, Monday to Friday).[127]

Against all the party political debates must be set the permanent, ingrained power of the Treasury. Keynes, its most respected and influential adviser, had brokered a deal in which he would allow the

Treasury to sanction the Beveridge report as long as a £100 million pa ceiling was put on pensions funding for the first five years of the programme from 1946. In effect it meant that the pensions system became PAYG, although the public were never enlightened on this change of accounting. As Lowe puts it, the concept of national insurance became a 'fiction'.[128] In the post-war period the Treasury remained determined to squash whatever public spending it could:

> The growth of private pension schemes is to be encouraged; it produces social stability. In the long run, moreover, it should reduce the individual's dependence on the Government scheme and perhaps even enable the Government to get away from the expensive doctrine of 'universality' – and perhaps lead to the adoption of benefit payments according to need.[129]

In 1959 Titmuss produced a provocative essay, 'The Irresponsible Society':

> When I was young what some of us argued about was the democratic process. We wanted to know in our academically illiterate way whether more dialogue, more democracy, was possible. We thought it a dreadful crime to prevent other people from speaking up. We realised that the poor (whether they numbered two million or ten million), the mentally ill, the disabled and other casualties or failures in our society were penalised, not only by their poverty, but because they were denied the social rights of protest and full membership of society. We believed in the possibility of an alternative government. We did not understand that government by the people could mean that power in government, the Cabinet and the City, could lie almost permanently in the hands of those educated at Eton and other public schools.[130]

At the end of the 1950s Brian, Titmuss and Townsend were united by a shared intellectual and moral commitment. Since the beginning of their collaborations in 1953 they had forged strong public personas, taken on significant policy advisory roles and elaborated their vision of a fair society. They had achieved this by collective and individual activities, supporting one another through continual dialogue. Brian – a product one of those 'other public schools' of Titmuss's essay – was now defined as much by his committed socialism as by his family or class.

Health and happiness: 1956–64

Judgements and predictions: health and medicine in Britain
Funding health service research: collaborations and conflicts
Bedpans and balance sheets: managing the NHS
Friendships and partnerships
A natural historian: *The Hospitals 1800–1948*
In the public's eye

What really strikes 1990s eyes about those brave, semi-collectivist years of mid-century Britain is the combination of hope and public purpose. That sour law of unintended consequences, or change-can-only-make-things-worse, was scarcely visible in the land. (Peter Hennessy, 1992)[1]

Brian's interest in the NHS was academic, managerial and political. He researched how health services were planned and provided, he also served as a governor on several London hospital management committees and a regional board, and he advised Labour politicians, still out of office, on the risks to the future of the NHS. He published two landmark histories of hospitals and nursing, written with an overt statist philosophy of health and social welfare. It is important when reading this chapter to see it as but one part of his life. He spent as nearly as much time working abroad for WHO and on projects for former British colonies such as Tanzania and Mauritius as he did at the LSE, fitting these projects around his term-time teaching commitments. He began to develop contacts with other health economists, especially in the US. (It has proved easier to discuss his international work separately in the next chapter.) Despite this punishing work schedule, his private life always took precedence, especially after he met his life-long partner, John Sarbutt, in 1960. Their busy social life was carefully separated from Brian's public profile, which continued to grow through his regular appearances on television and radio.

Judgements and predictions: health and medicine in Britain

Brian could not have known, when he accepted the short-term research post at NIESR in 1953, how fortunate a move it would be for his subsequent career. His secondment to the Guillebaud investigation established him as one of the NHS's first 'experts'; few others could speak with such authority on its costs, problems and potential. The Ministry of Health treated him as a valued collaborator, with access to their files approved by the Permanent Secretary, John Hawton. He dined with the former Minister of Health Aneurin Bevan at the House of Commons.[2] He was in demand at events such as the Annual Conference of the Association of Chief Finance Officers, even before the Guillebaud Report was published. In the conference transcripts he comes across as a confident speaker on wide-ranging issues including population projections, Whitleyism (pay scales for public servants) and rational allocation statistics.

His article, 'Present and Future Costs of the Health Service. The Economic Evidence to the Guillebaud Committee', in *The Lancet* brought him further attention, especially from the medical profession. Referencing the specially commissioned 1951 Census analysis of the occupants of hospital beds, he asked whether the interesting questions it raised were being addressed: why were there relatively more single people in hospital than in the population at large? 'Is marriage a shield against high morbidity? Is high morbidity a shield against marriage? How far is the hospital service acting as a family substitute for those who are ill-equipped with husbands, wives and children?'[3] These, he suggested, were the types of questions that needed to be asked to help plan for the NHS of the future.

Brian had already decided that he wished to be more intimately involved with this future. He had accepted an invitation in March 1955 for a three-year appointment to the Management Committee of the Lambeth Group of Hospitals. In 1956 he was appointed to its parent body, the South West Metropolitan Regional Hospital Board. A year later, in 1957, he was appointed a governor of St Thomas' Hospital. This close involvement with the routine of healthcare delivery undoubtedly coloured his choice of research interests.

After the NIESR post finished, Titmuss had arranged for him to be appointed as Assistant Lecturer at the LSE in his new Department of Social Administration from 1 October 1955. From the outset Brian attracted attention from undergraduates for his brilliant teaching. He was particularly in demand for first year teaching of Economics, as his lively and understandable style was an improvement on some of the more staid lecturers in the Economics Department. Brian had vowed when he left Cambridge and the NIESR that he would no longer work as an economist, and he was loath to teach the subject at the LSE, but it took some years before he was able to persuade Titmuss to let him do this in favour of only Social Policy subjects. Brian also adopted a steady stream of postgraduate students, to whom he gave excellent supervision, renowned for the quality and promptness of his feedback.

Together Brian and Titmuss worked up a grant proposal to take to The King's Fund (founded in 1897 as The Prince of Wales' Hospital Fund for London; it changed its name in 1902 when Edward became King). It supported research into the improvement of English health systems (with a focus on London, while the Nuffield [Provincial Hospitals] Trust looked after the provinces), and was the logical body to support their work. Titmuss first wrote to Hawton at the Ministry of Health for permission to use the Ministry's files. He then wrote to A.G.L. Ives, Secretary of The King's Fund, asking for funding for a project, because: 'to make more intelligent guesses about the future we need more accurate "trend" data over a longer period of time'. He proposed a broader chronological study that would also include doctors' remuneration, which had not been covered by the Guillebaud Committee.[4]

Surely it is no coincidence that in January 1956, only a couple of weeks after they had raised the idea with The King's Fund of investigating doctors' salaries, Titmuss and Brian received an invitation from Bruce Cardew, General Secretary of the Medical Practitioners' Union (MPU), to an off-the-record dinner to meet a small group of doctors to discuss their Guillebaud book.[5] The MPU had been formed in 1914, and rivalled the British Medical Association (BMA) because it aimed to extend state medical care while retaining the independence of the GP.[6] Doctors were becoming increasingly unhappy with their incomes under the NHS. Brian was approached by T.F. (Robbie) Fox, editor of *The Lancet*, to write an anonymous editorial to comment on whether their claims were realistic in the current economic climate.[7] In June 1956 the BMA presented a formal demand to the government for an increase of 24 per cent, at a cost of £20 million.[8] The government, already feeling the effects of the economic recession, did not wish to re-open the unpleasant negotiations of the 1952 Danckwerts arbitration award. Later in 1956, as the doctors intensified their demands for a new pay settlement, the Treasury and the Ministry of Health finally agreed to appoint a Royal Commission to make a full investigation. The profession, sensing a *fait accompli*, only agreed by the smallest majority to cooperate. The industrialist Sir Harry Pilkington chaired the Commission.[9]

Titmuss judged this the ideal opportunity to force the collection and publication of information on doctors' pay and conditions. He had already accumulated a file of related material: everything from adverts in the *British Medical Journal* of medical (GP) practices for sale, to enquiries to *The Times* as to why there was a sudden absence of doctors' estate values listed in the probate section. His letter to *The Times* on 1 February 1957 criticised the failure of the government to replace the Spens Report calculation, made in 1946, with one that properly linked doctors' pay to the amount of work they did. He put Brian up to going to see Fuller, the Secretary of the Commission, to offer their assistance.[10] Brian was duly called to give evidence to the Royal Commission on Doctors' Pay on 24 April 1957. He saw this as a natural extension of his research for the Guillebaud Committee, and had already begun to collect statistical evidence on how the costs had changed since the creation of the NHS. He stated at the outset that he was giving evidence on behalf of Titmuss, who was then in New York, and himself; he later sent Titmuss a summary of the proceedings.

Brian opened with the historical context for the British capitation system, noting how Lloyd George had asked the government actuary in the run-up to the 1911 National Health Insurance Act to collect information on GPs' average income per patient per year. He discussed how although the amount had been greater before the NHS, BMA figures showed that practice expenses (which the GPs paid themselves) had increased from 15 per cent of gross income before the First World War to nearly 40 per cent now, but that this was, to some extent, an increase in notified expenses to offset the impact of the increasing rate of income tax. Brian suggested that this required further investigation: the reimbursement of practice expenses meant that 'It is possible for a general practitioner to charge appropriate parts of his house, his garden, and even his wife, to the Exchequer.'[11] He further proposed that the Royal Commission should investigate the amount of actual time GPs spent seeing their patients. The BMA had conducted a survey in 1952, but had not made public the results, suggesting that the annual number of patient visits may have actually declined. There was also suspicion about the quality of their assistants, some of whom were foreign, with poor English. The private Emergency Call Service, run in conjunction with the magazine *Picture Post*, was used by some London GPs for evening and weekend cover for nearly one million patients. This had also suffered from negative press, with stories of 'recently qualified doctors in fast cars unsupported by medical records or any knowledge of the patients they were visiting. It was further alleged that this development was leading to substantial increases in hospital admissions'.[12] On the subject of doctors' private earnings, Brian highlighted the fact that there was actually no firm empirical evidence. The BMA had vetoed the use of Inland Revenue returns in 1952/53 for this purpose, but there were alternative sources that could be used to circumvent problems of cash payments and non-declarations, such as use of the Household Budget Survey.

By May 1957 he was sufficiently convinced that the doctors were unfairly profiting from the NHS that he wrote to Titmuss in New York: 'I thought you would be interested to hear that we are organising an "anti-doctor lobby". Norman MacKenzie and I wrote the enclosed article. I produced the information and he did the writing. It represents a short summary of the evidence which I gave on our behalf to the Royal Commission. . . . I hear that the Royal Commission was "impressed and disturbed" by my evidence (source Sir David Hughes Parry).'[13] Their joint article had appeared anonymously in the *New Statesman and Nation* on 4 May under the title 'The Dilemma of the Doctors', with a thinly disguised attack on the profession: '. . . the doctors have a peculiarly privileged position in our society. They regulate the entry, the standards, the ethics, and, to a large extent, the structure of their profession. But they also deploy the monopoly power they thereby wield to strengthen their business interests. The *mores* of public service and self-interest are hopelessly mixed-up.'[14] Replies to the article, especially letters from GPs, sought to counter the article's 'undercurrent of hostility towards the doctors' with case studies on what it was like to work a 13-hour day, six days a week, with night calls, and with all costs paid from a relatively modest maximum income of £2,200 per year.

When the Royal Commission reported in 1960 it resulted in a 22 per cent award (on the 1955/56 level) which cost £12 million, including a pot of money ring-fenced to give bonuses to GPs along the lines of the 'merit' awards allocated to hospital consultants based on peer review. It also recommended a more permanent mechanism to conduct periodic reviews of doctors' (and dentists') incomes, which was established as the Kindersley Pay Review Body in 1962.[15] Yet only three years later, in 1963, Brian was invited to a high-level symposium at Magdalen College Oxford on 'Incentives in general practice'.[16] Once again he was analysing the weakness of the existing capitation system, the disincentives to modernise practice buildings or improve the quality of care given. He proposed that premises should be provided from government funds, and that doctors' remuneration should be linked to their age, continuing training and list size.

His friend and colleague Jerry Morris raised the taboo subject of salaried doctors, and suggested this might now be acceptable to the younger generation of GPs. Morris (1910–2009) was an epidemiologist who had been director (with Richard Titmuss as statistician) of the Medical Research Council's pioneering Social Medicine Research Unit established in 1948 at the Central Middlesex Hospital. He had pioneered research into exercise and health through a 1953 study of London bus drivers and conductors – the conductors had less heart disease because they constantly walked up and down the bus stairs. He published a classic text in 1957, *The Uses of Epidemiology*. The issue of salaried GPs has remained at the forefront of the NHS debate ever since.[17]

Funding health service research: collaborations and conflicts

In response to Titmuss's approach in January 1956, The King's Fund had agreed to award a two-year grant for research on the broad theme of 'The Demands for and Finance of Medical Care', to cover the cost of a research assistant and secretarial support. It took some sensitive discussions to get the Fund's administrators to see quite what Titmuss and Brian intended to study, and how they wished to do it. Brian wrote to Titmuss in April 1956: 'I am very upset about the attached letter [from Stone at The King's Fund]…. It is intolerable that I should be expected to be controlled by Stone (much as I like him). Surely it must be made clear I work to you and no one else…. I am not concerned with economy and efficiency … what we are concerned with is information needed for hospital planning….Why must all these complications waste all our time! PS. Please excuse the violent tone of this letter.'[18]

When these early misunderstandings had been ironed out, Brian began to solicit statistics from the Ministry on the pre-NHS costs of health services. By June he had prepared a first draft of a paper for The King's Fund, 'The Cost of Medical Care in 1938'. It confirmed that there was mileage in much more sustained historical research into British health services that The King's Fund could support. Titmuss was already supervising Frank Honigsbaum for a PhD on the history of the medical profession. Through the second half of 1956 and into 1957 Brian worked up parallel project proposals to be funded by The King's Fund on the history of nursing and the history of hospitals. Dianne Farris was appointed as a researcher in August 1956 to help Brian collect archive material, especially from the Royal College of Nursing. Brian also used his new position as a governor at St Thomas' Hospital to arrange access to their documents, and the assistance of Miss Turner, the matron of the Nightingale Nurse Training School.[19] The General Nursing Council proved less cooperative, refusing access to their papers on the grounds of confidentiality.

Both Brian and Titmuss had begun to look for alternative funding to The King's Fund. In the spring of 1957 they began discussions with Odin Anderson, director of the New York-based Health Information Foundation (HIF), which was funded by the US pharmaceutical industry.[20] HIF was actively looking for research to fund in Europe, and Anderson had put their four-part project proposal (two historical studies; a comparison of costs in the US and the UK, and a utilisation of medical services study) to his Board. Unfortunately, he had given the Board the impression that there was no restraint on professional freedom in the UK NHS, which 'upset a number of the firmly-held prejudices of Board members'.[1] Since then both Anderson and HIF's President, George Bugbee, had worked on 'softening up' individual board members to get them to re-consider a grant application from Brian and Titmuss.

Anderson visited London in August 1958, and held discussions both with Brian at the LSE and with Saunders at NIESR on potential collaborative projects. Titmuss had been seriously ill that summer and diagnosed with tuberculosis. He was on extended sick leave from the LSE and still suffering the side effects of the streptomycin treatment. Brian and Anderson met over dinner, which gave Brian a chance to suggest that HIF might also wish to enter into a partnership with the WHO, which was having difficulty raising funds for an ambitious multi-country study of healthcare costs.[22] Anderson seemed, as Brian reported back to Titmuss, 'delighted and flattered at the idea of participating even on an informal basis in a World Health Organization study'. Finally, in September 1958 they got their approval for a project on 'The History of the National Health Service', and were able to give their chosen researchers, Frank Honigsbaum and Bob Pinker, notice of a summer 1959 start date for the two-year projects.[23]

Brian and Titmuss were beginning to collect together researchers at the LSE who would stay with them for the next decade. Tony Lynes was already there as Titmuss's research assistant. In June 1960, as the HIF project entered its second year, Brian proposed moving Sheila Benson onto their funding. She later played a key role in the administration of the Rowntree-funded poverty study between 1964 and 1969. Brian's choice of researchers sometimes strayed from purely academic motivations. When Bob Pinker announced that he wished to leave the hospitals historical study in 1960 to return to a full-time studentship, Brian suggested to Titmuss that they should employ Norman Holly, a Harvard graduate he had met in Stockholm. He recounted to Titmuss that even though he had spent only a few hours in conversation with him and his wife, he was 'impressed by their moral purpose' and felt that employment in London would also allow them to access free NHS treatment for their chronic health problems, which had forced them to leave the US.[24] Holly was duly appointed to the HIF project in October 1960, initially on a six-month trial.

Anderson milked Brian for confidential information on the politics behind the NHS. In January 1961 he wrote asking for background to the Labour Party's plans for NHS capital expenditure. Brian replied, acknowledging that he had been a member of the Labour working party that had drawn up the manifesto policy document in 1959:'Most of the time the committee was devoted to the discussion of the future of occupational medical care. There were a number of people who were trying to develop a fourth stream of the Service, while there were others such as myself who were trying to prevent this happening. This letter is of course, for your eyes alone, but if there is anything else you would like me to tell you about the background of this pamphlet, do not hesitate to let me know.'[25]

By October 1961 Titmuss was able to send a report on the HIF grant to Anderson. Their US$17,133 had funded the research and preparation for two key books on the pre-NHS history of the health services (by Honigsbaum) and the history of hospitals (written by Brian, with the assistance of Pinker).[26] Brian had secured a book contract with Heinemann in March 1961 (and a £100 advance), but was temporarily diverted from finishing the writing up by an urgent secondment to Tanganyika.[27]

The history of nursing project had already reached a very successful conclusion. Under its original proposed title of 'Ladies of the Lamp', Brian's manuscript had been rejected in 1958 by Allen & Unwin for being too similar to existing books on the subject by experts such as (Mrs) Cecil Woodham Smith and Lucy Seymer. He offered it instead to Heinemann's, who persuaded him to change the title to *A History of the Nursing Profession*.[28] This was to be the start of a long publishing partnership, working through Alan Hill. The acknowledgements perfectly epitomise the era of publication. Brian thanked his research assistant Dianne Farris for typing up the drafts, and the librarian of the Royal College of Nursing for 'on occasions turning a blind eye to the author's nasty habit of smoking in libraries'. Brian was determined to present the history of nursing in its wider social and economic context. This perturbed some of its existing historians, who felt his drafts did not give enough prominence or credit to Florence Nightingale. In fact, Brian was keen to expose the bigoted attitude of Nightingale's band of nurses, who had effectively 'pulled up the ladder' into the profession for later women by imposing rigid entry requirements and elaborate working rituals.

When *A History of the Nursing Profession* was published in September 1960 it attracted reviews in all the national newspapers and professional nursing journals. Zachary Cope, reviewing it for the *British Medical Journal*, welcomed 'the excellent account of the long and bitter struggle for registration (it is the first time that such a candid and revealing account of that unfortunate struggle has been printed in a book)'.[29] Michael Young, writing in *The Spectator*, latched on to Brian's exposure of the ruthlessness of women: 'This book shows that if women had built the empire they would not have let it go'. Brian's former flatmate, John Vaizey, praised it: 'Mr Abel-Smith's history is good – solidly-based on statistics and original sources. Lovers of heroic figures will be disappointed. Princess A. empties no bedpans; Miss Nightingale – well, it's fairer than Lytton Strachey. His questions are radical. Do nurses need so long a training? Should they not be students? Should they live in? What is the job of the hospital in 1960?'[30] The *Observer* review noted that Brian had exposed the 'entrenched power and privileges' of the General Nursing Council, which had extended Nightingale's short probationary period into a three-year training, and failed to 'improve the working environment of nurses to make it less restrictive and status-ridden'.[31]

The other research project funded by the HIF took longer to appear, mainly because of the many competing interests for Brian's time by the early 1960s. *The Hospitals 1800–1948: A Study in Social Administration in England and Wales* did not appear until 1964.[32] Its production is discussed later in this chapter, and owed a huge debt to the first-hand experience that Brian gained of hospital life from 1956.

Bedpans and balance sheets: managing the NHS

When the NHS was created in 1948 it brought together into one system a disparate collection of hospitals and institutions, ranging from massive infirmaries originating in the 19th-century Poor Law, to the so-called 'voluntary' hospitals, which had evolved from philanthropic endeavours into businesses supported both by charitable donations and sickness insurance schemes. Although there were often informal collaborations through hospital boards in towns and cities before the NHS, hospitals were essentially independent institutions, and many valued this status. The NHS Act of 1946, by nationalising all hospitals, brought them together within geographical regions, and forced them to share a regional funding budget. Hospitals were now obliged to cooperate and negotiate with neighbours through Hospital Management Committees (HMCs), which reported to RHBs. The only institutions to escape this forced regionalism were the designated teaching hospitals, which were deemed to require a separate relationship with, and management by, the Ministry of Health.

In London, which historically had been served by a proliferation of relatively small, often specialist, hospitals, there was potential for various permutations, reflecting old alliances, recognised neighbourhoods and current local government boundaries. It formed the geographical nucleus for a much wider group of four 'metropolitan' RHBs, whose territories extended to the south coast, Kent, Essex and up as far as Bedfordshire. In 1956 Brian had been invited to join the South West Metropolitan RHB, whose patch encompassed the counties of Surrey, West Sussex, Hampshire, Southern Wiltshire and Dorset, as well as the 'South West' quarter of London. His fellow Board members included an array of titled individuals including Dame Elizabeth Cockayne (Chief Nursing Officer, 1948–58), Lady Brain and Lady Petrie. He served on a number of its committees until 1963, helping to steer the Board through its first attempt at restructuring the services inherited from the pre-NHS period, to fit with the Ministry of Health's ambitious 10-year hospital building plan, launched in 1962. Through the visits he made to various institutions, he encountered the appalling conditions in which geriatric and mental health patients lived. The sense of outrage informed his writing, especially pieces such as 'Whose Welfare State?' in the book *Conviction* in 1958.[33]

Brian's regional duties also included delegation to the Lambeth Group HMC, which covered central London services. In 1957, when it was decided to merge the Lambeth Hospital's services with St Thomas', Brian was asked to become a member of the governing body at St Thomas' to maintain good relations between the two hospitals.[34] HMC members played a very active role alongside the professional staff, and Brian soon found that it took up a considerable amount of his time. There were meetings most weeks, and a rota for visiting the various hospitals within the Lambeth district, which the Board members did in pairs. There were sub-committees for finance, planning, nursing and midwifery, and a group medical advisory committee that dealt with staffing and professional conduct. HMC members also served on the individual house committees for each hospital, which dealt with day-to-day issues such as staffing appointments and short-term budgets. There were also *ad hoc* working parties formed to deal with specific issues, which had medical, nursing and administrative representation. All of this relied on the presence of an efficient secretary, and the Lambeth HMC was fortunate to have the services of William Mayne Butcher, who appeared to be an NHS equivalent of a 'Sir Humphrey' of 'Yes Minister' television fame, with the skills and deviousness necessary to ensure that business got sorted.[35]

In December 1959 the chair of the No 4 (Chelsea) Group HMC, Admiral John Godfrey, retired. He had been very closely involved with the Board since its establishment, and also worked for The King's Fund. In view of an impending HMC merger, Brian accepted an invitation to become acting chair. He had three years' experience of the Lambeth HMC and brought to the role his usual enthusiasm. He got Butcher to send him a full array of background information, including notes on his new HMC members (company directors, doctors, ladies, retired judges, etc), waiting lists at the various hospitals and previous sets of minutes. The minutes of the finance sub-committee demonstrated the minutiae of the HMC's role: discussions were required on such decisions as purchasing three geriatric armchairs for St Luke's Hospital (£54), not a significant sum in the context of an annual HMC budget of over £0.5 million, but clearly the accountability ethos of the NHS had permeated to its lowest levels.[36]

The HMC, in addition to overseeing the operation of its institutions (St Luke's, St Stephen's and the Princess Beatrice Hospital, and the Cheyne Walk Centre for Spastic Children), also had to manage their development, in the light of Ministry of Health circulars such as the 1959 *Improving Efficiency in Hospitals*.[37] The planned merger with the Fulham and Kensington HMC, chaired by Lady Iris Capel, also required Brian to begin tortuous negotiations on which hospitals should have wards and departments closed. From February he began a programme of visits, meeting staff in all institutions, and discussing which site had potential for further expansion, and which might be closed completely. He put pressure on the Organisation and Methods branch of the Ministry of Health to conduct an investigation at St Stephen's Hospital into its domestic work, proposing a controlled experiment to see if costs could be reduced through more efficient working patterns.[38] He also pushed for the appointment of a planning officer for the HMC to oversee the all the current developments, a role that he was beginning to fall into himself.

Brian took a keen interest in all aspects of 'his' hospitals' work, personally scrutinising every plan. The re-building at St Stephen's, partly funded by The King's Fund, promised to create a state-of-the-art hospital, double its current size, with a three-storey streamlined outpatients department to 'channel patients through with a minimum of delay'; three new wards blocks each containing a minimum of 386 beds; and a new pathology department with space for 40 staff – to be 'the best-equipped in England'.[39] In the lead-up to the amalgamation he liaised with Lady Iris Capel to construct a new HMC. On the eve of his departure for a six-week trip to the US in August 1960 he wrote to Alderman Tunbridge who had agreed to deputise for him: 'Do please keep a very close eye on the finances.'[40]

This close involvement, and almost possessive attitude towards this small section of the NHS, gave Brian an unparalleled access and insight into the contemporary conditions inside its institutions. The notes he made of his visits to St Mary Abbots and the Western Hospitals in June and July 1960 describe dismal wards in a 'deplorable and dirty state', a shortage of furniture, patchy attempts at redecoration, with no apparent schedule of work. In the lavatories there were rubber bedpans lying on the floor filled with disinfectant as there was nowhere to store them, and the doors to the cubicles were not wide enough to admit wheelchairs. These two hospitals came under the remit of the Fulham and Kensington HMC; he was not impressed, and expressed his concerns about the supervision of domestic work to Lady Capel, the HMC Chair.[41]

After the merger in October 1960, the new HMC was known as the Chelsea and Kensington, and Brian assumed the role of caretaker Chair. Within days he was dealing with new crises: patients threatening to sue over their treatment; newborn babies incorrectly labelled at St Mary Abbots; problems with hospital laundry services; and dilemmas over whether the Western Hospital wards should be fitted with privacy curtains (he consulted Peter Townsend on this, who sent an emphatic 'yes', even if it meant reduced bed capacity). The former Chair Admiral Godfrey was causing problems at the Cheyne Centre, which he still regarded as his personal fiefdom, forcing Brian to install a new manager who would report directly to him. He conducted difficult negotiations with the RHB to increase his HMC's budget by meeting 90 per cent bed occupancy rates in all their hospitals. He persuaded Dr G. Sheerborn of the Kensington Public Health Department to serve on the house committee at St Luke's Hospital to provide a link between institutional and domiciliary services for the elderly. Throughout this frenetic period of consolidation he enjoyed the camaraderie of his fellow 'voluntary' workers, and saw several of them socially. They were, for the most part, dyed-in-the-wool Conservatives, but aware of Brian's family pedigree, they turned a blind eye to his now well-known socialism.

By February 1961 he was exhausted and he resigned, citing ill health, and reminding both the HMC and the RHB that he had only agreed to take on the role in the short term. The letters of thanks he received from his fellow Committee members and the RHB testified to his consummate skill in achieving not only a smooth merger, but in helping to develop ambitious and really quite innovative hospital building programmes. Dr J.H. Weir, Medical Officer of Health for Kensington, wrote to him 'In a fairly long experience of widely varying Chairmen of all kind of Committees, I have never served under one so able'. Butcher, Secretary to the HMC, finally dropped his formality: 'I shall treasure the note you sent to me…. Yours (for once) William'. Hilda Boleyne-Smedley's letter was equally sensitive and sincere: 'Your chairmanship cannot have been easy, but it was delightful for us to have someone young, stimulating and provocative yet with a deep interest in the welfare of patients and staff, thank you for all your help.'[42]

Brian had joined the Labour Party's working party on the NHS in 1958 – its 10th birthday year – and helped to develop policy drafts in readiness for the expected 1959 general election.[43] Through Brian, Titmuss also participated, providing briefing papers and attending working party meetings at the request of its chair Peggy Herbison. The working party discussed the drugs bill, waiting lists, arrangements for teaching hospitals, the cost of mental health services and relationships with the pharmaceutical industry. Two doctors who actively participated were Dr Horace Joules of the West Middlesex Hospital and Dr Bruce Cardew, a GP involved with the MPU. Brian subsequently recommended both of them to Tony Benn who was looking for 'telegenic' party spokespeople for election broadcasts.[44]

The 10th anniversary of the NHS in 1958 provoked a wide range of public discussions and assessments on its effectiveness and purpose. Brian was a guest lecturer at a three-day University of London extension residential course run in conjunction with the North West Metropolitan RHB: 'The problems of policy and administration in the hospital service'. His topic was optimistically entitled: 'The First Ten Years of the National Health Service'.[45] He also wrote an anniversary piece, 'After

Ten Years' for the *New Statesman*, in which he put his finger on what was wrong with the system. It could be summarised as a shortage of money and lack of leadership, but he elaborated a number of factors. First, there had been gross miscalculations of the original costs during the wartime planning stage. The NHS thus started life at a disadvantage, already getting a smaller budget than it really needed, and tainting all future allocations with a sense of profligacy. Second, the system was 'penny wise, pound wasteful': replacing tin mugs with railway china, wooden benches with Navy, Army and Air Force Institutes (NAAFI) chairs, and painting hospital wards, while ignoring the 'vast opportunities for saving running costs by capital expenditure on new boilers, new laundries and compact, well-designed buildings. The Treasury, like the Co-op refuses to pay the market price for entrepreneurial ability. For senior engineers, catering officers and lay administrators, the service exploits the sense of vocation of first-class individuals or recruits the dregs of managerial talent. Some £700 million of public money is spent with hardly any operational research to see if it is wisely used. There is no money available to apply on a wide scale the cost-reducing lessons which have been learnt by local experiment.'[46]

A third significant factor for Brian was political:

> None of the transitory Ministers of Health has seemed to want to plan, and the ministry itself … has rejected the role of a strong policy-making body. It does not regard itself as the top management of a national corporation. Nor have the unpaid volunteers that the minister appoints to hospital boards the time or energy for strong leadership, or the knowledge that they will be trusted to take decisions or supported if they do. The mainstay of the National Health Service is a group of able doctors and administrators (lay and professional) who have both the courage and the integrity to take their own decisions and act as their consciences direct.

He was speaking for himself and for his colleagues on the various NHS hospital management boards on which they served. He concluded,

> There can be no doubt that the patient has had much better care since the Health Service. There is abundant evidence of this. But this is not the only criterion for judging the success of a national service. Is the service responsive to the wishes of the consumer? Does it even know what the consumer wants? Does the consumer feel he is encouraged to complain and make suggestions? In

general the answer to these questions is in the negative, and this is perhaps the failing of the service which should cause Socialists the greatest concern.

His assessment of the NHS in 1958 was undoubtedly also coloured by his fact-finding trip to Canada in the summer of that year, when he stayed with his good friends Sandy Robertson, then Professor of Social and Preventive Medicine at the University of Saskatchewan, and his partner, Richard Moore.[47] Canada was in the midst of major unrest over the privatisation of some parts of its health service, driven by similar concerns about its cost and efficiency that had dogged the British service during its first 10 years.

In the early 1960s Brian's interests in health services encompassed the cost of drugs, medical emigration, conditions in hospitals and the slow rate of expansion of health centres. His expertise was valued both within the NHS and the Ministry of Health. He had remained on the Governing Body at St Thomas' long after the takeover of the Lambeth Hospital, and played a very active part, including, it was rumoured, helping to secure a greater allocation of funding from the Ministry than the hospital should normally have received.[48] Brian got on well with all the governors, including the Conservative-leaning ones such as Sir John Prideaux and Peter Lumsden. Socially, he was one of them, but politically they accepted his usefulness in forming a bridge to the very left-wing Lambeth Council. In 1962 Bryan McSwiney, clerk to the governors, introduced Brian to Walter Holland, an epidemiologist recently returned to St Thomas' after appointments at Johns Hopkins University in the US and the London School of Hygiene and Tropical Medicine (LSHTM). Holland was asked by the Ministry of Health to establish a new Social Medicine and Health Services Research Unit. This was to have not only research but also a teaching function. Holland created an Advisory Board under the chairmanship of Austin Bradford Hill, which Brian joined in a personal capacity but also as the official representative of the Board of Governors. Connections with the LSE were further strengthened when Holland established reciprocal teaching arrangements with Titmuss. He also staffed his unit with two epidemiologists, two economists, two sociologists and two medical statisticians, and arranged for the economists to have two days a week attached to the LSE Department of Social Administration, under Brian's supervision. Brian was very much *persona grata* with the Ministry of Health and St Thomas' Hospital and Medical School. He was an astute choice by Holland for his advisory board, and fulfilled this duty, later acting as chair, until the unit moved to the Brompton Hospital in 1994. Brian recommended Holland to the Ministry (later the DHSS, Department of Health and Social Security) for a range of advisory roles over the next few years, including serving on Crossman's NHS (regional) working party and on the Resource Allocation Working Party (RAWP).

Another of Brian's collaborations developed at this time also turned into a life-long friendship. He had been introduced by his brother Lionel to Archie Cochrane, while skiing in Davos in January 1960.[49] Cochrane was then a member of the Medical Research Council's Pneumoconiosis Research Unit at Cardiff, and Brian quickly proposed him for membership of the Fabian Society's planned Industrial Injuries Group.[50] Brian took Peter Townsend and his family to South Wales to meet Cochrane in April 1960 to discuss joint research interests and collaborations on data. Cochrane had just published a paper, 'Investigation into the Working of the "Death Benefit" for Coalworkers' Pneumoconiosis'.[51]

Friendships and partnerships

At a party in 1960 Brian met John Sarbutt, who became his life-long partner. Sarbutt, then 19, came from a large Norfolk farming family and had recently moved to London intent on starting an acting career. John – Johnny, as Brian called him – came from a very different social world. To some of Brian's friends, he was a 'bit of rough' and a counterfoil to his sophisticated culture. He did not initially fit easily into Brian's existing close social set. This included Roger Lockyer, the historian, and his partner, the actor Percy Stevens; Denzil Freeth, the Conservative MP; the barristers Milton Grundy and Peter Mansfield QC; and Cecil Gould, Deputy Director of the National Gallery. To a naïve country lad, some of Brian's friends appeared snobbish, old, unattractive and horribly camp. For a while relations within the group became strained, and Brian chose to entertain them when John was not around. To them it seemed that Brian had a masochistic streak, persistently trying to consolidate this relationship despite John's sometimes antagonistic behaviour. Brian, however, was devoted to John from the outset, refusing to believe stories about his rogue nature. Within a short time of their meeting he had bought John a red Mini for his birthday (parked outside the house to surprise him, decorated with ribbons). He indulged John's juvenile behaviour and spoiled him at every opportunity. Brian was fiercely protective, on one occasion cutting up a leather jacket given to John by an admirer. There was good cause for his concerns: John's boyish beauty attracted the unwanted advances of several of Brian's gay friends, who chose to visit when they knew Brian was not at home. John found himself in a difficult situation, and lacked the social skills to deal with these embarrassing and unwelcome encounters. When Brian found out, he made his loyalties very clear, choosing to cut ties with some long-standing friends to secure his relationship with John.[52]

There had also been other significant changes within the Abel-Smith family recently. In January 1958 Lionel had made the break from Vivée, having finally plucked up the courage to tell her that he was setting up his own home in South Eaton Place. She did not take the news well, and it exacerbated a return of her problems with alcohol and a nervous breakdown. Lionel, a barrister at Lincoln's Inn, was able to make the change as gentle as possible, continuing to visit her almost daily for tea or dinner. In April Lionel and Brian took Vivée to Switzerland for a short holiday. They spent time in Geneva before heading up to a ski resort. Perhaps this was the occasion that the 'boys' used to brooch the subject of her move from the Durward House flat, which was now bigger than she required. During the summer, while Lionel and Brian were holidaying abroad (Brian in Canada and Lionel in France), a nurse was employed to live in with Vivée. A smaller house was found at 2 Inkerman Terrace, in South Kensington, into which she moved in November 1958, taking her long-time 'sharer-tenant' Mrs Worthington with her. Lionel, despite feeling that he was taking the larger share of the responsibility for keeping an eye on Vivée, slowly settled into a new domestic routine, eating at the French Club before going on to other clubs with friends, or entertaining them at his new home. Brian and his then partner, the Hungarian boxer Laci Tomazi (who some friends referred to as Attila or Hungary), were Lionel's guests on several occasions during the autumn of 1958, but never at the same time as Vivée.

In June 1960 Brian moved out of 16 Vincent Square Mansions, his home since 1953. He bought the lease on 34a Elizabeth Street, a four-storey Victorian terraced house in Belgravia, just around the corner from Lionel's home in South Eaton Place. Although it appeared to be small from the outside, internally it was spacious and well proportioned. It provided the opportunity for John to live with Brian, and was big enough, should the need arise, to claim that this was a financial arrangement to help him cover the higher bills of a larger property – a necessary precaution when homosexual acts were still illegal and could be prosecuted even when they took place in private between consenting adults. The basement was ideal for parties, and he generously let the Young Fabians hold one or two events at his home each year.[53] From the ground floor the staircase passed John's bedroom, which looked onto a light well at the rear, and went up to the first floor where a long drawing room with full-length sash windows faced onto Ebury Street, next to a dining room and galley kitchen. On the second floor was Brian's study, his bedroom and a bathroom. Finally on the top floor, which would have originally been for the children and servants of the household, was a self-contained flat with a sitting room, two bedrooms, a very small kitchen and bathroom. Elizabeth Street provided a source of income through letting out either the basement or the top flat. The latter option was potentially tricky, as there was no separate entrance, and the occupants had to pass up the staircase through Brian and John's home. For this reason, Brian let it only to people whom he felt would not jeopardise their privacy. Brian and John shared Elizabeth Street with a number of tenants, including refugees from the Hungarian Revolution of 1956, an opera singer and several women who could be collectively seen as 'in need of support'.

Brian appeared at times to want to have it all: he wanted to be known as a flamboyant and sexually successful character within his gay community, known for his parties and handsome boyfriend, but also to have recognition as a pillar of the establishment. He wanted to be the sophisticated, eligible bachelor, ferrying important international visitors out to the Titmuss's home in Acton in his sports car, a Rothman cigarette constantly alight, but he also wanted a settled, domesticated (if mainly private) life with John.[54] This public–private tension at times caused real problems for Brian. In the early 1960s he was close friends with one of the daughters of the wealthy Weston family. She invited him to visit her parents at their Canadian mountain holiday home one summer, with the intention of promoting him as a possible husband. Brian went on the trip with the intention of soliciting a large research grant from the Garfield Weston Foundation that had been established in 1959. In the event, neither Brian nor the daughter achieved their mission, and Brian was taken ill with gallstones, which meant a lengthy and painful descent down from the mountains to the nearest hospital, and then return to England.

There were discernible routines to Brian's life – dining most weeks at the French Club, often with Lionel and his partner, and then moving on to gay clubs – usually the Rockingham, but sometimes the Calabash in Fulham, Gigolo on the King's Road or the Spartan in Pimlico. He regularly ate out, especially at restaurants that were known to be gay-friendly such as La Bicyclette, La Popote or La Poule au Pot, just round the corner in Ebury Street. His mother Vivée, however, was a continuing source of concern, which Brian and Lionel managed through an agreed rota of weekly visits – Brian usually taking responsibility for Saturdays, and Lionel for Sundays, along with at least one mid-week supper. They also took her regularly to the theatre and opera (Brian had arranged for Lionel to meet Hugh Dalton's wife, Ruth, who in turn got him elected to the board of the Sadlers' Wells Opera Company). They sometimes also took Vivée to the French Club to dine. Lionel was now adept at managing his trust fund, and chose to free up some capital by selling part of the Wendover estate in 1959. From this 'windfall' he made generous gifts to his mother and to Brian – who received £500 for his 34th birthday, the equivalent to over £8,000 at today's values, and inherited Lionel's Zephyr car when he bought a second-hand Rolls Royce.

Brian was a generous and gregarious person, and casual acquaintances from travels developed into long friendships. He met Gale Fisher, a Canadian academic, on his trip to Saskatchewan to see Sandy Robertson, and invited him to visit him in London. Through Fisher he met another Canadian, Rupert Schieder, Professor of English at Toronto University, who in turn mentioned Brian to two younger Canadian academics, David Blewett and Arthur Sheps, when they were planning a year-long European tour in 1964 after finishing their Master's degrees at Toronto. They arrived in London and telephoned Brian, who immediately invited them to supper. When they both obtained research fellowships in 1967 they returned to London and rented the top floor flat. This was to become the start of a decade-long tradition of extended summers based with Brian and John at Elizabeth Street. They shared meals and effectively lived as one household, moving into Brian and John's quarters if the top flat happened to have tenants. They also had mutual friends in Sandy Robertson and his partner, Richard Moore.[55]

David and Arthur also joined Brian and John on some of their annual skiing trips. Brian's love of skiing had continued after his lessons with General Winterton in Vienna in 1947–48. Most Januarys he persuaded Lionel to join him, along with other sets of friends such as Milton Grundy and Viacheslav Atroshenko, and the art historian, Cecil Gould. Their regular skiing resort was Davos in Switzerland, where they chose the Oxen Hotel because it would serve them supper at the relatively late hour of 8.00pm. Brian had developed a routine of eating late at home, to allow him to work up until 8.00pm and then have a drink while preparing supper for 9.00pm. But to ask the Swiss to accommodate a further postponement for Brian's habits was too much.

A natural historian: *The Hospitals 1800–1948*

It was not until October 1964 that his long-planned book, *The Hospitals 1800–1948: A Study in Social Administration in England and Wales*, was finally published by Heinemann.[56] This was the final fruit of the HIF grant that he and Titmuss had secured in 1958, and which he had researched with the assistance of Bob Pinker.[57] His *History of the Nursing Profession* had been published in 1960, and related medical history books from Frank Honigsbaum, Rosemary Stevens and Gwendoline Ayers were also in the pipeline.[58] *The Hospitals* was an ambitious, but clearly focused history, which 'attempts to analyse the changing role of hospitals for physical disease in England and Wales between 1800 and 1948 in relation to the needs and objectives of the medical profession'. Brian made clear in the preface that his concern was not with methods of treatment or changing medical knowledge and their impact on morbidity and mortality. It was to be a broader picture, concerned with national legislation, and the emergence of a socialistic approach to hospital-based healthcare from the various voluntary and Poor Law institutions which had provided care as individualised charity rather than as a comprehensive social right. The chronology risked accusation of Whiggishness, ending as it did with Bevan's triumphal creation of the NHS in 1948. Yet Brian was at pains to show this not as a natural evolution, but as the outcome of years of pressure group politics and social and economic developments. Over 500 pages he displayed a very natural talent as a historian. His sources were skewed towards the easily accessible – back issues of the *British Medical Journal*, *The Hospital*, *Burdett's Hospitals and Charities*, the *Hospital Gazette* and the *Poor Law Officers Journal*. He also drew on meetings with some of the most influential figures in the recent history of British medicine: Lord Beveridge, Sir John Charles and Sir Wilson Jameson. The 30 chapters pick out key turning points in British hospital history, especially the impact of the Royal Commission on the Poor Law Reports of 1909, the role of the two world wars as catalysts for change, and how Bevan pushed through his preferred brand of a nationalised rather than municipalised health service in 1946. This last chapter, discussing events of less than 20 years ago, demonstrated his historian's credentials – an aptitude for analysing and explaining complex events. As Dan Fox has discussed, Brian demonstrated that he had the skill to be an impartial analyst, yet without hiding his personal political stance.[59] This is what makes the book the classic that it is – it is now part of the history of the history of the emergence of the British NHS. It was one of the first history books to have a relevance to contemporary health policy, and to be written by someone whose authority on the subject came from several years of intimate involvement with hospital boards and NHS committees.[60]

Some reviewers found it difficult to judge. One of the most glowing came from M.R. (possibly Michael Rose) in the *New Left Review*: 'The labyrinthine developments of the hospitals, the extraordinary hierarchical dominance of the voluntary teaching hospitals and the armadilloid reactions of the medical "guilds" to social change are extensively discussed....This book is essential reading for those who wish to understand how the Heath Service has developed in the way it has.'[61] The *British Medical Journal* review rather predictably highlighted how Brian had acknowledged the beneficial role of the BMA in campaigning for a unified health system, and how he had relied extensively on its own archives for his research.[62] Asa Briggs, in the *New Statesman*, and Francois Lafitte, in *New Society*, commended Brian for his balanced approach, which gave due attention to the less glamorous Poor Law institutions as well as the voluntary hospitals, and for asking the persistent but necessary questions, 'On what financial and other terms should patients of different sorts be allowed to access hospital facilities? On what terms should doctors work in hospitals – and what sorts of doctors? How should hospitals be managed and pay their way?'[63] Lafitte asked, 'Is it possible to see points at which we might have taken a different turning? If Herbert Morrison, not Aneurin Bevan, had been Minister of Health in 1945, would nationalisation [of the hospitals] have been resorted to?'

Inevitably, some reviews picked up the minor errors and omissions. Brian had not acknowledged the key PEP report of 1937, which had done so much to stimulate the BMA and the Ministry of Health to work up their own plans to solve the financial and organisational crises that beset British healthcare. Ruth Hodgkinson (a doctor-medical historian) in *Medical History* commended Brian's 'clarity and brevity', but found some of the themes over-simplified: 'Legislation and policy have been recounted when practice was frequently quite different....The metropolis was not the typical area and the entire work leans a little too much on the London experience.' Her conclusion hints at the territorialism that later professional medical historians were to exhibit in their crusade against doctor-historians: '... the human angle is absent. While we give thanks and praise for the vast and expert assembly of facts and figures and the computers' accuracy, we miss the richness of the true historian or the truths of the social philosopher. A Sigerist would have mentioned the common man and his place in the development of this part of the welfare services. This book is valuable and very necessary and will be widely appreciated. But let us also still plead for the other historian who thinks deeply and writes alone and may we be fortunate enough to have the time and understanding to read him.'[64] Sydney Holloway, who reviewed it for the *British Journal of Sociology*, was the most critical: 'it is astonishing to discover that nothing of significance is said about the development of medical education.... *The Hospitals* is subtitled "a Study in Social Administration": it is certainly not a study in sociology.... Nonetheless this book does contain valuable empirical material which will prove useful to whoever ventures to write a sociological study of the development of hospitals in England during the period 1800–1948.'[65]

Despite Holloway's dismal predictions, *The Hospitals* was an enduring success. Brian had discussions with Heinemann on a new edition in 1979, which was to have been cut down to 250 pages with 20,000 new words to bring it up to date. This proposal appears to have fallen by the wayside. *The Hospitals* was, however, translated and published as a Japanese edition in 1981 with the assistance of Professor Kozo Tatara of Osaka University Medical School.[66]

The Hospitals had clearly benefited from Brian's close involvement in contemporary British healthcare. Although he had given up some of his governorships, he retained his position on the governing body of St Thomas' Hospital, and drew authority from his role to write a series of keynote articles in professional publications such as *Medical Care*, the *Stethoscope* and the *Journal of the American Hospital Association*.[67] His 1964 article 'Hospital Planning and the Structure of the Hospital Service' was a critical response to the White Papers *A Hospital Plan for England and Wales* (1962) and *Health and Welfare: The Development of Community Care* (1963).[68] He examined the historical context of the regional hospital system that the NHS had inherited, and highlighted the myopia of hospital service planning:

> How far is the scale of our hospitals being determined by the limitations of inherited sites rather than by the optimum for efficient operations? How far are our ideas of scale being determined by the catchment needs of the 1834 Poor Law administration?... Though our sites are, in general, too small, we tend to fill them in the process of meeting present needs and leave little space for the unrecognised needs of the future. We make grossly inadequate provision for the motor car – for the parking needs of 1963, let alone 1983. We make too little provision for changing medical developments. In the next twenty years out-

patient departments may double in size. The in-patient treatment of *all* mental patients may be at or near their district general hospital. How could our present sites and plans be adapted to demands on this scale? Our planners too often start with the sites and then look to see what can be fitted on them, rather than looking at the needs to see how best they can be met.[69]

According to Brian, research on hospital demand was too narrowly focused on statistics, and ignored real practices:

> We have rediscovered Say's Law. Within limits, supply can create its own demand. When general practitioners know that hospital beds are short, they send to hospital only those patients who are desperately in need; they treat the rest at home, and get used to doing so.... When hospital doctors know that beds are short, they reduce the length of stay. When they know they are plentiful they increase the length of stay. Many hospital doctors find it invidious and unsatisfying to reign over an empire of empty beds.

He urged a fundamental reassessment of the place of the hospital within medical care, especially the role of institutions in treating the chronic sick, elderly and those with mental illnesses. He highlighted the blinkered approach of the Ministry of Health (and therefore Enoch Powell, through his Hospital Plan), in pushing the concept of community care at a time when the local authorities that would pay for it had announced they were slowing their investment plans. His attack on London's healthcare was even more strident – observing the illogicality of dividing London into regions according to the location of its teaching hospitals (which saw themselves as exempt from taking on real health service provision): 'The doctor of the future should be trained less on the esoteric and more on what constitutes the bulk of a general practitioner's work.... It would be preferable to divide London into areas based on the new London Boroughs, since this would open the way to closer co-ordination between different branches of the health services and assist the transition towards an all-purpose health or health and welfare authority, which in my view is bound to come in the long run.'[70]

Coterminous with his piece in *Medical Care* on the British hospital system, Brian published a lengthy article in the *Bulletin of the New York Academy of Medicine*, a transcript of the lecture he gave there in March 1964 that compared the development of medical services in the US with other developed countries.[71] Returning to British issues, he provided a response in the *Nursing Times* in July 1964 to the Platt Report on nursing education. He argued for nurses to be given a core education on tripartite medical administration (the division of the NHS into hospital services, GPs and local authority services), if necessary within universities.[72] He also published, with Kathleen Gales, the results of their Nuffield Trust-funded study on the emigration of British-trained doctors. Based on a sample of doctors registered between 1925 and 1959, they showed that between 11 and 16 per cent had emigrated (depending on which cohort was examined), a far higher number than previous Ministry of Health estimates. The popular press picked up the story and claimed there was a crisis because of this 'brain drain' of 'doctors who won't come home'. This linked into concerns that there had also been a substantial reverse flow of doctors into Britain who may not have had the same quality of training.[73] This generated significant debate in the medical press. In 1965 he was writing in *The Guardian* about the discontent of GPs, suggesting that even if their large pay demand were met in full, they would still be 'unhappy creatures'. What was needed was a complete reform from their employment as 'independent contractors' to salaried posts, working in practices owned by the Executive Councils.[74]

In the public's eye

By the early 1960s Brian was viewed as an expert in more fields than just social welfare. There were invitations to private dinners at Browns Hotel with Harold Wilson to discuss the Robbins report on higher education.[75] He had been a member of Labour's working party on the NHS that drafted the policy statement 'Members one of another', and he knew the backgrounds and reputations of key doctors sufficiently well to be able to brief Tony Benn on which ones to use in election broadcasts.[76] His Elizabeth Street home was a regular venue for political soirées. Peter Shore – from 1964 Harold Wilson's Parliamentary Private Secretary – and his wife Liz were regular guests, and he was godson to one of their children, Piers. Brian impressed them with sophisticated suppers – a leg of lamb spiked with 30 cloves of garlic and plenty of good wine. After supper, when the conversation became more political and heated, Liz would curl up to sleep on the large bearskin rug which Brian had brought back from a Canadian trip, until Peter was ready to go home. The Benns were there too, but Caroline was not allowed to sleep through Tony's bombastic monologues.[77]

Increasingly during the late 1950s and into the 1960s Brian's name and face appeared in the British media. Nearly all of his articles, radio and television appearances were designed to drawn attention to his view of what was wrong with society, and how it could be fixed. He was by now skilled in generating suitably provocative headlines and sound-bites. He regularly appeared on BBC shows such as the 'Ten O'Clock News', 'Panorama', 'Twenty Four Hours', 'Home' and 'Tonight', at least once every two or three months on such topics as the NHS, pensions, smoking, solicitors' charges, the state of Britain's hospitals and the new GP charter. For each appearance he received a fee of between five and 21 guineas.

When he took part in Kenneth Allsop's prime-time BBC television programme, 'This Nation Tomorrow', broadcast on Sunday 5 May 1963, the *Radio Times*' brusque synopsis set the tone: 'Brian Abel-Smith asserts his belief that the Welfare State is a myth, and that the middle classes are hypocrites in their attitude towards it. His views are then critically examined by three people in the studio.'[78] The programme provided him with a unique opportunity to tell millions of viewers about what he felt was wrong with the British welfare state. Filmed as he walked around Ladywell, the former Lewisham workhouse that now served as a local authority old people's home, he berated the system for its penny-pinching meanness and failure to address underlying, but well-known causes of poverty. He also used the programme to criticise the NAB, and its wage-stop policy. He used his personal life to provide context on the inequity of the welfare state:

> All this talk about a Welfare State is a lot of nonsense. None of our social services are as good as they ought to be. And it is not the poorest people who are getting all the welfare in Britain today but the people with the best jobs – people with salaried positions in government and private industry – middle class people.
>
> I suppose I am one of them. I'm a university teacher. I am forced to be in the pension scheme for university teachers. The employer pays most of the cost. And I can expect with any luck, a pension of at least half pay when I retire. If I'm sick I get my full salary just the same. Indeed I am better off when I am sick as part of my pay take the form of sickness benefit which is untaxed. I am appointed until I am 62 and would have to do something very terrible to get the sack. I can hardly be chucked out for teaching badly. In manual jobs people get sacked for doing their work badly. This is not the case for many professional salaried jobs. You don't sack a judge for being a bad judge or a matron for being a bad matron. No, unless I do something almost criminal, I've got nothing to fear from unemployment.[79]

The Sunday Times reviewer of the programme was not complimentary, calling Brian an 'incorrigible sentimentalist' who 'foamed on unquenchably and with touching innocence about the shortcomings of our conspicuously decent society.... Perhaps because I have the advantage over him of remembering what life was like pre-war, I had some difficulty in recognising his picture of life today; and more, in trying to tot up the bill for his New Jerusalem. However, you have to admit that this series really does unearth 'em. Never a dull moment.'[80] The *New Statesman* reviewer said that Brian 'pulled out more emotional stops than was necessary to make his case, but made it all the same'.[81] Maurice Richardson, writing in the *Observer*, begged to differ: 'This was a really powerful polemic and deserved a heavier-calibre panel to discuss it. I hope we shall see more of Abel-Smith. He has the makings of a champion telly-disputant. If I had the handling of him I would match him first with some trusty old right-wing chopping block such as McAdden or Curran, just for the experience. Then I would try to promote a contest for him at Ministerial level. He would take Marples as a lizard takes a bluebottle.'[82]

Despite the cynicism of some of the journalistic reviews, the public response to 'This Nation Tomorrow' was immediate. Within days he was receiving dozens of letters via the LSE and the BBC from viewers eager to thank him for publicising the 'real' welfare state. 'WM' wrote from Great Yarmouth giving Brian details of how unfairly he had been treated by the NAB when he had tried to claim benefit through ill health in 1959: 'I can tell you the sordid truth sir. We are up to our eyes in debt and any time know [sic] the electricity will be cut off. The water rates are overdue with a further 7 days final demand or the pipes will be removed. HP firms are screaming and the whole world seems to be closing in on us. I know you can't help us but how good to hear someone rearly [sic] face the truth and talk with sincerity. I don't now [sic] your address sir but I will never forget the name.'[83] While 'WM' was happy for Abel-Smith to publicise his case if it would help to change the system, others requested anonymity. The wife of an injured mine worker in Tredegar in South Wales sent him calculations on how little money they lived on, but asked 'please don't reveal our name and address as this will only cause distress to our family. We pretend we're doing alright, they have enough worries without ours atop.'[84]

Brian's rising public profile generated letters from all parts of the country and all social classes on a wide variety of health and social policy issues. Most were handwritten, providing several pages of personal accounts. Some verged on the cranky, but he dutifully replied to them all and forwarded their cases to government ministers where he thought it would be effective. He wrote to Huw Wheldon at the BBC suggesting a series of half-hour programmes on Sunday evenings called 'Other People's Problems'. He provided a list of potential themes including 'the homeless, widowed mothers, mentally subnormal, teenage delinquents, homosexuals and psychopaths': 'I am not asking for a job. I would however be glad to help as a backroom contact if that were any use. If this is lunatic fringe don't bother to answer.' Wheldon did reply, expressing interest, but citing lack of BBC capacity for such a series.[85]

The BBC did, however, make a documentary series in 1964 called 'Studying the Social Sciences', which was based on the work of academics at the LSE. It focused in each episode on a different discipline. Social Administration was covered in Episode 3: 'Problems in a changing society'. Brian was a prominent figure, alongside colleagues such as Nancy Seear, Adrian Sinfield, Richard Titmuss and David Donnision. They were filmed in the LSE buildings, and also visiting interviewees for research projects.[86]

Not all his media appearances were judged as successful. The ITV programme 'The Drug Takers' was panned by critics, who deemed it 'sensational, timid and sanctimonial' or 'pathetic', 'inane' and 'boring'. Brian presented the basic facts about drug addiction and then the film cut to show just the mouths of a group of addicts who talked about their problems. One reviewer summed up: 'As he emerged from the programme, the addict was simply a sub-normal weakling who had acquired the habit as a compensation for lack of talent and self-confidence and the moronically inarticulate interview subjects seemed to have been hand-picked for their ability to embody this image....With matters as close to home as this there ought to be some way of presenting sufferers as people, and not as curiosities in a psychiatric menagerie.'[87] Sometimes Brian's writing appeared constrained by his fixation on the current issue. His *New Statesman* article 'The Voiceless Millions' used the case study of an unemployed Cornish lorry driver with eight children to highlight the inequity of the 'wage stop' ruling of the NAB, and to call for increased family allowances.[88] The reaction was mixed: why did he not see the bigger picture, and make available free family planning rather than supporting larger families, asked one correspondent.[89]

Brian was alert to new initiatives that fitted with his broader agenda for a fairer society. One such opportunity was offered to him late in 1964 by the newly formed Public Schools Committee. Founder members included the usual suspects – Titmuss, Townsend and politicians such as Peter Shore, Tom Driberg and Dick Taverne. Stimulated by Labour's manifesto document *Signposts for the Sixties*, it acted as a ginger group within the Labour Party to push for the merger of all schools within the state-maintained system, thus ending the public school's freedom to select by education ability or parental wealth. Brian agreed to be a sponsor of the organisation, and spoke at the inaugural press conference on 5 May 1965.[90] This was widely reported, along with the fact that he had attended one of Britain's elite public schools, Haileybury.

6

Lingua franca: 1956–67

Health economics

Mauritius: three is the magic number

Paying for Health Services

The unnerving discovery that every Minister of Health makes at or near the outset of his term of office is that the only subject he is ever destined to discuss with the medical profession is money. (Enoch Powell, 1966)[1]

Economese is, like English, an important *lingua franca* in international affairs – but skilled speakers are scarce. (Alec Cairncross, 1981)[2]

In 1956 Brian was invited to conduct a pioneering multi-country study for the World Health Organisation on the costs and financing of healthcare systems. From this first consultancy onwards, Brian worked for part of every year on international projects. He was one of the first of an emerging group of 'global' expert advisers – many of them fellow academics – who were contracted by international organisations and developing countries to devise new health and social welfare policies. Their work was supported by the emergence of a distinct network of health economists who were analysing new sources of data to respond to widespread concerns in the developed world about the rising costs of healthcare. Brian's first comprehensive system was designed (with Richard Titmuss and Tony Lynes) for the newly independent Mauritius, which he visited several times between 1959 and 1963. Dealing with contentious issues such as family planning opened Brian's eyes to the international politics of development, especially the role of organisations such as the UN. His trip to the former Soviet

Union as part of Milton Roemer's study group in 1961 provided a valuable insight into 'second' world healthcare systems.

Health economics

The Guillebaud study came to a rather unpleasant and unexpected conclusion for Britain's Conservative government in 1956: the NHS was actually very good value for money, and deserved a greater share of the GNP. A further outcome was the exposure of just how rudimentary Britain's official statistics were. Brian, working as Guillebaud's research assistant, had to make special requests for information not usually collected, and for more useful collations of data normally sent straight to Whitehall filing cabinets. It seemed that supply and demand were concepts best kept to the economists' desks, rather than employed in managing the NHS. It took until 1957, nine years after its creation, for the NHS to develop a Main Costing Scheme, and even then nearly a quarter of all hospitals were unable to supply information in a standardised format to the Ministry of Health. In practice this meant that it was not possible to adequately distinguish between long- and short-term costs, disentangle cost-effectiveness and technical efficiency, comment on the basis on which hospitals collected their data or provide estimates of demand in each catchment area.[3] The Ministry privately acknowledged its inadequacies, recognising that there was 'an appalling state of ignorance about the hospital service. Differences exist in hospitalisation which defy explanation, there is no real measure of need, nor any direct attempt to measure efficiency'.[4] Yet little was done: in 1964 a Ministry study group stipulated that computers should only be purchased if they saved more than 10 per cent in staff costs every year.[5]

The Ministry of Health, however, had made some attempts to develop its statistical expertise: setting up an Organisation and Methods Unit, conducting annual hospital in-patient surveys and collaborating with research organisations.[6] In 1960 the Nuffield Trust published a study of Barrow-in-Furness that developed the idea of the 'critical number' of acute care beds (using doctors' requests for hospital admissions and lengths of stay as tests of adequacy).[7] It was the one of the first in a new line of research that had direct NHS application, but also revealed new concerns. Subsequent studies, such as that by Harvard economist Martin Feldstein, suggested that Britain was allowing such simplistic analyses of demand and length of stay to push up the number of beds.[8] This argument resonated with politicians: Enoch Powell worried that 'there is virtually no limit to the amount of medical care an individual is capable of absorbing'.[9] There were, however, useful lessons to be learned abroad. American economists were pioneering the modelling of hospital admission rates, lengths of stay and costs, such as the large healthcare study carried out by University of Michigan in the late 1950s.[10] Roemer's Law, named after the public health expert Milton Roemer, had demonstrated that in a country operating a health insurance system, the ultimate determinant of the volume of hospital in-patient days, was the number of beds available. This is colloquially expressed as 'a built bed is a filled bed'.[11]

While ministers may have privately wrung their hands at their perceived statistical inadequacies, there was emerging evidence that Britain was not alone. The pioneering work that Brian had conducted for Guillebaud was to pay international dividends. This was only possible because of the WHO. Three months younger than the NHS, the WHO was the successor to the inter-war League of Nations Health Organization. It was one of a handful of organisations set up under the umbrella of the UN, with its headquarters in Geneva. After a slow start – its constitution had to be ratified by each UN country – it appointed its first Director, the Canadian psychiatrist Brock Chisholm. The WHO is funded through wealth-related contributions from member countries and donations from philanthropic bodies such as the Rockefeller Foundation, and in the first few years it established six regional offices and representatives in member countries. The fundamental ethos of the WHO was to improve health, mainly through direct campaigns. The first six priorities chosen to develop into work programmes were malaria, tuberculosis, venereal diseases, maternal and child health, nutrition and environmental sanitation. There has subsequently been criticism of the naïve approach to some of these issues, especially the malaria eradication campaign, in which the Americans championed programmes aimed at underpinning economic growth rather than more risky social reform.[12] In 1953 Chisholm was replaced by the Brazilian Marcolino Candau, who was to lead WHO for four successive five-year terms, and steer it through the Cold War machinations that saw the former Soviet Union and other Communist countries return to the UN in 1956, and a shift in the power balance away from strong US alliances at the WHO.[13]

Switzerland's long-held neutrality made Geneva the logical choice for the headquarters of the major organisations and their subsidiaries such as the WHO, ILO, UNICEF and the UN Development Programme (UNDP). This compact and picturesque city on the shores of Lake Geneva had established its reputation as the epicentre of international dialogue in the inter-war years. The urban fabric reflected these global ambitions, with the development of a 'UN' village on fields above the old town. Around the Palais des Nations were large office blocks for the various organisations set between monumental plazas and boulevards. Because many of these were staffed by national representatives, often on short-term contracts, it increasingly felt like a massive airport terminal: sterile and transitory. Indeed there were few places of its size that boasted direct flights to so many capitals, or such a variety of cuisines and languages.

In the spring of 1957, in the midst of 14-hour days working to get Crossman's national superannuation plan into print, Brian also found time to go to Geneva to consolidate plans for an ambitious WHO working party. He had been asked to produce a report, *The Practical Possibilities of Undertaking a Cross-National Study of the Costs and Financing of Medical Care Services*, which he presented in Geneva on 15 April.[14] This new line of work appealed on several levels – not only the academic challenge, but also the attraction of being back on the continent, where he had been posted during his National Service in 1949–50. His subsequent holidays from Cambridge had usually involved several summer months on long European driving tours. His love of skiing, developed while serving as an ADC in Austria, could now be easily fitted with his professional duties. He wrote to Titmuss, 'I enjoyed Geneva enormously.... I had four days skiing at 7,000 feet up. I am so sunburnt that I would be thought on the wrong side of the colour bar in the US.'[15]

In the previous couple of years the WHO had identified that health administrators in many countries, especially those that had recently introduced comprehensive health services, were having problems in developing and justifying 'reasonable and well-balanced' health budgets that their government's treasuries would accept. Highlighting the British Guillebaud study – and similar initiatives in the Netherlands, New Zealand, Canada, Chile and the US – it had proposed a long-term programme with the following objectives: to assess expenditure by the state on healthcare; to assess the financial burden for the individual; and to assess the availability of free or insurance-covered (prepaid) services.[16] This programme would require specific data, collected according to internationally agreed definitions, and was intended to build on existing research by the Social Security Division of the ILO and broader UN studies of maintenance of family levels of living. Professor Hernan Romero of Chile had been asked in June 1956 to prepare an introductory paper to complement Brian's, which was to focus on the practical aspects of organising a pilot study. Dr J.W. Mackintosh, a WHO medical consultant, was asked to comment on Brian's proposals, and the WHO regional offices identified which countries in their regions might be suitable to participate in the study.

Brian's 16-page paper acknowledged the daunting scale of the task, and drew on lessons from the Guillebaud study, especially the wide gap between expectations and the reality of government statistical sources. He addressed two main questions: (a) What concepts can be developed which are potentially capable of empirical application?, and (b) How far does statistical information already exist in the countries to be studied which can be assembled or collected to conform with the concepts developed in (a)? Once he began analysing types of 'costs' it proved difficult to draw lines: what is a hospital? what is a drug? what is health? Brian drew on Milton Roemer's study, *Medical Care in Relation to Public Health*, to suggest that the sample should include a country from each of Roemer's categories of healthcare systems: private initiative, social assistance, social insurance and public service. His timetable proposed convening a working party in the autumn of 1957, with a final report being presented to an Expert Committee for discussion in late 1959.

While the WHO was deciding how to proceed with the study, Brian entered into correspondence with Wilbur Cohen, then Professor of Public Welfare Administration at the University of Michigan, Ann Arbor, and later to become US Secretary of Health, Education and Welfare in 1968 under President Johnson. President John F. Kennedy had nicknamed him 'Mr Social Security', and he was widely seen as the brains behind the development of the Medicare system. Brian had met Cohen at Castle Tyrol in northern Italy during the 1957 International Gerontology conference, and as a result began to work up a paper on the costs of support of the elderly.[17] He and Cohen exchanged data sets on British and US expenditures, and began a life-long friendship.

In December 1957 Brian spent three weeks working in Geneva establishing the definitions to be used in the project. He sent Titmuss a copy of his working paper for comment, who returned it with some rather negative annotations, doubting the expectation that costs of personal healthcare could be broken down into 'preventive, promotive, diagnostic and curative' elements.[18] Brian was not solely responsible for drawing up the pilot study – his collaborator was Kalman Mann, Director General of the Hadassah Medical Organisation in Israel. In April 1958 they finished drafting the project questionnaire in Geneva (and Brian managed to fit in a few days skiing).[19] He returned in July to formally present the paper to the ILO/UN/WHO working party.[20] The group, chaired by J.S. Peterson, Director of the Division of Organisation of Public Health Services at WHO, agreed that a pilot study should proceed, but that it required the close direction of a consultant to ensure that the countries selected to participate produced statistics in the required format. Donald McGranahan, Chief of the Office of Social Affairs at the UN European Office, commented on a similar study that the UN had conducted in India as part of the 'Planning for Balanced Social and Economic Development' programme. He felt that there would be considerable difficulties, depending on whether expenditures were classified by the department responsible or by the purpose of the expenditure. The representatives from the International Social Security Association (ISSA) were equally wary of the proposal. Finally, it was agreed to commission a pilot study, provisionally to include Britain, the Netherlands, Bulgaria, the US, Chile, Costa Rica, Israel, Ceylon and Japan. Information was to be collected in the first instance just for one fiscal year, and if possible, to include an assessment of the spatial patterns of health expenditure in each country.

When Brian returned from his 1958 extended late summer holiday in Canada with Sandy Robertson, he was invited to act as the consultant on the pilot study. Teaching and research commitments at the LSE, especially on the Nuffield Trust grant on the development of British health services, meant that he could not find time to take this on until the end of the academic year in July 1959. He then embarked on an ambitious tour. The selection of countries had changed from the initial working party proposal: he visited Sweden (4–18 July), then travelled on to Czechoslovakia (19–29 July). As he was already committed to spend August in Mauritius on a British government mission, the next stage of the WHO project had to wait until September, when he travelled to Ceylon (10–21 September). For each of these trips he produced a visit report, required to release payment of the WHO consultant's fee.[21]

Brian's visit reports listed the individuals in each country who had helped him locate and interpret the diversity of statistics relating to healthcare costs and sources of finance. The Swedish visit provided reassurance that such material was available, even if some of the sub-categories on the questionnaire could not be completed. The steep learning curve of working on the British Guillebaud enquiry paid off – Brian could anticipate and plan for expected weaknesses. In Czechoslovakia, where 92 per cent of the population received their healthcare through insurance-funded services provided by the Ministry of Health, Brian arrived with the assumption that the questionnaire would be relatively easy to complete. He soon, however, discovered that separating out curative from preventive services was more complicated than he had expected. Even distinguishing between capital and recurrent costs proved difficult. Brian's September visit to Ceylon was the first since he had visited the island as part of the British Council universities debating tour in 1952. As in Czechoslovakia, he found that the government's accounting system did not quite correspond to the cost categories that he and Mann had devised. Some curative services, such as the school health service, were reported under the public health budget heading; no attempt had been made by the hospitals to distinguish between in-patient and out-patient expenditure. As a result of Brian's initial visit, the Ceylonese government debated whether they could find the manpower to produce more detailed statistics, in a format that would be compatible with the WHO study. Back in Geneva in late September the working party's document and questionnaire were further refined in the light of Brian's fieldwork.

The following year, 1960, Brian once again fitted consultancy work on the WHO project on the 'Costs and sources of finance of medical care' around his LSE duties and other commitments. In May he gave a paper at the Keppel Club, an informal study group that met monthly at LSHTM (based in Keppel Street), entitled 'The Economics of Medical Care'.[22] In September he returned to Sweden and Czechoslovakia to discuss their completed questionnaires. He was impressed by the Czechs' attention to detail and plans to establish a medical economics unit to improve future budgeting and reporting. However, in a confidential memorandum to WHO, Brian set out the sensitivities he had uncovered during discussions with the officials from the Ministry of Health: they were concerned that 'Eastern Europe' would come across poorly in any comparative study of healthcare, hence their desire to use 1959 statistics that would reflect their very recent improvements. For reasons of national security they did not wish to disclose their expenditure on military medical care. They also wanted Brian to secure for them a more favourable breakdown of expenditure categories that would show their actual provision of maternal care, and acknowledge that their spa treatments, of which they were very proud, were bona fide medical costs. He promised them he would raise these matters with WHO Geneva, in the hope that an informal understanding could be reached before the Czech government was officially asked to participate in the main study.[23]

Brian's experiences on the WHO project undoubtedly coloured his rapporteur duties at the 12th International Hospital Congress held in Venice in June 1961, where he had the unenviable task of drawing together 60 contributions from 16 different countries. He wryly noted: 'We had a mass of information – some revealing the facts, some distorting them. It was often hard to distinguish statements of aspiration from statements of achievement. And often the discussion was clothed in heavily emotive language. On a number of occasions, these deceptive phrases were torn open by ruthless questioning.... I learnt that not only the word "voluntary" but also the word "insurance" had a special meaning in America.'[24] Later in June he travelled to Israel to resume the WHO project fieldwork, spending 12 days visiting hospitals and healthcare facilities.

The end of his 1961 summer vacation from the LSE was spent in the former Soviet Union, in a group of 12 British and US clinicians and social scientists put together by Milton Roemer for a two-week fact-finding tour. Brian had not yet met Roemer, despite having overlapped during respective assignments in Geneva in the late 1950s. When Sandy Robertson passed on Roemer's invitation, Brian was immediately enthusiastic.[25] Roemer and his group were interested to see the impact of the Gosplan agency's long-term planning strategy, which was reported as having achieved better population health than in the west. It provided free healthcare, aiming at a doctor–patient ratio of 1:333 by 1980 and 16.5 hospital beds per 1,000 population. By 1961, when the third Gosplan programme was started, the crude death rate was reported at 7.6/000 – lower than in the US – and the infant mortality rate of 36/000 was comparable with many developed countries. With its central planning system, the Soviet medical service was similar in many ways to the British NHS, although even this 'socialised system' was a model that the Americans felt uncomfortable with. Roemer and his group wanted to see if the reality matched the rhetoric.

Other members of the study group were Sandy Robertson, Bill Glaser and his wife Todd from Columbia University Bureau of Applied Social Research, Milton Terris, Head of the Chronic Disease Unit at New York City Public Health Research Institute, Henry Makover from the Albert Einstein Medical College, Mary Monk, a doctor from Indiana and Michael Kaser, who had been stationed in Moscow when he worked for the Foreign Office, but was now an academic at the University of Oxford with research interests in Soviet healthcare systems. Kaser's fluent Russian was critical to the success of the visit. Brian had studied Russian briefly between leaving school and doing his National Service, but that was nearly 20 years earlier. The visit had been booked through the official USSR travel agency, Intourist, which provided the group with a guide/interpreter, but Kaser's knowledge of the language and culture was invaluable in helping the group to read between official statements and explanations.

Brian and Kaser flew out to join the group in Moscow on 14 August. Kaser had last been in Moscow in 1957, and noted the immense changes in his diary. Although there was still a shortage of eating places, they were able to obtain caviar, Polish Śląska vodka and reasonable quality meals at the Metropole and the Berlin, two of the official tourist hotels. Their 'billets' in university accommodation were not up the standard they had expected for their £4 10s per night. Roemer had arranged visits through a contact at the Ministry of Health, but when they arrived they found that plans had been changed. They were unable to meet staff from the Ministry's Planning and Economics Department as they had requested, and suspected that this was a polite way of making it clear that questions about sensitive financial and planning issues would not be welcome. Their visits to the Semashko Institute of Public Health and the Moscow Sanitary Epidemiological Station were more successful and informative. The group spent a full day at the Botkin Hospital – the 'Hammersmith Hospital of the USSR', as Sandy Robertson called it.[26] As with many Russian hospitals, the legacy of Pavlov permeated both design and operational philosophy, with great attention to the colours of rooms, systematic physical exercise for almost all patients, a programme of sleep therapy and much health education.[27] When not on official visits, the group walked in Gorky Park, visited museums, the Lenin-Stalin Mausoleum and Red Square. They took a boat on the river to a pontoon, from where they enjoyed a beer watching the sunset behind the domes of the Kremlin. Brian, Robertson and Kaser were invited to the British Embassy for a very formal lunch with H.E. Frank Roberts, served on silver plates. The tinned gooseberries were served with tinned cream – a sign of the current food shortages – but accompanied by champagne and an excellent Chateau Lynch-Bages from the embassy's cellars.

After six days in Moscow the group flew to Kiev in the Ukraine, accompanied by their Intourist guide, Rita. She was unable to resolve their problems at the Ukrania Hotel, which told them flatly that as tourists they had to sleep three to a room. Kaser's Russian secured them a relatively better deal after the first night. They visited the Ukrainian Academy of Sciences, where their questions on public health administration were answered very fully. Their persistent questions on economics were difficult to explain to officials whose bureaucratic delineation was solely focused on health. As in Moscow, their pre-arranged itinerary was abandoned, and Kaser tried to negotiate new plans on the crackly telephone line with Ministry officials. Their request to visit a policlinic based in a factory was refused (too sensitive). They visited a Kiev hospital, where Roemer volunteered to test the acupuncture service, a skill that the USSR was rapidly disseminating into its regions, having sent doctors to China to be trained. They were taken by bus out into the countryside, slipping on the muddy, potholed Russian roads, to visit a rural hospital – not the one usually shown to foreign visitors, which was unreachable after flooding. This was a lucky re-arrangement which let them see an authentic USSR rural hospital, surrounded by poor houses which Kaser described in his diary as little more than hovels. Their week in Kiev was marred by near-continuous rain, which frustrated sightseeing (Brian had no raincoat or umbrella with him). The food was less abundant than in Moscow, and caviar unobtainable, but the plentiful supply of Ukrainian champagne and Polish vodka ensured pleasant evenings in restaurants followed by dancing to local bands.

At the end of the fortnight most of the group travelled onwards from Kiev to the International Epidemiological Association conference at Korinla in Yugoslavia. Brian and Kaser flew to Moscow to connect with a flight for London. Kaser took Brian on a tour of some of the sights they had not seen in the previous week, educating him on the impact of recent Soviet culture – hotels used for centuries by visiting Europeans had been rebranded – the Savoy was now the Berlin, the Aurora was the Budapest, the Europa was now the Armenia. The former English Club was now the Museum of the Revolution, only its grand staircase indicating its former social status. Brian was particularly delighted to see the Eliseev Store, Moscow's pre-1917 pre-eminent grocers and wine merchants, with its stunning gold fretwork and crystal chandeliers, the equivalent of London's Fortnum & Mason.

Brian attended the second WHO study working party meeting in Geneva in December 1961, which approved further refinements to the questionnaire and definitions, and requested that he present another report the following spring. The reaction at Geneva was enthusiastic: 'An excellently presented study that would require very little editing – its clarity is positively dazzling'.[28] Reaction to a further paper, *Balanced Social and Economic Development*, which Brian sent to McGranachan, was less positive. Perhaps Brian had hoped this would be his entrée into the wider world of UN social policy, but McGranachan was disappointed that it was not as provoking as he had expected, and wondered how it would fit with the recent UN New York Social Commission resolution.

Brian already had an established network of international contacts, many of whom were friends as well as colleagues. After attending the Fifth Gerontological Conference in San Francisco in August 1960, he had taken his holiday to drive up to Saskatoon to meet up with Sandy

Robertson and his partner Richard Moore. Robertson (now at the Milbank Memorial Fund in New York) came to stay with Brian in London the following summer; he entertained Wilbur Cohen later that year, and Ida Merriam was pushing for him to sort out his invitation to spend a term at Yale Law School. The LSE had recognised his growing international reputation by promoting him to a readership that summer (with a salary of £1,675 and an £80 London allowance). This academic base gave him a flexibility to take up the most appealing and useful offers that came along. On accepting an invitation to give a keynote speech to the Milbank Memorial Fund in September 1962, he wrote to Sandy Robertson setting out his plan to integrate holiday and work: 'I am anticipating that I will be able to have the little flat in the Village which I used when I was in New York last time.... I am very happy there.'[29] However, it was Geneva that was increasingly central to Brian's work and social life. When Red (Herman) Somers and his wife Anne arrived there in September 1962 for a year's secondment from Haverford College, Philadelphia, US, to the Social Security Division of the ILO, Brian took pleasure in introducing them to one of his favourite restaurants, Au Fin Bec.

Mauritius: three is the magic number

Brian's contract after he finished working on the Guillebaud report in 1957 had been a full-time lectureship at the LSE. Its three academic term structure (10 weeks each) left plenty of time for research. The LSE had a long tradition of international relations, and this was visible through the activities of several of its directors and leading figures. Harold Laski's close relationship with India resulted from teaching many of its politicians at the LSE in the 1930s. His influence was such that one Indian Prime Minister said 'there is a vacant chair at every Cabinet meeting in India reserved for the ghost of Professor Harold Laski'.[30] Sydney Caine, LSE's Director between 1957 and 1967, secured a (then) major grant of £250,000 from the Ford Foundation in 1958 to extend teaching and research on developing countries. Caine had previously been Vice Chancellor of the University of Malaya, and subsequent LSE directors had held appointments in Rhodesia, the European Commission and the UN. The student profile of the LSE in the post-war period was also increasingly multinational, with many returning home to take up senior positions in former British colonies: Jomo Kenyatta in Kenya, Kwame Nkrumah and Hilla Limann in Ghana, Goh Keng Swee in Singapore, Erroll Barrow in Barbados, Michael Manley in Jamaica, Shridath (Sonny) Ramphal in Guyana, and later Secretary

General of the Commonwealth. This illustrious roll-call stimulated Daniel Moynihan, an American Ambassador to India, to comment in 1975 that the LSE was 'often said to be the most important institution of higher education in Asia and Africa'.[31] More specifically, what many of them took home was a brand of Fabian socialism, which dominated political systems throughout the developing world: 'it was an inspired cartographic convention ... which decreed that the British Empire should be coloured pink'.[32]

Seewoosagur Ramgoolam and Veerasamy Ringadoo were two such disciples who took LSE's lessons to Mauritius. Ramgoolam (1900–85) was an Indian-Mauritian of Bihari descent. He left Mauritius in 1921 to study medicine at University College London, surviving on meagre rations and spending his free time developing a left-wing political consciousness through his involvement with the Fabian Society. He also attended lectures at the LSE, and when he returned to Mauritius in 1935, established the newspaper *Advance* in addition to setting up a medical practice and working within the Labour Party. By the late 1950s he was one of the most influential politicians on the island, serving in the Labour government as *de facto* Prime Minister, and leading the campaign for independence from Britain. When this was achieved in 1968, Ramgoolam was appointed as Prime Minister, a position he held until he retired in 1982, when he was appointed Governor General. Veerasamy (known as Nades) Ringadoo (1920–2000), a Tamil Hindu, followed the same path to Britain as Ramgoolam, to study Law at the LSE. He returned to Mauritius to hold various offices in the Labour government, and in 1986 succeeded Ramgoolam as Governor General. When Mauritius became a republic in 1992, he was elected as its first President. From 1959 these two men developed a relationship with Brian and Titmuss which was to last the rest of their lives, and helped transform Mauritian society.

Mauritius was a classic 'third world' country, according to the 1950s Cold War terminology. It lies in the Indian Ocean east of Madagascar. It is a small island of 720 square miles – as big as the county of Surrey, as the 1956 British Society for International Understanding helpfully suggested in its pamphlet guide. It also noted its relative obscurity – the man in the street would struggle to pin its location to the Indian Ocean. Indeed, when Queen Alexandra wrote to thank the Mauritians for the floral wreath they sent to the funeral of Edward VII, it was addressed to Mauritius, British West Indies.[33] With its borderline tropical-temperate climate, lush green vegetation, palm trees, white coral sands and clear blue waters, it has been seen as a modern-world

Garden of Eden. When the Dutch first colonised the island in 1638 they found it uninhabited. They brought with them sugar cane to cultivate, and imported slaves from Madagascar and Africa. Within a few years the island's most famous inhabitant, the Dodo, was extinct, and the Dutch abandoned it in 1710. The French claimed the island in 1715, rejuvenating the sugar industry. Mauritius was lost by the French in 1810 when British troops occupied it during the Napoleonic wars, and it then became a British colony in 1814, with English added to French as one of the official languages. By 1835, the year that slavery was abolished, the population had reached 100,000. The freed slaves remained on the island, but were reluctant to continue to work on the (mainly French-owned) sugar plantations, so indentured labourers were imported from India.

By the late 1950s Mauritius had a population of nearly 600,000, of which 67 per cent claimed Indian descent (both Hindu and Muslim). Four per cent were Chinese and the remainder a mix of French, English and African, most of whom were Catholic. The *lingua franca* was a Creole, but the authority of the sugar barons on the island ensured that French remained the language of business and culture, with English as the language of government. In the absence of any significant mineral reserves or manufacturing industry, sugar was the lifeblood of the island, and accounted for 98.8 per cent value of exports in 1958. It was also its Achilles' heel: the plantations, the largest source of employment, but shunned by all but Indians, could not offer continual full employment to their workers, and were regularly devastated by tropical cyclones. Despite this somewhat precarious existence, the population thrived: the 'phenomenal' 36 per cent increase between 1947 and 1957 was mainly due to the eradication of malaria and a surge in the birth rate, one of the highest in the world at 47/000.[34]

Mauritius had often been the subject of investigations into its economic and social conditions. Experts sent from Britain such as Dr A. Balfour reported back to the Colonial Office in 1921 on the pervasive poverty, lack of basic sanitation and a sub-culture based on a very non-British system of bribery and extortion. Although under the Poor Law some basic welfare services had been established, they were insufficient to tackle the structural faults that existed. Primary education was provided, but for more advanced education there was no choice but to leave the island to study in Britain or another developed country. Many who made that journey were reluctant to return. Housing on the sugar plantations was usually in round straw huts; in the urban areas, such as the capital Port Louis, overcrowding in tin shacks was the norm for the majority of the Creole population. The small society of sugar barons lived in relative luxury in their estate mansions, and the sizeable government workforce was located in the better quarters of Port Louis or in the mountainous centre of the island at Curepipe (although this was plagued by persistent cold drizzle).

Political representation had only recently caught up with the developed world. The March 1959 election – the first to take place with universal adult suffrage – elected a newly empowered Executive Council, in which Ramgoolam as Ministerial Secretary fulfilled some of the typical duties of a prime minister. The Labour Party in effect held office, but with significant powers retained by the Governor, Sir Colville Montgomery Deverell. The relationship with Britain was closely managed, with frequent visits to and from the island by Colonial Office staff and Mauritian politicians and civil servants respectively. Although Mauritius was a relatively prosperous colony (its annual GNP per head at Rs1,000 [£75] provided a higher standard of living than in India or African colonies), there was a clear need for support for economic and social development. The output per head fell 14 per cent between 1953 and 1958, while at the same time levels of unemployment were rising. In the absence of an effective social insurance system, the burden of support was shifted to other benefits. Sickness claims in 1959 were over six times higher than they had been in 1953. Part of this rise was owing to genuine sickness, as the WHO survey of nutrition found in 1959 when it estimated that over 50 per cent of some groups in the population suffered from anaemia, which made then unfit for the typical hard work of sugar plantations.[35] The government's doctors resented the fact that 'they are forced into a situation of having to administer what they recognise to be a disguised, inefficient and morally discreditable system of unemployment benefit'.[36]

From the British perspective Mauritius was but one of a handful of its colonies that required assistance. With the aim of stimulating investigations and new initiatives, a series of Colonial Welfare and Development Acts were passed after the Second World War. Yet, as Frederick Cooper has shown, 'development' was then usually seen as something to be done *to* and *for* these countries, not *with* them, and explicitly linked to economic growth.[37] Colonies were valued for the potential contribution they could make to the imperial economy. Macmillan's request to civil servants in 1957 makes clear the 'make or break' British perspective:

> ... to see something like a profit and loss account for each of our Colonial possessions, so that we may be better able to gauge whether, from the financial and economic point of view we are

likely to gain or lose by its departure. This would need of course,
to be weighted against the political and strategic considerations
involved in each case.[38]

In the post-war period most imperial powers such as Britain, France
and the Netherlands shared a view of development as implicitly
'modernising', in which former colonies would be supported in
their move away from the 'primitive' or 'traditional' towards approved
standards and methods. If explicit didacticism failed there was the hope
of 'permeation' of 'modern' forms of governance and society. The Acts
also facilitated and funded a number of collaborations with British
academics, to supplement the already significant expertise that existed
within Whitehall. For ministers in the colonies, it was a time to renew
old acquaintances and exploit networks. By the mid-1950s Mauritius
had already gained over £2.2 million of British funding to improve
water supplies and irrigation and for anti-malarial projects. A further
initiative was taken in September 1957, when a Committee of Ministers
was appointed by the Governor, Sir Robert Scott, to investigate the
feasibility of a contributory, compulsory and comprehensive system
of social insurance. It recommended the appointment of an expert to
develop a more detailed policy, and Scott put in a request to Lord Perth
to ask Titmuss to 'appraise the nature and implications of the scheme'.[39]

Titmuss was the recognised expert in social policy, his name currently
widely in circulation as the brains behind the British Labour Party's
schemes for national superannuation and reform of NAB. Through
Harry Hall at the Colonial Office he negotiated wider terms of
reference to allow him to consider the whole field of social security,
health and welfare, and to have the assistance, both in Britain and during
the investigation in Mauritius, of Brian and his research assistant Tony
Lynes. It is indicative of the novelty of such academic/government
investigations that Titmuss was at a loss initially on how to cost the
project. The Mauritian government had agreed to pay air fares (his,
first class; Brian and Lynes, by tourist class), a clothing allowance (they
assumed that academics would not have the appropriate wardrobe for
a sub-tropical climate) and an honorarium. Titmuss eventually decided
on £900, apportioned £400 for himself, £300 for Brian and £200
for Lynes. Caine, Director of the LSE, agreed to their conducting the
study during vacation time.

One significant obstacle to carrying out this project was Titmuss's
health. He had been diagnosed with tuberculosis in 1958 and had to

continue with his course of treatment well into the summer of 1959, making travel to Mauritius impossible. It was agreed that the first visit would be made in August 1959, if necessary just by Brian and Lynes, and that a report would be ready by summer 1960, after Titmuss had had the opportunity to visit the island. He formally accepted the invitation on 24 February, and after ratification by the Mauritian government of the terms of reference, an announcement was made in the British and Mauritian press. The language was choice: it was from the outset called the 'Titmuss Mission'. The connotation of religious missionaries engaging in conversion campaigns seemed appropriate for a figure who inspired disciple worship in Britain for his pronouncements on social welfare.

Titmuss's 'Mauritius Mission' fits within a wider post-war movement in which economists were brought into a developing (then 'third world') country: 'As the managers of that country's economy go, hat in hand, to external sources of credit, it is necessary to clothe requests with rationales, plans, predictions and promises.'[40] It was hoped that economists and other external experts would 'rise above (or be blind to) local political realities'. Furthermore their real and perceived independence of judgement ensured legitimacy for their policy proposals – 'science' as the ultimate source of authority in an era of uncertainty – where shifting responsibility from politicians to experts became an increasingly fashionable option.

Yet Titmuss and Brian were not the only pioneers in acting as consultants for developing countries. Archie Cochrane, the epidemiologist who headed the Medical Research Council's Pneumoconiosis Research Unit at Cardiff, was already involved in work which inspired Titmuss: 'What you had to tell me about the Jamaica project has made us very curious to learn more. It has given me – that is, Brian Abel-Smith and myself – the beginnings of some ideas about the proposals we are making for the government of Mauritius in relation to medical care, family planning and social welfare in general.'[41]

In May 1959 Brian attended a briefing at the Colonial Office to begin to collect background paperwork. He was cautioned about the attitudes to family planning held by the Catholics and Muslims on the island, and some of the weaknesses of the civil service. In his summary for Titmuss he noted: 'I was immensely impressed by the whole attitude of the Colonial Office. I felt that I had attended a meeting of the Fabian Colonial Bureau. Perhaps I had. The Colonial Office seemed particularly anxious that we should break new ground in our report. We are booked to leave on August 4th.'[42]

A few days before Brian and Lynes left, Titmuss met with Ramgoolam (Ministerial Secretary to the Treasury), Ringadoo (Minister of Labour and Social Security) and Beejadhur (Minister of Education) while they were on an official visit to London. His memorandum notes their frustrations that they had not also been given the Economic Mission (a type of investigation arranged and funded by the British government for its colonies) they had urgently requested, and the time it took to get anything done through the Colonial Office. But these appeared relatively minor gripes compared to their summary of the laziness of the civil service on Mauritius, and criticisms of the French sugar magnates who lived in luxury maintained through tax avoidance and who bitterly resented suggestions that their workforce should be de-casualised.[43]

The Mauritian LSE Society were disappointed not to be able to welcome Titmuss at the airport as they had planned, but he was not well enough to make the journey in August. Brian and Lynes arrived from the overnight flight via Paris to an official government welcome, and were driven to the best of the island's sparse hotels – Park Hotel at Curepipe. Nearly every evening they were invited to an official reception or dinner. Brian had insisted on having a self-drive car rather than a chauffeur; Lynes' request for a bicycle was declined. In his first airmail letter to Titmuss, sent on 8 August by the first plane to leave the island since their arrival, Brian reassured him that they were getting access to all files and as much assistance as they needed. They had a civil servant to act as their secretary, who typed up reports of their surveys. The extent of the Mauritian government's support was uncomfortable: they were constantly accompanied by a messenger, but they could not think of things for him to do, except buy Brian's cigarettes. He walked in front of them, carrying their briefcases into meetings, and disconcertingly also accompanied Brian to the lavatory to open the door. Lynes had his own cultural difficulties as he struggled to find vegetarian food at the official functions. But Brian ended his letter to Titmuss with reassurances: 'Don't worry about us. We have a formidable job to do in a month but the fears I once had about closed doors and opposition are quite unreal. The top people want us to have every facility and everyone knows it. So everything is at our disposal. We are gradually accepting our high place in a rigidly hierarchical society … love to you all.'[44]

They had begun, partly out of courtesy, with interviews with the 'top people' on 7 August. The first was Robert Newton, Colonial Secretary since 1954, and acting Governor. In his council room in Government House, sparsely furnished with only a French-style table and chairs and some large heavy oil paintings, they discussed the 'extremely low' standard of administration on the island and the problems of getting people to cooperate with the government. He appeared to have little confidence that Mauritian politicians could be left to run the island unaided, and felt that Ramgoolam was partly in charge of the Labour Party because 'he could exercise an extremely fiery temper from time to time'. He confirmed Lynes' suggestion that some of the ministers had financial interests in the sugar industry.

They then met George Wilson, Financial Secretary – in effect, the second most senior civil servant on the island (he had previously worked in Britain at the Ministry of National Insurance). Lynes' memorandum was pessimistic:

> Mr Wilson talked at us for about 40 minutes without stopping. During the interview Brian spoke about twice. I did not speak at all. He warned us that we should not take any notice at all of how things were supposed to work in theory in Mauritius ... he doubted whether the money [public assistance] was really going to the people it was supposed to.... The difficulty is to keep up standards. Mauritians can do things as long as there is somebody to tell them what to do, but once you leave them to themselves they slip back into inefficiency. There are, he said, only five UK Officers in the Central Secretariat in Port Louis.... He said that it is inevitable in any colony that the people should think that the government is there to be swindled.[45]

The meeting with the Minister of Works was equally depressing: 'Mr Walter was a self-important lawyer in his late 30's. He had seven years in England and had practised in Lincoln's Inn. He had absorbed all the mystique of the British Bar and had copied its manners.... In a way he seemed to be the Lord Hailsham of the Mauritius Labour Party, very bumptious and not all that penetrating. He addressed us as if we were a public meeting.'[46]

Their requests for contact with the sugar estates proved more difficult to arrange, and they only succeeded in making three visits to plantations. Newspaper announcements requesting written and oral evidence helped to fill in some of the gaps. Brian was experimenting with using a tape recorder to make notes during their meetings and visits. At the end of each day they dictated summaries of their activities to send to Titmuss – in total over half a million words.[47] Titmuss fretted back in London, unhappy that he had not been well enough to travel with them, and concerned that they were not getting enough contact with people who had 'constructive ideas or considerations of the practical level of administration.'[48] On some official visits Brian and Lynes also felt that they were not getting to see the reality, as, for example, when visiting to the Père Leval Infirmary:'Everywhere I went Mother Superior induced the inmates to say good morning to me in chorus and to thank me for my visit when I left....Anyone I spoke to was asked to tell me that they were happy here which they duly did.'[49] On some of their tours of inspection it proved impossible to hide the real poverty and misery. At Currimjee Jeewanjee Infirmary in Port Louis Brian's memorandum recorded: 'The most unpleasant sight I have seen here or anywhere else was a paralysed man lying on a bed covered with flies. Flies were drawling around his eyes, his nose and his mouth. Mr Catherine pointed this out to the man in charge who called an attendant to chase the flies away which he did. Presumably they had returned again within half a minute. This was the most blatant case of neglect that I saw, but it was typical of the atmosphere of the place.'[50] Through days and weeks of visits like this Brian and Lynes were able to verify the concerns of both the Mauritian government and the Colonial Office – that unplanned rapid population growth and indiscriminate welfare aid for the large numbers of unemployed were creating a dangerous social and economic situation.

Brian met with Dr Stott who was concluding a three-year WHO study of nutrition on the island. Brian's idea of increasing the importation and consumption of dried skimmed milk provoked a sardonic response: 'the school milk programme had had difficulties when it started. It had been said that skimmed milk is what is given to pigs. Why should the schools feed the children like pigs? Dr Stott's reply to this criticism was that the children of Mauritius would be much better off if they were fed like pigs.'[51] Their reports back to Titmuss, later incorporated into the official mission report, voiced the obvious, yet hitherto unmentionable: 'By economising on relief for the genuinely unemployed, the Government has fostered a costly form of indiscriminate aid which penalises the honest, encourages disrespect for the Government, lowers the morale of the Government Medical Service, spreads corruption, creates waste of scarce medical resources and imposes a heavy strain on the budget ... paradoxically, the establishment of social insurance is needed to limit the abuse of public assistance.'[52]

Titmuss was determined to extend his terms of reference to include healthcare. Mauritius was relatively fortunate in already having a virtually free service, but the distribution of resources between overcrowded government dispensaries and hospitals and the private healthcare sector was inefficient. Brian and Lynes were sent confidential memos alleging abuse of public funds and a general lack of ethical standards in the medical community. For example, poor quality French penicillin was imported, and then marked up to an extortionate price by traders who hawked it door to door; doctors injected their patients with local anaesthetic to relieve rheumatic pains, which they knew would return a few hours after the patient left their surgery; and some doctors owned pharmacies and prescribed drugs that only they stocked.[53] The government medical services were not above reproach. They failed to invite sufficient tenders for pharmaceutical supplies and turned a blind eye to hospital staff who extorted money from patients for drugs and treatments which should have been free. The sugar estates were required to provide their own hospital facilities, but most plantation workers resented this as they were used to justify excessive compulsory deductions from their wages. Underlying most of these problems were the facts that there was no General Medical Council, no professional consensus on enforcing ethical behaviour and a chronic shortage of doctors and nurses on the island.

Brian left Mauritius on 5 September, leaving Lynes to stay until the 17th to tie up loose ends. Back in London, Titmuss had been fortunate to have as a visiting student at the LSE, Edith Adams, a demographer from the UN in New York. He secured additional funding to employ her to do the population modelling needed for the report. The Titmuss team were also able to draw on the expertise of Dr Burton Benedict, who had just completed an ethnographic study in Mauritius.[54] Adams' first projection, which allowed for constant fertility and declining mortality, showed the current estimated population of 594,000 reaching 1.3 million by 1982, and 2.8 million by 2002, with a potential density of 4,000 per square mile. Even her third and most optimistic projection, based on rapid fertility decline, showed a growth to 983,000 by 1982.[55]

In the midst of soliciting rigorous and impartial information, Titmuss was also receiving unsolicited advice. In December 1959 he received an invitation from G.J.M. Schilling, a partner at Blyth, Greene, Jourdain & Co Ltd, one of the largest sugar traders in London (based appropriately at Plantation House in Fenchurch Street). Schilling, who had first-hand knowledge of Mauritius, asked Titmuss to lunch at the Viceroy Restaurant in Colonial House to 'discuss some of the island's problems', and he subsequently sent Titmuss a list of Mauritian personalities he should talk to during his forthcoming visit. The short pen portraits of selected sugar plantation owners, doctors, barristers, members of the Chamber of Agriculture, make quite plain the sugar industry's wish not to damage their lucrative set-up or the island's strong French-Catholic culture. His summary of the Roman Catholic Bishop Daniel Liston is a rather bizarre non sequitur: 'a charming, understanding and intelligent Irishman. I always found him most helpful in all Boy Scout problems.'[56]

On 19 January 1960 Mauritius was hit by Alix, one of the worst cyclones in its history. Cyclones were a frequent event in Mauritius, but this one was on an unprecedented scale, passing straight over the island and causing huge damage. This intensified the need for Titmuss's social welfare reform, and helped the case for greater British aid. Lynes asked Titmuss for permission to travel ahead of the planned March visit to help with relief work, and he flew out on 23 February. Lynes used his connections with the International Voluntary Service to recruit British volunteers to come and work with Edwin de Robillard of the Compagnons Batisseurs on the post-cyclone reconstruction.[57] A second cyclone, Carol, arrived on 29 February, finishing off the wrecking job that Alix had started, and leaving over half the houses on the island damaged or destroyed and a substantial part of the sugar crop lost. Lynes, holed up in his small Chinese-run hotel in Port Louis, watched from the window as the corrugated tin roofs were ripped from neighbouring buildings. Relieved when the wind subsided he ventured out, only to be told that this was the calm eye of the storm. When the wind returned, from the other direction this time, it capitalised on the structural damage, flattening even substantial buildings. Lynes sent a telegram to Titmuss and Brian telling them to delay their arrival, as their research would be impossible. They came anyway.

Brian had sent a diplomatic letter in advance of the trip to Nades Ringadoo, the Minister of Labour, who had become their closest ally in the Mauritian government:

> I have been doing a little thinking about the plans for Professor Titmuss when he comes to Mauritius. I have discussed it with Mrs Titmuss, who is in touch with his doctor. The important thing is that we must not let him get over-tired. I assume from the great kindness which you all showed to Tony and myself while we were in Mauritius that the Professor will receive a number of invitations to dine in the evenings. Late nights are not good for him and I think it would be best if we could see that he does not dine out more than four nights in the week, and on those nights, that he has several hours in the afternoon to lie and rest or sit on the beach. He does not know that I am writing to you in this way and would probably be displeased if he did know. But I did want a quiet word with you about this in the hope that it

would be possible to prevent too exhausting a programme being arranged for him.[58]

Brian travelled out with Titmuss, arriving on 2 March. They spent their time re-checking material from Brian and Lynes' first visit, and producing estimated costings. The first three weeks went very well, but then Titmuss contracted dysentery, an infection he took home to Acton and which laid him low for another few weeks. Some of the official statistics began to look less reliable when carefully scrutinised, and Brian accepted an invitation to call in at Geneva on the return journey to see Zelenka at the ILO, who had 'much more experience of social security in under-developed countries'.[59] Titmuss remained sceptical of the ILO's work, especially their intention to do a large-scale survey of Mauritius. Ringadoo had been pressing him to get the ILO to confirm their commitment: Titmuss instead had been liaising with the Colonial Office: 'We agreed that what Mauritius needs most of all is the building up of its own statistical surveys, rather than these elementary empire-building affairs from Geneva'.[60]

While Titmuss had been setting up his mission, the Mauritian government had been pressing the Colonial Office for a parallel Economic Mission. James Meade, the Cambridge economist, was appointed in November 1959, and Brian had successfully mediated between the Mauritian government ministers and the Colonial Office to ensure that Meade was allowed as much investigative freedom as Titmuss had secured.[61] Meade's mission was due to arrive on the island as the Titmuss mission was entering its writing-up phase, and the two teams held useful meetings to ensure that Meade followed up on issues significant to both parties. Brian sent Meade his own interpretation of the weaknesses of the Mauritian economy, highlighting the limited potential for new sources of employment, save perhaps for stimulating a pottery industry to make sanitary ware (currently imported by sea) or expanding its fledgling tourist trade. He could not understand why foreign firms had not attempted to break the hold of the small Chinese shopkeepers, or why the sugar estates did not become more entrepreneurial. 'The question which fascinated me for the whole of my stay in Mauritius was to try and work out what would happen in an economy like this if one applied straight Keynsian remedies to the unemployment situation.'[62]

The 'Titmuss Mission's' report was finally submitted to the Mauritian government on 24 February 1961, to coincide with the arrival of the 600 copies that had left Britain by sea before Christmas. It is a brilliant example of traditional colonial paternalism, meshed with the nascent skills of international expert advisers. The bulk of the inquiry and drafting had been done by Brian and Lynes, under the eagle analytical eye of Titmuss, who shared authorship with Brian (but Lynes was somewhat unfairly credited as 'assisted by'). This report, as with Titmuss's classic wartime study *The Problems of Social Policy*, was carefully built up from historical and demographic facts, and phrased in blunt language that left no room for doubt: 'The prospects opened up by these projections are alarming; more alarming than any previous attempts to estimate the future growth of the population. Frankly, they amount to economic, social and political disaster. We would be failing in our duty if we used any other word.'[63] They appealed to the Mauritian government not to let their report end up on the rejected heap of previous official inquiries, and to accept their recommendations in full – this was not a pick-and-mix set of policies, but a carefully integrated solution to the impending crises.

Both Titmuss and Meade were in agreement in their reports (published almost simultaneously for maximum effect): there was no way that emigration or increasing mortality would avert the over-population crisis, which they saw as the result of:

> … strongly-held beliefs; an apathetic and fatalistic attitude to life nurtured by custom and a long history of suffering and hardship; early marriage and child-bearing; the low status of women and the lack of education and occupational opportunities for girls and women; and an economic system by which a large proportion of the population subsist, seasonally and over the life cycle of the family, on irregular and unpredictable cash earnings. A system which quite literally engenders a 'hand-to-mouth' pattern of daily life is not conducive to restraint in family-building habits. Such uncertainty and instability in the finances of the family do not encourage the belief that man has much control over his future.[64]

The only option was the promotion of the three-child family as the new ideal (the current average family size was seven). This required easily available information about family planning, as well as access to suitable methods. Many Catholics and Muslims on the island privately agreed that such a policy should be promoted, but publicly the Catholic church opposed any form of contraception. Yet Mauritius was not alone in facing problems of rapid population growth. Japan had recently run a very successful birth control campaign which reduced the birth rates from 34/000 in 1948 to 18/000 in 1958. Puerto Rico, as another small developing country had also overcome strong religious opposition to birth control to tackle its crisis.[65]

Brian and Titmuss were painfully aware that their report would stand or fall on this one issue. They cited earlier studies by experts such as Dr R.L. Meier, who had used Mauritius as a case study in his book *Modern science and the human fertility problem*. Meier painted a bleak and frightening picture of the future Mauritius in which the surplus unemployable population would have to be housed in camps: 'Problems of petty theft and policing will probably lead to a demand by the independent residents of Mauritius that the camps be surrounded with barbed wire. The decay of the fabric in the tents will lead to the construction of barracks-type buildings. By that time it will not only feel like a prison, it will also look like a prison.'[66] From there it would undoubtedly be a swift descent into inter-racial violence, collapse of the overloaded welfare system, increasing malnutrition and consequential ill health and mortality – especially for children. Brian and Titmuss's language was less dramatic, drawing as always on their unshakeable faith in the core values of humankind:

> We are very conscious of the fact that in urging the need for a policy of family limitation we are challenging the attitudes and beliefs of a considerable section of the population. Nevertheless, we do so on the grounds that every man and woman should have the dignity of freedom to make the decisions for themselves in obedience to conscience; a doctrine of society in which men and nations are bound to care for one another, and to help one another to ease the present suffering, and avert the threatened cataclysm, of overpopulation....The tolerances and courtesies of a liberal society must be practised by all. The illiberalities of some must not thrive on the courtesies of others.[67]

Titmuss, Brian and Lynes recommended some radical reforms and extensions to the existing welfare services. The first priority was to establish a nation-wide family planning service; the second – as explained in the 'other report' by Meade – was for the government to deliberately create a 'reasonably high level of employment'.[68] With these two cornerstones agreed, the Mauritian government could then begin the process of introducing a family allowance – a universal fixed benefit not tied to the number of children in a family. The legal age of marriage should be raised from 15 to 18; payments made for couples who delayed marriage until the age of 21 and for those who maintained a gap of two years between pregnancies, which would also help to reduce the large family sizes. Conditions should be attached to benefits, requiring attendance at family planning and maternity and child welfare clinics to receive payments. Cinemas and newspapers would be required to display at least one advert per week for the free family planning services, and posters with details should be displayed in all villages and printed on all government record cards and income tax forms.

The chronic problem of public assistance was to be tackled by introducing a more effective work test, and setting up a system of social insurance that made payments only for genuine unemployment. This would reduce the current burden on government medical officers who were pressured to certify people unfit for work. The sugar estates health and welfare facilities should be taken over by the government; private doctors should be offered government contracts to act as GPs for specific districts, based on the Swedish incentive system, who would provide free treatment, and effectively reduce the demands for multiple medical opinions that were currently the norm. The traditional link between doctors and pharmacists, which had perpetuated extortionate overpricing and monopolies on the supply of drugs, must be broken. Titmuss, as was his style, pursued every sub-division of every failing. The lack of doctors (1 per 4,500 population in Mauritius compared to 1 per 1,000 in Britain) was linked to the funding the government provided for students to go abroad to study medicine. Mauritius had more medical students training abroad, and more Mauritian doctors currently practising abroad, than there were Mauritian doctors at home. If they returned, there would be no problem. But Titmuss and Brian spoke the unpalatable truth: most would not, preferring more lucrative careers in developed countries. The logic was therefore to recommend that the government end their generous subsidy and income tax allowances for overseas education, unless these medical students promised to repay the funds or return to the island to work.

Although their report deliberately avoided attempts at costing specific reforms, Titmuss, Brian and Lynes carefully and repeatedly demonstrated that efficiency savings in some areas would help to offset the costs of any new services they were recommending: 'To a considerable extent we are redistributing existing burdens so that they are borne more fairly and at less cost to the whole population. We are proposing the replacement of the costly, inefficient and demoralising loan-raising machinery which exists all over the island with a cheaper and more rational system of compulsory saving to meet the needs of sickness, unemployment and other contingencies…. Many of those who will be asked to pay more in the form of taxes and contributions will be relieved of part of the disproportionate charges which they are already paying in other ways.'[69]

The report ended with a direct appeal to the people of Mauritius:

> Our plan is one and indivisible. The problems we have described have been made worse by the neglect of the past. With every year of delay, the prospects of success with our plan or indeed any similar plan are diminished. We do not reach these conclusions or make our many recommendations in the interests of a far-off posterity. We are concerned with the problems of today; with those who are sick because they are poor and who become poorer because they are sick. The children, as always, suffer most. That is why we believe that social planning and family planning are indivisible. To be effective, both require vision; a quality which we are confident is not lacking in the people of Mauritius.[70]

Titmuss's team saw the potential for Mauritius to become a role model, to make a critical contribution to the struggle against poverty worldwide, perhaps through serving as a laboratory trial for the new oral contraceptive pills. But this would not be easy: 'Our plan does not only depend upon the willingness of the population to make financial sacrifices. From the government it calls for political courage of the first order, dynamic leadership and honest administration. From the people it demands tolerance and a high sense of moral conduct and national unity.'[71]

There were some similarities between what Titmuss, Brian and Lynes were proposing for Mauritius, and what they had already helped to achieve in Britain. Indeed, their report made direct reference to Beveridge's report, the historical development of the British NHS from earlier capitation schemes, and suggested that the consolidated public healthcare system might be called the Mauritian 'National Health Service'. Yet they had not plagiarised Britain for an identikit policy. They were sensitive to the uniqueness of this developing country, which did not have a tradition of stable continuous employment or an administrative system that could cope with national superannuation. But they saw no reason not to proclaim Mauritius as a potential model welfare state.

The full report was over 300 pages long, packed with every possible detail, and some classic Titmice dry humour: 'The diet of the people of Mauritius is not so generous that it can be shared with these [hook] worms.'[72] Brian and Lynes directed a British journalist – who normally worked on the *Mirror* – to draft the text for a popular pamphlet version, in suitably inclusive and simple language: 'Mauritius is heading for disaster....Why may this happen to us? Because there will soon be far too many people for our small island to support.... For every person that dies four children are born....'[73] There were also French and Hindi versions printed as newspaper supplements. These 100,000 popular versions were intended to get at least 50 per cent of Mauritian households to read it. The public reaction, as reported in the newspapers and collated by K. Hazareesingh, Director of the Mauritian Central Information Office, was generally positive, but *Le Mauricien* provided the most memorable quote, claiming that 'after months of labour, the rumbling mountain has given birth to a dead mouse'.[74]

The reaction in the Mauritian Parliament was more tempered, and when Wilson, Financial Secretary, built the April 1961 budget around the Titmuss proposals for a family planning service, the level of dissent was palpable. The three opposition parties called foul play when their combined opposition failed to block Ramgoolam's ruling Labour Party pushing through the budget. This was the second time that Wilson had made a faux pas on family planning. In March 1960, when Titmuss had sent a confidential draft of their report to the government, he had unexpectedly announced the start of an 'all-methods' family planning service. His timing (during Holy Week), and lack of consultation in advance with the Catholic Bishop, had sparked outrage. Wilson had grossly miscalculated, thinking that by making the service optional it would not provoke opposition. The government had to climb down and announce that no further action would be taken until the Titmuss report had been officially received. More significantly, Ringadoo wrote in confidence to Titmuss asking him to remove the passage on sterilisation from his draft report – this would be most certainly a step too far for Mauritius.[75]

Brian later learned that Bishop Liston had already been trying privately to initiate change within the Church. He had taken a memorandum to Rome setting out the island's population problem, but over a year had elapsed before he received an acknowledgement from the Cardinal at Madagascar – and no promise of action. Brian summarised the delicate situation the family planning issue created in Mauritius:

> The Church does not like being so obviously exposed as exercising temporal power over this matter. It is feared that in time public opinion might blame the Church for no action

being taken. Thus at present the Church is particularly keen to see some sort of family planning programme started – limited, of course, to 'licit methods'. Indeed, if the government did nothing, the Church might itself act. The Bishop is keen to use as many methods as possible. A Belgian Cardinal has been arguing that it is licit to use a pill to regularise the menstrual cycle and to extend the lactation period after pregnancy … assisting nature and in no way a contraceptive practice. The Bishop was keen to see the lactation process extended for 40 months. But this cannot be done at the moment because (1) there are said to be serious side effects with the pill in question and (2) the Cardinal is only prepared to wear this for 4 months, not the 40 months as the Bishop had imagined. The Church is terrified that if the government fought for free choice again, the Church would lose. Nevertheless, the government is obviously not going to fight. One reason for this is Ram's [Ramgoolam's] position in his own constituency. He needs Moslem support and some Moslems are opposed to birth control. He fears that this group of Moslems might deliberately unseat him at the next election.[76]

Although a Family Welfare Association had been formed on the island in 1957 which was affiliated to the International Planned Parenthood Federation (IPPF), it had lacked support because it recommended all forms of birth control, in direct opposition to the doctrine of the two significant religious groups – the Catholics (24 per cent) and Muslims (15 per cent).[77] The Titmuss report had dangled the carrot of significant international aid – possibly up to Rs200 million from foundations such as Nuffield, Carnegie, Ford and Rockefeller, for specific schemes to tackle the population problem. In September 1960 Titmuss had written to A.D.K. Owen of the Office of the Director General at the UN in New York, soliciting an invitation on behalf of Ringadoo ('a man of high principles and certainly the ablest member of the Government') who would be visiting in October, as part of a trip to explore emigration possibilities for Mauritians to British Honduras, British Guinea and Brazil. Titmuss hoped that the UN would set up appropriate connections for Ringadoo with New York-based foundations.[78]

In 1962 the Mauritian government eventually agreed to implement a family planning programme, but, bowing to religious and political pressures, it was conditional on being limited to the rhythm method. Guy Forget, Minister of Health, approached Titmuss and Brian to request their help in obtaining funding. Their negotiations with the

Planned Parenthood Organisation and the Population Council were unsuccessful – probably because the Mauritians refused to entertain the full range of birth control options. There was also a lingering taint in New York philanthropic circles on the Titmice resulting from Brian's after dinner lecture: 'Population growth and public health in Middle Africa', to the 39th annual conference of the Milbank Memorial Fund in September 1962.

This lecture – which he had been invited to give by his old friend Sandy Robertson – was written in the cold light of two months' intensive work in Mauritius and Tanganyika (now Tanzania), and demonstrates Brian's genuine sense of duty to illuminate what he felt was wrong with the world. His audience in New York's Plaza Hotel included the patrons and employees of major philanthropic organisations such as Rockefeller, Carnegie, Ford and the UN. The typed text shows that he made few last-minute alterations, fully aware of the impact his rhetoric would have. He opened with an acknowledgement that he was in the presence of population and development experts, but claimed to draw authority from his recent experience of 'real' Africa. His attack was on the system itself: 'As a Keynesian I wonder whether some countries are not kept poor when they receive some such Trojan horse as a malaria eradication campaign. It is indeed possible that the few millions which the United States gives for malaria eradication are lowering national incomes per head by as much as the billions of dollars which it gives in economic aid are increasing it.'[79]

Brian proceeded to detail Africa's uncontrolled population explosion, the lack of basic health services and the bitter irony of putting money into urban economic development programmes:

> The high survival rates of the towns can be kept balanced by the high mortality of the rotting rural areas. This indeed is what is actually happening in much of Africa. The pampered and privileged elite of unionised labour, with its minimum wages, social security and welfare services, its municipal housing and · municipal schools, is fattened up to pay the taxes from which development can be promoted. This is certainly one way to break the 'vicious cycle of poverty' and create 'a take off into sustained growth'.

He commented on the double-edged success of the colonial medical services in 'weaning the indigenous population from shrines and herbalists' only to see an enormous expansion of private (and ethically corrupt) medicine. He accused his well-fed audience of failing to address the key questions: 'Is it really better to die of malnutrition than disease? Is death at twenty years to be preferred to death at twenty months if life is wholly preoccupied with the battle to obtain sustenance? ... Seen through African eyes, being developed must be a very confusing business.... I have talked now for forty minutes without mentioning the overworked word 'challenge''. I am sure it belongs somewhere in any concluding sentence to this talk. Please compose it yourselves.'

Titmuss seized an opportunity to try to limit the collateral damage of Brian's lecture, writing to Henry Villard of the Ford Foundation:

> I am very troubled about these reports of the reactions to Abel-Smith's lecture. I have now read the verbatim script and cannot find anything politically contentious in it. Of course it was challenging and controversial, but that is precisely what, I understand, was expected of him. He is a relatively young man and is acutely conscious (as I am though slowed down a bit by age) of the urgency of these issues. He may have upset the demographers by what he had to say about population explosion in Africa, and I rather guess that some of them may have had difficulty in accepting him as an authority on such highly technical problems. And he may have upset the doctors by his outspoken comments on unethical practices in developing countries. Such questions were, however, publicly debated in Britain and the US half a century ago in much more colourful terms....Thinking about these reactions, I cannot help feeling that what is relevant is the fact that Abel-Smith is completely acceptable to the Mauritian government and other leaders out there. I believe they respect his frankness, honesty and enthusiasm and I have never heard from Mauritius one whisper of criticism. When – as frequently happens – Ministers come to London they often meet in his house and I have myself attended what could be described as Cabinet discussions there.[80]

Despite the ripples that Brian's Milbank lecture had caused, Titmuss enjoyed the continued confidence of Villard, as he reported to Brian: 'The Foundation is now giving $7 million in devious ways to India for its population control programme and has just decided to invest another $3 million in fundamental laboratory research on biochemical methods. Villard is partly responsible. He talked at length about this "most dangerous area of philanthropy" and is acutely aware of the risks of American experts telling the coloured races to have smaller families.'[81] Villard had explored with Caine, Director of the LSE, the possibilities of setting up a 'Population Control Institute' at the school to offer training programmes, and held preliminary discussion with the demographer David Glass, and the Titmice's close colleagues Jerry Morris and Archie Cochrane. Titmuss remarked that Villard 'would not be surprised if he received an application for $1 million for 2 years – or even more…. The cost of Pills and condoms *ought* to be borne by the government though part might be "concealed" aid.' Any application from the LSE would need a letter of commitment from the Mauritian government with (if possible) the support of the Bishop. He also agreed to fund a preliminary visit by Brian to Mauritius to plan a large-scale 'action and research study'.[82]

Brian asked the Ford Foundation to fund Dr Benedict Duffy, an American population expert, to accompany him. He had met Duffy in New York and highly valued his research. They agreed that Duffy would travel to London to meet Brian for a briefing with Titmuss, Lynes and Benedict over a supper at Brian's Elizabeth Street home, and then they would fly together to Mauritius for a month-long trip in March 1963. Brian advised Duffy on appropriate clothing (not tropical rig, just ordinary suits). There was no need to take a dinner suit – they would inform the Governor's ADC and he would ensure other guests at receptions would be dressed accordingly. He also asked Duffy for suitable reading on family planning, so that he could get up to speed on the latest research before the trip. Brian was to be paid an honorarium of US$500, with US$50 for preparation and a daily expenses allowance of US$25.

Mauritius was now under almost continuous surveillance for one scheme or another. Tommy Balogh, another British academic turned expert adviser, was seconded to the Mauritian Ministry of Agriculture and Natural Resources and spent January 1963 on the island. The Catholic Marriage Advisory Council had also been invited to provide family planning advice, partly to appease Bishop Liston. It had been arranged in 1962 that Dr O'Connor Moore, an Irish Senior Registrar in Obstetrics and Gynaecology from London's Hammersmith Hospital, would be seconded to the island for six months to develop a scheme based purely on the 'licit' Ogino rhythm method.[83] In January 1963, after Ford announced that they would fund an exploratory project by Brian and Duffy, Ramgoolam took the initiative of postponing Moore's trip, so that there would be no potential conflict of opinion.

Brian used his former partner Charles Schuller, now working at the United Travel Club on Albemarle Street, to make his booking on the BOAC plane, leaving on 3 March 1963, arriving in Mauritius the following day, with an open return. He had by now learned the trick of not telling the Mauritians the precise date of his planned departure from the island, so that he could claim an earlier date to speed up their deliberations. He and Duffy spent an intensive three weeks studying the feasibility of various schemes, and enjoying the island's hospitality. Harold Walter gave a farewell bachelor party for Brian, attended by His Excellency, the Governor, various visiting Colonial Office dignitaries and Mauritian government ministers at his bungalow. Sadly Duffy's flight left too early and Brian wrote to him about the 'pretentious meal of camerons, wild hare and champagne. You would have enjoyed it'.[84] For Brian this had been a very pleasant reunion with an island that he had become increasingly fond of. Such international trips had the added advantage of allowing him to indulge in wider friendships. When planning his flights he wrote to Professor Sarwat Badaoui of the Law Faculty of Cairo University: 'I have just discovered I will be passing over Cairo on March 26. Would it be convenient to drop down and see you about the 26th or 27th? I have got to rush back to London but I did want a glimpse of both you and the Pyramids.'[85]

The family planning programme remained the most politically sensitive issue on the island. The Colonial Office had offered Ramgoolam Mauritian independence *if* he obtained a large enough majority at the forthcoming election, but this required that he did not propose plans that conflicted with Catholic and Muslim beliefs. Titmuss felt that Ramgoolam should be made to sign an agreement in advance to adopt a family planning campaign if he got the necessary majority. He was also sceptical of Duffy's expert view that the Ogino rhythm method alone could be more effective than the rhythm and pill combined. He suggested, 'probably a crazy non-starter', that an alternative to government action might be to establish a 'quasi-official Family Planning Institute, representing the major racial and religious groups, including the Ministry of Health, and responsible for launching an island-wide propaganda rhythm and pill campaign'.[86] Titmuss's public statements on Mauritius were more cautious: in an article in *The Lancet*, 'Medical ethics and social change in developing countries', he avoided detailed proposals, focusing instead on the need for social and economic development to be fully integrated, and for non-western cultures to be respected and incorporated as far as possible when developing family planning programmes.[87]

When Brian and Duffy left the island (Brian to return to London via Cairo, Geneva and Paris), they felt they had made little progress. Their reports to the Ford Foundation noted the stalemate: the Catholic Church had little faith in the government, and the government itself had little confidence it could develop an implementable programme. The new Governor, Sir John Rennie, had offered to act as intermediary between Bishop Liston and the government, and Brian and Duffy felt they had done their best to 'build a bridge', having proposed a statutory authority along the lines Titmuss had outlined for a Population Council. They saw the arrival on 1 March of Dr Moore as a potential thin end of the wedge, especially if he could establish a pilot clinic to teach the rhythm method. They had also urged the Mauritians to apply for a Ford Foundation grant to conduct a baseline survey on attitudes to family planning.

Back in the UK, Titmuss discussed the effectiveness of the rhythm method with the population expert Francois Lafitte at the University of Birmingham. His view, in agreement with Clyde Kiser's 1962 book *Research in Family Planning*, was that there had been no useful comparative surveys on which programmes could be based, and he wondered whether the coitus interruptus method had been discussed with Mauritians, as he understood that this was considered a lesser sin by Catholics in the US than contraception, and that it was a sin on the husband's part only.[88] Meanwhile, Brian arranged for Duffy to visit him in London later that summer to discuss plans for a joint population control officer training programme, and to make him a member of Le Petit Club Français.[89]

Moore, on arriving in Mauritius on 1 March, had quickly learned that most of the 170 doctors on the island actually knew nothing about the rhythm method. Once they had been trained, tuition clinics were established in the existing hospitals and maternity and child welfare clinics, with Moore sitting in with doctors for their first 20 consultations. Both husbands and wives were encouraged to come to the consultations together, to impress the point that birth control was not purely the women's responsibility. Nurses followed up with the more practical aspects of the method. They realised that illiteracy need not be a barrier – as long as the couples could recognise figures on a clock they could be taught to read a thermometer and mark a temperature chart to identify fertile from infertile periods of the monthly cycle.[90]

So, for the immediate future, Mauritius looked set to adopt a rhythm-only programme of family planning. Behind the scenes the government continued with their initiatives to get more reliable statistical data, requesting a demographer from the UN to conduct a fertility survey, and allowing Mauritians such as Reggie Lan Po Tang to participate in the WHO fellowship scheme on his anaemia research. Ramgoolam continued to meet with Brian and Titmuss for help with his applications to The World Bank in Washington, and several Mauritian ministers such as Ringadoo and Walter remained close friends. Brian was not officially invited back to Mauritius again until 1974, when his expertise was needed to develop a new pensions policy.[91]

Mauritius was one of the first countries to appear under the microscope of the increasingly influential international agencies such as WHO, ILO, UNDP and The World Bank. This symbiotic relationship thrived on discovering the extent of poverty and inequality and expanding the capacity for further monitoring, and, it was hoped, intervention. Agencies that had been in existence for only 10 years were able to demand massive increases in their funding from developed countries, and to use this money to employ the growing army of consultants. Many of these had backgrounds in economics, which in the early post-war years seemed to be the panacea to cure all ills, social as well as economic. The policy community was to later turn a critical eye on the trend for economic experts:

> Economists, depending on one's outlook, may be held to rise above (or be blind to) local political realities. Abstraction from the local is congruent with international communication....The defensive but visible appointment of economists is particularly compelling when one party is a fairly desperate Third World country.[92]

In some regions of the developing world, the 'almost mystical belief in the power of planning' to solve problems meant that economists were the default choice of expert.[93] Brian was the model consultant *par excellence*. On the strength of his work for the Guillebaud report on the cost of the British NHS he had secured a number of WHO consultancies, and through his academic liaison with Titmuss at the LSE he had been one of the key experts used by the Mauritian government to develop its health and social welfare policies. What becomes clear through a study of the Mauritian project is just how much Brian was valued beyond his economist's skills. His acute sense of diplomacy and ability to liaise between government ministers, Colonial Office officials and vested local interests made him indispensable in getting the Titmuss report and its successors into a practical and useable shape. These were the same skills that he was now regularly using for WHO, ILO and the other international agencies.

Brian was now in a position to choose the projects that interested him and to negotiate the terms of engagement. An offer from George Rohrlich at the Social Security Division of the ILO in 1960 for a six-month Asian study could not be fitted within the LSE's offer to give him one term's research leave. Brian, however, also felt that such a long study would be too exhausting:

> But for how many months can one continue to be really effective on such a demanding assignment? It takes a lot out of one to meet new problems and new people every day, quite apart from the continuous strain of changing climate, hotels and food (with all the obvious health risks). I claim to be as energetic and physically robust as any European but there are limits to what one's body can stand of this sort of thing. One month in Mauritius was a wearing assignment and I doubt if I could take more than three months of this sort of work without a drastic reduction of pace and efficiency.[94]

Although these international consultancies increasingly took precedence, they still required LSE authorisation, and had to be fitted into his teaching commitments. His close personal and professional loyalty to Titmuss helped to steer him through such choices, and he always sought his mentor's opinion before accepting new projects. Occasionally he attempted to juggle too much. Writing to Titmuss in June 1961 about his invitation to teach for a term at Yale Law School, he confessed that he had not yet completed enough teaching terms, or given enough notice at the LSE to qualify for leave that autumn: 'I am afraid I have got myself into an awful muddle about Yale....This is very bad administration.'[95] He had no choice but to postpone his position as a Visiting Associate Professor of Social Administration until the spring term 1962.

Paying for Health Services

During the intensive period of work on Mauritius between 1959 and 1963, Brian had made a number of parallel study tours, including the one to the former Soviet Union in the summer of 1961, discussed above. He had also continued to participate in the WHO study: 'Medical care in relation to public health: A study of the costs of sources and finance'. As discussed earlier in this chapter, he had been the leading consultant for the pilot study and for developing a workable set of definitions and categorisation of costs. The Expert Working Party accepted his report in 1962 as the basis for a more substantial study, aimed at standardising health accounting practices internationally. Brian's pilot study was published by WHO in May 1963: *Paying for Health Services: A Study of the Costs and Sources of Finance in Six Countries.*[96] He introduced it as 'an exercise in social accounting, which it is hoped will be of use to the health administrator'. The first chapter discussed the economic concepts, especially those of 'cost'. The second chapter attempted some standardisation of how to define medical concepts, especially in five borderline areas such as between environmental public health measures and those which were regarded as public utilities; between health services and ordinary care of the body; between promotive healthcare for children and ordinary child welfare arrangements; and how to distinguish between residents in long-stay institutions, especially the elderly and the sick. He proposed a broad three-stage division of medical costs between domiciliary, ambulatory and in-patient, although acknowledged that not every country would share the same definition of a hospital, or of the 'specialists' working within them. He presented the results of the six pilot studies, standardising costs into US dollars to show the wide spectrum of experiences. Ceylon had the worst population rate per hospital bed at 300, the US rate was 110 and Sweden had the best at 90. Some comparators were even more skewed: Ceylon, one dentist per 59,000, Israel, one per 1,400. The per capita GNP ranged from US$135 in Ceylon to US$2,722 in the US.[97] Not all the six pilot countries could provide the required breakdown of data: Chile was unable to supply any figures for capital expenditure, or to divide recurrent by sources of finance. Ceylon's returns included estimates of expenditure made by the large corporate agricultural estates, which were known not to be accurate. Czechoslovakia was unable to separate medical care services from public health services. The US had to estimate in-patient costs as physicians and surgeons did not record where they had performed their activities. Defining 'pharmaceutical' was equally problematic. Only Israel and Sweden appeared to be able to provide the data in the format that Brian required.

Despite this analysis, Brian concluded that the study 'was not unsuccessful'. It had stimulated some countries to consider how they might improve their national accounting and budgeting; it had illuminated for health administrators how other countries allocated resources between domiciliary, ambulatory and in-patient care. Future studies would have to grasp the nettle of how to deal with marginal issues such as whether tonics and sunglasses were really pharmaceuticals, and whether medical education should be treated as an educational cost. An improvement in WHO data collection might be to ask not only for the number of bed days provided in hospitals, but also the numbers of patients discharged or dying in hospital, to allow the average length of stay to be calculated. Likewise, rather than just collecting information on the number of prescriptions issued, it would be more meaningful to know what the quantity of drugs were issued on a single prescription – enough for a week, month, year? It opened up bigger debates, such as on how the culture of payment for medical services might influence how patients presented for care and were allocated resources. Brian concluded by asking some key questions:

> Cost is only one problem that concerns the health administrator. Does a country which spends more on health services have a higher level of health? How far does higher expenditure in a country improve the level of health? What meaning should be attached to the phrase 'level of health'? What is the quality of health services in different countries? These questions cannot at present be answered. But it seems helpful to approach them from a body of knowledge about what is actually being spent in different countries.[98]

Paying for Health Services received mixed reviews. Dennis Lees, Professor of Applied Economics at Swansea, writing in the *British Medical Journal*, found the results 'so hedged around with qualifications as to be well-nigh meaningless'. He judged that although this had been a pilot study, it would have been better to develop domestic 'languages' with an operational use to health administrators:

> We must learn to walk at home as well as to fly abroad. Nor will the basic method of this study yield fruitful hypotheses. Dr Abel-Smith continues to rely exclusively on the social accounting technique, which is a limited and inflexible tool. It leads too readily to Lees's Law, which I now pronounce: a meaningless numerator divided by a more meaningless denominator yields a meaningful quotient. Instead, we need a rigorous application of the apparatus of price theory, which has proved a powerful explanatory tool in other fields. The truth is that there is no such animal as 'the economics of medical care' unless we use that as shorthand for 'economic theory as applied to medical care'.[99]

The Medical Officer, by contrast, found that his study 'constitutes almost textbook reading on the subject of assessment of costs and resources of health services'.[100]

During the LSE's 1963 long summer vacation Brian was contracted by R.F. Bridgman, Chief Medical Officer for the Organisation of Medical Care division at WHO Geneva, to visit seven countries in Africa and West Asia for the studies on costs of health services and hospital utilisation. His consultancy fee was US$700 per month, along with travel costs and a daily subsistence rate. Beginning with a briefing on 23 July by AFRO (the WHO African region office, which was actually based in Geneva and run by Europeans until the mid-1960s), he spent between three and six days in each of his destinations: Abidjan (Ivory Coast), Dakar (Senegal), Salisbury (Southern Rhodesia), Dar-es-Salaam (Tanganyika), Nairobi (Kenya), Karachi (Pakistan) and Kuwait. He returned for a de-briefing at Geneva on 28 August. In each place he met local government officials and tested their accuracy in completing the questionnaire. He found unhappiness with the imposition of classifications: 'Countries did not like to see their "district hospitals" – some with more than a hundred beds downgraded (as they saw it) by WHO into "cottage hospitals" just because they had a few beds under medical and nursing supervision.' He suggested this could be avoided in the future by using terms such as 'major and minor in-patient units'.[101]

After a belated summer holiday in France and Italy in September 1963, Brian resumed discussions with Bridgman on how the health costs and hospital utilisation project should be developed. Even the US Public Health Service (USPHS) had returned its questionnaire with significant sections left blank, because it was unable to give a breakdown of hospital bed use by specialty. Brian replied to Bridgman elaborating the difficulties of internationally acceptable definitions, using his recent experiences in Africa, where a small hospital might not routinely have a resident doctor (one of their potential criteria for defining a 'hospital'), or might treat a mix of tuberculosis, mental health and maternity cases in one building (which would prevent classification of beds by medical speciality).[102]

Brian had tried to stimulate British interest in participating in forthcoming World Health Assembly technical discussions on 'National health planning', but the Chief Medical Officer, Sir George Godber, was not persuaded. This was in contrast to the enthusiasm of colleagues such as J.S. McKenzie-Pollock, Chief of the Pan-American Health Organisation (PAHO, the regional office of the WHO for the Americas): 'The appropriate relative place of health in development

1. Brian Abel-Smith's father, Lionel Abel-Smith (1870–1946)

2. Brian Abel-Smith's mother, Geneviève (Vivée) Abel-Smith (1898–1988)

3. Brian Abel-Smith with Lionel and their mother Vivée (early 1940s)

4. Brian Abel-Smith in his early teens

5. Brian Abel-Smith as Haileybury School head boy in 1945, sitting to the right of the headmaster E.H. Bonhote

6. Haileybury School's Elysium club, Spring 1945

7. Brian Abel-Smith [back row, far right] with fellow recruits of the Nonne Boschen Platoon, Oxfordshire and Buckinghamshire Light Infantry at the Gujarat Barracks in Colchester, Essex, December 1945

8. Brian Abel-Smith at his desk in the Schönbrunn Palace, Vienna, 1947

9. Brian Abel-Smith in Positano, Italy, 1949

10. Brian Abel-Smith in Wengen, Switzerland, with Susan Hamilton and Tony Bambridge, 1949

11. Brian Abel-Smith on Middle East holiday, 1951

12. Cambridge Labour Foot Beagles Ball, November 1950. Brian Abel-Smith's 'female companion' in the long dress is Edward Greenfield. The man holding Greenfield's hand is Anthony Buck.

13. Cambridge Union Society, 5 June 1951. Brian Abel-Smith is sitting in the secretary's chair in the absence of Douglas Hurd. The retiring president, Donald Macmillan, is shown proposing the motion. In the chair is the newly-elected president Julian Williams, and seated to his right is the vice-president Greville Janner.

14. Brian Abel-Smith speaking at a debate on the British Council universities debating tour of India, Pakistan and Ceylon, 1952

15. Brian Abel-Smith, 1950s

16. Brian Abel-Smith and Richard Titmuss, 1950s

17. Brian Abel-Smith and Peter Townsend at the LSE, 1956

18. Brian Abel-Smith with Sue Holman (Vivien Leigh's daughter, in white shirt) and Shirley Worthington, *House Beautiful* article, September 1956

19. Brian Abel-Smith with Edith Summerskill, Labour Party annual conference, Brighton, October 1957

20. Brian Abel-Smith and Hugh Dalton (centre) on holiday in Italy, August 1957

planning is at last receiving considerable attention and the role of the economist interested in the analysis of the health sector will soon be better appreciated....The planning fever is assuming epidemic proportions in Latin America.'[103] McKenzie Pollock took his expertise to Manila the following June for the first regional seminar on 'National health planning'.

Brian's travels in 1964 were again fitted into his teaching commitments at the LSE. During the Easter break he gave a lecture at the New York Academy of Medicine: 'Major patterns of financing medical care services outside America'. In preparation for this he had solicited help from James Hogarth at the Scottish Home and Health Department (who had published a study on the development of general practice in European countries), and from John Griffith at the School of Hospital Administration at the University of New South Wales in Sydney. The latter request was for accurate information, as Brian was aware that there was work to do in 'convincing the Americans that all is not in Australia as the AMA [American Hospital Association] paint it'.[104]

During the 1964 summer holidays he spent a fortnight working in the Netherlands and Sweden helping government officials to complete the WHO questionnaire, contracted at the highest WHO consultant pay band of US$700 per month *pro rata*. In addition to fieldwork, the WHO also contracted him for US$100 to write a chapter 'The Cost of Hospital Services' for the forthcoming *Manual on Hospital Planning and Administration*. He was always generous with his advice, writing to Peter Ruderman at the PAHO to suggest that Miguel Flores Marques, based at the Bank of Mexico's Department of Economic Studies, would be the ideal expert to undertake the survey of Mexican healthcare costs.

Despite the scepticism of fellow economists such as Lees, the questionnaire began to stimulate some interesting discussions. In June 1965 the working group that met in Geneva included Ruderman from PAHO, Leo Kaprio, Director of the Division of Public Health Services at WHO Geneva, and W.P.D. Logan, Director of WHO Health Statistics, as well as representatives from the ILO, the ISSA, the UN Research Institute for Social Development and the UN Economic Commission for Europe. The other consultant in attendance with Brian was Michael Kaser of St Anthony's College, Oxford, who had been with Brian on Milton Roemer's study trip to the USSR in 1961. They discussed the relationship between their cost and financing study, and the proposed revision of the UN system of Standard National Accounts, ending with a broader discussion on the future of health economists in the WHO, and ideas for future health economics studies. Over the next year Brian worked up another draft report based on the questionnaire returns, and correspondence with Ministries of Health. His becoming ill with jaundice (probably hepatitis) in May 1966 delayed further progress till he could return to Geneva that autumn, but while convalescing at home he received useful comments from individuals including Leonardo Bravo (Chief of Medical Care for PAHO), Ida Merriam (Assistant Commissioner for Research and Statistics at the American Social Security Administration in Washington DC), and even Surgeon General James Watt at the USPHS.[105]

It was not until 1967 that Brian was able to publish his book, *An International Study of Health Expenditure*.[106] Leonardo Bravo, who had initiated the project more than 10 years earlier at WHO Geneva, sent his congratulations to Brian, and an invitation to stay with him in Washington DC where he now worked for PAHO. Brian replied: 'It is amazing to think how long it is since you first sent for me. I greatly appreciated your having confidence in me at a time when I was so young and inexperienced.'[107]

7

Distractions and diversions: 1964–68

The disappearance of national superannuation

The professors of poverty

Child Poverty Action Group

The new Supplementary Benefits Scheme

Managing the Poverty Survey

A legal interest

(Only) Just Men

There is nothing a government hates more than to be well-informed; for it makes the process of arriving at decisions much more complicated and difficult.' (John Maynard Keynes, quoted in Titmuss, 1938)[1]

In Britain 'poverty' was essentially a statistical concept. The poor did not make themselves visible; they were discovered at the bottom of income tables by social scientists. (Keith Banting, 1979)[2]

When Labour returned to government in 1964 after a 15-year absence, Brian was one of their closest advisers, working with ministers to shape new social welfare benefits, and attempting to introduce the pensions scheme he had helped to devise in the 1950s. His academic work was driven by a belief in social justice. He extended his research interests to co-author two provocative books on the English legal system, exposing its antiquated unfairness. His most important research, however, during this period was on redefining poverty. Working with Peter Townsend, he directed a major study which showed that Beveridge's welfare state had not helped millions of families. In 1965 they were founding members of the campaign group Child Poverty Action Group (CPAG). He continued to travel widely, but also found an enjoyable sideline in setting up Just Men, a chain of boutique stores, at the height of London's fashion boom in 1965. He and his partner John also decided they needed a country home and bought Tanglewood in Kent.

Social welfare, as a policy issue in the late 1950s, had intermittently pushed national obsessions with economic growth from the top of the political agenda. But often the debates for ideologists such as Tony Crosland remained a by-product of an increasingly obsessive focus on GDP (gross domestic product) growth, and its ability to reduce social tension.[3] The emergence of an economic analysis of politics was 'based around the idea that governments were responsible for the course of the national economy'.[4] It must also be remembered that during the inter-war period the authority of the Treasury was relatively poor to the extent that the Chancellor of the Exchequer was not a member of the first years of the wartime government. From the 1940s the engagement of economists as government advisers, such as the brilliant John Maynard Keynes and Nicky Kaldor, and Brian's Cambridge tutor Joan Robinson, enabled the increasingly favoured 'macroeconomic' philosophy to take root. In 1940 Richard Stone and James Meade constructed the first comprehensive estimate of national income and expenditure, and the 1941 budget used their work to determine the amount of taxation that might control spending and inflation.[5] From 1957 quarterly national income and expenditure data was published, followed by data on factor income and price statistics in 1959 and a national income time series in 1960.[6] All this newly available data, along with the development of the first computers to replace the punch card analyses that social scientists were currently using, meant that academics like Brian could now address more ambitious research questions.[7]

Politically minded academics such as Brian, Titmuss and Townsend could force government policy makers to react to their research. Kenneth Stowe, later the Permanent Secretary at the Department of Health and Social Security, recalled this new impact:

> Richard Titmuss was very active at that time; he was held in very considerable respect. I remember going down with Allan Beard to listen to a debate at the House of Commons, and the Opposition was winning all the arguments. Fed by the Titmice, they were coming out with facts and figures which made the Ministers' answers look thin.[8]

Both Kenneth Stowe and Allan Beard were well-placed to recognise the authority of the Titmice on the emerging issue of social welfare. Beard was an official at the NAB, and in the early 1960s had been involved with a secret internal review of the National Assistance scale rates. This had been commissioned by Sir Donald Sergeant, who became Chair of the NAB in 1959; Stowe was a member of Sergeant's new Information and Research Unit specifically established to help counter the attacks of Titmuss and his team.

By this time the Titmice were like a well-oiled machine, developing a public presence in a variety of well-chosen media. Tony Lynes and Peter Townsend's letter to *The Guardian* in November 1960 publicised the fact that NAB scales had fallen well behind the increases in average earnings, which had been pledged as the benchmark by the new Conservative government in October 1959.[9] They further suggested that the government had now effectively abandoned the subsistence principle of National Assistance, but without establishing an alternative. Lynes continued the attack with his pamphlet *National Assistance and National Prosperity*, which provided more evidence that scale rate increases had not kept up with rises in average incomes.[10] Furthermore, Townsend and Dorothy Cole (Wedderburn) had discovered that the NAB was collecting but not publishing critical information, and that many people were not claiming support they were entitled to.[11] In a Young Fabian pamphlet Howard Glennerster put his finger on the NAB's problem: 'It seems afraid to raise its voice too much in case too many people hear.'[12] The NAB's own internal review aimed at not just establishing the correct physiological basis for minimum subsistence, but also acknowledging the social relativity of the concept, with the aim of reducing the stigma attached to the system.[13] It established that there was a significant number of people, many of them elderly, who needed long-term assistance, or, as the jargon for the subsequent changes styled it, a 'minimum requirement'. Also, from a detailed study of cases, it concluded that there was a wide variation between NAB offices in giving exceptional needs grants, and that assessments of nutritional needs were being made often on social rather than physiological values. As Stowe bluntly summarised:

> If one probed into it one found things went very, very differently according to the temper of the local office manager and the local office staff, and it simply justified the criticisms that were made in support of the income guarantee case, that discretion was not found to be discretion but arbitrary judgement, highly personal

arbitrary judgement. Which was the Ark of the Covenant knocked over in terms of the Poor Law.[14]

Although this was an internal review, it is interesting for its admissions:

> To expect people on national assistance to spend only on an arbitrarily restricted range of goods and services is to expect them to live as a class apart. And today we believe the community at large does not wish or expect those on national assistance to live in such a way. Provision should be made to enable the individual or family to live as a member of the community.[15]

One of its main conclusions was that the level of benefit would have to rise to remove the excessively high rate of discretionary awards that were being made. It coincided with and confirmed the Ministry of Pensions and National Insurance's (MPNI) survey *The Financial Circumstances of Retirement Pensioners*, which concurred that reducing the administrative load would only be possible if 'one deliberately ignored needs but granted rights, in the true legal sense, to a given level of resources'.[16] This review had been commissioned – at least in part – in the hope of discrediting Townsend and Utting's earlier study of pensioner poverty.[17] For the new Labour government raising benefits was not a financially viable proposition, and knowledge of this pioneering in-house government survey of social security adequacy restricted to only a handful of civil servants.[18]

The disappearance of national superannuation

Labour's election victory in 1964 had ended its 13 years in the wilderness. Wilson's election campaign was memorable for his speech welcoming the 'white heat of the technological revolution'. His optimism may have been misplaced, yet Britain went through a number of mini revolutions enabled by his government's libertarian and egalitarian reform agenda which abolished the death penalty and legalised abortion and homosexual acts. This new, and for some, 'permissive society' was enabled by a period of low unemployment, rising incomes, consumer culture and new freedoms for women through the contraceptive pill and work opportunities.[19] There was a new interest in discussing current affairs and exploring Britain's post-war status, as Anthony Sampson captured in his widely read book, *The Anatomy of Britain*.[20] Publishers such as Penguin Books found a market for readable academic research and the weekly magazine *New Society* offered a forum alongside the national broadsheet newspapers for social policy debates. Social scientists such as Brian and his LSE colleagues felt welcomed and respected for their labours. They had the ear of editors, who were usually willing to take a 2,000-word article and get it into print within a fortnight. Furthermore, in 1965, Wilson's government established the Social Science Research Council (SSRC), which funded a wide range of social policy projects. Some social scientists also found themselves in influential positions in government agencies, and appointed to Royal Commissions and Committees of Inquiry.[21]

During the 13 'wilderness years' Labour had intermittently attempted to develop its social welfare policies. The development of the national superannuation policy in 1957 had not been enough of an electoral selling point to win the 1959 general election, and since then even Crossman had lost enthusiasm for government issues of all kinds, not even bothering in 1962 to write his backbench diary. His relationship with Gaitskell had deteriorated and he resigned as frontbench spokesman on pensions and national insurance in 1960. After that, other issues such as Clause Four, defence policy and leadership crises prevented social policy from receiving sustained Labour Party attention.

In Harold Wilson's new Cabinet in 1964 the responsibility for coordinating all the social security services was given to Douglas Houghton. He had been a member of the Study Group on Security and Old Age since 1959, and had contributed the innovative proposal that the Inland Revenue could be involved in assessing and delivering an 'automatic minimum income'. Crossman saw him as a threat and rival.[22] Some commentators, such as Howard Glennerster, have seen Houghton as the explanation for disappearance of national superannuation – which had been an apparently water-tight policy commitment until Labour's election to government in 1964.[23] Tony Lynes considered him 'hopeless', with no useful ideas of his own, but equally unable to use his Cabinet authority to push through other people's ideas.[24] Perhaps also ministers now felt the scheme was too redistributive, and this decision should be seen as a 'milestone' in the Labour Party's move 'away from any serious concern to increase equality in British society'.[25] It also needs to be understood in the context of the newly predominant revisionist tone of Party thinking, especially Crosland's belief that 'saturation point' had been reached 'so far as taxation of income was concerned' and that further redistributive policies were unlikely to be successful.[26] Wilson's slim majority at the 1964 general election also required that more easily achievable policies were prioritised.

After the 1959 general election failure, Crossman had acknowledged that his focus had been too narrow: 'if we concentrate solely on the old age pension we are neglecting a large part of the problem of poverty'.[27] He reformed the Study Group and requested it also review the operation of National Assistance. This fitted well with Brian and Townsend's current research interests, and benefited from the enthusiastic labours of Tony Lynes. The Study Group had arrived at a critical decision in 1960 to recommend that the existing contributions towards sickness and unemployment benefits (which were Beveridge's flat-rate ones) should be replaced with a single earnings-related contribution. This idea had initially been floated at a dinner party Brian gave for the Crossmans, Titmusses and Townsends in March 1958. There was, however, considerable trade union concern over shifting responsibilities for such benefits between employers and employees, and Douglas Houghton worked on re-drafting the Study Group's proposals to overcome these barriers. The LSE was closely involved in this phase of policy formation – not only through the presence of Brian, Lynes, Titmuss and Townsend on the Study Group, but also through the commissioning of Christine Cockburn to make a survey of social security systems in Belgium, Germany, Sweden and the US.[28] The Study Group agreed on 'twelve principles' as the basis for future discussions including index-linking benefits and developing an earnings-related formula that would allow for some element of wealth redistribution. After negotiations with the TUC's Social Insurance Committee, Lynes had managed to produce a draft scheme that formed the basis for the party's National Executive which was issued as *New Frontiers for Social Security* in 1963.[29]

Crossman was more circumspect with the launch of *New Frontiers*, having seen how *National Superannuation* had been, in his words, 'shot to pieces' on its publication in 1959.[30] This time, no estimates of the cost of the planned 'income guarantee' were published, only the commitment to end the stigma of means-tested relief. When Peggy Herbison introduced it at Labour's 1963 annual conference, she was at pains to stress that it 'is based on the most detailed and rigorous technical, financial and actuarial advice'.[31] Dorothy Cole (Wedderburn) and J.E.G. Utting's 1962 report, *The Economic Circumstances of Old People*, had added weight to Townsend's 1954 research by showing that a significant number of pensioners were living in poverty because they were not claiming the supplementary benefits they were entitled to.[32] Although national superannuation, if adopted, would address this in the long term, a more immediate solution was needed. Lynes tinkered with various options including a flat-rate housing benefit, but although such solutions might work well in Sweden, they could not cope with the diversity in British rent levels. It was Douglas Houghton who had hit on the idea of the 'Guaranteed Income'.[33] He proposed piggybacking on income tax returns to calculate which pensioners would receive support to reach a set minimum income – 1962 was therefore an 'important moment in the long, tortuous quest for social policy's "holy grail": a scheme to combine tax and benefit into a single transaction, taking from those who could afford, paying out to those who could not – the latter a kind of "negative" income tax.'[34]

While Labour in opposition were actively considering such schemes, an internal Treasury Working Party had been formed to review the social security system in February 1963. This was partly in response to the emerging consensus view that a new 'Beveridge Report' was needed. Yet when Labour came into office in 1964, substantial parts of their *New Frontiers* manifesto were not implemented. 'We stress that, with the exception of the early introduction of the Income Guarantee, the key factor in determining the speed at which new and better levels of benefit can be introduced, will be the rate at which the British economy can advance.'[35] As the Labour MP Lena Jeger wryly noted, 'This must be one of the least prophetic sentences ever to have come down the mountain.'[36]

The excitement raised by 'income guarantee' morphed into political pressure to do something immediate to relieve existing pensioners in poverty, but Labour's Study Group had not progressed far from Houghton's bright idea into detailed costings for the scheme. Wilson appointed Peggy Herbison as Minister of Pensions, and Houghton was given the role of social policy 'overlord' through his non-departmental Cabinet post of Chancellor of the Duchy of Lancaster. There was no rapport between them, and it did not help that their offices were in different buildings rather than on the same ministerial corridor.[37] Houghton was to conduct a review of social security policy, an odd decision given the supposed detailed plans that Labour had worked up in opposition. *The Times* and the Conservatives pointed out his lack of staff and ministerial authority (although he was in the Cabinet and Herbison was not). Significantly, there was no role for Crossman, perhaps an indication that Wilson did not value his initiatives. Soon after coming into government Labour announced an unprecedented 18.5 per cent increase in National Insurance benefits (against the advice of the Chancellor, James Callaghan). This was to be administered in the existing flat-rate scheme to fulfil the widely anticipated manifesto pledge, but it coincided with a period of economic crisis, thus making more radical changes increasingly unlikely.[38] As Houghton himself put it, the Income Guarantee foundered 'on the rocks in the economic gales of July 1965'.[39]

The locus of policy making also changed after the arrival of the 1964 Labour government. The existing Study Group on Social Security and Old Age was reincarnated as the Social Policy Advisory Committee – still a sub-committee of the National Executive Committee's Home Policy Sub-committee and with some of the original members – but it was now interdepartmental committees of civil servants that took the initiative in progressing the detail of ideas. Why were they able to do this? Possibly as a safeguard reaction to the nature and scale of criticisms from the MPNI of Crossman's national superannuation plan, particularly over 'inflationary dangers' and lack of detailed figures.[40] A new interdepartmental Working Party on Pensions (later renamed the Official Committee on Social Security Review) was established by the Ministry's Permanent Secretary, Clifford Jarrett. This working party quickly decided that the flat-rate pension had to go, and a formula arrived at that 'if necessary [could be] weighted in favour of the lower-paid'.[41]

There were similar structural weaknesses in Crossman's planning for national superannuation and Houghton's income guarantee – in both cases Labour's policy advisers had failed to actually deal with the practicalities of such a scheme. Houghton might have had the bright idea of using the Inland Revenue, but with its annual returns it was not suited to coping with short-term changes in benefits, or more fundamentally, giving out money rather than collecting it. The scheme would have required a 'formidable programme of inter-departmental planning' to bring together the NAB, the MPNI, the Board of the Inland Revenue and the Post Office. A subsequent academic review was damning: 'However enthusiastic and expert they may be, a group of academics and politicians doubling up as part-time policy planners and a handful of staff servicing the whole range of policy committees, cannot be expected to devise workable proposals; but they are expected to do so.'[42] Commentators have since reflected on how the Study Group's re-focus on the 'national minimum' was a distraction away from progressing national superannuation.[43]

Even this observation misses the more fundamental criticism, made by Titmuss at the time, that Labour's policies lacked a vision of the bigger picture of social welfare. How much of this was due to the style of the Wilson administration has been widely debated. It seems to have lacked the capacity for micro-managing policy development as well as for longer-term planning.[44] What is surprising is that Titmuss and his team failed to persuade the Study Group, and through them government ministers, to consider related issues such as the coordination of services for the main users of national assistance – the elderly, the chronically sick, the long-term unemployed and single-parent families.

Some of the explanation for the slow development of an effective National Insurance benefits blueprint lies within the situation at the LSE, which was heavily relied on not only by Crossman, but also by other Labour policy makers both before and after they regained office in 1964. The LSE Department of Social Administration had expanded steadily through the 1950s, and Brian wrote up a glowing account of it for the *Sociological Review* in 1962, highlighting the research topics and their origins and funding. He was keen to stress that nearly all of the Department's research began with some historical context, and that many of the projects had been exclusively historical studies. At the end he listed by year, since 1956–57, the publications of his colleagues. Each year there were between 10 and 13 staff producing outputs on topics as diverse as care of the elderly, the emigration of British doctors, industrial issues around female employment, truancy and the juvenile courts. Alongside his close collaborators such as Titmuss and Townsend, the Department also included up-and-coming social scientists such as David Donnison and Nancy Seear.[45] Teaching was as important as research, and the Department welcomed students who might not have previously considered taking a university course. Brian's lectures were always eagerly anticipated, for his enthusiasm, and sheer sense of energy. They were usually on Friday afternoons and were held in one of the old science lecture theatres. Adrian Sinfield, who took the Diploma course in 1962–63, remembers Brian's performances, which would begin with him standing behind the long wooden experiment bench. Before long, he would be sitting on it, and on days when his bad back troubled him, he would lie along the bench.[46]

But Townsend moved from the LSE in 1963 to create a new Department of Sociology at the University of Essex (at Colchester) shortly after its foundation. This had left a number of research projects short-staffed, and strained relations with both Brian and Titmuss. The planned book, *Two Nations in Old Age Policies*, which all three had agreed to write, never made it past an outline structure.[47] Although they remained in regular contact by telephone, their socialising grew less frequent. Brian continued to give his badly-wrapped extravagant Christmas presents for their children, but the parties that brought Brian, the Crossmans, Shores and Benns together at the Townsends' Hampstead home became less frequent.

The professors of poverty[48]

Even if the Titmice did not push forward on these specific social policy issues in the early 1960s, to their subsequent critics' satisfaction, their broader research interest on poverty was to have a greater impact in the long run, and the LSE became the epicentre for the poverty debate. Poverty had been at the heart of Titmuss's research from the 1930s.[49] His 1962 book, *Income Distribution and Social Change*, highlighted the shocking inadequacy of information on income distribution, and the government's inability to develop appropriate policies.[50] Brian had written a draft manuscript, 'The Definitions of Poverty', in January 1952, as a newly registered PhD student at Cambridge, in which he proposed a survey that would include data on family nutrition levels.[51] In the same year Townsend's pamphlet, *Poverty: Ten Years After Beveridge*, was published. In 1954 he sent Brian a copy of his article 'Measuring Poverty', inscribed with the dedication 'with affection and appreciation for what I learn from you'.[52] Their relationship was symbiotic: both were absorbed with challenging the classic Rowntree definition, which was routinely interpreted as seeing poverty as an absolute condition.[53]

One of the key mechanisms of Beveridge's welfare state intended to reduce levels of poverty was the introduction of family allowances (there was already a child tax allowance which was automatically allocated to married fathers). From 1945, this new (taxable) benefit was paid weekly to mothers, in cash, at Post Offices, for all second and subsequent children in a family, regardless of its income or socioeconomic status. Yet this radical innovation had been allowed to deteriorate, becoming little more than a token of Beveridge's intention – he himself had been persuaded to abandon family allowances for the first child to appease the Treasury (and halve the cost of the scheme), and the principle of 'adequacy' had never been accepted. Despite a small increase in 1952 it did not generate political attention, even within the Labour Party. Indeed, some politicians claimed off the record that family allowances were a handicap, because ordinary Labour voters saw them as 'handouts to the large feckless family'.[54]

Through the 1950s, as the real value of family allowances fell, there was growing recognition, especially among social workers, that an increasing number of families with young children were struggling to maintain their living standards. Although Rowntree's third survey in 1951 had found that levels of absolute poverty had decreased, further analyses were now being done, using more accurate guidelines on nutrition requirements. Another new data source was also available: the Family Expenditure Survey. From the early 1950s this government-run survey of a national sample of households had collected information on family income trends. From 1957 it became an annual exercise.[55]

For the Titmice poverty was fundamentally a relative concept, and they saw the government's reliance on an outdated poverty 'line' as deeply damaging. They recognised the need for substantial new research on family poverty to inform Labour's policy developments. In March 1960 Townsend had prepared a briefing note for Labour's Study Group on Security and Old Age, *A Note on the Definition of Subsistence*, in which he noted the lack of research since the war into the concept. He proposed the calculation of a 'relative' formula, based on the average wage of the lowest quartile of earners. The subsistence percentage of this adequate wage could then be varied according to whether it was applied to a single person (30 per cent), a married couple (50 per cent) or a married couple with children (80 per cent).[56] He had stimulated academic discussion around this issue at the 1962 British Sociological Association conference at Brighton, where he read his paper 'The Meaning of Poverty'.[57]

In 1961 Brian and Townsend obtained some internal LSE funding to re-analyse the Family Expenditure/Income data for 1953/54 and 1960, using the questionnaires kept by the Ministry of Labour at Colindale. Caroline Cadbury (of the chocolate manufacturing family) was employed to do the tedious analysis, which in the days before computers used punch cards and paper tapes. Brian only later cottoned on to why Townsend kept Caroline under such close supervision: 'Peter's dedication was not motivated only by concern for academic accuracy'.[58] To maintain political credibility, they took the government's basic minimum income or subsistence level (which set the level below which National Assistance benefit would be paid) as their starting point, and this usefully became the accepted benchmark for subsequent poverty studies. Their work was also informed by visits to the US that they separately made in 1963 and 1964, where Townsend read Michael Harrington's 1962 book *The Other America*.[59] They spoke at various meetings and learned that the Americans were also beginning to research the concept of a 'poverty line'.[60]

The re-working of the Family Expenditure Survey data showed that when using the basic NAB level, the problem seemed relatively small – 4.7 per cent of households containing 3.8 per cent of the population would be classed as poor. Brian and Townsend argued that a more realistic line would be to take not only the basic benefit, but also to include the additional special needs payments and small amounts of informal income some families received. If this was used to set a poverty line of 140 per cent of basic NAB rates, their calculations produced a new estimate of 14 per cent of the population: 7.5 million people living in poverty in Britain. And these were not just the elderly, as commonly assumed, but included over two million children. These shocking figures were wildly at odds with the Rowntree findings of 1951 and the government's own more recent estimates.

In addition to re-working the Family Expenditure Survey data, Brian and Townsend submitted an application to the Joseph Rowntree Memorial Trust (JRMT) in March 1964 for a study grant 'to find out, among other things, how far increases in prosperity are shared equally among the whole population'. It proposed to find out how many and what categories of persons were in poverty and relative deprivation, to describe and explain their living conditions and problems, and to review the methods used in social policy to alleviate hardship. The four-year project was to have four main research themes: large families; fatherless families; the chronic sick; and the aged. In each of the studies they proposed to do between 100 and 200 pilot family interviews to inform interim reports. The second stage would involve at least 5,000 households, using a specially trained team of interviewers, or the government's own Social Survey staff, and a sub-sample would be asked to keep detailed accounts of income and expenditure.[61]

Brian wrote to Titmuss in May, on hearing the outcome: 'You will be staggered to hear that Peter Townsend and I have been granted £32,000 by the Rowntree Trustees for our major study of poverty. We are staggered too and have now got to start some serious planning. The initial letters from Waddilove [JRMT secretary] were so discouraging.'[62] It was agreed that the grant would be held by Townsend at his new base at the University of Essex, but two of the research staff would be based with Brian at the LSE, and that an advisory committee would be appointed by Rowntree. The 'Poverty Survey', as it was to be known, was officially announced in June, and generated considerable press coverage and letters from the public.

Three research assistants were appointed in September 1964 to staff the project. Hilary Land had a degree in Mathematics, Psychology and Physics from the University of Bristol and had then taken the one-year Diploma in Social Administration at the LSE. She was based at the LSE in Skepper House to work on the large family theme. She also had responsibility for the design of the main survey's three-stage stratified sample (which drew on electoral registers, supplemented by hand searches of rates records), and she undertook the majority of the cleaning and preliminary analysis of the questionnaires. John Veit-Wilson was appointed to work on the chronically sick theme, initially at Skepper House and then moving to work with Townsend at Essex. His career after reading Economics and Social Anthropology at Cambridge had been in a variety of management consultancy roles. Brian's initial reservations about him were quickly overcome: 'I am glad that we have appointed Mr Wilson. I found him rather civil servantish, but I feel there is commitment underneath and he has become the way he is as a result of four years in civil servantish sort of jobs'.[63] He was already known to both Brian and Townsend through his mother, the sociologist Harriet Wilson. Denis Marsden, a Cambridge Natural Sciences graduate, was persuaded to move from the Liberal Studies Department at Salford to work with Townsend at Essex, with responsibility for the fatherless families research.

The invitation letter drafted by Brian for the large families sample was simple but effective:

> Dear Madam, We are research workers from the University of London who are trying to study the financial problems of people who have large families, like yourselves. When we know the facts we hope to write a book because we feel that people do not know enough about the special problems of bringing up a large family and how you manage. Of course we shall not mention any names, and nothing you tell us will be passed on to any Ministry or to the tax authorities. Would you be kind enough to let us come and visit you and explain more about what we are trying to do and how you can help us? If so, please post the enclosed postcard.[64]

However, initial enquiries to the London County Council's Education Department to permit Hilary Land to extract details of large families from school registers did not bode well. Their request was lost in a labyrinthine committee system and risked delaying the start of the project.[65] When the team held their first meeting at Colchester in November 1964, they were beginning to appreciate the difficulties of such large-scale collaborations. In the early months of 1965 Brian and Townsend entered into long negotiations with the MPNI to obtain their pilot sample families. The delays were becoming such a concern that they considered an offer from Walter Holland, an epidemiologist at St Thomas' Medical School, to use his sample of 10,000 school children in Kent and 2,500 families in Harrow instead.[66] Considerable time had already been invested in the questionnaire designs and survey methodology. When the invitations were eventually sent out to the large families sample, the acceptances were worryingly low: only 35 replies from 150 letters.[67] The Ministry was persuaded to write again to the remaining large families in the sample and this time to ask them to reply if they did *not* want to be interviewed. Land eventually interviewed 86 of the sample of 150 families.[68]

It took a long period of concerted effort from Brian, Townsend and their research team to advance the sampling and interviewing, using all the pressure they could apply to their contacts in government. In June 1965 Brian wrote to Townsend: 'The position is getting desperate for us, as we have two staff members waiting with virtually nothing to do.'[69] It took much longer than expected to get the pilot study into a fit state to reliably inform the second stage. On the plus side, however, were the experiences the project brought. Brian recalled in 1995:

> I have some happy memories of the fieldwork. Peter and I decided to visit all the interviewers on their home ground. I remember visiting one in a beautiful village in Scotland. She was the wife of an excise man at a small whisky distillery. After our discussion, she offered me what she described as "a wee bit" to sample. She became so involved in her [project] work that when I happened to be giving a lecture at a polytechnic a few years later, she was in the audience, having decided to train for social work. I took her out to the pub afterwards to repay her splendid hospitality.[70]

But one wider benefit that the Rowntree grant provided was the creation of an expert advisory committee. This included Titmuss (somewhat reluctantly, as Chair), the nutritionist J. Yudkin, Leonard Nicholson from the Central Statistical Office and F. Forsyth from the Ministry of Labour. Brian and Townsend exploited this group to give feedback on the first draft of their reanalysis of the Family Expenditure Survey data from 1953/54 and 1960. Initially called *Low Levels of Living*, this was later to become *The Poor and the Poorest*.[71]

Child Poverty Action Group

Early in 1965 the Social and Economic Affairs Committee of the Society of Friends (the Quakers) held a series of public talks on the theme of 'current social problems'. Brian was invited to give a talk on child poverty. Using the new findings of his research with Townsend, Brian's talk at Toynbee Hall on 13 March 1965 initiated a more sustained debate on this issue.[72] He recalled at a witness seminar held in 1993: 'When I gave the *Poor and the Poorest* findings, Harriet [Wilson] said what are we going to do about it, and I remember replying that nobody represented a pressure group. I came out with exactly the same idea, and I felt a great air of enthusiasm around that room.'[73]

A follow-up meeting was held on 5 April under the auspices of the Family Service Unit (FSU), directed by Fred Philp.[74] Although Brian could not attend as he was in the US, Tony Lynes went along to meet with Harriet Wilson (Lecturer in Sociology at Cardiff University), her son John Veit-Wilson, Audrey Harvey, Fred Philp and other interested individuals.[75] They devised a memorandum, 'The Alleviation of Family Poverty', to present to Douglas Houghton, the government's new 'overlord' for social services, calling for a commitment to address the poverty issue. They presented two main suggestions: an increase in family allowances and the introduction of a negative income tax (which Tony Lynes had developed).[76]

When he returned to the LSE in April, Brian also tried to maintain pressure on Peggy Herbison, Minister for Pensions and National Insurance, who was revising the National Insurance system, now a critical issue as wage-stop cases were becoming more common. He had evidence from New York State of a system that allowed people to continue to receive benefits even if they had some low income from work. His letter to Herbison demonstrated his valuable historical and international contextualisation, which appeared to be lacking in government circles: 'If the Americans, who are so anxious to preserve the work incentive, are able to do it, it would seem possible for us to do it. I recognise this is Speenhamland all over again, but something might be done by way of subtle disregards.'[77] Her unenthusiastic reply, along with Houghton's tardy and weak response to the group's memorandum, confirmed that there was a need for a permanent pressure group, a decision justified further by Callaghan's announcement on 27 July of the official postponement of the income guarantee.

Brian, now Professor of Social Administration at the LSE (from 1 October 1965), remained closely involved with the group's development. He and Townsend toyed around with potential names: the first one – the Advisory Council for the Alleviation of Poverty – evolved into the Family Poverty Group. Finally, in October 1965, Harriet Wilson's suggested name of Child Poverty Action Group was chosen, from the outset branded as CPAG. Timed for maximum conscience impact in the season of goodwill, Brian and Townsend published *The Poor and the Poorest* on 22 December. This slim 78-page book has since been described as a 'major turning point in British post-war social policy'.[78] They questioned the status quo:

> Two assumptions have governed much economic thinking in Britain since the war. The first is that we have 'abolished' poverty. The second is that we are a much more equal society; that

the differences between the living standards of the rich and the poor are much smaller than they used to be. These assumptions are of great practical as well as theoretical importance. They form the background to much of the discussion of social and economic policy. But are they true?[79]

A press release from the new CPAG announced that they would deliver a memorandum signed by leading academics and politicians (including Lady Wootton of Abinger, Lord Simey of Toxteth, Sir John Maude and Dame Eileen Younghusband) to Harold Wilson on 23 December at 3.00pm, calling for an end to child poverty in Britain. Wilson did some hasty diary reshuffling to find ten minutes to see them in the Cabinet room, knowing that there were television cameras outside in Downing Street. Led by Fred Philp (CPAG Chair), Brian, Peter Townsend, Walter Birmingham and Harriet Wilson presented the memorandum and made their case.[80] As Brian explained to Nicholas Kaldor, one of Wilson's closest advisers:

> Money might be found for improving family allowances from reductions in tax allowances for children. As far as I can see, the existing concept of public expenditure used in the National Plan tends to confuse the issue by making it impossible to do this sort of thing....Am I right in saying that there is already a precedent for regarding tax allowances and cash grants as inter-changeable in the recent substitution of investment grants for investment tax allowances? I do hope you will be able to make some sense of all this. As I said when we met, it was such a shame that the Royal Commission on which you sat was not concerned with all taxation rather than solely with income tax.[81]

The Downing Street meeting was followed by a press conference at Toynbee Hall, in which poverty was personified through individual accounts of how families were failing to make ends meet. On Christmas Eve an emotive BBC television programme on family poverty was broadcast. It featured a number of case studies that demonstrated the diversity of poor family types, and the genuine need for support. One single mother was filmed saying that she had no money for toys. Christmas would have to be like any other day for them. All she could give the children that day was the most nourishing food she could afford. After the interview the camera crew went out shopping and came back with a hamper of toys and Christmas food. As well as the pre-recorded documentary, Brian was interviewed live on the ITV

9.00pm television news, and on the 'Ten O'Clock' radio programme on the BBC's Home Service. Commissioned articles from Maurice Peston (Professor of Economics at Queen Mary College) and other influential figures appeared in *New Society* to coincide with the launch of the campaign. The difficult task was to keep it in the public eye. There were other campaigns launched at this time, which focused on related aspects of poverty. Shelter, which tackled the problem of homelessness, built on public sympathy raised through the emotive television programme, 'Cathy Come Home'.

Responses to *The Poor and the Poorest* continued to appear in the press into the spring of 1966. *The Times* carried an article on 22 March under the headline 'Sponging on the State' by a 'Director of Welfare Services', which disputed Brian and Townsend's estimate of the extent of poverty in Britain, claiming that the 11 increases in National Assistance benefits since 1948 favoured the low paid and casual working man, but also acted as an incentive to employers who knew that the state would meet a shortfall in their low wages.

> Politicians and the public in general simply do not appreciate that utter chaos now symbolises the welfare state. Such words as poverty and hardship are glibly bandied around by politicians, from the leaders downwards, as though academics like Professor Abel-Smith and Professor Townsend have proved that chronic indigence is the settled state of large groups in the community. In fact the poorest members are better-off than they have ever been. Those living in real poverty or suffering hardship are rarities indeed.[82]

Correspondence in the *British Medical Journal* focused instead on the rising number of large families – a 45 per cent increase in those with six or more children since 1953–60: 'it is the families (social classes 4 and 5) who can least afford it who are so prolific. Until a family planning service is included in the National Health Service this tightly packed island will become increasingly uncomfortable – physically and psychologically – to live in.'[83]

In order to have an impact, CPAG needed a proper base. The founder members solicited support from a variety of related organisations, and in January 1966 set up a first office in the FSU's offices, before transferring to LSE's Skepper House in Endsleigh Street. Tony Lynes, who had been Brian's student and worked as Titmuss's research assistant for seven years, was appointed as CPAG's full-time secretary in March, a role that suited him perfectly. It also offered him a way out of an unsatisfactory position as a temporary 'Principal' to Peggy Herbison,

Minister of Social Security, who used him as an 'irritant to stimulate ideas', but failed to give him direct ministerial access, independent of the Whitehall bureaucracy. So Lynes already had good relations with the media and politicians, and, through the new journal *Poverty*, he could direct effective campaigns.[84] From an initial membership of 13 in December 1965, CPAG expanded to 450 within the year. There was, however, a charming naivety about CPAG's early work. The core group decided that they would not actively fundraise, and even turned down offers from LSE colleagues. They refused the suggestion of setting up local branches, and believed that Tony Lynes beavering away with his editions of *Hansard* and academic research to produce bulletins that he then distributed by bicycle to the Westminster community was all that was needed to achieve an immediate government anti-poverty policy. Yet they persisted with this strategy for the next four years.

But there was also a growing international interest in poverty. In the US President Johnson had set up a task force on income maintenance during the year-long 'Great Society' debate in 1964. UNESCO chose to 'sponsor' the issue of poverty in the same year, coinciding with meetings of the International Committee of Poverty Research, which Townsend was closely involved with. Was this to be the beginning of the end of poverty in the developed world?

The new Supplementary Benefits Scheme

The Supplementary Benefits Scheme, created through the 1966 Social Security Act, was 'salvaged from the wreck of the Income Guarantee'.[85] The NAB was replaced by the Supplementary Benefits Commission, operating from within the new Ministry of Social Security, which was directly responsible for all types of social security schemes, both contributory and means-tested. It simplified insurance and assurance systems and placed a new emphasis on benefits as *rights*.[86] Titmuss was uncomfortable with the use of the word 'rights', sensing that it would lead to more antagonism between claimants and social security officials, as he had witnessed during his visits to the US. Even if some of the resulting changes were more cosmetic than functional – the 'test of need' was replaced by the 'test of requirement' – there was a rise of 365,000 claimants in the first year.[87] Yet the cost of the scheme was considerably cheaper than the income guarantee option would have been. The timing of the announcement, just before the expected 'consolidating' general election, was seized on by the Conservatives as a face-saving measure. Herbison justified the reform of National Assistance as something 'on which my Department has been working for a considerable time'.[88] While in opposition before 1964, Labour had amalgamated their attention on two related problems – that of old age pensioners living in poverty with the issue of their unwillingness to ask for legitimate support. But there was an emerging tacit political agreement, underpinned by the Titmice's research, that benefit rates were not just a problem of the elderly.

Yet, although Herbison's review acknowledged the contemporary awareness of the deficiencies of the NAB 'wage-stop' practice, and its failure to cope with *family* poverty, there had actually been very little research into why National Assistance was not fulfilling needs, either of pensioners or other disadvantaged groups in society.[89] No pressure groups had really targeted National Assistance as a concept, or forced parliamentary debate on its structural deficiencies. There was no public consultation on how 'clients' viewed the social services they used. This was very much in contrast to the US. Tony Lynes, on a visit to New York, had discovered a groundswell of public interest in what they called 'welfare rights' – a term that subsequently pervaded British social policy rhetoric.[90] The American Welfare Rights Movement was a campaign by the people for the people to make themselves heard, not like CPAG which, up to that time, had very little direct involvement from poor people. In some ways, this lack of British public interest was useful to Labour, excusing it from a broader study of the poverty issue and from acknowledging that the income guarantee pledge had been broken until a replacement offer was ready to be launched. It was woefully short of the vision of a comprehensive social welfare review that many had expected a Labour government to undertake after so many years of discussions with people like the Titmice.

There had been regular informal discussions on social policy issues in the mid-1960s held at Tony Lynes' flat in The Cut, close to Waterloo station, which brought together academics and civil servants to exchange ideas.[91] Della Nevitt and Tony Lynes had also been drafting papers on the linked issues of housing and poverty and specifically how local authority housing allowances had an impact on other benefits.[92] When the Social Security Bill was in preparation, Lynes wrote to Lena Jeger with practical suggestions. Adrian Sinfield, who had been one of Brian's students on the LSE Diploma course in 1962-63, and who was now working with Townsend at Essex, was also active in drafting potential amendments.[93] Brian, along with Sinfield and Townsend, wrote a letter to *The Times* to highlight the government's intention to continue with a 'wage-stop' policy in the new Bill: 'Surely now is the time to abandon the "wage-stop" which sentences to statutory deprivation some hundred thousand children for "sins" which the vast majority of their fathers have not committed and would not contemplate committing.'[94] He also wrote to Timothy Raison, editor of *New Society*, and gained his agreement to take an article by Hilary Land on the first results of the pilot study on large families.

The Titmice maintained the public pressure on Labour throughout 1966. Brian appeared on the BBC's 'Panorama' programme on 26 September, along with the Minister of Health Kenneth Robinson, to discuss the state of the NHS. In November he translated his Fabian lecture 'Labour's Social Plans' into an article for the *Observer*: 'Do we care so little about poverty?' By comparing Britain's expenditure on health, housing and welfare with other countries, he showed how little priority such areas seemed to hold for the Labour government, and called for an increase in taxation to fund the overdue improvements.[95] Townsend gave the last of the three 'Titmice' Fabian lectures on the theme of what the welfare state meant in 1966 in the aftermath of the new Social Security Act: 'The real lesson is that the government does not try hard enough either to find poverty or to measure it, it does not question critically enough the workings of its own new system. It does not ask itself often enough what it means by "subsistence" – which is a governmental word for poverty. "Subsistence", as Townsend points out, is a changing value....'[96]

On 23 November Crossman used his speech at the Caxton Hall to launch a 'massive attack' against the Titmice, sitting in the audience in front of him, for their criticisms of Labour's failure to achieve a robust poverty policy. With 'great gusto and considerable humour', he castigated them – Brian and Townsend by name – for their failure to 'bring political realities into their considerations'.[97] The following day Lena Jeger, a Labour MP who had been closely involved with the poverty issue, chided Crossman for his attack, and called for more dialogue and even 'confrontation' of the government's methodology and schemes: 'How to mobilise the army, the soldiers of thought, the sergeants of research? Break the rules and ask them to dinner in the mess? Expose administration to the enthusiasm of thinkers? Let down the drawbridges of Whitehall? Labour Ministers, above all, need to cherish the impatience, the passion for excellence, of those who support them. Maybe all we need, like the latest pirate transmitter, is another wavelength of communication.'[98] Brian also featured in the press that day, with an article in the *Telegraph* magazine: 'How Poverty Could Be Eliminated Tomorrow', which would have been whirring round the print room as Crossman made his Caxton Hall attack.[99]

'Child poverty, which until a few months ago was hardly talked about outside the claustrophobic confines of the LSE (I speak of the school's physical characteristics) is now a political issue.'[100] This was the view of Alan Watkins writing in *The Spectator* in April 1967. Brian, Townsend and Lynes, on behalf of CPAG, had renewed their public criticism of Labour's performance. They sent an open letter to Wilson 'to appeal to you to help restore the Government's sense of social priorities. The Chancellor of the Exchequer's Budget speech suggests that the Cabinet is not offering prompt and just solutions to Britain's current problems of poverty and social inequality because it is not being presented with the right questions.'[101] After the Fabian lectures in November 1966, CPAG had launched a campaign for an increase in family allowances, sending a memorandum to the Chancellor on 15 February. Brian followed this up with a talk at the Association of Child Care Officers conference in April. He highlighted the appalling number of children who were taken into care because their families faced eviction over rent arrears, or because of poor housing conditions. He called on social workers to 'mobilise the poor' to flood their local authority social services offices with applications for help with claiming benefits, and also suggested that a rational rent plan, based on the tenant and not the house, was urgently needed. The social workers' response was cautious, fearing the probity of such a political action. Brian, however, saw it as in the spirit of other professional campaigning such as that by the BMA.[102]

By June 1967 CPAG's strategy of careful diplomacy had not produced the desired rejuvenation of Labour's commitment to tackling the poverty issue. The various memoranda to the Prime Minister and the Chancellor had elicited only cursory replies. With hindsight, it is possible to see in them Wilson's pragmatism in the face of relentless economic crises. At the time, it was becoming apparent to the CPAG executive that their 'close' relationship with the Labour Party was perhaps naïve wishful thinking, and that a stronger, more critical approach was needed.

Managing the Poverty Survey

Brian's public statements on child poverty were not vague incitements to action. They drew on long-running discussions with Fabian colleagues such as Shirley Williams and Tony Crosland, and on collaborations with fellow academic researchers such as Mike Reddin and David Donnison. As early as November 1957 Brian had drafted a policy document for the Labour Party on educational maintenance allowances.[103] In May 1966 he had discussed with Donnison the paradox of school meal provision: that the means test for free school meals actually worked as a disincentive for the poorest children to take them. Using research from Hilary Land's large families study on the stigma of free school meals, he proposed a voucher system, perhaps operated via the Post Office, so that the stigma of receiving free school meals might be removed if all children had to pre-buy (or be given) vouchers.[104] In February 1967 Reddin sent Brian material he had solicited from local education authorities (which was collected but never published) on the patchy provision of free school meals and educational maintenance allowances.[105]

The formation of a poverty studies panel by the SSRC, chaired by David Donnison, was another useful development. Brian was a member, along with A.H. Halsey, Alan Little, Norman Dennis, Richard Lipsey, J.B. Cullingworth and Richard Dale (Head of the Social Insurance Department at the TUC). The idea was to link social studies departments at universities with those of local authorities prepared to take action against poverty in their areas. This initiative coincided with an awareness of the growing wealth inequalities in Britain.[106] Although such collaborations could be rewarding, there were also disadvantages. Brian asked the LSE to give the Poverty Survey as little publicity as possible in its annual round-up of research in December 1966 to deter '… the stream of casual foreign visitors attached to the school coming to talk over what one is doing, usually without any real knowledge of the field….The problem for myself and many other research people is that one finds oneself eventually landed with enormous public relations work at the cost of actually doing any research. It is dangerous to take one's sabbatical in England. If only we could move the whole unit to some remote Scottish island, well off the route of PAN AM and TWA!'[107]

Earlier in 1966 Brian had acted as an adviser for the Ministry of Social Security's own poverty survey (The Circumstances of Large Families), hoping that in return he might get the government's social survey team to carry out the questionnaire on their behalf.[108] This role also gave Brian an opportunity, as he put it, 'naughtily' to send a copy of the Ministry's own draft questionnaire to Townsend: 'I am not clear whether it is or is not under the Official Secrets Act, but I think you ought not to admit that you have seen it.'[109] The civil servants refused to cooperate, despite Brian and Townsend's leaning on Ministers such as Shirley Williams. They then tried applying pressure through the recently ennobled social scientist Tom Simey: 'Our final intervention with the Minister only secured that the non-respondents in the original sample would be told that they would be visited if they did not write to ask not to be. As you know well, persuasion on the doorstep secures much better co-operation than any type of letter "contracting in" or contractin [sic] out'.[110] Simey's reply, claiming to have 'clobbered the Assistance Board good and proper' and secured behind the scenes Treasury support, generated more worries than it allayed. Brian forwarded it to Titmuss: 'Tom is rather odd isn't he? I hope that this wouldn't happen to anyone who became a Lord!' Titmuss replied: 'It is frightening and sad. I fear he may be doing some harm.'[111]

By mid-summer of 1966 Brian and Townsend therefore resolved to hire and train their own team of interviewers for the main survey. Now they had to persuade the Rowntree trustees that they needed a further extension to their funding. Ford Longman, who was overseeing their research at the Trust, had concerns about the progress of the project, which had suffered further delays in the spring when both of them were ill – Brian suffering with jaundice for two months. There were significant methodological problems. The General Registrar's Office constituency and enumeration district data (local authority-based), which they wished to use, did not coincide with the boundaries of health districts.[112] Brian worried that they were missing key poor groups, including immigrants and gypsy travellers, and so persuaded Alan Stuart, Professor of Statistics at LSE, to join their Advisory Committee to allay some of Rowntree's fears. They were also experimenting with computer analysis – something so new to social science that special sessions had to be booked to use the University of London's computer at Imperial College (at a cost of £15/hour). Walter Holland recommended a 'marvellous pre-pack computer programme' from IBM called Introduction to SRG, and Brian encouraged Hilary Land to develop her computing skills so that the project could try it out.[113]

One potential problem that Brian and Townsend decided to keep to themselves at this stage was the subjective style of Denis Marsden's analysis of his interviews with fatherless families.[114] In the event it turned out to be a relatively minor issue: Brian and Townsend had sent a carefully worded progress report to Rowntree on 2 October 1967, confessing their problems with achieving sample sizes and processing the data without a further injection of funding. On 23 October Ford Longman replied, relaying the Rowntree Trustees' 'grave concerns' and stating that they would be 'unable to make a further grant'.[115] As they had already taken on additional staff at the end of 1966, including Christopher Bagley and Sheila Benson, in the hope of meeting their revised interviewing targets, they quickly worked up an alternative grant application to the SSRC.

Although Rowntree had declined to fund an extension to the Poverty Survey, they were prepared to support CPAG, and made a £500 donation along with Lord Sainsbury's Charitable Trust in 1967 to replace the £1,000 which the group had obtained for its first year from the Sembal Trust.[116] In May 1967 CPAG had used this funding to move out of Skepper House into more suitable premises on the top floor of 1 Macklin Street, from where Tony Lynes continued to orchestrate their attacks on issues such as NHS charges, and to collaborate with other new pressure groups such as Shelter. Brian also thought up a novel scheme for a CPAG legal department, in which second and third year LSE law students, under supervision from Michael Zander, would act as counsel for supplementary benefit tribunals.[117] CPAG claimed two small victories later in 1967. In October a small increase in family allowances was finally announced, and in December the NAB/Supplementary Benefits Commission agreed to relax the administration of the wage-stop. Yet the basic principles remained unchanged, and the Fabian mantra of permeation of policy groups and intellectual arguments for change appeared weak.

A legal interest

In the early 1960s Brian had been involved with the Fabian Society's Industrial Injuries Group, along with his new collaborator Archie Cochrane of the Medical Research Council's Pneumoconiosis Research Unit at Cardiff. This led to an invitation to be a member of the Justice Committee on Compensation for the Victims of Crime and Violence, which reported to the Home Secretary in July 1962. Chaired by Lord Longford, other members included the barrister Louis Blom-Cooper, several MPs, solicitors and social science researchers.[118] Joining the Justice Committee also fitted well with Brian's growing interest in legal matters, including his sabbatical as Associate Professor at Yale Law School for three months in 1962. All his work, academic and lobbying, was founded on his concern with promoting social justice, which can be seen emerging even in the mid-1940s, through his voluntary work at the Stepney Boys' Club.

The Justice Committee was in part a critical response to the White Paper *Compensation for Victims of Crimes of Violence* published in June 1961. Over the course of 15 committee meetings from October 1961 there was considerable disagreement on what responsibility the state should take. Some members favoured payments of lump sums and weekly benefits relative to victims' earnings. Yet Brian spoke out from the outset against compensating victims of violent crime, believing that there were other social casualties more deserving of benefit:

> At our last meeting we tried to base an argument on the likelihood or feasibility of insurance. But how many people insure their children against accidents? How many people insure against having a child made mentally subnormal by bad obstetrics? How many adults insure themselves privately against chronic disability? Which of these risks will the insurance industry cover and for how long? It seems, therefore, that it would be quite wrong to fall into the trap of giving special help to those whose disability happens to arise in a newsworthy way and ignore those whose case is equally strong but less sensational. What is needed is a general improvement in our social security provisions. And if these cases which happen to gain disproportionate public sympathy are singled out for special treatment, this general improvement will never be made.[119]

Through his brother Lionel, a barrister at Lincoln's Inn Chambers, Brian already had some insight into the legal world. While at Yale in the spring of 1962 he met Robert Stevens, a former member of Gray's Inn, who had moved there to take a Master of Law degree in 1958 and remained as a member of faculty.[120] They met again in 1963 in Dar es Salam in newly independent Tanganyika (Tanzania) where Stevens was seconded by Yale to help establish a law school for the new University College.[121] He was accompanied by his wife, Rosemary Stevens, whom Brian had already met when she was a hospital administrator at the Princess Beatrice Hospital in London. Brian and Richard Titmuss had been invited to Tanganyika by Julius Nyerere to conduct a study into its health services.[122] Brian and Titmuss stayed at the Stevens' home, and Robert was impressed by their philosophy on social welfare, which provoked discussions on the current state of the British legal system. Brian and Stevens decided that an investigation would be timely. From his new American perspective Stevens was acutely aware that existing studies were either sycophantic or so vague as to be useless: there was no tradition in Britain of academic research into legal administration, and there had been no study of the Legal Aid and Advice scheme – 'possibly the most important development in English law in the twentieth century'. Stevens exhibited a 'sardonic eye', 'lack of reverence for outdated traditions' and 'posture of calculated disrespect' which Brian would have found refreshingly in sympathy with his own views.[123]

Together they constructed a plan for a book that would discuss issues which the legal profession had considered sacrosanct, and show how badly served the public were by this 'least adequate' of all the social services, which remained based on an outdated and now inappropriate historical tradition. Stevens had already arranged to spend 1963 as a Visiting Lecturer in the Law Department at the LSE, and he applied to the SSRC and the Rockefeller Foundation for additional research funding. They found enough to pay for a few months of a research assistant's time. They employed an LSE law graduate, Rosalind Brooke, who had also taken a course with Brian in Social Administration. A former head girl at the English boarding school Benenden, she had an upper-class demeanour, which in some ways matched Brian's own. Some members of staff at the LSE, however, felt uncomfortable at her persistent attempts to 'make a good man' of Brian.

What made Brian and Stevens' study unique was the integration of strong historical context with rigorous social science methodology. They conducted (often together) over 400 interviews with judges, lawyers and academics to complement the detailed archival surveys. Many useful discussions were held at Brian's home, over dinners, when he brought together old friends such as Geoffrey Howe with his more recent political colleagues such as Tony Crosland. Stevens returned to Yale in 1964 and they sent each other chapter drafts. Stevens enjoyed working with Brian, impressed that his writing was not only prolific, but also near perfect at first draft. They decided to split the research into two books.

Their first joint book, *Lawyers and the Courts: a sociological study of the English legal system, 1750–1965*, published in 1967, was the essential historical precursor to their contemporary policy attack: 'In this field, history repeats itself – *ad nauseam*. But we thought it right to tell the story in full, in order to expose the whole graveyard of rejected reforms.'[124] It was 'groundbreaking, pioneering, original, innovative, well-researched, refreshing, inspirational and highly readable'.[125] It exposed how little legal education the legal profession actually had – most lawyers and virtually all superior court judges had learned their law through practice, not a university degree. As Anthony Sampson put it in his popular book, *The Anatomy of Britain*:

> The Law still clings to its old fashioned authority and prestige, rather than to interest itself in the exciting developments of society. The Law, more than any other profession, is imprisoned in its own myths and shibboleths, and while the benchers preserve their traditions, and the solicitors tie up their thick paper in pink

tape, their protected world has become increasingly irrelevant to the great corporate world outside.[126]

The reaction to *Lawyers and the Courts* was predictably mixed: some saw it as 'the most important study of the legal system, and in particular of the profession, to appear in this country for many years'.[127] The Bar Council, having previously welcomed Brian's proposal for a collaborative study on the social background of judges, now withdrew its permission.[128] Members of the legal profession, including Brian's own brother Lionel, were bemused by the book's focus on financial aspects of legal practice (ungentlemanly), its contextualisation of law with politics, its suggestion that law was a social science and its popular style. It was 'insufficiently deferential' and written by an ex-pat legal academic and a young socialist social scientist. The scale and pace of the reforms they proposed were touted as a direct threat to wider English traditions and society. The sub-title 'A sociological study' was equally disturbing and confusing, and with hindsight, both Brian and Stevens regretted giving their critics this easy target, which allowed them to say the book was reductive or mono-causal, and to ignore its thorough analysis. In fact, the book drew on strong English research traditions, emulating the reformist approach of Chartists and Fabians. The reaction from the legal profession was so strong that Stevens was told that he would never get an academic job in England.[129]

The second book, *In search of justice*, published a year later in 1968, advocated creating a commission to consider whether the public had fair access to the legal system, and whether it should be self-policing:

> We are taught to have a confident faith in British justice. We learn at school that all men are equal before the law.... We are brought up to respect the laws of England, to trust the integrity of its lawyers and to revere the impartiality of its judges.... This book questions the complacency of some of these assumptions about the law in England. We argue that there are some who never obtain justice and others who obtain it only after a struggle lasting several years or at considerable financial sacrifice. We do not suggest that judges or lawyers are dishonest or corrupt.... The faults of our system lie deeper.[130]

In search of justice came out in the same week as Michael Zander's *Lawyers and the Public Interest: a study in restrictive practices*.[131] Zander was a colleague of Brian's at the LSE (in the Law Department), and the two books together helped to stimulate further public debate on how the legal profession might begin the process of reform. Brian sent copies of the book to colleagues such as Geoffrey Howe – his Cambridge friend who was now a QC and budding Conservative politician. The reaction to *In search of justice* was similar to that of *Lawyers and the Courts*. Reviews in the legal press attacked its 'misconstruction of motives and disregard of realities' and suggested that research into the English legal system 'requires tact' and should 'avoid hurt feelings as much as possible'.[132] In the mainstream press verdicts were wide-ranging. Louis Blom-Cooper's review in the *Observer* was titled 'The Indictment of a Profession', and talked of the book being 'brimful of great good sense'.[133] *The Listener's* review, 'The bar at the Bar', extensively misrepresented their points. It was judged by Brian 'rather nasty', but he wrote to his publisher Charles Clarke that although he would be quite happy to fit in with any action he had in mind, 'my general inclination is to ignore this type of criticism'.[134] William Plowden, Professor of Politics and Modern History at the LSE, writing in *Book World*, summed up the tone of much of the criticism of Brian and Stevens' proposals: 'But perhaps modernity, by itself, is not always relevant. It is also the task of the law to express the collective judgement of society in imposing sanctions – and to do this in a way that commands general respect. If the society concerned is still in many ways a traditional one, respect may well depend on some of the traditional flummery which the authors deplore. The High Court judge asking "Who are the Beatles?" or the courts bringing their full majesty to bear on the inoffensive pot smoker may look frankly ridiculous; but one may still feel that – regrettably maybe – in England the bank robber and spy at least do call for the full wig and Oxford accent.'[135]

The positive legacy of these two books was seen (after a considerable interval) in better training for judges, an expansion of the legal aid system and other reforms. Their more radical ideas, such as removing the process of divorce from the courts, have not been adopted.

(Only) Just Men

Somehow, alongside his huge academic and political workload, Brian found time for some entrepreneurial activity. Quite why he did this is not clear, but it perhaps reflects the deep-seated concern with money which he had inherited as part of the Abel Smith banking family, and especially his experience of being the 'spare' not the heir to their branch's own relatively modest family trust. Lionel, having inherited at 21, had regularly given Brian what he called 'Wendover Windfalls', named after his Lordship of the Manor of Wendover in

Buckinghamshire, which came with the Trust. Through his university years these gifts helped Brian to cover his tailors' bills and holiday costs. He had also had his own family inheritance from Uncle Harold that helped him to buy his first leasehold property, 34a Elizabeth Street, in 1960. Yet he remained conscious of Lionel's relative wealth and success, which allowed him to retire from the Bar in 1965 and move from South Eaton Place to Groves, a house he had renovated near Peasmarsh in Sussex, where he farmed sheep.

Lionel also helped Brian in 1965 to establish a men's clothing business, called Just Men.[136] Brian's motivation for this was not only entrepreneurial but also personal. His relationship with John Sarbutt was happy and stable. John's acting career was successful, and he had regular work. Brian and John had been together for five years, but Brian still felt a loyalty and sense of duty towards one of his former partners, Charles Schuller. By creating Just Men, he was able to give him a steady job to replace the temporary ones he had held after leaving the Royal Ballet. This was especially important now that Schuller had married and started a family.[137] Schuller managed the first shop in Tryon Street, just off the King's Road. Brian got great pleasure from going on regular buying trips to Italy to source suits and accessories, and it quickly became known for its high quality and sense of style. Further shops were opened in Beauchamp Place and in Jermyn Street at the heart of London's exclusive tailoring district.

Just Men, or as Brian sometimes referred to it, 'Only Just Men', was of its time, offering 'with it' and 'way out' high fashion. Friends such as Milton Grundy saw it as an upmarket version of Carnaby Street, priced for the King's Road set. Its faintly outrageous items such as see-through black shirts, were popular with both gay and straight men.[138] At the King's Road flagship store there was a resident tailor, Nicky Kahn, and, in the 1970s, a barbers shop. Regular customers included Roy Strong, who bought there the brown cotton velvet jacket and waistcoat later chosen for display by the V&A gallery to mark his directorship. For him Just Men reflected the 'huge explosion of dandyism between 1965 and the oil crisis of 1974'.[139] Pete Townshend and Keith Moon from The Who helped to boost its cult status when photographed buying their suits in Just Men in 1966. Warren Beatty and his then girlfriend Julie Christie were also regulars, and Joan Collins bought her jeans there. Along with other King's Road shops like Lord John, Take 6, John Michael, Mary Quant and Biba, Just Men was at the forefront of mass market fashion. In 1967 the company diversified into Just Men (Tailors) Ltd and Just Men (Shirts) Ltd, and sales were now over £60,000 pa.

While Charles Schuller had day-to-day responsibility for the shops, Brian maintained a close interest. John was also involved, and went with Brian on some of the buying trips to Italy. The success of the shops also brought headaches. They were over-staffed by Schuller, and there were chronic high levels of theft. On one occasion items of clothes were found hidden in a dustbin at the rear of one of the shops, waiting for staff to collect them when their shifts had finished. There were the occasional fashion disasters, such as the hundreds of suits chosen by John which failed to sell. But, despite these issues, Just Men thrived, giving employment to one of Brian's close friends, and another source of income for himself. New branches later opened in Cheltenham and in New York and even a short-lived one in Philadelphia.

In 1967 John got a small part in Tony Richardson's classic film, *The Charge of the Light Brigade*. Brian went out to visit him during the filming in Turkey several times during that summer. John had been 'adopted' by Trevor Howard (who played Lord Cardigan) and his wife Helen Cherry (they had no children of their own). On non-filming days they toured the Turkish countryside in their car, always taking John with them and Brian too during his visits. Other actors on set included John Gielgud, Vanessa Redgrave and David Hemmings. John's farming background worked to his advantage, allowing him to use his excellent riding skills for his character as one of the British cavalry during scenes for the ill-fated 1854 battle of Balaclava against the Russians in the Crimean War.

After the disjointed summer of 1967, John persuaded Brian to buy a country retreat where they could relax and indulge their shared love of gardening. They opted for Kent, to be within an easy drive of Lionel's farm at Peasmarsh in Sussex. At Westwell near Ashford they found a modest house called Tanglewood, set in nearly 12 acres. The plan was to spend all available weekends there, creating a garden and entertaining friends. It was only 60 miles from their London home, and John would collect Brian from the LSE on Friday evening for the drive down. The modern house was small for the size of the land, which included paddocks and fields. Several months after they bought it they discovered there was an abandoned horse, living off the grass in one of the paddocks. John was delighted, and took to riding to the neighbouring village to do their shopping. At Tanglewood they could see their closest friends, especially those with whom John felt at ease, and who shared his love of gardening. Regular visitors included Peter and Ruth Townsend, Richard and Kay Titmuss, Bob and Jennifer Pinker, and Alistair and Camilla Sampson, whom Brian had known since Cambridge, and who was now a successful antiques dealer. Political friends were also welcome, including Geoffrey and Elspeth Howe. They became good friends with 'the Peters' – Peter Knight and Peter Garden – who lived nearby. Tanglewood was the epitome of Brian and John's relationship. It flourished with their mutual love, respect and support. Brian involved John in as much of his life as he felt he could comfortably get away with before the legalisation of homosexual acts in 1967. He was determined not to make compromises for his sexuality. Their domestic lives in London and at Tanglewood were little different from those of other long-term couples, except perhaps for Brian's hectic work schedule. This was about to become even busier, and could only be sustained by having John as his practical and emotional support.

8

Values: 1968–70

Policy from the inside: advising Richard Crossman

Health enquiries

AEGIS and the Ely scandal

Restructuring the NHS

The LSE, 1967–69

The end of the Titmice

'The Poor Get Poorer Under Labour'

In 1969, the editor of *New Society* remarked: "Shouldn't one talk about the Cautious Sixties, rather than Swinging Sixties?" Given the increasing concern with declining standards and law and order in the late 1960s, perhaps the "Anxious Sixties" would be just as appropriate. (Peter Thompson, 1993)[1]

In 1968 Richard Crossman became Secretary of State for the new Department of Health and Social Security (DHSS). He invited Brian to become his special adviser – one of the earliest such posts within British government. It was recognition not only of Brian's academic expertise but also of his political usefulness and integrity. The part-time position gave Brian a powerful base to help steer Labour government policy on health and social welfare issues. This chapter looks back to some of his earlier informal expert adviser work with the Health Minister Kenneth Robinson, linked to concerns about the costs and structure of the NHS. Brian was also at the centre of an emerging pressure group, AEGIS, which used the Ely Hospital scandal of 1967 to push for better treatment of the elderly and mental health patients. During his political secondment, Brian retained a part-time position at the LSE, but found himself immersed in institutional and personal conflicts, including the student riots and the breakdown of the relationship between Richard Titmuss and Peter Townsend. The outcome of their poverty research project risked undermining the Labour government which they had actively supported since 1964, and caused an irrevocable split in the 'Titmice'.

Policy from the inside: advising Richard Crossman

Richard Crossman was finally appointed as social security 'overlord' in April 1968, after the position had passed quickly through the hands of Patrick Gordon Walker and Michael Stewart following Douglas Houghton's departure from the Cabinet in January 1967. He had been in the Cabinet since the formation of Wilson's government in 1964, initially as Minister of Housing, which immediately exposed his prejudices:

> ... already I realise the tremendous effort it requires not to be taken over by the Civil Service, My Minister's room is like a padded cell, and in certain ways I am like a person who is suddenly certified lunatic and put safely into this great, vast room, cut off from real life and surrounded by male and female attendants.... Of course they don't behave quite like nurses because the Civil Service is profoundly deferential – "Yes, Minister! No, Minister! If you wish it, Minister!"[2]

This distrust of his civil servants underpinned the whole of Crossman's ministerial career.

Crossman had chaired the Ministerial Sub-committee on Earnings-related Pensions since February 1967 through which discussions continued on the rates of returns that contributions would generate. It was suggested that there should be two earning 'bands', the main one generating a pension benefit of 60 per cent of earnings, and the upper band generating only 25 per cent. What became known as the 60/25 benefit formula formed the basis for all pensions policy discussions for the rest of the parliamentary term. Crossman moved quickly to reconnect with the LSE team, also known as the 'Pensions Circus', to form 'The Lord President's Group of Academic Experts'. His Whitehall officials dimly viewed this as a 'last-minute "think-in"' and ensured that they attended armed with the best of briefings.[3] Titmuss had been called to a meeting at Crossman's Privy Council Office on 8 March.[4] Soon after, Brian and Titmuss began to attend regular meetings, along with the Hungarian-born economists Thomas Balogh and Nicholas Kaldor (nicknamed Buda and Pest). This group became Crossman's main source of policy advice, as he had 'stood down' the Jarrett Committee.

Brian played an active role in the Lord President's Group, providing policy notes for Crossman throughout the summer of 1968.[5] His role as adviser had been informal, and if one looks back, he had effectively been Crossman's adviser since he joined the Working Party on Security and Old Age in 1955, after he and Townsend had published their Fabian pamphlet *New Pensions for the Old*. His new allegiance to Crossman did not, however, stop his speaking out against the Labour government for their inability to develop a coordinated policy for the social services. In the BBC Radio 3 programme 'Personal View', broadcast in May 1968, he was typically blunt: 'The Government is certainly at its lowest ebb. Chastised by Cecil King and the *Mirror* newspapers, quarrelling with the trade unions and abandoned by many of its former supporters in last week's local elections. Why has the government got in such a mess?... Part of the reason is, of course, the economic situation. But there is another, perhaps subsidiary, reason which should not be overlooked. And it is about that which I want to talk tonight. It's the lack of a co-ordinated policy for the social services.'[6] Brian saw himself as the person to correct that situation.

In Britain elected politicians have traditionally been supported in the process of governing by civil servants – the non-political permanent Crown employees whose task is to implement the policies agreed by Parliament. Following the Northcote-Trevelyan Report of 1854, the civil service developed a professional culture, with rigorous selection procedures and hierarchies. Senior civil servants – mandarins – became valued for their generalist qualities, rather than specific technical ability in any one area of government. By the early 20th century the civil service was firmly entrenched in the British establishment, and managed a more complex set of state functions. What the civil servants could not do, however, was to initiate policy. This task remained firmly in the control of the politicians who increasingly engaged with a variety of external experts. Early examples of this include Lloyd George's 'garden suburb' of temporary advisers in 1917 housed in huts behind 10 Downing Street, and the formation of the Economic Advisory Council in 1930 to ensure that governments had access to the highest quality advisers.[7] But until the Wilson government of 1964 the employment of such advisers was rare. Although Wilson's ministers never employed more than a dozen or so special advisers (a small number when compared with the 100+ of 21st-century governments) they crucially represented a sea-change in parliamentary attitudes to policy formation. In part they reflected a growing concern about the calibre of advice available from the civil service, which continued to value abstract intelligence rather than specialist skills and knowledge.[8] This had been articulated in 1959 in *The Establishment*, a collection of essays edited by a former civil servant, Hugh Thomas. The economist (and one of Wilson's closest advisers) Thomas Balogh, used his essay, 'The Apotheosis of the Dilettante', to provide a withering critique of British mandarins and to set an agenda for change. He was also a member of the Fabian Society's Working Party that produced a blueprint for reform in 1964.[9] It was not until 1968 and the Fulton Report that the civil service got the overhaul Balogh proposed.[10]

It has been suggested that, along with the generalist issue of the civil service, Wilson saw their institutional obstructiveness as a justification for bringing in outside experts. Another possible explanation is that the 13-year period out of government had left the Labour Party with few people who had experience of ministerial office and who knew how to effectively use the civil service.[11] As the number of special advisers employed increased, the role became formalised. An implicit assumption was that they would be sympathetic to the political party that appointed them, but the extent of their politicisation varied. Peter Shore, Head of the Labour Party Research Department between 1959 and 1964, thought that special advisers should be the 'guardians of the manifesto'.[12] Wilson later sketched a list of duties that he thought special advisers could provide, some of them more political and expertise-based than others. It included 'sieving' government papers for their ministers, 'devilling' (checking facts and opinions outside Westminster), preparing 'think pieces' on potential policy issues, assisting with policy development, liaising with the political party, writing speeches and general research.[13] The first qualification remained, however, their undivided personal loyalty to their minister – their 'sheer availability' and role as a personal confidant made them uniquely valuable.[14]

Brian's long and active involvement in the Fabian Society and Labour Party meant that his research interests and expertise in health and social welfare were politically coloured. Indeed, his open socialist stance had denied him funding by the Nuffield Foundation in 1955 who judged him not impartial enough for academic research. It is interesting to consider why he was not appointed as a special adviser to Kenneth Robinson in 1964, however. He was on first name terms with him, but maybe he was not yet seen as sufficiently senior to be of use? Maybe the Minister (and Ministry) of Health was not deemed sufficiently important to justify the expense of appointing a special adviser? By 1968, when Crossman was appointed Secretary of State to the newly created Department of Health and Social Security, the circumstances were different.

Crossman, in a Fabian lecture in 1963, had already made plain his admiration for bringing in external expertise to government. He attributed Britain's wartime successes, and its anticipated return to glory, to an 'army of outsiders, uninhibited by civil service procedures ... in the technological revolution to which we are now committed ... we shall permanently need the marriage of established civil service and outside expertise that we developed as a temporary expedient in World War I and perfected in World War II'.[15] Crossman's diaries reveal the extent of his reliance on Brian, and his limited ability to work with civil servants.[16] His biographers have tended to paint a rather hagiographical picture of his late flourishing in government, as he had held relatively insignificant roles before 1968.[17] More recent analyses have questioned whether he really had the ability to fulfil such a demanding role at the DHSS. He appears to have been more reactive on policy issues than his diaries suggest.[18] Theakston goes further: '... he simply had no idea how to use the civil service machine properly in order to reach his political goals. His combative and contemptuous attitude antagonised his officials; he misinterpreted their actions and motives. He was amazingly ignorant of some of the basic features of the Whitehall set up....'[19] Perhaps also his acknowledged weakness in economics made it essential to have an economist on hand to give both credibility and status to his policies. This is a trend which has proliferated since the Second World War on a global scale – most countries have dramatically increased their employment of economists, often valued for their common sense, judgement and wisdom as much as their technical abilities.[20]

Following an official invitation in May 1968 to be a senior adviser to Crossman, extended negotiations began with the LSE so that they retained Brian's services on Wednesdays, Thursdays and Fridays. Brian stressed to Sir Walter Adams, the Director, that the School would benefit financially over and above the cost of buying in a replacement lecturer. He indicated how he would cover his research commitments. The Law and Poverty Survey funded by the Ford Foundation would be written up during the summer with Zander; the Ministry of Health study of nursing, which Dr MacGuire was doing under Brian's supervision, was nearly completed; the study of pathology services funded by the Ministry was co-directed with Hilary Rose, who took principal responsibility; and Sally Sainsbury was the principal researcher on the study of disability financed by the National Fund for Research into Crippling Diseases and did not need much supervision. The Poverty

Survey, funded by the Joseph Rowntree Memorial Trust and jointly conducted with Peter Townsend, would prove a bigger problem. The fieldwork was half-complete, with the analysis designed for the first report and the programming completed, but another six months of fieldwork remained: 'Undoubtedly this will mean placing a larger burden on Professor Townsend but he is prepared to shoulder this.'[21]

After security vetting, Brian began working for Crossman on a half-time basis in September 1968. He seemed quite relieved to be able to give up his council membership in CPAG: 'I am very anxious to release myself from as many outside commitments as possible and it is much more comfortable and time saving to be able to inform bodies that one cannot rather than one will not.'[22] In June he resigned as Treasurer of the Fabian Society, but put a lot of effort into finding a suitable replacement. In October he also resigned as a governor of St Thomas' Hospital. It isn't clear whether this was to prevent potential conflicts of interest, but the Clerk to the Governors, Bryan McSwiney, sent a handwritten letter, thanking Brian for his services over the past 11 years, and acknowledging his very significant impact on the development of the hospital, especially the re-building project.[23] John Prideaux, chair of the Board, also wrote, expressing the hope that 'whilst formally you will no longer be a Governor, we may be able to call upon your advice from time to time, and that perhaps your membership of the Board should be treated rather being in abeyance, to be resuscitated at a time when your present commitments allow'.[24] Brian was relieved, however, that the civil service rules allowed him to continue as a director of the limited company for his chain of men's clothes shops, Just Men.

Despite initial concerns that there would be sufficient work to keep him occupied in his new room at Adam Street, he quickly became essential to a number of Crossman's activities. After signing the Official Secrets Act he was given civil service clearance to see all ministerial red boxes, and he provided briefs on a wide range of issues that appeared in Cabinet papers. Much of his time was spent in briefing Crossman on the political implications of his decisions, offering alternative viewpoints to those provided by his civil servants, and drafting speeches and White Papers. Here his ability to write quickly and fluently was particularly valuable. Meetings with Crossman fell into a routine – either breakfast with him at 8.00am at 9 Vincent Square, or late afternoon/early evening at the House of Commons. Occasionally they would meet for supper at Crossman's club, The Garrick.[25]

Robin Wendt, who was Crossman's Parliamentary Private Secretary at the time, witnessed Brian's indispensability to Crossman. Both Wendt and others viewed him as a *de facto* additional civil servant. He was given the nominal civil service rank of Deputy Secretary – the number two position in the DHSS civil service hierarchy after Clifford Jarrett, the Permanent Secretary, and Sir George Godber, who also ranked as a Permanent Secretary, but who managed the medical civil service parallel hierarchy. Brian knew 'instinctively' how to handle civil servants and developed a cordial and happy liaison with them. Because he was constantly at Crossman's side he was very highly regarded, both by civil servants and outsiders. His upper-class pedigree and connections with the royal family were also well-known in the DHSS headquarters, and helped to consolidate his establishment image.[26] The ministerial pace was relentless, but Brian absolutely revelled in this closeness to the seat of power. His loyalty to Crossman during this period was unquestioned. He prioritised his availability at the DHSS above all other aspects of his life, from fitting his holidays into Crossman's holiday schedules, to waking at 5.00am most mornings in anticipation of the first pre-breakfast telephone call. His close Canadian friends, David Blewett and Arthur Sheps, were living in the upstairs flat at 34a Elizabeth Street in the late 1960s. They would often also be woken by the telephone ringing, and the sound of Brian sorting out the day's agenda with Crossman.[27]

What made Brian invaluable to Crossman in these two years was not only his academic expertise and ability to stand up to his minister's bullying style, but also his extensive network of contacts. Brian's archives contain a wealth of correspondence with NHS officials, members of the public and other academics, all keen to access the Secretary of State for the DHSS. Soon after his appointment, in October 1968, he arranged for Crossman to visit the Wessex Regional Hospital Board who wished to discuss the relationship between the NHS and postgraduate medical education. John Revans, their dynamic chair, expressed their gratitude to Brian: 'I think we took advantage of every minute of the time made available to us, we would have liked to have him for a week to have shown him more of our problems and how we meet them but, clearly with his responsibilities this would have been asking too much.... The Lord President [Crossman] had some exciting proposals to make and I would like to reiterate that if there are any pilot studies to be undertaken in the Hospital Services we down here would like the opportunity of being considered at an early date. With many thanks for letting us have him on our own....'[28]

Brian was consulted on potential members for Royal Commissions and RHBs, and smoothed Crossman's relations with his senior civil servants.[29] Through Brian's academic position, Crossman had access to sets of statistics on health and social welfare of unparalleled quality to inform his policy development. Brian's friendship with people of the status of Wilbur Cohen, US Secretary of Health, Education and Welfare, ensured this knowledge network was truly international. He also privately invited academic colleagues from the LSE and the LSHTM to comment on pertinent issues that appeared in Cabinet papers, and fed their comments back to Crossman.[30] At times, his position also allowed him to plead on behalf of acquaintances, such as the social psychologist Michael Schofield, who was called on to resign from the Government Advisory Committee on Drug Dependence because he published his personal views in an article.[31] Crucially, Brian also offered a critical extra-Westminster perspective on public values in what was seen as an 'affluent' society. This was central to Crossman's understanding of public expectations and experiences of the NHS and other aspects of the British welfare state in policy development.

Although Brian and the Pensions Circus provided a strong source of external policy advice, Crossman could not ignore internal and very legitimate policy interference from his junior ministers. Judith Hart, Peggy Herbison's replacement as Minister for Social Security, in July 1967 brought a fresh review of the policies that Crossman had intermittently championed since 1957: 'I have been examining the implications of the present planning assumptions in the field of social security generally. They are unsatisfactory.' She proposed to re-focus on 'the pockets of poverty which have recently and rightly become the focus of pressure groups, and, therefore of the press and public attention'.[32] Crossman found her proposals to make the scheme 'more redistributive' disquieting, and not in tune with either his ideas or those of the DHSS officials.[33] In the event, Hart was promoted out of Crossman's ministerial team in November 1968 to become Paymaster General. Yet her comments indicated the government's sensitivity to public opinion, and recognition of the success of pressure groups. Although unidentified by Hart, she undoubtedly was referencing the Child Poverty Action Group, which had generated a constant stream of publicity since its formation in 1965, much of it before September 1968 from Brian's pen. The government had in fact commissioned a survey of public views on social welfare in 1968. Beveridge had commissioned a similar one in 1942 that was carried out by G.D.H. Cole and the Nuffield Reconstruction Unit when planning his report on social insurance and allied services. The 1968 survey, however, was kept secret. The handful of officials who knew about it were asked not to make its existence known. When José Harris questioned Brian about it in 1973, he replied '… as far as I remember Dick Crossman who seems to have leaked nearly everything that happened when he was in office has apparently forgotten to leak this yet. So I must ask you not to use this information. I told Howard [Glennerster?] in confidence. You can of course word your statement cautiously, eg "No publically acknowledged survey of this kind has been undertaken since [Beveridge]".'[34]

Despite the rapid turnover in his ministerial team, Crossman's civil servants produced a White Paper – *National Superannuation and Social Insurance* – in January 1969.[35] This scheme had changed considerably since the Titmice's 1950s proposals. The two-tier benefit system had been replaced by a fully graded scheme incorporating a redistributive element. The plan had been scaled down from the 1957 draft – originally employers would have had to make contributions on employees' earning up to four times the average wage – in the White Paper a more modest one-and-a-half times average earnings was used as the 'ceiling'. It contained proposals for 'abatement' – a contracting-out scheme specifically designed to appease the powerful private insurance industry – going as far as proposing a 'partnership with the occupational schemes'.[36] It was too late in the political day to return to the strict contracting-out conditions that Titmuss had advocated in 1956, in his personal battle to 'break the power of private insurance'.[37] It also recognised that by the mid-1960s over half the working population already contributed towards some form of occupational pension, and bowed to significant pressure not only from the insurance industry lobbyists but also the trade unions.[38] Funding for each element was to be ring-fenced: a national superannuation fund and a social fund. This was an appeasement to the perceived investment risks that had beleaguered the 1957 national superannuation plan. As Paul Bridgen has observed, most of the framework for the 1969 White Paper was in place by the middle of 1966, and it bore the hallmarks of the almost autonomous 1964 Whitehall inter-departmental committee of officials rather than Labour ideologists.[39]

Tony Lynes, one of the main architects of the scheme, hastened to stress not its novelty but its re-positioning role: 'It is twelve years since proposals of this kind were first put forward by the Labour Party, and what was once a pioneering scheme will now do little more than bring Britain into line with our European neighbours in the provision made for income maintenance in retirement.'[40] Reaction to the White Paper was mixed. *The Spectator* viewed the scheme as a 'series of hoaxes, woven together in a system of immense and totally unnecessary complexity, simply to try and persuade people that the higher taxes are not really higher taxes at all'.[41] Arthur Seldon, writing in the *Sunday Telegraph*, remained pessimistic: 'People in a private scheme are more likely to feel they are paying for something *out of* their earnings; compulsory contributors to a State scheme would regard the additional contribution as a tax *deducted from* their earnings, especially as it will be paid with PAYE.'[42] For others, the plan was not radical enough: 'Was it really not possible to introduce a more radically redistributive scheme with some flat rate element in the benefits?', *The Guardian* lamented.[43] Tony Lynes, who followed the press assessments, put his finger on the underlying issue: 'It is perhaps unfair to criticise *The Economist* too harshly for an off the cuff reaction to the White Paper which, when examined at leisure, turns out to be impractical nonsense. In fairness one must admit that *The Economist* showed an infinitely better grasp of the issues than did *The Times*, which carried a leader (29 January 1969) consisting largely of fanciful arguments so divorced from reality as to suggest political motives unworthy of a once great newspaper.'[44] Titmuss, as expected, made plain his opposition to this appeasement to the private pensions industry in an article in *New Society*.[45]

Crossman found it a struggle to produce the White Paper, and he took until September 1969 to make crucial decisions on issues such as abatement. During his period as 'overlord' he had felt at odds with the civil servants who were supposed to support his policy, recording in his diary: 'In the course of all these consultations I have found (it's a sad thing to have to admit) that my own personal position had been fatally undermined. I am fighting both the Ministry [of Social Security] and the Treasury in support of a properly funded scheme.'[46] After his promotion to social security 'overlord' in April 1968 he was acutely conscious that time was running out for national superannuation. It required a swift progression from the White Paper (January 1969) to the publication of the Bill in time to get the legislation on the Statute books before the expected general election in October 1970. A second White Paper in November 1969 showed how the government was prepared to bend over backwards to appease the private insurance industry: there would be no inspectorate or central registry.[47] Brian's constant presence at Crossman's side during the last few months of negotiations was critical. It left him exhausted, and in need of his annual skiing trip, which he managed to ring-fence from 27 December to 5 January at Davos with Milton Grundy and his partner Viacheslav Atroshenko and his Canadian friends David Blewett and Arthur Sheps.[48]

The Bill went through Committee very easily in May 1970, partly because it reflected some of the Conservatives' own aspirations for pensions policy. It was only a few weeks away from receiving Royal

Assent when Wilson's Cabinet took the decision to bring forward the general election from October to June. Crossman was devastated. In his retrospective assessment, *The Politics of Pensions* published in 1972, he noted: 'it fell, totally … fifteen years of work were wasted'. But, he acknowledged, 'The great changes in British society have not been thought up either in the House of Commons or the political parties. They have all been brought into politics from outside by individuals or pressure groups running their own crusades outside politics and impinging on politicians who are the hucksters, the mediators. Politicians make good by borrowing ideas.'[49]

Health enquiries

On returning to office in 1964, Labour inherited a National Health Service that was in the process of considerable rejuvenation. Enoch Powell had launched an ambitious Ten Year Hospital Plan in 1962, to replace the essentially pre-war (and much of it pre-First World War) fabric with fit-for-purpose facilities. The plan epitomised the government, the medical profession and the public's narrow gaze on hospitalised medicine, the strongest element within the 'tripartite NHS'. Brian had been at the epicentre of the 1953–56 study by Guillebaud into the apparent rising cost of the NHS, and his research had helped to disprove the myth that it was inefficient and over-funded. Since then he had maintained a close involvement with healthcare, serving on the Lambeth HMC (1956–61), the Chelsea and Kensington HMC (1961–62), the South West RHB (1956–63), as a governor at St Thomas' Hospital (1957–68) and at the Maudsley Hospital and Institute of Psychiatry (1963–67). He had also published, to widespread acclaim, a comprehensive history of hospitals, which drew on his inside knowledge of the NHS.[50] During this period there was increasing criticism of the quality and quantity of NHS provision, as expressed through the emergence of the term the 'national health lottery' in 1966.[51]

Kenneth Robinson was Labour's keen but constrained Minister of Health from 1964 to 1967. He had no Cabinet seat, and relied on Douglas Houghton, as Chair of the Social Services Committee, to plead his case for increased NHS budgets and improved facilities. Robinson had appointed Brian to his Advisory Committee (sometimes called Advisory Group or Study Group) on the Long-term Development of the NHS. This was established in July 1965, and comprised senior Ministry officials and external experts and academics: George Godber, Professor W.J.H. Butterfield, Sir Edward Collingwood, R. Huws Jones,

Sir Peter Medawar, Professor M. Roth and Miss M. Scott Wright. It met regularly, if not frequently, until 1968, but 'exercised very little influence'.[52] This was partly because Robinson himself set tight limits on what it could investigate: he was happy for them to develop ideas for administration based on the Porritt report, but not to consider anything that might involve wider (and extra-manifesto) reorganisation of the NHS.[53] As Charles Webster, the official historian of the NHS, puts it: 'Robinson was increasingly swimming against the tide. His negative response towards reorganisation was at odds with the ethos increasingly prevailing in planning circles....Reorganisation overtook co-ordination as a dominant theme in social administration.'[54]

Robinson faced a number of public expectations of his management of the NHS, including the abolition of charges, which he duly announced in December 1964, but which met with strong BMA and Treasury opposition. The Treasury, and the Public Expenditure Survey Committee, were already in the process of tightening the screws on the NHS budget and expansion plans. It demanded efficiency savings and cuts to the Hospital Building Plan (Robinson had to scale down his plans for 134 major reconstructions to 59 and other large schemes from 356 to 318), and a renewed attempt to curb the unrestricted growth of the pharmaceutical industry. Other Labour manifesto commitments, such as introducing an earnings-related pension and social security plan, meant that there was further pressure to raise the flat-rate NHS contribution from National Insurance. The devaluation crisis of November 1967 also triggered demands from the Treasury to re-open previously rejected schemes, such as the introduction of a GP consultation fee, and funding the NHS through compulsory insurance. In the event, Wilson's beleaguered government agreed to reintroduce prescription charges, although there were so many exemptions (up to 40 per cent of the population) that it was difficult to administer and raised less than they hoped (£25 million instead of £50 million).

One major area of concern was the cost to the NHS of pharmaceuticals. This expanded from £52 million in 1957/58 to £90 million in 1963/64. Over the same period the cost per prescription had increased by 122 per cent and the ingredient cost by 170 per cent.[55] Although there was a Voluntary Price Regulation Scheme (VPRS), set up with the pharmaceutical industry in 1957, it was due to expire in June 1964. A three-year extension was agreed, but the Treasury pressed Robinson for a more fundamental solution. The TUC was also expressing dissatisfaction with what it saw as excessive profit levels in the industry, and called for an enquiry to consider nationalising key companies to obtain better prices for the growing numbers of prescription medicines. It highlighted the increasing advertising budgets of pharmaceutical companies, and raised ethical concerns over some of its sales practices. There were other ethical issues emerging too – the recent Thalidomide disaster, and a growing awareness of problems with prescription drug dependency.

Robinson bowed to pressure, and announced the appointment of an investigative committee. It was chaired by Alan, Lord Sainsbury, Chair of the supermarket chain, who had extensive experience of governmental committees. The final line-up, drawn from academia, general practice, law and industry, was announced on 31 May 1965. Brian was one of the 10 appointed.[56] The Committee's terms of reference were: 'to examine the relationship of the pharmaceutical industry in Great Britain with the National Health Service, having regard to the structure of the industry, the commercial policies of the firms comprising it, to pricing and sales promotion practices, to the effects of patents and to the relevance and value of research; and to make recommendations'. Brian had relevant experience: he had been on Henry Cohen's Sub-committee of the Central Health Service Council on Prescribing Statistics between 1960 and 1964 – Cohen had undoubtedly selected him because of his earlier ground-breaking research for the Guillebaud Committee on the cost of the NHS.[57]

The Sainsbury enquiry took longer than expected, and did not produce its report until 28 September 1967.[58] It was deliberately scheduled to follow the White Paper on legislation on the safety of drugs which was published on 7 September 1967.[59] Webster judged the Sainsbury report 'an eccentric and not entirely adequate product'. The Committee had had access to the huge US Senate Sub-committee on Antitrust and Monopoly that had investigated the US situation.[60] The text amounted to only 98 of its 232 pages, and it reprinted the 85-page Government Social Survey Report on Information for the Prescriber to no useful end. Sainsbury suggested a number of new regulation and pricing strategies, but did not find in favour of nationalisation. Its relatively moderate tone (in contrast to the US Senate report) was still radical enough to antagonise the domestic industry. It wanted more accurate evaluations of research and development costs to ensure that these were properly reflected in final product pricing, and greater use of the 1949 Patents Act, which gave the government a 'disregard' option on patents when purchasing for the NHS (Enoch Powell, when Minister of Health, had used this clause to buy cheaper foreign supplies of antibiotics for use in British hospitals in the early 1960s).

The Committee's most significant recommendations were the establishment of a new independent regulatory body to be known as the

Medicines Commission; a new Economic Development Committee for the pharmaceutical industry to consider issues such as the length of patents (currently 16 years); and no further use of brand names for products licensed by the proposed Medicines Commission (they estimated that 14 per cent of the value of NHS sales was promotion expenditure). The Committee even suggested that the Medicines Commission should act as an intermediary between doctors and products to prevent direct marketing. They were less concerned than might have been expected with the issue of profits within the pharmaceutical industry. There was no attempt to define 'reasonable' profit, but some recognition that profits were essential to maintaining Britain's cutting-edge position in research and innovation.

The critics of the pharmaceutical industry, such as the TUC, found the Sainsbury report too timid. Predictably, the industry thought it went too far down the route of government regulation, and rang alarm bells over emigration of top scientists and economic collapse. The DHSS and the Treasury found it 'disappointing and inadequate'.[61] Brian wrote a piece for the *New Statesman*, entitled 'Sainsbury and the Drug Industry', which was published on 6 October. He was scathing of the industry's crude PR campaign: 'The very real contribution of the industry to research has been coated with sentimentality. They are only in it to help mankind! And the whole economics of the industry have been overlaid with calculations of the economic benefits of better drugs – an argument wholly irrelevant to the issue of drug prices. (Should we pay motor manufacturers the value of time saved by travelling faster than on horseback?)'[62] Brian highlighted that the Sainsbury Committee had not been allowed to investigate the essence of the problem – doctors prescribing any drug they wished on the NHS: 'If Kenneth Robinson is really under pressure to save money on drugs to spend on other health needs, it might be better to do so by limiting this freedom.... Most countries with comparable health schemes allow doctors to give *free* drugs only from a limited list.' He also expanded on the logic behind the Committee's recommendations on reducing patent life and brand advertising: 'Price competition therefore is what the industry fears most of all. The more competition there is, the less need for the Ministry to control prices – the less need for what the industry calls state control! ...The root of the problem is that product competition with a 16-year patent life and an unlimited brand-name life is not enough.' He finished by highlighting the wider implications: 'But the Sainsbury report is not just about money; its most important recommendations are vital to the health of the nation. Modern drugs are too dangerous to allow expensively-trained doctors to be exposed to drug literature and pressure salesmen, both indirectly paid for by the taxpayer. This is a question of principle and the government would have no difficulty in explaining to the public what is really at stake.'

Despite Brian's bullish optimism that the Sainsbury Committee had got it right, when the government commissioned further analyses of its findings, the economic conclusions began to appear weak: the Committee had not considered such issues as long-term profit trends, risk levels or profitability of comparable industries. Further, if the pharmaceutical industry was forced into publishing its 'standard cost returns' (how much profit was made by each drug unit over the raw material costs) and into dropping brand names, it would give a competitive advantage to foreign producers. As Webster concluded, the long-term impact of the Sainsbury Committee on pharmaceutical policy was minimal: most of its novel recommendations were watered down, and most would have happened anyway in due course: 'The Sainsbury tree was therefore destined to bear only scantlings'.[63] Robinson, embarrassed by the outcome of this enquiry, delayed issuing the government's formal response statement until June 1968, and even then prevaricated on key decisions such as the branding of medicines.[64]

AEGIS and the Ely scandal

Brian had accepted an appointment to the boards of the Maudsley Hospital and the associated Institute of Psychiatry in 1963. Established in 1923 in Southwark, South London, this became one of Britain's leading centres for the treatment of mental illness, and for training specialist staff. In 1965 the hospital and institute merged with the infamous Bethlem Hospital to form a specialist hospital board. Brian initially refused the invitation to stay on the new board for another three years, suggesting to its Chair, Viscount Sandon, that he wished to concentrate his work at St Thomas' Hospital: 'I have decided on the latter because I feel that change is most needed and is most important in the undergraduate teaching hospitals. I feel I have not been pulling my weight at the Maudsley as a Governor, and it is quite wrong for one to continue to occupy a place if one cannot really give the time to it.'[65] Robinson wrote personally to Brian to ask him to extend his term of office. Brian initially refused but eventually 'yielded to pressure'.[66] In the event, he offered his resignation again to Sandon in November 1966: 'Since I last tried to resign I have been loaded with a lot of other things. The Minister of Health, after twisting my arm about Maudsley, then put me on the Sainsbury Committee, and now I'm getting immersed in the committee structure here [LSE] and have to take over the administration of our department in a year and a half's time. I am also due to go on sabbatical leave from next April. Thus I cannot see how I can be of any help in view of these commitments.... Unfortunately the job one is paid to do has to come before all one's voluntary work – however important and interesting.'[67] This time Robinson reluctantly accepted his resignation: 'In your various capacities you are already doing so much work for the health service – much of it I confess with my encouragement – that I am sure you are quite right to concentrate your efforts by retrenching a little.'

Despite his retrenchment, Brian was still seen as at the heart of the British NHS. In May 1967 he was featured in *Hospital Management*, in a conversation piece with the journalist Stanley Hill. In response to the question what would he do to improve the NHS, if he were Minister of Health, Brian had a ready checklist, which included increased funding; a re-organisation of the service at the local level to bring the management of hospitals and GPs and local health authorities under a common local administration; smaller hospital management committees 'more closely resembling a board of directors'; and, parallel to the management committees, committees of patients, providing a constant lobby to present the viewpoint and interests of patients to the official committee. This last point he had presciently lined up with the comment: 'there is too little, rather than too much discussion of health service matters.... Most hospital authorities are reluctant to show their black spots on television. I think they should co-operate in every way with programmes of this kind, to bring home to the taxpayer what still needs to be done. Instead there is something amounting to a "conspiracy of silence" which is not only undesirable in a public service, but also seriously inimical to its interests.'[68]

Only a few months after Brian gave that interview, a major health scandal was revealed at Ely Hospital in Cardiff. In August 1967 the *News of the World* published serious allegations about the inhumane conditions and procedures within this long-stay mental health institution, which had been given to them by one of its nursing assistants. Robinson was dismayed and genuinely shocked. He was viewed as a progressive and well-informed minister, with a keen awareness of medicine and health: his father had been a GP and his mother was a nurse. He had a long-standing interest in mental health, having introduced the first House of Commons debate on the subject for 20 years in the run-up to the 1959 Mental Health Act.[69] This made his response to Ely all the more surprising. Instead of immediately launching a full inquiry, his Ministry sought to refute the allegations of institutionalised negligence and brutality.

Yet the Ely revelations were not the first: they joined a long list of recent allegations about long-stay institutions from across the country. Many of these were channelled through the campaigning group that Brian was closely associated with: AEGIS, Aid to the Elderly in Government Institutions.

AEGIS originated in a letter to *The Times* published on 10 November 1965:

> We the undersigned have been shocked by the treatment of geriatric patients in certain mental hospitals.... The attitude of the Ministry of Health to complaints has reinforced our anxieties. In consequence we have decided to collect evidence of ill-treatment of geriatric patients throughout the country, to demonstrate the need for a national investigation.... We shall be grateful if those who have encountered malpractices in this sphere will supply us with detailed information, which would of course be treated as confidential.

It was signed by the peers Strabolgi, Beaumont and Heytesbury, alongside Brian, Daniel Woolgar (a Dominican friar), the illustrator Edward Ardizzone, the socialist reformer John Hewetson, and citizens' rights campaigners Audrey Harvey and the Reverend Bill Sargent. The initiator of the letter was Barbara Robb, a former ballerina from an upper-class family, who had been shocked to see the conditions one of her elderly relatives was experiencing in a state-run nursing home. Robb and Brian had met socially, and she recognised the value of his position. He provided a potential channel of communication into the Ministry of Health. He could also use his expertise on social welfare policy to direct how the campaign should target reforms. On a more practical level still, he was willing to advise individuals of their rights (he was active in the London Citizens' Advice Bureaux). The stream of letters that flowed to Robb's Hampstead address following *The Times* letter in 1965 resulted in the book *Sans Everything: a Case to Answer.*[70] This brought together emotive case histories with clear, focused analyses, including a contribution from Brian, who advocated the appointment of a hospital ombudsman to investigate such allegations of mistreatment.

The formation of AEGIS and the publication of *Sans Everything* had generated significant public and press attention, including a full episode of the BBC television programme '24 Hours' on 30 June 1967, but there was no policy change from the government. Robinson had been briefed that *Sans Everything* was about to be published, and as a pre-emptive measure he was persuaded by Ministry officials to set up teams of investigators at the regional level, rather than establish a full enquiry. Most of the AEGIS witnesses wished to remain anonymous, fearful of their job security or the welfare of relatives still in these institutions. Robinson tried to play this to his advantage, speaking in the House of Commons about 'totally unfounded or grossly exaggerated' allegations, and promising only specific, reactive, investigations to individual allegations. This further fuelled public outrage: *New Society* judged Robinson's comments as 'shockingly complacent'.[71]

After the exposure of the Ely Hospital scandal in August 1967, Robinson eventually agreed that it required a more substantial response, and Brian suggested to him that his Cambridge friend (now a QC and recent Conservative MP), Geoffrey Howe, be appointed to conduct an independent inquiry. This began under Robinson's watch in 1967 and was not yet ready when he found out in the summer of 1968 that he would soon be out of office, to make way for the Crossman empire of the DHSS. He was gracious in defeat, and invited Crossman to the celebration of the 20th anniversary of the NHS held in July. Crossman noted in his diary:

> He [Robinson] did have the courtesy to introduce me to the Secretary of the BMA and one or two other bigwigs. When I get into my new job I shall find myself in a completely new world, nothing like local government. Nobody knows me by sight and I don't know them. What's worse, they all know that I am working Kenneth Robinson out of a job and by all their tests he was an excellent Minister.[72]

Ely, for Crossman, triggered painful personal memories. His mother had died in a poorly-run nursing home, and his second wife, Zita, only received hospital attention for her terminal illness because the physician had assumed that Crossman intended to cover the costs privately. Howe need not have been anxious that Crossman would bury his Ely report, but he took the precaution of speaking to Brian to make sure that it reached Crossman's desk without Whitehall interference.[73] Crossman overruled his civil servants and published the 83,000-word Ely report in full. It showed that nearly a quarter of a million patients were housed in pre-NHS 'Public Assistance' buildings – many of which originated as 19th-century Poor Law workhouses.[74] Introducing the report in the Commons, Crossman defended his unusual decision to publish it in full, and promised immediate action. In the privacy of his diaries he acknowledged another rationale and its wider implication:

I could only publish and survive politically if in the course of my Statement I announced necessary changes to policy including the adoption by the Ministry and the RHBs of a system of inspectorates, central and regional, such as there are in almost every other Ministry and such as the Health Service has never yet permitted itself.[75]

The Ely report actually met with little opposition within the DHSS: there were already internal moves towards reform of mental illness and mental subnormality institutions, and Wilson agreed to the creation of a permanent inspectorate. The regional authorities remained, however, to be convinced that their already pruned budgets should be skewed towards these less than fashionable areas of the health service.

The suppression of the facts was one of Crossman's main complaints: he had discovered that reports of abuse and poor conditions at Ely had been received by the Chief Nursing Officer at the Ministry of Health as far back as 1953. He set up a post-Ely policy working party (known as PEP), initially intended to run for three months. It was soon extended to cover community mental health services, to consider Brian's suggestion of creating a Health (or Health Service) Commissioner and Hospital Advisory Service, and to look into producing guidelines for minimum standards in the NHS. Its membership shows all the signs of Brian's personal connections. In addition to himself and the Chief Medical Officer, George Godber, there were his old friends Peter Townsend and Geoffrey Howe; from his days as a governor at the Maudsley he included Eileen Skellern, Superintendent of Nursing; he also knew Dr Gerald O'Gorman, Physician Superintendent of the Borocourt Hospital in Reading, and Dr Albert Kushlick, Director of Research in Sub-normality at Wessex RHB, and Lady Frances Williams. Pauline Morris, author of *Put Away: A Sociological Study of Institutions for the Mentally Retarded* completed the eclectic group.[76]

Brian had known Eileen Skellern since 1963, and highly valued her opinion. They entered into a private correspondence, Eileen writing from her home to Brian's, to allow her to send him uncensored personal comments on the reality of conditions inside mental institutions. She had extensive experience, having served on inspection teams, and lectured at St Thomas' Hospital on the Sister-Tutor Diploma course. Brian solicited her views not only on the long-stay institutions. He also sent her a copy of the Carter report on the function of the district general hospital, and when she responded with her handwritten comments, he got his secretary to type them up as an anonymous memorandum for the Ministry.[77] She also wrote up her views on community care for the mentally ill. Skellern fed Brian with useful information from her extensive network of professional colleagues. One of Crossman's planned improvements was the creation of a Hospital Advisory Service, and Skellern alerted Brian to the nurses' 'distrust and distress' about what was in essence a proposal for a powerful inspection mechanism. She privately acknowledged that reports of unsatisfactory conditions had been sent to RHBs for many years 'but no one wanted to know. There is a lot of disillusion around I'm afraid'.[78]

Ministry officials tried to terminate the working party once its initial (narrow) remit had been fulfilled, but it continued to meet, and Crossman was content for it to develop into a study group on the future of mental handicap services (a term increasingly favoured over mental sub-normality by the late 1960s). In keeping with his approach to other policy developments, Crossman chose to steer his own course, and excluded the Mental Health Standing Advisory Committee, which was well-equipped with experts to provide him with support. From mid-1969, at Crossman's request, Brian worked on drafting a White Paper on mental handicap. He had already produced memoranda on the principle of amalgamating sub-normality hospitals with district general hospitals, and the DHSS's own Mental Subnormality Sub-committee had produced an 'Approach to comprehensive policy' document the previous year. His continual refinement of the draft illustrated his determination that even the smallest improvements should be addressed, for example, allowing incontinent patients to wear normal clothes, but to have more of them (and the necessary staff to change them), and domestic-style washing machines that would not destroy ordinary clothes, as happened with the industrial hospital laundry machines.[79] He persuaded Crossman to host a two-day conference on sub-normality in October 1969, partly so that mental health professionals could have the morale-boost of contact with their minister. By December 1969 he had produced a nine-chapter draft White Paper.[80] This went through five further editions, and also responded to feedback from a leak to a *Guardian* journalist, Ann Shearer, who wrote an article 'New Deal Planned for Subnormal'.[81] With the fall of the Labour government in June 1970, Crossman lost office, and was replaced by Keith Joseph as Secretary of State for Social Services. Brian's draft White Paper on mental handicap was passed over to Joseph, who thanked him for his work and expressed the hope that he could call on him in the future for advice. The post-Ely working party was, however, disbanded.[82]

Yet as a trigger, the working party was one of the most influential initiatives ever to have been created. The NHS Hospital Advisory Service came to life (as a 'thin end of the wedge' approach to regional opposition to a formal inspectorate) on 15 October 1969. Brian's ideas for a health commissioner began to take shape in the spring of 1970 when a consultation paper was circulated, although this was to be a more tortuous process.[83]

Restructuring the NHS

Along with the Ely scandal, Crossman had inherited from Robinson a Green Paper on the structure of the NHS. This had been published in July 1968 (to coincide with the 20th anniversary of the formation of the NHS) with the ambitious timetable of a complete NHS reorganisation by 1970.[84] The deficiencies of Bevan's 1948 NHS were apparent by the late 1950s. Indeed, Brian's work for the Guillebaud Committee report, published in 1956, had been one of the first indicators that it was structurally flawed. The tripartite division between hospital services, GPs (executive council) and local authority services emerged as the key obstacle to improved efficiency. There was little coordination of these three branches of the NHS within its areas, and resources were not allocated on the basis of need, but on pre-existing biases towards hospitals, especially those within the metropolitan area (and teaching hospitals in the provinces). The 1962 Porritt report had found little optimism for improved coordination within the existing system, but at least served to stimulate longer-term deliberations.[85] The Joint Consultants Committee (JCC) had approached the Ministry of Health in 1965 to discuss 'matters affecting the efficiency, development and reorganisation of the NHS'.[86] They were appeased with the innovative 'cogwheel' initiative started by the Chief Medical Officer, Sir George Godber, which reported in 1967 on medical personnel management in hospitals.[87] Underlying all discussions of potential reorganisation was the Treasury's fear of increasing expenditure. Any suggestion of innovation to them seemed to imply an unnecessary and unaffordable cost. The only proposal that gained their serious consideration was for an independent NHS board, which had been discussed by a number of organisations including the Acton Society Trust, the Guillebaud Committee, and by Enoch Powell when he was Minister of Health (1960–63). It failed to gain sufficient support at that time, amid worries that it would undermine parliamentary accountability for the NHS, and was quietly dropped.

The Ministry of Health had formed, without the Treasury's knowledge, a small committee to look at reorganisation in June 1967, headed by Sir Arnold France, the Permanent Secretary. It came within the remit of the recently formed ministerial Long-term Planning

Division.[88] Its first attempt at a plan (LP(67)9) was circulated within the Ministry, based on full integration with the existing local government framework, but it remained primarily concerned with meeting hospital requirements. Robinson was not persuaded by this internal document, but neither would he permit external knowledge of, or consultation on, his reorganisation plans.

Robinson's eventual Green Paper had proposed a single tier administrative system of between 40 and 50 authorities, to be known as area health boards, and coterminous with local government districts, from which they *might* absorb public and environmental health duties. The reaction from the medical profession and hospital administrators was that the regions would be too small for planning purposes but too big for effective management. Senior doctors were concerned that their influence on the boards would be diluted. GPs feared loss of status relative to hospital doctors. Crossman immediately decided to design a two-tier structure. He called and chaired a conference for RHB chairs and officials – some 100 people – on 17 January 1969, and used it to test out his theory. No one spoke in support of Robinson's one-tier structure, which Crossman took as carte blanche to develop his own plan. As a way into this issue, and partly triggered by the Ely scandal, Crossman asked Brian to produce a briefing paper with a statistical analysis of how the NHS regions spent their monies, and especially how they prioritised certain services. Brian demonstrated how resources were skewed towards acute clinical care, and advised that there should be a minimum 1.25 per cent shift in expenditure towards 'subnormal' hospitals.

Crossman also began discussions with Labour colleagues on transferring responsibility for the NHS to local government. This had been one of the options that Beveridge and then Bevan had debated before the creation of the NHS in 1948, and it harked back to substantial local government control of healthcare (municipal hospitals, the remnants of the old Poor Law infirmaries and various specialist clinics) from the 1930s. But Crossman's sounding out of Tony Crosland, which had been done through a letter sent from this DHSS office in April 1969, had provoked his ever vigilant civil servants into a state of alarm. He received an urgent request for a meeting from Sir George Godber, Chief Medical Officer, and Alan Marre, Second Permanent Under Secretary, to discuss it. Crossman's diary account reveals just how little he understood of the niceties of the civil service, or the sensitivities of the medical profession:

I had been given a flatulent answer by the Department [to Crosland's initial enquiry], which I had re-dictated to explain how we were genuinely trying to get a much more community-based Health Service and how I had thrown out Kenneth Robinson's Green Paper of a highly autocratic, centralised structure. I had added that the obvious reason why we couldn't transfer things to local government was that the doctors objected and also that there were difficulties in financing it. I also told him that anyway the tripartite system was working badly, everybody agreed on that.... It was obvious that Marre and Godber, solemn, busy men who had come across to rebuke me, were warning me that I was stirring up a hornet's nest. It's true that Serota [Lady Bea Serota, Minister for Health] and I have made it pretty clear that we are baffled and bewildered at what these 4,000 people in the Department can be doing and that we think previous Ministers have just been carried along with the Department, whereas we want to get a hold and have a policy. The Department is warning me, "Take care. We will ditch you if you are a trouble. We will see to it that you have two or three stumbles and we have registered that we disapprove of you".[89]

Crossman pressed ahead anyway with consultations, calling a meeting of the chairs of the RHBs. They rejected Brian's 1.25 per cent proposed redistribution of their funds to subnormal hospitals, and also rejected Crossman's offer of their own post-Ely inspectorate – a clear sign that they wished to take no greater responsibility for these institutions.[90] Concurrent with his scheming was Crossman's bungled announcement that there was to be a 25 per cent increase in charges for dentures and spectacles. His own Party members were annoyed, as he allowed the House of Commons to schedule the statement immediately before the local elections, in which the public had a golden opportunity to tell Labour what they thought of yet another attack on their precious NHS. The increased charges were supposed to generate another £3.5 million in NHS revenue – a small drop in the ocean of its total budget, but symbolic of chronic problems with health service financing.

A couple of days after Crossman was attacked for his charges announcement, Brian gave a dinner party at Elizabeth Street to allow him to discuss the reorganisation ideas with Serota and Jerry Morris, Professor of Public Health and Director of the Medical Research Council's Social Medicine Unit, at LSHTM, and one of Brian's closest academic colleagues. Crossman noted the dinner in his diary: 'An astonishing fellow, Brian, with his house full of antique furniture, his modern portraits, somehow slipping out and in ten minutes producing a brilliant meal. It was a pleasure I could enjoy even in all my misery.'[91] Brian regularly used Morris as a sounding board for DHSS policy issues, and offered him opportunities to put his own expert opinion to minsters like Crossman. Soon after this supper Brian sent Morris an advance copy of the long-awaited report of the Central Health Services Council Committee on the functions of the district general hospital, which had been established in 1966 (the Bonham-Carter Committee). Morris's verdict was scathing:

> At times its blandness verges on the ridiculous ... the main conclusions of the committee are that (a) all hospital facilities should be gathered together on a single site and (b) they should serve larger populations than at present envisaged – 300,000 plus if possible.... However the needs of the acute and the chronic hospital are different. The model for the former is medical-technological, for the latter medical-social, with day hospitals, rehabilitation, etc.... Out-patients are scarcely mentioned nor how the centralisation would help them grow.... The Committee confuses integration of management with location.... What we want in the NHS are some clear and strong strategic principles, and beyond that the utmost flexibility for a varied and unstable situation. The proposals of this Committee would tie an even heavier millstone than the 1962 plan around the department's neck. The Report will be of no help to the Department whose thinking already is way ahead of the game – eg in "best buy". Its main importance is to illustrate again the need for proper planning machinery in the Health Service. Incidentally, once again a high power committee, not particularly equipped, has disposed of a chunk of general practitioners' time and, characteristically, without reference to the different things the other hpcs have recently said.[92]

Morris's views undoubtedly steered those of the ministers and advisers on the post-Ely working party who worried that the Committee's proposals were 'more oriented to the needs of the hospital consultant than of his patients'. The Bonhan-Carter Report, when finally published, carried ministerial reservations.[93]

Morris and Serota had both served together on the Seebohm Committee on the future of the personal social services, and it was likely that either Brian or Titmuss had suggested Morris's name to Kenneth Robinson when the Committee was established in 1965.[94]

Brian certainly knew its Chair Frederic Seebohm (1909–90), who also chaired the JRMT that had funded a number of his research projects with Titmuss and Townsend. The Seebohm Committee's investigations were constrained by the almost coterminous (Todd) Royal Commission on Medical Education and the (Redcliffe-Maud) Royal Commission on Local Government. Seebohm proposed a much greater coordination between various professionals and organisations, and a restructuring of local government personal social services, to end what Titmuss had called the 'Balkanised rivalry' between local authority departments and their leaders, especially the Medical Officer of Health and the Director of Social Services.[95] What it did not do, as some had hoped, was propose a full integration of health and social services. Instead the Medical Officers of Health (MOHs), having lost their control over personal social services, were to be redefined as 'community physicians' with administrative and health surveillance briefs.[96] So by 1969 there was a state of impasse, as the government received, considered and judged on a variety of key reorganisations, each one intimately dependent on the outcomes of the others, especially on the delicate issue of service control and boundaries. There were several Green Papers (a new parliamentary technique first used in 1967 to test opinion on potential areas for policy development), and ministers such as Crossman began to find their loyalties seriously divided.[97]

Brian's Elizabeth Street dinners played a key role in the development of Crossman's own NHS reorganisation Green Paper. Again, in August 1969, he hosted Crossman, Serota and Morris, this time joined by John Revans, Senior Administrative Medical Officer for Wessex RHB, and Jim Sharpe, who had begun his career at the LSE before moving on to be Assistant Commissioner to the Redcliffe-Maud Commission between 1966 and 1969. They discussed the difficulty of persuading doctors to accept joint (NHS and local government) boards for managing the health services, and Crossman admitted that, despite all the good intentions, the opportunities for local participation in the NHS remained small, with most decisions still taken at the top. His affection for local government was balanced by a natural disinclination to favour what he called the 'self-perpetuating oligarchies' of the medical establishment. His officials worked hard to incorporate his wishes. Godber proposed a two-tier arrangement of some 300 small districts, which were to become known as 'Godber bricks', under the control of around 20 regions.[98]

During the summer of 1969 Brian worked up several policy papers for Crossman, which included some innovative proposals for increasing

NHS revenue, such as levying accident patients. But in Cabinet meetings, at which the Chancellor, Roy Jenkins, was proposing a six-month freeze to capital programmes for new hospitals to make the required NHS saving of £22 million, there appeared to be little room for discussion. The Treasury stand was now that it would oppose any plan that lacked the essential strong managerial factor at both regional and district level. NHS staff, picking up on these conflicting accounts of what reorganisation might entail, were becoming increasingly demoralised. It is important to recognise that although Brian was Crossman's senior adviser, Crossman was stimulated by discussions with a wide range of people, from the Labour Party, trade unions and the medical profession. As an indication of the extent of interest in the changes, some 400 sets of written comments had been received after the publication of the first Green Paper, and meetings had been held with over 50 organisations. Yet Crossman's domineering personality and determination to leave a restructured NHS as a sign of his political achievements meant that he pushed his advisers to follow his policy whims, and there were often multiple policy papers in circulation and at varying stages of favouritism.[99] His diary entry for Monday 4 August 1969 is a classic example of how, like Toad of Toad Hall, he expected everyone to follow his bright idea:

> … now my mind is fixed on the idea of a joint board, like the Metropolitan Water Board or the Gas Board used to be. We might have a joint board, appointed from both a Regional Health Authority and the local authorities. The whole of this afternoon I fought with the Department in an obstinate way and made them go through it again, poor things. They had their own elaborate plan they wanted to put but I wasn't going to listen to it because I said the joint board was all I wanted to hear about.[100]

Brian put effort into making Crossman think carefully about the impact of his plans on the central management of the NHS. In a briefing paper in September 1969 he alerted Crossman to the lack of central (civil service) knowledge of how the NHS actually operated:

> The more I work at the Elephant [and Castle, DHSS HQ] the more I am worried about the Department and its role in the top management of a large public service. I suppose it is inevitable that an organisation run by the Civil Service will be more defensive than aggressive. In theory the Central Department helps you formulate your broad policy while the actual operation of it is

in the hands of Regional Boards, Executive Council and Local Health Authorities. But creative leadership is still needed at the top. It would be needed more still in a combined service with up to 90 districts. Loading the Elephant with heavier responsibilities would make it less agile in exercising them.[101]

He also highlighted the very limited opportunities for staff to move between the DHSS and the NHS regional and district offices. Brian acknowledged that a fully integrated management system for the NHS was impossible, given the requirement that the minister retain final responsibility, but he suggested that a health service council might work, with shared responsibilities. Medical, nursing and administrative staff could move between the centre and the regions, and a requirement for senior posts would be that they had served a substantial amount of time at the local level. He also proposed bringing in 'outsiders with relevant experience elsewhere (eg the supplies manager of a large hotel chain, a tycoon from the building industry)'. His idea was well in advance of Margaret Thatcher's invitation to Roy Griffiths, Managing Director of Sainsbury's supermarkets, to advise on the NHS in the 1980s.

In December 1969, at a meeting at Prescote, Crossman's constituency home near Banbury, Brian shocked Crossman by announcing his dislike for the structure of the Green Paper as it stood. Brian offered to go away and re-draft it. On 11 December, again at Prescote, 10 senior members of the Department gathered in the dining room to discuss his revised draft. Crossman reported: 'We found this a splendid room for a policy meeting, with an excellent atmosphere, because one can't be rude to one's host.... Of course I now realise our tremendous loss in not setting up a Royal Commission on the Health Service as we did on local government. This would have been first-rate because no one really knows how the health service is run.'[102]

Brian had tried during the previous months to alert Crossman that there was considerable opposition to his (Crossman's) proposal to have a two-tier NHS structure by abandoning the regional tier and leaving area boards and district committees. This was intended to move power back into communities and allow some local government involvement. At this Prescote meeting on 11 December, Brian arranged for Liz Shore, Deputy Chief Medical Officer, and a number of other senior civil servants to tell Crossman that his idea to remove the regional tier just would not work. He eventually conceded, but only on condition that the retained regional level would have a significantly reduced role. Everyone present understood that the biggest issue, the requirement to have coterminous district boundaries with local government, had been brushed under the carpet. It was not until 2 January 1970, when Crossman attended a meeting in the other 'half' of his DHSS empire to discuss the Seebohm Committee Bill for defined social services districts, that he recognised that his compartmentalisation strategy was untenable. He simply could not progress plans on the social services side, knowing that the NHS Green Paper wished to keep the issue of boundaries for future discussion.

Despite considerable Treasury disquiet, and unhappiness from BMA and local government representatives, Crossman forged ahead, producing a very speedy second Green Paper on the NHS on 11 February 1970, entitled *NHS: The Future Structure of the National Health Service*.[103] As Geoffrey Rivett puts it, Crossman's scheme 'wobbled' between the dichotomous solutions of either local government service integration or new health authorities.[104] It exhibited the triumphant authority of the CMO, George Godber: his district-level 'bricks' were explicitly planned not to be coterminous with local government districts to prevent any future discussions of local government control of the NHS. It received a mixed reception, with many commentators complaining that it had failed to take advantage of this golden opportunity to completely integrate health and personal social services. Crossman's attempt to give power at all levels worried the Treasury. In a Fabian pamphlet, Maurice Kogan, Professor of Government and Social Administration at Brunel University, said that the Green Paper should 'not unfairly be characterised as syndicalism run wild'.[105] The RHBs launched an immediate and vociferous attack on their apparent demotion, to which Crossman responded by re-balancing some of the authority between areas and districts, essentially creating a three-tier NHS.

Crossman determined to push ahead with producing a White Paper by July 1970 without further consultation, conscious that time before the general election was running out. His thinking still oscillated between having five and 25 regions, and he tried to prevent other government departments, especially the Treasury, gaining knowledge of what he was planning. Of course, when the document was leaked the Treasury responded with a predictable damnation, especially of Crossman's failure to apply any basic management principles.[106] With the fall of the Labour government, it was left to the incoming Conservative Secretary of State Keith Joseph to publish the White Paper. This appeared, with the re-insertion of a strong third regional tier, in August 1972.[107]

In his final year as Secretary of State Crossman also had to cope with an increasingly unhappy medical profession. Although the Pilkington Committee on remuneration for doctors and dentists had recommended an improved Pay Review Body for Doctors and Dentists, which was set up in 1962 (chaired by Lord Kindersley), within a few years there were renewed calls for improvements. A new contract for GPs was introduced in 1966 which went some way to meeting their demands, but the Kindersley Committee repeatedly turned down the annual demands of hospital doctors. Its 10th report in February 1969 had, however, recommended an 8 per cent increase, justified on the grounds of comparability with salaries for other groups with professional qualifications such as teachers. Yet the government stalled its acceptance and implementation, partly because Barbara Castle was trying to push through the creation of a new Prices and Incomes Board that would deal with all claims, from which the doctors would not be exempt.

Crossman was working hard in private to retain the Kindersley Committee for 'his' doctors, but even he was flabbergasted when the 1970 report, which the government received (in confidence) in February, recommended a 30 per cent increase in pay – far more than even the BMA had dared to ask for. The Treasury wanted an outright rejection of the report; the senior staff at the DHSS, including Godber, recognised that the 30 per cent recommendation was unrealistic, but that something had to be salvaged to present to the doctors. By 26 May the doctors' organisations accused Crossman of dragging his feet in publishing the report. They threatened industrial action – breaking off contact with the government and refusing to sign sickness benefit certificates – unless they were given the report, and the government's view of it, within 24 hours. Crossman met their representatives and agreed a stay of execution by proposing that they hold a meeting with Wilson. In the final weeks before the June election Crossman, with the help of Brian, wrote a statement announcing that he was going to refer the doctors' pay award to the Prices and Incomes Board. He met the doctors' representatives, and told them they would only have £57 million of the £85 million proposed by Kindersley, because the impact of the full award might produce a 'perilous situation' for the economy. The doctors' leaders took this private statement to the Conservatives, who made good political mileage out of it in the final campaigning. The Kindersley Committee, only given this news 30 minutes before Crossman told the doctors, resigned en masse, leaving Crossman, who already knew he was on his way out of politics, with a nasty mess to hand on to the next Secretary of State for Social Services.

The LSE, 1967–69

Despite his contract to work as an adviser to Crossman, Brian maintained his workload at the LSE, compressing most of his academic duties into the periods he was not officially 'on call' for the DHSS. This often meant returning to the LSE in the early evening to catch up on paperwork and give lectures. The range of courses now offered in social administration (and its satellite subjects) would have impressed the small team that Titmuss had joined in 1950. When the Department celebrated its 50th anniversary in 1962 it had over 300 students.

By the mid-1960s the LSE had an enviable reputation for the quality of its research and teaching. It was attracting large numbers of international students, and from 1967 it benefited from the new differential fees charged for overseas students, initially set at £250 pa, which universities were now allowed to retain rather than passing them to the government, thus introducing a 'private' interest into these traditionally public sector institutions. Dahrendorf, writing as an LSE historian after retiring as its Director, saw this as the beginning of a period of considerable change at the LSE: 'Staff and students found the School a less homely place; they felt lost but also exposed to masters whose bureaucratic power they could neither permeate or control. Teachers became more competitive; students wondered about their opportunities.'[108] Given its specialist status in political and economic science, the LSE naturally attracted politically active students. Because most of its courses were at this time postgraduate, it meant a more mature and vocal student body than that found at traditional universities. The Student Union witnessed increasingly vitriolic debates as various political factions experimented with techniques of direct action, including sit-ins and boycotts. CND, the expulsion of South Africa from the Commonwealth in 1961, and other international issues provoked passionate debate. Keeping the peace in such a volatile atmosphere was never going to be easy. A specific catalyst for action came in 1966 when the committee appointed to find a replacement for Sydney Caine as Director chose Walter Adams, then Principal of the new University College in Rhodesia. This was to be the first of two significant 'troubles' the School faced.

Adams' appointment was viewed by the student body as the culmination of a conspiracy of powers, and they thought that they should have been consulted on the selection process. They objected to his tacit acceptance of the racist culture of southern Africa, and by compiling a dossier on his background, judged him a weak character, not in keeping with the ethos of the LSE. The School reacted by disciplining the president of the Student Union for publishing these views and the students responded by accusing the School of restricting freedom of speech. Divisions began to emerge among the staff, some of whom supported the students, but Adams' appointment was ratified by the Academic Board. The students called a 'Stop Adams' rally, to be held in the Old Theatre, the heart of the LSE, on 31 January 1967. Caine banned the meeting, and attempted to stop the students entering the theatre. He even took the precaution of having the light fuses removed so the windowless room remained pitch-black. In the ensuing struggle, the students gained access. A porter, who was not present at the 'storming', and who was not subject to any form of abuse, died from a heart attack. Caine closed the School, and went to the Union to comfort the distressed students. In the following weeks there was an official enquiry into the conduct of four of the students which dragged on for several weeks, and the atmosphere remained tense and unpleasant. It became clear that this first 'trouble' was not just the work of a small band of activists: over 40 per cent of students had participated in the sit-in and boycotts that followed the Old Theatre siege and the disciplining of their colleagues. In March 1967 it was the site of the first major student strike in Britain:

> During those eight days the School presented an extraordinary spectacle to people used to its normal ordered appearance. The lobby and corridors of the main building were filled with student sitting on the floors, holding seemingly endless discussions, listening to distinguished outsiders who they thought had the solution to the problem of LSE, reading, singing, eating or just sleeping.[109]

But the sit-in was in essence a peaceful affair. Staff and students who wished to work were not obstructed, although in practice most lectures were cancelled. It was good-humoured and, according to Professor John Griffith who supported the students, 'great fun'.[110] It was not so good for the LSE's reputation. Fleet Street, just around the corner, sent reporters and television news cameras to cover the 'Rebellion at the school for rebels'. When the summer term ended and the students departed, Caine finally retired, having made some cosmetic changes to the School's staff–student liaison through new committee structures. He was replaced by Walter Adams, who arrived to a relatively 'quiet year' at the LSE.

The School's strategy for these difficult years, from the first protests in March 1967, was to try to involve student representatives in the deliberations of its Academic Board. This worked up to a point, but in October 1968, when it emerged that some students intended to hold a mass occupation of the School during the forthcoming large anti-Vietnam demonstration, the Student Union fragmented along previously submerged fault lines. As Colin Crouch, then president of the Union, puts it, 'the issues in this debate were central to the whole framework of the new left's concept of both the university and the political system. For the new left such activities as the Vietnam occupation were not only acceptable uses of a university, but about the only uses worth accepting.'[111]

Adams issued a statement in the name of the Board of Governors (a lay body that had already lost the students' trust over representation issues) claiming that he had the authority to close the School to prevent damage to property from such an occupation. This move was seen as an unwarranted intervention in the running of the school by its governors. The occupation went ahead and caused minimal damage. But unlike the 1967 dispute, when relations between students and staff had remained relatively friendly, this time the atmosphere was unpleasant, and worsened by the School's decision to discipline two members of staff who had supported the students. Other flashpoints that year included a talk by the distinguished historian Hugh Trevor-Roper, which Marxist students tried to disrupt because of his stance on the Greek colonels' regime, and a resurgence of the opposition that had been expressed on the appointment of Adams because of his links to South Africa. There were teach-ins on the situation in Rhodesia and a demand that the School declare any investments it held in that country or South Africa. Adams refused to appear before the Student Union, which in retaliation occupied the senior common room. Lectures were boycotted and staff verbally and, at times, physically attacked. The final straw for the students was when the School installed gates in the Lent term of 1969 to enable shutting off parts of buildings from potential sit-ins. The Academic Board had also issued instructions to members of staff on what to do in the event of future disruption, including a requirement to identify those students involved. This exacerbated an already tense atmosphere and, according to Crouch, worked to the advantage of the revolutionaries.[112]

The students responded by wrecking the gates (which had actually been in place for some time without attracting attention) with pick-axes in January 1969. Adams closed the School indefinitely, and it remained closed for 25 days. The LSE effectively went into exile, holding classes at other University of London buildings around Bloomsbury. The protest triggered a statement in Parliament by Edward Short, Secretary of State for Education: 'The real perpetrators are a tiny handful of people – fewer than one half of 1 per cent of the 3,000 at LSE. Of these, at least four are from the United States. They are subsidised to the extent of between £1,000 and £2,000 for their one year master's degree course by the British taxpayer. These gentlemen are clearly not here to study but to undermine British institutions.'[113]

Brian was one of the staff who attempted to mediate between the LSE Standing Committee and the students. Titmuss, on the other hand, used his position on the Standing Committee to mount a strong attack on the students, motivated by what Dahrendorf considered a real fear that the School's existence was threatened. After the main school reopened, there continued to be small 'guerrilla' attacks by radical students, often targeting the offices of staff they judged hostile to their cause. With the LSE's internal authority damaged, Adams resorted to taking out criminal summons against student 'ringleaders' and Nicholas Bateson and Robin Blackburn, the lecturers who had supported them, which provoked a further night of student occupation.[114] Despite this, he was seen by colleagues and outsiders as too weak for such a role, and suffering from the domineering presence of Lord Robbins, now the LSE's Chair. Slogans were spray-painted all over the school buildings, which old Marxist factions attempted to clean off before the end of the sit-in. It did not temper the School's decision to dismiss Bateson and Blackburn. It was a much stronger response than to the 1967 protests, and shocked many of the staff. The confrontation eventually dissipated in the summer term. Dahrendorf considered that at this time academic freedom had been at serious risk, and that it was the School's unhappiest year, but that the LSE had weathered these student disputes better than some institutions such as Berkeley.[115]

The end of the Titmice

The Poverty Survey, begun in 1964 with £32,000 funding from the JRMT, entered its final stage in the summer of 1969. It had been beset by delays, some caused by Whitehall intransigence on access to the interview sample, others by Brian and Townsend's initial naivety on how much work such a substantial project would require. They had not expected their draft application to be accepted literally by return of post, before they had done the full costings. Their request for top-up funding from JRMT in October 1967 had been refused, and John Veit-Wilson's contract had not been extended.[116] They then secured £26,700 from the SSRC, for a related study on the sub-employed in three local communities, and the Rowntree fund eventually relented and provided an additional sum of £22,400 to complete the original project.[117] Hilary Land published the results of her section of the project in 1969: *Large Families in London: A Study of 86 Families*.[118] Adrian Sinfield, who had joined Townsend at Essex during the project, also produced linked research on the long-term unemployed.[119] Although this had begun as a joint study, Brian had increasingly handed over responsibility to Townsend, especially in September 1968 when he began to work as Crossman's part-time special adviser.

This fulfilment of a desire for a more active political life stemmed from Brian's decision not to stand as an MP as he had contemplated in the early 1950s. He had discussed his options with Townsend then, late into the night at his Vincent Square flat. However, when Brian accepted Crossman's offer to become his adviser, he was effectively reneging on a substantial commitment to one of his closest friends. Townsend was 'devastated by his decision, which left me holding the baby. We'd planned an extraordinary and over-ambitious survey book ... it would be a joint effort ... when I found out that I had to do the whole thing it was almost crazy of me to expect to try and do that.'[120] The impact on their research team was equally demoralising. They witnessed the painful dilemma of balancing research and political commitments, the diverging opinions of Brian and Townsend, and felt that it was wrong for Brian to go and work for Crossman.[121] They went as far as to draft a letter to Brian, telling him that they thought he would be more effective in achieving policy change as an academic than as an adviser.[122] When Townsend's book, *Poverty in the United Kingdom: a survey of household resources and standards of living*, was finally published, he sent a copy to Brian, with an invitation to the launch.[123] Brian replied: 'Your acknowledgments are very generous and I always feel very guilty about having to withdraw from the project when I got absorbed with Dick Crossman, and left you holding such a heavy baby all on your own.'[124]

Townsend had always been sympathetic to Brian's position. He tried to understand this move to the DHSS as a potential short-cut to getting a more effective input into health and social welfare policy. They both naïvely felt that 'the facts alone, if they were constantly remembered, would change political decision making'.[125] Townsend was prepared to see the best in every situation. When the CPAG Committee decided that its members should staff weekly welfare rights stalls in high streets and markets, Brian was excused on the grounds that he could be more effective through other campaigning work. He had tried to work on the stalls, but Townsend understood that as a gay man with no children, Brian could not engage as naturally in conversations with the public about the problems of school meals or family allowances. Likewise, Townsend justified taking on the lion's share of the poverty survey pilot interviewing because he knew that Brian would feel uncomfortable visiting poor families in their homes.[126]

At the same time, Townsend's increasingly distant relationship with Richard Titmuss further deteriorated when Titmuss became Deputy Chair of the Supplementary Benefits Commission (SBC) in December 1966. This position was a double-edged sword for the Titmice: it gave them a better insight into how the SBC functioned, and Titmuss gave Brian some very useful feedback on the draft policy papers he prepared for Crossman on benefits and means testing, but it also split Titmuss's loyalties.[127] In 1968 Townsend criticised the SBC's ethical conduct in Northern Ireland, where its office had been effectively stuffed with Protestant staff, who were unsympathetic to claims of Catholics for housing allowances and other benefits. Titmuss took Townsend's public criticism of the SBC badly, sending him a 10-page typed letter, no doubt with some of the detail drafted by SBC civil servants, but very personally topped and tailed.[128] Townsend was devastated by Titmuss's reaction: 'I was so thrown by this that I started a reply but never fulfilled it because I couldn't quite comprehend why a close friend would suddenly ditch me, as I saw, or rather ditched what we had both believed in – that's better put – ditched what we had believed in. I was baffled by it.'[129] They were also poles apart on their support for (Townsend) and criticism of (Titmuss) the student uprisings of 1968–69.

With Townsend based at Essex, commuting weekly from his home in Hampstead, and Brian's new post with Crossman further reducing their opportunities for contact, the Titmice could no longer be considered 'an item'. They had been so close, emotionally, socially and intellectually in the 1950s and early 1960s, to the extent that Townsend had been allowed to make the decision for all three of them, that they would reject any formal offer from Wilson of life peerages.[130] Kay Titmuss's anger over this decision had strained their friendships, but the disciple–mentor relationship was already beginning to crack. Townsend had begun to question more deeply Titmuss's position and modus operandi: 'he was a bit unsure of himself, and lacked a certain scientific or intellectual, or educational, or university confidence, and wanted rather desperately his very closest associates, like Brian Abel-Smith, David Donnison and myself, to prop him up in certain major particulars. And the truth is that the propping up, it was more than that. He depended on people for making some of the overtures and taking some of the initiatives, for which, then, he became noted as being the older person, being the leader.'[131]

As the component Poverty Survey studies neared completion, Brian was forced to re-engage with some difficult issues. The Rowntree Trustees decided at the eleventh hour they were not happy to be publically acknowledged in Marsden's forthcoming book *Mothers Alone: Poverty and the Fatherless Family*.[132] Their decision followed on from Titmuss's, who, as Chair of the Advisory Committee, had objected that he had not been shown the draft. Nor had it been signed off by the DHSS and NAB civil servants who had had it for several months for comment.[133] Titmuss took issue with Marsden's extrapolation of results from the small pilot study interviews he had conducted four years earlier. He could see no evidence that the SBC of 1969, of which he was Deputy Chair, deserved Marsden's criticism: 'I have always held the view – and still do so – that the results of pilot research studies (whether methodological or otherwise) should not first be published in a popular form. They are less likely to be appraised by one's peers. Others, however, may disagree with me. But when I do hold to this view – basically in the interests of maintaining academic standards – it should not be thought that by doing so I am defending the Government, the Department, The Commission, and its officials.'[134]

Brian and Townsend had already attempted to pacify Titmuss on this issue, and reiterated that they had already cleared publication with the Trustees, but with little effect. Brian decided to privately disassociate himself with this impasse, and wrote to Lewis Waddilove, Secretary to the Trust: 'There is much that I could tell you about the Marsden incident which I should hesitate to put on paper. This might make you take a better view of all that has happened. Is there any chance of having a quiet word with you when you are next in London? I am not sending a copy of this letter to Peter Townsend and am not telling him that I am writing. I think I know more about the inside story than anyone else concerned with it at all.'[135]

Brian and Townsend were also forced by their respective university finance departments to discuss how the project overspend of £5,272 should be reported to JRMT, who had declared that there would be absolutely no further money forthcoming. The Rowntree budget had always been managed by Townsend at the University of Essex, with the LSE reclaiming from them cost of the researchers based at their site. But Brian and Townsend had not factored into the original 1964 proposal the cost of punch card and computer analyses. The LSE also now expected some reimbursement for the use of its rooms. Brian again approached Waddilove to mediate, hoping to draw on his enthusiasm for their research.[136]

It was not that JRMT were not happy with the project; it had produced extremely useful data sets, which were already being requested by politicians and policy makers. Sir Keith Joseph had written to Brian in November 1968 to ask for information on the number of single women with dependants in the UK. Brian was able to say that there could be any number between 98,000 and 210,000 households with single female heads – a factor that he also relayed to Richard Crossman, and cemented his desire to tackle this issue while still Secretary of State for Social Services. He set up a departmental committee in November 1969 with the influential barrister Morris Finer as its Chair.[137] The committee's report provoked a new attitude to the legal responsibilities of fathers and the support of single mothers. It was clear therefore that the Rowntree project was producing data in a format that the government did not currently have, and that could provoke new policy discussions.

'The Poor Get Poorer Under Labour'

During the late 1960s the Child Poverty Action Group (CPAG) had developed into an efficient professional pressure group, but saw diminishing impact on the government and struggled to finance its activities. It constantly sought novel ways to inform the public that the problem of family poverty had not disappeared. They asked permission to make a charity collection at the Odeon in Leicester Square at the premiere of the film *Oliver*, but were refused. Undaunted, the Committee urged local branches to try similar initiatives at their cinemas.[138] Lynes' resignation in November 1968, after two years in post, personified the group's sense of disillusionment with Labour's record in office, and their capacity to effect change. Lynes' departure marked a watershed at CPAG. He had been increasingly unhappy at the proliferation of CPAG branches, which had transformed his role into an organisational one, rather than the lobbying and editorial one he had developed from 1966. Only a month earlier Brian had resigned from the Committee, ostensibly because he felt that his membership was not compatible with his new employment as Crossman's adviser. Soon after, the chairmanship passed from Fred Philp to Peter Townsend. There was a real sense that a sea change in approach was required. The Management Committee decided that CPAG should explore expanding into the 'public relations' field, and advertise for a director instead of a secretary.

Frank Field's appointment as Director in February 1969 brought a number of benefits. He was fresh to the poverty issue, had not served on

Labour's Social Policy Study Groups or been active within the Fabian Society.[139] In a sense he was thus free of some of the traditional *modus operandi* that had set CPAG in its original tracks. It allowed him, to the delight and relief of the group, to develop a much more provocative campaign on Labour's failures in government, with the challenging title: 'The Poor Get Poorer Under Labour'.

Although the government had made a token increase in family allowances in 1967, this was almost negated by also increasing the price of school meals and the subsidised milk scheme. Labour had failed to see social policy as an integral element of its general approach to taxation. The traditional strength and authority of the Treasury and the Inland Revenue made CPAG's suggestions in this area useless. Tony Lynes had proposed that an increase in family allowances (and their extension to the first-born child) would be both affordable and efficient, if a similar amount was 'clawed back' by removing the child tax allowance. James Callaghan, Chancellor, considered this a politically risky strategy, which might alienate working men (they would lose the annual tax allowance: their wives would gain the family allowance in weekly cash). He very reluctantly came round to accepting the claw-back principle in 1968, but this became a relatively minor victory for CPAG in the aftermath of the devaluation crisis, the reintroduction of prescription charges, and the hard-hitting Review of Public Expenditure announced in January 1969.

With the general election due in 1970, CPAG, under its new management team of Townsend as Chair and Field as Director, decided to run a campaign highlighting Labour's lack of achievements on poverty during its term of office. This was a risky strategy – attacking the party traditionally associated with equality, and drawing further attention to the claw-back family allowance arrangement that had antagonised many in both the working and middle classes. Townsend was hesitant, and took some persuading by Field.[140] CPAG had built up a group of parliamentary supporters – mainly Labour – whom they could use to put forward questions; there were still some close associations with Labour's Social Policy Sub-committee and Labour activists were also instrumental in forming relationships and fundraising within constituencies and the trade union movement. A group of backbench MPs, including David Marquand and David Owen, issued an alternative policy statement called 'Change Gear', which proposed a tax on wealth, a Value Added Tax (VAT), and shifting the tax burden from families to single people. It was with some trepidation, therefore, that they put together their argument that poverty had increased under the Labour government, and began requesting meetings with the government to inform them of CPAG's intentions. As became evident to Field, Brian's withdrawal from the group to work with Crossman exposed the relative weakness of Townsend.[141] He was unable to produce costed examples of the claw-back policy, and other CPAG academics were asked to help. If Townsend's supporters had felt aggrieved that he never got the accolades that Brian received, here perhaps was some justification for seeing him as the junior partner in the Titmice team.

Wilson declined to meet with Field and Townsend as CPAG representatives, but on 27 January Crossman gave them 90 minutes of his time, and insisted that Brian be present. Brian called this 'the biggest embarrassment I ever had … it was the only time I ever thought of resigning'.[142] The meeting is recorded both by Crossman in his published diaries, and by Field in his book *Poverty and Politics*. Crossman noted that he had had a 'trying time … we are in trouble here because the attack is on our most sensitive point, our humanity'.[143] Field gives a more vivid insight, through his 27-year-old eyes, which had probably not seen the inside of the Cabinet Office before:

> Crossman began what can be only described as an extraordinary "performance". He banged the table, he shouted, and he mocked. There was an endless machine-gunning of sarcastic jokes to which the civil servants responded as if part of a medieval court. For an hour Crossman behaved like a spoilt child unable to get his way. He played almost every trick in the book in order to keep attention to himself and away from the argument…. Peter Townsend quietly argued back against this torrent of abuse. I was uncertain how to react … he [Crossman] said that nobody would believe what we were saying.[144]

Brian felt awkward, sitting across the table from his long-time close friend Townsend, and seeing the group which he had been a founder member of under such a sustained attack. Writing in 1979 to Townsend he recalled the meeting: 'I always remember that awful session you had with Crossman when he dismissed, in front of me, the whole concept of relative poverty. I longed to crawl under the table.'[145] But his first loyalty had to be to Crossman, his employer.

A few weeks later, the government tried to refute CPAG's now public claims, with David Ennals, one of Crossman's junior ministers, writing a reply. This counter-attack needed to hit hard to stem any potential haemorrhage of voters in the lead-up to the general election. Ennals claimed that CPAG's conclusions could only have been reached 'by the most selective and misleading use of statistics'.[146] CPAG responded by persuading 16 leading social scientists to sign a letter to *The Times*.[147] Brian and Titmuss declined to sign. In April, in an attempt to mend bridges, Ennals agreed to give a talk at CPAG's annual general meeting. Brian and Crossman helped him to revise his 'long, intricate defensive speech'.[148] He fared little better than in February: 'To say that the poor are getting poorer is a cynical comment which stands the truth on its head. The incomes of low earning families with several children have increased much more than average earnings.' He never actually said that the group had sold out to the Tories; he just said that scarcely a day passed without some opposition member chucking the group's arguments at him. Townsend responded, using the BBC radio programme 'The World this Weekend' to vent his anger at Ennals' 'disgraceful' and 'mud-slinging' speech.[149]

On 18 May Wilson announced that the general election would be held on 18 June, much earlier than expected. CPAG issued a press release soon after: 'The poor worse off under Labour'. The Conservatives saw the potential for capitalising on this attack, and Iain Macleod met with CPAG representatives to tell them that if they formed the next government they would increase family allowances and operate the 'claw-back' policy. It was such a surprising manoeuvre that they had to ask Macleod to repeat himself.[150]

After the election, the right-wing press niggled the new Conservative government on this promise: 'Open support by responsible Tory leaders for the theories of crackpot Leftists ... gives rise to profound misgivings among the Conservative rank and file. If Mr Heath wishes to allay their fears that Conservatism is being insidiously corrupted by Socialist influences he must ensure that the many pink spots do not develop into a rash of a deeper hue.'[151] Townsend's surprising victory with the Conservatives further damaged his reputation with Labour. For a long time after the election he endured vicious attacks for what was seen as his naïve strategy. The fallout was felt in the academic world too, with Townsend entering into long and intensely negative disputes with colleagues such as John Veit-Wilson. At times he appeared unwilling to listen fully and digest people's criticism of his work, despite significant international collaborations such as his 1970 edited book *The Concept of Poverty*.[152]

In the week before the general election Crossman travelled to Oxford to give a speech to the city's Labour Party and the University Labour Club. David Piachaud, who had put it together for him at Transport House, the Labour Party's London headquarters, sent a copy to Brian: 'You will observe 80% BAS, 20% Transport House sociology. Your help was greatly appreciated. DP.'[153] Crossman used his speech to outline Labour's achievements in social policy since 1964, highlighting improved family allowances, supplementary benefits scheme, pensions and better conditions in long-stay hospitals. He outlined how much more there was to do – for one-parent families, divorced and separated wives and tackling high rents.

Harold Wilson and his government have been viewed as having 'left office with little credit'.[154] Peter Hennessy goes further, blaming Wilson for behaving 'as if he were the bureaucratic equivalent of an experiment-crazed boffin'.[155] This is perhaps a little unfair, and fails to fully reflect the economic restraints the 1964–70 government worked under.[156] Wilson was aware of the challenges he faced, establishing the Department of Economic Affairs (DEA) in 1964 specifically to facilitate a coherent development plan. Despite its demise in 1969 it helped to consolidate the precedent of external expert advisers, especially economists such as Brian, being brought into Whitehall.[157] Furthermore, Labour did manage to achieve regular increases in benefits and to introduce new earnings-related supplements for widows, the sick and the unemployed. Yet these achievements came amid chronic ministerial tensions and re-shuffles, which were duly exploited by Whitehall mandarins intent on steering through their preferred policies. The Fulton report on the Home Civil Service in 1968 may have criticised the 'philosophy of the amateur' but the scheming of some 'Sir Humphreys' ensured that it remained an effective block on unwanted policy development. Remember how they attempted to limit the influence of Crossman's various committees, especially his 'Pensions Circus' and 'Brains Trust' for the NHS?

Was Crossman the right person for Wilson to choose to steer these health and welfare reforms in the late 1960s? His late arrival at this senior level of government appears to have bemused him at times. He enjoyed the attention it brought, especially from the media and public, but also found himself powerless to control the agenda and chronology of change. However sulky his diary entries were about his civil servants, he was honest enough not to blame them for the failure of his policies. With hindsight he advised: 'Where you have good things well worked out do not trust to providence. Do them straight away. Do them early. I will tell you why. First of all your impetus is much greater early on. Governments get terribly comfy....The fault, dear Brutus, lies not in our civil servants but in ourselves.'[158]

By March 1970, while intently watching Wilson for signs of when the election would be called, Crossman had already lined up an alternative (and he felt more stimulating) career to politics. Brian was the first person he told – in confidence – of his agreement to become editor of the *New Statesman*. Brian 'was sharp and clear-headed and thought it was crazy. He said, "You can either go on in government or you can retire and write a book but to go out of government and waste your energies on all that ephemeral journalism makes no sense at all." He may be right.'[159]

Brian's influence with Crossman may have wavered during their long association from 1953, when he first drafted his Fabian pamphlet on reform of social security, but never by much. Crossman had got over the Titmice's 1966 disloyalty and appointed Titmuss as Deputy Chair of the SBC. Townsend's 'Poor get poorer under Labour' attack in 1970 was, however, a step too far for Crossman. This tested long-held friendships and placed Brian in a difficult situation. Crossman held firm to his belief that Brian put his role of special adviser above all else, recording in May 1970: 'He has been my closest personal friend and without him I could have done very little in the past two years.'[160]

9

Patriarchy and authority: 1970–74

Health and social policy: theory and practice

Enquiries: abuse of social security, NHS management, thalidomide

'Quite like old times': pensions

International interests: health economics

Development, poverty and population control

Losses

———

The best doctors for improving population health were the
economists wielding their economic growth model of Rostovian
take-off for each and every national economy. (Simon Szreter,
2005)[1]

*When Labour lost office in 1970 Brian also lost his part-time special adviser's
position. He returned to full-time work at the LSE and a heavier administrative
and teaching load that restricted his capacity for international work. This 'London
confinement' gave him the opportunity to engage more fully with some of the
emerging health economics debates. He began to write up his own ideas on cost
benefit analyses, and on poverty from a development perspective, including the
role of family planning. He was a member of several inquiries, and watched closely
as the plans for reorganising the NHS took shape. The key event of this period
was the untimely death of Brian's mentor and close friend, Richard Titmuss.*

Health and social policy: theory and practice

Brian greeted the arrival of 1970 in the same way as he had 1960
– and most years in between – with a 10-day skiing trip to Davos

in Switzerland. Later that month he attended a very select country house party at Ditchley Park, owned by a foundation established by the tobacco magnate Sir David Wills to give the British elite a venue in which to hold informal discussions with international powers. The theme of the eighth conference for US senators and congressmen was 'Welfare and incentives/citizens and government'. Titmuss was also present at these high-level debates. From June 1970, when Edward Heath's Conservatives replaced Wilson's government, life became a little less pressured. His employment as Richard Crossman's special adviser automatically terminated with the change of government and he returned to his full-time LSE professorship; in theory he had 'free' time to devote to his other interests.

His chain of men's clothes shops, Just Men (managed by his former partner Charles Schuller), absorbed a lot of his attention. It had expanded from its first Chelsea shop to include other London branches and, for a short time, outposts in Cheltenham and in the US in New York and Philadelphia. Brian got great satisfaction from sourcing the clothes, even learning how shirts were constructed for their off-shoot company, Just Men (Shirts) Ltd. He commissioned his DHSS colleague David Piachaud, who had learned how to write basic computer programmes as a student in the US, to set up a pioneering stock system for the shops. Sales peaked at £172,299 in 1970, but the following year saw a dismal performance, with sales of only £30,938, and they continued to decline, with some years not even reaching £5,000, and the net losses steadily rising. Staffing problems remained a source of irritation, and Brian increasingly gave control of the business to Schuller. He poured any spare energy into gardening at Tanglewood, his country retreat in Kent, with his partner John Sarbutt. John was developing his landscape gardening business, as well as continuing to take on some acting work, and modelling for advertisements.

Brian's involvement with social policy planning after the change in government was ongoing, if more reactive. Paul Odgers (who had been Richard Crossman's Assistant Under Secretary in 1968 and was now in the Cabinet Office) wrote him a personal letter in May 1971 to say that the working party set up in 1969 to develop a multipurpose means test was now bearing fruit: 'The road is proving to be a long one, but let me once again express our appreciation of all the help you gave during the first difficult stage of these proceedings.'[2] Brian had also been involved with drafting Sir Keith Joseph's classic paper, *The cycle of deprivation*, in 1971. In June 1972 he was sent an advance copy of Joseph's speech to be given at the Pre-School Playgroup's Association meeting at Church

House, Westminster, in which the concept was introduced to the press. Joan Cooper, Director of Social Work Service at the Department of Health and Social Security (DHSS), who had helped Joseph to draft the report, was particularly grateful for Brian's input, and hoped that he would be involved in any evaluation of the impact of the speech and the Social Science Research Council's planned research.[3]

In a series of articles in *New Society*, however, Brian took issue with the lack of progress that Joseph was making on promised reforms such as establishing a hospital ombudsman, and he highlighted the inherent weaknesses in the anticipated NHS restructuring. He could not see the benefits from bringing in 'businessmen' to manage the NHS, and felt there were more effective reforms that needed to happen – the extension of Crossman's Hospital Advisory Service into a Health Advisory Service, and the amalgamation of the statistical and economics branches of the central DHSS staff.[4] He was particularly scathing of Joseph's plans for a stronger regional tier of health authorities, and emasculated community health councils that would be 'a handpicked coterie of docile local worthies invited to a cosy chat over tea and biscuits once a month – a charade of local consultation'. His article concluded: 'Sir Keith's consultative documents should be opposed by all general practitioners who really want a unified health service and believe in community care. They should be opposed by all consultants who want to get their patients out of hospital and are frustrated by inadequate provisions made by local authorities. They should be opposed by all doctors who believe that the National Health Service is chronically underfinanced. They should be opposed by all of us who believe that we have a right to a say in the running of our local health services.'[5]

Brian continued to work in partnership with Titmuss, but the partial estrangement from Townsend damaged their collective authority. Titmuss was now producing some of his most stimulating writing. Books such as *The Gift Relationship: from human blood to social policy*, published in 1970, consolidated his reputation as an international heavyweight in social policy theory.[6] The Child Poverty Action Group (CPAG) provided a mechanism through which Brian and Townsend could continue to have some communication. Townsend, as Chair, sent Brian copies of his correspondence with Keith Joseph in October 1970, in which he tried to correct the Conservative Party's understanding of CPAG's proposals. Brian forwarded the letter to David Piachaud for comment, who replied that he found Townsend's discussion 'sheer nonsense', drawing as it did on data from 1968, which was before the introduction of the 'claw-back' policy (which increased universal family allowance, while reclaiming this from those who earned above a threshold through the income tax system).[7]

By late 1970 Brian appeared unhappy with the strategic direction of CPAG. Sending a copy of its latest press release to David Piachaud he asked, 'Is this also all wrong [?]. If so I would like to write a polite but critical letter to Peter and Frank [Field, CPAG Director] & suggest that [they] discuss it all with us. It seems such a waste of time for them to put up good schemes for John Stackpoole to shoot down. We must now all work together on schemes which merit serious attention.' Piachaud replied with a 'few disgruntled thoughts'.[8] Under Frank Field's direction CPAG had launched campaigns highlighting the impact of the Conservative government's new social policies, especially the planned Family Income Supplement (FIS). This had been intended to help 190,000 low wage-earning families, but only 13 per cent had registered for it despite a government advertising campaign costing £340,000 in the summer of 1971. Brian highlighted that FIS would only pay out an extra £7 million, whereas Iain Macleod and Heath, when negotiating with CPAG before the 1970 election, had promised to spend £30 million on increasing family allowances. Brian also had predicted the low take-up, particularly among immigrants and unmarried mothers.[9] On his 'restricted' copy of the August 1970 DHSS internal memo introducing the FIS he wrote, alongside his pithy deconstruction of the scheme, 'Joseph's fig leaf'.[10]

A loose collaboration, including Nicholas Bosanquet, Ruth Lister, Tony Lynes, David Piachaud, Mike Reddin, Frank Field and Paul Barker, maintained a relentless public presence through articles in *New Statesman*, *New Society*, *The Listener* and the daily broadsheets, which evaluated the impact of new Conservative policies on the poor.[11] Virginia Bottomley wrote a pamphlet for CPAG, 'Families with low income in London'.[12] When Margaret Thatcher, Minister of State for Education and Science, increased the price of school meals, they monitored the reduction in take-up, especially among poorer families. Thatcher's Bill to restrict free school milk to medical need cases stimulated further research. When Anthony Barber announced in his budget statement in March 1972 that he intended to launch 'the most radical reform, improvement and simplification of the PAYE and social service systems for a quarter of a century – the tax credit scheme', Brian collaborated with colleagues to identify its potential impact on inequality and poverty. Michael Meacher, Labour MP for Oldham, drafted an article 'Tax Credits: The Modern Answer to Poverty?'[13]

David Piachaud and Brian drafted a paper on how to calculate age relief and child relief within a tax credit system.[14]

Brian also re-engaged in debate with DHSS civil servants about Barber's plans, asking for information on tax credits for the children of the self-employed. John Stackpoole wrote to Brian: 'Thank you for your letter of 11th October about the tax credits Green Paper. I am so glad that you like the scheme – it obviously has enormous potentialities, and it is one of those proposals that once they have been made seem to be the almost inescapable consequence of previous developments.'[15] Brian's collaborations with the DHSS during the 1970–74 Conservative government perfectly illustrate both his enduring value and the unwieldy nature of DHSS systems. Earlier in 1972 two other senior civil servants, Bryan Ellis and Tony Crocker, had taken it on themselves to go to see Brian at his LSE office. They urged him to push Labour to adopt a policy for paying out unused tax allowances as positive cash credits. Ellis was unaware, until he read the draft of this chapter, that his DHSS colleague Stackpoole was also informally involving Brian in a similar fashion in policy discussions.[16]

Brian spent a considerable amount of time quietly working up his more radical 'Negative Income Tax' policy over the next two years before Labour returned to government. In parallel with developing his own proposal, he was called to give evidence to the Select Committee on Tax Credits. He told his Oxford friend and colleague Michael Kaser that he viewed it as a 'terrifying experience'. He also took the opportunity to propose to Kaser that they make another visit to Eastern Europe together again (they had been on a study tour organised by Milton Roemer to the USSR in 1961): 'Your knowledge of how to handle these countries makes the life of a bon viveur tolerable.'[17] Titmuss had also returned to DHSS collaboration, phoning Stackpoole after reading the Green Paper to suggest that tax credits and family allowance (FAM) should be paid to the mother, not the father.

Titmuss coordinated comments from Brian and from David Piachaud on the DHSS policy paper on the Guaranteed Maintenance Allowance in 1973. Brian called on his friendship with Sir Claus Moser, Director of the Central Statistical Office, to try to get advance access to the 1971 Census data on married women's economic activity and dependent children to support their analysis, but neither that nor the General Household Survey had the precise breakdown of data required.[18] Tony Lynes, now secretary of the working party on single-parent families (having also worked as a welfare rights officer for Oxfordshire County Council's Children's Department) was also actively engaged in preparing briefing papers. Collaborations between the LSE and the

Centre for Environmental Studies, such as the 'Distribution of income' conference, provided another forum for discussion.[19] Della Nevitt, another of Brian's colleagues at the LSE, was also active on related issues, publishing briefing papers wearing her hat as a member of the National Council for the Unmarried Mother and her Child. Women's rights were beginning to enter serious public debate in the early 1970s, alongside discussion of other areas of discrimination in British society.

In an article in the LSE magazine in May 1971 Brian summarised the activities of the Department of Social Administration. Accompanied by a photograph of the staff (in which Brian is sitting next to Titmuss, uncannily copying both his dress and pose), the article discussed how the Department had grown from its initial staff of two in 1912 to a staff of 33. The courses had evolved from the original one-year Social Science Certificate to meet both British and international needs, and there was now a clear distinction between basic courses of study in Social Administration as an academic subject and courses that provided professional education (mainly for social workers). Its two-year Diploma in Social Administration remained one of the few university courses that could be taken without passing through the usual hoops of A-levels, giving 'a good hope to people who left school early and attracts mature students, many of whom are of considerable academic ability'. The one-year Postgraduate Diploma in Social Administration had now been running for 30 years, and in 1965 a degree centred on social administration had been introduced (called rather confusingly Branch III of the BSc Sociology). This was followed in 1966 by a one-year taught MSc.

When Brian wrote his review in 1971 there were 44 students registered for the MSc, who completed dissertation research projects alongside five research officers and five research assistants. The series of Occasional Papers in Social Administration, which had been established by the Department in 1963, had just published its 43rd manuscript. The LSE produced more professionally qualified social workers than any other British university. It had pioneered amalgamated social worker courses from 1953, offering training options for probation officers, social workers, family case workers and childcare officers: an experiment that anticipated by 17 years the demands of the new combined social services departments. In 1971 the combined Diploma in Social Work Studies had 75 registered students. New courses were also being developed for experienced qualified social workers and directors of social services departments, in collaboration with the new National Institute of Social Work Training. Three of the LSE staff were also teaching on the MSc in Social Medicine at the London School of Hygiene and Tropical Medicine (LSHTM), and there were plans to move into teaching undergraduate medical students. There were also ambitious plans for new areas of study: community work, 'race' relations and the relationship between law and social administration. International links, especially with developing countries, were being strengthened, with three staff currently seconded abroad to Ghana, Hong Kong and the US.[20]

Enquiries: abuse of social security, NHS management, Thalidomide

Between 1971 and 1973 Brian served on the Committee on Abuse of Social Security Benefits, known after its chair, Sir Henry Fisher, as the Fisher Committee. This had been established by Sir Keith Joseph to examine persistent rumours that there was widespread benefit fraud.[21] Tony Lynes, no doubt at Brian's instigation, submitted a paper on his experience of how the four-week rule of the Supplementary Benefits Commission was inconsistently applied. When it reported, the Committee provided a very full analysis of methods of fraud limitation, but avoided providing what everyone wanted – an objective assessment of the actual amount of abuse that existed. It dismissed ideas that Commonwealth immigrants were perpetrating large amounts of abuse, but discovered an 'exceptional' amount of fraud by Irish immigrants who 'worked and signed'. It attempted to address the sore question of concealed cohabitation, which had brought charges of invasion of privacy against the SBC in 1971.[22] Instead of the suggested random sampling to uncover systematic problems, the government opted instead for 'intensive local drives'.[23] One of Brian's colleagues at the LSE, David Piachaud, was openly critical of the Fisher Committee's verdict. In a letter to *The Times* he stated that there was no evidence of the extent of abuse or of its causes; that the social security system was already known as the 'SS' for its style of interrogation, and that it would be disturbing if the Fisher report led to the appointment of more 'special investigators'.[24]

Brian also served on the Hunter Committee on NHS management. Crossman had set up a working party in April 1970 at the request of the Society of Medical Officers of Health (MOH) to consider NHS management arrangements. During the protracted investigations into social services, the NHS and local government in the late 1960s, public health had been batted between various homes in the draft permutations of reconfigured services. MOHs were based in local government departments, and controlled an eclectic range of staff and services, from vaccinations and family planning to the provision of home helps and some social workers. Crossman veered between wishing to relocate them in health authorities, and giving hospital services to local government, which would have increased the role and status of the MOH. By the end of the Labour government it was apparent that as in 1948 in planning the NHS, the fate of their discipline would be the last, essentially default, decision.

Crossman's Committee was chaired by Dr R.B. Hunter, Vice-Chancellor of the University of Birmingham, and Brian was one of its 15 members, along with his old friend Jerry Morris, Professor of Epidemiology at the LSHTM. However, the Committee had no women, or social scientists with an interest in primary care, and no community representation. It was understandable, given the DHSS's current preoccupation with NHS efficiency and management, that the Hunter Committee's deliberations were conducted with this subliminal steer. Joseph had allowed Hunter to slightly expand his Committee's remit to also consider training for public health professionals, and it produced an interim report which recommended the immediate creation of short courses in medical administration (clearly now seen as the new *raison d'être* for the discipline) as an effort to raise morale. Charles Webster found it 'extraordinary that the interim report was handled in a casual manner', with a delay of six months from ratification to publication, given the crisis in public health medicine.

The final report was published on 31 May 1972, with the portentous title, *Report of the Working Party on medical administrators*. At 50 pages (excluding appendices) it was a brief and 'uninspiring' document, constrained by concurrent indecision on NHS restructuring. It very broadly outlined possibilities for what the 'specialists' might do in their new 'community medicine' territory: coordination of health services, and a limited health surveillance function, and a new concern with efficiency in the use of resources. Yet the report was vague on the discipline's management and hierarchy – there was no indication how it would sit relative to the proposed three tiers of the NHS. The power base of the old MOHs appeared to have been removed from under their feet (along with the publication of their annual reports). There was a widespread belief that 'community physicians would evolve into ancillary management functionaries alienated alike from other medical professionals and their local communities'.[25] The Hunter report did, however, further support the view of the 1965–68 Royal Commission on Medical Education (known after its chair as the Todd Report), that there should be continuing professional development for all medical specialties, which stimulated the formation of the Faculty of Community Medicine within the Royal College of Physicians, London.[26]

In 1973 Brian was also a member of the Panel of Financial Advisers for Thalidomide Children, chaired by Sir Gordon Newton (retired editor of the *Financial Times*). This was established to adjudicate on appropriate compensation payments for those left with severe disabilities after their mothers took the drug thalidomide during their pregnancies (it had been marketed as providing relief from morning sickness in 1957, and was withdrawn in 1961). The company that manufactured the drug, Distillers Co (Biochemicals) Ltd, had initially offered a payment of £5,000 to each child affected. Brian's involvement in the Financial Panel helped the families to push for a collective fund of £20 million with inflation protection, based on his calculations of what social services for disabilities would be likely to cost during their lifetimes.[27] As another of the key campaigners for the thalidomide families was Jack Ashley, whom Brian had known since their time together at Cambridge, it is possible that this was how he had become involved. Ashley, who was by this time disabled himself through total deafness, was a very active campaigner for disability rights, and adept at involving individuals who he knew would be effective at achieving justice.

Brian also returned to the debate on legal reform which he had begun in the mid-1960s through his collaboration with Robert Stevens. This time, he worked with Michael Zander, Professor of Law at the LSE. They had obtained a US$25,000 research grant in 1968 from the Ford Foundation for a study of access to legal services in three London boroughs. Zander valued Brian's social science methodologies, and they employed Rosalind Brooke to assist their research programme, which involved 1,651 members of the public completing a 43-page questionnaire. Contact with members of the legal profession was easier this time, having gained the personal (and publicised) support of the Lord Chancellor, Lord Gardiner. A further sign of Brian's authority on legal administration was his participation at the All Souls College Oxford conference, 'The future of law reform', in September 1972.

The resultant book from the Abel-Smith and Zander project, *Legal Problems and the Citizen*, published in 1973, demonstrated that there was as much unmet need for civil legal services as there was for criminal ones, and exposed the large number of cases that went to court with no legal representation.[28] Despite the fact that law centres had been established in 1970 (partly as an outcome of the Society of Labour Lawyers petitioning through their *Justice for All* pamphlet in 1968), it was usually still the poorest people who failed to gain access to justice. Although the Law Society again resented this intrusion into their closely controlled world, as they had in 1967, they continued to send Brian and Zander invitations to lunches, allowing, as Zander puts it,' the enemy to come and feed among them'.[29] Brian also served on the Labour Party's legal aid working group, when it was established in January 1974, at the invitation of its chair Sir [Frederick] Elwyn Jones.[30] It was linked to Labour's Legal Action Group, on which Brian also served, and looked at how legal aid could be reformed to make it easier to obtain assistance. He took advice from Francis Deutsch of the Paddington Neighbourhood Advice Bureau and Law Centre on what changes would be useful. He also was a sponsor of the Labour 'Campaign for mental health'.

'Quite like old times': pensions

During its period in opposition Labour sought to mend the fences with the trade union movement following the breakdown in communications over its proposed incomes policy and reform of industrial relations. This had been fractured by their 1969 White Paper, *In Place of Strife*.[31] In working towards a 'social wage' within the Social Contract, discussions naturally extended into pensions territory. Jack Jones, General Secretary of the Transport & General Workers' Union, was leading a campaign for a substantial increase in basic pensions, and to index them as a protection against inflation. There were significant changes in how Labour now accessed social policy advice. Unlike the 1950s and 1960s, when the National Executive Committee (NEC) tightly controlled this through its Home Policy Committee and Social Policy Sub-committee, the TUC now had a significant input through a new TUC/Labour Party Liaison Committee. It has been suggested that the magnitude of the TUC's influence at this time left the NEC unwilling or unable to question trade union priorities, and how they fitted into the wider policy debates.[32] Yet Labour saw such collaboration as essential to repair the relationship with the trade unions if they were to stand a chance of winning the next election.

At the 1972 Labour Party conference Jack Jones had summed up the TUC's feelings about earnings-related pension plans:

> One of the prime difficulties about many of our past proposals is that they were incomprehensible. I do not think even the people who drew them up really understood them. Much of this was because of the idea that pensions always had to be based on the contributory principle since this was supposed to establish the right to a pension. I believe we have to up-date our attitude on

this, because so far all the contributory principle has established is the right to an abysmally low pension.[33]

The outcome of Jones' powerful conference speech was that by late 1972 the Social Policy Sub-committee was instructed to re-evaluate the principle of superannuation. At a series of meetings policy papers were presented by Judith Hart, Bill Simpson and Tony Lynes which acknowledged that Labour had to have a comprehensive analysis, not just an uncritical continuation of a Crossman-style earnings-related policy. Lynes drew attention to the limited capacity of such a scheme to really address wider inequalities in old age, and the risk the financial instability of a small fund would create for its long-term security.[34] This helped relations with the trade unions, which were already improving, partly as a consequence of Labour's commitment through the Social Contract to an 'immediate' increase in pensions to £10 per week for a single person (£16 for a couple) when it returned to government.[35] This, Barbara Castle and the Social Policy Sub-committee were at pains to stress, did not mean, however, that an earnings-related national superannuation scheme had been completely abandoned.

The TUC's appeasement came in the form of the planned retention of the flat-rate pension, but with the introduction of a second tier of earnings-related pension. This ensured that the Crossman scheme lived to see another parliament, but allowed a substantial re-thinking of its key elements. Tony Lynes worked overtime on reconciling demands to look after existing pensioners with the introduction of an earnings-related scheme, and devised a 'crediting-in' mechanism. In the end it did not make it into Labour's election manifesto in February 1974, but it provided valuable negotiating power to the Social Policy Sub-committee.

Was this subjugation of Labour's Social Policy Sub-committee apparent at the time? Possibly not, but perhaps some inkling of this shift in policy power lay behind Brian's decision to decline an invitation to participate in its healthcare working party in June 1972, claiming pressure of his other commitments. He did, however, join the tax credits working party. This was formed to evaluate the Conservatives' October 1972 Green Paper *Proposals for a Tax Credit System*.[36] The working party was chaired by Barbara Castle, and fellow members included Peter Townsend and Brian's LSE colleague David Piachaud, along with the economist and special adviser Nicholas Kaldor, whom Brian had known since their involvement with Crossman's pension planning in the late 1950s. They batted ideas among themselves, and produced proposals for Labour to submit to the Select Committee, which also received submissions from pressure groups such as CPAG and the National Joint Committee of Working Women's Organisations.

Brian saw this as an opportunity to correct some of the systemic weaknesses of the welfare state. His proposal for a 'Negative Income Tax' credit system (similar to a proposal then circulating from Arthur Cockfield) was 'the only way of replacing FIS [Family Income Supplement] and extending the benefit of income tax allowance to those below the threshold, and that the party should not reject the opportunities for redistribution which such a scheme presented'.[37] Brian's proposal was opposed by Kaldor, who considered it too expensive, and favoured a minimum wage, or a modified tax allowance scheme.[38] Their debate extended into the summer, culminating in Brian writing to Castle making the case for tax credits as not only the cheaper claw-back mechanism but also the most equitable.[39] He publicly aired his views at an International Fiscal Studies conference. In a seminal paper entitled 'Equity and dependency' he proposed some 'controversial suggestions': family allowances for all children, including the first; combined tax and social security systems that neither encouraged nor discouraged marriage; wives to have the same right to claim a tax credit as a single person; and all those over 16 to have the right to claim maintenance allowances if in full-time education.[40]

In November 1973 Brian, Tony Lynes, Peter Corfield and David Piachaud were invited by Brian O'Malley to join a Labour working group to produce a detailed social security scheme with a draft bill and costings, for the tight deadline of the third week of January 1974. Brian relayed this invitation, noting that 'It is quite like old times.' Lynes was pessimistic because of the ongoing disputes around an earnings-related scheme, and he predicted that the 'flat-raters' would absent themselves from meetings where they knew they would be out-voted, confident in their belief that the war would be won in the NEC anyway: 'Brian O'Malley and Barbara Castle may be kidding themselves they have won, but I am sure Jack Jones doesn't think so. Nor does Terry Pitt…. You will gather that I'm a good deal less optimistic about the whole exercise than you appear to be.'[41] Michael Meacher put up questions in the House of Commons to Joseph, Secretary of State for Social Services, on what the costs would have been for modifying the existing social security benefits. What, for example, would the Exchequer gain from abolishing both family allowances and child tax allowances and replacing them with a 'child endowment cash benefit'? David Piachaud spent long hours calculating the impact of the Conservatives' White Paper *Strategy for Pensions*, and how various permutations of contributions would affect the levels of pensions. Along with Brian, he engaged in debates with Paul Barry, who had produced an alternative costing scheme.[42]

International interests: health economics

While Labour were out of government between 1970 and 1974, Brian was effectively unemployable in Britain as a special adviser. Although he played an active part in helping Labour develop a number of health and social welfare policies, what is surprising is his apparent failure to get more involved with the work of international agencies such as the WHO, the ILO and The World Bank during this period. After the success of his 1967 book, *An International Study of Health Expenditure*, he participated in a 10-day WHO-EURO Health Economics Seminar in Moscow in June 1968, where he was employed as a temporary WHO adviser, and also tasked with preparing the seminar summary. Sixteen European countries (including the USSR) were represented, as well as senior WHO staff. Brian's own contribution, a paper entitled 'Economics and health services', drew on his now extensive involvement and knowledge of the British NHS, and international comparisons. Yet he still felt unable to explain what determined the level of a country's health spending, or why the percentage of GDP spent on healthcare continued to rise, with the likelihood of reaching 10 per cent in the near future.[43] He considered in his paper whether quantifying a number of days of 'effective life' might be a useful criterion for establishing budget priorities. He also discussed possible efficiency measures, such as delegating tasks to lower-paid health service workers, and highlighted the importance of close cooperation between doctors and economists. Other contributors spoke on topics that included cost benefit analyses, and the importance of health manpower planning.

From September 1968 to June 1970, however, Brian had been sucked into Crossman's Westminster world. His continuation part time at the LSE ensured that he kept abreast of the latest publications and academic networks. His archive files are full of papers by economists such as Robert Grosse, Burton A. Weisbrod and the statistician Dorothy Rice – all with detailed annotations. He was in regular contact with US colleagues such as Ida Merriam who led the research and statistics branch of the Social Security Administration, and George Silver, who, as Deputy Assistant Secretary at the Department of Health, Education and Welfare, had overseen the introduction of Medicaid and Medicare. Brian also followed emerging debates on cost benefit analysis closer to home in the work of Alan Williams at the University of York and Jenny Roberts at the LSHTM. But in terms of participation at international meetings and consultancy work, he had little flexibility. There had been occasional invitations that he accepted, and he kept up with colleagues in Geneva, but the intensity of his international work in the late 1960s seems to have ebbed.

By the early 1970s the WHO was no longer the close-knit network that Brian had found so exhilarating as one of their first freelance consultants in 1957. Through the 1960s it had continued to expand to disseminate western medical orthodoxy – both its methods and standards of acceptable healthcare. Historians have since remarked on how this was actively encouraged by developing countries such as India, who saw it as their entitlement under the post-war new world order to have access to westernised medicine and healthcare of the quality they saw operating in countries like the UK and the US.[44] It was not until 1973, when China finally joined the WHO, and demonstrated to the world the efficiency of its socialist 'barefoot doctors' programme, that this ideology began to be widely challenged.

One developing country that made an early move towards reforming its health and welfare systems was Chile. The election of Salvador Allende as president in November 1970 brought a new enthusiasm for change, which the WHO wished to support. Within a year, Brian was asked to join a working party to Chile organised through the Pan American Health Organisation (the American regional office of the WHO). He travelled via New York, to link up with Vicente Navarro, whom he had first met in London in 1965, where Navarro had been helped by Richard Titmuss after his political exile from Spain. Navarro subsequently moved to Johns Hopkins University, where he was encouraged by Brian to establish the *International Journal of Health Services*, to provide an alternative to the more conservative US health publications.

On arrival in Santiago, Brian and Navarro, following a formal audience with Allende, worked intensively with Ministry of Health officials, and with Hugo Behn, Dean of the School of Public Health, advising on potential funding and organisational systems. Brian's public praise for what the Chilean government was achieving was important for its international reputation, although many of the reforms were reversed after the coup in September 1973 that brought in the military regime of General Pinochet. Navarro and Brian continued to collaborate, both on the journal (Brian was a member of the editorial board) and on other projects. Navarro found his calm personality and elegant dress disarming. He learned that Brian's facial expressions were far more revealing at times than his words (as, for example, when he indulged Brian's request for a tour of the Bronx district on one of his

New York trips) and he admired Brian's ability to make strong, and often controversial, statements while smiling. [45]

In December 1972 Brian, employed as a temporary WHO adviser, participated in the joint Statistical Commission and European Commission for Europe Conference of European Statisticians Consultation on Health Statistics. This four-day meeting in Geneva focused on the health sub-system within the system of national accounts and balances. Delegates discussed the integration of health statistics with social and economic statistics, and reconciling differing approaches with the UN System of National Accounts. Brian, who also acted as rapporteur, made a number of proposals that the conference accepted, including establishing a separate classification for environmental health services; a method for distinguishing between hospitals and welfare institutions; and definitions for what constituted pharmaceutical products.[46] In July 1973 he participated in an inter-regional seminar on 'Health economics' at Geneva, giving a paper, 'Basic Concepts: Macro-Economic Aspects of Health Care'.[47]

WHO was also beginning to extend the application of health economics within its work programmes. Brian had participated in 1971 in a WHO working group on the economics of medical education.[48] He was also keen to demonstrate how health economists could be usefully brought into debates on disease control policies. His article 'Cost effectiveness and cost benefit in cholera control' resulted from his participation in a WHO inter-regional seminar on 'Cholera and smallpox in Malaysia and Singapore' in November 1972. It shows the progression of his intellectual interests, and how he brought them into the WHO policy environment.[49] Slowly, over these years, he was consolidating his views on what health economics was and what it could achieve. They are clearly set out in his entry 'Health and disease, economics of' in the 1974 edition of the *Encyclopaedia Britannica*.[50]

Development, poverty and population control

Although he would probably not have identified himself as such, Brian was one of an emerging band of development economists. He had progressed from studies of British health and welfare services to investigate and advise on developing countries, coloured by his experiences in Tanzania and Mauritius in the early 1960s. Through assignments he came into contact with this rapidly growing academic community, in new institutions such as the Institute for Development Studies at the University of Sussex, and with intellectuals such as Gunnar Myrdal, who were producing radical development theories to challenge the 1950s pioneers lead by Arthur Lewis.[51] As Martha Finnemore puts it, 'Before 1968 being "developed" meant having dams, bridges and a (relatively) high GNP per capita. After 1973 being developed also required the guarantee of a certain level of welfare to one's population.' Her tight periodisation might be a little naïve, but it highlights the speed with which the development debate had moved. One of the key trends within the international development community was a re-focusing of the poverty debate. Gunnar Myrdal and other development economists now deemed neoclassical development orthodoxy as a failure where it had left poverty untouched. Their position was supported by changes within The World Bank – one of the major development policy funders – after the arrival of Robert McNamara as its new president in 1968. Like Brian, he was 'an internationalist driven by internationalist morality and optimism'.[52] Unlike his predecessors, he talked about 'the poor' as individual human beings rather than as countries.[53] He enabled poverty-oriented lending – small grants to developing countries that were not stymied by masses of paperwork and complicated cost benefit analyses.[54]

Population control was an issue which bridged the poverty, development and health debates. Brian had been one of the first policy advisers to try to develop an integrated approach to population control and economic and social development through his work in Mauritius in the early 1960s, with Richard Titmuss and Tony Lynes. He had established collaborations with members of the UN Population Commission, and lobbied on behalf of the Mauritian government for aid to implement a family planning programme. He was therefore well aware of the activities of the International Planned Parenthood Federation (IPPF) when it asked him to be the special rapporteur for its ninth international conference, held in the English seaside resort of Brighton in October 1973.

The IPPF had been founded in 1952 in Bombay, with eight founding partners: the Netherlands, Hong Kong, India, Singapore, Sweden, the UK, US and West Germany.[55] At that time the only government to actively promote family planning was India; there was no support from international organisations such as the UN. Only Japan, China, Pakistan, Fiji and Korea had followed India's lead by 1962. The IPPF facilitated the foundation of family planning associations in new member countries, and conducted a survey of 'unmet needs' in 209 countries, mainly those classed as 'developing' – or 'third world' in the terminology of the period. The UN sent a field mission to India in 1965 led by Sir Colville Deverell, former Governor of Mauritius, to review its family planning programme. On 10 December 1966 –

Human Rights Day – the UN Secretary General issued a declaration: 'We believe that the majority of parents desire to have the knowledge and the means to plan their families; that the opportunity to decide the number and spacing of children is a basic human right'. It also passed a landmark resolution to assist countries with developing family planning programmes and research, which was helped by the designation of 1968 as Human Rights Year, and the UN conference held in Tehran had family planning as one of its key themes.

Presenting family planning as a 'human right' related to the health of mothers and children was the key breakthrough. In 1965 the IPPF was given consultative status at the ILO and UNICEF, with the WHO in 1966, and UNESCO and Food and Agriculture Organization (FAO) in 1968, thus consolidating their reputation and authority. It was also greatly helped by a donation of US$300,000 from the Swedish government in 1965, along with a bequest of US$150,000 from the Victor-Bostrom Fund, which was matched by 30 US private individual donors – giving the IPPF an income of US$3.6 million for 1966–68. The UN Fund for Population Activities also received increasing support – contributing countries increased from 23 in 1967–70 to 132 in 1973. Other UN agencies such as the WHO began to build family planning into maternal and child health programmes, and UNICEF into its nutrition and other welfare schemes. The World Bank began to give grants for family planning programmes, and USAID (US Agency for International Development) made having a family planning programme a prerequisite for its grants. Parallel to these initiatives was an emerging sense of 'overpopulation'. Publications appeared with titles such as *The Population Bomb*.[56] Overpopulation was increasingly presented as a medical problem that could be tackled with vertical disease programmes such as those now being used to tackle malaria and smallpox:

> Overpopulation is a malady of society that produces wasted bodies, minds and spirits just as surely as have other familiar scourges – leprosy, tuberculosis, cancer. [The] problem in India [is] of epidemic proportions.[57]

By the time of the 1973 Brighton conference (the first since Chile in 1967), the IPPF was a major player in the population control field. Its annual budget was more than £30 million. Some 600 representatives from 84 countries attended the Brighton conference. It was timed to coincide with the launch of the 10-year World Plan of Action, to be initiated in 1974, designated World Population Year. These grand gestures and titles alluded to the increasing global concern at rapid (and essentially uncontrolled) population growth. It was estimated that the total spent on population control worldwide was US$3 billion, and that in developing countries governments were now beginning to step in to provide clinical services and training for personnel previously provided through IPPF-funded national associations. Despite these significant developments, Brian summarised the state of affairs in 1973:

> Only half the world's population is believed to have access to organised family planning programmes. Less than a third of the 500 million women at risk of pregnancy are regularly practising any means of contraception, and about half of these users are employing relatively ineffective methods. Organised services are a tiny part of total activity. Non-users are heavily concentrated in the rural areas of the developing parts of the world to which knowledge is not easily conveyed or services delivered. Last, but not least, population growth is making the task so much more difficult to perform ... by 1975 the world population is expected to be four billion ... and by 1995 six billion.... IPPF must be concerned not only *about* but *with* world poverty – economic poverty, social poverty and poverty of rights.[58]

In his inimitable style, Brian stressed the importance of disassociating family planning from medical services: 'in the long run contraceptive supplies must be stripped of all mystery and most of them provided through similar distribution channels to salt or soap. Family planning should become part of ordinary living. The target groups are men as well as women, the poor as well as the rich, senior citizens where they legitimise social change as well as the young. It should never be forgotten that the capacity to reproduce comes with the threshold of adulthood. The earlier in life the message gets across, the longer the impact within the woman's limited period of fertility and the greater the impact on the period of man's greatest potency.'

Brian recognised that in many countries 'a heavy load of legal and cultural barriers will have to be removed' and that 'in many societies, the key message is essentially a feminist message: family planning cannot progress until the status of women is changed.... For what is needed is for the male to accept the female as an equal partner and not a junior partner in the marriage contract.' To make family planning work, Brian concluded that it had to be made into a 'popular movement', like adult franchise or trade unions, and ideally a self-help movement: 'At least it is clear that community pressure of the type used in China can be a very effective force in promoting the acceptance of family planning.' He identified four key roles for the IPPF's national associations, including pushing their governments to take responsibility for family planning, taking the 'next step', whether that was establishing a legal age of marriage or providing services for the unmarried. These associations, he thought, should 'operate right up to the edge of what is legal and sometimes even beyond where the law is uncertain or out of tune with public opinion. While a government gains short-term respect by being respectable, a voluntary body may gain long-term respect by being responsibly disreputable.... The work will not be finished until no child is unplanned, unsought or unwanted, and until there is a safe and prosperous future for every child born on this planet.'[59]

Losses

By the autumn of 1972, despite his relentless workload, it was clear to his family and friends that Richard Titmuss was again ill. He had suffered periods of ill health from the 1950s, both physical and mental.[60] This delicate man, who had been lovingly referred to as 'God' by Brian, Townsend and other disciples since the mid-1950s, was now entering a prematurely final stage of life. Titmuss had successfully survived treatment for tuberculosis in 1957, but his damaged lungs were further stressed by heavy cigarette smoking, and the large doses of streptomycin left him partially deaf. His intense pace of work had remained possible because he was supported at home by Kay, but this 'one-man information retrieval system' was increasingly in pain. Clinical examinations in 1972 had focused on muscular problems, and by the time his lung cancer was diagnosed it was incurable. He persisted with his teaching through the course of debilitating radiotherapy into the spring of 1973, sometimes travelling straight from the Hammersmith Hospital to give his lecture to a silent, empathetic audience. Even after the prognosis, he continued to see members of government committees at his Acton home, in the hope of concluding their investigations before his death. A final example of his enduring sense of duty is the vivid and moving account he wrote of his NHS treatments, and his in-patient stay at the Westminster Hospital, which was published as a postscript to a collection of his essays, *Social Policy: an introduction*, which Brian edited with Kay.[61] He did not recover from the operation designed to make him more comfortable. After the last semi-conscious days, during which his demands for cigarettes were met instead with peppermint, he died aged 65 on 6 April 1973, in the Central Middlesex Hospital, with Kay and Ann at his bedside. Brian was sitting on a bench in the corridor with Mike Reddin. Kay went out to tell them that he'd gone, and Brian went in to see him. They joked that it was characteristic of his awkwardness and rebellion against bureaucracy that Titmuss had died one day into the new tax year.[62]

Brian was devastated. He had lost his mentor, friend and father-figure. They had been in almost daily contact since Brian's appointment as a research assistant at the NIESR in 1953. In the early years, if face-to-face contact was not possible, they wrote long newsy letters, usually signing off 'with love'. They had a rare depth of understanding of each other's intellectual lives. Over a thousand people attended the memorial service held on 6 June at St Martin-in-the-Field's Church in central London. There were speeches by the Right Reverend Trevor Huddleston (Bishop of Stepney), Richard Crossman and Wilbur Cohen (former Secretary of the US Department of Health, Education and Welfare, and known as 'Mr Social Security'). 'Jerusalem' was sung, and Brian read the passage from I Corinthians 13: '… beareth all things, believeth all things, hopeth all things, endureth all things. Charity never faileth….'

Brian had promised Titmuss that he would take care of Kay, now living on a widow's pension. This filial loyalty was clear in the very practical ways in which he now supported her. Within a matter of weeks he had begun to sensitively make enquiries about her financial position. He arranged for his stockbroker (at his friend Denzil Freeth's firm) to invest Richard's legacy for her. Kay also had been ill for some time, and too frail to entertain the friends she wanted to see. She couldn't travel to see Peter and Liz Shore, so Brian instead invited them to Kay's Acton home, where he catered and cooked for all of them.[63] She may have privately mocked his love of new gadgets (Ann Oakley remembers his garlic press being one such object of mirth), but Kay increasingly came to depend on Brian over the next 15 years. He visited regularly, and always rang her on Sunday morning. After her death in 1987, reminiscing with Oakley about Kay's cooking – how he had always left the Acton house feeling hungry – he admitted to her that he had not really liked Kay. Perhaps it was his love of Richard that made his devotion to her tolerable.[64] The LSE established the Titmuss Memorial Fund in June 1973, which was announced in national newspapers, and details were sent to his overseas contacts. Its purpose was to provide financial support for LSE students, especially mature students and those from developing countries. This resulted in some very generous donations, including a substantial one from the Mauritius government. It was suggested that this might pay for part of the LSE library to be re-named after Titmuss and hold his collection of books.[65]

The year 1973 also saw Kit Russell's retirement from the LSE after 24 years as the coordinator for fieldwork for students taking the Diploma or Certificate in Social Administration. It added to the sense that this was the end of an era. Her colleagues (with her help) undertook a commemorative survey of all the students who had passed through the courses since 1949.[66] Over 87 per cent responded, and the analysis, published as *Changing course*, highlighted not that these courses had enabled student social mobility (two thirds of the nearly 2,000 students were from middle-class backgrounds), but that social welfare work was becoming ever more professionalised. A diploma or certificate was no longer sufficient: these students wanted – and their employers increasingly demanded – a Master's degree.[67]

This 24-year survey also served as a near coterminous account of how the Department had been transformed by Titmuss. From his arrival to lead the Department of Social Administration in 1950 he had almost single-handedly steered its development. Although he had handed over its management to others during the 1960s (Brian and Donnison), he retained the general authority to sanction any significant proposed change. His tenure had paralleled the creation of the welfare state and the transformation of social policy from its charitable origins into an international academic and professional discipline.

Brian was Titmuss's anointed successor in more ways than one. The Department increasingly looked to him for leadership, and external colleagues in the social policy community talked about him as 'Titmuss's earthly representative'. He was also asked by the joint editors, William Robson and Bernard Crick, of the *Political Quarterly* if he would take Titmuss's place as an editorial director of the holding company. There was a poignant symbolism in sending back Titmuss's share certificate and receiving one in his own name. From November 1973 he participated in this new set of editorial meetings, alongside an eclectic mix of academics and politicians, including Amartya Sen, Merlyn Rees, Shirley Williams and Michael Zander.

10

'Such marvellous fun': 1974–76

Chocolate soldiers: the rise of the special adviser

Private concerns

'One of us': advising Barbara Castle

Labour's policy machine

National Health Service: 'The ark of our covenant'

Pay beds

Resource Allocation Working Party

Mental illness, mental handicap and disability benefits

Pensions: third time lucky

Throughout its history, the NHS and its staff have been dogged
by a sense of doing better and feeling worse. (Brian Edwards,
Administrator, Leeds Area Health Authority, 1974–76)[1]

*This chapter is defined by Brian's re-appointment as a part-time special
adviser to the new Labour government of 1974. This time he worked for the
charismatic, strong-willed Barbara Castle amid deepening tensions between the
government, the Labour Party, the trade unions and NHS staff. He helped
to smooth negotiations with the medical profession over Castle's controversial
plan to remove all private medicine (pay beds) from NHS hospitals. He was
instrumental in setting up the Resource Allocation Working Party (RAWP)
to introduce a more equitable system for allocating funding between the NHS
regions. Some of the policy ideas that he had helped Labour to develop over
the previous 20 years reached fruition, including an earnings-related pension
plan. Although the international economic crisis was beginning to have an*

impact on government spending, Brian's sideline business, Just Men, continued to thrive, and he balanced a hectic working life with weekends with his partner John Sarbutt at their country home.

Chocolate soldiers: the rise of the special adviser

Brian had lost his position as special adviser when the Labour government fell in 1970. Among other interests, especially his growing international consultancies, he continued his health and social welfare research at the LSE until Labour's return to government in March 1974. Almost immediately he was offered a special adviser position by the new Secretary of State at the Department of Health and Social Security (DHSS), Barbara Castle, based on the reputation of his work with Crossman and his ongoing close involvement in Fabian and Labour circles. Crossman had predicted this in the run-up to the June 1970 general election:

> This evening I had a long dinner with Brian and from 8 until 11.30 we discussed his future. He has been my closest personal friend and without him I could have done very little in the past two years. He knows that I am getting out and sees there is a case for my going. Should he stay on? I said, "If I could see to it that Barbara took my place, it would be worth your while to stay. She is good with research people. If it's Denis [Healey] I wouldn't stay". After a splendid dinner at a little restaurant just by Brian's house I came back home.[2]

So, after a four-year Conservative government, Brian returned to the DHSS at the Elephant and Castle. By this time special advisers were a permanent fixture within Whitehall. Castle was allowed up to five, an indication of the prestige of the DHSS and her bargaining power with Harold Wilson. In addition, the Joseph Rowntree Social Service Trust had initiated funding for research assistants – 'chocolate soldiers' – for government ministers in 1971, and Wilson subsequently made this a government-financed scheme. In just over 10 years the whole culture of Whitehall had changed and with it the process of policy formation. In May 1974 *Hansard* reported that there were 31 special advisers in government. Nineteen of these were academics, five of whom were from the LSE. Wilson formalised and institutionalised the role of the special adviser, granting them civil service status, and through individuals such as Brian, exploring how they could best fit within the Whitehall machine.[3] The relationship was mutually beneficial: top advisers such as Nicholas Kaldor (now Lord Kaldor) could command £11,000 pa – double a professorial salary – and a room at the Treasury.[4]

The substantial increase in the number of special advisers in Wilson's 1974 administration called for a clear grading and pay structure. There were inherent difficulties in linking these 'temporary' posts to the civil service hierarchies in which age played a larger role in determining salary point than experience. Adrian Ham, special adviser at the Treasury, attempted to collate information on salary and conditions of service. Discussions were further coloured by the worsening economic climate. Tony Lynes wrote to his colleagues in January 1975: 'It is my view that special advisers, as a whole, are generously paid and that, in the present economic situation, it would be appropriate for us to accept a cut in our salaries'. He knew, however, that this was unrealistic and proposed instead that they decline the annual increase in cost of living allowance. He held firm to his convictions. Other special advisers such as David Lipsey felt that these gestures might not be domestically feasible.[5]

The rise of special advisers also needs to be seen in the context of the proliferation of other channels of policy advice. A telling example of the increased competition in this area can be seen in the Labour Party's decision in 1973 not to allow the formation of any more policy study groups: it could not effectively cope with the products of its existing 50 or so groups.[6] Another problem that the rise of special advisers sought to fix was the increasing sense of 'overload' in British government.[7] Ministers could not handle the vast amount of paperwork that arrived on their desks on a daily basis. Special advisers signed the Official Secrets Act and could therefore see all confidential (especially Cabinet) papers, which were not open to Parliamentary Private Secretaries. They identified priority areas and issues that their minister needed to be aware of. 'They clearly saw themselves as the Minister's alter ego, extending his capacity for work.'[8]

One further way in which Wilson's new government attempted to streamline the policy-making process was through the creation in 1974 of the Policy Unit. This was Labour's take on the Conservatives' 1971 Central Policy Review Staff, the first of the 'think tanks'. When David Piachaud was seconded to work in the Policy Unit he observed that nearly all of the social policy advice given to Wilson bore the intellectual hallmark of LSE. Policy Unit briefings had to be printed on green paper so that Wilson could quickly find them amongst his voluminous paperwork.[9]

Private concerns

Brian's special adviser status had also opened up a potentially damaging line into his private life, which became a real threat when Richard Crossman announced that he planned to publish his diaries. This flouted the civil service and parliamentary convention that memoirs should not discuss the previous 30 years. In 1973 Crossman already had in preparation his early ministerial diaries from 1964. He was aware that he had serious health problems and that he might not have long left to finish them (and thereby secure funds for his young family). He died of cancer of the liver on 5 April 1974, aged 66. His memorial service was held on 15 May 1974, at which Brian gave a surprisingly intimate eulogy based on his experience of working with Crossman:

> He would cross-examine us, upbraid us and even insult us but always without malice. And thus also without remembrance or remorse. Nothing mattered but the search for truth – at least as he currently saw it. He would have an idea in his bath and rush into the sitting room at Vincent Square wet and nude to challenge a point I had made at breakfast or to argue the precise opposite of what I had drafted for him at his request for a speech, statement or White Paper. As long as you knew not to take the pyrotechnics seriously it was all such marvellous fun. It was also education on the most magnificent scale. It was all part of what he called the charm of politics.[10]

Barbara Castle wrote in her diary that it was 'a polished and very charming' tribute.[11]

Crossman's pioneering diary publications were political and social dynamite, but also potentially lucrative, and Brian had concerns over how much he (and his relationship with John) would appear in them. He was aware that they needed Cabinet Office clearance (indeed, Whitehall launched a legal battle to try to stop publication), and he wrote to the Cabinet Secretary Sir John Hunt for clarification. Hunt clearly did not understand how far back Brian and Crossman's friendship extended: 'You would not enter the story until the summer of 1968 and I am a little reluctant to answer hypothetical questions when I do not know what, if anything, Dick Crossman has said about you! However I can say that I would regard information derived solely from the Positive Vetting process as something to which confidentiality attaches. And this, I think, is all you are really asking me.'[12]

In the event, the first volume of Crossman's diaries (*Minister of Housing 1964–66*), which appeared in 1975, made no reference to Brian. For the second volume (*Lord President of Council and Leader of the House of Commons 1966–68*), published in 1976, Janet Morgan, Crossman's assistant, completed the editing after Crossman died, as she did with the third volume (*Secretary of State for Social Services 1968–70*), published in 1977, in which Brian had his most sustained appearances. *The Backbench Diaries of Richard Crossman*, which covered the period up to 1964, were edited by Janet Morgan and published in 1981.[13] These dealt with how Crossman had first come across Titmuss and the Titmice, and their early collaborations on pensions and National Insurance policy developments. In all his diary references to Brian, Crossman was genuinely impressed by his intellectual abilities and political skills. He appreciated Brian's willingness to go beyond the usual support offered by special advisers, sometimes hosting dinner parties at his home, where he displayed his excellent cooking skills and facilitated sensitive off-the-record discussions.

During his period away from Whitehall, between 1970 and 1974, Brian had focused his energies not only on the LSE and his overseas commitments, as discussed in Chapter 9, but also on developing his men's clothing business Just Men. Although Brian, to his gay friends, jokingly called it 'Only Just Men', it catered for a wide audience, and in the early 1970s was thriving in the booming fashion market.[14] In November 1974 they sold the flagship King's Road shop and opened one in the heart of London's gentlemen's club-land in Jermyn Street. The original shop in Tryon Street, just off the King's Road, continued to do well, with a resident barber as well as a bespoke tailoring service.[15]

Domestic matters were less plain-sailing. Their lodger, Carmen, who initially rented the basement at Brian and John's Elizabeth Street home, had moved into the top flat. Relations became strained, and there were rows between her and John, with Brian choosing not to get involved. By the spring of 1974 the situation had become intolerable and Brian asked her to leave. She tried to fight this, claiming 'squatters rights', but eventually left in April and the flat was renovated. Brian wrote to their Canadian friends (and regular summer tenants) David Blewett and Arthur Sheps to ask for help in finding temporary tenants. He provided a checklist: 'We would like an occupant who: (a) knew the facts (b) did not care (c) did not gossip…'.[16]

In the spring of 1975 Brian and John had decided to move. Brian wanted a freehold property, and John a London garden. Unless Brian was overseas for work, they spent their weekends at Tanglewood, the home that Brian had bought at Westwell, near Ashford in Kent in 1967. Brian shared John's love of gardening, and took every opportunity on his overseas travels to visit gardens, often bringing back seeds, cuttings and ideas for Tanglewood. In the summer of 1975 he planned to use Tanglewood as a writing retreat with Archie Cochrane, with whom he was writing a book on medical economics. Despite having known Cochrane since meeting him skiing in 1960, their relationship had been essentially professional. In making the invitation to Tanglewood, he felt it necessary to share some personal confidences, which it seems Cochrane reciprocated. Writing in June to their mutual friends Blewett and Sheps, who had originally met Cochrane through Brian when they had all been together on a skiing trip, Brian recounted: 'He [Cochrane] came to dinner with me & John here recently and now we have no secrets. But Archie's story is not what we thought. Very unusual. Sad but not unpleasant in any way. But not for a letter. For when we meet. Incidentally he sends his best regards & of course had no illusions.'[17]

In the autumn of 1975 Brian and John found an almost suitable new home at 11 Westmoreland Place off Lupus Street in Pimlico. It didn't have John's desired garden, but there was a roof terrace, and their new tenants in Elizabeth Street wished to move with them. As Brian described it to Blewett and Sheps: 'The new house is staggering with lots of room for you both (it has four bathrooms!).'[18] But when the sale of Elizabeth Street fell through just before Christmas Brian hoped that they might give him an easy solution: 'why not buy Elizabeth Street for yourselves – £25,000 including carpets and curtains. Then you can let the house to friends & keep the top flat for yourselves. The lease has 27 years to run.' Although they had been looking to buy a London flat for their summer trips, this was beyond their means and not entirely logical, and they declined. Finally, the move to Westmoreland Place happened in spring 1976.

'One of us': advising Barbara Castle

Edward Heath had gambled on calling an early general election on 28 February 1974, which was held in what Charles Webster has called 'an atmosphere of crisis reminiscent of 1931'.[19] The miners were threatening to call out other unions in mass strikes, inflation was out of control, and a whole host of other economic problems were waiting for the next government. Harold Wilson thus formed his third Labour government since 1964 but, as in 1931, a minority one. As Bryan Ellis, a DHSS civil servant, so neatly put it:

The policy files of the Conservative government were put away, and those relating to topics which might interest a Labour administration were taken out and dusted over. On Monday 4th, things looked rather different. Mr Heath had not resigned and had been talking to Mr Thorpe about a coalition. The Labour files went away and the Conservative ones came out again. On Tuesday 5th, the new position was clear once more. A new Government had arrived. The Labour files came out and remained out.[20]

Wilson called a further general election on 10 October, but only managed a majority of three seats – subsequently lost at by-elections. Through alliances with small parties, Labour managed to last the full term to May 1979. Heath, after two election defeats, was finally replaced as leader of the Conservatives by Margaret Thatcher on February 1975.

During Heath's 1970–74 government, Labour's shadow health and social security spokespeople had been Shirley Williams and then John Silkin. Neither had really raised much 'opposition' to Keith Joseph's policies, and Labour's wider policy groups seemed similarly unenthusiastic to engage in debate. When Wilson came to fix his senior ministerial team in February 1974 he offered the position of Secretary of State for Social Services to Barbara Castle. Castle had been out in the cold from Wilson's inner circle after the furore around her controversial *In Place of Strife* White Paper in 1969, which had tried to curb the power of the trade unions. It had divided Wilson's Cabinet, causing lasting damage to Labour's relations with the unions, and contributing to the 1970 general election defeat. Some commentators have speculated that it precipitated the infiltration of local Labour groups by Trotskyite factions like Militant, which further undermined the authority of the Labour leadership. It also lost Castle the opportunity to lead the left of the Party – a role that was subsequently fought over by Michael Foot and Tony Benn. Wilson's 1974 Cabinet, therefore, was an opportunity to rehabilitate Castle and give her the long-sought big ministerial post (she was then 63).

Castle had one of the longest parliamentary careers of the 20th century. She was born in Chesterfield to a tax inspector and his wife, who later moved to Bradford where they became active members of the Labour Party, and where her mother served as a Labour councillor. Castle achieved a third class Philosophy, Politics and Economics degree at St Hugh's College, Oxford, where she was closely involved in running the Labour Club. Her political activism continued after she moved to London to enter the civil service, also serving as an ARP warden in

London during the Blitz. After the death of the socialist-intellectual journalist William Mellor, with whom she had a 10-year semi-public affair (and whom she had helped to set up the newspaper *Tribune* in 1937), she married Ted Castle, night editor of the *Daily Mirror*, in 1944. At the 1945 general election she was elected MP for Blackburn, a seat she held until her retirement in 1979. Anne Perkins, Castle's official biographer, summarises her as 'clever, sexy and single-minded ... the most important female politician the Labour movement has yet produced ... she was an unflagging champion of an ethical socialism that she believed should shape every aspect of life. In one of the ironies of politics, she paved the way for Margaret Thatcher to capture the commanding heights of government.'[21] Michael Foot called her 'the best socialist minister we've ever had'.

Castle ran a tight political ship, calling on her years of experience both in government and opposition. Her ministerial team included Brian O'Malley for social services (who had served under Crossman in Wilson's 1964–70 government), Alf Morris, the first ever Minister for the Disabled and David Owen for health (Castle rejected Shirley Summerskill, who had been a shadow spokesperson for health). Owen was medically qualified and ambitious for promotion. Castle had to persuade Wilson to give him the rank of Minister of State in July 1974, an upgrade from the initial offer of Parliamentary Secretary. She appointed Jack Ashley as her Parliamentary Private Secretary. Her ministerial team was not initially liked by the civil servants, but their professional ethos ensured that they followed through Labour's policy agenda. Castle recognised that she had to quickly assert her authority, and her civil servants seemed to accept this approach more readily than Owen's, which Castle thought they found 'irritating', and other colleagues found 'rude'. She was willing, however, to acknowledge his strengths: 'I like David and am glad of his endless policy initiatives, even if some of them are only half thought through and, having started them, he drops them suddenly. I would far rather have someone who thinks for himself and stirs things up, for out of this good always comes.'[22]

On coming into office one of Castle's first actions was to appoint her team of special advisers to support her ministerial and civil service staff. Her diary shows the ease with which Brian slipped back into this familiar territory: 'I rang up Brian Abel-Smith this morning and said simply, "Will you come to me?" to which he replied equally simply, "Of course". What a relief! He is unmatchable.'[23] Having filled this crucial post she then appointed Jack Straw, former President of the National Union of Students, then a barrister and Islington Labour councillor, as her political adviser. Tony Lynes and Paul Chapman, who had completed the Diploma in Social Policy and Administration at the LSE the previous year, were also appointed.[24] When Paul Chapman resigned to return to his PhD studies, Brian recruited another of his top-scoring Diploma students, Geoff Alltimes, to replace him.[25] He used Chapman and Alltimes – 'bright young things' – to extend his capacity to support other DHSS ministers, especially Alf Morris, who was seen as the weakest member of Castle's team. Chapman recalls that it took the civil service some time to discover that he and Alltimes were little more than Brian's 'handmaidens', with no specific policy expertise.[26]

Castle's Monday lunchtime team meetings were compulsory for junior ministers and advisers, but she excluded the DHSS civil servants. They were occasions for her team to put up policy submissions and to fix the strategic direction in which she wished to steer the DHSS, and an opportunity to talk about upcoming events in her diary.[27] The relationship between Castle's special advisers and their relative positions within the department needed careful management. In October 1975 an updated DHSS circular on ministerial responsibilities clarified the arrangements. Brian had drafted the text relating to what he saw as 'his' team:

> Professor Brian Abel-Smith advises over the whole range of the Secretary of State's Departmental interests and co-ordinates the work of the special advisers. He is assisted by Mr G. Alltimes. Professor Abel-Smith should be invited to attend most important meetings held by ministers, and will otherwise be consulted by them. It is important, therefore, that he should receive copies of all submissions on important matters of policy when they are made to Ministers. Mr Tony Lynes assists Professor Abel-Smith on social security questions … he has access to the papers sent to Professor Abel-Smith who will arrange for his attendance at appropriate meetings held by Ministers. Mr Jack Straw assists the Secretary of State in carrying out her duties as a Minister. In particular he acts as a link between her non-Departmental duties (eg by briefing her on Cabinet papers in which there is no Departmental interest), as well as advising on certain aspects of Departmental policy. He also assists with speech writing and DHSS correspondence involving the Secretary of State's constituency and some other people and organisations.…The Special Advisers are outside the departmental hierarchy and have direct access to the Secretary of State. They have access to Departmental papers except any dating from previous Administrations.…[28]

Tony Lynes objected to being described as Brian's assistant, but the term stood, dictated by his relative position on the civil service salary scale.[29] Yet colleagues in the DHSS and wider social policy circles understood that it was usually Lynes who put the meat onto the bare bones of ministerial policy ideas. He had been performing this function quietly, with great competence since he was Titmuss's research assistant in the 1950s, when they devised Crossman's first national superannuation scheme. Jack Straw's job description belied the nature of his activities. When Castle appointed him she made her expectations clear: 'I have appointed Brian for his brains and you for your guile and low cunning'.[30] Brian fitted instantly and easily into Castle's team. The DHSS establishment had retained a favourable impression from his time with Richard Crossman. Civil servants viewed him as almost one of them, and appreciated the good manner he had with Castle, who carried a faint air of drama queen about her business and Whitehall relationships. As Patrick Nairne, who replaced Philip Rogers as DHSS Permanent Secretary in 1975, put it 'You needed a certain amount of social skill to get on with Barbara Castle. People used to sympathise with me … wrongly actually.'[31] Nairne recognised Brian as a man of quiet charm who could comfort Castle, and who could be relied on to quickly produce eloquent and effective speeches for her. David Owen also saw how much she liked Brian, and his relaxed and pleasant manner. Their friendship was strong enough to allow him to boss her in a way she would not have accepted from others.[32] This was due to his academic superiority on health and social welfare matters, but also smoothed by his upper-class charm, which he was well aware appealed to women of a certain age.

Castle's tenure as Secretary of State was always going to be controversial. She was still a 'formidable and impressive political force', who was expected to put up a strong fight for her interests, but she inherited some significant issues on both sides of her department. Keith Joseph's NHS reorganisation was due to come into effect on 1 April 1974 (April Fool's Day) and was already facing criticism; the junior doctors and hospital consultants were looking for better remuneration packages, spurred on by the nurses' recent victory; and the Conservatives had not achieved a satisfactory state pensions system. Castle's very public image was also likely to cause her some difficulties. She had fought election campaigns consistently on the issue of removing the last vestiges of private medicine from NHS hospitals, and now she had her opportunity to put this into action. Her idealistic passion pushed her at times to ridiculous posturing statements, which were to ultimately undermine her authority with her Cabinet colleagues and the wider Labour Party.[33]

Brian's experience of standing up to Crossman undoubtedly served him well when Castle hit such moods. When she proposed to make private patients pay for their blood transfusions both Owen and Brian told her this was contrary to the whole ethos of the British Blood Transfusion Service, which Richard Titmuss had championed so recently in *The Gift Relationship*.[34] Yet she pursued this issue for some time, until her team found ways to stymie the idea. Brian's response was to laugh at her – a tactic not many of her staff would have been brave enough to try.[35] He learned, as did Owen, that he had to respond to her intellectual as well as her political brain. The trick was to put more appropriate, nearly finished, proposals to her which she could then 'stiffen' (as she put it) to make her own.

It was Brian who suggested to Castle when she became Secretary of State that she should revive her tradition of holding weekend departmental conferences at Sunningdale, the Civil Service College near Windsor. So in April 1974 Brian accompanied her to the magnificent neo-Georgian country house (with its rather spartan modern residential annexes) to discuss how the Treasury's proposed expenditure cuts could be accommodated within their policy agenda. Castle recorded in her diary: 'we ended on a happy note, Brian A-S being the most enthusiastic of all about the value of the exercise. I certainly cleared my own mind and learned a lot of facts.'[36]

Labour's policy machine

Brian had been involved with the Labour Party's policy machine since 1955 and had an expert understanding of how it operated. Under the umbrella of the National Executive Committee (NEC) there were a number of broad policy committees. He was most familiar with the Home Policy Committee, which in turn oversaw a number of sub-committees. As policy issues arose, sub-committees were empowered to establish working groups (parties), and to co-opt members with relevant expertise. Resolutions were fed upwards through the committee hierarchy (and from the Constituency Labour Party branches) to the annual October conferences for approval as policy targets. Here also the TUC, one of the main Labour Party funders (which had its own research department and policy committees) had an influential block vote. In theory, ministers and shadow ministers received regular policy advice from the NEC committees and from the parliamentary Labour Party (Labour MPs and peers). In practice, there were growing concerns that the leadership were going their own way. The MP Ian Mikardo claimed that Wilson treated the Labour Party 'as one would treat an elderly, boring aunt, sending her a birthday card (in October) every year but never inviting her to visit and never listening to what she said'.[37]

The Social Policy Sub-committee's remit was to work up long-term policy strategies that covered all areas of social policy (and in the process touched on related issues such as employment, housing and environment, which were the remit of other sub-committees). The structure of its early evening meetings, held in the House of Commons committee rooms, had not changed since Brian's first participation in the 1950s – policy papers were allocated sequential 'RE' numbers as well as titles so that one could keep track of them as they passed up the committee hierarchy. Yet the sub-committee (chaired by Castle) had fallen into a sporadic meeting pattern – it did not meet between July 1974 and March 1975. After his re-appointment as Castle's special adviser, Brian sought to rejuvenate it as an active policy forum. In March 1975 he suggested which members should be removed, either because of poor attendance or for failure to express themselves clearly and cogently in committee. He liaised with Jack Straw to identify potential new members. Brian's list included Nick Grant and Bernard Dix as union representatives. He favoured Ruth Lister over Frank Field as a CPAG representative: 'she is less aggressive and knows better than Frank does all the detail of means tested benefits and welfare rights'. Tony Atkinson, an economist at the University of Essex, would bring expertise on taxation. Other possibilities were related to new policy issues that he had identified for the Social Policy Sub-committee to investigate. He proposed Paul Sighart, Chair of the Justice Committee, 'an eloquent advocate of the cause of no-fault insurance' (recommended to him by Antony Lester), and Robert Holman of the University of Birmingham (suggested by Tony Lynes), who had expertise on fostering and other provisions for the under-fives, 'a keen supporter of the Finer cause' and a general interest in welfare rights. His other suggestions came with limitations, for example, Jonathan Bradshaw from the University of York, who had a good knowledge of social security and means-tested benefits, but was unlikely to be able to attend easily. Jack Straw was also keen to select an active Labour regional health authority representative, and backbenchers who had an interest in social policy.[38]

Castle took up most of Brian's membership suggestions, and in April 1975 the Committee was refreshed. NEC members were Barbara Castle, Renee Short, H. Hickling and Tom Bradley. Co-opted parliamentary Labour Party members were Jack Ashley, Alf Morris, Bruce Douglas-Mann, Bruce George, Michael Meacher, Alf Bates, Brian O'Malley,

David Owen and Laurie Pavitt. Co-opted 'others' along with Brian were Tony Atkinson, Nicholas Bosanquet, Mary Cohen, Bernard Dix, Nick Grant, Valerie Guttman, Peter Jacques, Ruth Lister, Tony Lynes, David Piachaud, Audrey Prime and Peter Townsend.[39] Committee members were asked to take responsibility for leading on new issues. Brian played an active role, writing many of the policy papers himself, providing briefings on other papers for Castle, and liaising with civil servants to develop detailed costings for the papers that were to be further developed.

In 1975, when Brian re-joined the Social Policy Sub-committee, most of its attention was focused on social welfare issues. There was an overt parallel strategy to the formal programme of work which was established at the first meeting of each year: to develop the medium and long-term policies while at the same time putting them into a campaigning format ready for inclusion in Labour's next manifesto, which Jack Straw began to coordinate on behalf of Castle less than a year after Labour came into office. The Committee decided to investigate a number of issues. Jack Straw's policy paper RE195: 'Under fives: Care and education' looked at the potential for expanding the number of nursery places, which would benefit women in returning to work. Brian liaised with Muir Gray, a community physician, to investigate the effectiveness of providing nurseries at places of work. The National Labour Women's Advisory Committee also produced proposals for greater day care for pre-school children. These were, however, firmly squashed by John Stackpoole, a senior civil servant in the DHSS Children's Division. His minute perfectly judged the 1970s culture – childcare was essentially the mother's responsibility whose work should fit around the child and not vice versa:

> It surely does not need an expert to see that it would be wrong for a three year old to be left in one group at 8.00 in the morning, passed on to a nursery class at 9.30 or so, and returned to the first group at 12.30, there to await his mother's return at 6.00 in the evening. If the mother must be away so long it would be far better for the child to be left in one setting, and preferably a homely one.... But in any event health and general wellbeing are surely more important than academic achievement for three year olds and four year olds, and for their later development?[40]

Brian produced a paper, RE151: 'The Social Wage: Health, Personal Social Services and Social Security' in May 1975, which proposed a radically different funding system.[41] He worked with Bryan Ellis, a junior official at the DHSS, on the detailed strategy. Tony Atkinson wrote to ask what Brian meant by an 'acceptable' level of child benefit – could this be quantified as a percentage of average earnings? Figures also needed to be attached to the 'raised levels' of benefit for pensioners. Atkinson also queried (as Brian himself as a smoker must have done) whether his proposal to reduce cigarette smoking would work: 'I am not sure that this should be a priority or that preventive work is likely to be very rewarding. In terms of health costs, the pay-off – at least in terms of lung cancer – is not very large and overall it is probably negative. If one is concerned about people undertaking activities which shorten their lives, then there are many others which are also candidates for campaigns.'[42] Brian replied: 'I accept that I have fluffed the level of child benefit and the level of benefit for pensioners but it seems to me unhelpful to try and produce some academic criterion. There are so many other margins on which to operate that I doubt whether we can expect to reach the ideal on more than a few of them with the public expenditure which a future Labour government may find tolerable in the late 70s or early 80s.'[43]

Ruth Lister also submitted a paper to the working group, RE250: 'The Means Test', for a 10-year phased plan to reduce substantially dependence on means testing by extending and raising universal pensions and benefits. These would include free school meals, the introduction of child benefits to replace FIS (Family Income Supplement), and the abolition of the distinction between short-term and long-term benefits. Brian wrote a briefing for Castle: 'Her plan is typical of the aspiration of many of our socially committed supporters and I think you would find it helpful to have it costed to show what would be involved in tax levels if anything like this were implemented. I think the costing would show that to pay for it, it would be necessary to have very high tax/NI [National Insurance] contributions indeed. Showing the costing would lead the committee to face priorities more realistically. The acceptance of a 10 year programme does not solve the problem as she wants the single pension to be one third of average earnings in ten years time – whatever the rate of economic growth. And of course other services will be needing more money over the next 10 years – particularly health and PSS [personal social services] as you know only too well.'[44]

At the September meeting of the Social Policy Sub-committee, papers by Nicholas Bosanquet and Tony Atkinson (RE272: 'Taxation and Labour's Social Policy') and two by Brian (RE115: 'The Integration of Tax and Social Security' and RE 279: 'The Costing of RE250: Means Tests') were discussed. Bosanquet had been optimistic that his proposals would not require a massive restructuring of taxation and social security, but could be achieved by removing special tax allowances, using that revenue to raise the level of social security benefits, taxing social security benefits and then introducing reduced tax rates. Brian pointed out the accounting flaws, and Lister drew attention to the fact that if child tax allowances were withdrawn, many more families would fall into the poverty trap. The meeting agreed not to pursue Bosanquet's idea of taxing child benefits, but that Brian would begin to work on alternative costings. Brian wrote to Castle in October: 'The main choice is between a policy aimed at reducing means testing by the negative income tax approach or a policy concentrating on extra help for particular groups and new help for such categories as one parent families.... I think you will find the paper of considerable interest.'[45] Over the next six months Brian's paper was discussed by the Social Policy Sub-committee and DHSS officials and generated some heated discussion. Michael Meacher, now Parliamentary Secretary, wrote a critical minute, suggesting that Brian's proposed Negative Income Tax scheme was unfeasible. Brian challenged all of his points in a robust 'rejoinder' to Meacher's minute to Castle.[46]

During the summer of 1975 Brian had written another policy paper, RE326: 'A Benefit for One Parent Families: alternatives to the Guaranteed Maintenance Allowance'. Castle asked him to delay submitting this to the sub-committee until after the second volume of the Finer report on one-parent families had been published in June.[47] The late Morris Finer's team had estimated that there were 620,000 one-parent families in Britain (of which 520,000 were headed by women), with over one million children. About a half of the fatherless families received supplementary benefit. Even when lone mothers were able to work, their earnings were much lower than for two-parent families. There were, however, ten times as many two-parent families who also received supplementary benefit because of their low incomes. Brian attempted in his paper to re-work Peter Townsend's policy proposals for one-parent families in such a way as not to appear to be giving them preferential treatment over poor two-parent families or those with a disability. It was a sensitive balance to maintain, and one which was essentially a paper exercise given the lack of funding for any benefits improvements.[48]

A working group on short-term benefits was also set up to take the discussions further, through which Brian worked with Lynes, Townsend, Lister and Castle. Meetings were held with the TUC, Stan Orme was co-opted and a programme of work adopted. Brian had also been appointed in September 1975 (as a Labour Party nomination) to the new joint TUC/Labour working group on the retirement age. This attempted to mediate on the TUC's demand for a reduced male retirement age of 60, which the government considered economically unfeasible. Brian briefed Castle on the costs of various scenarios, and provided European case studies of flexible and occupation-related retirement age schemes.[49] The group attempted to negotiate a phased reduction of one year every five years. TUC representatives pressed hard for priority for miners and other heavy industry occupations. Brian continued to act as a gatekeeper to the DHSS on this issue for some years, for example, seeing union officials on behalf of Castle, passing on feedback from Peter Jacques, Secretary of the TUC's Social Insurance and Industrial Welfare Department, and constructing replies from draft text supplied by officials such as Bryan Ellis at the DHSS.

At the January 1976 meeting of the Social Policy Sub-committee the debate continued on Brian's papers 'Tax Credits and NIT [negative income tax]' and 'The Gap between Short Term and Long Term Social Security'. David Piachaud also contributed a paper, RE417: 'Future social security strategy'. Through the spring Brian worked up a first draft of the social policy chapter for the next Labour manifesto, liaising with Liz Arnott, Secretary to the Sub-committee. David Donnison and David Piachaud (the latter now in the Policy Unit at 10 Downing Street) provided supporting information on the impact of introducing a minimum wage, using new data from the Family Expenditure Survey that showed a remarkably low 0.5 per cent of low-paid families had an income below the Supplementary Benefit level. Peter Townsend also submitted material on disability benefits, but Brian reworked it before sending it on to Castle: 'as it was full of inconsistencies and errors … and, being Peter, asked for the sun, moon and stars in the next Labour government'. He prepared a revised draft on priorities: 'I still feel it gives too much stress to cash over services. Would you like something added specifically on buildings? If it is not, we leave ourselves open to a Tory election bid to rebuild Britain's slum hospitals after four years of Labour neglect!'[50]

On 13 February Brian had lunch with Peter Jacques, Secretary of the TUC Social Policy Committee. They had a good working relationship, and Jacques used the occasion to suggest that Alan Fisher might be appointed to the new independent board being set up to administer the Goodman deal, which 'would help to silence his opposition to the package'.[51] Yet the relationship between Labour and the trades unions was becoming more stressed by the production of the draft social policy chapter. Brian sent Brian O'Malley, Minister for Social Security, a post-lunch briefing: 'He [Jacques] is unhappy that there has so far been no discussion between the key TUC people and you and the Secretary of State about the priorities to be given to the different options. This is not in the terms of reference of the Joint Working Party, now re-established to deal with short-term benefits.... He suggested the possibility of a dinner and thought my home would be a suitable setting. If you wished I would be very glad to put on such a dinner for 5 each side invited.... Do you think this would be useful?' O'Malley forwarded the minute to Castle, adding, 'I think this is extremely important. TUC have reservations about the NEC Social Policy sub-cttee. I therefore recommend strongly we ask Prof A.S. to arrange urgently.' Castle replied 'Delighted! I think this is an excellent idea!'[52]

The dinner date was fixed for 1 March and Brian worked with O'Malley to draw up the guest list. He suggested Jack Straw attend to take minutes as he would be busy coping with the meal. Alf Morris and O'Malley made up Castle's DHSS team. On 27 February Brian wrote to Castle: 'Peter Jacques tells me that the TUC envisages this almost as a <u>negotiation</u> of priorities. Once agreed it is expected that both sides would support them in the NEC and in the trade union movement. With the Minister of State's agreement I am sending out the enclosed paper on costed options to the TUC in the hope of keeping the discussions within economic realities.'[53] The TUC representatives (Terry Parry, Audrey Prime, Harry Urwin and Peter Jacques) clearly came to the dinner at Brian's Elizabeth Street home with a hidden agenda. According to Castle's diary entry, they got her to tell them about her plans for Child Benefit and then they requested an increase in married pensions of £3.50 – not a large sum, but significant in the context of agreed pension increases and the Chancellor Denis Healey's firm insistence that no further concession be made. Castle offered no promises.

Parry summed up the mood of the evening: 'We ought to have one of these every month' – a testimony to Brian's cooking as much as to the off-the-record discussion with government ministers.[54] But the speed with which the DHSS staff had put together Brian's costed options paper had produced some large errors, which only came to light after the dinner. They also failed to tell the TUC representatives at the dinner that the DHSS had introduced a new method of pensions uprating, which would affect all their calculations. Brian wrote to O'Malley: 'I am sure you found this discussion of the next uprating acutely embarrassing. The TUC may well feel even more heavily let down when the bombshell bursts in view of the fact that you were unable to give them a hint of what was intended even on such an intimate occasion. Is there any way that the TUC can be told before the announcement to soften the blow.'[55] It was Brian who was given the job of conveying this bad news to Jacques two days later.

By 29 March 1976 Brian was able to send Castle the third draft of the social policy chapter but was still waiting to hear from Transport House [Labour Party headquarters] which type of costings should be used. The following day the Social Policy Sub-committee met. This was its last chance to make amendments before it was sent up to the Home Policy Committee. They went through the draft line by line before approving it. Brian worked with DHSS staff to prepare the final figures, and he then sent Castle a further draft, with suggestions for areas that might be emphasised or removed.

Brian had a long-standing interest in pharmaceuticals policy, having been a member of the Sainsbury Committee in 1965–67. The remit had been far too narrow, and did not consider the relationship between pharmaceuticals and wider economic issues. Its limited recommendations were further weakened by industry lobbying, and little progress had been made. In 1974 the DHSS were still dithering about what do, despite acknowledging that this industry had a special social responsibility towards prescribers and consumers. The Labour Party had included commitments to greater public control of the pharmaceutical industry in its recent manifestos to 'enable the government to control prices, stimulate investment, encourage exports, create employment, protect workers and consumers from the activities of irresponsible multinational companies, and to plan the national economy in the national interest'. It agreed to work in parallel with the DHSS to look at how the Sainsbury proposals could be implemented. Brian joined the Home Policy Sub-committee working party on the pharmaceutical industry (chaired by David Owen) in spring 1974. Various proposals were under consideration, including forming a state holding company and establishing a 'cost-efficiency' unit within the Medicines Commission which would have the authority to withhold licences for drugs until the price was 'right' relative to other products. The members of the working party also wished to look at wider issues such as patent law, and the implications of European Economic Community (EEC) legislation.[56]

During 1975 the working party received and discussed papers RE120: 'The Distribution of Medicines under the NHS'; RE88: 'Notes on the Industrial Common Ownership Movement' (Bob Edwards MP); and RE106: 'Research and the Drug Industry' (Nicholas Bosanquet). One of the members of the working party, Professor D.G. Wibberley, Professor of Pharmacy at Aston University, spoke at length at the April meeting about his recent reading of literature by Ivan Illich, Rene Dubos and E.F. Schumacher, and what he had learned at the 'Limits to medicine' conference held at Davos in Switzerland. Brian drafted a major policy document, RE71: 'Public Control of the Pharmaceutical Industry', which he continued to revise during the summer, with contributions from Bosanquet. The 10 substantial chapters covered issues such as the options for public control and the capacity to stimulate research and development. Brian's commentary on the relationship between the pharmaceutical industry and the medical profession reiterated the views he had tried to put into the Sainsbury report in 1967:

> The pharmaceutical industry spends about 14 per cent of its turnover in the UK on sales promotion. The level of expenditure has risen as sales have risen. For 1973 sales promotion cost about £32m and the overwhelming proportion of this cost fell on the National Health Service ... it is grossly excessive expenditure to influence the prescribing behaviour of only some 56,000 doctors ... at present rates the average doctor can expect to have nearly £30,000 spent on his 'education' by the pharmaceutical industry – about twice the cost of his original medical education. Doctors are showered with literature sent through the post. It is impossible for them to give careful attention to all the items they receive which have been prepared at great cost. Subscription journals are loaded with glossy advertising matter. In addition no less than 30 give away journals and newspapers are sent to doctors. There are some 3,000 representatives paid almost exclusively to visit doctors in their offices. Small gifts are sent to doctors and firms vie with one another to provide free hospitality.... Samples normally consist not just of the odd pill but of enough medicine for a whole course of treatment.[57]

Brian highlighted the problems with the Voluntary Price Regulation Scheme (VPRS), which was intended to claw back excessive profits from the pharmaceutical industry. Companies were avoiding this by putting some of their profits into sales campaigns. The draft policy document therefore proposed banning all gifts and free samples. A blanket ban on advertising would, however, be detrimental – not all doctors could be relied on to read professional journals or to attend refresher courses to hear about latest drug developments, and journals relied heavily on companies for sponsorship. A compromise would be to regulate all adverts to ensure their claims were genuine and accurate, and to place a cap on the percentage of turnover that could be spent on sales promotions. Brian suggested that the government also needed to be more sophisticated in using its licensing powers to withdraw drugs that had become obsolete.

The conclusion, drafted by Brian, was blunt: 'The analysis made in this report has shown that taken as a whole the pharmaceutical industry does not operate in the public interest. While it has a good export record, the pursuit of profit in the home market has resulted in grossly excessive expenditure on sales promotion at the cost of the NHS, the provision of misleading information to doctors which distorts the practice of medicine and the encouragement of excessive prescribing.... The specific abuses which we have identified must be dealt with by specific solutions which apply to all companies operating in Britain irrespective of their national ownership.' Radical policy suggestions included allowing the government to participate in the activities of large UK pharmaceutical companies (possibly to even buy a company). During the drafting of the working party's document, Brian, David Owen and Audrey Prime had attended meetings with representatives of the Industrial Policy Committee, and liaised on how to amend the draft to avoid policy conflicts at NEC level.

In addition to his roles on the policy sub-committees, Brian was always looking for opportunities to make links between policy areas and his extra-curricular interests, even if they potentially opened up further tension within the Labour movement. Wearing his hat as Deputy Chair of the Greater London Citizens' Advice Bureaux (CAB) group, in 1976 he wrote a memorandum for the Conservatives on how the CAB had set up legal centres, which employed lawyers to give free legal advice to those people who could not afford to pay for it. Geoffrey Howe had thanked Brian for initiating it, and Brian was spurred on to write to Jack Ashley: 'I do wish we could get the Party more interested in legal services for the poor.... It seems to me that the Party could take an enormous initiative here. So much help could be provided for the underprivileged by a national service costing only some 50 million pounds. One of the problems is, of course, that the trade unions would be worried about such a development. They see their legal departments as one of the services that members get. If members can get what in many cases would be a better service for free, then what are people joining the unions for?'[58]

These sub-committee case studies illustrate how effectively policy could be worked up through formal and off-the-record discussions. Brian's role was critical: facilitating contact between ministers, Labour's NEC and the TUC. Yet in 1976 Wilson tried to limit the participation of special advisers in Labour Party committees, arguing that they should abide by the same rules on refraining from political activities as applied to mainstream civil servants. This provoked protest letters from a number of politicians, including Barbara Castle (drafted by Brian) and from Shirley Williams, who pointed out how useful such attendance was for keeping ministers in touch with party views on policy, and ensuring that economically unrealistic suggestions did not emerge from the Labour Party.[59] If Castle had not had Brian as her eyes and ears at some of these meetings, contributing his own policy papers for discussion, she would have been severely handicapped in promoting issues such as social security benefits.

National Health Service: 'The ark of our covenant'

Once in office in May 1974, Castle and Owen had worked quickly to develop a plan for the NHS which many saw as a desire to return to Bevan's 1946 initial vision. The 'Democracy in the NHS' project aimed at strengthening Community Health Council and local authority representation on area health authorities and, as announced in the 1974 manifesto, the issue of private medicine was to be fully addressed. Although Owen soon pushed for the elimination of the regional tier in the newly reorganised NHS, Castle was advised to leave well alone until Joseph's new system had had time to settle down. The most that was achieved was a reduction in the number of NHS districts to 205. The 12 London teaching hospitals, which the 1973 NHS Reorganisation Act planned to incorporate into the mainstream regional structure, were given a temporary reprieve.

But the overriding determinant of all their plans was the Treasury's sanction of budgets. Castle was clearly told that she could not have her cake and eat it: she had to prioritise either social security or health. There were existing commitments to improving pensions, reducing NHS waiting lists and renegotiating consultant contracts. Her room for manoeuvre was further constrained by uncontrolled wage inflation which effectively halted any plans for increases in NHS expenditure. Castle fought the Treasury on every single issue, and won many of the fights she picked, including raising the age of prescription charge exemption from 15 to 16 and reducing that for women from 65 to 60.

These small concessions were, however, insufficient to stem mounting public and professional concerns that the NHS was facing a real crisis, possibly imminent collapse. The British Medical Association (BMA) and other representative bodies demanded meetings with Wilson and called for an independent enquiry into the NHS, and an immediate increase in its budget. Although senior DHSS medical staff warned that the morale of NHS staff had fallen to a dangerous all-time low, Healey refused to bow to pressure, reminding Castle that the NHS was already protected in the wider programme of cuts to public services. The Treasury also opposed any independent enquiry, mindful that previous ones such as Guillebaud in 1956 had invariably strengthened the case for increased expenditure. Yet the BMA worked itself and other representative bodies up into what Charles Webster has called an 'almost hysterical attachment' to the demand for an enquiry.[60] Castle felt that an enquiry should be established, as it might help to mollify the medical profession and lead to more favourable negotiations in the ongoing junior doctors' dispute (as well as halting the very personal and vitriolic campaign against her).

Wilson finally announced the creation of a Royal Commission on 20 October 1975, and it received its Royal Warrant in May 1976. It was to be chaired by Sir Alec Merrison, the experienced academic scientist who had previously also chaired a committee investigating the regulation of the medical profession. The remit was sufficiently wide to assure the medical profession that it would consider the balance between the NHS and private medicine, but the membership was decidedly skewed against hospital specialists. Many of the members were very senior, and some retired from their fields of interest in health authorities, social work training and trades unions. Even at the outset the expectations of this Royal Commission were not high. It did not have the innovating personalities that had served on the mental health and mental education Royal Commissions or some of the more effective independent committees such as Briggs (nursing), or Lane (1967 Abortion Act).

The OPEC oil crisis hit the British economy harder than other western countries, and with each year that the recession bit, the government imposed even greater cuts to reduce the Public Sector Borrowing Requirement. Ministers explored all possible alternative funding options, including establishing lotteries to raise NHS funds. As sterling continued to decline into 1975 and terms for a further International Monetary Fund loan were negotiated, Castle held out for a minimum 1.5 per cent growth rate for the NHS, and 2 per cent for personal social services. Supported by briefing papers from Brian, she negotiated some shifts in her budget by agreeing to increases in ophthalmic and dental charges (manifesto dreams of a complete elimination of charges were long gone). In July 1975 Brian's speedy dissection of Healey's surprise second-stage budget-cutting proposal (cunningly sent to the DHSS to coincide with Castle's attendance at Cabinet to agree to a first reduction in her budget) allowed him to warn her in time not to make any concessions until Healey had laid all his plans on the table. Even with Brian's special adviser tactics Castle felt exposed and vulnerable: 'And we are under this difficulty: that none of us are equipped with the sort of economic advice that enables us to stand up to the dubious expertise of the Treasury....As Brian put it to me this afternoon, "I could talk to Worswick of the NIESR [National Institute for Economic and Social Research]; he's a friend of mine. But how could I disclose a Treasury document to him[?]".'[61]

Yet the Treasury had been partly mollified by the introduction of a DHSS departmental planning system, designed to work in harmony with the Public Expenditure Survey Committee. It submitted its first 'planning submission' for the 1974/75 cycle in February 1975, with the ambition to become fully operational in 1976/77, and was supported by the landmark consultative document, *Planning for Health and Personal Social Services*, which finally appeared after much internal wrangling, on 24 March 1976.[62] This presented, for the first time in the NHS's history, an overt statement of its objectives and projected expenditure. This development had also been partly facilitated by the increase in economic expertise within the DHSS. Previously the Economic Adviser's Office had been thinly staffed, headed by Leonard Nicholson and with much of the NHS work being done by the health economist David Pole. Jeremy Hurst, who was appointed in 1971, helped to strengthen the team and contributed to the *Planning for Health* document, along with Ron Akehurst. Brian was also involved in plans to use external health economics' expertise in evaluating the NHS. He and the Chief Scientist Sir Douglas Black supported Alan William's bid to establish a Master's course in Health Economics at the University of York to generate more interest in this neglected area.[63]

Pay beds

In this dire economic situation, Castle's ambition to eliminate the 4,500 private pay beds from NHS hospitals – which generated £20 million a year – should have been off the agenda. Yet she remained doggedly fixed on this goal from the outset of her time as Secretary of State. Her passion for this issue went beyond that of most of her party, and certainly went against the 1948 agreement that Bevan had forged with the medical profession. Despite an initial decrease in private health insurance after 1948, from the 1960s there had been a steady trickle of new business, mainly through the British United Provident Association (BUPA), which was the biggest of the health insurance providers. Part of the explanation for this lies with the more expensive surgical procedures that were now possible, but it was mainly due to the expansion in company schemes – an attractive bonus for workers at a time when salary increases were economically unfeasible. By 1970 almost two million people were covered by private health insurance. When Labour came into government in 1974 this had increased to 2.4 million, two thirds of whom were in company schemes. Insurance patients were treated in some 3,700 beds in private hospitals; the remainder used pay beds in NHS hospitals, which could offer access to high-technology operating facilities, and treatment by consultants who were often on full-time NHS contracts.

Brian was well informed about the treatment of private patients in NHS hospitals. He was still closely involved with staff from St Thomas' Hospital, where he had been a governor between 1957 and 1968. The consultants had begun to develop a model called 'geographical full time', meaning that they pledged to do all of their private work on site, which would give the hospital consultant availability 24 hours a day rather than seeing patients off-site at private hospitals. Consultants such as John Richardson and John Pullen stood to lose some of their considerable private practice income through this scheme of work, but were prepared to consider it for the greater good of the hospital.[64] When Castle began her campaign to phase out all private medicine from NHS hospitals, this goodwill was withdrawn, and consultants instead stuck rigidly to their NHS contract hours. Walter Holland and others who briefed Brian privately on this hoped that he would use his influence with Castle. The impact was long term and deeply damaging: the next generation of younger consultants never had the same sense of loyalty and obligation to their hospitals.[65] Jack Straw considers the private medicine issue as the one area of Brian's special adviser's role with Castle where he 'had the greatest reservations ... the department were very reluctant [to phase out pay beds] and so was Brian'.[66]

Yet phasing out private medicine had been central to nearly every Labour Party manifesto since the creation of the NHS in 1948. Although health had been a relatively minor issue during its 1970–74 opposition period, Labour had produced its own 'Green Paper' (albeit with no firm expenditure commitments or alternatives to Joseph's scheme). Castle had given a public assurance of Labour's determination to 'eliminate private practice from our NHS' at the Party Conference in October 1973 but it was not a main feature of the February 1974 election campaign. Even for the October 1974 campaign Labour's health manifesto was 'less adequate than its Conservative equivalent', with limited discussion of reducing regional inequalities of standards, more emphasis on prevention and primary care and priority for spending on services for the mentally handicapped and mentally ill.[67]

The private medicine in NHS hospitals row had rumbled around Parliament for some time. A Commons Expenditure Committee in 1971 investigated complaints of queue jumping, inappropriate use of NHS equipment and consultants skimping on their NHS patients. It had found, however, much to the dismay of Labour, that there was insufficient evidence to substantiate these pervasive claims.[68] There was some substance, however, behind the allegations. The fees paid to the NHS by the health insurance companies were a gross approximation of the actual costs of private patients. There was also a sense of inequity in the system, as the nurses, technicians and junior doctors involved in the provision of treatment did not usually share in the consultants' private patient income (although some gave a Christmas 'bonus' in recognition of this work).

David Owen recalled that Labour's manifesto pledge caused immediate alarm in Whitehall, and that Sir Philip Rogers, DHSS Permanent Secretary, had also tried to warn Castle off the idea:

> Sir Philip deployed a strong case against our taking any action. He warned us that the mood of the medical profession was very brittle and said that the considered judgement of himself, the Chief Medical Officer [Sir Henry Yellowlees] and all the top officials was that, in the best interests of the National Health Service, we should avoid a confrontation with the doctors on this issue. Rather movingly he insisted that if the Secretary of State, having heard him out, came to a different conclusion then that was the last she would hear of it and everyone in the Department would carry out her policy faithfully and to the best of their abilities.[69]

Castle, after listening to Rogers' advice, pressed ahead with her plans. The pay beds issue was to be a chronic distraction from advancing other, more achievable, objectives during her two tumultuous years as Secretary of State.

Any initial hopes that the pay beds policy could quickly be achieved through discreet negotiations early in Labour's term of office were shattered by a dispute in June 1974 at the new Charing Cross Hospital, where trade union activists refused to attend to patients in the two private wards. They threatened industrial action if these pay beds were not made available for NHS patients. The amount of private medicine undertaken at this hospital was considerable, earning it the nickname 'the Fulham Hilton' for the comparative luxury of its facilities.[70] The 10-day dispute attracted considerable media attention and forced a showdown between the DHSS and the BMA. Although a local settlement was reached (which allowed for unused beds on the private wards to be used for NHS patients), the timing of the dispute was unfortunate, coinciding with negotiations (chaired by Owen) on a new consultants' contract. Castle was tempted to use more stick than carrot in persuading some consultants to accept whole-time contracts with the NHS by threatening to only consider 'whole-timers' for merit awards. She used her opportunity in the debate on the Queen's Speech on 1 November 1974 to reinforce the commitment that she would phase out pay beds and introduce shared NHS and private waiting lists.

Brian, as he often did, saw the bigger picture in the aftermath of yet further protest from the medical profession. At the regular Monday ministerial lunch meeting he attempted to bring some element of control to her phasing-out strategy by inserting phrases such as 'over a reasonable period taking into account local circumstances'. Part of his logic, which departmental officials had not thought of, was to allow enough time for the government to get the necessary power to control the inevitable expansion of private medicine that would follow Castle's expulsion of it from NHS hospitals.[71] By December 1974 some consultants were working to contract in protest, claiming that Castle's proposals amounted to the extinction of private medicine in Britain. Walpole Lewis, Chair of the BMA's Council, declared in *The Times*: 'We are fighting for the independence of the profession.'[72]

The year 1975 opened with a 16-week working-to-contract protest by hospital consultants, swiftly followed by disagreement with the junior hospital doctors over their promised reduced hours contract. The GPs were also threatening mutiny, collecting 16,000 signed but undated resignations to be used if Castle reneged on their imminent pay award. The BMA expressed its concerns about lengthening waiting lists and possible harm to patients and appealed directly to Wilson, who refused to override Castle. Castle pushed on, ignoring the advice of Brian, Owen and her senior DHSS staff. She announced that there would be legislation for a phased reduction in pay beds. Brian supported her using a strategy that had worked with Crossman – hosting private, off-the-record dinners at his Elizabeth Street home. On 12 May 1975 Castle went there with Owen and Straw to meet Alan Fisher from NUPE, Audrey Prime from NALGO and Peter Jacques from the TUC to 'put them in the picture' about developments on the pay beds policy. After Castle and Owen returned to Westminster for a 10.00pm vote, Brian worked hard on getting the union officials to see

Castle's logic, and by the end of the evening he had managed to talk Jacques round to supporting the government line.[73] Barbara sent him a handwritten note of thanks the following day: 'You certainly put those trade unionists into a mellow mood with the food, drink and general ambience....Where did you get that exquisite red wine? And was it as expensive as it tasted? I would love to know the name of your wine merchant.'[74] At its annual conference the following month NALGO came out firmly against private medicine and called on its local branches to oppose all planning applications for new private hospitals.

The consultation document on the separation of private practice from NHS hospitals was published on 11 August 1975, while Castle was on holiday in Corfu.[75] She returned to one of the most personal campaigns ever launched against a government minister, spearheaded by the Tory press, which cited rumours that her Permanent Secretary and other senior officials and advisers would resign over this issue. This undoubtedly contributed to her ill health during the autumn. On one occasion she spent an evening 'sharpening and humanising' a speech that Brian had written for her to give the following day to a community care conference. But stomach problems meant that Brian was sent off in the morning to deliver her speech for her.[76]

Castle doggedly continued to initiate new policy discussions, in the hope that the pay beds row would blow over. She was even willing to entertain commercial support to lift the efficiency of the NHS, if that was what was needed. On 7 October she hosted an intimate dinner in the private dining room at the Stafford Hotel for Derek Rayner of Marks & Spencer. Brian was there too, along with Owen, her Principal Private Secretary Norman Warner and James Collier from the DHSS, to hear Rayner's vision for a centralising procurement policy for the NHS, and the possibility of developing an export market for medical equipment.[77]

Despite Castle's impression of business as usual, the pay beds crisis was deepening. Brian accompanied her to give a lecture at the Oxford Union, in which there was an ominous row of doctors from the Radcliffe Infirmary in the audience. Castle was forced to read the speech 'for safety's sake'. Brian reassured her afterwards that she had done 'marvellously'.[78] But the medical profession was meanwhile putting aside internal differences to unite, claiming that the NHS was facing a crisis on a scale unseen since its creation in 1948. The Royal Colleges issued a rare collective press statement, calling the consultation document a 'serious threat to the care and safety of patients and to the standards of medical practice in this country now and in the future'.[79] By December 1975 the junior doctors had joined the consultants in all-out industrial action, forcing casualty and other departments to close in hospitals throughout the country.

Wilson was forced to step in and meet representatives from the BMA and the hospital consultants. He tried to delay the progress towards the introduction of a parliamentary Bill by asking his favoured political fixer, the lawyer Arnold Goodman, to arbitrate between Castle and the doctors. Goodman was proficient in handling such matters (and indeed had been consulted by BUPA in August 1975 on the pay beds issue). Yet even he felt it necessary to brief Wilson that Anthony Grabham, Chair of the Central Committee for Hospital Medical Services, was 'a tiresome man with terrifying influence – a Napoleon of the medical profession'.[80] After an initial set of evening meetings held at Goodman's flat, which involved Wilson, Castle and medical representatives, Goodman took the initiative, and moved to exclude Castle from the final negotiations. She was offended, and feared it would damage her political authority. Yet she could not really complain, having herself excluded the Chief Medical Officer, Sir Henry Yellowlees, from the closed meetings, which had a decidedly negative impact on his standing with his medical peers.[81] Goodman achieved some reconciliation with the medical profession – enough for them to allow Castle to begin drafting the Health Services Bill in January 1976, which proposed a slow transfer of pay beds to the NHS and, in return, a light touch on licensing of private hospitals (to exclude those with fewer than 100 beds in London and 75 elsewhere).

Resource Allocation Working Party

By 1974 life expectancy at birth in Britain was 69 for men and 75 for women, a continuation of the progressive increases since the late 19th century. Yet as well as the difference between male and female life expectancy, there was growing recognition that there was an unacceptable discrepancy in standards of health between regions and social classes, exacerbated by inequalities in the allocation of resources within the NHS. At the start of the NHS in 1948 45 per cent of the hospitals had been built before 1891 and 21 per cent before 1861. Although there was a capital allocation scheme, it favoured those Regional Hospital Boards that had vociferous governors who could generate a lot of fuss about 'their' hospitals, especially those governors who were members of the House of Lords. The London teaching hospitals were the most successful in attracting a higher calibre of members than Hospital Management Committees, and they also benefited from having skilled administrators.[82] Brian, of course, had intermittently served on a number of London HMCs and on St Thomas' Hospital Board of Governors since the late 1950s.

Although there had been no attempt to hide the inherited inequalities of the pre-1948 systems, there had been no specific reference to the issue in the 1946 NHS Act, and it failed to attract serious academic or political attention during the early years of the NHS.[83] Indeed Webster has suggested that Brian and Titmuss deliberately downplayed the issue of inequalities in access to healthcare in their report for the Guillebaud Committee in 1956, because they realised it risked drawing unwelcome Treasury attention to the existing inefficiencies in the NHS.[84] Ann Oakley suggests that if true, it was more likely to have been driven by Brian, whom she saw as making more politically focused decisions, than her father, Titmuss.[85] Titmuss, however, regularly returned to the issue of health inequalities in his lectures and publications, as did his collaborators such as Jerry Morris, through his pioneering 1959 *Lancet* paper, 'Health and Social Class'.[86] The Guillebaud Committee conceded that it could not recommend the use of a resource allocation formula because 'any rational formula would have to be weighted to take account of such a wide range of variables in Hospital Regions that it cannot be considered as a practical proposition at least for the present'.[87] It also acknowledged the problems that were emerging in variations in hospital costs, and with inter-regional patient transfers.

As discussed earlier in Chapter 7, Brian and Townsend had highlighted the interrelationship between health inequalities and poverty in their book *The Poor and the Poorest*, which provided the launch for the Child Poverty Action Group.[88] They demonstrated that the NHS actually reinforced inequalities in access to healthcare by social class. Within the NHS and BMA there were also mutterings of discontent as it became apparent that the heavy bias of teaching hospitals in the metropolitan area caused considerable inequity in allocation of funding. The provincial RHBs, supported by independent research from bodies such as the Acton Society Trust, were, by the mid-1960s, using weighted beds formulas to demonstrate the unfairness of the allocations based, as *The Lancet* put it, 'on nothing but the administrative convenience of an outworn formula'.[89]

Richard Crossman, during his 1968–70 DHSS administration, had been steered by Brian to develop a new approach: the Crossman formula.[90] This was intended to achieve redistribution of hospital budgets over a 10-year period, beginning in the 1971/72 financial year. The formula allocation was based 50 per cent on area population, 25 per cent on existing hospital bed provision and 25 per cent on in-patient admissions. Crossman was insistent that this was only possible if the NHS was adequately supported by the Treasury: 'I can only equalise on an expanding budget.'[91] But it did not include the allocations to the teaching hospitals (which had boosted bed provision in the metropolitan regions), non-hospital healthcare or consider capital expenditure. It did not recognise that some regions were more efficient than others, and some had more ill health. Furthermore, it used historical data to predict future trends.[92] Brian later admitted to his colleague Walter Holland, a member of the RAWP group, that the Crossman formula had been crude and that it actually exacerbated inequalities in healthcare.[93] Some hospital authorities were even suspected of trying to increase their allocations by setting up temporary wards with additional beds.[94] Labour had also been addressing the issue of inequalities as part of its plans for NHS reorganisation, and had included a commitment to a new method of resource allocation in its 1970 Green Paper, but this required the construction of geographical authorities below the level of the region.[95] It is perhaps significant that Brian never participated in the Health Economists Study Group, established in 1972 by academics at the University of York's Department of Health Economics, which then included, among others, Tony Culyer, Alan Peacock, Jack Wiseman and Mark Hauser.[96] Had Brian been involved with this group, he might have been encouraged to re-work the Crossman formula in a different way.

There had been emerging interest in geographical inequalities in health in the 1960s, with the work of the US economist Martin Feldstein, who was then a fellow at Nuffield College, Oxford.[97] Furthermore, by the early 1970s, Ann Cartwright's tentative research findings that the higher social groups made disproportionately more use of NHS GP services were confirmed by a study by the economists Cooper and Culyer, who were commissioned as a BMA working group.[98] It was a South Wales socialist GP, Julian Tudor Hart, who attracted most attention to inequalities in class access to healthcare with his memorably titled 1971 *Lancet* article: 'The inverse care law'.[99] In 1972, in a book of Fabian essays, Nicholas Bosanquet calculated that metropolitan NHS regions had 24 per cent greater revenue funding per person than regions such as Sheffield.[100] A study by Noyce, Smith and Trickey estimated that the regional variations in NHS spending were even higher than Bosanquet had suggested. The range in 1974, on the eve of reorganisation, was from the South West Metropolitan RHB at 41 per cent above the mean to Sheffield RHB at 23 per cent below the mean.[101] Yet the emergence of these studies came at a time of increasing financial constraint for the NHS, with the international economic recession following the OPEC oil crisis. The Labour Party tried to focus attention on this issue, with its opposition 'Green Paper' in August 1973.[102] Barbara Castle had been a member of the working party that produced it.

When Castle became Secretary of State in 1974, she was therefore well-briefed on the issue of health inequalities. The NHS reorganisation, which introduced the smaller geographical units of area health authorities under regional health authorities made possible a reinvestigation of targeted resource allocation. Indeed, the 'shadow' area health authorities had already prepared area profiles in 1973, supported by a new regional group within the DHSS headquarters. With her Junior Minister of Health, David Owen (who had first-hand experience of issues of access to healthcare by social class and region from his former career as a junior doctor), in May 1975 Castle established the Resource Allocation Working Party (for England), immediately known as RAWP. It was composed of 12 NHS representatives and nine DHSS members, and chaired by John (J.C.C.) Smith. The balance was strategic to ensure NHS engagement, but DHSS control over the general direction of the recommendations. However, the failure to include clinicians irked the medical profession.

Brian played an active role in the formation of RAWP, advising on the selection of members and bringing to its debates his long-standing expertise in inequalities, as well as his ongoing research on efficiency in health services. Indeed, he took a short break during this busy period to deliver a keynote speech on the subject at the Helsinki Health Economics Seminar in June 1975.[103] The remit that guided the working party over the next 14 months was: 'To review the arrangements for distributing NHS capital and revenue to RHAs [regional health authorities], AHAs [area health authorities] and Districts respectively with a view to establishing a method of securing, as soon as practicable, a pattern of distribution responsive objectively, equitably and efficiently to relative needs and to make recommendations.' An interim report was published in November 1975, followed by a final report in September 1976. With a stated aim to achieve 'equal opportunity of access to health care for people at equal risk', its philosophy has underpinned all subsequent policy on health spending.[104]

What was different about RAWP was that it developed formulas to relate 'target' allocations to objective measures of a region's need. This involved sequential consideration of demographic indicators and standardised mortality ratios as a proxy for morbidity rates for the hospital allocation. Population size was the sole factor used for the allocation for community care. It initially produced results that showed that London was receiving a bigger share of NHS resources (even allowing for its expensive teaching hospitals and higher cost of living) than it would be entitled to when the RAWP timetable was fully operational. It improved on the Crossman formula by excluding the distribution of hospital beds (which in effect represented historical inequalities in funding), and including separate allocations for medical teaching and research. There were safety valves to allow for existing commitments to capital expenditure, for the quality of the existing hospital infrastructure and for regional deprivation. The key innovation in the RAWP formula was to identify and address 'relative' need. It signalled a fundamental change in ethos, from 'muddling through' to 'rational planning' within the NHS.[105]

The actual amount of redistribution to areas identified by RAWP as underfunded, such as Trent and East Anglia, was capped at an increase of 2.5 per cent. Losing regions were equally protected by a 2.5 per cent maximum RAWP reduction but hit again by the overall reduction in NHS budgets. Owen, as Minister with responsibility for RAWP, felt that the key to its success was the time they had taken to give the DHSS staff a sense of ownership. This ensured they were confident with both the structure and the methodology before it was sent out to NHS authorities on 21 February 1977. He was surprised, however, at Brian's relative ambivalence in helping to establish the RAWP methodology, given his previous experience with Crossman. He would always respond to Owen's calls for assistance, but perhaps feared a political backlash to this really quite radical policy, or recognised the impact it would have on St Thomas', to which he still felt a great loyalty.[106]

There were, perhaps inevitably, complaints about the principle and practice of RAWP: it did not attempt to use morbidity data, and it failed to acknowledge that health inequalities within regions could be as big as variations between regions. There was no mechanism to require NHS regions to apply RAWP formula to their internal allocations, and in areas with teaching hospitals there was often such a prioritisation of their funding that community health services suffered.[107] Nick Bosanquet, judging the impact of RAWP in 1980, considered it have been the 'least worst' of Labour's options, but that its blinkered focus on acute medical services wrongly took priority over inequalities between client groups and between social classes.[108]

Mental illness, mental handicap and disability benefits

When Brian had been special adviser to Crossman between 1968 and 1970 he had devoted an enormous amount of time and effort into drafting a White Paper on mental handicap. This was partly stimulated by the Ely Hospital scandal and subsequent enquiry, and by Brian's involvement with the AEGIS (Aid to the Elderly in Government Institutions) pressure group. As the 1970 general election approached Brian worked through six drafts of the White Paper, which reflected his own views and those of the post-Ely working party. The final draft was handed to the incoming Secretary of State Keith Joseph, who was determined that it should be published without much further alteration. His officials, however, found Brian's draft 'too euphoric, idealistic and vague', with its lengthy case studies of the poor state of some facilities. It did not go far enough to appease those who wanted an immediate closure plan for the largest long-stay institutions and a move towards care in the community.[109] The eventual White Paper, *Better Services for the Mentally Handicapped*, was published on 23 June 1971, with an added costed timetable, but a retrenchment: the role of district general hospitals as sites for mental health services was downplayed. This gave a temporary stay of execution to the long-stay establishments, as Joseph had to agree to a 20-year programme to appease the Treasury and local government, which had to develop replacement community facilities.[110] Peter Townsend, a long-standing critic of Crossman's (and therefore of Brian's) policies, found little in the White Paper that was an improvement on the 1957 Royal Commission on Mental Illness.[111] Few local authorities really welcomed the White Paper as an opportunity to develop their services.

Related to the issue of services for the mentally ill and handicapped was the chronic problem of inspection of institutions. Even after the exposures of AEGIS and the Ely scandal there were several further instances of poor conditions and unacceptable staff treatment of patients. Joseph had belatedly agreed, under pressure from Brian and from Barbara Robb, to ask Mr J. Hampden Inskip QC to investigate the death in 1969 of Robert Robertson at South Ockendon Hospital. One of Castle's first actions as Secretary of State, which she credited to Brian, was to publish Inskip's 1973 report in Parliament, and to make an official visit in April 1974 to inspect the hospital herself.[112]

Brian had proposed to Crossman in 1969 that long-stay institutions should be routinely inspected, and that an ombudsman be appointed to deal with complaints. The Hospital (later Health) Advisory Service had been created by Crossman in October 1969, and its first director was Dr A. A. Baker, a psychiatrist from St Mary Abbots Hospital, a large mental handicap institution with a psychiatric unit in Kensington, which had come within Brian's territory when he was Chair of the Lambeth Group HMC between 1956 and 1961. Crossman made the Hospital Advisory Service administratively separate from the NHS and the DHSS central department. It sought to achieve a fine balance between critical inspections and positive support for improvements. Baker found, however, the new Conservative regime under Keith Joseph less tolerant of the demands for reform that his inspection teams proposed.[113]

The creation of a comprehensive NHS complaints procedure took longer to come to fruition. The Conservatives made a tentative commitment to such a scheme in their 1970 manifesto, and since then Joseph had been privately considering how to implement such an initiative without antagonising the medical profession. But when the consultative document on NHS reorganisation was published in May 1971 there was no reference to the much-discussed creation of a health service commissioner.[114] There was considerable objection, including an article by Brian, 'A hospital ombudsman', which was published in *New Society*. He re-iterated the need for such an individual, whether called an ombudsman or a health service commissioner.[115] Another batch of negative hospital enquiries forced Joseph's hand, and he appointed Sir Michael Davies QC to chair a committee to investigate the hospital complaints procedure in February 1971. This had been another of Brian's recommendations that emerged from the post-Ely working party that Joseph had initially declined to consider. Although the Davies Report was not published until December 1973, it paved the way for clauses to be included in the NHS Reorganisation Bill which received Royal Assent in the summer of 1973.[116] This gave the existing parliamentary commissioner for administration the duties of a health service commissioner, and Sir Alan Marre duly took on this new role on 1 October 1973.

When Labour returned to government in 1974 it sought to widen the remit of the Hospital Advisory Service, which until then had focused its inspections on psychiatric and geriatric institutions. Owen suggested renaming it the 'Health Advisory Service' (HAS), which was adopted from 1 April 1976. The linked proposal that it integrate its work with that of the Social Work Service provoked some serious objections, and it was agreed to retain two separate but liaising inspection services. The Davies Committee had considered the role of the HAS as well as the new Community Health Councils, when drawing up a draft code of practice for a complaints system. As was to be expected, the medical organisations were deeply suspicious, and even the health service commissioner's staff had concerns that a Code of Practice might interfere with their own investigations. Owen's response, sensing that further uncertainty would be damaging for the NHS, was to refer the issue to the Select Committee on the health service commissioner, which published its report on 1 December 1977.[117] Evidence of the profession's intransigence and strength can be taken from the fact that there was no effective progress on this issue until the launch of new procedures for handling complaints in Circular HC(81)5, issued in April 1981. This appears to have been one area in which Brian was unwilling or unable to invest his time to make policy change happen.

Brian also appears to have withdrawn from Labour's discussions on the development of Keith Joseph's draft White Paper on the mentally ill. Owen took the initiative on this in 1974, but because of substantial Treasury opposition to any policy that might have budgetary implications, a much less radical White Paper was finally published, *Better Services for the Mentally Ill*, on 16 October 1975.[118] There was still indecision over the transition from large institutional services to new integrated mental health services, now vaguely given a 25-year timescale. It was 'a rambling document, considerable in length, commendable for its pious expressions, but deficient in practical content'.[119] It was much more satisfactorily summarised in six pages of the *Priorities for Health and Personal Social Services* document than its original 91 pages could achieve. This predicted that the population of long-stay mental hospitals would fall from 90,000 in 1974 to 75,000 by 1979. It was short-lived optimism, squashed by the revisionary document, *The Way Forward*, the following year. In view of this continued hiatus in planning for the mentally ill, a working group was set up in 1977, chaired by Timothy Nodder, Deputy Secretary in the DHSS, who had been closely involved with NHS reorganisation. Even his immediate enquiry did not produce a report until September 1980.

Alongside these initiatives, there was a further DHSS initiative, this time to review, as promised, the 1959 Mental Health Act. The review was announced by Owen in January 1975, and carried out by an internal panel, producing a report in August 1976. It caused tension with organisations such as the National Council for Civil Liberties, MENCAP and the National Association for Mental Health (later known as MIND), which had been pushing for a new White Paper which re-balanced the issue of treatment and detention, and establishing a clear legal framework for compulsory treatment of the mentally ill. When it finally appeared on 12 September 1978 it was deemed unsatisfactory, and required the publication of a further White Paper in 1981 before the final Mental Health Act of 1983. Alongside these slow manoeuvres, there were some more positive developments. Castle established an enquiry in July 1975 into services for the mentally handicapped, especially children, who were routinely housed with adults in long-stay institutions. This was chaired by Peggy Jay MP, a prominent advocate for children's welfare and rights, and a known supporter of community care. Its report, published four years later in March 1979, was a groundbreaking, if very belated, policy document.[120] The Committee proposed that even those with the most severe mental disabilities should live in the community, but that this would require substantial investment in training carers (based on a social work rather than nursing model) to meet the expected doubling in workforce – not welcome news to the Treasury's ears.

In other policy areas Brian helped Castle to achieve significant and quick progress. Within a month of coming into office Castle took Brian to a meeting at 10 Downing Street with Wilson. She wanted cars for disabled people to be made cheaply and in bulk, but the cost was prohibitive. Brian explained his alternative plan for providing cash allowances towards the cost of buying cars. Even this had potentially large financial implications as there were up to 500,000 people who would qualify. But Castle found his plan discriminatory: many disabled people could not afford the full cost of buying a car, even with a government mobility allowance. Brian came back to her a few weeks later with a rent-a-car policy. The non-contributory Invalidity Pension (NCIP) was introduced in 1975 for people of working age who were not covered by invalidity benefit because of low contributions, or who had not been able to work for at least six months. The following year the Invalid Care Allowance (ICA) provided support to men and (single) women of working age who were unable to work because they had to stay at home to look after a severely disabled relative.[121]

Yet some policy issues, such as health promotion, touched on ministerial and advisers' personal beliefs. Joseph had tried to make progress on smoking during his four years in office, but only achieved the warning notice from the Chief Medical Officer on the back of cigarette packets. Both Castle and Brian were heavy smokers, and did not see further legislation as appropriate. Owen took the initiative, by proposing to ban sponsorship of sports events by cigarette manufacturers, which Castle referred to as his 'pet campaign against smoking'.[122]

Pensions: third time lucky

Richard Crossman died just after Brian's return to Whitehall, which had provided a glimmer of hope that his long-planned pensions policy might finally make the statute book. Brian, and Tony Lynes, were pre-eminently suited to advise on pensions. They initiated Labour's national superannuation plan in 1957, which Crossman used as the basis for a Bill during his 1968–70 DHSS leadership. Wilson's decision to call an early general election in 1970, which Labour lost, had cost Crossman his legislation, only a few weeks before its expected parliamentary approval. Keith Joseph then obtained consent in 1973 for an alternative two-tier state pensions system, in which employees would have to qualify for the second pension by belonging to an approved private scheme (for which Joseph had set low requirements) or by becoming a member of what was viewed as an inferior 'State Reserve Scheme'(SRS). One of the main deficiencies of the SRS was that it would be funded, that is, the contributions were to be invested and the pension determined by the yield. Labour were vociferous critics of Joseph's 'modest scheme', especially because the pension payments were not guaranteed through Exchequer subsidy.[123]

Labour's 1974 election manifesto, *Let Us Work Together: Labour's Way out of the Crisis*, attempted to initiate a departure from the old rhetoric: 'Clearly a fresh approach to the British crisis is required, and Labour insists that it must begin with an entirely new recognition of the claims of social justice.'[124] The scope of this relatively new term of 'social justice' included the elimination of poverty, increasing social equality, fairer deals for housing tenants and disabled people, and better levels of benefits such as pensions and family allowances (which Labour proposed to replace with a new system of 'child cash allowances' for every child).

When Labour returned to government in March 1974 they honoured their commitment to the TUC and immediately increased the flat-rate pension. Castle overrode the conventional timetable for such benefits upratings, and new pensions books were issued to reflect the 29 per cent increase: from £7.75 to £10 for a single person, and from £12.50 to £16 for a married couple. Yet this was a stop-gap measure, and a more durable pensions policy solution was still required. At a meeting soon after her appointment as Secretary of State in March, Castle was presented with two choices by her senior civil servants. It was by then impossible to cancel or defer the introduction of Joseph's earnings-related contributions from 5 April 1974 because all the preparations, instructions and new PAYE (pay-as-you-earn) cards had long since been printed and distributed to employers, and there was no time to replace them. In any event, the National Insurance scheme's finances depended on these new contributions. Castle thus had the choice of either letting the Joseph earnings-related benefits start to accrue *pro tem* until she could replace them with something devised by the new Labour government, which on past form would take several years, or of cancelling the accrual of new benefits and continuing with the existing flat-rate ones *pro tem* in return for the new earnings-related contributions.

Unsurprisingly, Castle was not attracted by either option. Given Labour's previous attacks on Boyd-Carpenter's 1959 graduated scheme as a 'swindle' for not providing a good earnings-related return on its earnings-related contributions, Castle was especially wary of the second option. When Michael Partridge, Assistant Secretary at the DHSS, suggested that it was at least the more socialist re-distributive option, she replied 'Young man, you can have too much of a good thing. The British people would not stand for it.'[125] Nevertheless she finally preferred it to implementing the Joseph scheme in full, given the uncertainties of how long it might take to persuade the Treasury of the virtues of a revised national superannuation scheme. The result was that ministers and civil servants were under exceptional pressure to produce a new scheme, a White Paper, legislation and implementation in record time before the next election, to avoid the fates of Crossman and Joseph.

From May 1974 Brian worked closely with Castle's other trusted 'Brian' – Brian O'Malley, Minister for Social Security. Brian had sounded out the department, and felt that the younger staff were keen to consider a modified Crossman scheme. However, the possibility of linking the existing flat-rate pensions to a national superannuation scheme was sidelined, perhaps because the Labour Party/TUC Liaison Committee had no strong allegiance to Crossman's scheme which was now in its 19th year of gestation. Policy debate had moved on, without Crossman. National superannuation had never been seen as an integral part of the Social Contract. Castle announced in May 1974 that only limited parts of Joseph's 1973 Act would be implemented. Labour's own White Paper, *Better Pensions*, appeared in September 1974.[126] Her Bill would also address an issue ignored by Joseph: how to tackle the pension inequalities faced by most women, who invariably retired on smaller pensions than men.

With the resultant Social Security Act of 1975 Castle finally achieved what had eluded Crossman: a State Earnings-Related Pension Scheme. SERPS, as it was known, came into operation in 1978. The traditional bias towards male pensions was halted, and women were awarded the same pension, despite their greater longevity, earlier retirement at 60 and selection of their best 20 years' contributions. A person would begin to earn, on top of their basic flat rate, an upper-tier pension of up to about a third of average male earnings, so that the half of the workforce who were not previously in schemes now found themselves coerced into greater saving and thus better retirement incomes.[127] The state went further, actually underwriting certain private schemes: 'a move that extended public liability in an unprecedented fashion (thanks to the fact that SERPS pensions were index-linked), which governments have been trying to reduce ever since'.[128] This assistance was timely – many schemes were at the point of collapse following the OPEC oil crisis which reduced the value of their investments, and by that time some 11 million people were contracted-out. But SERPS did not address the problem of the poorest, who were never in a position to make contributions to pension schemes. It also failed to credit in existing pensioners. Castle firmly rejected this proposal from the Social Policy Sub-committee because of the current poor economic situation, but she also insisted that the Act make provision for it, with no need for new legislation, should better times allow.

Despite all these very positive developments from her team at DHSS, Castle herself was increasingly the subject of negative public and political debate. Her antagonism towards the medical profession and failure to pacify the trade unions on the private medicine issue fuelled rumours as early as May 1975 that Wilson was going to replace her with Tony Benn. In January 1976 the new rumour was that Brian O'Malley and David Owen would both be promoted to the Cabinet to replace her.[129] In an uncharacteristic slip of political nous on 4 March 1976 Castle told Wilson that she was considering resigning after she had seen through the pay beds legislation. Wilson told her that he also expected to resign in the 'near future'. Her diaries show that she had no idea just how soon that would be, or the potential impact it would have on her future.[130] Wilson announced his retirement to the Cabinet on 16 March, and MPs selected Jim Callaghan, her long-standing arch-enemy, as his replacement on 5 April.

11

Disillusionment: 1976–79

Ennals, 'Deep Throat' and the Cabinet papers leak
The Castle Diaries
The Royal Commission on the National Health Service
The 30th anniversary of the National Health Service
Inequalities: the Supplementary Benefits Review and the Black Report
Peter Shore and the Department of the Environment
Labour in 1979: assessments and strategies

If the start of the 1970s saw the apotheosis of paternalistic nationalism, with the 1974 reorganisation of the NHS as its monument, the second half of the decade produced the politics of disillusionment. (Rudolf Klein, 2001)[1]

Brian remained a special adviser to the Labour government after Barbara Castle's departure in 1976, working for her successor, David Ennals. Staffing, structural and funding crises finally resulted in the appointment of a Royal Commission on the NHS, to which Brian gave evidence. He also steered the formation of a committee to investigate Britain's persistent health inequalities, chaired by Sir Douglas Black. In 1978, with a general election due within a year, Brian accepted an invitation from his old friend Peter Shore to work as his special adviser in the Department of the Environment (DoE). This provided a new perspective on his longstanding interest in social justice, especially on housing policy. During the 1974–79 Labour government Brian spent at least three days a week working in Whitehall. However, he maintained a large teaching load at the LSE, and also took on new international projects and advisory roles (discussed in the next chapter).

On 8 April 1976 Jim Callaghan sacked Barbara Castle from her position as Secretary of State for Social Services, ostensibly on the grounds of bringing in younger ministers to reduce the average age of the Cabinet. She had been scheduled to introduce the Health Services Bill to Parliament the following Monday (which would enact her precious pay beds policy). But Callaghan (who held Castle partly responsible for Labour's defeat at the 1970 general election) could not see beyond achieving this very personal and immediate insult to allow her the extra couple of months to announce her own resignation. Brian knew that a change of Prime Minister, especially when it turned out to be Callaghan, might mean the end of his term as special adviser. When Castle was summoned to Downing Street he and Straw remained behind, waiting outside her office at the Elephant and Castle. When she returned, and broke the news, they helped her to write her reply to Callaghan, and then planned a farewell office drinks party. It was an emotional occasion, interrupted by the farce of Norman Warner trying unobtrusively to remove Castle's personal papers and ornaments before the ministerial room was made ready for the next Secretary of State. All her team were there, apart from Henry Yellowlees, still sulking about his exclusion from the pay beds negotiations. She recorded in her diary that evening that Brian said it had 'been such fun', an odd phrase for a man who could usually be relied on to have the appropriate words to hand.[2]

Castle was stunned and insulted to find that her replacement was David Ennals. Ennals had limited government experience of health, although he had served as Minister for Social Security in Wilson's 1964–70 government, and Richard Crossman had valued him for his hard work and loyalty. He lost his seat at the 1970 general election and returned to work for the charity National Association for Mental Health (later renamed MIND). He was elected again as an MP in 1974 and Wilson had appointed him as a Minister at the Foreign and Commonwealth Office (FCO). The senior DHSS civil servants did not welcome Ennals with enthusiasm; they saw him as 'not in the same league' as Castle. As soon as Brian heard that Castle's replacement was to be Ennals, he went immediately to his office to offer his services. Ennals, aware of the impending crises, decided to keep him on.

Castle, already tearful with the brutality of Callaghan's manoeuvres, was hurt by Brian's apparent disregard for her feelings. Yet Brian was a pragmatist. He also recognised that it would not be beneficial for Jack Straw, ambitious for a political career, to remain with Ennals. He went to see Liz Shore, then also at the DHSS as Deputy Chief Medical Officer, and asked whether Peter Shore would take on Straw at the Department of the Environment (DoE). Liz liked this idea, and persuaded Peter to offer him one of his special adviser positions, which Straw readily accepted.[3] Straw was replaced at DHSS by Mike Hartley-Brewer, a former journalist, who had unsuccessfully stood as a Labour candidate in 1970 and was keen to develop a political career. David Owen also left the DHSS a few months later for the more glamorous world of the FCO. There was no period of grace to let Castle's wounds heal: she and Brian had to meet again the following week, when they travelled by train together to Rotherham for the funeral of Brian O'Malley, who had died after a brain haemorrhage. Their shared grief at the sudden loss of a friend and colleague eased the awkwardness of this new political configuration.

Ennals, 'Deep Throat' and the Cabinet papers leak

Ennals' first task was to put through the Health Services Bill. The medical profession had had such a tough time with Castle that anyone else could seem an improvement. The Act, given Royal Assent in November 1976, was less inflammatory than Castle's initial Bill, and the number of pay beds to be lost in the first cut was 1,000, leaving 3,500 for an undetermined later cull. The Act also established the Health Services Board to supervise the next phase, and to introduce common NHS and private waiting lists. By the end of the Labour government in 1979 there were still some 2,800 pay beds within NHS hospitals. As Webster has noted, Labour's concerted effort to get rid of private medicine within the NHS actually helped to stimulate its growth in the private sector, facilitated by the creation of the Health Services Board.[4]

Ennals also faced the difficult task in April 1976 of reversing the planned introduction of Labour's new Child Benefit Scheme, which was to replace both family allowances and child tax allowances. Castle, from the backbenches, gave one of her most devastating Commons speeches, attacking the 'abandonment of one of this Party's major reforms'.[5] In the new economic crisis it was one of the first casualties of the spending cuts. In the months leading up to Wilson's resignation, the government had attempted to find a way out of this long-running commitment to child benefit. It had been a manifesto pledge in 1974, and welcomed by the Child Poverty Action Group (CPAG), which had campaigned since its formation in 1965 for greater support for families. Yet, despite a 35p increase in family allowances in 1968, there had been little further attention by Labour to the issue. Wilson, when he returned to government in 1974, had not increased family allowances. As Frank Field points out, poverty did not even merit an index entry in Wilson's retrospective account of this time in office.[6]

Brian had been a founder member of CPAG, and on its Management Committee until May 1968 when his appointment as special adviser to Richard Crossman presented a conflict of interests, and he resigned. Since then he had retained an unofficial interest, which waxed and waned, affected by his relationship with Peter Townsend and his increasingly heavy international work commitments. After the controversy of CPAG's attack on Labour in the run-up to the 1970 general election, when he had sat at Crossman's side facing an angry Townsend and Field across the Cabinet Office table, he seemed to find less time for the group. He was still consulted on its campaigns, but failed to re-engage with its activities even when his position as special adviser ended with the fall of the Labour government in June 1970.

Brian had been closely involved in helping Castle to prepare the child benefit scheme. He long argued that the seven million first or only children in Britain should be acknowledged and supported by the state's welfare system. The public also welcomed the planned scheme, albeit if some disaffected men would suffer in the movement of benefit from 'wallet to purse'. It was going to prove tricky for the government to cancel this reform. Castle had already in 1975 reluctantly accepted two postponements to its introduction, even while the Child Benefit Bill passed through Westminster. After she was sacked there were heated debates in Cabinet, and Brian briefed members such as Tony Benn on the importance of the scheme in the run-up to the crucial vote.[7] It was narrowly agreed to abandon the scheme altogether. Castle reacted furiously, blaming the 'stubborn masculine bias of British politics'.[8] Callaghan had effectively out-manoeuvred Castle in the preceding months, announcing a rise in the child tax allowance, which then 'forced' a compensatory rise in family allowance. He then argued that it was trade union pressure on this unpalatable outcome that had forced the government to cancel the scheme.

On 17 June 1976 *New Society* published an article by Frank Field, Director of CPAG, which laid bare Callaghan's scheming.[9] It drew on leaked Cabinet papers from April and May, shortly after Callaghan became Prime Minister, and Ennals had replaced Castle. Field has never disclosed who leaked information from the Cabinet papers to him. He referred to the person as 'Deep Throat', the pseudonym given to the Washington informant in the Watergate scandal of Nixon's 1974 administration. Who was Field's 'Deep Throat'? It had to be someone with access to Cabinet papers – either a member of Cabinet or one of their senior staff. *The Sun* accused Tony Lynes. Brian certainly also had a motive in exposing how his and Castle's hard-won scheme had been trashed. There was a police enquiry that involved interviewing and fingerprinting all members of the Cabinet and their staff (240 in total), and forensic analysis of the 34 copies of the leaked document (apart from the Queen's copy). Sir Douglas Allen led a Civil Service Department internal enquiry. The prime suspect seemed to be a member of staff at the DHSS. Allen questioned all of Castle's advisers.

The transcript of Brian's interrogation shows a certain degree of logic:

> He considered that the article could not have been written by someone who had seen the full DHSS memoranda as these indicated that the department was well behind in the printing of the books [for collecting the benefit]. The article ignored the administrative problems which were well known to all in DHSS closely connected with the scheme. Moreover the CPAG had not worked out the cost involved in getting an improved benefit in real terms, another fact well known to the DHSS. Professor Abel-Smith knows Mr Field but had had no recent contact with him. He had no suggestions to make as to how the leak had occurred beyond the impression (for reasons given above) that it came from outside the DHSS.

There appeared to have been some connection to the LSE. When David Piachaud was interviewed he said that he had learned about Field's article through a colleague at the LSE who in turn had heard that another LSE colleague had been shown a draft the week before publication.[10] After weeks of questioning, both the police and internal enquiries arrived at dead ends.

Brian's appointments as special adviser, to Crossman in 1968, Castle in 1974 and Ennals in 1976, gave him unprecedented access to government papers. Of course the civil service, before permitting this, had put him (and his partner John) through rigorous security checks, and he had been required to sign the Official Secrets Act. Yet there is evidence that he was prepared to bend the rules when he felt he could either gain valuable expert policy advice by showing confidential papers to colleagues, or when he could provide information that would advance specific policy issues. Thus Crossman's blueprints for the NHS owed an unknown debt to one of Brian's colleagues at the London School of Hygiene and Tropical Medicine, and in 1972 he sent Judith Marquand a copy of Ennals' inflammatory speech to CPAG from April 1970 to 'give useful leads but I should prefer you not to quote from it directly as I do not think that the text has been published anywhere in its entirety'.[11]

The leaked Cabinet papers from April and May 1976 exposed the fact that the trade unions had been manipulated. They had been told that a survey of backbench MPs showed deep opposition to the Child Benefit scheme, because it would affect men's take-home pay by removing the child tax allowance. In view of this news, the TUC agreed to support a postponement of the scheme. Callaghan reported back to back-benchers only the last part of this – that the TUC now opposed the scheme, and thus got Cabinet to 'agree' to postpone.[12] From her new position outside the Cabinet Castle now mustered her trade union contacts into a campaign for the re-instatement of the scheme, exploiting their sense of humiliation at how Callaghan had misused them. By late summer the various campaigns began to have an effect, and on 23 September Ennals was able to announce that the government would phase in the full Child Benefit scheme between April 1977 and 1979.

When Ennals replaced Castle as Secretary of State for Social Services, Callaghan tried to cut back on the agreement for DHSS special advisers that Castle had enjoyed. He refused to allow the part-time appointments of Tony Lynes and Geoff Alltimes to account for a full-time equivalent, and stipulated that the total number of special advisers be limited to two. As Jack Straw had moved to be adviser to Peter Shore, Ennals would have to lose either Lynes or Alltimes if he wished to replace Straw. A possible solution offered (but not adopted) was that Brian could be re-classified as an 'expert' rather than 'special' adviser, although the civil servant who suggested this solution did not further elaborate on what the difference (if any) between the two terms was.[13]

One of Brian's first initiatives as Ennals' special adviser was to set up an off-the-record meeting for him with TUC representatives in June 1976. Brian offered to host a dinner at his new home at 11 Westmoreland Place, which Ennals duly accepted, no doubt aware of Brian's reputation as a fine cook. Brian subsequently submitted a rather chutzpah bill for the costs of the dinner, as he had done when entertaining for Castle. In a typically bureaucratic civil service response, however, he received a stern warning that such an event might arouse the 'hostility shown by the press, radio, etc towards hospitality at public expense. We might find it difficult to defend home entertainment, however satisfied we are of its desirability in certain circumstances, and I hope that these are not gatherings likely to occur too frequently or to excite any kind of publicity.'[14]

Brian loved entertaining, and took pleasure in his guests' admiration of how he managed his hectic schedule. He could arrive home at 7.00pm from a long international flight and have drinks served to guests and supper ready by 8.00pm, before departing early the following morning on another flight out of Heathrow. What many guests to his home did not appreciate was that although Brian did the cooking, John was responsible for the shopping and aftermath cleaning up. Close friends such as Roger Lockyer and Percy Stevens were aware of this, but at semi-formal functions such as the TUC dinner John would disappear before guests arrived. Brian had the option of introducing John as his lodger to London guests. When they travelled together overseas, Brian would usually introduce John as his godson.

Pat Nairne, DHSS Permanent Secretary, appreciated the value of Brian's extra-curricular hospitality. He wrote to thank him the day after another off-the-record dinner party on 25 April 1977: 'your lovely house & superb dinner gave the "enterprise" the best possible start.... P.S. I assume that you will be recovering all your costs via Mike Malone-Lee.'[15] It is not clear from the handwritten invoice that Brian submitted to the departmental Hospitality Fund exactly how many people had attended, but the catering was impressive: salmon trout followed by duck, strawberries and cream, and cheese. This was accompanied by five bottles of red wine (@£1.75), three bottles of white wine, 1 bottle part gin, part whiskey and half a bottle of cognac. Brian also included an estimate of '(say) £1' for use of electricity and hot water. The total cost of £54.37 he had run past a friend who was a management trainee from Rank Hotels who 'assures me that commercially the dinner would have cost £12 to £15 per head. So the Department cannot complain that it's not getting a bargain.'[16]

The Castle Diaries

Barbara Castle forgave Brian for his swift transfer of allegiance to Ennals, but she returned to the backbenches with no intention of slipping into quiet semi-retirement. She planned to exert her influence in a variety of ways, and began by editing her diaries, which she anticipated would bring her renewed attention and financial gain. Unlike Crossman, who had usually dictated a full week's worth of diary entries during weekends at his country home (with consequential errors), Castle made a habit of writing hers every night. The events – and emotions – of the day were still fresh in her mind. Each entry summarised the mood of the moment, unlike some of Crossman's, which were tempered by the knowledge of what was to happen during the following few days. This was critical in the fast-moving political world, where there were often parallel meetings, subtle shifts of allegiances and agreements brokered on partial knowledge. When Castle fell and injured her ankle she refused to be taken to hospital, insisting that David Owen and Jack Straw drive her to her flat (and carry her up the stairs) so she could write her diary entry for that day.[17]

Castle asked Brian if he would read draft sections of her edited diaries. His written feedback was carefully constructed, as if for a student, beginning with some positive comments and gently, slowly, unleashing the underlying negativity:

> I had a very exciting weekend reading the section from your diary. It is a gripping story and a major contribution to history. The descriptions of the NEC and the wheeling and dealing between Ministers are magnificent. You might like to consider whether too much is said about how your speeches were received and what people said to you about them. It is inevitable that this sort of thing was recorded in the diary but it does stand out a bit much when you read entry after entry on particular speeches. It does give rather the impression that a top politician's life is rather like a one-performance repertory company.... Personally I would like the diaries to have analysed a little bit more the reasons why you reached particular decisions at office meetings. This is what would interest students of social policy most of all....
>
> If you published within the next year I do not see how it would be possible for you to continue to play a leading role in Labour Party politics. Moreover, if I were in politics, I personally would feel very uncomfortable to lose friends because they thought you had shown them up in an unfavourable light and done so as they would see it unfairly. Any quoting or reporting is inevitably selective. Moreover they did not know that they were verbatim on the record. Jim [Callaghan] appears as weak and ineffective on a number of occasions, Harold [Wilson] comes out as devious, as many people think he is, Shirley [Williams] appears nice but not very effective, Wedgie [Tony Benn] comes out very badly indeed – like some irrelevant Old Testament prophet. The forthright statement of David Owen's Rightist views on public expenditure won't do good to his political career. Possibly more damaging, he appears irresolute, inconsistent and undecided (it is always much easier to be No 1 than No 2) and as for Alf [Morris] – alas poor Yorrick! And so on....
>
> There would be little here to shock the politically sophisticated. Dick [Crossman] has done that already insofar as they were not

sophisticated enough already. But most people do not fall into that class. Your diary would further disillusion the idealistic intelligent young and make them less likely to want to enter politics. It would further upset the loyalist rank and file who need heroes and heroines. Most important of all it could be used by the Tories with devastating effect at the next election. There are enough quotes here to destroy the credibility of many of your colleagues. What if Central Office [the Conservative Party headquarters] gutted the book and gave a potted version of what each Cabinet member was recorded as saying to the Tory candidate in his constituency? What if Central Office compared what Ministers said in Parliament announcing decisions with your account of how decisions were reached?...Thus I do not think it could be published before the next election or after it if we were returned to power....The price paid for early publication if you wanted a reasonably comfortable life would be immediate departure from Parliament but I am sure that you would not contemplate that – a by-election and all the feeling of the Blackburn people that they had been let down. Then you would have to face all the nasty questions about the price you were paid by your publisher and the *Sunday Times* for those revelations....Thus my advice is that this needs to remain on the shelf for several years and have careful editing when you finally think the time is right to publish. I have discussed all this with Jack Straw and I gather he takes the same view. You asked for my honest opinion. Here it is.[18]

The Castle Diaries 1974–76 were finally published in 1980, after Labour's defeat in the 1979 general election.[19] Many of the leading characters were no longer actively involved in politics when Tony Blair formed the next Labour government in 1997.

Just before Christmas 1976 Brian wrote to David Ennals for permission to take his annual skiing holiday, and sending a list of external commitments he wished to undertake the following year. These included spending time at WHO in Geneva in March to finalise the draft of a book on the economics of health policy for developing counties and participating in a WHO Euro working group in June on controlling the costs of healthcare. In November he wished to attend an international conference related to the WHO book. Brian also asked Ennals' permission in February 1977 to take a fortnight's assignment in Colombia advising on their adoption of a UK-style health service, which 'could set a precedent for the rest of Latin America now that

Chile, the previous progressive health country, is in such bad hands'.[20] He had already solicited the FCO's approval, which was 'extremely keen to develop British links'. Ennals agreed to Brian's absence during the Easter parliamentary recess. Yet his special adviser role clearly came first: 'Inevitably the discussion will turn to how to get value for money in health services. We may learn something from the experiences of other countries.... I have committed myself to none of these visits saying that I cannot undertake them without your permission. I will quite understand if you want me not to be away at any of these times.' Ennals replied: 'I am very happy you should carry out these WHO engagements. We benefit so much from your knowledge and experience and it would be churlish to deny this to others. In any case we gain indirectly.'[21]

Brian managed to withdraw from some projects, such as the proposed Sandoz Institute study of health economics in developing countries, to free up sufficient time to undertake his DHSS responsibilities. Sometimes these overlapped with his ongoing LSE position: in May 1977 he was part of the small organising committee for Senator Edward Kennedy's visit to the UK. After a breakfast meeting with Ennals to discuss pharmaceuticals policy, Brian then accompanied Kennedy in his car to a meeting with the DHSS Medicines Division. He used this opportunity to talk about the LSE's fundraising appeals for its library and studentships programme, having been briefed that Robert Kennedy Jr was about to come to the LSE to take the MSc in International Relations. Later that year Brian also hosted Joseph Califano, US Secretary of Health, Education and Welfare, when he visited the DHSS as part of his UK visit.[22] A month later, when Brian was in Washington DC, he arranged for the friends he was staying with to invite Karen Davis from Health, Education and Welfare to dinner so that he could plant the 'idea of an DHSS/HEW exchange of thinking about health policy planning' which would involved a handful of DHSS staff visiting Washington DC for three or four days. He explained the logic of this to the DHSS Permanent Secretary Patrick Nairne: 'There is always a danger that our thinking will get in a groove and I always find my visits to the USA refreshing. They plan more than they can implement.... If you felt that it was worth taking further, a letter from the Secretary of State to Califano suggesting a visit in say May or June 1978 might be the next step. I understand that Califano has great goodwill for us and it might be sensible to strike soon while the memory of his UK visit is still fresh.'[23]

In addition to these overseas commitments, Brian also brought value to Ennals' team through his ongoing participation in Labour's NEC

Social Policy Sub-committee. He was particularly interested in its discussions on the deterioration of the NHS, but he also contributed to discussions on occupational pensions and child benefit. He reported back from his European Economic Community (EEC) meetings on how new draft directives on equal treatment of women in social security would affect the UK. He was involved with the collaboration between the Social Policy, Regional and Local Government, and Town and Country Planning Sub-committees to discuss regional authorities and local government administration. When he found that he couldn't attend a key meeting he wrote to Ed Miller, Local Government Officer of the Labour Party, expressing his concerns that the draft consultative document was not clear enough on what Labour were trying to achieve for the NHS. The Social Policy Sub-committee also gave him continued contact with Barbara Castle, who had maintained her role as Chair. In March 1978 he wrote to advise her on committee members: 'You have only one social worker – Mrs Cuttsman, though others like Nicholas Bosanquet have experience of social services committees ... you might consider asking Tom White (Director Coventry) to join the cttee.'[24] White subsequently joined, and produced Working Paper RE1884: 'Minimum standards in the personal social services'. Brian also supported Ennals in his consultations with county council staff following the publication of the Sub-committee's report RE1589: 'Organic change in local government: the social services', which debated returning social services to local council control. Tony Lynes, Peter Townsend and Nicholas Bosanquet also remained regular and vocal members of the Social Policy Sub-committee. During 1978 they continued to debate NEC statements on local government reform and the transfer of the NHS, crediting in existing pensioners to the new pension scheme, short-term benefits and one-parent families.

Britain's health services were under increasing scrutiny during this period. Castle, in response to ongoing dissatisfaction with the 1974 NHS reorganisation, had initiated a review by a group of Regional Hospital Board chairs, which reported to Ennals in July 1976, This in turn prompted a wider-ranging investigation of the management of the central DHSS department, which was seen to be operating two very different administrative cultures for its health and social security sides. It stimulated the creation of a Health and Personal Social Services (HPSS) Strategy Committee in 1978 with a supporting policy unit.

The DHSS's seminal planning document, *Priorities for Health and Personal Social Services in England*, which was produced in March 1976, had signalled some improvements to the NHS. The 'Cinderella services' such as mental health, geriatrics and services for children were to gain substantially more support.[25] But the economic climate was not favourable, and the follow-up publication that appeared in September 1977, *The Way Forward*, was more guarded in setting priorities.[26] It included a table illustrating how regional inequalities in health service funding had remained virtually unchanged since 1958. This applied to funding for general practice as well as hospital services. General practice had been recently more successful in attracting more doctors, and they were now looking after smaller lists (an average of 2,331 patients by 1977), increasingly within purpose-built health centres. But there was still huge disparity between regions. This was one of the concerns about the new RAWP scheme, which had no capacity to allocate GP budgets more equitably. The Treasury was concerned that it would be used as a way to demand further resources, and it put pressure on the DHSS to soften its introduction. Although Ennals' team replied that they had never intended to base allocation solely on the RAWP formula, they bowed to pressure to cap the redistributions, so that no region would have to bear a growth rate of less than 1 per cent in its annual budget, and no region gained by more than 5 per cent.

The Royal Commission on the National Health Service

Wilson had established a Royal Commission on the NHS in October 1975, partly to appease the demands of the medical profession. It was chaired by Sir Alec Merrison, and began a four-year process of taking evidence. Brian knew several members of the Commission well, including Peter Jacques and Audrey Prime, trade union representatives who were members of Labour's Social Policy Sub-committee. It is possible that Brian had also had a hand in the nomination of other members such as Professor Alan Williams, a health economist at the University of York, who had been seconded to the Ministry of Health in the 1960s to introduce some planning. The Labour Party established a linked working party, chaired by Barbara Castle, through the Social Policy Sub-committee to prepare its evidence.[27] At its first meeting in September 1976 a programme of work was agreed that focused on (i) the case for central financing of the NHS; (ii) the case for more resources to be allocated to the NHS; (iii) the need for geographical equality in the distribution of financial and manpower resources; (iv) complaints procedures within the NHS; and (v) the hospital sector career structure, medical education and the role of the different medical professions in healthcare. Brian agreed to coordinate the collection of supporting materials. He wrote to Ennals on 1 October expressing his concerns:

> Barbara is clearly determined on tough evidence to the Royal Commission. How far do you wish your team on the Committee to help with the evidence? I am sure that Barbara hopes that I will dig out facts and figures to document the case via the Department. This will make the paper more forceful and also make it clear that Ministers have assisted in preparing it. The Prime Minister wants us all to work closely with the Party. But the price paid in strained relations with the doctors over the two years after publication could be high. Barbara will presumably want the evidence to be published. The happiest solution would be for the same evidence to be given to the Royal Commission by the Fabian Society rather than the Labour Party. The doctors would then be forced to see that the Fabian Society is wholly independent of the Government. I doubt if there is much chance of your persuading Barbara to accept this (assuming I could sell it to the Fabian Society). Meanwhile do you wish to amend the synopsis? If the more contentious points were removed, Barbara would smell a rat. I hope I am not being unduly worried. You will remember that Barbara simply caved into the doctors on Service Awards and feels very sore about it. I am not copying this to CMO [Chief Medical Officer, Henry Yellowlees], but you may wish me to ask for his opinion.[28]

Brian drafted large sections of the working party's submission himself, drawing on his years of experience as a hospital and RHB governor. He also used his medically qualified colleagues such as Muir Gray and Walter Holland as sounding boards. Holland was dismissive of Brian's proposal that future medical students should complete a year's work experience as a nursing assistant/aide in a psychiatric hospital, or as a porter in an acute general hospital to make them better doctors. His proposal to create a new sub-clinical grade of specialist nurse also received short shrift, and Holland felt that Brian was unduly negative towards those consultants who had incomes from private medical practices: 'Your comments about the attitudes of part-time consultants are perhaps a little strong. I do not think it is true for the majority.'[29]

Working papers by Derek Senior and Dick Wilson were discussed by the working party, which focused on devolution and reorganisation issues. Muir Gray submitted a paper 'Personpower considerations'. Brian was also aware of, and tried to influence, associated policy issues.

He was involved with the evidence submitted by the University of London, which had interests through its affiliated medical schools. He also monitored what was happening at Cabinet level. He wrote to Roland Moyle, Minister of Health, in December 1976 about the Ministerial Group on Urban Policies GEN 38(76)15:

> I am worried by the despairing tone of Annex A on the Inner City Family Practitioner Services. General practice in inner city areas is admitted to be pretty poor....There is a further problem – not spelt out in the paper – that while there is no statistical shortage of inner urban GPs there may well be a shortage of GPs willing to take new patients. Aged GPs may keep their list size low and some Kensington/Chelsea/Westminster doctors exploit the NHS payment system by taking 1,000 patients which gives them considerable cash advantages while their main work may be private practice, occupational health, insurance work, etc. Then there is the problem of the poorly trained and poorly equipped lock up surgery and the proportion of poorly trained and poorly committed immigrant doctors. All in all there are a whole battery of obstacles to effective primary care team working. But the problem is presented as virtually unsoluble....There is a desperate need for health centres attached to the teaching hospitals for the medical students to get good experience of general practice – yet even these may be vetoed by the Medical Practice Committee as they generally involve bringing new good GPs into the area. Surely there is a case for some sort of working party to consider this whole question as I suggested in my "The Agenda for a Strategy" paper?... I cannot see that a solution need require more money. The state of inner city general practice is an obstacle to community care and your general aim of getting better value for money.[30]

Moyle agreed to set up a meeting to see what more could be done with Brian's suggestions. During the spring of 1977 Brian collated draft sections from other members of the Social Policy Sub-committee working party, and wrote a piece on regional government and the NHS in which he worked up alternative funding and management models for regional and area health authorities.[31] He also prepared a briefing and speaking notes for Ennals' meetings with the Joint Consultants' Committee (JCC) on the proposed new Code of Practice on NHS complaints procedures. This was a response to the tense and unproductive negotiations that the Chief Medical Officer, Henry

Yellowlees, had held with the JCC the previous summer, on their refusal to accept the recommendations of the Davies Committee that reported in December 1973.

In all of Brian's work related to the Royal Commission on the NHS he relied on DHSS staff to provide him with supporting materials and feedback on his drafts. They were critical friends, quite willing to tell him when he had been too vague or possibly 'perjorative'. On the issues of NHS complaints procedures, modernisation of primary care and private pay beds Brian took great care to ensure that he had 'the clearest, crispest statement' on why the government had taken certain actions, and that these were consistent with earlier negotiations with the medical profession. He was constantly alert to the historical precedents of the current review, asking DHSS staff to confirm what Aneurin Bevan had agreed in 1948, and checking *Hansard* for speeches by Castle and Ennals on the pay beds issue. He collected press cuttings about the trade unions' call for the abolition of all private medicine and the nationalisation of pharmacists.

The final draft of Labour's evidence to the Royal Commission on the NHS was discussed by the working party in February 1977, before its submission to the NEC Home Policy Committee. Brian had to incorporate diverse views, and position their evidence carefully with regard to other possible developments such as devolution and reorganisation of local government, and the EEC harmonisation project. He had read and synthesised for his ministers the draft evidence that the TUC planned to submit to the Commission. But above all, he was concerned about the doctors, and expecting a 'torrent of opposition in any attempt to negotiate what I am proposing with the profession'.[32]

When Brian gave the sixth annual Rivers Lecture to the Institute of Chartered Secretaries and Administrators and the London Chamber of Commerce in 1977 he was following in distinguished footsteps – previous speakers included Lord Redcliffe Maud and Lord Hailsham.[33] He chose to discuss the interim recommendations of the Royal Commission on the NHS. These included such trite phrases as 'People should be prevented from becoming patients' and 'Hospitals need to be more closely integrated with community services', although the ninth recommendation, 'Encouragement should be given to provide practice outside the NHS', with hindsight seems a thin-end-of-the-wedge comment. His provocative speech focused on doctors as a significant source of inefficiency in the NHS, which he felt the Royal Commission had not yet adequately addressed:

Should our aim be to make available to each hospital clinician information on the cost of what he authorises as he authorises it? Should our aim be to inform every clinician of the total cost of what he has authorised at the end of each week or of each month and how he stands in this respect compared to his colleagues? Should such information be built into the process of audit as it develops? The technology to provide this would seem to be readily available....One gains the impression that the Royal Commission saw no really urgent need to increase health service spending because of international comparisons which show that nations which spend more of their resources on health services do not necessarily have better health as indicated by mortality rates. Comparisons of this kind may be seriously misleading ... in my view the largest single weakness of our health service is that in its primary care services it behaves largely as if it were just another health insurance scheme [as in Germany, the US]. It does far too little to grasp the advantage it could obtain from being in name at least a health *service* scheme. Improvement implies to me much more than the passive role of waiting for consumers to come through an open door. It implies the active role of seeking out under-users of health care and securing, wherever possible, use in line with need.[34]

Judging from the length of Brian's typed lecture script, he must have spoken for nearly an hour, working through an unremitting catalogue of the Royal Commission's omissions and weaknesses: its failure to introduce geographically defined GP practices (with coterminous health visiting and community nursing services); its failure to eliminate single-handed GP practices; and its failure to take up Ennals' (probably Brian's) idea to build and lease out health centres to salaried GPs in deprived inner-city areas.

Despite this very critical public lecture, Brian was viewed as a valuable expert on the NHS, and on the evening of 19 December 1978 he attended a private dinner at Commission House to provide a confidential briefing to three of the commissioners: Sir Thomas Brown, Professor Sir Ivor Batchelor and Dr Christopher Wells.[35] They discussed a number of themes. On the NHS Brian made the points that it was poor at experimenting with policies before they were advocated nationally; there was still too great an isolation between GPs and hospital doctors; the programme of continuing education for GPs was inadequate; and district general hospitals were about a third bigger than they needed to be, and were hindering the construction of small-scale hospitals, which was also exacerbated by professional uncertainty about the role of a community hospital. He highlighted recent research published in the *Journal of the Royal Statistical Society* which demonstrated a correlation between decreases in employee morale and increasing size of workplace: this was also reflected in the NHS, where small units such as local maternity hospitals often reported the highest staff morale.

Brian also talked about the 'right amount' of money to spend on the NHS. He cited his recent book on European health services, which showed that the Netherlands and West Germany spent a substantially higher proportion of GNP than other countries on health, but it was difficult to evaluate the returns, and many of the problems that health services dealt with were affected by wider socioeconomic factors. Brian suggested that RAWP was hindered by lack of support, even from those who had gained from it, and that the Royal Commission should highlight this good practice, along with Britain's world-leading expertise in health service planning. However, dialogue between the localities and the centre could be further improved, and greater clarity of information was needed – for example, the difficulty of defining the elderly as a client group because it spanned across the chronic and acute hospital sectors. On the structure of the NHS, Brian told the commissioners that it was likely that personal social services had even more important links with housing than they did with the NHS. This was a major advantage of the 'Organic Change' proposal, although the changes risked reintroducing part of the old structure of local government within the new. He saw a disadvantage of local authority control of the NHS in the possibility that doctors would be restricted from sending their patients outside their authority's area. He had witnessed this in both Denmark and Sweden. They discussed how the DHSS senior civil servants functioned, especially how the Permanent Secretary was constrained by his role as NHS accounting officer, which prioritised budgeting over policy problems. Although the DHSS had explored devolving some financial responsibility to regions, there was little potential given ministerial accountability. Brian proposed a possible long-term structure for the NHS in which top-tier authorities would contain a mixture of local government, trade union and professional members and directly elected members in equal proportions. The accountability problem could be addressed if there were surcharge powers to deal with gross over-spending by members of these authorities.

Brian did not want his advice to be part of the official (published) evidence. The Secretary to the Royal Commission sent Brian a copy of the notes from this private conversation, noting, 'We should be happy to ensure that this record has a thirty year embargo on it. It will certainly be regarded as highly confidential within the Commission.... I know that everyone very much appreciated the discussion we had with you and thought it provoking. I hope you enjoyed it too.'[36] It took another two years before the final report was published which, of course, made no mention of Brian's influential role.

The 30th anniversary of the National Health Service

Ennals lacked Castle's fighting instinct for his DHSS budgets. At crucial Cabinet negotiations he failed to push his department's case. Although he was subservient to Treasury pressure for further cuts, he seemed incapable of achieving the required economies, which further increased the Treasury's wrath. He had fond hopes that the 30th anniversary of the NHS in 1978 would provoke some generosity and that he would be given his desired 3 per cent increase, but this was short-lived when the Salmon Report laid bare the widespread inefficiencies in supplies procurement and waste in the NHS.[37]

By now, press reports of ward and hospital closures, unemployed nurses and lack of care for critically ill patients were regular occurrences. Although Ennals had plenty of evidence of such NHS crises, he appeared unable to put together a coherent plan for how he would invest the £50 million that he had urgently requested from Callaghan. The Treasury was convinced that he would pour this precious bailout money into hospitals rather than targeting other pressing needs. Ennals' attempts to pacify them, by announcing a campaign to save £30 million a year on pharmaceutical costs by educating the public on responsible consumption of medicines, were unsuccessful. A further embarrassment was the arrival of a report into the 'excessive' costs of re-building St Thomas' Hospital, where Brian was known to be very closely associated.[38]

One of the areas that Ennals failed to adequately focus on was care of the elderly. This is odd, given the mounting statistical evidence that it was this age group that was putting increasing pressure on acute hospital services. As discussed in Chapter 8, Crossman had finally faced up to the chronic abuse of elderly patients in long-stay institutions, as publicised by Barbara Robb's pressure group AEGIS (Aid to the Elderly in Government Institutions). Brian was active within this, and led the post-Ely working party in formulating policies to redress the structural faults of the welfare state in this area. Yet despite featuring as one of the pioneering programme analysis and reviews by the

Conservative's new Central Policy Review Staff in 1972, there was little real policy development. When Labour came back into office they issued a White Paper, *Prevention and Health: Everybody's Business* two years later in 1976, with the subtitle *A Reassessment of Public and Personal Health*.[39] As Webster has noted, it 'confined itself to homely advice, rather like a parish magazine, telling the elderly that they would benefit by wearing "well-fitting shoes, a rubber ferule at the end of a walking stick, the avoidance of slippery polished surfaces and loose mats or carpet edges"'.[40] The elderly, having waited so long for a useful White Paper on their needs, were told that a further White Paper was then required to plan their services. Ennals continued to stall on any meaningful investigations right through his term as Secretary of State. The long-promised consultation paper, with the dubious title *A Happier Old Age*, finally appeared on 27 June 1978.[41] It was 'vacuous and patronising'.[42] The larger typeface, ostensibly chosen to make it easier for its elderly subjects to read, had, officials admitted, also been chosen because otherwise the document 'would look too short with normal type'.[43] The White Paper was again deferred, pending the next general election.

Brian's feelings about working for such an embattled and ineffectual Secretary of State can only be gauged indirectly. With his long-standing determination to achieve more equitable and efficient health and social welfare policy he must have found it deeply frustrating to be in a department so constrained by budget cuts and lack of political clout. It is perhaps surprising that he could not steer Ennals as effectively as he had done Crossman and, to a lesser extent, Castle, through the Treasury's devious bargaining process. He did not appear to encourage Ennals to return to key issues, such as the place of teaching hospitals within the NHS structure, apart from establishing a study group in September 1977, followed by a small conference. A decision on their fate was postponed for a further three years.

Recording the history of the NHS for the 30th anniversary was perhaps a strategy to bolster staff morale in the hope of surviving to better times. Ennals asked Brian to produce an official history of the NHS in January 1978, which required producing a draft by Easter, if it was to be printed in time for 5 July. He had plenty of personal experience to draw on, beginning with his work on the Guillebaud enquiry into the cost of the NHS in 1953–56, and an almost continuous engagement with both the policy planning and delivery of health services through his governorships of St Thomas' and the Maudsley Hospitals, and membership of various local and regional hospital boards.

In classic Whitehall tradition, when the project began, Brian sent a minute to the upper echelons of the DHSS, suggesting some themes which he might include, such as tuberculosis, infant mortality and diphtheria, if supporting statistics could be provided. Liz Shore, one of the Deputy Chief Medical Officers to Sir Henry Yellowlees, and a long-standing friend of Brian's since the 1950s, replied to Brian's minute with the collated response of her team of medical civil servants: 'You will see from the attached minutes that we do not find it at all easy to identify many health changes for which the NHS in its role as a preventer of disease can claim a considerable part of the credit even though we can produce statistics showing that mortality rates for a number of conditions have been dropping over the last thirty years.... On infant mortality we are vulnerable to the criticism that our fall is now lagging behind other developed nations. I think the maternal mortality story would be more useful for your purpose....'[44] Polio was suggested as an alternative good news story. Dr A. Yarrow, one of Liz Shore's medical staff, replied that 'Sir George Godber [Chief Medical Officer 1960–73] once attempted this sort of exercise and came to the conclusion that the only statistically valid reduction he could definitely adduce to the NHS was in the incidence of blindness....'[45] This tentative success story was quashed by a later minute from the medical officer responsible for collating statistics on blindness. Brian sought out information on the contributions of voluntary organisations, such as leagues of hospital friends and voluntary service organisations, to the NHS. The DHSS collated information on the number of patients treated, prescriptions issued, health centres opened and pathology tests performed. He was advised not to say too much about the recent changes to junior doctors' pay, which had brought the medical profession again close to industrial action.

The first draft was sent to several of Brian's friends and DHSS acquaintances, including Dame Enid Russell Smith (1903–89; Deputy Secretary, DHSS) and Dame Elizabeth Cockayne (1894–1988; Chief Nursing Officer, 1948–58). Dame Albertine Winner (1907–88), former Deputy Chief Medical Officer, acknowledged that it was 'conscientiously and carefully researched', but found that in the first chapter 'your strong socialist predilections have rather run away with you. This would be fine, if it were a Labour Party document, but I think a DHSS history ought to be a bit more objective. In some ways I really did not recognise the Health Service I worked in before 1948 and I would question whether so lurid a picture is wise in our present depressed state of Health Service morale....'[46] Sir John Hawton (1904–81), who had been Permanent Secretary at the Ministry of

Health from 1951 to 1960, replied: 'My main comment must be that creating the NHS service wasn't like that at all. So I don't feel that any textual amendment by me would serve any purpose.'[47] John Pater, another senior civil servant who had been closely involved with the planning for the NHS, advised Brian to use the example of Middlesex Local Authority, which had provided the best hospital service prior to the NHS. George Godber, retired Chief Medical Officer, sent some constructive comments but noted that balance of the draft was too much towards the machinery of the NHS and not enough on the people who worked in it or used it.[48]

The booklet was launched at a seminar on the anniversary, 5 July. As hard as Brian tried to remain upbeat about its achievements, he was forced to respond to the parallel media stories on NHS crises. Writing in the GPs' magazine *Pulse*, he highlighted the efficiency of the British system compared to US and some European insurance-based schemes: 'These countries are even more worried than we are about how to reduce unnecessary admissions to hospital and over-long hospital stays, how to cut out excessive use of pharmaceuticals and surgery and avoid the wasteful duplication of expensive equipment and the staff needed to use it.'[49]

Reaction to Brian's anniversary booklet was mixed. Keith Mills, General Administrator for Greenwich and Bexley Area Health Authority, wrote to him to correct his misrepresentation of the origin of the new Greenwich Hospital, which Brian had said was due to dissatisfaction with the 'matchbox on a muffin' design. Mills had also worked on both the 'Best Buy' and 'Harness' projects within the NHS. He corrected Brian: there had actually not been any 'Harness' hospitals built, despite the time invested in that initiative. The NHS's 30th anniversary was also acknowledged internationally. *Time* magazine ran a feature article, in response to the US's enduring fascination with Britain's 'socialised medicine'.[50]

Professional responses to the 30th anniversary of the NHS varied. The presidents of the Royal College of Nursing and the Royal College of Midwives, along with prominent trade union leaders, exploited it to send an open letter to Ennals. They accused the government of failing to support their dedicated staff through lack of resources. As Webster has highlighted, however, the letter lost its potential power when it emerged that it had been written in collusion with Ennals' own departmental staff at the DHSS.[51]

Inequalities: the Supplementary Benefits Review and the Black Report

In 1976 the DHSS began a comprehensive review of the supplementary benefits scheme.[52] This was a stymied investigation, pinned down by the Treasury to secondary issues of claims and appeals procedures rather than being allowed to explore the critical issue of the relationship between National Insurance and Supplementary Benefit levels. Yet estimates of the numbers still living in poverty continued to cause concern throughout Labour's government. In 1976 there were over one million living below 90 per cent of the Supplementary Benefit level, and some 10 million who lived below the 140 per cent level – the marker which Brian and Townsend had used in their 1960s research. Expressed another way, 15 per cent of families lived below the Supplementary Benefit level, and another 8 per cent within the 100–120 per cent band.[53] Despite significant increases to Supplementary Benefits since 1974, it was still a 'harsh enough poverty level by any standards'.[54]

After the split from the Titmice, Townsend had made poverty research his personal domain. Working at Essex, he meticulously processed the accumulated evidence from the Rowntree project, and developed his hypotheses on relative poverty. By the summer of 1976 the draft of his magnum opus was complete. He sent it to Brian for comment, who replied in September with detailed feedback. He had one general criticism:

> I think it is very unwise to go far beyond the data and attempt interpretations which do not arise directly from the data. You will see that I have marked the passages where it seems to me that you have done this. I am not saying that I necessarily disagree with your interpretation, but it cannot be proved from the data. There is a risk therefore that your sociological colleagues who are not greatly motivated to struggle through the mass of hard data will focus on your theoretical interpretations and write reviews disagreeing with it. Thus your book might well be judged by theoretical discussions which are not essential to it rather than by those important facts which you have documented and interpreted. I also suggest a somewhat cooler tone in criticising the work of others. You make your opponents look devils, which they certainly are not. Some were attempting to answer different questions. You have, of course, every right to point out that you consider your approach more *relevant*. But can one say that the United States definition of poverty is 'wrong'?... You must be

very pleased that such great results have come from such long and heavy work. My main advice is, therefore, the same advice as Titmuss used to give me. Let the story tell itself, keep your polemics for another type of publication. The cooler approach is much more devastating.[55]

Brian was not personally much involved with the 1976 Supplementary Benefits Review, which was carried out by a DHSS team which worked closely with David Donnison, who was appointed chair of the Supplementary Benefits Commission (SBC) by Barbara Castle, with the valuable freedom to produce its own Annual Report.[56] Nevertheless, the review made use of the innovation of using outside experts, especially from the LSE, pioneered in the Crossman review, and Donnison exploited his freedom of comment and action in ways reminiscent of Brian's involvement with DHSS over many years. The review broke new ground in several ways. The team, led by Geoffrey Otton and Michael Partridge, who became successive Permanent Secretaries of Social Security, and including Jack Straw's future wife, Alice Perkins, discussed ideas monthly with Donnison and outside experts such as Tony Lynes, David Piachaud, Richard Layard, Jonathan Bradshaw and Ruth Lister. It also discussed its papers monthly with the SBC, which exposed them to public debate through its Annual Report. When the proposals were published in July 1978 the team and Donnison held public meetings across the country and with local SBC office staff. The Commission published its own comments and was free to comment on wider questions of National Insurance and welfare benefits.

All this was 'open government' with a vengeance, and a new experience for civil servants in making policy in public, in marked contrast to the traditional ways of operating behind closed doors. This had led to problems such as the leak that was bedevilling the review of Child Benefit taking place at the same time elsewhere in DHSS (see the beginning of this chapter). It was a neat and effective way of tackling the problems that Brian encountered on other occasions of how much of the government's thinking could be shared with experts whom an adviser wished to consult. It was not approved of by the Treasury or some senior civil servants, but it paved the way for more open government in the subsequent decades. The Supplementary Benefits Review also resulted in fundamental changes to the centuries-old system of granting poverty relief at the authorities' discretion, beloved of Finance Ministries and The World Bank, replacing it with entitlements and welfare rights modelled on social insurance, a principle for which Brian fought long and hard in many countries (see Chapters 6, 12, and 13 on his international work). In the event, the well-informed public debate led the incoming Conservative government in 1979 to adopt the proposals and legislate speedily, so that Supplementary Benefits did not become a political football as successive pensions reforms had.[57]

In 1977 Brian was instrumental in setting up the working group on inequalities in health. He had never lost his long-standing interest in the subject, which began with his undergraduate studies at Cambridge. With Peter Townsend, from 1953, he repeatedly demonstrated that poverty and health were closely associated, and that inequalities in health (and access to healthcare) had not been eliminated by the creation of the NHS in 1948, which was shortly to celebrate its 30th birthday (with all the retrospection that such occasions generate). The recent development of RAWP had re-invigorated his interest, and there were other like-minded individuals beginning to make public noises about the persistence of health inequalities. Richard Wilkinson, an economic historian who was then taking the MSc in Community Medicine at the University of Nottingham, wrote a two-page article in *New Society* entitled 'Dear David Ennals …' in December 1976.[58] His research demonstrated the close association between low income, poor diet and higher mortality rates, and how this had actually worsened since the arrival of the NHS. He wrote to Ennals to ask for an urgent enquiry, but in March 1977, only a week before Ennals' announcement of the Black Inquiry at a speech to the Socialist Medical Association, his suggestion was rebuffed.[59]

Brian, as Ennals' adviser, would have been privy to this correspondence, and also alert to the political mood of the public and media coverage of the story. It is therefore likely, if impossible to prove, that he briefed Ennals that a new enquiry into inequalities in health was necessary and timely. Brian was also most likely responsible for suggesting that Sir Douglas Black, Chief Scientist at the DHSS since 1974 and then President of the Royal College of Physicians, might be approached to chair an enquiry.[60] Brian certainly proposed to Ennals who would be ideal to sit on the working party, naming two of his closest friends and colleagues, Peter Townsend and Jerry Morris, Professor of Epidemiology at the London School of Hygiene and Tropical Medicine. Together with Dr Cyril Smith (Chair of the SSRC), Brian steered the creation of an effective team that could produce a practical, policy-ready report.

Although there were only four people on the working party, Black ensured that they had access to the very best technical support, and almost constant dialogue with the Office of Population Censuses and Surveys (OPCS) on the use of longitudinal studies. Yet even with this support, it proved a more lengthy and difficult exercise than they had anticipated. As Morris explained at the 1997 witness enquiry: 'We faced the standard problems of the epidemiology of social medicine, and were trying for instance to produce testable hypotheses of causal relationships between the social conditions and health, working almost entirely on observational data and grand natural experiments on data which had been largely produced for quite other purposes.'[61]

An interim report was circulated and discussed at a meeting at The King's Fund, which threw up a range of new questions and issues over the style of analysis that Black's team were using. It was decided that instead of rushing to produce a report that would be guaranteed to be published within the life of the current (Labour) government, they would take their time to rewrite sections. In the event, Callaghan was indecisive in setting the election date. It was expected to be held in autumn 1978, but he unwisely delayed until May 1979, which followed the 'winter of discontent'. The Black Report was unfinished when Callaghan's government fell and was replaced by a new Conservative administration led by Margaret Thatcher.

Although the authors, especially Townsend, felt that it had been worthwhile taking longer over getting the report right, and including new research and policy suggestions for tackling area deprivation, it meant that would almost certainly face a more hostile reception. Liz Shore saw this coming, and had urged Black: 'can't we have some quick and dirty general recommendations to be getting on with?'[62] This did not happen, and from 5 May 1979 the civil servants found themselves adjusting to the new regime that was openly ambivalent about the inequalities in health issue. When the Black Report was finally submitted to the DHSS in May 1980, attempts were made to publish with the least possible public attention. Instead of a proper government professional publication, only 260 photocopies were made and sent out to the usual media on the Friday before the August Bank Holiday weekend, a time when Parliament was still in deep summer recess and most politicians (and some lucky journalists) were enjoying long sunny European holidays. Patrick Jenkin, the new Secretary of State for Health, had done the bare minimum: his disingenuous foreword to the report noted that '... while it is disappointing that the Group were unable to make greater progress in disentangling the various causes of inequalities in health, the difficulties they experienced are perhaps no surprise given the current measurement techniques.... I cannot, therefore, endorse the Group's recommendations. I am making the report available for discussion, but without any commitment by the government to its proposals.'[63] Jenkin later reflected on his actions at a witness seminar held in 1999, but did not manage to overturn the impression that he had quashed the report's publication.[64]

Black, despite his reputation as a 'canny Scot ... a brilliant political person', refused to believe that this was a deliberate Conservative strategy to bury his report.[65] It was only when a subsequent report, Margaret Whitehead's *The Health Divide*, suffered a similar fate in 1987, that he was willing to concede he had been duped by Jenkin, no doubt under pressure from his domineering boss. Despite the attempted suppression, Black, Townsend and Morris, with the support of journalists such as Jill Turner from *New Society*, managed to organise their own press conference at the Royal College of Physicians and disseminate the working party's findings very effectively. The Black Report was quickly turned into a Penguin special paperback and attained the status of a health classic.[66]

Peter Shore and the Department of the Environment

Brian had given an interview to *The Lancet* in February 1978 about his work:

> I think the job of the special adviser is often to widen the options available to Ministers, to try and think of ideas which have not in practice been put to Ministers. I suppose it's one task to think of things which have not been done and alternative ways of doing things....There is a loneliness about power. There are certain things a Minister can talk to his private secretary about, certain things he can talk to his Permanent Secretary about, certain things he can talk to his junior Ministers about. But there are some things about which he just wants somebody to talk to in total confidence and somebody to give him reassurance if he is feeling low.... Dick [Crossman] always needed an awful lot of this. Although he was apparently the most self-assured of people, privately I felt he was not and was very vulnerable, strangely enough very easily hurt.

He told *The Lancet* interviewer that he had found Crossman '"very stimulating, very rude, enormously creative" and Barbara Castle "every bit as sharp", but with different areas of concern. But when it came to David Ennals Civil Service discretion took over.'[67] Ennals was increasingly seen as ineffectual at the DHSS. He was a 'nice chap', but his frequent periods of ill health did not help his reputation. He spent several long periods in hospital, but tried to maintain his Cabinet and DHSS duties by holding meetings at his bedside. As Barbara Castle's successor, his lack of dynamism was all the more conspicuous. Although Callaghan had set up joint NEC/Cabinet working groups in November 1977 (partly to assuage NEC jealousy over the TUC's relationship with the government), Ennals had not taken the initiative to use the Social Policy and Education Working Group to push for his policies as Brian had suggested.[68] Reading the minutes sent to Ennals by Brian and his other special adviser, Mike Hartley-Brewer, confirms the impression of a man who did not know what he wanted to achieve as Secretary of State for Health and Social Services. Is it significant that Brian, having supported Ennals through two-and-a-half difficult years, moved to replace Jack Straw as special adviser to Peter Shore at the DoE? In classic civil servant speak, Liz Shore tactfully provides an explanation for their defections: 'I got the feeling both of them felt that there was more likelihood of action in that department than the department they left.'[69]

There were other sources of discontent in Brian's life in 1978. The move he and John made to their new home at Westmoreland Place the previous year had not worked well. They both felt that the house was too large. The rooms were enormous, and the industrial-size fridge was excessive, even for Brian's love of catering. John cultivated a roof garden, but his project to install a lead-lined pond backfired when it broke the ceiling, sending water flooding through all floors of the house into the basement. Brian was abroad when it happened, and John managed to get most of the damage repaired before he returned, but they both felt the house did not feel like home. In 1978 Brian sold 11 Westmoreland Place and bought 30 Bloomfield Terrace – a smaller Georgian house in Pimlico, which had a garden. They remained here for 10 years, again with paying guests.

Brian had known Peter Shore and his wife Liz since the early 1950s when they were part of the younger contingent of the Fabian Society. Peter was at the Labour Party's Research Department, and was instrumental in bringing Brian's 1955 Fabian pamphlet, *New Pensions for the Old*, co-written with Peter Townsend, to Richard Crossman's attention. When Peter and Liz's son Piers was born in 1957, Brian was chosen as one of his godfathers, a role that he fulfilled very well.[70] Sadly this later brought the awful task of speaking at Piers' memorial service on 16 September 1977, where he read poetry by Wordsworth and Donne.

Peter Shore had entered Parliament at the 1964 general election and been chosen by Harold Wilson's as one of his 'kitchen cabinet' advisers. He was promoted to Minister at the Department of Economic Affairs (DEA), until its abolition in 1969 when he was downgraded to office of Minister without Portfolio and Deputy Leader of the Commons. In Wilson's 1974 government he became Secretary of State for Trade, and was transferred by Callaghan in 1976 to be Secretary of State at the DoE. Labour colleagues saw Shore as a 'backroom boy', excellent at using his intellectual talents to draft policy, but perhaps promoted beyond his abilities as a politician.[71] Unlike some of his Cabinet colleagues, however, he made effective use of both his civil servants and his special advisers (when Straw left Shore's team he was allowed to appoint David Cowling as an additional adviser). Perhaps Brian also saw Shore's interest in local government reorganisation as a possible way to continue to influence the NHS. Shore was a keen supporter of the 'Organic Change' review that had been announced in January 1978 and intended to redress some of the significant weaknesses that resulted from the Local Government Act of 1972.

Shore had first invited Brian to join him at the DoE in July 1977, to replace Straw who had stepped down when he was adopted for Barbara Castle's safe parliamentary seat in Blackburn. But Brian had decided that his recent commitment to take up a part-time adviser role with Henk Vredeling, EEC Commissioner for Social Security, would not make it possible to move from his role with Ennals at the DHSS.[72] Shore instead appointed David Cowling, who had been working at the Greater London Council (GLC) in Reg Goodwin's Leader's office, until Labour's disastrous results at the May local government elections. In December 1978 Shore got approval to appoint a second special adviser, and again invited Brian, who this time accepted. He joined Shore's office in Marsham Street in December 1978. He was immediately thrown into debates on reforming the assessment of land and property values, studies of vacant land use in urban areas and plans for the future of docklands (London and other large ports such as Liverpool). Labour's NEC Town and County Planning Sub-committee had produced Working Paper, RE1899 'A new system of current use values'. Shore was unclear how this policy proposal (which contained four different potential methods of land valuation) could be developed, and relied on Brian and David Cowling to work with civil servants on producing a DoE response.

Brian adopted the style of engagement that he had used so successfully at the DHSS when asking civil servants for help: 'S of S has only a limited grasp of the problem.... I have had a shot at such a paper.'[73]

He attended the sub-committee meeting on 12 December on Shore's behalf and sent him a post-meeting briefing on the membership of its new working party on current use value, and the ongoing uncertainties on their section of the draft Labour election manifesto. This contained the commitment: 'We will also introduce a new system of land valuation to ensure that disused and under-used land is either brought into socially acceptable use or is acquired by local authorities at a price much more closely in line with the income generated by the land rather than being based on hope value and the way the land has been zoned for use.'[74] Brian liaised with Andrew Broadbent from the Centre for Environmental Studies on schemes for rating valuation systems. In preparation for Shore's meeting with the NEC he prepared him an aide memoire of the issues that affected the DoE: 'You might like to have by you a list of <u>omissions and fudges</u> from the NEC draft and some notes for arguments.'[75]

Other significant issues that the DoE was handling in early 1979 included investigations into establishing an anti-corruption agency and register for the building materials industry, which Reg Freeson, Minister for Housing and Construction, was leading. Shore's earlier suggestion that a competitive public sector building company might be established led to opposition from CABIN, the Campaign Against Building Industry Nationalisation. It had commissioned a report from the Economist Intelligence Unit in January 1978 in response to the Labour Party document 'Building Britain's Future'.

Some of Shore's proposals also met with opposition from the public and from experts in local government and housing. Although Labour were open to the idea of selling council houses – indeed Cowling had drafted a policy proposal on this for inclusion in Labour's election manifesto – the now Conservative-controlled GLC proposed a mass transfer of its housing estates to the London boroughs. In September 1978 the GLC Labour Group issued a critical report on the 'Impact of Transfer', which called the plan 'The Sale of the Century'.[76] The DoE had issued press releases in January and February 1979 about council tenants' rights to housing mobility and rights to improve, expressing a broad agreement with the GLC's 'Homesteading' scheme to sell off uninhabited council houses. But in March Shore announced in the House of Commons that he was going to restrict the type of property that could be sold under the 'Homesteading' programme. Horace Cutler, GLC Leader, wrote to Shore telling him of disappointed people who had camped outside County Hall, some for almost a week, in order to qualify for a house on 8 March, when the scheme was due to begin. Brian helped draft the damage limitation press statement that

Shore issued the following day. He also helped to edit Shore's speech on the publication of the National Dwelling and Housing Survey. This had provided further uncomfortable publicity for Labour as it exposed the disproportionate numbers of minority ethnic families who were living in the worst housing conditions.

Working as a special adviser rarely caused conflicts of interest for Brian. He had declared his business interest in Just Men when he became Crossman's adviser in 1968, and he had stepped down from active roles in CPAG and the Fabian Society. He probably did not expect to have any potential conflicts when he joined Shore at the DoE, but within a matter of weeks he found himself caught between the department and an organisation he belonged to: the Belgravia Leaseholders' Association. This represented residents like himself in one of the wealthiest parts of London, where much of the freehold was still owned by the Duke of Westminster, Britain's largest landowner. Under the 1967 Leasehold Reform Act the rights of leaseholders with lower rateable values to acquire their freeholds was established, but the 1974 Housing Act which dealt with higher rateable value properties was drafted in such a way that those leaseholders faced expensive court cases to establish valuations on their properties. The Belgravia Leaseholders' Association, along with the Leaseholders' Association of Great Britain, began a campaign to repeal the offending section of the 1974 Act. A Labour Housing Bill had been drafted which would have achieved this, making the valuation process as simple as for properties with a lower rateable value, but the Bill was abandoned when the 1979 general election was called.

In March 1979 the Belgravia Leaseholders' Association invited Brian to join its committee, no doubt aware of his position as Shore's special adviser at the DoE. Brian attended its meetings, but appears to have refrained from close involvement until after the general election, when he then advised the Association based on personal discussions he held with Jack Straw, who was on the new Housing Bill Committee to consider Michael Heseltine's revised Bill. He also drafted letters to be sent to Conservative MPs and peers in the House of Lords, using phrases such as 'home ownership' in a deliberate play to their manifesto commitments.

Labour in 1979: assessments and strategies

Arriving at the DoE in December 1978, Brian knew that there would be a general election within a year, and that Callaghan would most likely call it in the spring of 1979. If Labour did not win, he would only have a few months of working as Peter Shore's special adviser. As soon as he arrived he began to work with Cowling on the draft election manifesto. Shore felt that it was weak on priorities and did not say enough about the problems confronting Britain. Brian was asked to provide some ideas. By April 1979 Labour's election plans were well advanced. Brian worked with Cowling and other special advisers to finalise the housing sections of the manifesto, and assisted Shore in resisting Eric Heffer's re-wording.

Shore's key objectives as Secretary of State were to cut waste in public spending, revitalise the inner cities, and more generally, to develop the environment as a stand-alone political issue. His department bore the brunt of the 1978–79 'winter of discontent'. Widespread strikes by local government trade unions, angry at Callaghan's public sector pay freeze to control inflation, left bodies unburied and mountains of uncollected rubbish lining the streets of Britain's towns and cities. The DoE's strategies came under further attack when Leslie Chapman, who had been a DoE civil servant for 35 years, re-issued his book *Your Disobedient Servant* which exposed the waste within Whitehall, and gave the Conservatives further ammunition.[77] Brian and Cowling produced a response for Shore to use. Together they planned an itinerary for an election tour that would cover as many marginal seats and manifesto issues as possible in the month leading up to the election date of 3 May 1979.

Brian drafted speeches for Shore on cutting taxation and public expenditure, social justice and social services, organic change, unemployment and the inner cities. He and Cowling accompanied Shore on the long train journeys and to the meetings in school halls and community centres up and down the country. Poll results showed that Labour were falling behind the Conservatives, who had a 65 per cent share of the predicted vote, and that key issues such as membership of the EEC would not work in Labour's favour. On 15 March there was a major radiation leak from the nuclear plant at Windscale in the Lake District. As this was the responsibility of the DoE, Shore was diverted into dealing with plans for the clean-up and how to handle the press. He initially decided not to issue a press release, which caused some difficulties for his team when he was forced to issue one on 23 April.

Two days before the election Shore was booked to speak on BBC Radio 4 on a special issue of 'Your Saturday Programme' called 'Destination Downing Street' along with Lady Seear for the Liberals and Norman St John-Stevas for the Conservatives. Brian briefed Shore: 'I question whether this is the time and the place to float fundamental and challenging ideas about the future role of the trade union movement.

Great care would be needed to draft what you said in a way which was not misunderstood by them. Much better for a set speech later on where every sentence could be carefully drafted (so as not to sound offensive if taken out of context) and a preamble of praise of their many achievements added to precede what could seem to be criticism [of the trade union movement]. You know better than I what a tetchy lot they are. Thus I attach at "B" something much more mundane and much more what I assume they expect from you.'[78] He also summarised for Shore what he thought Margaret Thatcher's key government strategies would be (less government, U-turns on some issues such as pension rises linked to earnings, and watering down legislation on the trade unions). When Shore was due to go on a live panel show on Capital Radio, Brian briefed him on its young audience, some of whom would be voting for the first time: 'I would suggest that in your opening remarks you try to underline the essential radicalism of Labour policies and their concern for improving the quality of life of many people with less advantage than others.'[79] He chose a number of issues for Shore to discuss which would appeal: government initiatives for the young unemployed, the introduction of child benefit and women's rights.

Ministers such as Shore clearly got great value from their special advisers in all sorts of areas. However, there were other channels of policy advice that were beginning to be developed, especially think tanks. Some of these were more formal and transparent than others, with a pedigree going back to the inter-war period; others owed their emergence to specific policy vacuums. The Joseph Rowntree Reform Trust had established the Outer Circle Policy Unit (OCPU) in 1976. Its name reflected not only its location in Regent's Park, but also its political situation, and it focused on a variety of contemporary issues, including taxation, the welfare state and freedom of information. Its first Director was James Cornford, who Brian knew through *Political Quarterly* (Brian was Director between 1973 and 1994; Cornford was its Literary Editor, and later Chair between 1976 and 2001). In 1978 the OCPU established the 'Hidden Economy Group' that included Frank Field, Michael Hill, Alan Lewis, Hermione Parker, Cedric Sandford, Robin Simpson and Adrian Sinfield. Brian was sent an advance copy of their report, *Beyond Beveridge: Taxation, Welfare and Poverty*, in June 1978. This complemented the internal DHSS review on the anomalies that had arisen from current income maintenance and taxation policies.

But special advisers remained central to political life, although by 1978 they were increasingly unhappy about their terms of service. Callaghan had agreed to improved terms in 1977, which gave those over the age of 35 three months' severance pay instead of the contractual five weeks, but there was no agreement on pay structures. As their spokesperson Roger Darlington summarised: 'The existing pattern of pay of Special Advisers is a mess. The explanation lies in the rather unexpected timing and result of the General Election of February 1974 followed by the rapid appointment of almost 40 Special Advisers. Individual Ministers and Establishment Officers, as well as the Civil Service Department, had little experience of the employment of Special Advisers and therefore there was a random series of individual decisions rather than a co-ordinated and coherent system.'[80] Since 1975 pay rises had been on an ad hoc basis, and Darlington proposed a single pay scale, age-related with annual increments.

Special advisers were now recognised by the public as integral parts of the government's policy machine. Wilson had even insisted in 1974 that Castle's advisers were filmed at work by the BBC for a documentary to show the public exactly how useful they were. She was flattered yet concerned how it would turn out, and gave Brian and Jack Straw the right to veto any clips they did not think appropriate. In the event it was a great success, with the cameras following one of her regular Monday lunchtime meetings, at which the discussion was on how to use the EEC 'butter mountain'. In the run-up to the 1979 general election Brian participated in meetings of special advisers to aid the fine-tuning of Labour's campaign. They had been commissioned as a group by Michael Foot to provide a briefing on where they thought Labour were getting it wrong – especially their failure to maximise good publicity. Elizabeth Arnott at No 10 solicited information on departmental policy developments through each special adviser, and reluctantly concluded that 'there are few, if any, major new policy initiatives in the pipeline.... Can we do more to make the government look active and more forward-looking? Without money, we can really only indulge in window dressing which will be easily exposed.... I suggest we should do better pushing forward on publicity and the Manifesto than thinking up last minute policies which may be seen as gimmicks.'[81]

At meetings convened by David Lipsey the advisers discussed the gloomy poll forecasts, how the TUC might be able to assist Labour with a credible long-term approach on pay and prices, and how the forthcoming pay negotiations with nurses and miners would make it difficult to fight on a 'responsible government' platform. Brian's practical approach to the possible impending crash of Labour was to think of how other advisers (who did not have academic posts to return to) might be helped. He had served on the board for the Institute for Fiscal Studies in the mid-1970s and still offered advice when asked.

Its new Research Director John Kay was looking to recruit staff, and Brian suggested he consider Gavyn Davies, who was working in the Prime Minister's Policy Unit: 'He is an extremely able economist, and his knowledge of how government works could be invaluable to the Institute. If there is a change of government, he would suddenly be looking for a job, and you might be able to snap him up if you had contacted him about the possibility in advance. I am not the only one who thinks very well of him.'[82]

One good news story was Labour's enduring financial commitment to social welfare during its period in office. Between 1973/74 and 1978/79 total expenditure on social security nearly tripled, to £15,361 million per annum. Although this figure was distorted by inflation, it still represented a real increase of 30 per cent. As a proportion of total public expenditure it rose from 18.4 per cent to 21.5 per cent, and expressed as a percentage of GDP it increased from 7.9 per cent to 9.8 per cent. As David Piachaud has noted, this was a major achievement at a time when many departmental budgets were being cut, and real incomes were static or declining.[83] The introduction of RAWP had also had a marked impact on reducing the gap in regional NHS budgets: by 1979 the worst-off region was about 9 per cent below its target allocation and the best-off was 13 per cent above. Brian had remained on the joint TUC/Labour Party working group on short-term benefits since its creation, and was also involved in discussions on the joint TUC/Labour Party document 'Into the Eighties', which called for economic growth rates of well above 3 per cent. However, these good news stories were lost in the aftermath of the 'winter of discontent', and their impact in the May 1979 general election was predictably insignificant.

12

International commuting: 1975–79

Value for Money in Health Services: A Comparative Study

Return to Mauritius

The European Economic Community

A new European advisory role

Basil Fawlty: We're all friends now, eh? All in the Market together, old differences forgotten and no need at all to mention the war. (John Cleese and Connie Booth, Fawlty Towers, 1975)

This chapter runs parallel to Chapters 10 and 11. It shows how one of Brian's key books, Value for Money in the Health Services, was stimulated by the emergence of new interests in health economics, especially on the costs of healthcare. It was the fruition of 20 years of policy development experience in both developed and developing countries. The explicitly comparative approach drew praise from the growing community of health economists in Europe and the US. Despite his heavy work as a special adviser to the British Labour government, Brian also returned in the mid-1970s to help the Mauritius government develop new social welfare programmes. International development projects were increasingly open to commercial exploitation, which began to alter the role of traditional academic expertise. Brian's close relationship with the British government and with international organisations such as the World Health Organisation and the International Labour Organisation helped to consolidate his reputation as an influential expert adviser. He was invited in 1975 to advise the European Economic Community (EEC) on social affairs and in 1977 he was appointed as adviser to Henk Vredeling, the European Commissioner for Employment and Social Affairs. These European roles brought bureaucratic frustrations as well as valuable opportunities to use academic research to generate new health and social welfare policies.

By the mid-1970s international organisations such as the WHO and The World Bank had steered the development of health and social welfare policies for a quarter of a century. In the process some had matured into powerful agencies, which were as political as they were scientific. Chapter 9 discussed how Brian had chosen to pick up various international projects for such organisations while Labour were out of government in Britain between 1970 and 1974. Relative to the intensity of his work when he was a government special adviser (1968–70 and 1974–79), it seems odd, in retrospect, that he did not choose to do more consultancy work for the WHO, the ILO and The World Bank, given their established positions of authority in health and social welfare, areas of work that were close to his heart. Perhaps their growth into such large and bureaucratic organisations led Brian to suspect that they might no longer be as effective as they had been in the 1960s, and he was content to remain an interested outsider. The explanation might also be personal – a wish to spend more time at home with his partner John Sarbutt, expanding their garden at Tanglewood, or preoccupation with his clothing business, Just Men. It is more likely that he had to reduce his much-loved travelling because colleagues at the LSE were expecting him to pick up more administrative roles to compensate for his absences during the Crossman years.

If one looks at his written output from the 1970–74 period, there also appears to be a hiatus. There were no significant books between *In Search of Justice* (1968) and *Legal Problems and the Citizen* (1975). His British press articles (mainly in the *New Statesman* and *New Society*) begin to appear again from November 1970, after the fall of the Labour government. With titles like 'Poor Kids and Rich Kids', 'Poverty and the Budget', 'A Hospital Ombudsman', 'Managing the Health Service', 'The Politics of Health' and 'Social Security and Taxation', they reflect his enduring interest in British health and social welfare.[1] There are relatively fewer articles between 1970 and 1974 that are internationally focused. The explanation again might be pressures of his return to a full-time professorship at the LSE.

Value for Money in Health Services: A Comparative Study

There was, however, one book in production. The idea for a text on health economics originated in a conversation with Archie Cochrane on a ski lift in Davos, Switzerland (where they met each winter). It was to be jointly authored and, although it started out that way in 1972, by September 1973 Brian sensed that Cochrane was pulling out: 'I really did not expect you to be able to do much writing this year. Perhaps at some stage you could spare the time to read through and comment on what I have written. I found it a bit ominous that you referred to it [in his last letter] as my book rather than as our book.'[2] Cochrane was in the process of winding down his Medical Research Council Unit in Cardiff and was also President of the new Faculty of Community Medicine affiliated to the Royal Colleges of Physicians (for which Brian had agreed to serve on the examining board). He admitted to Brian 'I find it increasingly hard to write when I am under stress in all directions. In point of fact I do write quite a lot but I always tear it up. What I can promise to do is to criticise, and I will make a very big effort to produce something on the history of medical research but I am getting more and more frightened of making any promises.'[3] They found a compromise: Brian helped Cochrane with writing his three prestigious Dunham lectures that he was due to give at Harvard, and Cochrane commented on Brian's chapter drafts.

Brian also called on a number of international colleagues to read draft sections of his book. George Rohrlich, who was now Professor of Heath Economics and Social Policy at Temple University in Philadelphia, and who had been one of Brian's main contacts at the ILO in Geneva, was very helpful. In return, Brian was able to supply Rohrlich with some useful information for his current Puerto Rican study.[4] So, too, was Ida Merriam, the economist who headed the US Social Security Administration's research and statistics branch with whom he had been liaising since the early 1960s. Brian explained what he hoped to achieve:

> I had hoped to write a timeless and placeless book on health economics and health planning which would be of use to medical and other health administrators in both developed and developing countries. I imagined this being a useful textbook for schools of public health, etc. I thought that the underlying problems of a developing country would be brought home most vividly if one included developed countries in the same book. Obviously this strategy has not come off and I must think very carefully about what to do as a result. I will work through all your suggestions and ponder deeply on it.[5]

In April 1974 Brian first used the phrase 'Value for money in health services' which, in its 1976 book title version, was to epitomise his intellectual philosophy of social welfare. The occasion was the inaugural lecture in the Robert M. Ball Lecture Series, established as a tribute to the former US Commissioner of Social Security. It was subsequently published in the *Social Security Bulletin* in July 1974, and as an almost verbatim transcript, it is imbued with his now characteristic provocative rhetoric. He began with five propositions, some controversial, some well-accepted.

> First ... the supply of hospital beds generates the demand for them ... second, unregulated competition in a free health care market can lead to a loss of quality ... unnecessary surgery, excessive prescribing ... an excess of specialists means a lower average experience in specialist work; third, that the free forces of the market under an unregulated fee-for-service payment system do not secure an even geographical distribution of physicians.... Fourth, the physician is trained to buy the best rather than find the best buy. After training he is exposed to conflicts between the interests of his paymaster and those of competing commercial interests. His doormat is piled high with drug firm literature, and his doorstep shaded by drug house retail men. Over his shoulder looms the risk of malpractice litigation.... My fifth proposition is that where the physician is not cost-conscious and the patient acts on his advice there is no pressure on those from whom he purchases to be cost-conscious either. The drug market is carved up by patients and branding: competition is by product and not by price. Unless they are regulated, nonprofit hospitals enjoy what almost amounts to the arbitrary taxing powers of medieval princes. They use these powers to finance the twentieth century palaces that dominate both cities and suburbs – palaces with almost the same proportion of underoccupied bedrooms and a much higher proportion of underoccupied powder rooms.[6]

Brian went on in his lecture to advocate evaluations of the effectiveness of new medical techniques (as developed by Archie Cochrane), replacing commercial medical advertising with non-commercial continuing medical education and control over drug pricing. He outlined three possible paths to intervention: the regulation of services, planning the system of delivery and action to change the behaviour of those who control the system. In his conclusion he urged his American audience to ask the bigger questions about the ethos of health workers' responsibilities:

> The central questions are not so much of value in its narrow sense but of social value in its widest sense. We are not just concerned with the justification of medical acts and the price tag they should

carry. Nor are we simply concerned with the technical quality of services rendered by teams of professionals. We are concerned with equity in the distribution of health resources, with their deployment in the promotion of health, and with the integration of health and social care. Value for money in this last sense cannot be achieved by fragmented providers or pluralistic financing agencies. Somehow a socially responsive organisation is needed that can mobilise the resources needed to promote these values.[7]

His trip to the US in April 1974 to give the Ball Lecture was timely. He recycled the lecture title for his imminent book, *Value for Money in Health Services: A Comparative Study*.[8] Brian had established a good working relationship with his publisher Alan Hill at Heinemann, who steered the production of his first major commercial book, *A History of the Nursing Profession*, in 1960. Hill had subsequently helped Brian to secure contracts for *The Hospitals*, *Lawyers and the Courts* and *Legal Problems and the Citizen*. Brian's books reached a wide enough audience to be deemed 'popular'. By 1973 *A History of Nursing* had sold 6,652 hardback copies (including 500 through a contract in the US with Springer). *Lawyers and the Courts* had sold 4,573 hardbacks (including 1,500 in the US through Harvard) and 492 in its 1970 paperback edition. *The Hospitals*, just between 1969 and 1973, sold another 2,950, of which 1,000 were in the US through Harvard. Later a paperback version of *A History of Nursing* was launched, and *The Hospitals* was translated into Japanese.

Hill intermittently entertained Brian to lunch to discuss potential publications. In January 1973 Brian told him about the 'half draft' of a text on health economics that he had written with Cochrane. In July 1974, after Cochrane had pulled out, he approached Heinemann with a firm proposal for a book. When he finished writing it in January 1975 (without a contract) he told Hill. 'I am convinced I have a book here with a considerable international sale. I have worked very hard to keep it short and within the capacity of the general reader. Thus, I have not assumed that my reader is trained in economics, or knows much about health services. I hope it will be possible to produce the book quickly … this is a field where material dates very quickly; so much is happening to change health services throughout the world. It could be called "Health Planning and Health Economics", but this is a bit forbidding. Hence the title "Value for Money in Health Services".'[9]

Brian worked quickly to incorporate Heinemann's readers' suggested changes, and comments from Dorothy Rice (then Deputy Assistant Commissioner at the US Department of Health, Education and

Welfare), and batted it back with a request that it come out as soon as possible. He was even prepared for it to go straight to page proof stage, if this meant it could be published faster. Hill did all he could, even jumping it up the list of Heinemann books scheduled for production in 1975. He also brought forward more of Brian's agreed advance to £400 on signing the contract, and £150 on publication. *Value for Money in Health Services: A Comparative Study* was finally published on 24 April 1976, a few months later than Hill's promised 'autumn 1975'. Brian worked with Paul Richardson at Heinemann to put together a publicity campaign. He asked for free copies to send to influential international contacts. He astutely reckoned that by sending personalised signed copies the recipients would feel obliged to read and comment on the book, rather than relegating it to their reading piles.

The 240-page book appeared in both hardback and paperback. The cover blurb proclaimed Brian's intimate knowledge of the British health service, special adviser role and international profile: 'He has visited the health services of eighteen countries, advised four countries on different aspects of their health services and served for many years as a consultant to the World Health Organisation for whom he has written two books on the financing of health services.... Although the book draws upon economics, sociology, epidemiology, public administration and politics, it is aimed at the general reader and studiously avoids jargon. Despite its immense breadth, it is short, extremely readable and written with a deep concern to improve the health of peoples all over the world.'

Brian acknowledged in the Preface how much Cochrane's ideas had influenced his thinking, especially from his book *Effectiveness and Efficiency*.[10] Embarrassingly, however, Cochrane's name is consistently misspelt throughout the book, even in Brian's Preface acknowledgements. But this book was essentially the cumulative experience of his 20 years of academic, political and advisory roles. His innate historicism is evident in the structure – the first part of the book is devoted to describing the evolution of the organisation and financing of health services in different countries (he naturally chose Britain, with some limited European, North and 'Latin' American comparisons, and occasional references to Japan, India and the USSR [the former Soviet Union]). The next section of the book focuses on key questions – how useful are health services in promoting health? On what principles should they be organised? How can the services be improved? Specific chapters tackled hospitals, the pharmaceutical industry and prioritisation of health services. The last main section of the book deals with planning, with separate chapters on developed and developing countries. It finishes with a chapter on education and training.

The conclusion refines the themes he had aired in his 1974 Ball Lecture:

> Will there come a time when the working population says 'So much is enough'? How long will it be before the working population demands hard evidence that it is really getting value for each day devoted to working to pay for health services? How much is spent to establish a diagnosis which if established could not lead to effective treatment? How much is spent in costly efforts to save life which had only a remote prospect of being successful and no prospect of achieving anything approaching recovery? How much is spent in postponing death by days or weeks without providing an extension of conscious life or the prospect of doing so? As Dr Mahler, Director General of WHO said recently: '... the major – and most expensive – part of medical technology as applied today appears to be for the satisfaction of the health professionals than for the benefit of the consumers of health care'. These questions bring us face to face with the difficult ethical dilemmas of health care....[11]

As he predicted, international colleagues immediately wrote with comments, most of them offering praise for his new book. What he really wanted was truthful critique. This came from Peter Ruderman, now Professor of Administrative Studies at Dalhousie University in Canada, who had worked with Brian at WHO in the 1960s: 'The book surprises rather than annoys me because you seem to show a certain reluctance to take sides and it is all terribly balanced.... I wonder ... whether your temporary status as an advisor to government blunted your usual knife edge.... I also wonder why you did not choose to devote some space to alternatives to health care such as self-diagnosis and medication, modifications to life style or the environment, or simply lowering individual demand by getting people accustomed to some degree of unwellness as normal as suggested by the Office of Health Economics.'[12] Brian replied: 'I expected you to be annoyed in precisely the opposite way. I expected you to write and say what hard evidence have you to support all this criticism of fee-for-service payment. In this chapter I had you very much in mind. The truth is there is so little hard evidence. Similarly, surely hard evidence on hospitals is hard to come by. Facilities may be duplicated and under-utilised, but are they of lower quality? How can one prove that the wealthy consumer would not rather have a facility nearby, even if it is much more costly to provide it? I have stated the theoretical reasons why I suspected under-utilised facilities will be of poor quality. But this is different from proof.'[13]

Despite his discussion with Ruderman, in fact the quality issue is not covered at all in *Value for Money in Health Services*. He makes no reference to the work of academics such as Avedis Donabedian, who pioneered the study of quality in healthcare and medical outcomes research. His seminal 1966 paper, 'Evaluating the Quality of Medical Care' had stimulated a new line in research, which he subsequently developed to include systems management in health services. Brian must have been aware of this work on the quality debate, but perhaps did not see it as relevant to his focus on 'value'.[14] He also chose to ignore the newly fashionable Diagnosis-Related Group (DRG) methodology developed by John D. Thompson and Bob Fetter in the US. DRGs enabled collective purchasers to set a price for a bundle of services and escape the trap of arguing with providers about how to calculate the cost of care. In the first Reagan administration DRGs were the primary tool with which the Medicare scheme (established as a social insurance scheme for older people in 1965) set the prices it would pay for hospital services.[15]

Other recipients of his personalised copies replied, as he hoped they would, that they intended to use it for teaching – from Tehran to Hong Kong. He sent it to old acquaintances – Ida Merriam, Wilbur Cohen, George Silver – and to individuals with whom he would later work closely, such as Halfdan Mahler. In total he placed personal copies into more than 14 countries, and used Heinemann to solicit further contacts. Within two years it had sold out its first print run of 4,000 in the UK, but Brian was not happy with the sales through its US publisher, St Martin's Press. He sent Hill a copy of a favourable US review by I.S. Falk, Emeritus Professor of Public Health at Yale, suggesting that as Falk was known as 'the main brains behind Senator [Ted] Kennedy's main Insurance Bill', that Heinemann might provoke St Martin's Press into another publicity campaign.[16] For Falk, Brian was 'widely regarded as one of the world's foremost authorities on social welfare and health services.... Since Abel-Smith is knowledgeable about the complexities, "value" has many meanings, and the criteria and parameters are diverse – they extend to the need of the services, demand, availability, quantity, quality, cost and prices, sources of the money and equity in impacts, capacity of the providers, care and amenity as well as cure ... and overall, the contribution of the health services to human welfare and social polity.'[17] Falk applauded his 'wholesome respect for diversities in practices....The book deserves a wide audience'.

Reviews in professional journals were equally favourable, if more nuanced. Alan Maynard, in the *Journal of Social Policy*, found the book in parts 'too mild', and missing key references (which he used his review to provide). Why did Brian not draw attention to fundamental issues of equity, for example, the failure to get medical students to repay the costs of their expensive training from their above-average salaries? Why did Brian not fully discuss all the mechanisms available for regulating the pharmaceutical industry – control of physicians' prescribing, use of anti-monopoly policy, voluntary pricing regulation? Why had he not discussed what rationing mechanisms might be used if the state found health expenditure too high (odd given that Brian had been closely involved with the development of Crossman's earlier RAWP scheme)? In summary, for Maynard, this book was 'useful but it should be used with care in part because it is slightly dated and in part because it is incomplete'.[18]

Rudolf Klein, reviewing the book for the *British Medical Journal*, found it an 'admirable introduction' which did not break new ground, but was 'ambitiously and successfully comprehensive in its review of the issues'. Although he acknowledged that Brian had been upfront with the reader about his own personal values and preference for a British model health service, Klein felt that this had led him to 'make some debatable assertions and to underplay the complexity of some problems. For example, his *ex cathedra* statement that "Charges of any kind frustrate the objective of securing that health services are readily available to all" requires more supporting argument than he provides. And again, the question of how to reconcile planning by experts with responsiveness to the wishes of consumers is unsatisfactorily brushed aside in 2½ pages.'[19] Kenneth Boyd chose to review *Value for Money in Health Services* alongside Robert Maxwell's new book, *Health Care: the Growing Dilemma*, in the *Journal of Medical Ethics*. Both authors, he thought, were, in their quest for understanding how health resources should be allocated, similar to the 19th-century explorers of Africa – 'they go in as specialists, economists, epidemiologists, sociologists. They return somewhat less convinced. Health care, like Africa, is different.'[20]

Return to Mauritius

It is a surprise, looking at the index for *Value for Money in Health Services*, to find only one entry for Mauritius. It had provided Brian (and Titmuss) with his first 'laboratory' to design a health system from scratch in the early 1960s. It enabled him to develop evidence-based ideas on the relationship between health and economic development, and provided an entrée into a wider policy community, through his new contacts at the UN and the Rockefeller Foundation. In *Value for Money in Health Services* Brian insisted that planning alone was not enough: 'Value premises must underlie any choices of priorities … ideally each community should be enabled to participate in the choice of its priorities.…What is needed is the political will to redistribute resources. In some developing countries, particularly in Latin America, this will is absent.'[21] He was soon offered another opportunity to test his ideas – this theory – again in Mauritius.

The production of *Value for Money in Health Services* coincided with his return as a special adviser, this time to Barbara Castle who was appointed as Secretary of State for Health and Social Services in Wilson's March 1974 Labour government. Despite this sudden intensification of workload, which lasted until Labour fell from power in 1979, Brian always found time to pursue his international interests, albeit that he now had to seek permission from his ministerial bosses. In February 1975 Nades Ringadoo, now the Minister of Finance in Mauritius, wrote to Barbara Castle to request the services of Brian and Tony Lynes to develop a new pensions plan. Ringadoo had been trying unsuccessfully for some time to persuade the British government to second Brian again: he had not been back to the island since he worked on the Titmuss Mission of 1959–61. Then their recommendations for social welfare hinged on getting the colonial government to adopt a family planning policy. As discussed in Chapter 6, progress was fraught because of strong opposition from the Catholic and Muslim communities.

Brian had remained in touch with Ringadoo, Prime Minster Ramgoolam and the other Ministers such as Harold Walter, seeing them regularly when they passed through London. In the intervening decade Mauritius had gained independence from Britain, and was successfully addressing its population control issue. The Titmuss social welfare proposals were phased in, with support from the ILO, and the government now wished to introduce a new pensions scheme and had three conflicting proposals to choose from. Brian briefed Castle on the history behind the relationship and why Ringadoo was so insistent on having Brian rather than Tony Lynes alone: 'The word "Professor" carries some magic in Mauritius … neither Tony nor I are now particularly keen to get involved because of the delicacy of having to do what is really the Prime Minister's job of reconciling different viewpoints among his Ministers.'[22] Barbara Castle initially refused the request to let two of her closest advisers be diverted from their work at the DHSS, where they were mid-way through reforming Britain's own pensions policy. By late May, however, the workload eased and Castle released them on official leave to travel to Mauritius.

By this time the novelty of official receptions and dinners was wearing thin for Brian, who declared in advance to Lynes that they would spend all possible time on their investigation and writing up the report. He had, however, made a small request to Ringadoo: 'You know we are both swimming addicts. I understand there is now a hotel on a swimming coast not too far from Port Louis. There is nothing I like more than a swim before breakfast and last thing at night. If we can be fitted in somewhere which is good for swimming nothing would make our stay more enjoyable.'[23] They arrived on 19 May (first class, courtesy of the Mauritian government) to find several formal dinners already planned in their honour. Brian adamantly declined the invitations for both of them: for Lynes this was a sad indication that his status was still as Brian's junior.[24] They were met at the airport by the Minister for Social Security and an old associate, Percy Selwyn, who had been at the Colonial Office during the 1959–61 Mission and was now Director of the Mauritius Economic Intelligence Unit in the Ministry of Finance. They were put up at Trou aux Biches, one of the new beach-front tourist hotels, as Brian had requested. The first day was like old times – a series of meetings with government ministers, cocktails at 6.00pm followed by dinner with the Governor General at his official residence, Le Reduit.

The ILO had funded a report in 1970 by the British social security expert A.E. Goddard under its United Nations Development Programme Technical Assistance scheme. He recommended a social insurance scheme, and the ILO had subsequently funded the secondment of G.D. Stredder from the DHSS in November 1971 for a year to work out a detailed plan (which would also include benefits for sickness, maternity and employment injury) in the hope of pushing the government into committing to a specific scheme. Nothing happened, and the government continued to explore other social welfare innovations. Russell Prosser, Senior Adviser to the Ministry of Overseas Development, visited the island in November 1974 to make a preliminary survey on public assistance and to identify where British technical assistance might be usefully employed. He found significant weaknesses in the existing system, which had failed to adopt some of the Titmuss Mission's key recommendations, and he proposed a more detailed survey to gauge the real level of poverty on the island.[25]

Brian and Lynes set about evaluating the various schemes, and assessing the capacity of the administrative system to implement a new scheme. A major stumbling block, as in 1959–61, was the sugar industry, which was reluctant to abandon its own occupational pensions scheme. Brian and Lynes worked closely with Sandrasegaram Mootoosamy, Assistant to the Minister of Social Security. They wrote a draft White Paper, a report and secured the preparation of draft legislation, before leaving on 5 June. They worked literally up to the last possible moment. In fact, Brian did not leave enough time to drive himself and Lynes to the airport and they arrived too late for their Air France flight. British Airways refused to accept their first class Air France tickets, and they travelled home in economy class. Of course the Mauritians could not let their favourite adviser leave the work at that unfinished stage, and by June Brian was again writing to Castle for permission to return in August, en route to his holiday in Tanzania (which Mootoosamy had helped to set up).

On arrival in August, Brian encountered a series of diplomatic and more practical difficulties. Word had got out that the Mauritius government only had four computers (ICL), invoking a hard-sell visit from the Chair of IBM to Ramgoolam, the Prime Minister. It was becoming clear that complicated machinery was required to cope with the proposed stamp and card insurance system for daily-rated plantation workers. Brian was also unhappy with the calculations produced by the Mauritian actuaries, and privately requested that British officials check the figures. One of the main stumbling blocks was the private sector, who objected to the Mauritian civil service continuing with their lucrative pensions arrangements while the sugar industry would be forced to close its own scheme. Ramgoolam asked Brian to prepare for him a briefing document for discussions with representatives of the private sector, and to make a presentation to point out the actuarial difficulties of bringing the civil servants into the planned scheme, and he spent several hours on the day of his departure in this mediating role. But despite these difficulties, the Mauritians made every effort to support his work. Mootoosamy was especially attentive to his needs, finding him 'real milk to make real English tea' and sending him off on his Tanzanian holiday with a bottle of Green Island Rum.

In September Brian sent their report via the diplomatic bag of the British High Commission: 'I have typed it in large type to encourage ministers to read it!'[26] He also held talks with Ringadoo while the latter was on a visit to London. By October 1975 the Mauritian government had progressed to amending some of the finer detail, but still required assistance. Brian was unable to get away from teaching and special adviser commitments, so Lynes was despatched with full authority to make any necessary changes to their plan. On this trip he was accompanied by his wife Sally, a social worker, who was commissioned to make a survey of the island's social welfare institutions that Brian and Lynes had visited 15 years earlier. The Mauritian government arranged their first class air travel and accommodation at the beach hotel that Brian favoured, but apart from these indulgences, it was an intensive working trip. Lynes managed to resolve the final sticking points on the pensions scheme, before moving on to consider the public assistance issue and producing a joint report with his wife. Brian regretted not being with them: 'If there were any work to do during an odd week in February it would make a marvellous break but I say this as the November weather descends upon us and I think of you enjoying the first fruits of flamboyant. We miss you.'[27]

The wheels of Mauritian administration turned painfully slowly, and seemed to require a British push at every stage. Brian liaised between the DHSS and the Ministry of Overseas Development to get them a suitably senior specialist on secondment. Throughout the summer of 1976 he vetted various officers, finally arranging for a retiring civil servant, Tom Stephens, to travel out in August to help with drafting the Bill and associated regulations. The Mauritius Sugar Producers Association put up a strong fight, engaging Bacon & Woodrow, a London firm of actuaries, in an effort to rubbish the Abel-Smith/Lynes pensions scheme. They claimed that is was inappropriate for Mauritius – a crude copy of the new British scheme that both Brian and Lynes were so closely involved with developing. Ringadoo came to London to take advice from Brian and Lynes, cabling back to Ramgoolam that they could compromise on the earnings ceiling for contributions and other points in the aim of getting an agreement. Having finally passed the Bill, it was then arranged for Mootoosamy and another Mauritian government civil servant to travel to Britain for a month-long training programme at the DHSS to help them implement the new pensions scheme.

The Mauritians continued to seek Brian's involvement in their health and social welfare development intermittently. In 1977 he prepared a report for the Mauritian Ministry of Health on a free GP national health service.[28] This was a follow-up to reports by N.R.E. (Rex) Fendall of the Liverpool School of Tropical Medicine in 1975, and Donald Chesworth in 1976 to attempt to redress the balance in favour of primary healthcare on the island. Although free access to GPs had been recommended in the Titmuss/Abel-Smith report in 1961, it had not been possible to implement it with so few doctors on the island. From the 1960s the numbers slowly increased: in 1972 there were 140 doctors, and by 1975 there were 258. Since 1970 the country used five-year development plans, and it was hoped to include free GP services in the 1975–80 plan.

In April 1978 Brian was invited by the Mauritian government to give the first Titmuss Memorial Lecture. In his opening address to Brian's lecture, Ramgoolam, the Prime Minister, recalled Titmuss's long service to the island before his death in April 1973. Not only had he provided the initial report for social welfare development, Brian disclosed that Titmuss had also helped privately with the critical negotiations for independence.[29] Brian used his lecture to talk about how Titmuss's early career in the insurance industry had provided insights into how to study social policy, and about how he (Brian) had personally been inspired by reading *Problems of social policy* as a student in the early 1950s. He described how Titmuss had developed much wider ways of looking at inequality, that the real measure of inequality was access to all forms of resources – capital and income – over a whole lifetime. Brian also talked about how Titmuss had introduced a radical approach to health policy in 1960s Tanzania, putting a new emphasis on training para-medicals to work in rural areas in the spirit of equity, giving these populations their fair share of government expenditure.[30] The lecture was the final event during a week-long stay, in which he also gave lectures and seminars at the University of Mauritius, and held meetings with senior government ministers. It had been hoped that Kay Titmuss, Richard's widow, would accompany Brian, but her increasingly frail health, including vertebral fractures due to osteoporosis, made this unrealistic.

As Mauritius developed, Brian was asked to return to tailor the services to the emerging social and economic conditions. He later used his European experience to advise on the practicability of introducing user charges, which he felt would be both unpopular and inefficient, but one solution to the increasing cost of the health service on the island. The Mauritian friendships continued during the intervals between his visits to the island, and he advised a number of Mauritian ministers and friends on their children's applications to British universities. He also facilitated a very generous donation from the Mauritian government to the Titmuss Appeal, which helped to secure dedicated library space for book collections on social welfare development, and to catalogue Titmuss's papers. The very practical, hands-on knowledge that Brian had gained through advising the Mauritius government since 1959 provided the bedrock for his joint WHO book in 1978, co-authored with Alcira Leiserson, *Poverty, Development and Health Policy*.[31] This was written primarily for senior health service administrators and teachers of health personnel in developing countries to tie in with the 29th World Health Assembly's directive in 1976 'to take appropriate steps to ensure that WHO takes an active part, jointly with other international agencies, in supporting the national planning of rural development aimed at the relief of poverty and the improvement of quality of life'.[32] Brian's key role in WHO's strategy reorientation is discussed in detail in Chapter 13.

The European Economic Community

'Europe' was a concept and place about which the British had recently reviewed their ideas. The first Commission of the European Communities (CEC) was formed in 1951 and developed into the executive arm of the EEC, after its creation in 1958 with six founding member countries. Britain deliberated on whether to join, and the first application was suspended, mainly due to French opposition. A new application was re-submitted in 1967 and membership granted from 1 January 1973, leading to some bitter divisions within political parties, especially over concerns that it would dilute British independence. The Commission, staffed by its own hierarchy of civil servants in Brussels, produces draft legislation for the Council and Parliament to approve. Its work is divided between Directorates-General, with similar interests to national government departments (for example, DG V, that is, group five, is responsible for social affairs). Although it was designed to maintain *European* interests, it had two representatives from each member country, which brought some national political flavour, with one of the Commission members elected as President for a five-year term of office, and member countries taking it in turn to direct its activities. Legislation, approved by the Council, has had varying degrees of authority – a Regulation has the force of law in all member states and overrides domestic law; a Directive or a Decision is brought into force by each member state as it finds appropriate; Recommendations and Opinions flag up areas for potential policy change.

In May 1975 Brian received a letter from Patrick Hillary, Vice-President of the Commission. He referred to the Council's Social Action Programme resolution of 21 January 1974 and now wished to create a 'group of independent experts, composed of an equal number of government experts, top level civil servants employed in the field of social protection, and of non-government experts. Each member state will thus be represented by two experts, both of whom sit in their own right.' The group was tasked to examine all proposals relating to social protection emanating from member countries and the Commission. It would meet four or five times a year, with experts paid 50,000 Belgian francs a year for their services. Hillary 'would be very pleased' if Brian would agree to join the group (presumably as a British non-government expert, given that the invitation was sent to his LSE address).[33] Brian wrote to Brian O'Malley, Minister for Social Security, about this offer, 'remembering how enraged you were to discover about the role of independent experts in social policy in the EEC, I was rather amused to receive the attached letter'.[34]

Britain, however, was about to hold a referendum on whether to stay in the EEC, in response to continuing public concerns, and the worsening economic crisis. Brian's response was therefore guarded: he recognised the potential conflict of interest with his post as special adviser to Castle, and the political embarrassment it might cause if he were to accept a European post before the referendum scheduled for 5 June. Furthermore, Castle was leading Labour's campaign to withdraw from the EEC. He wrote to Castle suggesting that he use his LSE contract as a delaying tactic by replying that he would have to ask permission from Dahrendorf, Director of the LSE, to take on this role. Dahrendorf approved it, to be reviewed after a year.

An internal DHSS memo from F.B. (Freddie) Hindmarsh of the International Relations Division provided a bit more context to the offer than Hillary had given in his letter of invitation, especially on the general European objective of 'harmonisation' of social policies mentioned in Article 117 of the Treaty of Rome. Little had been achieved despite good intentions, because member countries could not agree on what 'harmonisation' meant. Hindmarsh noted that the Commission's civil servants and experts were authoritative, and that Britain should look to send someone of Permanent Secretary rank to fill their allocated slot – possibly Sir Philip Rogers.

The Commission was also responsible for the Social Budget. The first one met with severe British criticism, who considered the whole exercise a 'largely meaningless comparison of expenditure'. They had attempted to veto the creation of a second budget, but by 1975 their strong objection was being accommodated by a proposed shift to a biennial exercise which compared expenditure patterns in depth and the measures taken by member countries to solve particular problems. It was hoped that this might prove a useful study aid on social questions and 'further remove the suspicion – always strongly denied by the Commission – that the Social Budget will be used to pressurise member states towards introducing similar programmes'.[35]

Brian sent a letter of acceptance the day after Britain's referendum decision to remain in the EEC. He was an archetypical Europhile, having enjoyed frequent holidays (especially his annual skiing trips) on the 'Continent' since his first visit to Paris in 1947. He spoke reasonable French, and some German, and appreciated a less stuffy class hierarchy than in Britain. He no doubt also saw this as opportunity to achieve social welfare reform on as wide a scale as possible. As his experiences with the WHO from 1958 demonstrated, he relished engagement with people from different nations and participating in complex organisations, even if they advanced (if at all) at a glacial pace.

Brian's contract specified that he was commissioned to work on the 'concertation of social protection policies' – the bespoke terminology signalled an immediate immersion into Brussels culture.[36] He would be paid £588 for his year-long engagement, based in DG V Social Affairs, headed by Director-General Michael Shanks. His more enduring contact was with Leo Crijns, Head of Sub-directorate C that had responsibility for matters relating to social security and the European Social Budget. A very helpful memo by Hindmarsh outlined the prospect of increasing involvement of DHSS policy divisions in EEC matters: 'A good deal of influence can often be brought to bear on the Commission's ultimate proposals by officials indicating what their Governments might regard as practicable and acceptable.'[37] Proposals which the Commission decided to pursue were then sent to working groups, which DHSS officials frequently attended as specialist advisers, following departmental clearance and liaison with other British government departments via the Committee on European Questions based in the Cabinet Office. Staff of the International Relations Division briefed those going to Brussels, in particular on tactics and Community procedures, and how to work with the UK representative in the Commission.

Brussels had some cultural and architectural similarities to Geneva. It had around 12,000 permanent staff – similar in size to the British Foreign and Commonwealth Office. They were accommodated in monumental buildings, designed around public spaces, and all named to consolidate its young heritage, especially its founding father, Jean Monnet. The Parliament and Court initially sat in neighbouring Luxembourg, before moving to Strasbourg in 1952. Brian felt quite at home in Europe, possibly more so than some of his DHSS colleagues. A telling example of this is his letter to Shanks on how he might make practical arrangements for attending Brussels meetings: 'It might be easier to drive over as I have a cottage not far from Dover.'[38] In the 1970s there could not have been many people who saw the English Channel as a commutable route.

The first meeting of experts that Brian attended was held on 21 November 1975. With the aid of a hand-drawn map supplied by one of the DHSS International Relations Division staff, he made his way to the Commission headquarters on Rue de la Loi. He was invited to a wide range of meetings. Some, such as the 'Third meeting on hospital legislation in the nine countries of the European Economic Community', he sent apologies for:'I am very much at the beck and call of my Secretary of State, as you can imagine. It really is impossible to be away for two days, quite apart from teaching commitments here.'[39] He relied on briefing notes compiled by Alec Atkinson, Deputy Secretary in the DHSS, who was the British government expert appointed at the same time, and who had attended the first working group meeting on 10 October:'On the whole, the representatives of the member states were refreshingly realistic in their approach and there was a very healthy resistance to over-elaborate procedural arrangements or to swelling still further the flood of paper.'[40] At this meeting Atkinson had confessed that he did not yet understand the difference between harmonisation and concertation, and he was probably not alone. The introductory note that they had been sent defined the aim of social protection policy as 'The improvement of living and working conditions so as to make possible their harmonisation while the improvement is being maintained'.[41]

Brian and Atkinson were given copies of the Green Book, which every British government official attending EEC meetings was issued with. They were also carefully briefed by Hindmarsh on the procedure for entering 'reserves' during negotiations:'it is difficult to hold out indefinitely in a minority of one – or even more than one – and I should have thought that in the working group which you are attending we shall need to go along with the majority even though we may ask for time for reflection. It is I think important in this immediate post-referendum period that we should give no grounds for criticism that we are being unnecessarily obstructive.'[42] The government representative sub-group met first and decided that the working group would have four priorities: pension age, demographic considerations in the development of social security, benefits for invalidity and provision for non-working mothers. It was agreed that the two types of experts – government representatives and independent experts – would meet separately.

After attending the first meeting of his sub-group on 21 November, Brian sent a briefing note to Atkinson.'There was a certain amount of feeling about the fact that the tasks for the independent experts had been selected by your group. It was suggested that this procedure was intended to keep the independent experts off controversial ground.' It had been agreed that they would meet every two months, and that for the next meeting each member would 'prepare a 5 page presentation on our social security system and health services financing system and some of the current problems (a tall order for 5 pages!)... In view of our "box and cox" relationship I volunteered a paper [on cash provision for invalidity and disability]. I am beginning to think that this could be a useful forum for exchanging information and comparing ideas and approaches.'[43] Brian also used the meeting as an opportunity to suggest to one of the Directorate-General staff that Professor John Greve of the University of Leeds would be a better UK independent expert for the EEC Anti-Poverty Committee than Professor Holman. Greve had extensive experience in studying homelessness, and was currently a member of the Royal Commission on the Distribution of Income and Wealth. He had also made special studies of Scandinavian housing policies.

Brian's paper was discussed at the next meeting on 6 February 1976, along with similar national studies for the other member states. He meticulously summarised all the British benefits, and outlined areas in which there was pressure for change, including from the trades unions on pensions, and to improve disability compensation payments and benefits. Tony Lynes commented on his draft, which he then had re-typed in single space but still failed to meet the stipulated five pages. The French representatives seemed the most worried about EEC 'harmonisation' of pensions, as they were already under enormous political pressure to reduce the pension age to 60 and to provide 50 per cent of the average wage. Brian was appointed (perhaps at his suggestion) as convenor of a separate group dealing with invalidity benefits. He wrote to Atkinson that there was 'no advantage in summarising what I gathered through the interpreter. I find great risks of inaccuracy with oral presentations simultaneously translated.'

Throughout 1976 Brian and Atkinson continued to attend Brussels meetings, using DHSS staff to prepare briefing papers for them in advance. The debates widened and re-focused as different member state representatives pushed their personal agendas. At the meeting on 7 May Brian presented the British concerns over European policy for the disabled, and as a result of the following discussion he found himself instructed to summarise the discussions and prepare plans for a linked research project. He worked up a paper on social security provision for chronically sick and disabled people (usefully defining terms such as 'incapacity', 'disability' and 'rehabilitation'), and drafted a questionnaire to solicit comparative information from member states. He tabled this at the next meeting on 20 July. In September his one-year contract was extended for a further year, and he began to plan with DHSS staff how they would complete the Disability Benefit Survey. He persuaded Brussels to pay for one of his PhD students, Paul Chapman, to do the bulk of the data analysis. His report justified the need to explore areas where it was hard for traditional social insurance to enter, such as minor disability, housewives, those not insured, congenital disabilities, or disabilities resulting from criminal injury.

'Dynamisation' entered EEC parlance in 1977 in the context of social security benefits, and Brian's attention widened to include discussions on retirement age.[44] He expected that declining birth rates by the 1980s would require incentives to keep people at work until the age of 70, and asked Bryan Ellis of the DHSS to solicit the TUC and Confederation of British Industry (CBI) views on British retirement age. Ellis replied that the TUC wanted to see a common (that is, for both men and women) retirement age of 60, but that Jack Jones saw pension value increases as a higher priority over reducing the pension age; the CBI were more flexible – they wished to see an age band approach spanning 62 to 70. Ellis suggested to Brian that they use the recent OPCS (Office for Population Census and Statistics) questionnaire on retirement to respond to the EEC questionnaire. Brian reported this back to Leo Crijns.

There were also moves towards 'codification' – to systematise the assorted rules in operation in member countries, as discussed at the meeting of experts held on 1 April (as Ellis wryly noted to Brian, April Fool's Day in Britain, if not in Brussels). From 1 July 1977 the first three volumes (of a proposed nine) of a code book would come into force throughout the EEC to achieve this objective. This had implications for the various sub-groups: Mr Veldkamp's on humanisation of social security and Professor Coppini's on social security and demography. At the working group meeting held on 7 January 1978 the experts discussed a paper prepared by H. Markman, 'A Model for Making the Retirement Age Flexible'. This used data from *Eurobarometer*, and proposed that it should be possible to retire gradually – moving to part-time work to maintain income levels if necessary when pensions would be lower from an early retirement. Markman noted that 'The "cult of youth" is still predominant in our society. However, there are already clear signs that "senior citizens" are becoming of greater importance to society, and particularly to the economy, even if primarily as a consumer group with purchasing power.'[45] Brian was not persuaded that some of the papers discussed by the working group really grasped reality. Writing to Crijns in February 1978 he commented diplomatically that M. Dupeyroux's paper failed to acknowledge the complexities of the British pensions system, and contained some basic analytical errors.

A new European advisory role

All these trips to Brussels, and European-wide studies, brought Brian into contact with some of the most senior people within the EEC Commission. In June 1977 he received an invitation to become special adviser to Henk Vredeling, European Commissioner for Employment and Social Affairs. Vredeling's staff telephoned Brian on several occasions asking him to accept. Brian wrote to Ennals informing him of the offer, and that he had been on the point of refusing it. However, he changed his mind after a conversation with Freddie Hindmarsh, who headed the DHSS's International Relations Division: 'He attached enormous importance to the offer of appointment and said that the British Representative [to the EEC] would also. To turn it down could be interpreted as further evidence of the cool attitude of HMG [Her Majesty's Government] to the Community. Thus Britain would have lost an opportunity to influencing [sic] EEC policy at its roots in an area where several new initiatives are expected.'[46]

There were, however, some Whitehall concerns. Sir Douglas Allen, Head of the Civil Service Department, and Sir Patrick Nairne, DHSS Permanent Secretary, made it clear that if Brian accepted the post it would have to be on condition that his advice to Vredeling remained confidential, and on the understanding that it would not compromise his position in Britain as special adviser to Ennals. He would have to find about 30 days a year to work for Vredeling. He proposed to do this by reducing his special adviser post from three to two-and-a-half days per week, and by asking Dahrendorf to release him from half a day of his two LSE days per week. He would also be resigning from the Commission's Working Group on Concertation of Social Protection Policies.

Vredeling assured Brian that there would be ways to accommodate his concerns, and reiterated that he was hiring him for his own 'eminence' as a university expert, not because of his closeness to the British government. However, Brian did consider it appropriate to ask Nairne to secure him a contact with the Department of Employment (at Under Secretary level) as his new role would also focus on alternative schemes to reduce unemployment. Having gained final approval from Downing Street via Sir Ken Stowe, and having carefully worded a press statement to indicate Ennals' approval for this new appointment, Brian signed his new European Commission contract.[47] In the obligatory CEC application form he gave his social activities as skiing and swimming; and under parents he listed his mother, then living at 28 Queen's Gate, London. The section marked 'marital status' he marked as single. There was no option, had he so wished, to identify his partner, John.

He began a new routine that would last until 1980. On his contracted three days per month for EEC work, Brian would take the Underground from Sloane Square, a 10-minute walk from his Westmoreland Place home, to Heathrow (or train to Gatwick), fly economy class to Brussels, then take the airport bus to his meetings. If he needed to stay over he always used the Hotel Bedford, on Rue du Midi.[48] The resulting paperwork typified all that the sceptical British suspected of the EEC – everything submitted in duplicate, matched 'mission' request forms with expenses 'claims', which had to show the time he left home as well as the times of each flight. Thankfully he had his LSE secretary Eileen Ellis to make the reservations and type up each form. He then waited (up to six months) to be reimbursed for his travel, hotel bills and services.

On 1 September 1977 Brian joined Vredeling's new advisory group; the other members were Jean Vincens from Institut d'Etudes de l'Emploi, Toulouse; Professor Wouter Siddré from the Erasmus University in Rotterdam; and Professor Dr Burkart Lutz from the Institut für Sozialwissenschaftliche Forschung in Munich. At their first meeting with Vredeling on 20 September (held at the Berlaymont Building), they were joined by some of Brian's former colleagues – Leo Crijns and Jean Degimbe (Director-General of DG V: Employment and Social Affairs), and also by Mr Cohen (Chef de Cabinet) and Mr Tavitian (Director of Employment and Vocational Training). The civil servants at the DHSS were more than happy to meet Brian's enlarged briefing needs. McGinnis wrote to him: 'Having a friend at court could clearly be of value to the rest of us, and we would want to be as helpful as goodwill and (in the opposite direction) resources allow.'[49]

In November the advisers met again to thrash out the practicalities of how they would prioritise their work and collaborations. They were briefed on the relationship between the advisers, the Commissioner, the Cabinet and the Director-General. Brian's handwritten notes from the meeting show that they acknowledged their existing workloads, that they could not be expected to be experts on everything, and that they had to get to know one another. Vredeling urged them to use 'brainstorming' to separate out daily from long-term problems. He stressed to them the newness of the Community, and that there was no fixed way of working. Crijns commented on the need to react quickly to the Community's agenda, and proposed a trip to Geneva to see how the ILO's personal advisers operated; Brian might have thought his considerable experience of Geneva's organisations would have exempted him from this training. Crijns also reflected on how difficult it had been for the EEC to develop contacts with the OECD, and to understand the attitude of the Americans.

Henk Vredeling's personality emerges from the correspondence between Nel Barendregt (his Chef de Cabinet, equivalent to a Parliamentary Private Secretary in Britain), and Bill Nicol, Deputy to Sir Donald Maitland, UK Permanent Representative to the European Union. Nicol wrote to Hindmarsh in the DHSS's International Relations Division with feedback on his recent paper submission, which had raised Ennals' proposal that health affairs within the Commission should be reorganised and placed under the control of a single body: 'First the Commissioner [Vredeling] wants discussions to be the basis of and prelude for action. By temperament he is not interested in studies and information collecting and he is also not inclined to usurp or duplicate work done by WHO, the Council of Europe or the OECD.'[50] Vredeling had considered forming a health advisory committee within the European Commission, through which he would be able to extend his influence within member states, but the Public Health Committee of the Partial Agreement of the Council of Europe already existed, and there would have been opposition to such large-scale reorganisation, and to increased staffing costs.

Other simmering issues at the European level in the mid-1970s now had a greater resonance for Brian. In 1975 the radical Marjolin Report had proposed economic and monetary union of the EEC by 1980. Two years later a study group on the role of public finance in European integration (the MacDougall Report) reiterated one of the Marjolin proposals for the creation of a Community Unemployment Fund (CUF). In August 1978 the Second European Social Budget was published. It forecast that the level and rate of growth of British expenditure on all aspects of social protection were well below the average for the community as a whole. Although British civil servants at the DHSS considered it an improvement on the first Social Budget, there were still difficulties with international comparisons. They decided not to send the 'voluminous' Second Social Budget to the Minister, but to put it on file if wanted.

Brian maintained some involvement with the Working Group of the Concertation of Social Protection project, which had given him his first entrée into EEC activities in 1975. In April 1978 Crijns and Degimbe asked Brian to referee the draft healthcare study report by Professors Prims and Groot that he had earlier been involved with. He sent it to Teddy Chester in the Department of Social Administration at the University of Manchester to validate his assessment. Chester replied: 'I could not agree with you more.... I think it is awful from every point of view and can only assume it was put together by some young research assistants and not by the putative authors, both of whom are well known to me as quite shrewd interpreters of the health scene in many parts of the world.'[51] Brian sent his verdict (with a copy of Chester's letter) to Crijns: 'I am extremely disappointed with the result of so much work....The structure of the report has been unsuccessful.... Statistics are extremely poorly handled.... In general I feel that the authors have set about their task without any clear definition of what they are looking for. They hadn't started with any hypotheses.... I feel that the approach we adopted in the Pharmaceutical Consumption Study was much better. We decided on what information was relevant and attempted to collect it.' Brian suggested to Crijns that it would be more valuable if he were to prepare a summary report and identify crucial missing data. The intimation was thinly veiled: 'why not let me conduct a more satisfactory report on healthcare in the nine European countries?' Following the meeting of Health Ministers in November 1978, Brian's contract was extended again so that he could take on his preferred task.

Brian's new role expanded his expertise into adjunct issues to his usual concerns with pensions and healthcare. In February 1978 he provided a detailed critique of the Community Unemployment Insurance (CUI) scheme. He accepted the advantages of establishing such a scheme, and focused on problems such as definitions of unemployment, how to harmonise the length of unemployment before which a CUI payment should be made, and whether to base the top–up on gross or net last wage. British administrative systems, he pointed out, worked on the previous tax year – the CUI would be unpopular as it would require lengthy recalculations and balancing payments. The draft CUI criterion made no mention of benefits ceilings, or how to cope with large families, wage stops and so on. In Britain it would 'require very controversial legislation which might not be supported by Parliament. Again the community would be blamed'. The UK and Ireland paid the same benefits for the sick and unemployed, unified so as to create no incentive for the unemployed to conceal sickness so as to pretend that they were available for work and no incentive for the unemployed to pretend they were sick; if the government were forced by Europe to pay more to the unemployed, it would also have to adjust its sickness benefits. Brian could see no signs from governments of the Community for a desire to improve the level of unemployment benefits: indeed, there was active support in Britain for other reforms, such as higher pensions and child benefits, and better support for people with disabilities. His fifth objection was the lack of any redistribution in favour of the poorer: 'This would be contrary to basic concepts of social justice as seen in the UK and Ireland and I would expect it to be strongly resisted.... The problems of making a transition, if one decided to do so, from a Beveridge type [flat rate] scheme to a percentage scheme would be formidable. Some claimants would be better off than new claimants. Would that be tolerable?' He concluded by noting that he hadn't even analysed the most fundamental European aspect, whether the scheme 'really would at all times redistribute from the richer countries to the poorer and whether poorer parts of countries necessarily have higher rates of unemployment'.[52]

Back at the DHSS there were similar concerns about this latest European initiative. Blunt wrote to Brian: 'Our position is that we are wary of minimum standards proposals'. It was felt they would 'interfere with our own assessment of priorities in social expenditure … and could lead to significantly increased public expenditure on social security benefits.... Our information is that there is considerable doubt within the Commission (especially in DGV) about the merits of such a proposal.'[53] The following month Brian was able to relay some reassurance to his DHSS colleagues: 'you will be pleased to hear … that Community Unemployment Benefit [CUB] as suggested in earlier reports will not be taken out of the cupboard and given another run. Mr Ortoli does not like it because it is negative rather than positive and Mr Vredeling clearly accepted the priority I pressed of using community money to support the creation of jobs rather than the maintenance on those without them. I had also submitted some months earlier a paper on the formidable political and technical details of CUB.'[54]

Thankfully, Brian appeared to be spared direct involvement in the politics of the Commission. Maitland, the British Permanent Representative on the Commission, sent telegrams to the FCO which Brian was copied into, on the sensitive negotiations involved in setting up meetings of Health Ministers, and also a 'Council' meeting of representatives of member states. Agreeing venues and agendas seemed to take as much negotiation as the actual meetings achieved. Discussions on items such as proposals on colouring of pharmaceutical products vied with broader issues, including economic aspects of healthcare. Vredeling claimed he had insufficient staff to prepare contributions on other items that member states wished to put on agendas.

When meetings of health members did take place, the outcomes were not always useful. An internal memo by Henri Etienne, following such a meeting in November 1978, noted: 'The Commission was given instructions which were incomplete and often ambiguous. Several delegations – Denmark, France, Britain – repeatedly voiced hostility to any community harmonisation or regulation of public health and unwillingness to let the commission have the necessary funds to engage in further operations....' Vredeling had led the discussion on the agenda item 'Economic aspects of health', and had outlined a possible programme of work on the cost of healthcare (quite likely at Brian's suggestion), but disagreement emerged 'even as to the very concept of health costs'.[55] Roland Moyle, British Minister of Health, commented that one of his previous suggestions had not been adequately pursued. The Commission was forever holding all sorts of meetings, which officials from his Ministry had to attend, on foodstuffs, the environment, industrial health, cosmetics, pesticides, microbiology, public information, and so on. He felt it would be better for there to be a permanent body of public health experts attached to the Commission.

Brian agreed with the Commission's officials that progress was slow and not always adequately supported with data. He had been invited to attend a meeting of the Social Budget Committee in February 1979 and afterwards wrote to Crijns with his concerns that it had too narrow a concept of healthcare costs, and lacked data on areas such as capital expenditure and the private sector. Returning to an issue that he had been passionate about since his first WHO study in 1957, he noted: 'the main problem is the vagueness and imprecision underlying the definitions of the basic data. I could make quite a long checklist of problems if required.... If our task is to examine critically the data which has already been collected either for the Social Budget or for the Maynard/Abel-Smith study and extend develop and update it and produce a commentary, I wonder whether the main Social Budget Committee is the right forum for such detailed specialised work or indeed whether they would think they were.'[56]

Vredeling used Brian to prepare a number of briefing papers and speaking notes, which he used to direct Commission discussions and draft legislation. Topics included the development of primary healthcare which discussed the increasing role of GPs in preventive work, an aim for a joint declaration by Health Ministers of shared principles, and some plan for speeding up the rate of convergence towards their agreed aims. Brian worked up a detailed paper on the need for a European Health Card, to supplement the E111 form that gave free medical treatment to EEC citizens in other member states when travelling away from home. The introduction of a wallet-sized card would make it easier to see who was eligible for treatment, and tighten up on how non-EEC people could gain treatment during holidays. He told Vredeling that 'It would also show that the Community cares about the health of its citizens and not just about the health of agriculture and industry'.[57]

Regulation of pharmaceutical prices was also a topic on which the Commission had been trying to make progress for some time. The Bureau Européen des Union de Consommateurs (BEUC) had recently published its report, exposing widespread drug price fixing, based on what the pharmaceutical companies thought each country could afford. The Commission also wished to introduce 'limited lists' of drugs that could only be prescribed by doctors in member states, and another list of products that could be paid for by social security. Brian briefed Crijns in July 1979 on how he saw problems with these issues: 'As you know I am worried that if the Commission gets tough about price discrimination in this area, the result will be a trend for production to be moved to high cost countries thus damaging employment not only in the UK and Italy but in Ireland which is at last seeing the fruits of many years of effort to attract foreign pharmaceutical companies to manufacture there. Frankly I do not yet see a long term solution and the moves made so far by DG III suggest to me that they have not thought through the long term implications of what they have been tending to encourage.'[58] He could be caustic when dealing with these European 'harmonisation' proposals, but this lengthy quote illustrates that he was skilled at thinking through the ramifications of potential policies:

> There are health questions here which may be important in the case of some products. But Mr Vredeling is not likely to get much of a mention in history books for making a few more products "Prescription only" throughout the Community. I do not see this as a cost-effective way of using DG V's limited staff resources … we would face a whole wormsnest of arguments: 1. Cutting out ineffective products now used as a placebo could raise costs if doctors prescribed effective products when all they intended to prescribe was a placebo. 2. Should we destroy the bulk of the home market for effective but costly products which are already or could earn major export revenue for the Community? 3. There would be awful arguments on what really was biologically equivalent. 4. Most major firms get most of their revenue from one product at any [one] point in time. A decision to strike a product off the list of all nine countries is a decision to cripple a whole firm with possible drastic employment consequences for towns where the firm is the largest employer.[59]

Yet Brian appreciated that his value to Crijns and Vredeling was not just in demolishing weak proposals, but in offering appropriate alternatives. In the covering letter Crijns sent with the pharmaceuticals briefing he requested that Brian put further suggestions on how to implement the proposed health treatment cards. Brian also expressed disappointment to Crijns that he had not been given the go-ahead to update and improve estimates of healthcare costs in the 'nine': 'It will be years before the Euro-statistics can do a better job. It would be possible to do this without putting any strain on you and your team. The most cost-effective way of doing it would be for me to visit chosen experts in each country to examine existing data and collect up-to-date figures. I could make 2 or 3 round trips to cover the eight countries other than the UK. We would change some of our experts. I have the right man for Italy (Brenna).... I could fit in the trip in November to February and hopefully have better data by the summer of next year. The only strain on the Commission resources would be (a) translation of the final report, (b) my travel and subsistence. This would be my main assignment as special adviser (or expert as Nel [Barendregt] is now thinking of grading me).'[60]

Alongside these primary interests in health costs, Brian had also agreed to take on the preparation of a second report on social security provision for the longer-term disabled, which he submitted in 1979. He highlighted the persistently wide differences in the extent of provision for the disabled in different countries of the Community, even for people with exactly the same degree of disability, depending on how the disability arose, the age, insurance and family status of the individual. He judged that the insurance approach left too many holes in provision, which were inadequately filled by social assistance schemes.

Following the meeting of Health Ministers in Dublin in December 1979 he returned to the issue of pharmaceutical pricing, outlining a selective but useful study that would focus on the 100 products in each country on which most was spent each year. He estimated that this would produce a Community-wide list of about 300-400 products. He suggested that before beginning the study, the European Pharmaceutical Manufacturers Association should be given an opportunity to see a description of the proposed method and allowed to comment on it, to prevent criticism afterwards.[61] He also prepared a briefing paper on the potential for a Community scheme of parental allowances (distinct from child benefit), for parents who took leave from work to care for children. This could commence immediately following statutory maternity leave, and run for up to six months (12 months for single parents), and be used by both mothers and fathers.

21. The WHO/ILO working party on the costs of medical care, Geneva, 1958

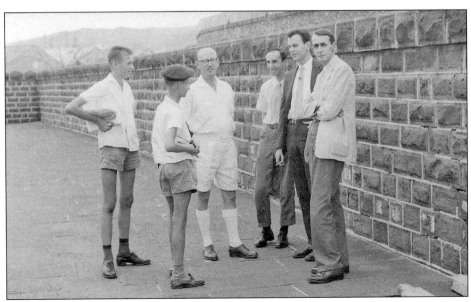
22. Brian Abel-Smith with Richard Titmuss, Tony Lynes and Edwin de Robillard (in white shorts) of the Compagnons Batisseurs in Mauritius, shortly after Cyclone Alix, March 1960

23. Brian Abel-Smith visiting a hospital in Kiev, Ukraine, in 1961, as a member of Milton Roemer's working party visit to the USSR

24. LSE Department of Social Science and Administration, 1971
Seated left to right: Muriel Brown, Howard Glennerster, Kit Russell, Roger Hadley, Kay McDougall, Brian Abel-Smith, Richard Titmuss, Garth Plowman, Zofia Butrym, Peter Levin, George Goetschius, Angela Vivian, Don Gregory.
Standing left to right: Andrew Howell, Tessa Blackstone, Joan Edmonds, Beata Blair, Ruth Griffiths, Sally Sainsbury, Mike Reddin, Doreen Wilson, Christine Stander, Leone Kellaher, David Piachaud, Vivienne Gilby, Rosalind Brooke, Jackie Shreeve, Anne Edwards, Helen Burns, Judith Benjamin, Maureen Mulvany, Dianna Wories, Charlotte Sutton, Kathleen Hill, Janie Thomas, Roberta Gillingwater, Irmi Elkan, Geoffrey Sage

25. Brian Abel-Smith and John Sarbutt on holiday in Malta, 1972

26. John Sarbutt, 1980s

27. Brian Abel-Smith with Alf Morris (centre), Minister of State, DHSS and Sir John Donne, Chairman of South-East Thames Regional Hospital Authority at the 30th anniversary of the NHS, July 1978

28. Brian Abel-Smith with his brother Lionel and mother Vivée at a Christmas lunch, 1970s

29. RHDAC meeting at WHO EURO Copenhagen, 24–26 April 1984

30. First Health Economics short course, LSHTM, 1986. Anne Mills, course director, is standing to the right of Brian Abel-Smith

31. Meeting of the Academic Advisory Committee of the Center for Public Health Research [forerunner of the National Institute of Public Health of Mexico], Mexico City, circa 1987. Front row l to r: Carlos Cruz, Henry Mosley, Harvey Fineberg, José Luis Bobadilla, Enrique Ruelas, Victor Cárdenas; back row l to r: Robin Badgley, Brian Abel-Smith, Avedis Donabedian, Miguel Angel Gonzalez-Block, Julio Frenk, D. A. Henderson. [I am grateful to Julio Frenk for providing the identifications.]

33. Brian Abel-Smith accepting his LSE award of Honorary Fellow, 14 July 1995 at the Savoy Theatre

32. Brian Abel-Smith at the Euro-Pharma meeting, 1993

34. At Beatrice Webb's desk, LSE, 1995

35. Brian with his Battersea rescue dog, Nicky

36. The house and garden at Tanglewood, Westwell, Kent

37. Mauritius stamp

Despite all these good proposals, they were small fry in the bigger European scheme of things. The report, *Better Health at Lower Cost*, produced by the Commission's Work Programme on Health in November 1979, epitomised the scale of the problem.[62] On page 27 it noted 'Aid from DGVI in support of tobacco production under the CAP [Common Agricultural Policy] amounts to 262 million EUA whereas Community expenditure to combat all social diseases including smoking totals to only 200,000 EUA'.[63] Next to which Brian had written one word: 'wow'.

Part 3

SHIFTING THE BALANCE OF POWER, 1979–96

13

In and outers: 1979–91

Health for All by the Year 2000

HFA2000: health, wealth and health economics

Making a Financial Master Plan

Special adviser to Mahler

Health promotion

HFA2000: targets and assessments

The rise of The World Bank

The Commission on Health Research for Development

Kenya

———

Tell the Ministry of Public Health that it only works for fifteen per cent of the total population of the country and that this fifteen per cent is mainly composed of gentlemen, while the broad masses of the peasants do not get any medical treatment.…The Ministry of Public Health is not a Ministry of Public Health for the people, so why not change its name to the Ministry of Urban Health, the Ministry of Gentlemen's Health, or even the Ministry of Urban Gentlemen's Health? (Mao Zedong, 26 June 1965)[1]

Brian had worked intermittently for the World Health Organisation since 1956, developing a reputation as a freelance consultant and expert adviser who could quickly produce sensible policies based on robust academic research, drawing on his extensive international experience. After the fall of the British Labour government in 1979 (which was not in office again during Brian's lifetime) he had the capacity to re-engage with international projects. Although he returned to his full-time position at the LSE, he accepted an invitation from

*Halfdan Mahler at the WHO to help develop the Health for All by the Year
2000 (HFA2000) strategy. During the 1980s, at a time of global economic
recession, Brian travelled widely to advise on country-level and regional policies.
He continued to advocate policies based on socialist and egalitarian principles,
which increasingly brought him into conflict with staff at The World Bank,
whose policies seemed to threaten core values of risk sharing and social capital
in health and social welfare systems. The Kenyan case study shows how Brian's
academic authority was matched against the narrow dictates of the powerful
World Bank on how healthcare should be organised and funded.*

In May 1977, at the 30th World Health Assembly, the WHO had
formally announced a change of policy direction. It approved the
resolution for 'the attainment by all the people of the world by the
year 2000 of a level of health that will permit them to lead a socially
and economically productive life'.[2] At its meeting in Alma Ata, USSR,
the following year it issued a declaration, putting primary healthcare
at the centre of a strategy to achieve 'Health for All by the Year
2000'.[3] The declaration stated that 'the existing gross inequality in the
health status of the people, particularly between the developed and
developing countries as well as within countries, is politically, socially
and economically unacceptable'.[4] One of the powers behind this
move (alongside key WHO insiders and experts such as Ken Newell
and Carl Taylor) was China, which had joined the WHO in 1973 and
subsequently pushed to rebalance the preferred model of healthcare
away from expensive high-technology secondary care towards its
'barefoot doctors' model. Between the launch of Mao's scheme in
1965 and 1972 over one million 'barefoot doctors' had been trained to
provide low-cost healthcare for rural communities.[5] However, it was
the Soviets (USSR) who led this latest campaign within the WHO,
insisting on hosting the 1978 meeting on Russian soil (which led to
the Chinese refusing to attend).[6]

The world had changed since 1948: the break-up of empires
meant that the language and strategies of paternalism were no longer
appropriate or as tolerated. The WHO, which was mainly funded
by income-related member levies from developed countries (with
additional extra-budgetary donations for specific campaigns), had been
a useful channel to air grievances and ease tensions. The ex-colonies
demanded their share of their former rulers' accumulated wealth. As
the WHO Ceylon delegate had put it in 1951: 'South East Asia is not
receiving as much aid as it ought ... the European nations of the world
owe to the South East Asian nations a duty that they shall undertake to

raise the living standards and the health conditions of the people [of] those areas, whom they have exploited for over 200 years.'[7]

Through the 1950s, 1960s and 1970s the emphasis had been on spreading formal western-style medical education. The WHO provided fellowships for students from developing countries to travel to Europe for medical training, before returning to their homelands. The professional dominance at WHO, both in Geneva and in its regional and national offices, was overwhelmingly medical. The common criteria that was used to evaluate the healthcare potential of developing countries was the number of medically qualified staff available. The WHO also embarked on ambitious 'vertical' disease-specific strategies. There were some successes such as the yaws, BCG and smallpox campaigns (smallpox was declared officially eradicated in 1980). But the more common experience was a dawning realisation that some of WHO's goals, such as for the malaria eradication campaign, were unachievable. As the size of the WHO increased through the 1960s when the newly independent African and Asian countries began to join, pressure to abandon what was seen as the arrogant diffusion of western dogma increased.

The WHO's mission was further complicated because of the diversity of views on how health fitted with the process of 'development'. Although the US, the USSR and their allies organised specific health campaigns, health was often seen in the 1950s and 1960s as a by-product of wider development policies. This also applied to campaigns developed by the international non-governmental organisations (NGOs) such as the Ford Foundation and the Population Council. Yet publications such as John Bryant's 1969 book *Health and the Developing World* publicised the fact that 'Large numbers of the world's people, perhaps more than half, have no access to health care at all, and for many of the rest, the care they receive does not answer the problems that they have ... the most serious health needs cannot be met by teams with spray guns and vaccinating syringes.'[8] There was also recognition that health was determined not only by access to doctors and hospitals. The 1974 Lalonde Report, named after the Canadian Minister of Health, identified four main determinants of health: biology, health services, environment and lifestyles.[9] In the developed world, too, there was a new scrutiny of what doctors were doing in the name of 'health'. Some of the most extreme anti-medical views were expounded by Ivan Illich in his 1975 book *Medical Nemesis: the expropriation of health*, which suggested that some medical care was actually done for the benefit of the medical profession, not the interest of the patient.[10]

Although the WHO had already begun to move towards projects that were focused on 'basic health services' – from 85 in 1965 to 156 in 1971 – there was no effective momentum for change. The creation of the Division of Strengthening Health Services in 1972, headed by Ken Newell, a public health expert with a strong interest in 'basic' health services, stimulated a reappraisal. This was further supported in 1973 by the WHO Executive Board's report *Organisational Study on Methods of Promoting the Development of Basic Health Services*.[11] It facilitated the collaboration between Newell's division and UNICEF (UN International Children's Emergency Fund) in a major study published in 1975 as *Alternative Approaches to Meeting Basic Health Needs in Developing Countries*:

> ... history and experience show that conventional health services, organised along 'western' or other centralised lines, are unlikely to expand to meet the basic health needs of all people.... Some countries will need to make drastic or revolutionary changes in their approach to health services....The remodelled approach must be linked to the prevailing human attitudes and values, which differ from community to community, and it will require a clear motivation and commitment on the part of the people who have the knowledge and political and economic power to make change.[12]

Newell published his own personal interpretation in the same year in a book, *Health by the People*.[13]

A further sign of the shift can be found in the appointment in 1973 of Halfdan Mahler as the WHO's third Director General. A charismatic Danish-born doctor, he had been with the WHO since 1951, first with its Indian tuberculosis programme and then from 1962 in the Geneva headquarters where he moved on to directing the Project Systems Analysis. Mahler quickly acknowledged the pressure to prioritise 'primary' healthcare. In 1975 his addresses to three of the WHO's regional committees were titled 'Health for All by the Year 2000'.[14] The following year he used this phrase again for his address to the World Health Assembly – this time as an overt goal. He was critical of the assumption that western medical systems were the universal panacea. He signalled his support for a complete re-think by adding a new heading to the Director General's annual reports: 'Traditional medicine'. Over the next two years he put forward increasingly detailed definitions of primary healthcare. Meetings in 1977 helped to sharpen the focus, in preparation for the conference planned for September 1978 at Alma Ata, the capital of the Soviet Republic of Kazakhstan. The 3,000 delegates from 134 governments and 67 international organisations were marshalled into discussions by the organiser, David Tejada-de-Rivero, WHO Assistant Director General. Mahler challenged them at the opening ceremony with eight compelling questions that required immediate action, calling for radical change in existing health delivery systems, a readiness to fight political and technical battles and to overcome social and economic obstacles and professional resistance.[15] Yet already the vested interest of the medical profession in secondary healthcare was beginning to flex its muscle, and there were concerns over whether there was sufficient recognition in the conference background papers of the link between health and poverty.

Health for All by the Year 2000

After the 1978 Alma Ata Declaration – which comprised 10 key statements on primary healthcare, rights and duties – the WHO launched the global strategy, Health for All by the Year 2000 (HFA2000) at the 32nd World Health Assembly in 1979. The preliminary document stressed the need for national and regional plans of action and agreed targets to 'improve health as an integral part of social and economic development' and provided some basic guidance and a timetable.[16] In December of that year the UN General Assembly formally adopted a resolution on 'health as an integral part of development' and reiterated the WHO's call for all countries to respond to the Alma Ata Declaration. It reflected the rhetoric of the late 1970s and formalised the subtle ideological shifts that had been happening not only within WHO, but also within all the major international organisations.[17] From an academic viewpoint, too, there had been increasing research on the mechanisms of development. Buzzwords that were now in wide circulation included 'inter-sectoral', 'multi-dimensional' and 'trickle-down', linked especially to Reagan–Thatcher economics. Some of it emanated from the developing countries: Latin American theorists now talked about the concept of 'under-development', which argued that since the 1960s the process of international trade had widened the gap between rich and poor countries. This was mirrored in Africa and in the emerging 'dependency theory'.[18] Much of this new development terminology reflected its origin within the offices of economists – both academic and consulting. They were at the top of their game, ready with solutions to the world's problems. Economists had proved useful as generic experts because they provided 'the real and perceived independence of judgement that makes the visibility of professionals in power into vehicles for conferring legitimacy'.[19] Certainly this is how Brian's continued employment by developing countries such as

Mauritius must be seen. The success of their pensions and social security policies in the 1970s owed much to his ability to deliver schemes that did not take political sides.

In 1980 – two years after the Alma Ata Declaration – an alternative strategy for improving health in developing countries was formalised. Its identifier adjective was to prove political and divisive in the global health community. *Selective* Primary Health Care advocated targeted low-cost interventions, of the sort that Brian had seen effectively used in countries such as Tanzania. It had emerged from a conference hosted by the Rockefeller Foundation at its Bellagio Conference Centre in the Italian Lakes the previous year. Rockefeller's Chair, John H. Knowles, was inspired mainly by the lack of primary healthcare in the US, but his concerns were shared by Robert S. McNamara, the new President of The World Bank, who saw selective primary healthcare as a realistic and achievable model for developing countries. The conference used as its case study an article by Julia Walsh and Kenneth S. Warren entitled 'Selective primary health care, an interim strategy for disease control in developing countries'.[20]

Although they did not openly criticise the Alma Ata Declaration, Walsh and Warren suggested 'entry points' that would provide attainable goals, allow for cost-effective planning, and be easy to monitor and evaluate. They were focused on low-cost technical interventions for the main disease problems in developing countries, which led to the acronym GOBI (Growth monitoring to fight malnutrition in children, Oral rehydration techniques to defeat diarrhoeal diseases, Breastfeeding to protect children and Immunisation).[21] The selective primary healthcare model was strongly championed by James P. Grant, who was Director of UNICEF from 1980, and had been present at the Bellagio meeting. It appealed to McNamara's World Bank people as a destination for its funds because it showed quick results. Mahler, who was also at Bellagio, subsequently distanced himself from Grant and from UNICEF.[22] After Bellagio, the WHO Alma Ata model found itself with its own defining adjective: 'comprehensive' primary healthcare. In the ensuing debates some experts portrayed selective primary healthcare as an efficient variant of the Alma Ata model. Others viewed it as a dangerous dilution of the accumulated political momentum for health in developing countries, and its narrow 'technocentric' approaches such as oral rehydration solutions to tackle infant diarrhoea, as a 'band aid' instead of investing in supplying clean water and sanitation.[23]

Yet HFA2000 was intended to be a truly global initiative, as relevant to developed as to developing countries. In Europe the response to

the Declaration was the creation of a WHO-EURO Regional Health
Development Advisory Council (RHDAC) which Brian was asked
to chair. He had a long history of working with WHO-EURO and
its Regional Director, Leo Kaprio. This invitation initiated another
period of Brian's close involvement with European health policy, and
began in traditional style, with a planning meeting to plan the first
meeting, which was held at WHO-EURO's Copenhagen offices in
March 1980. Among the 18 participants and 12 WHO-EURO staff
who attended were Jo Asvall, then Director of Programme Management
for WHO-EURO, who chaired a parallel set of meetings on Country
Health Planning (CHP), an 'approach' that had been used by WHO
since the early 1970s. A key issue was how to integrate CHP into the
broader HFA strategy. Brian was also well-acquainted with Herbert
Zöllner, WHO-EURO Regional Officer for Health Economics.

Brian's handwritten notes from the meeting acknowledge the scale
of the challenge, and the importance of liaison between health and
other policy areas such as education and environment as part of the
inter-sectoral approach advocated by WHO.[24] Although preliminary
initiatives had included sending a questionnaire to all member states of
the European Union to elicit some basic information to supplement
the UN Demographic Yearbook, a much greater level of information
and technical support would be required. Some WHO regions,
such as the Western Pacific, were quick off the mark in producing
guidelines for regional health strategies which addressed such issues
as regional information exchange and creating a regional network of
health development centres. There was also an HFA2000 group for
industrialised countries, of which Brian was a member. But reading
through the voluminous paperwork that accompanied the annual
Health Assemblies, regional meetings and various committees, the
general impression is that there was considerable debate but a reluctance
to take action for the first few years of HFA2000. Brian was present
when the draft WHO-EURO regional strategy document was
discussed at the 30th Regional Committee meeting at Fez, Morocco
in October 1980 (returning home with a 'nasty bug' which developed
into pneumonia), and in Copenhagen in November when a regional
planning meeting was held on the study of the influence of economic
development on health, at which he commented on the list of targets
and approaches.

At the April 1981 RHDAC meeting at Copenhagen, again chaired by
Brian, discussions revolved around how to fit HFA2000 with the WHO-
EURO's contribution to the forthcoming Seventh General Programme
of Work. These were the WHO's main planning mechanisms, and the

seventh, due to begin in 1984, had HFA2000 as its main focus. The council agreed that several basic concepts needed clarification: 'The term "lifestyle" seemed to imply that individuals were responsible for, and in control of, their own way of life (behaviour), whereas all too often their way of life was governed by their environment and society (structure)…. It was important to decide which types of individual health-related behaviour and government or commercial activities should be regulated through legislation and which should be left to people's own decisions. It was also necessary for WHO to take a firm stand against possible pressures to deflect the Organisation from preventive policies.'[25] The RHDAC welcomed the proposal to have a programme on disability prevention and rehabilitation (one of Brian's favourite issues), as well as other traditional public health and preventative issues. The minutes are full of good intentions and 'tick-box' phrases about political commitment and educating the public.

The outcome of the meeting was a resolve to ensure that work done in the Regional Office on health indicators would be closely coordinated with the development of regional targets, and to work towards making the HFA2000 strategy a more effective tool for aligning national health programmes with 'a view to resolving common problems'. Yet there was already tacit recognition that some of the targets would be politically unattractive to some European countries, and that they would have to be revised, or diluted within a wider menu of pick and choose targets. The council did, however, agree to consult specialist groups such as the European Advisory Committee for Medical Research (EACMR) which might help to 'moderate' on the choice of targets, and to involve political scientists, psychologists and social scientists in the process.

In September 1981 Brian presented a progress report on the regional strategy for HFA2000 to the Regional Committee at its 31st session in Berlin. This listed the additional meetings that had been held: 'Possible contributions of sociology to EURO programme development', a 'Consultation on self-help and health' and a workshop on 'Research on health of the elderly'. It further discussed the task of target setting and the choice of relevant health indicators. Brian continued to chair regular meetings of the RHDAC and to represent it at WHO-EURO meetings, including the consultative groups on programme development and budgetary questions. The Regional Committee agreed to establish five working groups of 6–10 temporary advisers each, to deal with those areas of the HFA2000 strategy identified as suitable for target setting. The themes were: Health lifestyles, Reduced risks, Adequate care, Support measures, and Equity, which Brian was asked to coordinate.

The intention was that Brian's Equity Working Group would cut across the other themes to try to answer the question 'How to do it *for all*'. The Equity Group first met in London in June 1982. It included representatives from Hungary, France, Portugal, Sweden, Italy, Turkey and Germany, with Zöllner from the WHO-EURO office. As expected, the group discussed key targets around access to healthcare, and specific issues around children, women, the elderly, socially deprived groups and people with functional restrictions due to ill health (chronic sick, mentally ill, disabled and handicapped). The group also discussed the frequency at which progress towards targets should be measured, whether at national or regional level, and how targets should be refined. Göran Dahlgren, the Swedish representative on the working group, recalls that they initially suggested there should be an integrated equality dimension for most of the targets. This was rejected and they had to formulate one single equity target for the whole European HFA strategy, without any time for in-depth analyses. This became one of the very first targets of the strategy: by the year 2000, the actual gap in health states between countries and between groups should be reduced by at least 25 per cent.[26]

Alongside his involvement with WHO-EURO, Brian took on other HFA2000 commitments. In March 1983 he was seconded to WHO South East Asia as a consultant to help prepare the inter-country seminar on financial planning for HFA2000. This was attended by 17 participants from eight South East Asian countries, along with agency staff from UNDP, UNICEF, USAID, Asian Development Bank (ADB) and WHO. It discussed the concerns around the impact of inflation on the health sector. He also continued to be involved with the International Social Security Association (ISSA), attending its Asian Regional Roundtable meeting on the extension of medical care programmes under social security in Seoul, South Korea, in April 1983 which took priority over the RHDAC meeting in Copenhagen. In his absence this reviewed progress and agreed that clearer wording was needed rather than phrases such as 'reducing by half' for various mortality or morbidity rates. Again, the language of the minutes is tentative and vague: 'The RHDAC felt that there should be a sound mixture of future dreams and today's realities in setting the targets ...'.[27] Yet there was still disagreement on the number of targets included in the regional strategy, and the sequencing of the document sections. Some members felt that the section on lifestyles was 'somewhat long'. The

Council got as far as agreeing that the regional targets may not be able to be set until 1984, but stressed that all documents should be treated as preliminary, pending further analysis of epidemiological data and further research on how to improve methods by which countries might reach the targets. When Brian returned from Seoul he made a trip to Copenhagen in May to finalise the targets document. This was then sent to the Consultative Group on Programme Development. There was not much that could be achieved at the 33rd session of the Regional Committee in Madrid in September 1983 other than re-endorsing the need for countries to 'continue to analyse, develop and reorient their national health strategies'.

HFA2000: health, wealth and health economics

Parallel to these target-setting working groups there was a drive to stimulate research on the links between poverty and health, especially the effects of unemployment. By the 1980s there was a clear 'hub' of expert advisers, most of whom had followed a similar career trajectory, from a PhD in Health or Development Economics, followed by an academic position and then secondment to an international organisation. Ted Marmor calls them 'in and outers', and Brian is a pre-eminent example. Understanding their function, loyalties and motivations is key to understanding the 'globalisation' of health policy.[28]

The WHO-EURO Study Group on the Influence of Economic Development in Health held a second meeting at Munich in September 1981. Brian helped Raymond Illsley put together the WHO-EURO consultation on poverty, unemployment and health, which was held at the Medical Research Council's Medical Sociology Unit at Aberdeen in November 1982. Brian agreed to present a paper at the Aberdeen meeting, drawing on his pioneering work with Peter Townsend in the 1960s: 'The differential meanings of poverty and their relation to health', but was pessimistic about the chances of finding data or speakers on poverty for European countries that equalled the British expertise. He told Illsley how the EEC had struggled to put together its nine national reports on poverty, and that his request to Leo Crijns (Director of the EEC's Social Security Division) had also drawn a blank. As a compromise he suggested inviting Professor Giovanni Sarpellon from Venice to give a paper on the non-British perspective, and perhaps inviting the Chief Medical Officer for Algeria who 'is always talking about the relationship between poverty and health at WHO meetings … to put some flesh on his constant emphasis on the connection'.[29] Despite Brian's pessimism, the Aberdeen meeting produced some good discussions and papers. Roy Carr-Hill and Mildred Blaxter's briefing paper, 'Indicators of Health, Poverty and their Joint Variation', drew on Blaxter's cutting-edge research from the 1970s, which had rebutted Keith Joseph's damaging 'Cycle of deprivation' concept.[30] They highlighted the long heritage of 'social indicators', contrary to the health economist Tony Culyer's hypothesis.[31]

The WHO Study Group on the Influence of Economic Development on Health had commissioned a research project in 1981 from Professor Harvey Brenner at the School of Hygiene and Public Health at Johns Hopkins University in the US, 'The influence of economic instability on health in Europe'. His pilot project, using linear multiple regression analysis to link health status and health risk variables for France and Sweden, had shown that countries could in fact reach the HFA2000 targets if broad action was taken on all fronts. But the methodology was problematical for rolling out region-wide. Zöllner involved Brian in meetings to discuss what to do about the 'Brenner problem'. At an informal discussion at the Regional Office in April 1984, following the fourth meeting of the RHDAC which reviewed the revised (and reduced) regional HFA2000 targets, it was agreed that Brenner's methodology was only one possible solution, and that there needed to be clearer discussion on empirical support for the HFA2000 targets.

An implicit assumption of the HFA2000 discussions, at global, regional and national levels was that money would have to be found to pay for projects linked to the chosen 12 targets. Although there was extensive discussion on the choice of the targets and indictors, there were less well-coordinated initiatives to discuss the economic impact of this strategy to prioritise primary healthcare. The lack of interest in this critical aspect is evidenced by the small numbers of economists actually working on the HFA2000 strategy. Although the WHO's use of health economics had become more sophisticated, it was still inadequate. The WHO projects undertaken in the 1960s had not routinely had economists as team members, and some economists had produced unworkable methodologies.[32] In 1973 WHO appointed its first full-time economist. Ralph Andreano, who was on leave from the University of Wisconsin, and who was selected by Mahler and Ken Newell. Brian made a point of going to introduce himself soon after Andreano's arrival in Geneva, and to offer assistance and advice on how to exploit this opportunity.[33] The HFA2000 target that countries should be looking to spend 5 per cent of their GNP on health services brought health economics into sharp focus. Yet the WHO had only one economist at its Geneva headquarters with responsibilities for the

HFA2000 programme (on a two-year appointment), and only one of the five WHO Regional Offices responsible for developing countries employed a health economist.

Since the 1970s, however, both developed and developing countries had been forced to respond to the concern that spending on health – both primary and secondary care – appeared to be on an unstoppable upward trajectory. Governments had already begun to look for ways to place some limit on their healthcare budgets. Brian was closely involved with such debates at an international level. In 1973 he had participated in the WHO inter-regional seminar on health economics, presenting a paper: 'Basic Concepts: Macro-Economic Aspects of Health Care'. A number of organisations were established at this time that were commissioning studies of healthcare. Most of these had strong national biases, owing to their funding sources and staff allegiances, but there were increasing attempts to give their outputs an international value. Brian was a fellow of the Institute for European Health Services Research, based at Leuven University in Belgium. In 1974 he participated in a study with André Prims, Professor of Hospital Administration at the University of Leiden, on hospital legislation and organisation in the nine EEC countries. In 1975 he worked with Jef van Langendonk and Jan Blanpain on a study of the relationship between national health insurance and health resources development, which was commissioned by the US Department of Health, Education and Welfare. Simone Sandier, at the Centre de Recherche, d'Études et de Documentation en Économie de la Santé (CREDES) in Paris, collaborated with Brian on several projects, including a comparative study on the remuneration of GPs commissioned by the German government. When Sandier moved to work for the OECD she continued to turn to Brian for advice and information.

Brian's 1976 book, *Value for Money in Health Services* resonated with health economists with similar interests, such as Alain Enthoven, who delivered the Shattuck Lecture in 1978 on the theme of 'Cutting cost without cutting the quality of care'.[34] Enthoven had asked his Stanford colleague Count Gibson for an introduction to Brian, so that he could spend some time in London researching British healthcare financing. In March 1979 Brian and Enthoven both attended the international sharing health costs seminar held at the Wolfsberg Management Centre in Switzerland, at which Enthoven spoke on 'Health care cost control through incentives and competition', and Brian was the rapporteur.[35] The seminar was organised by the National Center for Health Services Research. This was a US government programme established in 1968 through the efforts of Paul Sanazaro and Evelyn Flook, with support from Philip R. Lee, Assistant Secretary for Health in the Johnson Administration, Kerr White and a number other of influential individuals.[36] White had been on the landmark WHO Expert Committee on Health Statistics in 1970 which had usefully refined the definitions of 'efficiency', 'effectiveness' and 'efficacy' in healthcare.[37]

Brian had been a member of the WHO Expert Advisory Panel on the Organisation of Medical Care since 1976, a role he fulfilled through renewals until 1985. He also participated in smaller, but equally effective networks. One of these was the Council for International Organisations of the Medical Sciences (CIOMS). This had been formed in Geneva in 1949 as a collaboration between WHO and UNESCO and had some 55 international scientific member organisations, including the Sandoz Institute. CIOMS advised on a wide range of issues, including bioethics, health policy, drug development and use, and maintained the International Nomenclature of Diseases. Brian had first attended a CIOMS roundtable (on medical care and society) in Rio in 1974. In November 1979 he participated in the CIOMS roundtable conference in Geneva on economics and health policy. Archie Cochrane had also attended, paying his own way, which entitled him to complain to the organisers afterwards about the unsatisfactory discussions he had heard there.

In 1979 Brian also published, with Alan Maynard, a study for the Commission of the European Communities, *The organisation, financing and cost of health care in the European Community*.[38] This explored the increasing pressures placed on national budgets by rising costs since 1961. In their comparative study of Belgium, Denmark, Germany, Ireland, France, Italy, Luxembourg, the Netherlands and the UK they hoped to elicit which policies were effective in restraining costs. They highlighted that despite the diversity of national experiences, there were some shared themes on which a useful understanding of factors influencing healthcare budgets could be built.

Brian had provided the backbone for such national comparative analyses through his pioneering work for the Guillebaud enquiry into the cost of the NHS in 1956, which led to his appointment by the WHO later that year to lead the first project to develop a system of national health accounting (NHA).[39] He continued to refine NHA methodologies, and to collaborate with colleagues undertaking similar exercises. His role as 'grandfather' of NHAs has slipped from health economists' memories. However, Jean-Pierre Poullier, who is more usually given credit for their creation, acknowledged Brian's role in a letter to him in 1982 when sending him the latest OECD data: 'This work owed much to your studies for WHO and the International Community has to be grateful to you for launching quite a few people on that track, but after several months of work on health accounts – my feeling is that we are still a decade or more away from genuine international comparisons. The work being sent to you is thus only an intermediary product.'[40]

Making a Financial Master Plan

In 1981 Brian was asked by Edward Mach, from the Division of Strengthening of Health Services at WHO headquarters in Geneva, if he would advise on a new edition of the 1978 manual, *The Economic Basis of Health Programmes*. New draft sections had been written on explaining health policies, reasons for undertaking financial studies, methods of data collection on health expenditure, how to analyse data in relation to policy objectives and recommendations on financial planning. Brian was blunt in his response. Although he praised Mach for the greatly improved text and addition of tables, he found it 'a forbidding document. The style is heavy and academic with long and complex sentences. I now feel the volume needs tough editing, not just to improve the English, though this is needed, but to make the presentation easier to grasp using a crisper style.... I do not think this can be done simply by a professional editor.... Someone who really knows what they are doing could knock this into shape within a week of work and make it much more likely to be used by those at whom it is aimed.'[41] Brian of course anticipated Mach's response: would Brian be willing to edit it?

The contract for editing *The Economic Basis of Health Programmes – An Experimental Manual for Studying Financing and Expenditure of the Health Sector in Developing Countries* was signed in March 1982, for a fee of US$2,000. Brian put far more effort into the editing than he had anticipated. He wrote to Mach in April:

> I am afraid [Brian's favourite expression to impart unwelcome news] that the changes I am proposing are fundamental. You will see that I have taken the liberty of rewriting what are now chapters II, III and VII.... After a lot of heart searching I have come to the view that your chapter II cannot stay in the main text and must sadly be relegated to an Appendix ... it does not illustrate what we want to show [again, note the use of 'we'].... Most important of all you will note the suggested new title – Making a Master Financial Plan [sic]. Need we go on being so

tentative and apologetic? If the [HFA2000] strategy says that there ought to be a Master Plan, then no one else is suggesting how countries should do it.... Don't ring me up and tell me off for <u>ruining</u> your manual until you have put it in a drawer for few days and read it through a second time. <u>Some</u> of what I have done <u>may</u> then seem a logical development. Or have I thrown both of us into the jaws of some rival division concerned with planning who will bite our heads off and kill our manual rather than have us trespass on <u>their</u> territory. Obviously this letter cannot go on a registered file. But I am inclined to think that Dr Mahler himself would rather like the revision if he were not stopped from ever seeing it by some rival camp![42]

There was a postscript, carefully placed at the bottom of the page as if a genuine afterthought: 'If by any chance you like what I have done, you might consider joint authorship. I have rewritten nearly half the book and perhaps the most important parts.' There is no reply from Mach in Brian's archives, but their continuing friendship suggests that Mach accepted the editing in good faith. Their joint book, with the new title *Planning the Finances of the Health Sector*, was published by WHO in 1984.[43] Brian had further ruffled feathers by reprinting some teaching materials that had been jointly developed by the Botswana Ministry of Health and the Sandoz Institute. Adrian Griffiths, an economist at the Sandoz Institute, took exception to the way in which it had not been given full credit, and also because the Abel-Smith/Mach manual competed with Sandoz's own sponsored manual which had just been published, *Money for Health: A manual for surveys in developing countries*, which he had edited with Michael Mills.[44]

Mach and Brian collaborated again on a special issue of the *World Health Statistics Quarterly* devoted to health costs and financing, published in 1984. They solicited articles on the European cost containment study from Zöllner, and on the WHO's past and future work in health economics from A. Kühner (their co-editor). Other WHO divisions were asked to provide articles on how their programmes linked with health economics, and Häkan Hellberg was approached for a paper assessing experience with global indicators in the first round of reporting progress towards HFA2000. The papers were designed to 'not merely be interesting', but to discuss problems and solutions in different parts of the world, including country case studies from the USSR, Colombia, Malawi, Sri Lanka and China. David de Ferranti from The World Bank was asked to contribute a paper. Brian wrote the concluding article, drawing out lessons from the other contributions.[45]

The WHO belatedly re-activated the Health Economics Programme which it had formed in 1978. A meeting of the Advisory Committee was held at Funchal, Madeira, in October 1983, with 22 experts from 18 countries. Brian was elected as Chair. It recommended much greater involvement of economists at all levels and stages of WHO-EURO work, especially on HFA2000. It also identified a need for training activities in health economics (in collaboration with the programme on health manpower development). It proposed running courses to 'train the trainers' to ensure that the importance of health economics was understood by all involved in policy making. A number of potential new projects were identified: research into the economics of nutrition; economic assessment of medical technologies; and economic aspects of medical demography. Collaboration with the programme on health planning and evaluation and the programme on information systems was also proposed, and a new study on cost containment policies. The Committee also discussed target 78 of HFA2000 – that 5 per cent of GNP should be spent on healthcare. It was agreed that this target should remain, but be more carefully monitored. Health economics needed a greater representation at the Regional Office to achieve this.

A direct outcome of the Madeira meeting was a request from Zöllner to Brian in May 1984 to help develop a training course in health economics. He was asked to review existing materials, and advise on the content of teaching units which could be put together to customise courses for different client groups. This would support the work of the study group being coordinated by Antonio Brenna at the Institute for Health Economics Research at Milan, and to build on the study group working papers already circulated by Greg Stoddart (McMaster University, Canada) and Antonio Brenna, as well as the learning packages of the WHO training workshops. These had been put together by Gavin Mooney and Michael Drummond (1982 course – English), and by Jean Sabatini and Gérard Duru (1984 course – French). Zöllner had already selected a number of health economists to lead on developing learning modules: Steve Engleman from the University of Edinburgh was leading on the relationship between the health sector and the economy; Ralph Andreano of the University of Wisconsin, Madison, on health policy implementation and performance; Frans Rutten of the University of Limburg, Maastricht, on harmonisation of consumer and provider interests; Michael Drummond of the University of Birmingham on priority setting and strategy selection; and Juan Rovira Forns of the University of Barcelona on equity, equality and reduction of status differentials. Each module would contain a small number of units that provided a set of illustrative cases and defined exercises for students, reference material, a short write-up of the key messages and suggestions for teaching methods.

Through the 1980s Brian regularly accepted invitations to speak and advise on aspects of health economics, especially on how it linked to HFA2000 and related issues. In June 1981 he lectured on the first international course on 'Education for health services administration', held in Lisbon. He was also actively involved in advising countries on how to finance healthcare delivery systems. He was contracted by WHO to spend a fortnight in Sri Lanka in December 1981, returning for a month during the summer of 1982. In 1983 he made two trips to India in the spring (returning ill from the first one, which required emergency admission to St Thomas' Hospital in London). He presented a paper, 'Economic Efficiency and Health Care Delivery', at an ISSA research meeting at Turku in Finland in September 1982.[46] Following the ISSA meeting in Seoul in April 1983, Brian travelled to Greece, Israel and Portugal, and then spent a month of the summer in Indonesia as a WHO consultant on health services development, conducting a health financing policy and practice review, returning there in December to advise on the expansion of health insurance coverage, and again for two substantial trips in the spring and summer of 1984.

In 1986 Brian was invited by Julio Frenk to join the Advisory Panel for the Centre for Public Health Research that had been established in Mexico in 1984 (re-established as the National Institute of Public Health of Mexico in 1987). This had been enabled by the change of government in 1982 and the appointment of an enlightened Minister of Health who was keen to reform Mexico's health systems. Frenk saw Brian as 'the father of health economics' and was delighted that he accepted the invitation and was willing to travel to Mexico in early summer each year for the group meetings. Brian and Anne Mills, from the London School of Hygiene and Tropical Medicine (LSHTM), helped to develop the country's first programme in health economics and conducted the first study on healthcare financing, which had a direct influence on Mexico's decision to introduce universal coverage. Equally significant was the encouragement he gave to Mexican students to travel to take courses at the LSHTM, and to return to share their knowledge in Mexico. For Frenk and his staff, Brian's annual visits were eagerly anticipated and enjoyed by all. He could be 'extraordinarily excitable' about projects and brought a valuable wider intellectual perspective to their activities.[47] Brian always tried to find a few extra days on these trips to travel into the countryside, keen to experience

Mexican culture and especially to see the plants, and his appointment was renewed several times, until 1992.

In November 1984 Brian agreed to go to the South East Asia Regional Office in New Delhi to participate in a conference, and to gain an update on what the region's countries had done to 'promote realistic financial plans for health for all', with the request 'for a booking preferably at Claridge's hotel as I am a swimming addict'.[48] He returned the following month to attend the fifth annual conference of the Indian Society of Health Administrators, where he gave a paper: 'Global Perspectives in Health Care Financing'. He also published a version of this paper in the journal *Social Science & Medicine*.[49] His chapter in the book *Financial Planning for HFA2000* illustrates the messianic role he saw for himself and the HFA2000 Financial Master Plan he had helped to create:

> It is a custom in the Christian religion to start a talk by referring to a section of the Bible, our holy book. Thus I will begin with a quotation from the WHO holy book – the *Global Strategy for Health For All by the Year 2000*: 'Ministries of Health will present to their governments a master plan for the use of all financial and material resources'.... The crucial thing here is the words 'master plan'. The word 'master' covers everything which has a relation to health. Further, notice the use of the word 'all' financial and material resources, ie not just from the Ministry of Health, but also from other government departments, voluntary health insurance, private sector, external aid, etc. Similarly, notice the subtlety of all financial and 'material' resources, and not just money....[50]

Some 20 countries took up the WHO's first call to establish financial master plans, and were helped to cost their plans as part of what were called 'country resource utilisation reviews'. However, many of the cost projection plans lacked credibility because of the haste with which they were put together and the lack of data on existing expenditures. Some countries struggled even to estimate what percentage of GDP was currently spent on health services, and naïvely assumed that holes in their budgets would be filled by foreign donors. The world economic crisis of the early 1980s, following on from the oil shocks of the 1970s (which affected the debt loads of developing countries far more than those of industrialised countries) stymied many nascent financial master plans. There was a fall in GDP and living standards in most Latin American and sub-Saharan African countries. Even in Europe and North America there was a massive increase in unemployment.

Problems with high interest rates and devaluation made debt charges an unbearable strain on government budgets, and many developing countries found themselves with between a third and a half of their export earnings being sucked up in this way. The only option was to cut public expenditure on services such as healthcare, and to cut imports of medicines and equipment. In some African countries extensive drought exacerbated already weakened economies. They began to lose faith in Health for All, at least by the year 2000. It was suggested that the year 2100 might be more appropriate.[51] Despite these set-backs, planning for HFA2000 continued.

Brian also remained engaged with other WHO HFA2000 initiatives. Target 32 required member states to 'formulate research strategies to stimulate investigations that improve the application and expansion of knowledge needed to support their Health for All development'. This was addressed through the creation of the European Research Action Plan (ERAP), coordinated at Ulm University in Germany by K. Gerdes and S. Biefang, and overseen by Hannu Vuori, Chief of Research Promotion and Development at WHO-EURO. Brian was on the editorial sub-committee for ERAP, along with T. Fliedner, Z. Pisa and Margaret Stacey. They helped to produce the first volume of *Research for Health for All* (RHFA), on research policy, which was sent to the European Advisory Committee on Medical Research who were preparing the second volume on research needs and actions.

Special adviser to Mahler

The preceding sections have shown that HFA2000 meant different things to different audiences, and had a wide variety of responses. The aim to establish strategies at national, regional and global levels that were interrelated and fed off the same set of targets was hugely ambitious, and opened up more fundamental dichotomies – of funding sources and project priorities. Brian had been at the centre of so many of these separate yet parallel initiatives since the announcement of HFA2000 in 1979 that he had built up a good working relationship with the WHO's Director General, Halfdan Mahler. It was no surprise then when he was invited in September 1984 to join Mahler's Geneva-based staff for a short consultancy in the spring of 1985. This had to be agreed with Ralf Dahrendorf, Director of the LSE, so that Brian could take a sabbatical for the Lent term from his teaching commitments, as he had done in the 1960s and 1970s when employed as a special adviser to British Labour governments, and when he worked with the EEC. After he secured Dahrendorf's permission, Brian began to discuss his aims and objectives with Mahler. His title was to be Senior Consultant and Advisor to work up a new project that had the 'somewhat uninformative' title 'Economic Strategies to Support the Strategy of Health for All'.[52]

Working in collaboration with Häkan Hellberg, Director of the Health for All Strategy Coordination Programme in Mahler's office, Brian planned a series of research trips to investigate the practicalities of designing and implementing HFA2000 at country level, based on the first pilot group of countries to produce financial master plans – Sweden, Finland, the Netherlands, Indonesia, Zimbabwe and Costa Rica. In February 1985 he spent 10 days in Zimbabwe, assisting with their National Health Insurance Scheme. He then travelled to Washington DC to visit The World Bank, where he met with David de Ferranti. Brian congratulated de Ferranti on the quality of The World Bank Health Sector Review, and learned that because some of the teams had not included an economist, the financial side had not been properly addressed. They discussed the new WHO strategy for promoting financial master plans (initiated by Brian and Edward Mach), and the provisional selection of countries to trial them. De Ferranti recommended Jordan because of the work done there by Godfrey Walker and Anne Mills (of LSHTM) for the UK Department for International Development (DFID). They talked through what was happening in a number of developing countries: in China, pilot insurance schemes were selecting villages from poor and rich counties, but they had not yet decided whether they would be voluntary or compulsory; in Malawi, the government had not welcomed the advice they had been given to simplify and reduce the health service charges, or the introduction of charges for curative services; in Pakistan, as a result of a study, the fee schedule had been changed; and in Indonesia, The World Bank had financed the Volpatti study, para-medical manpower development, nutrition surveillance and long-term manpower development, and Brian was able to provide de Ferranti with an update on Indonesia's health insurance scheme. The World Bank reviews of Brazil, Morocco, Costa Rica and Colombia had all led to policy recommendations, and Brian was given a copy of the Brazilian and Costa Rican working papers.

At the USAID offices Brian met with Anne Tait for an update on their study of health financing in Honduras, as well as their studies in Egypt, Lebanon and Kenya. In Indonesia staff from Johns Hopkins University had been helping to strengthen public health education. They discussed potential centres for developing health economics training, including the University of the West Indies, which already offered courses on the subject, and the University of Hawaii. Brian reported back to

Mahler that USAID were keen to jointly finance WHO projects such as conferences and case studies, especially studies that identified unit costs. He agreed to send his recent papers on Zimbabwe to Mike Mills (in confidence).

The meeting at PAHO (Pan-American Health Organisation, the name for the WHO American Region, based in Washington DC) discussed the selection of pilot countries for the financial master plan project. While the potential for Costa Rica was accepted, PAHO staff felt that it would not carry much weight as an example for other countries of the region. Many countries were ruled out because of the formidable rates of inflation, the overwhelming problem of crisis management of the health sector, or because of political problems. The possibilities were Brazil after it had settled down to its new government, or Peru after the August elections. The timing was thought inappropriate for Uruguay, but Colombia, Mexico and Argentina might also be considered. PAHO staff had completed the study of Uruguay's 1982 data and there were ongoing studies in Peru and Argentina. Brian was given an update on efforts to coordinate training in health planning and financing in schools of public health. He was asked if he would be available in September to return to PAHO and assist with developing guidelines for health economics teaching. From Washington DC Brian travelled on to Costa Rica at the request of their government, and proposed a new capitation payment system to help save money in urban areas for redeployment to rural areas.

In his assignment progress report of 21 March 1985 Brian was able to outline an impressive set of achievements over the previous three months. In addition to visiting the Netherlands, Indonesia, Zimbabwe and Costa Rica, and providing very practical help as discussed above, he had advised the United Arab Emirates on cost containment, written a second draft of the Executive Board briefing paper on economic strategies in support of the HFA, arranged the curriculum for a three-week course on health sector financing at the LSE/LSHTM for spring 1986 and had planned a parallel French-speaking course.[53] His WHO progress report exemplifies his thoroughness and enthusiasm:

> I have checked on the shockingly poor information developing countries sent in on percentage of GNP spent on health services for the monitoring exercise. I am working with HST [Health Situation and Trend, a WHO division] to make sure that their data in the evaluation exercise is properly monitored by HQ and compared with other sources of data.… Policy Implications for WHO: The Global Strategy can be read as implying that you

cannot have HFA unless you spend 5 per cent of GNP on the health sector and that the North will pay for any financial gaps in the South, if a good enough case is made. Should the new thrust be that HFA is possible if you redeploy your own resources and tap every possible source of internal finance as well as taking what external support you can get? Organisational Implications for WHO: If financial planning catches on, WHO will need: (1) to strengthen its capability to support it both in HQ and Regional Offices so as to be able to respond quickly and flexibly to country requests; (2) to increase its credibility in this field of work (eg compared to the World Bank); (3) to be seen to speak with a single voice and to have coordinated all relevant activities – integrating financial planning with health resource mobilization and the management process for National Health Development. In specific terms, I would suggest: (1) that the overlap in work between HSC and SHS needs to be clarified with a definite line of demarcation of responsibilities; (2) that reports on country resource utilisation (CRU's) are made as high a quality in this field as the World Bank Health Sector Reviews. To do this every team would need an expert on health finance and reports will need tougher editing. Wouldn't it make sense for World Bank Sector Reviews and CRUs to be done as a joint exercise by the two organisations? (3) that teaching on the management process extends into issues of affordability and sources of finance and pursues these issues at depth on top of the specialised health financing training effort.[54]

Brian's paper, 'Economic Strategies to Support the Strategy for HFA project', was a main item for discussion at the WHO Executive Board in January 1986 and then at the World Health Assembly in May 1986. The following year it progressed as a technical discussion at the Assembly. Brian's work with Mahler's team had facilitated getting HFA2000 back on track, through a systematic analysis of how pilot countries were faring. He had demonstrated through his field visits in 1985 that there were obvious (and avoidable) dangers. Some countries were training expensive medical staff who they could not afford to employ; expensive buildings such as hospitals were not properly costed, or money diverted from primary care to cover their running costs; there may be trained staff and buildings, but insufficient supplies of medicines, or petrol to distribute them; and plans were not looking far enough into the future. Despite this gloomy assessment, Brian could see possible solutions: encouraging non-profit organisations to provide services, introducing modest charges for drugs and levying charges at urban centres to pay for rural services. Most significantly, it made him re-evaluate the merits of compulsory health insurance.

By the time he wrote his chapter for George Teeling-Smith's 1987 edited book *Health Economics: Prospects for the Future*, Brian was able to provide a much more positive assessment of the use of health economics within the WHO. He noted the transition: 'In the early days of cost benefit analysis when some health economists had arrogantly assumed that all that mattered was the economic benefits of health programmes – lost earnings as against direct costs of health intervention – the subject was not surprisingly given a cool reception in Geneva.'[55] He identified 1983 as the point at which financial planning at the macro level had moved to centre stage at WHO (the year he and Mach had published their manual on health economics parallel to the Griffiths and Mills manual). His experiences over the previous four years had been critical in helping him to push the message of the value of health economics:

> Beneath all the rhetoric, the Health for All programme is essentially about the application of health economics to health policy making. The problem is how a society can maximise health out of limited resources and secure the equitable distribution of health benefits…. Health economists will only be accepted in the long run in the WHO, Health Ministries and health insurance agencies if they have the humility to accept that they still have much to learn.[56]

Health promotion

In September 1985, the WHO-EURO adopted a proposal for a campaign to promote HFA. This was to consist of three components: increased awareness of HFA2000 among different audiences; promoting the development of HFA policy and programmes in member states; and promotion of 'concerted actions' throughout Europe in selected HFA target areas. At the fifth annual meeting of the RHDAC held in Copenhagen in April 1986, Brian's team proposed that the first target to be developed into a concerted action should be 'tobacco', linked to target 16 on positive health behaviour. This supported Mahler's report on tobacco to the WHO Executive Board in October 1985. The proposal was endorsed at the Regional Committee meeting in Copenhagen in September 1986, which also proposed a HFA charter, linked to a European-wide health promotion campaign, to be developed 'stepwise' during 1986–88, to stimulate discussions on health and health policy.

Parallel to these European developments were global initiatives. The outcome of a conference in November 1986 was the Ottawa Charter for Health Promotion. This was sub-titled 'The move towards a new public health'. Its main author was Ilona Kickbusch who led the WHO's Global Health Promotion Programme (and who had been WHO-EURO Regional Director for Health Promotion). She had sent Brian an earlier confidential draft of her document: 'Health Promotion: to put an idea into action' for his comments in 1984. The Ottawa Charter specifically linked to the Alma Ata Declaration, the HFA2000 strategy, and to recent discussions at the World Health Assembly on intersectoral action for health. It was based on a vision of health that saw people as active participants in their own well-being. The Charter used key phrases, which were to underpin public health philosophy for the next generation: building healthy public policy, reorienting health services, creating supportive environments, strengthening community action and developing personal skills. It required three basic actions: to enable, mediate and advocate. A second international conference on health promotion, held in Adelaide in April 1988, focused on identifying practical ways in which public policies might be coordinated in health-promoting ways. It refined the concept of health promotion to include the vision that the potential health impact of all public policies must be considered, and that a concern for equity and government accountability should be central to all public policy. These ideas had first been aired in the work of academics such as Nancy Milio in her 1981 book *Promoting Health through Public Policy*, and the work of Trevor Hancock in Toronto, who is credited with inventing the term 'healthy public policy' in the early 1980s.[57] Hancock had been the brains behind a conference in Toronto in 1984 which inspired the 'Healthy Cities' project, launched by WHO-EURO in 1986.

HFA2000: targets and assessments

The WHO-EURO HFA2000 selection of targets was a tortuous exercise, especially for Brian's RHDAC. It culminated in 1985 in the adoption of 38 targets. These included:

1. By the year 2000, people should have better opportunity to develop and use their health potential to live socially and economically fulfilling lives.

2. By the year 2000, disabled people will have the physical, social and economic opportunities to use to the full their capabilities for a socially and economically productive life.
3. By the year 2000, the actual gap in health states between countries and between groups should be reduced by at least 25 per cent.
4. By the year 2000, the average number of years that people live free from major diseases and disability should be increased by at least 10 per cent.
5. By the year 2000, there should be no indigenous measles, poliomyelitis, neonatal tetanus, congenital rubella, diphtheria, congenital syphilis or indigenous malaria in the region.
6. By the year 2000, life expectancy at birth in the region should be at least 75 years.
7. By the year 2000, infant mortality in the region should be less than 20 per 1,000 live births.

Some governments were more willing than others to engage with the WHO's HFA2000 initiative. Britain's Conservative government, led between 1979 and 1990 by Margaret Thatcher, was not one of them. They were notoriously resistant to any policy initiatives that touched on 'inequalities', to the extent that the term had been replaced by 'variations in health' in all government publications and correspondence. Civil servants were not allowed to mention the Black Report, the seminal study on British health inequalities that had been quashed by the incoming Conservative government in 1979, but which demonstrated in very blunt terms that ill health was strongly associated with poverty and provided a list of policy solutions. Few of these ideas had been followed through.[58] At the November 1983 WHO conference on 'Primary health care in industrialised countries', held in Bordeaux, the official British line was that broadly all such problems had been sorted out. Depressingly, this appeared to be a common nationalistic trend. Brian, irritated by these dubious official pronouncements which were a trait of international conferences, presented the data that his British civil servant colleagues dared not: that babies were twice as likely to die in the first month of life if they were born in social class V (working class) as those born in social class I; that this inequality continued right through life in Britain – those in social class V were two-and-a-half times more likely to die before they reached 65 than those in social class I. Jill Turner, a health journalist and friend of Brian's, captured his thinly-veiled sarcasm:

It was not, indeed, that Professor Abel-Smith wanted to wash Britain's dirty linen in public: he simply wanted to ask other countries whether their linen was really so clean. One after another, countries in the eastern bloc announced that they had eradicated various diseases, including venereal diseases. One after another, the delegations from western Europe reported that they had de-medicalised primary care…. France kept talking about its success in integration [of primary and secondary care], then showed delegates around a hospital so isolated, so dehumanised and so empty of patients that one wit remarked that their community prevention policies were clearly highly efficient! It was all very far removed from the 'bottom-up' approach to action in the health care system that Professor Abel-Smith advocated. Not only should money and manpower be distributed according to need, he suggested, but the *best* people should be attracted to provide community care in the *most needy* areas. Health professionals should be trained to communicate better with the less articulate users, make their services more accessible and to search out those in need in their homes…. 'Can we really hope to educate and change behaviours when we have taken away from people so much responsibility for health by making them dependent on the health care system, rather than partners in the struggle for health?'[59]

A year later, the British position had not changed. Brian spoke at the TUC's 1985 conference on HFA2000. He heard there from Nigel Lee, Chair of Nottingham's Policy and Resources (Health) Committee, of how he and Michael Meacher had resorted to putting parliamentary questions to the Minister of Health to gain information on what the Thatcher government had submitted to the WHO as the British HFA2000 plan. The response was that, five years after it had been requested to develop a plan, the government were 'still considering how the WHO's strategy for achieving health for all may best be drawn to the attention of the NHS and other interested authorities and organisations'.[60] Yet most other European countries were making progress with their plans, and some had already adopted the suggested indicators and targets. In Britain it was left to cities such as Liverpool and Nottingham to by-pass official government intransigence and develop their own HFA2000 plans.

Mahler was not blind to the weaknesses of comprehensive primary healthcare. He had been a constant critical friend to HFA2000 since its inception in 1980. In 1982 he voiced his concerns that the WHO was spreading its efforts too thinly, that it was 'still looking for other magic words to solve our problems, and listening to the ad hoc advice of well-meaning supporters and not so well-meaning adversaries'.[61] In 1983 he talked about 'red herrings' such as single-issue disease campaigns that diverted effort from the HFA focus. He used his address to the World Health Assembly in 1986 as an opportunity to reflect on what had happened since HFA2000's launch in 1980:

> … we find ourselves up to our necks in verbal mud, fighting all sorts of conceptual alligators eagerly poised to eat us alive. We are told that health for all is an empty slogan, an unrealistic dream based on romantic ethics, and that primary care is too unwieldy a vehicle to reach that ideal; that health for all strategies are not as cheap as we thought, and that in any event we have chosen the wrong time to launch our initiatives because of widespread financial crisis; that there is no way of modifying the pattern of resource allocation within the health sector and between it and other sectors; that it will take a whole generation to modify the attitude of the medical profession, and that non-professional health workers do not inspire the confidence of people; that health activities are a mere consumption of resources and do not contribute to social and economic development; and that governments are only pretending to be faithful to the principles of the Alma Ata declaration, while in reality they are setting up primary health care projects as small additions to existing ministry of health structures in order not to rock the ministerial boat. The alternatives being proposed? There are as many as there are health theorists and pushers of vested interests, often jumping on the same primary care bandwagon that they seem so intent on derailing. So governments of developing countries are being confronted with all sorts of remotely concocted proposals to pursue other kinds of health activities – often presented with seductive promises in neat self-contained packets. The most gigantic slur of all is that we are afraid to evaluate what we are doing.[62]

Mahler went on highlight the achievements in the face of these criticisms – good evaluation by most countries, a higher level of political will to improve people's health. But the bigger ongoing problems of poor infrastructure, hunger and illiteracy were hindering progress; the spread of unhealthy lifestyles from the developed to the developing countries; the ageing population. Echoing Brian's words to the Bordeaux conference in 1983, Mahler reiterated what primary healthcare was all about – that it required people to be actively engaged, not passive recipients of healthcare from above. Self-reliance, for Mahler, was critical to the success of HFA2000, and he used his speech to warn of the dangers of organisations like his own WHO: 'Attempts by anybody outside the country to decide for people what health care they should have, however genuine the motives, attempts of that nature are nothing short of mis-guided neo-colonialism and have no place in primary health care.' He proposed a strengthened focus on leadership development for HFA, on management and on building up district infrastructures.

At the CIOMS conference 'Health manpower out of balance: Conflicts and prospects', held in Acapulco, Mexico in September 1986, Brian made his own assessment of the progress of HFA2000. His paper, 'Economic Implications of Health Manpower Imbalances', discussed how the worldwide economic crises of the early 1980s had thrown the HFA2000 agenda off course, and stressed the need to reduce the number of doctors trained, as well as shifting the emphasis of training towards preventive healthcare. He noted the reluctance of developing countries to 'move beyond the colonial legacy of curricula' and to devise courses more appropriate for their own healthcare needs. He also discussed the problem of international migration of medical manpower: 'A net loss of 50,000 doctors from the developing countries to the developed, even at the Canadian cost of educating a doctor, was a gift of 10 billion Canadian dollars from the poor to the rich.'

Yet underlying this problem was, according to Brian, a more fundamental issue. The training of large numbers of doctors was leading to high levels of unemployment. It would be better, he argued, to extend the Egyptian and Pakistani trials which converted medical schools into training schools for para-medicals – thus shifting the balance from expensive acute medical care to more efficient primary healthcare: 'Unless there is resolute action, the world faces the prospect of 150,000 to 250,000 unemployed doctors by the year 2000 – a wasteful mockery of Health for All.' He concluded with his favourite historical context agenda:

> Earlier plans were often made on the tacit assumption that if some ideal staffing pattern were established, the money would be bound to be made available to finance it. The developing countries are not short of demonstration projects and model health centres built to earlier specifications. The fact that these

models were never generalised demonstrates that they proved to be economically unrealistic. Let us hope that future generations accumulate no further graveyards stocked with good intentions. Economic realism must now be the order of the day.[63]

The following year, in July 1987, Brian was invited to participate as an International Labour Organisation (ILO) consultant in a joint ADB/ILO Social Security Department regional seminar on 'Health care financing', in Manila in the Philippines. He presented a joint paper with Ajay Dua: 'The Potential of Community Financing of the Health Sector in Developing Countries'.[64] They drew attention to the limitations as well as the potential for community financing, and the need to educate the public in its function – that financial participation was but one form of participation in the provision of healthcare. He used the week-long seminar as an opportunity to talk to the delegates from countries such as China, India and Burma about their successes and failures, and ongoing projects, which he found were increasingly being influenced by the dominant international institution: The World Bank.

The rise of The World Bank

From the mid-1970s The World Bank, founded in 1946 to assist post-war reconstruction, began to expand its interest in health.[65] It increasingly had more clout than the WHO: it dealt with Treasuries rather than Ministries of Health. It could persuade governments to invest in its favoured campaigns to control population growth and combat malnutrition, which it deemed the most effective route to economic development.[66] In contrast to the rise of The World Bank's influence, the WHO's influence appeared to be waning – mired by internal problems. The World Health Assembly froze its budget in 1982, and powerful donor countries such as the US withheld some of their contribution – a response to pressure from their domestic pharmaceutical companies who disliked the WHO Essential Drug Programme.[67]

Although there had been attempts to bring together Mahler with James Grant of UNICEF to discuss GOBI, especially by Carl E. Taylor (the founding father of international health at the Johns Hopkins School of Public Health), by 1988 the internal WHO discontent between the rival programmes of Comprehensive Primary Health Care and Selective Primary Health Care had become public.[68] In the same year, Mahler retired after 15 years at the head of the WHO, to be replaced by Hiroshi Nakajima, a Japanese expert in drug evaluations from the

WHO Western Pacific Regional Office in Manila.[69] His appointment was not supported by the Americans or several European and Latin American countries, and the WHO entered a decade of crisis.[70] One feature of this was the growth of extra-budgetary funding that came from multilateral agencies or 'donor' nations, which in turn expected a greater say in where their money was spent.[71] In 1986/87 the regular budget was US$543 million and the extra-budgetary funds totalled US$437 million. As Brown, Cueto and Fee put it, The World Bank 'moved confidently into the vacuum created by an increasingly ineffective WHO.... By 1990 the Bank's loans for health surpassed the total budget of WHO.'[72]

The World Bank's strategy (but never a formal 'policy', as Brian sometimes disingenuously stated) required that its loans to developing countries were an efficient use of resources and that country-level policy makers should evaluate private as well as public financing options. This, in effect, forced governments to reconsider their role in the provision of health and social welfare services. Developing countries that had previously emulated western (often British Imperial) state-funded systems, now found that they were being strongly urged to look to private companies for such services.[73]

There were several factors at play behind The World Bank's new-found interest in health. Part of the explanation lies with the dominance of economists and development strategists within its staff. Within national governments economists were also moving from traditional territories and taking an interest in areas such as health. In Latin America some governments in the 1980s viewed social security as more driven by macroeconomic policy than social policy.[74] Another significant factor in the rise of new ideology on health financing, both at The World Bank but also at other international organisations, was the ongoing global economic crisis, which put pressure on all governments, but especially those of developing countries, to reduce their expenditure on health and social welfare.

In 1985 David de Ferranti, with whom Brian had been liaising on the WHO's economic strategy for HFA2000, wrote a research paper for The World Bank: *Paying for Health Services in Developing Countries: an Overview*.[75] It discussed the Bank's options for funding healthcare through a variety of mechanisms, which included user fees/charges. This internal document was not intended to be taken as a public signal of a shift in World Bank policy.[76] Two years later, in 1987, Nancy Birdsall, who headed the Bank's research group on health, decided to publish a formal statement: *Financing Health Services in Developing Countries: An Agenda for Reform* (co-written with John Akin and David de

Ferranti, who had recently moved on to other duties within The World Bank). This clearly articulated the increasing pressure it placed on governments taking its loans to introduce user fees as a cost-recovery and cost-sharing mechanism.

The 1987 World Bank paper was linked to a collaboration between WHO and UNICEF called the Bamako Initiative, formally adopted at a meeting in Mali in 1987. This was a direct response to the impact of heavy debt loads and of structural adjustment programme cutbacks on health services in sub-Saharan African countries. It aimed at tempering 'cost recovery' from health service users by combining user fee initiatives with government subsidies and external financing. Only certain health service interventions would be subsidised, and the user fees generated were to be used at the local level for community investment. Although it was progressively rolled out to cover 33 developing countries, the long-term results were decidedly mixed. Reviews highlighted that it had not achieved the promised sustainability, failed to achieve its promise of greater female involvement in community development, and often allowed the countries to be 'flooded' with unnecessary pharmaceuticals.[77] There was general agreement that those who needed the Bamako Initiative the most – the rural poor – were actually left no better off.[78]

The Bank argued that user fees were affordable and expected by most users, and that they would improve access, efficiency and quality of care. Despite, however, recommending that there should be exemptions for the poorest users, subsequent reviews of such schemes illustrated that fees introduced significant barriers to care. Users were less willing than The World Bank anticipated to pay the fees, and there was a strong correlation between income levels and demand for fee-based health services.[79] In practice, countries did not introduce effective exemption policies for low-income users. This resulted in greater inequity – deterring those least able to pay.[80] Where user fees were introduced they resulted in a 40–50 per cent reduction in health service use, especially for adherence to long-term treatment regimes such as those for tuberculosis and HIV.[81] Reviews commissioned by The World Bank unsurprisingly found widespread verification of their user fee strategy.[82]

The Commission on Health Research for Development

There was, therefore, a clear need for an impartial, evidence-based review of effective healthcare policies for developing countries. In 1988 an independent commission was formed, with funding from major international organisations such as the Ford Foundation, to conduct a two-year study. Based in Boston, it had a panel of 12 international experts, who collected and reviewed over a thousand sets of evidence from workshops and hearings. Its lengthy report, *Health Research: Essential Link to Equity in Development*, was published in 1990 and triggered a three-year task force to investigate more specific issues. In 1993 this was replaced with a permanent Council on Health Research for Development (COHRED), as part of the UNDP.

Brian participated in the Commission's priorities for health economics research workshop held at the LSHTM in May 1988.[83] A version of his paper was subsequently published in the *Journal of Tropical Medicine and Hygiene*.[84] It is worth discussing his presented paper in detail, as it provides an excellent survey of how his thinking on healthcare for developing countries had matured, especially in the aftermath of implementing the HFA2000 strategy. Brian concluded that because of the ongoing worldwide economic crisis – which had forced brutal plans of 'structural adjustment' on most developing countries – the HFA2000 target of 5 per cent expenditure on health services was damaging: 'Some developing countries produced absurdly expensive health plans in which the cost was not clearly indicated or no attempt at all was made to cost them. These exercises are increasingly recognised in the countries concerned as what they were – window shopping.'[85] He did acknowledge that the WHO's Executive Board had commissioned a paper (from him) on economic strategies for HFA2000, which, when tabled in January 1986 highlighted the issue of resource availability.[86] Yet there was already considerable wider concern about the strategy, as evidenced by the technical discussions at the World Health Assembly in 1987.

Brian noted that unlike the slow response of the WHO, The World Bank, USAID and the Asian and African Development Banks had recognised the importance of this area and were beginning to give grants or loans to pay for teams of foreign consultants and for local studies. But, he said,

> This switch in funding has had disadvantages. Some Ministries of Health are suspicious of World Bank policies. And some see themselves as forced to accept help in this area from consultants that they have not chosen, when a large loan sought for another purpose contains a clause that a small part of it will be used for work on financing. Normally USAID only uses American nationals as consultants. There are however few consultants of this nationality with wide experience in developing countries

outside Latin America. As a result there are too many examples
of short term consultants who give highly theoretical advice
and fail to come to grips with the administrative and political
realities of the country they are advising or who present solutions
wholly based on American experience. The use by the Asian
Development Bank of tenders from consultant firms is unlikely
to produce good results. The most experienced consultants are
not available to spend long periods in a country within weeks
of a tender being accepted. There is now a tendency to imagine
that solutions to deep seated problems can be found by throwing
a pile of dollars at them which have to be spent within a short
period of time. Some countries are now clearly suffering from
consultant fatigue.[87]

He suggested that the most valuable help came from consultants who
made regular visits to a country over a period of years

... becoming sensitive to what countries find acceptable and
the problems they are likely to encounter in implementation
... there is now suddenly too much money chasing too few
experienced consultants.... At present there is no clear career
structure for consultants. Many earn their living in universities
and cling to this in view of the uncertainties of demand for
consultant services. Many have entered the field by chance and
gained experience over a large number of assignments. They were
not systematically prepared for this work. Few academic courses
are available in the health economics of developing countries
and some give little attention to questions of financing or public
sector management.... Possibly the development of consultant
firms will fill the gaps. But many simply 'head hunt' for particular
assignments. This issue may be outside the terms of reference of
the Commission but it is of vital importance for the development
of the field.

Brian also used his 1988 Commission workshop paper to highlight that
more could be done to increase the involvement of health economists,
and to improve the capacity of local health economics in developing
countries. This was vital if these countries were not to have unrealistic
expectations of what health insurance could do for their health sector.
He suggested that the focus of research should be on the fundamental
determinants of health – nutrition, education, water, sanitation – not
just the provision of medical services. This would require 'further

exploration of the historical experiences of different countries', a research area close to his own heart. On primary healthcare Brian declared: 'The list of key elements was hastily put together for the Alma Ata conference, and one wonders whether the list does not contain elements which are far less cost-effective than others included because of the inherited, but not empirically tested, wisdom of medical practice. What, for example, is really cost effective in maternity and child care services? There is some evidence from the United Kingdom that ante-natal care became a widespread practice without having any impact on maternal mortality.'[88] This criticism of the Alma Ata list was perhaps unfair, and did not acknowledge that the list was intended to be more relevant to low-income countries than to the UK.

Brian was critical of the planning for delivering primary healthcare in many developing countries, especially as his research showed wide variations in the number of staff employed per 100,000 population: 'Some seem to have designed a Mercedes Benz model which cannot afford to be provided for half the population while others have designed a Volkswagen model which can be afforded and can reach nearly all the population. It looks as if some models have been designed according to professionally desired utilisation and not actual utilisation.... Once a country has adopted a model and trained people to operate it, there appears to be a great reluctance to rethink the economic viability as against the effectiveness of affordable alternatives.' Research was also needed, according to Brian, on the sensitive issue of drug procurement and distribution, which acknowledged the realities of 'kick-backs', pilferage and pressure from large international pharmaceutical companies to stymie global bulk purchasing schemes.

This workshop paper, which he knew would be taken seriously by the Commission, provided him with an effective platform from which to begin his attack on the 1987 World Bank strategy, *Financing Health Services in Developing Countries: an agenda for reform*.[89] 'The agenda is clearly intended to apply to all developing countries. It prescribes one solution.... It is essentially a theoretical model setting out policies which virtually no developing country has implemented ... what the World Bank has produced is an agenda for further research not an agenda for action.' He was particularly critical of the Bank's stated position on financing healthcare in developing countries, whilst acknowledging that he shared their views on recouping private patient costs, and levying bypass charges for those not referred through the primary healthcare system:'Indeed it was the author who invented the terminology for it. It should also be said that the author is not in favour of free services. As early as 1964 he was a member of a committee which recommended user charges in Tanzania, if more modest than those favoured by the World Bank, similarly arguing from theory rather than empirical research.'[90] But he disagreed that there was now sufficient reliable data for all countries on which to base such schemes, and posed a set of key questions:

> Even if willingness to pay modest charges were proven, it begs the question of the long term effects of choice. How far do health bills once paid add to the problem of rural debt which is an obstacle to rural development? How far do they add to the problem of landlessness? A Thailand study quoted orally at an international conference was said to have shown that 60 per cent of involuntary sales of land were due to medical debts. In Thailand charges can be said to be modest in the sense used by the World Bank policy statement. The weakest section in the whole policy statement is on protecting the poor.[91]

According to Brian, the voucher systems to exempt people from user fees/charges had not been properly evaluated by The World Bank: how could means testing work with such problems as 'illiterate street traders and farmers who keep no accounts'? Discretionary collecting schemes, as in Zimbabwe, were found to lead to the accumulation of bad debts on a scale too vast for the courts to handle. The World Bank had not listed the issue of protecting the poor as one of its six subjects selected for research. Brian therefore proposed an alternative set of research questions: 'What are the income and price elasticities for health services? Do they vary between countries because of beliefs in the effectiveness of Western medicine or the assumed quality of what is locally available or why? Do higher user charges reduce 'trivial' use or use which is of medical importance?... How effective are existing systems (eg Korea, Costa Rica and Ethiopia)?' A manual was needed for developing countries contemplating health insurance schemes, which avoided the confusion of the US terminology of HMOs. 'Countries need to understand the role which voluntary health insurance has successfully played in different societies at different times particularly how it evolved in Europe when it was a developing area and how it became regulated by government and why.... They need to understand why risk rating evolved in the USA and was largely prevented in Europe and how many European systems provided for dependents … (incidentally this is a manual the author would like to write if he could be enabled to find the time to do so).'[92]

Brian's integration of historical context into contemporary health policy development was by the late 1980s one of his standard methodologies. He wrote survey papers for *Milbank Quarterly* that analysed the background to European health financing. His paper, 'Who is the Odd Man Out? The Experience of Western Europe in Containing the Costs of Health Care', explained for his mainly American readers how 'prospective' budgeting operated, and debated the effectiveness of restricted prescribing lists and planned hospital closures.[93] Longer-term measures were also needed, for example, closing the European loopholes of Belgium and Italy which did not have quotas for training doctors, and thus took in students from countries such as Greece, who subsequently returned home and pushed up medical manpower costs. He concluded that more comparative studies were needed as well as attention to the finer political nuances of healthcare. He demonstrated that 'Soviet' medicine was actually not as radical as the earlier 'czarist' (possibly he meant the 'zemstvo' system of local government) medicine. Without putting it into direct words, he implied that the American people might quite like a national health service, if only they could overcome their politicians' fear that this was the thin end of the socialist wedge.

In his 1988 *Milbank Quarterly* paper 'The Rise and Decline of the Early HMOs: Some International Experiences', he demonstrated that HMOs were not invented in the US in the 1970s, but had European ancestry: 'President Nixon reinvented a very old wheel'.[94] His paper 'Financing Health for All' in the *World Health Forum* went through several drafts, and formed the basis for his input to the WHO-EURO Copenhagen series of meetings on financing of health services in the late 1980s.[95]

Kenya

Brian's consultancies placed him at the epicentre of several struggles between various international organisations. A classic example of his involvement – and the wider use of his authority – is seen in Kenya, when the country began to search for a healthcare financing strategy appropriate to its limited budget. As one of the poorer African nations, independent from Britain since 1963, Kenya had regularly received aid from the WHO and other UN organisations. Yet by the mid-1980s, with very limited public financing, it still lacked an effective and comprehensive healthcare service. Symptoms of underfunding included inadequate and unreliable drugs, lack of transport, problems paying healthcare staff and lack of ancillary support staff. A new strategy was needed to generate funds, ideally through the public sector, such as user charges or the creation of a contributory National Insurance scheme. However, with chronic high levels of poverty and income inequality, this was a difficult proposition. Furthermore, the existing healthcare systems, as Brian had found in so many of the developing countries he visited, were plagued with inefficiencies.

The Kenyan government decided to pursue the twin options of introducing user charges (although this could cover only 10 per cent of the healthcare budget if the service was to remain accessible to all) and a pooled public insurance fund, which might cover about 25 per cent of the healthcare bill. It opened up questions about what type of user charges might be introduced and who should contribute to a health insurance scheme. In a continuation of discussions with organisations such as USAID, in 1988 the Kenyan Ministry of Health received a new proposal (IBRD-I) from a World Bank team which assumed that 90 per cent of users would pay charges, with a predicted cost recovery of 20 to 30 per cent of the budget.[96] Yet the high levels of Kenyan poverty meant that many experts, on evaluating The World Bank proposal, felt that more than 40 per cent of Kenyans would not be able to pay the high charges.

Kenya had a long-standing bi-lateral care development cooperation programme with Sweden. In July 1988 Brian received a letter from SIDA (Swedish International Development Agency). SIDA was considering the possibility of co-financing a joint Kenya/World Bank health financing project to improve the balance between primary and secondary care in the country, and to expand the revenue base for the health system. The proposed project was expected to be a blend between traditional investment operations and a sectoral adjustment credit with SIDA support. Part of the explanation for SIDA's invitation to Brian to act as project consultant was apparent in their letter: 'However the documentation available so far raises some doubts with regard to equity issues; a matter of major concern to SIDA.'[97] Göran Dahlgren, then working as senior adviser for SIDA within the Kenyan Ministry of Health in Nairobi, helped to arrange Brian's trip, which was to include meetings with Ministry of Health staff and a seminar with health economists and planners from the Ministry and Kenyatta University. He sent Brian all the relevant background papers in advance of his visit planned for January 1989.

During the January mission for SIDA Brian spent time getting to grips with Kenya's political and economic situation. He was accompanied by two Swedish economists: Göran Berleen from the Karolinska Institute and Eva Juhlin from the University of Göteborg. He held meetings with USAID and UNICEF staff and visited district health services and Nairobi's shanty town. He did not learn until he had arrived in Kenya that The World Bank's own review, which he was supposed to link into, had been cancelled. Brian prepared a discussion paper on issues and options in health financing. He focused on two issues arising from the first World Bank report, and linked to SIDA's concerns about equity: (1) How can the poor be protected if user fees are raised substantially?; and (2) What is the potential for health insurance as means of raising more money for the government health service? He estimated that at least 33 per cent of the rural population and 15 per cent of the urban population were poor, and the proportion unwilling to pay user charges would be higher:

> Willingness to pay will depend on whether the policy is to refuse treatment to those who say they cannot pay or to treat first and seek payment later. It is argued that it is costly and impracticable to attempt to issue annual certificates of inability to pay in rural areas.... Attempts to exempt the poor at the time of treatment are bound to involve rough justice. Hence it is argued that charges must be kept modest to minimise the time devoted to trying to assess poverty and the inequitable results which will inevitably result from such procedures. Private health insurance operated in Kenya has very high overhead costs (about 55 per cent of premium), insurers make no attempt to control prices for health care and have grossly inadequate procedures to control abuse and fraud. It is therefore an unsatisfactory vehicle on which to promote the extension of health insurance. The approach favoured by this consultant is to develop the existing hospital insurance fund into a compulsory health insurance scheme financed by 4 per cent of earnings split equally between employers and employee subject to a floor and a ceiling of contributions.[98]

Brian also proposed that part of the National Hospital Insurance Fund (NHIF) should be redirected to fund the public health system. He based his advice on local experiments. For example, in one rural area of Kenya an increase in dispensary outpatient fees from 2 to 4 Kenyan shillings had been shown to reduce demand for its services by 50 per cent, and introduced new managerial and administrative problems on fee waivers. In his separate mission report to SIDA Brian suggested that it should renew its offer to fund an ability to pay study, and he provided them with a draft methodology. SIDA could also offer to co-finance a loan to the Kenyan government to upgrade its healthcare services, subject to some conditions on what to do with revenue from the NHIF. He also suggested that SIDA should do its best to persuade USAID to maximise the proportion of the US$10–$15 million it had earmarked for investment in Kenya's health services to the health service management training of Kenyans.[99]

His report was not welcomed by the Bank.[100] It sent in another team in early 1989, which returned to the proposal for high user charges, and dismissed the idea of redistributing NHIF money, or of employer contributions. Dahlgren wrote to Brian in May 1989 to let him know what was happening in Kenya: 'No reference is made to your report in the draft Aide Memoire presented by the World Bank mission. Their focus – not surprisingly – is instead on user charges and a NHIF primarily "benefitting" the private sector. USAID did appreciate your ideas of focusing upon the NHIF as the main source of financing. In fact they rewrote their programme proposal completely and developed many of the ideas presented in your report further into quite an interesting comprehensive strategy for health financing.' Dahlgren went on to explain the current lack of clarity in the Ministry of Health's policy-making process, and that The World Bank, and to a lesser extent USAID, had a 'good chance to "railway" their ideas through the present structure directly to the top level without too much of a professional dialogue.' He intended to complete an affordability to pay desk-study as their 'next effort to reduce the risk of accepting proposals without fully realising their social consequence'.[101]

The Kenyan government was persuaded to adopt the revised World Bank scheme, which was introduced early in 1990, and told to 'wait and see' its impact on equity and poverty. Yet within a month President Moi intervened to reduce the user charges to make services accessible to more people, specifically the fee for hospital childbirth and the daily cost of in-patient care. Within six weeks of the start of the scheme the national newspaper, *The Nation*, was reporting: 'General hospitals across the country, once notorious for over-crowding, now find themselves in the unfamiliar position of being deserted. It is not illnesses that have mysteriously disappeared, it is the assumption that every sick person can afford 20 kshs which was way off the mark. The introduction of cost sharing therefore except in terminal cases, made the common illnesses a luxury. People simply choose not to seek treatment.'[102] The official Kenyan policy was to treat people and to seek recovery of charges later. This meant that by the summer of 1990 the media were reporting patients being locked up in hospitals after their treatment for being unable to pay the new fees. Responding to increasing public anger, Moi abolished all the new user charges at public hospitals. The modified financing strategy was a 'second best' compromise, and failed to raise the redistributive funds that Brian had identified.

Brian had written to SIDA in May 1990 to check on whether the report he had completed for them was confidential. He was informed that it was a 'public document' and he was free to use it as he wished. It is no coincidence, therefore, that Göran Dahlgren's forthcoming article, 'Strategies for Health Financing in Kenya – the difficult birth of a new policy', in the *Scandinavian Journal of Medicine*, made extensive use of Brian's report.[103] Dahlgren sent a copy of his article to Edward Jaycox, Vice-President of the African Region of The World Bank (based in Washington DC). Jaycox replied, taking issue with Dahlgren's findings, claiming that differences in the 'time frame involved' may have resulted in the 'differences in perception'. He stated that the Bank 'most certainly did not ignore Professor Abel-Smith's very useful paper' but that the Bank's concerns were more with efficiency than equity.[104]

Dahlgren's courteous reply picked apart Jaycox's disingenuous phrases. He highlighted how the Bank's 'short-term' strategy was encouraging the Kenyan government to introduce damaging schemes (such as abandoning employer NHIF contributions and introducing free healthcare for civil servants), which would result in additional transfers of financial resources for health services from the poor majority of the population to middle and high income groups: 'A health service policy only focusing upon the efficiency of existing institutions is – against this background – "a health for few" rather than a "health for all strategy".' Jaycox had suggested that the fee structure developed by the Bank for Kenya had been 'illustrative'. Dahlgren disagreed: 'The representatives from the Bank certainly did not present their fee structure as "illustrative" when presenting and discussing it with the Ministry of Health. I can even recall US-AID contacting me expressing their worries that the Bank was not willing to present the fee structure as illustrative.' Jaycox tried to back-track on the issue of whether acceptance of the fee structure was a 'prerequisite' for a loan from The World Bank, claiming in his reply that 'framework for such lending' was a better phrase. Dahlgren replied: 'it would be very useful if future missions could be more precise as regards the meaning of the two concepts'.[105] Dahlgren sent Brian a copy of this pedantic yet critical correspondence.

What is disturbing about the Kenyan case study is that The World Bank staff went against the widely accepted development strategy that linked economic and social issues and aimed at strengthening rural healthcare through redistributing funds away from the over-served urban areas. This is what lay at the heart of Brian's proposal, and the concerns of SIDA and USAID. Yet The World Bank insisted on perpetuating a system which left nearly half the Kenyan population with virtually no access to modern healthcare. Its scheme favoured the well-off, by allowing them access to healthcare without subsidising services for the majority of Kenyans. As such, it fitted within the 'overall structural adjustment programme' it had designed in collaboration with the International Monetary Fund. This might have been the best solution for the Bank, but in terms of equity, efficiency and structural objectives, it was the second best solution for Kenya.[106]

Dahlgren had hoped that Brian, or 'Professor Brain as a Kenyan friend appropriately called you', would have a chance to come back to Kenya: 'your professional competence is highly needed'.[107] That view was shared by David Nabarro, based in Nairobi for the British Development Division in Eastern Africa. He was keen for Brian to return for a lengthier health financing project in Tanzania with himself and Gillian Holmes from the British Overseas Development Administration of the FCO. Later in 1989 Brian visited Dar-es-Salam on a preliminary fact-finding trip to explore alternatives for healthcare financing, including introducing user fees, recouping costs from motor insurance for traffic accidents, or a wider health insurance scheme. He was also approached via Anne Mills of the LSHTM to see if he would undertake an urgent consultancy in Uganda in 1989 on their capacity for new financing arrangements and to advise on the employment and evaluation of consultants. Mills had been approached by Sally Fegan-Wyles who worked there for UNICEF: 'SIDA are also very keen he [Brian] should keep an eye on Uganda as he is very central to similar process in Kenya.'[108]

This was the reality of health and social welfare policy making in the developing world in the 1980s: personal contacts counted for as much as, if not more than, what went on in ministerial meetings, but nothing could surpass the financial clout of The World Bank. It took several years for evidence of user fee policy failure to effectively filter back through to senior levels within the Bank. de Ferranti explains this as being due in part to the devolved structure of the Bank: staff set out their competing policy ideas in the style of a bazaar – in which economists had only recently taken interest in health issues. It lacks an equivalent to the WHO's World Health Assembly, which formally and publicly approves its resolutions, The Bank, suggests de Ferranti, has often been wrongly interpreted as a single-voice proponent of neoliberal health policy. He admits, however, that its fixation on user fees in the 1980s was damaging – both to the developing countries that experimented with them and to The World Bank's own reputation. It was not until the tenure of James Wolfensohn as World Bank President between 1995 and 2005 that there was some acknowledgement and discussion of its policy failures.[109]

This chapter has demonstrated Brian's pragmatism in trying to accommodate conflicting principles and employers. There were tensions between his various roles: as an analytic evidence-based academic expert adviser; as a Fabian socialist with egalitarian goals for health and healthcare; and as an influencer of officials and ministers, some of whom were cynical and corrupt. There were very few people who could play all these roles, often simultaneously, while retaining individual integrity. Brian had a chameleon-like aptitude for these challenges.

14

The end of the party: 1979–90

Labour in opposition

Reform or dissolution? The National Health Service in
Conservative Britain

London's health services

The new academia: a business of knowledge

There is something distinctive and recognisable in English
civilisation ... it is somehow bound up with solid breakfasts and
gloomy Sundays, smoky towns and winding roads, green fields
and red pillar boxes. It has a flavour of its own. Moreover it is
continuous, it stretches into the future and into the past, there
is something in it that persists, as a living creature.... And above
all it is *your* civilisation, it is *you*. However much you hate it or
laugh at it, you will never be happy away from it for any length
of time. (George Orwell, 1941)[1]

*This chapter, which focuses on Brian's British interests, begins with the end of
the Labour government in 1979, when he returned to a full-time position at
the LSE and developed a number of new collaborative teaching courses in the
years leading up to his retirement in 1991. He continued to take an active
interest in British health policy, especially the development of London's health
services, working through his position as a governor at St Thomas' Hospital
and Medical School and taking on new roles at The King's Fund. Although
he remained a key figure within the Fabian Society, he was less involved
with the Labour Party as it entered a difficult period of reconfiguration. As
the previous parallel chapter has shown, he increasingly looked abroad for
intellectual stimulation.*

Brian's mother, Vivée, died on 20 January 1980, aged 81. Her cremation was held at Hastings on Friday 25 January, close to the Folkestone nursing home where she had lived during her final years. Up until the late 1970s she had been living semi-independently in various London hotels, including the Eden Hotel in Harrington Gardens and another in Queen's Gate, Kensington. Brian's partner John collected her once a week to go to their home so that she could do her baking. She became increasingly fond of John, who she had initially referred to as the 'farm boy' when their relationship was revealed to her in the early 1960s. Brian and Lionel, with their respective partners, took great care to make sure she was living comfortably, although Brian was disappointed that Lionel had not offered her a home in the small bungalow next to his house on his farm at Peasmarsh. At times they stepped in to prevent her eccentricities threatening her well-being, and they also took the difficult decision to check her into rehabilitation clinics when her dependency on alcohol became a serious concern. She had outlived her husband by 34 years, and lived through her boys, sustained by the rituals of Sunday lunches and weekly telephone calls. Brian's friends, such as Robert Stevens, remembered her fondly: 'an upper class lady of a certain age and a certain type'.[2]

Through the 1980s, as seen in the last chapter, Brian travelled frequently on international consultancies, relying on John to look after their home in Bloomfield Terrace, where they lived from 1978 until a move to Denbigh Street in 1989. The other significant change in Brian's life was the closure of Just Men, his business of clothes shops. By the mid-1970s it was plagued by staffing problems, and struggling to keep up with the fickle London fashion scene. Since 1965 it had served its founding purpose in giving steady employment to Charles Schuller, the former Royal Ballet dancer who had been Brian's partner in the mid-1950s. But now both Brian and John did not have the time and energy to go abroad to buy stock, and they wanted to spend their weekends relaxing at Tanglewood. In 1976 Brian had resigned as a director of the affiliated companies of Just Men (Tailors) Ltd and Just Men (Shirts) Ltd, and annual sales were averaging only £2,500. A hairdresser was employed to work within the Tryon Street branch in 1978, which brought in around £4,000 a year, and helped to cover the running costs. Despite a small rally in sales in the early 1980s, the expenses of maintaining some of the branches, such as the one in London's exclusive Beauchamp Place, were escalating, and the company's debts increased, financed by an overdraft and investments from Brian. In the last year of trading as Just Men (London) Ltd, the sales were £22,538, but the small profit of £3,387 made little in-road into the accumulated debt of £18,927. Brian and Schuller, as joint directors, took the decision to close the business at the end of 1986.

Labour in opposition

Labour lost the general election in May 1979, and Brian lost his position as special adviser to Peter Shore. The Conservatives' majority of 44 seats gave them a comfortable position. Labour's share of the poll was 36.9 per cent – its lowest since 1931 – and James Callaghan resigned as leader to be succeeded by Michael Foot. The Party quickly degenerated into a bitter civil war, and values that had underpinned it (and which Brian held dear), such as transparent policy making and a commitment to analysing past trends, appeared to be increasingly irrelevant. The 'horrific ugliness' of the in-fighting, which focused on issues such as Britain's membership of the EEC, drove out many of its stalwart members. Some stayed in the hope of turning round the election defeat and rebuilding the Party's ideology. Shore, despite attempts to de-select him in his constituency by entryist Militants, was seen as a 'coming man', and went on to hold positions as shadow Foreign Secretary and shadow Chancellor. He blamed Tony Benn's faction for 'stirring up the demons of the deep' in their attempt to move the Party further to the ideological left. These political manoeuvrings left Brian cold, and although he continued to advise Peter Shore on his personal political strategy he reduced his involvement with Labour's committees and working groups. In the special issue of *Political Quarterly* to mark its 50th anniversary (Brian was one of its directors between 1974 and 1991), he wrote:

> I am one of those who believe that the election was lost rather than won – lost by the ruthlessness of the public sector strikes, which outrages the British sense of decency and fair play. This was all summed up in the most brilliant headline of the year: '*They* won't let *us* bury *our* dead'. The words in italics tell the whole story…. For years we have taken pride in being a compassionate society. Do people really want a lower standard of social services so that they can have more money in their pockets? The question was not put to the British electorate. Mrs Thatcher is taking a gamble for which she has no mandate. Is this a turning-point in British post-war history? Or will the Government U-turn before it goes too far? If it does not, what will be the judgement at the next election? How deep do cuts have to go before a service ceases to be seen as universal? How much unemployment can a

country stand without it leading to violence? These are the key social questions facing Britain now.[3]

Brian did, however, continue to be active in the Fabian Society (he had served on the Executive between 1956 and 1960, as Chair in 1963–64 and Treasurer in 1965–68). He was therefore at the epicentre of the fallout when the 'gang of four' left the Labour Party to establish the Social Democratic Party (SDP) in 1981.[4] Benn, who chronicled the episode in his diaries, saw Brian as an effective non-parliamentary politician, as well as a political academic, whose views carried weight in both the Fabian Society and the Labour Party: 'There was a self-standing authority about him which I respected very much….There was no arrogance about him at all. He was modest, but you knew that underneath there was a really tough character. He knew exactly what he wanted to do and he'd put it forward and argue for it, but there was no sense of pride about him at all that I ever came across.'[5]

Shirley Williams' resignation (and others) from the Fabian Society Executive in March 1981, because of their new affiliation with the Council for Social Democracy, triggered much soul searching. Dianne Hayter, the Society's General Secretary, invited the solicitor Bruce Douglas Mann to advise on whether the Society would be at risk of prosecution if it expelled them as members. Benn and others felt strongly that as they were an overtly political society allied to the Labour Party, they should be allowed to block the membership of those who had contrary allegiances to the conventional Labour Party one. John Parker, the new Chair, felt that they should be allowed to remain as associate members, but without voting rights.[6] It was agreed to ballot the members, and in the meantime the vacancies left on the Executive were filled, with Brian taking up the position of Treasurer from John Roper.

Only a month earlier Roper had set out for the Executive the dire straits that the Fabian Society was in, with a worsening deficit, declining membership, overly-long pamphlets that failed to attract a wide audience. The Labour Party, which gave the Fabians an annual subscription, was also facing financial struggles, and its own Executive had debated reducing or stopping this altogether. The Fabian Society paid £900 to the Labour Party, which 'bought' it 4,000 votes at conference, but it then got £300 back as a grant. A Labour Party constituency, on the other hand, paid £500 per vote. There was growing trade union disaffection with the Society's lack of public support for Labour. This had fuelled a damaging story in *The Guardian* in February

1981 suggesting the Society might even choose to disaffiliate from the Labour Party.

Brian also inherited some dubious financial dealings. A 'Dartmouth Street Trust' had been established in 1942, named after the location of the Fabian Society's London offices. It had no overt affiliation with the Fabian Society: its declared purpose was 'the promotion of studies in political, economic and social sciences and cognate educational subjects, and for the promotion of education and dissemination of knowledge in such sciences and subjects'. Charitable donations could be made to the Trust using a seven-year covenanting scheme, on which the tax was recovered. Yet the Trust was in effect just a front for the Society – all the donations were passed straight over to it. When the SDP was established, one of the key Fabians to leave the Society was David Sainsbury, who also cancelled his generous donation to the Dartmouth Street Trust, and stepped down as one of its trustees. Hayter relied heavily on Brian's personal financial acumen to adjust the Society's budgets and planning.[7] Other trustees such as David Lipsey, were not so impressed. Although he valued Brian's social policy expertise, he thought his financial knowledge 'was on the level of a poorish provincial stockbroker'. But it was impossible to fall out with Brian. He was 'very charming, very gentle, very persuasive – an exceptionally convivial man'.[8]

In the event, the Fabians voted to stay loyal to Labour. The SDP set up its own intellectual think tank, the Tawney Society, which faded in sympathy after 1988. Brian continued to be involved with Fabian events and publications, contributing a chapter 'Social Welfare' to *Fabian Essays in Socialist Thought* in 1984, which Ben Pimlott edited.[9] Brian was surprisingly self-critical when drafting it, writing to Pimlott:

> The trouble is that it needs a book not an article. Perhaps one day I should try to write it…. You may say that I have wasted too much space on analysing the past. But I thought the non-specialist reader needed this to grasp what I was proposing. You may wish to strike out the personal reference to my time as a special adviser. You may say that crime is not my brief. You may say that I have too much detailed social engineering and too little philosophy. Well that is me. You may say that it looks too much like a short term agenda. You may say that I cannot get away with such a single assumption that there is a solution to unemployment on the basis of the Shore plan. Well say what you think. Sorry not to have done better.[10]

Labour's 18 consecutive years out of government from May 1979 (Brian died a year before their return in 1997) meant that there was little further opportunity for him to be closely involved with government health and social welfare policy development. The Royal Commission on the NHS that Wilson had established in 1975 finally reported on 11 July 1979, just after the change of government.[11] It was perhaps an indication of how little energy Ennals had for the NHS that he failed to speed up the report to have it published while Labour were still in office. It has been suggested, however, that its Chair, Sir Alec Merrison, deliberately 'trod water' so that it should not be seen as a political document in the run-up to the general election, but be given its due attention by the new government. The consensus view is that it was 10 years too late to really have an impact on the structure and function of the NHS. Crossman should have followed his instincts and called for one in 1969 when he was dithering over the restructuring issue. As Charles Webster notes, although the BMA had been pushing hard for this Commission, they appeared to lose interest, leaving the government with 'an unwanted child.... In government circles it was rarely mentioned. It was treated more as a gesture of piety than as a determinant of policy.'[12] Although the Commission held 35 meetings (and its sub-committees held many more) and had taken evidence from 70 organisations, it was seen as less useful than the spin-off investigations that it initiated. It lacked clarity on whether it should commission or respond to new research.

The final report of July 1979 was 491 pages long, including 117 pages of recommendations. It did not include, as common with previous Royal Commissions, verbatim transcripts of the oral evidence. It was, however, the most unpretentious and accessible review that the British NHS has ever experienced. Its nearest comparison, according to Webster, is the Royal Sanitary Commission of 1871.[13] It consolidated the status quo of state funding through taxation rather than switching to an insurance model, or local government administration.

Brian's reaction to the new Conservative government's initial health policy and to the outcome of the Merrison Royal Commission was articulated through a series of articles for New Society in July and August 1979. No longer one of the Whitehall special advisers, he spoke freely about his concerns, putting the British dilemma of rising healthcare costs in a wider European perspective, and suggesting effective cost-control measures. For Brian, 'the great strength of the Royal Commission's report is that it looks at the service primarily from the consumer's point of view rather than the provider's.... Sir Alec Merrison is to be congratulated on securing a unanimous report which is in so many ways imaginative and forward-looking. But unanimity usually has to be bought at a price. Which issues appear to have been ducked or fudged to get it?' Brian found three areas: failure to tackle the relationship between occupational health services and the NHS, cautious wording of statements about abolition of charges and ambiguous phrasing on the issue of pay beds: 'Those who hoped that the Royal Commission would find some startling new way forward are bound to be disappointed. But the facts of life are disappointing.'[14] In a companion article the following month, he discussed the Royal Commission's proposals for the NHS's administrative structure, and found it did not face up to the difficult questions that its proposed regional health authority accountability to Parliament would create.[15]

In the spring of 1980 Brian returned to Labour Party policy discussions, but he no longer appeared to be so committed. He had been re-selected to the Social Policy Sub-committee (apparently without a formal request to him), along with many of its former members, such as David Piachaud and Peter Townsend, but he frequently sent his apologies to its meetings. He contributed research papers on inner-city primary healthcare (building on Donald Acheson's recent report on London), and on benefits for survivors and one-parent families, which contributed to the drafting of Labour's programme for 1982.

On occasions when he did engage with the Social Policy Sub-committee's debates he demonstrated his old passion. In 1982, when the Committee were to discuss a paper, 'Responsiveness in public services', he wrote at length to the Committee Secretary, Jenny Pitkin. He offered a paper on how issues such as rights were discussed on the Continent – he had used the term 'humanisation' for a report he produced for the EEC with international colleagues: 'a word which does not yet really exist in English', but which sought a solution by defining rights in the broadest sense, for example, covering delays, referral to other agencies and other issues for the public accessing services. He wrote about how he saw contemporary British social welfare, and the need to strengthen organisations such as Citizens Advice Bureaux (CABs):

> CABs are used by all social classes. And they can and do play a critical role as advocates for the disadvantaged – those least skilled in fighting bureaucracy – the less educated, immigrants with language problems, widows whose late husbands did all the coping with officialdom etc. Still many communities lack services and they are used almost entirely by local people. Most are under-staffed. And it is largely only in London where trained professional staff are employed. We must grasp this issue. Last

time it was discussed it encountered tough opposition from the trade union movement. People join unions to get advocacy. Strong publicly financed advice services would make people less keen to join unions. But what about those who have no unions because they are not at work?... I have always thought that the restriction of access to an ombudsman via councillor or MP is wrong. Why not have direct access or allow recognised services or law centres direct access to ombudsmen? Beyond all this, remedies differ for different services. In council housing, real decentralisation is critical. Could each estate have its own budget for repairs and the upkeep of its environment run by its own elected local committee? This would encourage 'do it yourself' (materials paid for by the local budget) and employing people on the estate to do small repairs, maintain the common garden etc. If the gardener is a resident, he will mobilise support to fight vandalism of his work. The problem is how far one could go in making each estate, in effect, a cooperative.... I am convinced that the key problems of social security are under-staffing and counter staff at clerical officer level with rapid turnover. If all counter staff were executive officers, there would be much less turnover, substantial training could be justified.... In Denmark the first line staff are five-year trained!... In the NHS, I think the way forward is to strengthen CHCs [Community Health Councils] still more by giving them a larger budget and more staff. They should be able to refer cases to the Health Commissioner. The powers of the latter should be widened to take appeals from FPCs [Family Practitioner Councils] which now go to the Secretary of State and to investigate clinical matters. Nine years after the Davis Committee report, the doctors have still managed to block action, despite a select committee reporting in favour of it. All that has so far emerged is a mild code of practice, for what that is worth! I hope these thoughts are of some help.[16]

He joined the Sub-committee's Working Group on Primary and Community Care organised by Frank Dobson, and Michael Meacher's Working Group on NHS Structure and Organisation.[17] The group discussed demoralisation of NHS staff, the implications of the Conservatives' structural changes, lack of effective complaints channels for patients and the possibility of using a local tax base to finance the NHS. In 1985 Brian accepted an invitation to join the new Labour Party Joint Policy Committee on Health and Social Services. This discussed, among other things, papers by Julian Tudor Hart (originator of the 1973 Inverse Care Law) on primary care, and Frank Dobson's proposal for a campaign charter on community care for use in the forthcoming county council elections.

Reform or dissolution? The National Health Service in Conservative Britain

Increasingly, Brian saw the British NHS through the comparative lens of the European Community. In 1979 he had published, with Alan Maynard, a study for the Commission of the European Communities, *The organisation, financing and cost of health care in the European Community*.[18] For several years Maynard and Brian had regularly travelled together to Brussels for project meetings. Maynard marvelled at Brian's well-honed travelling skills – his tiny suitcase contained no more than a change of underwear and shirt (always expertly folded by John), a shaving kit and a bottle of whisky.[19] Their project explored the increasing pressures placed on national budgets by rising costs since 1961. It must have been frustrating for Brian to find that some 20 years on from his call for an international health accounting language, there were still basic problems in defining hospitals, treatments, even in defining 'health service'.

They found the highest rates of growth in relation to GNP in Ireland; the lowest in Denmark and the UK. User demand had increased in those countries that had increased services provided under compulsory health insurance schemes since 1966, for example, the introduction of free family planning in the UK in 1974. Improved public knowledge about healthcare, particularly through the media, had increased pressure to seek out what was perceived as the best or most sophisticated healthcare, and people were less willing to tolerate pain or long waiting periods before treatment. The ageing European population was contributing to higher healthcare costs: in 1961 11.7 per cent of British people were aged over 65; by 1975 this had increased to 14 per cent and was projected to reach 14.9 per cent by 1980. Also, it had been calculated that the cost per head of the British NHS was six times greater for a person over 75 than for someone aged 16 to 64.

Brian and Maynard acknowledged the impact of lifestyle factors – increase in motor accidents, increased consumption of alcohol and the long-term effects of heavy smoking (although this evidence did not have an impact on Brian's smoking habits). Their menu of solutions were organised into short and long-term cost control. Initiatives included tighter restrictions of the number of medical practitioners and increasing user charges for items such as prescriptions. Long-term measures ranged from complete reorganisations of healthcare financing, as Italy had achieved, and new methods of paying for in-patient hospital treatments – moving from daily payments which did not encourage economy, to fixed rates per procedure, as had been tried out in Germany and France. A more radical solution would be to move as much medical care out of hospitals and into the community as possible. This might be achieved, they noted, by closing hospitals: 'In England, 134 hospitals have been closed over a period of three years with only a small minority of disputed cases.'[20] Brian also accepted an invitation to join a working party on expensive medical techniques, which was established in August 1979 by the Council for Science and Society. He produced a working paper on the proposed NHS Supply Council for the group, which included Derek Russel Davis, Douglas Black, Walter Holland, Margaret Stacy and Barbara Stocking.

Yet public–private collaborations to provide health services – which Brian found himself increasingly discussing at a global level through his work for international organisations such as WHO, ILO, UNDP and The World Bank – was not an open topic for debate in Britain. Brian, as evidenced in his work in Kenya and other developing countries, was amenable to persuasion that there was a role for private medicine, at least for countries other than Britain. In domestic politics he held fast to the Bevanite ideology of universal free healthcare at the point of delivery. Although he had tried to talk Barbara Castle out of her naïve policy of eliminating private pay beds from NHS hospitals in 1974, this was because he saw it as a deeply damaging political manoeuvre – private medicine could not be eliminated so easily. The plans swiftly implemented by Margaret Thatcher's Conservative government after 1979 appeared intent on facilitating the rise of this small core of British private medicine, despite the risk (or perhaps with the hope) of destabilising the NHS.

In the 1980s Brian's office files on 'private medicine' were regularly supplemented with newspaper clippings and articles. He joined NHS Unlimited: A Committee to Combat Private Medicine, chaired by the Labour MP, Frank Dobson. This had been formed in 1981, and quickly established a reputation as a small but effective pressure group that collected and disseminated information on where the Conservatives were allowing the core principles of the NHS to be eroded. It was supported by the Labour movement, especially NHS associated trades unions such as COHSE, NALGO and NUPE. It published regular bulletins, exposing how planning permission requirements were softened for new private hospitals, who the owners of these hospitals were, and their relationships with members of the government. Dobson, as shadow Health Minister, drew attention to the activities of hospital consultants, many of whom were on full-time NHS contracts, but who used substantial parts of their contracted time (and NHS facilities) to maintain large private practices. He deemed the monitoring of hospital consultants to be 'absurdly inadequate', and suggested that the government was effectively encouraging doctors to moonlight in the private sector.[21]

Brian was open to involvement in any forum that offered an opportunity to engage in discussions on health and social welfare policy. In February 1980 he was invited to join to the panel of honorary advisers for the Office of Health Economics (OHE). This had been established in 1962 by the Association of the British Pharmaceutical Industry (ABPI) to commission and disseminate research on the economics of health services. As its Director George Teeling-Smith's letter acknowledged, Brian had been offering informal advice to the OHE for many years. This was an opportunity to put his support on a more formal footing, which brought the added pleasure of attending the joint biennial OHE dinner with the ABPI, which that year was to be held at the Savoy Hotel. Brian accepted both invitations. He also continued to be a patron of the Disablement Income Group, which he urged to resist sponsorship by the Private Patients Plan precisely because disabled people would find themselves ineligible to hold private medical insurance.

London's health services

Brian's ongoing role at St Thomas' Hospital gave him a first-hand insight into the impact of the new Conservative policy for the NHS. He had first become involved with the hospital in 1957, when he was appointed to the Board of Governors. Although he stepped down from the Board in 1968, he maintained close links. In 1977 he accepted a three-year appointment as a representative of the University of London to St Thomas' Medical School Council, renewed in 1980, when he also became Vice-Chair. This coincided with the arrival of Brian Creamer as Dean in 1979, and the first discussions on a merger with Guy's Medical School following the report of the University working party, chaired by Lord Flowers. Brian represented St Thomas' during the amalgamation negotiations, which culminated in the formation of the United Medical and Dental Schools of Guy's and St Thomas' Hospitals in 1982, and Brian secured a place on the new board, which he held until 1989.

St Thomas' Medical School was also home to the Department of Community Medicine, where Walter Holland led the Social Medicine and Health Services Research Unit. When he had founded it 1962 he had been introduced to Brian by Bryan McSwiney, Clerk to the Governors at St Thomas'. Brian accepted Holland's invitation to join the unit's Advisory Board, and he also served as its Chair from 1975 until 1994. Brian's 'insider' status as a special adviser to the Secretary of State at the DHSS was useful to Holland's unit. They had responded to the call of interest issued by the DHSS in 1975 for research into 'alternative patterns of care for the elderly', part of David Owen's initiative to achieve economies through reducing residential care costs. Holland had submitted a proposal for a study involving Lambeth's elderly residents who used St Thomas' services, and had immediately begun a pilot study, which also involved an assessment of the potential for using health visitors to direct support services for the elderly. Yet communication with the Research Liaison Group at the DHSS who were handling the tenders became strained. It was not apparent to Holland that his unit was but one of several who were tendering for the research contract. When they were rejected in the summer of 1976, he used Brian to push Owen for a full explanation, and possible reconsideration.[22]

The structure of London's health services – both primary and secondary – gave particular cause for concern from the 1970s. The historical concentration of acute beds in the prestigious central London teaching hospitals (such as St Thomas') was judged at the time to be no longer tenable. They no longer had a such a large local population to serve because of the steady decentralisation to the Home Counties (although there were still between 7 and 8 million living in inner London, and a disproportionate number had poor health). The RAWP formula required a shift of NHS funding from these over-endowed metropolitan hospital boards towards areas of greater need in the north of Britain. A London Health Planning Consortium (LHPC) had been established to examine such issues. In 1979 it developed a methodology to calculate projected numbers of hospital beds and the demands for acute services in London, and produced reports on medical specialties.

Donald Acheson, Dean at Southampton Medical School, was subsequently appointed to chair an enquiry into London's primary healthcare. Acheson's report made 115 recommendations, and was informed by the new indicators of deprivation being developed by Professor Brian Jarman of St Mary's Hospital Medical School, but many of the proposals were dismissed by the government as too complicated to implement.[23] The LHPC's *Towards a Balance* report was produced in 1980. It recommended a 20–25 per cent reduction in acute beds in the central (mainly teaching) hospitals. This would have significant implications for how medical students could be trained, with greater use of hospitals outside London – into the 'wedges' of Home Counties that the four regions covered. Brian helped to draft the St Thomas' governing body's response. They judged the proposals 'yet another example of the inability of Central Government to adopt a unified and coherent approach to implementing social policies'.[24]

In February 1980 the Minister for Health, Dr Gerard Vaughan, rejected calls for an independent enquiry and instead set up a new advisory group on the future of London's health services to bring together the LHPC outcomes with those of the coterminous report on London medical education chaired by Lord Flowers.[25] Sir John Habakkuk, a former Vice-Chancellor of the University of Oxford (and at the time Chair of Oxfordshire District Health Authority) was appointed to chair these delicate discussions, in which there were so many conflicting vested interests. His London Advisory Group announced that a 15 per cent reduction in hospital beds was required, as well as the closure of small hospitals.[26] Yet after its report had been received by the DHSS, the Group was disbanded, and there was little incentive to force the pace. The Flowers proposals for merging medical schools slowly took shape during the 1980s, despite strong student and staff objections. But the London NHS districts still fell short of their efficiency savings targets, and there was a paucity of reallocation from acute services to other needy areas such as geriatrics and mental health.

The King's Fund – which had been formed in 1897 as the Prince of Wales' Hospital Fund for London – had evolved in the post-war period into an authoritative think tank with a wider focus on improving the quality of British healthcare, especially through practical training courses to improve skills and management. Alongside the Nuffield Provincial Hospitals Trust, it sponsored a number of significant studies, many of which were initiated by Robert J. Maxwell, its Secretary and Chief Executive. Brian had, for many years, been closely involved with its activities, including serving on its General Council, and he knew many of its staff well (indeed, he had supervised Maxwell's PhD). He was regularly invited to small dinners held at the Fund's offices at 10 Palace Court to meet influential figures in the British healthcare world. One such invitation in May 1981 was to dine with Sir George Young, Joint Parliamentary Under Secretary of State for the DHSS, along with Lord Hayter and Hugh Astor, members of The King's Fund Council.

Maxwell wrote to Brian to explain that the dinner was to pursue ideas with Young about the London Project: 'Sir George is well liked in the House of Commons and among civil servants, with a reputation for quiet humour as well as for competence. He does not seem to share some of Dr Gerard Vaughan's wilder views.'[27]

Brian's most significant role at The King's Fund was as Chair of the London Project Executive Committee (LPEC), a role he took on in September 1980 from its founding Chair, Sir Francis Avery Jones (which also gave him membership of the Fund's Project Committee). The 'London Programme' had been launched in 1979 to strengthen King's Fund activities in relation to healthcare in London. The broad aim was to encourage and disseminate good practice in the inner-city areas through a coordinated programme of research projects, conferences, workshops, seminars, publications and other enterprises. For the next five years Brian directed a series of linked initiatives through the LPEC. He chaired the Fund's conference 'Primary health care in London', held in September 1981, at which he proposed setting up pilot group practice schemes to take advantage of the Inner Urban Programme run by the Department of the Environment for district health authorities. He steered the Fund's response to the Acheson Report, chairing a meeting with ministers and civil servants in November 1981 to 'help Professor Acheson obtain a response from the Government and maintain a degree of urgency' in the implementation of his proposals. Norman Fowler, Secretary of State for Social Services, announced a £9 million investment scheme for London's healthcare in October 1983, as a result of the Acheson Report. The LPEC discussed innovative schemes for community nursing services, and strategies for reducing the number of single-handed GP practices. The LPEC also funded the Medical Architecture Research Unit (MARU) to produce a design guide on improving practice premises. Other proposals, for example, for projects on the computerisation of GP practice systems, funding support workers for Haringey Greek Cypriot women's health group, and establishing a health centre for the homeless, were not successful.

When Acheson was subsequently appointed as Chief Medical Officer in late 1983, he was now in a position within the DHSS to help direct this investment, and to use the resources of The King's Fund. However, government ministers were unhappy at the idea of allocating significant sums of research money to such external research organisations because of the difficulties of planning expenditure for projects over more than one financial year. Brian then pursued an alternative approach, facilitating discussions between the Fund and the DHSS on new research to strengthen academic departments of general practice. Linked to this was his suggestion to Malcolm Godfrey, Dean at the Royal Postgraduate Medical School at the Hammersmith Hospital, that he and The King's Fund might find a way to persuade Ken Newell, an innovative community medicine academic, to return from the Liverpool School of Tropical Medicine to a London position – perhaps by establishing a new department of community health at the Hammersmith. He also helped to develop plans for a joint LSE/ King's Fund collaboration for a major review of health services (Doreen Irving and Brian Jarman took the respective institutional leads).

From 1983 Brian was also involved in the discussions to establish a King's Fund Institute of Health. An idea for a British institute, independent from government, was not new. Sir George Godber, former CMO, had recently written about the benefits that such an organisation would have for British health policy. Brian urged Robert Maxwell to make it take on a wider remit, and to consider using it to monitor British progress on Health for All:

> I would hope that the Institute would not just engage in policy analysis in the UK context but look abroad and see which countries were doing better than us in particular fields, try and find out why, and see what lessons this had for us. But my main point is that some issues are hard for government to handle because there are conflicts of interest – the health aspects of tobacco and alcohol and the contribution to the balance of payments and to jobs in Britain of the tobacco and alcohol industries, the promotion of sport and the sponsorship of it by tobacco firms, rational prescribing under the NHS and the sponsorship of the British based pharmaceutical industry, the dairy and sugar industry and reducing the consumption of animal fats and sugar. At the very least the Institute could bring these dilemmas out into the open for public discussion.[28]

His proposal did not appear to resonate with King's Fund staff. When Greg Parston of the King's Fund College produced a first draft for the proposed institute's focus, Brian was quick to try to steer him:

> My criticism of your draft is that while it pays lip service to being concerned with health policy it is still overwhelmingly concerned with health service policy. This is shown by ALL the examples on page 4 and the narrow tokenism of the examples in brackets on page 3. Is it [sic] 70% or 90% of health problems which are generated outside the health service AND on which

the health service can do little to help. The main underlying causes of premature mortality and much associated morbidity are smoking, alcohol and accidents – none of these key health problem areas figure even as examples in your paper. I would assess DHSS devotes a tiny amount of time to considering them compared with the time devoted (however ineffectively) to considering precisely the type of issues listed on your page 4. Now we have a heroin epidemic. How many of the guessed 400,000 young people now on heroin will be alive at age 30? How serious are the health consequences of glue sniffing? What can be done about these newer challenges to health and what are the <u>deeper</u> underlying causes?... I hope an Institute will focus on <u>what matters most</u> in terms of the health of the population and not that of the NHS which is already relatively over-explored.[29]

Brian was subsequently appointed to the new Institute's Advisory Committee in 1986 for a five-year period.

The new academia: a business of knowledge

From the beginning of his academic career as Assistant Lecturer at the LSE in 1955 Brian was well known for his provocative lectures and charismatic lecturing style. Annabelle Mark, one of his former students, describes Brian's lecturing style as 'extraordinary'. His keynote lecture, 'The Finances and Economics of Social Services', made a stunning case *against* public welfare, more effectively than even the right-wing think tank the Institute of Economic Affairs could have achieved. He taunted students with his sharp analysis of the problems of state pensions and the NHS. Passing Howard Glennerster, the course tutor sitting at the back of the lecture hall on his way out, he would chuckle, "Well, that set them going!" His academic style had always retained something of the Cambridge Union debate – he could easily take the opposite view and push people very hard to defend their positions. Students and colleagues alike loved this interchange.[30] Much of his teaching was done using case studies of policy initiatives that he had been personally involved with developing. Because of his wide expertise, he could talk easily about all aspects of health economics and planning: from price control of pharmaceuticals to manpower issues and price barriers to health service access. He was less comfortable on econometrics and the more abstract aspects of health economics.[31]

An eclectic mix of students was attracted to study at the LSE on the strength of knowing Brian and the wider reputation of his courses.

One of his most unusual mature students was Elspeth Howe, the wife of his old Cambridge friend Geoffrey Howe, who was Chancellor of the Exchequer between 1979 and 1983 (then going on to be Foreign Secretary, Leader of the House of Commons and Deputy Prime Minister). Brian had known Elspeth Howe since her marriage to Geoffrey in 1953. They regularly dined together, and he had put her name forward for several non-executive board positions in health authorities and other public bodies. She had served as Deputy Chair of the Equal Opportunities Commission between 1975 and 1979. After taking up residence at 11 Downing Street, she was looking for alternative occupations to replace public appointments that might now cause conflicts of interest with the new Conservative government. In 1981 she asked Brian if she could register to take a Degree in Social Policy at the LSE. Brian was enthusiastic, and he helped her to fill in the UCCA forms that Geoffrey's secretary anonymously obtained for her. It was a source of great amusement that when Elspeth needed introductory economics textbooks for a module, and found them already out on loan at the LSE library, she got Geoffrey to borrow them for her from the House of Commons library – somewhat unconventional reading material for the Chancellor of the Exchequer.[32]

Brian had long-standing collaborations with the LSHTM, just up the road in Bloomsbury from his LSE office. His good friend Jerry Morris was Professor of Epidemiology there, and he and Richard Titmuss had jointly taught programmes with LSHTM through the 1960s and 1970s. Brian liked LSE's ethos of encouraging students from less privileged backgrounds (especially local London students) onto its courses. This was less easy for LSHTM to achieve given the nature of their interests, but Brian worked with Jenny Roberts of the LSHTM Department of Health Services Research to secure funding from the Rockefeller Foundation to establish six scholarships and staff funding for a new MPhil research degree programme in Health Planning and Financing.

Jenny Roberts had previously suggested that LSHTM and LSE staff should develop a joint postgraduate degree programme, but had met with a lukewarm response. When in 1984 another University of London institution, Queen Mary College, proposed something similar (but without the requisite staff expertise), Roberts pushed Brian again to take the initiative. After many months of difficult university meetings to establish how a joint degree would fit into the existing academic systems, they got approval. In 1986 Roberts and Brian launched the new joint LSE/LSHTM MSc programme in Health Planning and Financing (HPF), working with their LSE colleague John Carrier, and at the LSHTM with Patrick Hamilton and Anne Mills (who had joined the

LSHTM in 1979 and was appointed to the linked 'new initiatives' joint lectureship set up between the LSHTM and the LSE).[33] It coincided with the launch of a new journal, *Health Policy and Planning*, edited at the LSHTM by Patrick Vaughan and Gill Walt. Brian served on its advisory panel, helping to solicit papers from his extensive network of international colleagues.

The joint MSc was immediately popular, attracting an initial cohort of 18 international students, many of whom were already senior within their organisations, and brought to the classes their diverse experiences. Over the next few years there were social scientists and clinicians, senior civil servants as well as recent graduates. Keen students would turn up for both developed and developing country seminars. The nine-month course had two core courses: 'Basic community health' (mainly taught by Nick Black) and 'Health planning and financing' (mainly taught by Brian). He would often fly in to teach on precisely the issues that he had been advising on the previous day in developing countries such as Kenya, Jamaica and Indonesia. His class discussions on cost-effectiveness and user fees were real-time, not paper exercises.

Brian initiated the tradition of end-of-course parties for the students and staff, which he hosted at his home. Anne Mills remembers him serving whole poached salmon, beautifully decorated.[34] From 1989 there was also an annual study trip abroad. The first was to Como in Italy and later ones visited the major international health organisations in Geneva. As student demand increased, new, more specialised courses were introduced. Health Planning and Financing alumni went on to significant careers in health policy, health service administrations and academia. In 1987 the LSHTM created a new Department of Public Health and Policy, headed by Patrick Vaughan. This established an MSc in Health Services Management and the LSE Department of Social Policy introduced an MSc in International Health Policy. The 'development' component of the core Health, Planning and Financing MSc reflected the increasing interest in health economics of developing countries – a trend that Brian had started long before it became fashionable. Some students returned to their home countries and then asked Brian and Mills to visit them to run bespoke courses, such as Carlos Cruz from Mexico. Brian and Mills went out and collaborated with Julio Frenk, who had been appointed as the first Director of the new National Institute of Public Health, and later became Minister of Health. They worked closely with him to build up Mexico's health economics expertise.

Brian was equally respected for his academic administration. The management of the LSE Department of Social Administration rotated every three years between senior staff. Brian's tenures as convenor were noted for their efficiency, proving the maxim that those who most hate administration are the best at it. Colleagues noted that Brian was most often seen leaving the department at 9.30am, having done two hours' paperwork before heading off to the DHSS or home to write. Sally Sainsbury, who worked at the LSE from the 1960s, described the Department as running like a Rolls Royce: 'it just purred when Brian was in charge'.[35] In his years as a special adviser he would routinely return to the LSE after 7.00pm, either to give lectures or to resume administrative tasks. He could be brusque when it was appropriate – not shirking from difficult decisions, and pushing junior colleagues in their research plans and publications. He was viewed as a dynamic Head of Department, totally prepared to give it the attention it demanded when his turn came.[36]

One of Brian's most valued qualities was the enthusiasm he brought to the Department from his consultancy work. On returning from the DHSS he would let slip snippets of gossip on ministerial plots and intrigues, or come straight to the Department from Heathrow, full of tales of exotic meals with African heads of state. There was no apparent resentment from colleagues tied to more mundane academic routines. On the contrary, in some senses they lived through Brian's 'other lives', and his repartee helped to make the Department a lively and stimulating environment for all who worked there. They recognised that this partly came from Brian's background: he had always had the social skills and supreme, almost aristocratic, confidence to be able to easily engage the world's elites in conversation. When he reached 65, the age at which he could retire from the LSE, he had some difficult decisions to make about how to plan for the next stage of his life.

15

On the move: 1990–96

Reform: the progressive rise of health insurance

LSE 'retirement'

Cost Containment and New Priorities in Health Care

Tanzania, Indonesia and Thailand: personal and professional interests

The new language of health and social welfare

Health: political and personal

The problem with this election is that these guys are politicians when we plainly need an economist as President. (Conversation overheard during the 1992 US Presidential campaign)[1]

Although this chapter covers less than six years, it was one of the busiest and happiest periods of Brian's life. It begins with his transition from being a full-time Professor at the LSE to a punishing but rewarding life of international consultancies. Brian used his status as one of the pre-eminent expert advisers on health and social welfare to provoke debate on the rise of neoliberal funding policies, and the failure to tackle fundamental inequalities – themes he had consistently engaged with since the 1950s. This chapter illuminates his pivotal role in a global network of expert advisers and health and welfare economists (many of whom had been his students at the LSE), and his enduring impact on policy development.

Reform: the progressive rise of health insurance

It is interesting to follow the changing language of health and social welfare over the course of Brian's career. Although there is a persistent, implicit focus on change, the word 'reform' is remarkably rare in the titles of his publications. He used it for his first, the Fabian research pamphlet, *The Reform of Social Security*, in 1953, but it does not appear again until an article in 1992: 'Reform of the National Health Service', in the journal *Quality Assurance in Health Care*.[2] Perhaps this reflects his own maturity, which paralleled that of many of the key health and social welfare policies of the post-war period. In the early 1990s 'reform' became a ubiquitous adjunct to health and social welfare – used for a variety of international conferences and publications. Discussions of health and welfare services less frequently talked about 'development'; they now were the subject of 'reform'. A possible explanation might be found in the ongoing debate on appropriate methods of financing health and social welfare.

Brian had a long-standing interest in the choice between taxation and insurance-based schemes. During the 1980s, stimulated by the worldwide economic crisis and concerns about cost containment, he turned his focus to explaining the origins of health maintenance organisations (HMOs) to highlight their weaknesses as a corrective to the glowing testimonies some countries were importing from the US. He also sought to temper the railroading tactics of The World Bank, which was increasingly influential in steering health policy in developing countries towards its favoured neoliberal models, and insisting on the adoption of specific financing packages as a condition of its loans. The bank was especially keen on user charges/fees, and shifting financing from public to private organisations.

By the early 1990s there was a clear tension between The World Bank and other international organisations such as the WHO and ILO over the best strategies for healthcare financing. Social *insurance* (with the potential for mixed funding options) was increasingly seen as the most appropriate mechanism through which to generate a viable social *security* policy. In November 1990 Brian was contracted by the British government's Overseas Development Administration (a branch of the Foreign and Commonwealth Office known as ODA) to attend the five-day World Bank seminar on health finance and the role of health insurance in Asia, held at the Bali Hyatt Hotel in Denpasar, Indonesia. The seminar had been organised because there was 'dissatisfaction' among World Bank officials with the ILO-organised seminar held in Seoul in 1989 (which Brian had attended), which had only presented the social insurance approach to healthcare financing, with no opportunity to discuss alternatives, or how it had been put into practice in Latin America. Brian's contract with the ODA required him to participate in the Bali seminar as a 'resource' and to prepare a report on its discussions and outcomes. As with similar contracts, there was the unspoken assumption that Brian would also feed back to the ODA and the other interested organisations, on the tone of the proceedings and the informal discussions. The ODA paid him £240 per day for seven days overseas and eight days in the UK, as well as a return club class flight to Indonesia and subsistence. It helped to strengthen Brian's confidence that his international travels and lifestyle would be sustainable after his retirement from the LSE.

The Bali seminar (which Brian considered to be unsatisfactorily modelled on one he had attended in Taiwan in December 1989 organised by Professor William Hsiao of Harvard), was attended by delegations from Fiji, Indonesia, Korea, Malaysia, Papua New Guinea, the Philippines and Thailand. Observers were present from China, Kenya, Morocco and Nigeria, along with seven USAID staff, eleven from The World Bank, two from the WHO and six resource people. Brian noted in his report: 'There were thus about 30 participants (excluding observers). They were supported by 29 others overwhelmingly from the USA. There were only three Europeans. This support seemed excessive and unbalanced (as the longest and strongest experience of national health insurance is in Europe).'[3] He did not, however, appear to see the irony that he had been one of the key instigators in the creation of this international network of experts in health policy (who also did primary research), that included people like Hsiao and himself.

The seminar discussed the experience of health insurance in six developed countries (four of which had achieved universal coverage). It then discussed the insurance options for developing countries: private, for profit; compulsory using the social security approach; local community-based insurance; or a hybrid/mixed insurance package combining two or more of the above. The Asian delegates provided summaries of their countries' initiatives. Most were developing health insurance under social security schemes, or planning to extend it, but nearly all were faced with a shortage of funds, and there was a major need for bilateral agencies to provide substantial technical help. Hsiao gave a keynote speech on financing systems in different countries and how to evaluate them ('not wholly accurately', according to Brian). Brian chaired several of the discussion panels, and also gave a historical context paper on the development of the British health service, including the problems with the 1980s Thatcher reforms, to complement Tony Culyer's paper on the contemporary British system.

For its money, the ODA received a candid report on the Bali seminar from Brian. He felt that there had been too little time for discussion, and too much focus on the experiences of Canada, Japan, the UK and Brazil. The resource people (of whom Brian was one) were given a dominant role each day, rather than allowing the Asian delegates to contribute:

> It seemed tactless not to give time in plenary sessions for the delegates to present their problems in financing … at no stage were the administrative problems of introducing health insurance schemes ever discussed or the pros and cons of different ways of providing the benefits apart from some mention entirely from the experience of the more developed countries. Among all the delegates and resource persons present there was not one who had managed a health insurance programme.… In the discussion there was constant reference to the experience of the USA and some World Bank staff members seemed to be making judgements for Asia on the basis of which might work or not work in that country, or even debating the best way ahead for it [USA] rather than the Asian countries.[4]

Brian summarised the details of Indonesia's five years of experimenting with health insurance schemes under guidance from five ILO consultants, three of them British. It was envisaged that the success of these pilot schemes would lead to compulsory health insurance for all employed persons. Brian noted that further consultant help would be needed to supplement that currently funded by USAID. On the Malaysian experience he commented that their 'expensive' study, which had been completed by a US firm commissioned by the Asian Development Bank, had subsequently been criticised by a team of three experts from the ILO, one of whom was British. The main criticism was that only one scheme had been presented to the Malaysian government, whereas there were others which might have been more appropriate. The government had not yet made a decision, but commissioned a third report.

The Papua New Guinea situation was worse. Brian learned from a World Bank member official that insurance was being sold by a New Zealand company, under whose plan those few who could afford it were flown to second-rate New Zealand hospitals for their treatment. The Philippines had problems with fraud in its two pilot schemes; but Kenya had finally initiated amenity wards in its government hospitals through the Hospital Insurance Fund, which would generate a welcome source of finance for the over-strained and under-financed public health services. Brian noted in his report to the ODA that this was what two

British consultants had separately recommended (he was one of them), but who had been ignored by The World Bank. He also alluded to his role as a consultant for the Nigerian government, which was just about to begin a pilot health insurance scheme in four states. Brian concluded:

> In view of decisions already taken by so many of the above countries to press ahead with health insurance, using the social security approach, the academic discussion at the seminar on whether health insurance had a role in health service financing and what form it should take seemed several steps behind the thinking of the participating countries themselves....The concern was that Asian countries were rushing to adopt a solution which had not been advised by the World Bank but was being encouraged to do so by ILO and its consultants (including this consultant) with profound consequences for equity. It was not readily accepted that health insurance could be designed not to have damaging effects on equity and allow tax funds to be diverted from the mainly urban areas to improve primary care in rural areas. In the view of this consultant, what the countries really need at this stage was detailed analysis of the administrative and design problems of health insurance. This the seminar did not provide. As indicated above, such help has been provided by ILO and to a lesser extent by WHO....The resources of ILO are now strained and it is finding it difficult to recruit consultants at the rates it pays. These have not been increased in dollars over the past ten years....What is remarkable is the extent to which British consultants seem to be in demand in this field.[5]

Despite The World Bank's obvious unhappiness, the consolidating trend towards compulsory health insurance schemes continued. In developed countries there were moves towards greater efficiency, through extending coverage, reducing the number of funds and greater geographical equity. Brian was closely involved with the development and implementation of schemes in several developing countries, some of which are discussed below, and also in assessing their achievements for international organisations.

LSE 'retirement'

Although Brian talked easily to his LSE colleagues about his international travels, he rarely shared details of his private life. There were persistent urban myths that he was 27th in line to the throne, that he had inherited a fortune, even that he had adopted a child in Thailand. He was known to have friends in high places and to have been a regular guest at No 11 Downing Street when his Cambridge friend Geoffrey Howe was Chancellor of the Exchequer. When questioned on his socialism, he would repeat a tale of cycling through North Kensington in the mid-1940s, where he witnessed real deprivation for the first time. Colleagues knew that he was unmarried, and to some he would talk about his mother, whom he had supported financially and emotionally until she died in 1980. He had also played a similar dutiful role for Richard Titmuss's widow Kay, until her death in 1987. Some knew that Brian was gay, and some made that assumption, but only a small handful had met his partner, John Sarbutt, even though they may have been entertained by Brian at their home in London, or attended the departmental garden parties he held at Tanglewood, their country home in Kent. Brian sometimes introduced John to his colleagues as his godson, a convenient story, especially for when they travelled together overseas, but one which must have made it harder to break as the years passed.

It was therefore significant that when Brian retired from the LSE in September 1991, just before his 65th birthday, he decided to have a farewell party at the Denbigh Street home to which he and John had moved in 1989. The party was the epitome of what Brian loved and excelled at – bringing together fun people with good food and plenty of drinks. Many LSE colleagues were there, as well as politicians and civil servants he had worked with. Special arrangements were made for Barbara Castle to attend: John and Sally Carrier were tasked with chauffeuring her, and looking after her during the party. Castle wrote in the card that circulated among the guests during the evening: 'You know you saved DHSS from ossification of the spirit and the brain. Thank you.'[6] When the party was well under way, Brian called for silence, and made a short speech. He asked John to stand by his side as he thanked him for the years of support that he had given him, saying, 'I could not have done anything like I have done in my life without my friend.' John felt this was a brave act: neither of them had ever felt the need to confirm publicly their relationship. He was surprised but delighted that Brian had effectively taken that step for both of them. Brian's speech was greeted by cheers and clapping. It was the beginning of a new phase, with one less private compartment to his life.

Retirement from the LSE effectively reduced his teaching load, but he retained supervision of his PhD students, some of whom had been with him for many years. He took a relaxed approach with them – responding quickly when they submitted draft chapters, but never chasing them or pushing for completion. For some, supervision meant an annual meeting, more of a social event, especially for the international students who would fly into London just for this occasion. Over the course of their (sometimes 15-year) PhD supervisions, Brian had become a good friend.[7] He was always willing to comment on research, even for those who were not his students or immediate colleagues, and his capacity to turn around drafts quickly was legendary.

His involvement with students lasted beyond their official registration at LSE or LSHTM. He remained in touch with many who went on to international careers in health and social welfare – in government ministries and in international organisations. Alex Preker is an excellent example of how Brian's students extended his influence globally, even after his death. Preker had arrived in the UK in 1984 after completing his medical qualifications in Canada. Initially registered for a fellowship to work on geriatric care with Arthur Norman Exton-Smith at St Pancras Hospital, Preker went to see Brian, who was dismissive of his chosen PhD topic. Instead he suggested that Preker do a review of the economics and social policy of scaling up universal healthcare in the OECD under his supervision. He arranged for him to meet Jean-Pierre Poullier at OECD in Paris, who had done so much to implement the system of National Health Accounts (NHAs) that Brian had pioneered through his work on the Guillebaud NHS inquiry, and at WHO in the 1960s. After he completed his PhD in 1990, Preker worked on Eastern European healthcare and frequently rang Brian for his views and advice. Brian's influence on him increased after Preker joined The World Bank in 1993, where he served as one of the principal economists for health until 2013. Preker's contribution to re-positioning the Bank's approach to healthcare financing was a direct result of Brian's country-level studies, and the conversations they had together, as seen in The World Bank's first sector strategy for health which he wrote (under the direction of Richard Feachem, former Dean of LSHTM) in 1997, the year after Brian's death. Preker is but one of more than a hundred such 'disciples' of the Brian Abel-Smith philosophy of health and social welfare.[8]

If Brian had intended to retire gradually, there was little sign of it. In fact, he once again picked up the pace of his international travels. Close friends say that he was genuinely surprised to be offered so much consultancy work after his LSE retirement. He spent less time at the LSE, and colleagues sensed a slight withdrawal. The feeling was mutually exacerbating: when Ann Glennerster asked him why he no longer shared the excitement of his overseas experiences with the Department, he replied "Well, they are not interested". She told him that she thought he had got that wrong. His assessment may have also been coloured by the way in which the LSE initially relegated him and his beloved Beatrice Webb desk (inherited from Titmuss after his death in 1973) to a tiny room on the ground floor of the main building, previously used to house a photocopier. It was so small that no one could be in the room with him at the same time, forcing awkward conversations held half in the corridor. It added to his sense of isolation from the institution that had been his intellectual home since 1955.

He was acutely aware of his long involvement in health and social welfare policy, and increasingly used it as the basis for his public speeches. In November 1992 he gave a lecture at the Royal College of Physicians, 'The cost of health services', in which he drew on his understanding of the early years of the NHS, from his work with Guillebaud, through to the 1980s negative discussions on the importation of US elements of healthcare financing: 'Personally I feel that these commentators dismiss too easily the potential advantages of competition in the British context, which is by no means the same as the American.' He analysed the contemporary problems facing British healthcare through a Dutch comparison, and urged long-term pilot schemes, to establish what a national health service should be legally obliged to provide.[9]

One new initiative at the LSE that did help to rejuvenate his interest was the creation of LSE Health. Brian played a formative role, bringing in long-standing colleagues such as Walter Holland, who had now also retired, but continued to work from the Royal College of Physicians, to serve on its Advisory Committee. Whereas Brian lent his considerable international reputation to the new Department, the practical management and energy came from Elias Mossialos, who had been attracted to study at the LSE in the late 1980s by Brian's reputation as an outstanding teacher, and as one of the few people who at the time was pioneering international comparative studies. He had arrived from his PhD studies in Athens with letters of recommendation from John Yfantopoulos and Spyros Doxiadis, both of whom had worked with Brian. After a little fuss in arranging that Brian should be his tutor on the joint LSE/LSHTM MSc in Health Policy, Planning and Financing, Mossialos was encouraged to become Brian's co-researcher. Together they learned how to work the European Union funding system, and began to develop longer-term research plans. The LSE climate was not initially warm to the idea of international comparative studies on health policy, and there was little interest from Brian's old Department of Social Policy. However, in 1992 they were welcomed into Howard

Machin's newly formed European Institute, and given desk space and administrative support. Within three years they had accumulated a critical mass of short-term researchers and enough grants to be acceptable to the Department of Social Policy.

Brian's commitment to LSE Health was fundamental to its survival. His reputation helped to secure major European Union grants, including 245,000 ECUs[10] for the project 'Fundamental Choices in Health Policy' in 1993. He provided guidance to Mossialos on long-term plans, rapid and specific feedback on working papers, and constant encouragement and support. They established a Health Policy Network at LSE which brought together research institutes from six of the European Union member states, and created a new publication, *EuroHealth*, which was initially distributed three times a year to some 4,000 people across Europe. There were plans too for a summer school in comparative health policy. All this had to fit around his frequent absences on international consultancies, but it was probably the happiest time of his academic life. He had close involvement with a unit that perfectly supported his research agenda, but without the hassles of administration.

Cost Containment and New Priorities in Health Care

The majority of LSE Health's research in the early years had a European focus. This developed from, and supported, Brian's long-standing European interests and activities, dating back to his first WHO studies in the early 1960s. In 1991 Brian published a useful book, *Cost Containment and New Priorities in Health Care: A Study of the European Community*.[11] With a small honorarium and travel budget from the Milbank Memorial Fund, he updated his 1977–83 study of public finance for healthcare in 12 European countries to cover the period 1983 to 1989.[12] He wished to see which measures of cost containment had been tried, which had failed, and why. A second aim was to see how far the WHO's Health for All targets, which he had helped to construct, had begun to influence priorities at a country level. In particular, was the balance of expenditure really shifting away from hospitals towards primary healthcare? He concluded: 'The lesson which stands out from the experience of Europe over the past fifteen years is that what was previously regarded as unthinkable cannot only come to be thought, but adopted as a policy once a government comes under strong enough pressure to act'.[13]

His analysis of the Thatcher reforms in Britain was surprisingly neutral, noting that despite innovations in general management and policies to reduce both supply and demand for NHS services (increasing dental and prescription charges, emphasis on generic drugs, restrictions on employment of foreign doctors and allowing some GP practices and hospitals to become budget holders), there had been a negligible long-term impact on efficiency. His list of 'some difficulties in implementation' of the 1989 *Working for Patients* White Paper was beguilingly short, but his six bullet points have proved to be icebergs in the path of the subsequent NHS reforms. They are worth repeating to demonstrate his pithy prescience:

> (1) The information base is not at present in place for hospitals to cost their services in detail. Thus many observers have condemned the decision to implement the reform in April 1991. (2) The attempt to assess and protect quality may prove very difficult. (3) It will be extremely difficult to find a formula for distributing money to the large practices which opt to receive inclusive budgets which fully reflect the characteristics of their patients. As general practitioners can pick and choose their patients, there are risks of attempts to 'cream off' low health risk patients and 'counsel out' high users of services. (4) Budget holding general practitioners will be tempted to do procedures themselves rather than pay for them to be done elsewhere. Some may exceed their competence. (5) The doctor-patient relationship will be fundamentally altered in a budget-holding practice. The patient may come to believe that he is being done a favour if sent outside the practice for care and suspect that, if not sent out, it is to save the practice the cost. (6) Many have argued from US experience that a group of general practitioners serving 9,000 patients is far too small to spread risks.[14]

Brian found that although there had been a clear switch of finance from hospitals towards primary care, six of the 12 countries (especially France, Italy, Spain and Portugal) had actually increased their prioritisation of hospital budgets. He concluded that the radical reforms of the UK and the Netherlands, which appeared to be inspired by the experience of 'Health Maintenance Organisations' of the US, were nothing new: 'Europe had thousands of similar insurers in the nineteenth century and early twentieth century'.[15] His main conclusion was that costs had so far been successfully contained mainly by controls on supply rather than controls on demand, and especially through hospital budgets.

Tanzania, Indonesia and Thailand: personal and professional interests

From the late 1950s, when he had made his first international working trip to Mauritius, there were a handful of developing countries in which Brian took a long-term interest – Indonesia, Tanzania and Thailand were enduring favourites, for a variety of reasons. The nature of the project work he undertook for them allowed him to spend considerable periods of time in each country, and to build lasting friendships, which in turn stimulated him to look for further opportunities to return.

Tanzania had excited Brian from his first visit there in 1963. He had stayed with Rosemary and Robert Stevens in Dar-es-Salaam while preparing his first comparative WHO study on the costs of healthcare, and working with Titmuss on their pioneering book, *The Health Services of Tanganyika*.[16] He had returned for a holiday in the summer of 1975, but not been involved with any further work until 1989 when he was asked by the ODA to conduct a feasibility study for a health sector financing scheme. Formal voluntary health insurance covered only 255,000 people and provided limited benefits. There were around 200 private and semi-public insurance schemes, which had a variety of contracts with private hospitals and doctors. Some employers provided clinics and dispensaries on their premises. Some of the schemes provided for the cost of drugs, others just for access to a clinic. Some schemes covered spouses and children, but this increased the cost to as much as 11 per cent of the payroll, and most schemes were subject to abuse by providers and those covered by them. In short, Tanzania had a very inefficient and inconsistent voluntary health insurance 'system'.

In March 1991 the Tanzanian government finally decided to proceed with the project, and Brian was appointed as ODA-funded consultant along with Pankaj Rawal, one of his junior researchers at the LSE. This involved several trips over the next three years. Brian was sensitive to the traditional African respect for age and seniority, and therefore spent time at the outset of the project in Dar-es-Salaam to introduce Rawal, and make sure he had appropriate support and access to senior government officials in Brian's absence. They planned and implemented five studies: the potential for income from special private wards at national and regional hospitals; the potential for income from charges on drugs; the potential for income from bypass charges (for those patients who chose to go direct to hospitals without primary care referrals); establishing baseline data on the use of health services by different socioeconomic groups (to be used to decide on charge exemption policies); and the potential for income from compulsory health insurance. As part of their mission they held high-level meetings with senior government officials and staff of international agencies, and ran dissemination seminars. Their 'tentative strategy' for the implementation of user charges was delivered in 1992, and contained a carefully phased timetable. The Tanzanian government then requested further help from the ODA to develop a linked scheme of compulsory national health insurance (to initially cover up to 800,000 employees), and Brian and Rawal returned to Dar-es-Salaam in 1993.

Their confidential report to ODA makes clear the frustration that often came with working with governments of developing countries. Although Brian and Rawal were being paid by the British government as part of its aid package to Tanzania, they seemed to expect a greater conformity by Tanzanian officials to their proposals. When they had returned to Dar-es-Salaam in January 1993 they found that the implementation team had not, as promised on their last visit, conducted interviews with potential insurance scheme administrators, but had instead sent out a questionnaire that they judged 'almost valueless in view of the inadequate explanation of what is envisaged', and only one had been completed by the time their three-week mission was finished. The planned seminar for the providers, which was to have been the focal point of their visit, had to be postponed to April, and their report still had not been accepted by the government. There was continued pressure from World Bank technical staff to adopt a multi-insurer scheme. Brian wrote to Charles Griffin following a particularly difficult discussion:

> I realise that the idea of multiple competitive insurers has become popular in the USA since Alain Enthoven's proselytising of them and gained a new lease of life in Europe following the Drekker and Simon reports in the Netherlands. Personally I am not convinced of the net advantage. Greater competition may have led to increased choice in the USA but it has certainly not reduced costs. I know protagonists now focus attention on the employers' subsidy. But I still think it would be mad to risk launching Tanzania on the road towards spending 14 per cent of gross domestic product on health services.

> I can name no country which uses competitive insurers for compulsory health insurance. Yet most used to have competitive insurers before compulsion came in. Thus I cannot help feeling that so many countries acting independently might have had good reasons for their action. Their aim was to save administrative costs

by economies of scale. This they achieved at the price of restricting choice to that of provider rather than insurer. No one knows what administrative costs will be under the Netherlands model if it is finally introduced. The price of choice in the USA is 25 per cent of the premium. I would call this market failure. Remember we are talking in Tanzania about only 700,000 insured persons. This is already rather small to get good economies of scale. And I am by no means convinced that greater efficiency would compensate for still smaller scale, as I do not see where the entrepreneurial dynamism is likely to come from.

To choose one of the poorest countries in the world (with a very small private sector), at the very time that the denationalised parastatals are about to try and scoop up such dynamic management as can be found, for an experiment which defies international experience, would seem to me rash to the point of folly.[17]

By the end of their mission, The World Bank staff had, however, accepted 'with hesitation' Brian and Rawal's proposal for one insurer rather than several.

Brian and Rawal had to work hard to convince the Tanzanian government that the existing National Insurance Corporation was not fit to provide their recommended compulsory national health insurance scheme: 'It is a slovenly organisation which lacks dynamic leadership and is justifiably scarred [sic; should read scared] of the competition to which it is about to be exposed.'[18] They advised that there needed to be a new organisation to collect the fees as well as to distribute them to healthcare providers. They were aware that their proposals would lead to opposition from private employers (who operated their own schemes) and the politically powerful trade unions, and cause complications with the existing pension/provident funds. There were issues over out-of-date computers and records (which they hoped the ILO would be able to fix), and a whole stack of questions which were as yet impossible to address: how to define dependants; how to meet the shortage of doctors in primary care; which hospitals could afford to be contracted to the scheme; whether some or all providers would gang up and try and boycott a capitation payment system; and what the scheme would cost. They wrote up their experiences in Tanzania in two articles for the journal, *Health Policy and Planning*.[19]

Indonesia was a similarly frustrating country, from a consultant's perspective, but had a number of attractions for Brian. This group of tropical islands, formerly known as the Dutch East Indies, had been independent since 1949, but economic development, heavily based on agriculture, had never really taken off, despite the introduction of five-year development plans – known by their Indonesian acronyms as Repelitas – in 1969. The country's budget deficits were routinely supported by loans from The World Bank and the International Monetary Fund, and its problems were exacerbated by endemic institutional corruption. Brian's first role in Indonesia was as a WHO consultant on health services development in March and July/August 1983, conducting a Health Financing Policy and Practice Review. He returned in December 1983 (spending Christmas there with his brother Lionel and his partner) to advise on the expansion of health insurance coverage as part of Repelita IV, and again for three substantial trips in the spring and summer and winter of 1984. He enjoyed the culture and the climate, especially the lush gardens that it produced. He also developed a close friendship with a young Indonesian, Djafar Tahar, with whom he initially corresponded using his brother Lionel as intermediary. As the relationship developed, Brian paid for Tahar to travel to stay with him in London for medical treatment. Brian felt sufficiently attached to earmark 5 per cent of his estate for Tahar when he made notes for his will in 1985.

Brian's professional involvement with Indonesia was resumed in 1987 when he assisted with the construction of a pilot health insurance scheme in Jakarta as part of Repelita V. In 1988 he followed up on the work of his long-time Israeli colleague, Aviva Ron, who had been in Jakarta assisting the parliamentary drafting committee with the fine detail of the Labour Welfare Bill. Brian's mission was to review the pilot healthcare scheme (PKTK), travelling around the country for 18 days, before submitting a report to the ILO and the Indonesian Ministries of Health and Manpower, and attending a two-day debriefing with ILO officials in Geneva.

Brian developed a number of other significant relationships with people through his international travels. Some became life-long friends, such as Sahib Fazilamed, whom he met in Harare, Zimbabwe, in the mid-1980s when he was developing the pilot HFA2000 Financial Master Plan, and to whom he left a bequest in his will. Brian and John spent several holidays in Zimbabwe staying with their friends Ann and Roger Hamilton-King. John enjoyed Africa very much, and also accompanied Brian on some of his trips to Mauritius where Brian introduced him simply as 'Johnny', and arranged for him to be seated at the official dinners next to people who he would feel comfortable with (or, on one occasion, next to the Japanese ambassador because he spoke little English). In contrast to Fazilamed, other foreign friends such as Renato Vilar, whom Brian met in Manila in the Philippines, saw him as an easy touch for financial help. Vilar wrote pleading letters, asking why Brian had not responded to his need for money to rent a room of his own, claiming he had no bedcovers or curtains and that the mosquitoes bit him at night. Brian attempted to keep such people at arm's length (and some private from John) by corresponding with them through Lionel's address in Sussex.

It was with Thailand, however, that he developed his most enduring overseas attachments. In the late 1970s Brian had met Anusora (Toi) Ounneharerk in Bangkok and, unlike Vilar in Manila, he did give him some financial support. In the 1980s Brian met Cheep Khemsuk in Chiang Mai, in northern Thailand. He had grown to love being in Thailand's hot and sunny climate during the British winter, and within a short time he had bought businesses for Khemsuk and his brother – a taxi for Cheep and a shop for Wichian. Brian also bought a home for himself in Chiang Mai through them (non-nationals at that stage were not allowed to own property in Thailand), and they looked after it for him. Brian used the bungalow, with its beautiful walled garden of mango and avocado trees, and nearby swimming lake, whenever he worked in Thailand. Lionel and his partner who visited him there disapproved of the way that Brian spent so much money on the Khemsuk brothers, feeling that he was again being exploited. John's reaction to this new section of Brian's life was to use his dislike of hot weather as a reason not to always travel with him to Thailand, and this arrangement seemed to suit everyone. As with Sahib Fazilamed, Brian acknowledged his long friendship with the Khemsuk brothers by leaving them substantial bequests in his will.

In 1990 Brian was asked to return to Thailand as an ILO/UNDP consultant for the implementation of the new Social Security Act, which established a social insurance fund to cover some 1.7 million insured workers. Working again with Aviva Ron, he assisted in the preparations for establishing the Medical Committee, conducted workshops with senior social security and public health officials, and reviewed potential problems on benefits payments methods. In 1991 he worked in Thailand from 28 February to 25 April, for 18 days in the summer, and returned again on 19 December, when he stayed through the Christmas holiday to 14 January 1992. Although the ILO/UNDP project finished in 1993, Brian continued to make personal visits to his home in Chiang Mai to see the Khemsuk brothers. It was this detailed knowledge of a developing country that gave authority to his keynote speeches to international meetings, and perpetuated his usefulness to organisations such as WHO, ILO and ODA.

In an article in *Health Policy and Planning* in 1992, Brian set out his conclusions on such case studies:

> Competition between providers, coupled with consumer choice, can go a long way towards creating both efficiency and consumer satisfaction. The methods of controlling supply and securing the equitable distribution of health resources and paying providers are central to the objectives of equity and cost containment. In choosing between ways of paying providers, the administrative cost of different systems should not be overlooked. The aim is not to minimise such costs, but to ensure that such costs are balanced against the efficiency gains which can be generated by them.[20]

Here was an ideological flexibility that increasingly flavoured his work. It shocked some colleagues, who had not been alert to how far Brian's intellectual development had moved from the pure Bevanite health service model, in which all health services were provided for the entire population, free at the point of delivery. Julian Tudor Hart, the Welsh GP who had coined the Inverse Care Law in the 1970s, found this out in 1993. He had always admired Brian, having first been introduced to his works by Archie Cochrane in the 1960s, for whom Brian was one of his reference figures for what a real socialist was, 'enhanced rather than impaired by his status as nephew or something of the queen'.[21] Tudor Hart spent three months in Kazakhstan and Kyrgyzstan, reviewing their disintegrating Soviet healthcare systems for a US aid agency. In no time at all, he was locked in argument with the US health economists who were subverting the new national constitutions in both states which guaranteed that healthcare would remain tax-funded and free at the time of use: 'I had the high moral ground until it was knocked from under my feet by my US director, who said that Brian Abel-Smith had just completed a study of services in Kyrgyzstan, and concluded that the first step had to be introduction of user fees. I replied that I simply did not believe him. Even weakened by his connection with royalty, Brian A-S would never do such a thing.' When Tudor Hart returned home he wrote to Brian to get his version of the story. Brian replied with a long letter, confirming that he had indeed recommended user fees in Kyrgyzstan. To Tudor Hart, Brian's explanation 'was no more and no less convincing than the lengthy excuses comfortable people always find themselves making when they pass beggars on the street'.[22]

Tudor Hart's ideological standpoint was at odds with Brian's new experiences. Working in Kyrgyzstan had given Brian access to a new set of social welfare case studies for this 'new frontier' of countries that had emerged from the break-up of the USSR. What he could see from his long involvement (his first visit had been in 1961) was the futility of trying to hold onto the old system. He made several consultancy visits to Kyrgyzstan between 1993 and 1995, some arranged through Gillian Holmes, a health economist in the Human Resources Division of The World Bank's Europe and Central Asian Department, who later moved to the British Foreign Office's new Know How Fund.

One of Brian's missions was to assist the new Minister of Health (Kyrgyzstan became independent in 1991) to appreciate the realities of the country's healthcare. The official line – that healthcare was only paid for by the state – was clearly not the case. Brian had evidence that many people were also paying doctors direct, partly because the state was failing to pay doctors' salaries. As he tried to explain to the minister, until these payments were acknowledged and quantified, it was futile to attempt to design a new healthcare financing system. In his hotel in the capital Bishkek, Brian ran into Jane Falkingham who was there on a World Bank-funded project assisting the state statistics agency. Over a drink one evening they discussed how to provide robust evidence to support the new Ministry of Health in devising a workable health service. Brian asked Falkingham if she would be willing to work with him on adapting his Tanzanian household survey for this purpose, using her contacts at the statistical agency.

Together they devised a suitable questionnaire, which asked about how much people were already paying for healthcare services, including 'under-the-table' payments to doctors. This was perhaps the easiest stage of the project – the actual fieldwork required some unconventional strategies. As the concept of randomised household surveys was not known in the former USSR (Soviet Union), they had to educate the Kyrgyzstan statistical agency on the principles of randomisation. Next, because of hyperinflation in the local currency, they learned that they would have to pay the statistical agency fieldworkers who were to conduct the household surveys in US dollar banknotes. This meant flying into Kyrgyzstan (a convoluted route at the best of times) with US$10,000 in one and five dollar bills in their suitcases.[23]

Brian was thrilled to be involved with evolution of this volatile new country. Part of his enthusiasm was due to the openness of its health ministry to designing a new system (which must have triggered memories of how receptive the Mauritians had been in the early 1960s), but it was also due to the adrenaline rush he got from such situations

– having to quickly assimilate a new geography and culture, along with the slight sense of risk that often came with potential political and social instability. Brian and Falkingham were but two of a growing group of international consultants working in Kyrgyzstan in the early 1990s. They had arrived to emergency budgets, the introduction of a new currency and outbreaks of cholera. There was 90 per cent unemployment, rotting factories, empty shops and little tax revenue to be collected. The health services were trying to manage with a 60 per cent cut in their budgets, staff were three months behind in their pay and nearly a quarter of the drugs bought were smuggled in and of dubious quality. More than 40 per cent of people lived in poverty. Of Brian and Falkingham's sample of 2,000 households, 30 per cent did not expect to be able to heat their homes for over half the winter, and 8 per cent would not be able to heat them at all. With a winter temperature of −20°C (and in parts down to −40°C) this was a desperate state of affairs.[24] After extensive field studies, Brian and Falkingham advised introducing a system of user fees for healthcare – part of which would be retained at the local clinic level to ensure that staff were promptly paid, and to make under-the-table payments to doctors unnecessary. He returned at least twice a year for the next three years to help with pilot health insurance schemes and re-structuring health services, each visit lasting between 10 and 20 days.

Brian's engagement with Kyrgyzstan exemplifies his philosophy, which was shared by many of his social policy colleagues, and was articulated so clearly by David Donnison: 'We should not explore and record human suffering unless we are trying to do something about it.'[25] Brian did not stop at the production of his assignment reports. He arranged for a group of 10 staff from the Kyrgyzstan Ministry of Health to travel to London and Stockholm on a study tour, funded by the ODA, in March 1994. He personally arranged the itinerary, including visits to London hospitals, and accommodation through his secretary Deme Nicolaou Frini's family (that would be cheaper than through hotel agencies). In the summer of 1994 he taught a group of 26 healthcare professionals from Kyrgyzstan, Kazakhstan, Turkmenistan, Tajikistan and Uzbekistan at the Boston University School of Public Health and Centre for International Health. He delivered a three-day module on healthcare financing, soliciting beforehand exactly what aspects of their own countries' problems the participants would like to use as case studies for reform.

This was a busy period of Brian's life, overlapping with his semi-retirement from the LSE. With the restrictions of regular course teaching lifted, he travelled most months of the year. Often the visits were interspersed with just a couple of days back home in London to re-pack his suitcase. It was physically and mentally exhausting – even more so considering that this was before the advent of the internet, and all correspondence was by telephone, fax or letter (likewise all travel reservations). Yet Brian found this work a necessary stimulus and John was happy for him to continue. They had always shared their homes with paying guests, some of whom became life-long friends such as the Canadian academics Arthur Sheps and David Blewett. These big Victorian terraced houses had plenty of space for attic flats and spare rooms – it made sense to use them so John would have company when Brian was away on his travels. In 1989 Nigel Cox, an artist in his late twenties, moved into their new Denbigh Street home. He was to become a close friend to them both.

Brian had always had an interest in housing, as both an academic and entrepreneurial activity. From buying his first house in Elizabeth Street in 1960 he had indulged in property development, buying houses to renovate with his former partner Charles Schuller, and running this as a business to gain the available tax breaks under the trading name of Lonsdale Road Properties Ltd. He was, however, acutely aware through his involvement with the Citizens Advice Bureau and the Child Poverty Action Group of the misery of low-income families, who often had no choice but to rent poor quality housing. The Conservatives' large-scale selling off of council housing stock after 1979 exacerbated this problem. Brian's appreciation of the intellectual issues behind low-income housing was helped by his friendship and collaboration with housing experts such as David Donnison. Brian agreed to assist one of Donnison's former students, Anne Power, who had gone on to work with estate communities in Brixton in the 1970s and 1980s. Her idea, to investigate how council estates coped with poor conditions such as vandalism and crime, turned into a PhD under Brian's supervision on the origins and management of social housing. He made her read widely: Ralf Dahrendorf's *On Freedom*, Florence Nightingale, Beatrice Webb's letters and Donnison's classic books on housing.

In 1979 a pioneering Priority Estates Project was set up to develop estate-based management and tenant involvement with local authorities to attempt to reverse the poor conditions on Britain's estates. A government review of cooperatives and tenant participation in 1988 created direct government grants to tenants, and helped to kick-start a new approach. Shortly afterwards, a new charity organisation was formed, the National Communities Resource Centre (NCRC). It now needed a home in which to provide free residential training for those living in low-income communities who wished to take an active role in their estates' management. Power found a potential property just outside Chester – Trafford Hall – a 20-room Georgian country house in desperate need of repair. It was derelict in parts, with leaking roofs and bat infestations, but with enormous scope for improvement. Power persuaded Brian to form a charitable company with herself and the architect Sir Richard Rogers as co-directors to buy the house for the NCRC. This would require £2 million in fundraising, to enable a full refurbishment and the construction of a 24-bedroom annexe. It got off to a slow start, and it wasn't until the government finally gave a partial grant in January 1995 that the project was secured. Rogers produced a much cheaper design for an innovative self-build bedroom annexe with a turf roof.

Working closely with a new National Tenants Steering Group, Brian used all his influence to raise funds and benefits in kind. He helped to persuade the hotel chain Grand Metropolitan Estates to buy Trafford Hall and give the NCRC a 10-year rent-free period; the building firm McAlpine's worked at a massively discounted cost on the project; the National Westminster Bank (in which Brian had a family interest through the former Smith's Bank) and John Lewis department store were asked to donate furniture. Brian even went as far as to buy and send back hundreds of metres of red and gold heavy duty silk from one of his trips to Thailand to make the floor-to-ceiling curtains needed for the big Georgian sash windows. He was insistent that Trafford Hall had to have good quality furnishings, not planned on the lowest common denominator of what tenants' groups would be used to – as he put it, 'no plastic tables and paper cups'. There may have been a touch of snobbery in his views, but it also reflected his strong egalitarian ethos – what was good enough for his class should be available to all, and it also had to be an attractive and income-generating conference centre to help fund NCRC activities.

Trafford Hall was officially opened by Prince Charles on 6 December 1995. In the final months of renovation Brian even engaged John's expertise in landscape gardening, and they had driven up from Tanglewood with several carloads of plants from their own garden. Its mission was to train 1,000 young people and 1,000 low-income tenants each year, and to provide innovative resource packs on issues such as Credit Unions, Local Exchanges and Community Businesses. Brian was enormously pleased to have been involved in this pioneering project which encapsulated his philosophy of giving people the knowledge to improve their own lives. He always saw the bigger picture – not only training the tenants, but also helping to establish a Diploma in Housing at the LSE to ensure that there was a way to train the much-needed professional estate managers.

In addition to the projects discussed above, in the early 1990s Brian was also working on schemes in Chile, Colombia, Ghana, Namibia, Nigeria, Turkey and Vietnam (to name just the largest ones). They were lucrative as well as giving him the constant intellectual stimulation and travel that he enjoyed. The health economist consultant Mark Wheeler joked that Brian was 'the most expensive man in the world', but most of these consultancy fees were paid straight into LSE Health's account to fund research projects and studentships. The WHO contract to work with the Nigerian Ministry of Health to establish a national health service was for US$11,972, and travel by business class flights. In the spring of 1993 he spent nearly a month in China as a WHO consultant, returning there again for a month in the summer. He accepted re-appointment to the Academic Advisory Committee at the National Institute of Public Health in Mexico (representing the WHO), and gave lectures in Hungary for Human Risk Management Ltd, and in Sweden on the reform of the National Health Service. In December 1993 he spent three weeks in Singapore as a Lee Kuan Yew Distinguished Visitor at the National University, giving two public lectures and four seminars, culminating with an official visit to Prime Minister Lee Kuan Yew.

Also in 1993, he was engaged by the OECD to write a synthesis and analysis of the healthcare reforms then happening in several countries. A previous review commissioned from Richard Saltman by the OECD had been judged unsatisfactory. Brian's honorarium covered participation in the working party on social policy meetings of National Experts on healthcare reform in Paris in November 1993, and in Washington DC the following March. As a result of his engagement, he was asked to undertake a longer project, 'to analyse the health care reforms implemented or planned in 17 OECD countries in recent years'. He presented a paper, 'The escalation of health care costs: how did we get there?' to the follow-up conference 'Managing effective health care systems'.[26] A publication from the project, *Cost Containment and Health Care Reform*, was co-authored with Elias Mossialos.[27]

In 1994 he was invited by the Prime Minister of Greece to put together a team of researchers to investigate the Greek health services. As well as Mossialos, he also involved Walter Holland, and they spent several weeks in Greece studying the existing systems. The project informed a further comparative study, for the European Parliament, published in February 1995 as *Health Care in Three Southern Member States (Spain,*

Greece, Italy). This made several proposals for reforms to increase efficiency and user satisfaction, and highlighted the poor information currently available on how these countries operated their services.[28] He was given an honorary degree by the Athens School of Public Health, recognition of the importance of the LSE team's research, which, as he put it in his acceptance lecture, 'has, I am afraid, ruffled a few feathers in important medical circles'.[29] No doubt this was stimulated by his proposals for 'a fundamental reassessment of medical knowledge', and the production and implementation of 'practice guidelines'.

Brian's worldwide connections helped to establish LSE Health as a major policy research centre. In 1994, together with a new researcher at LSE Health, Panos Kanavos, they produced a powerful report for Pádraig Flynn, the Irish European Commissioner for Social Affairs, who needed support to counter the plans of Martin Bangemann, German Commissioner for the Internal Market and Industrial Affairs, to liberalise the pharmaceutical market. Brian and Mossialos analysed the impact of unrestricted prices on the European consumer and concluded that this would be a detrimental policy. Their report was critical to the successful campaign to quash this proposal.

The pharmaceuticals report is a key example of what Brian did best – bridging the gap between rigorous research and policy formation by directly engaging with the policy networks. In essence, this is what Brian had been doing since 1953. His comparative analyses and direct dialogue with policy makers helped to reshape the British academic tradition. This contact partly helps to explain the difference from American social policy research, which had little direct contact between academics and policy makers, and thus embraced a more rigorous experimental evaluation of US policy interventions, especially from the 1960s.[30] But to establish an entire unit on a comparative and collaborative research premise was novel, and not entirely welcomed by some academic colleagues. Yet Brian's quiet confidence in his methodologies sustained him, and he did not succumb to pressure for diversions into what he saw as unnecessary theorisation. Within a few years comparative analysis had become part of mainstream academic culture – valued for its intrinsic logic rather than devalued for being 'theory-lite', or for getting into bed with 'the enemy'.[31]

This capacity to synthesise and to draw on a rich historical context in a policy-useful way placed Brian at the centre of contemporary international debate on health and social welfare. He was often the initial point of contact when organisations wished to put together participant lists for seminars and conferences. In 1994 he was invited by the Foundation for International Studies on Social Security to give a keynote speech at its international research seminar at Sigtuna in Sweden, and was subsequently asked to edit two volumes of conference papers. In 1995 he helped to organise the WHO Interregional Consultation on Health Insurance Reforms, held in Seoul, Korea. Many of the invited countries were ones that he had been closely involved with. Delegates from South Africa, Costa Rica, Egypt, Morocco, Thailand, Korea, Germany, Vietnam, Ghana, Indonesia, China and the Czech Republic were among those who discussed how to keep costs down, and the merits of different systems of organising services. Brian prepared summaries of each country's experience. He discussed the implications for the development of social insurance, noting that although each country had a unique culture, history and institutions, there were nevertheless some useful generic messages:

> Planning and implementation takes time: the Republic of Korea took only 12 years to move from inception of social insurance to complete coverage, in the perhaps most favourable economic conditions, with real per capita annual growth of over 10 per cent. Other countries (Germany, Japan, Czech Republic, Costa Rica) trace the evolution of their full coverage back for periods of 40 to over 100 years ... economic growth facilitates the development of insurance ... it requires an efficient national banking system and a high level of administrative capacity ... more skills are needed than can be produced through ad-hoc study tours: this requires a programme of continuous human resource development within developing countries.... Countries with national health insurance schemes can be characterised as having a high level of solidarity, which is more than a simply political issue, but is something which reflects the character of social relations in a country, and may not be easily influenced. Also required is a degree of integrity in public and corporate affairs.[32]

Although Brian noted that social insurance may offer a more equitable means of financing health services, he stressed that it was important to develop a better health infrastructure too, not just to shift the method of financing. He gave examples of projects he had been involved with: in Costa Rica, where the surplus from urban health insurance had been used to develop the rural infrastructure, and Vietnam, where the undistributed surplus from health insurance was used to buy basic hospital equipment. He highlighted that there were different ways of mobilising community resources to improve funding for healthcare.

Good examples of community financing included Thailand's rural health card scheme. Community rating, that is, sharing risks within a carefully delimited district (as in rural Vietnam or in large cities in Indonesia) was also a successful policy. A good strategy began with easily defined groups, such as company employees, before a phased expansion to cover other groups such as the self-employed. It was important, however, that there were enough health and welfare staff to operate new schemes without draining existing services, and both primary healthcare and hospital-based services should be included with appropriate referral systems. If co-payments were used (where the patient contributes to the cost), it was preferable to fix varying rates to encourage them to use primary care services. Quality assurance was seen as an integral part of insurance systems, to be put in place from the outset, with both treatment and service protocols that were regularly monitored.[33] 'Guided competition' among providers and insurers was felt to be desirable, to obtain best performance or value for money.

Brian's conference report finished with a warning:

> Insurance should not be seen as a way of shifting core responsibilities for overall regulation and policy making, and for ensuring access to services for the poor, away from the government. In many developing countries, the physical resources are inadequate, inequitably distributed and of poor quality. Staff in the health infrastructure are poorly trained, with inadequate resources. Their improvement makes a strong claim on public resources and skills a priority. The supporting conditions required for successful development of social insurance are stringent: time to properly design and implement the scheme, economic growth, capacity, solidarity and integrity.[34]

The new language of health and social welfare

Long-term policy reviews were also finding a place in the strategies of consultants in the 1990s. This was history, but by another name, although Brian had no problem with calling it that. Brian's 1960 report on Mauritius re-surfaced in 1994 as the basis for a new study by John Roberts, who had previously worked for WHO-EURO in Copenhagen, and now worked as a freelance consultant through his own company, AdHealth Ltd. Mauritius, now a relatively prosperous developing country, was still regularly importing external expertise. The Ministry of Economic Planning and Development had initiated a review of social services and a reform of the health service system, and secured funds from the Commonwealth Secretariat. Their initial request had been to Brian, who had carried out a study on the financing of health services in Mauritius through the WHO in 1990, but he was unable to take on this project, so suggested Roberts to them instead. The following year, in 1995, Brian was again involved with a proposal for Mauritius, when he joined a team put together by the international accounting and consultancy firm Coopers & Lybrand to bid for a contract to develop a health insurance scheme. Their invitation to him was in part a reflection of his long-standing knowledge of the island, but also an attempt to match the expertise of a rival Harvard team, who had won a tender for a cost-effectiveness study because they had joined forces with LSHTM. Staff from the Mauritian government had then hinted to Coopers & Lybrand that they should also look for an academic partner, perhaps the LSE.

This was one of Brian's last projects, and provides a somewhat crude financial assessment of his value as an international expert on social welfare – £1,800 per day (plus expenses). Coopers & Lybrand's proposal was for a two-phase project, each phase lasting 10 weeks, in which Brian would contribute to developing the methodology and writing the report. Their full tender of £180,000 is indicative of the sums being spent on such consultancy at the end of the 20th century. For a country such as Mauritius this remained a significant sum, but an essential budget element if their development plans were to benefit from the international expertise of people such as Brian. Coopers & Lybrand were but one of a growing number of businesses offering policy consultancy services. Governments were also beginning to see the benefits of out-sourcing such expertise. When David Nabarro was at the British ODA in 1992 he initiated the creation of an independent resource centre: HLSP Ltd by Ken Grant and Roger England (originally called Health and Life Sciences Partnership, it was later sold to Mott MacDonald Ltd), based on an advisory model the Americans had been using for some time. It entered into competitive tendering for ODA contracts along with academic institutions such as the LSHTM and the LSE.[35] Brian had also worked for a number of other such consultancies, such as INDEVELOP, based in Stockholm, who had handled his commission for a project in Vietnam in 1990.

By the early 1990s the language of health economics was almost unrecognisable from Brian's Cambridge studies of the early 1950s. New terms had come in and out of fashion – CBAs (cost benefit analyses) were being ousted by CEAs (cost-effectiveness analyses).[36] The discipline was awash with acronyms, many of them invented or refined by his friends and colleagues: Dorothy Rice had worked on QALYs in the 1970s (Quality Adjusted Life Years, a forerunner of DALYs: Disability Adjusted Life Years). The Yale academic John Devereaux Thompson had developed Diagnostic Related Groups (DRGs) as a way to manage the allocation of healthcare resources in the late 1960s. When Thompson spent the autumn of 1973 in London as a King's Fund visiting fellow, he had aroused Brian's enthusiasm with the potential for this new management technique. In 1993 the *World Development Report: Investing in Health*, issued by The World Bank, introduced the new concept of the 'basket' of cost-effective interventions which developing countries were allowed to choose from, depending on their budgets.[37] Items such as vaccinations, family planning and tuberculosis treatment were priced up, but strong determinants of health such as water supply, sanitation and housing were explicitly left out of the 'basket' for the private sector to supply. Although *Investing in Health* was welcomed for its analytical contribution by many health economists, some international health campaigners viewed it as a 'manifesto for neoliberal health finance reforms…. From Bolivia to Pakistan, these reforms began to dismantle already fragile public coverage of health services'.[38] The World Bank's strategy appeared to effectively disregard health as a human right. It threatened public services, which lobbyists such as Global Health Watch were trying to protect, and which Brian had spent his career building up.[39]

Brian continued to produce new books which reflected these changing times. *An Introduction to Health: Policy, Planning and Financing* was published in 1994.[40] His preface encapsulated his philosophy, developed over the previous 40 years of research: 'This book is about how to improve health in a cost-effective and politically acceptable way. It is not just about health services as they are not the most important determinant of health improvement.' History was still the foundation for his work, and the book begins with a new analysis of McKeown's theory for the 19th-century demographic transition. The bulk of the book draws on case studies from developed and developing countries, which Brian intended to demystify the complexities of how healthcare could be financed. He was especially keen to draw attention to the dangers of the blanket, and increasingly negative term, 'privatisation'. His chart, 'Common flows of finance', effectively encapsulated the sophistication of healthcare financing that he had witnessed over the previous 40 years. Alan Maynard's review called it 'Vintage Abel-Smith. Comprehensive and comprehensible, reliable and stimulating.'

Health: political and personal

In 1995 Brian stirred up debate yet again, with the *Fabian Review* article he co-wrote with his LSE colleague, Howard Glennerster: 'Labour and the Tory Health Reforms'.[41] They cautioned Labour against the 'gut reaction' of undoing all the changes that the Conservatives had made to the NHS since 1979, but advocated evaluating each change on its merits. Some they judged as effective, such as the abolition of regional health authorities (which Crossman had proposed in his 1970 Bill). They viewed the introduction of GP fundholding and greater hospital autonomy as positive steps: 'The hospitals now have to sit up and take notice as these GPs now have the power to give or withhold money. They can bully specialists about waiting times and waiting lists. They can insist that test results come back quickly.... Surely it makes much more sense to build on what has been achieved and induce more GPs to join the system....' They proposed to limit private practice fees, to use incentive payments to keep patients' treatment within the NHS, and to encourage hospitals to use their right to negotiate locally appropriate rates of pay, which would be protected if a national minimum wage were also introduced. There would be tough decisions needed, based on the price of hospital services, not traditional loyalties, for example, to the expensive inner London teaching hospitals: 'They were originally placed there so that specialists could readily combine their unpaid morning's work in a voluntary hospital with their well-paid Harley Street private practice in the afternoon, by using a horse-drawn coach.'

Although Brian and Glennerster acknowledged that some real healthcare needs were still unmet, and that this was partly the consequence of Tory under-financing of the health service, 'the more fundamental problem is that much of the treatment provided is inappropriate or unnecessary.... What are needed are clear guidelines based on hard data about what improves the outcome for the patient.' They applauded the introduction of the new Health Technology Assessment Panels, and urged more national pooling of information, and a review of local authority management of home care, perhaps with an increase in National Insurance contributions dedicated to long-term care for the elderly. They concluded:

> What is wrong with the health service is that there is no democratic input below the Secretary of State. Local authorities are shackled by financial controls.... If they were once again given real taxing powers they could perhaps replace district

> health authorities, purchase specialised services and fill gaps left
> by fundholding GPs ... enabling them to secure much better
> coordination between the community health services and the
> personal social services....These are real decisions which a future
> Labour government will need to consider. Markets give choice
> and eventually make providers respond to the choices made. But
> in public services, there needs to be a local democratic regulator
> and proper funding.This is what the health service at present lacks.

The *Fabian Review* article provoked some strong reactions. Walter
Holland sent Brian a very detailed critique of each of the 11 significant
points of the article. He disagreed with many of their arguments, and
suggested that initiatives such as locally negotiated pay would lead to
poaching of staff. Howard Stoate, a GP (in a non-fundholding practice)
published 'a riposte' in the *Fabian Review*.[42] David Piachaud waited until
August before sending his lengthy disagreement, copying it to Julian Le
Grand as well: 'I have forgotten who said that the primary requirement
in academic life is irreverence. I am aware that I am challenging a
mighty accumulation of evidence, expertise and wisdom and I am
acutely aware that it is many, many years since I attempted to keep up
with even a little of the health literature – "fools rush in ...".'[43] Like
Holland, Piachaud was unhappy that Brian appeared to have moved
so far from the key principles of the NHS to champion the beneficial
power of the market. If Brian replied to Piachaud by letter, there is
no copy in his archive, but a copy of Glennerster's is, unrepentant for
their endorsement of key Conservative NHS reforms.

Brian's attitude to his own health was rather cavalier: he smoked
incessantly, and his lifestyle naturally involved lots of hospitality with
long meals and heavy drinking. Alongside his shirts, so expertly folded
for each trip by John, Brian packed a bottle of whisky, so that he could
be sure to have his usual nightcap. His occasional swim at the RAC Club
in Pall Mall was a token gesture towards these significant health risk
factors. In late 1995 he was clearly not well. He thought that it might
be a tropical bug – perhaps bilharzia (schistosomiasis) – that he could
have picked up swimming in an infected lake on his last trip to Thailand.
For several months he delayed seeking proper medical attention, in the
hope that the situation would improve of its own accord. A colleague
from the LSE asked John to persuade Brian to take a holiday. They went
to Tenerife, but Brian did not swim – a sure sign that he was not well.
In January 1996 he was in Brussels with Mossialos, attending meetings
at the Social Affairs Directorate. One evening, over a drink in a local

bar, he confided that he felt very tired, and had arranged for some tests in London. Brian had recently taken out private health insurance with BUPA. Colleagues who knew seemed shocked that one of the NHS's greatest advocates could have committed such treason. Brian justified it as a practical issue, to ensure that he could get medical care if needed on his frequent international travels.[44] After a further delay while the tropical bug theory was discounted, he was referred to the London Clinic for exploratory surgery at the beginning of March. It was discovered that he had advanced cancer of the pancreas, beyond treatment.

After the happiness of only four post-retirement years, in which he had reconciled all aspects of his life, the brutal swiftness of this illness seemed unfair. He returned home from the London Clinic and began to tie up work projects and domestic affairs. John drove him each day into the LSE until the final week of March. John was struggling to cope – he would now have to be the strong one who took the initiative and supported Brian, a role he had not often had to play during their long relationship, which had begun when he was 19. Their close friend Nigel Cox, who had lived with them in the early 1990s, moved back into their Denbigh Street home. Brian had initially worried that Nigel was a threat to his relationship with John, despite Nigel's assurances that it was in fact complementary. But Brian had also accepted that there would be a need for Nigel's support in the future, and an opportunity for his relationship with John to resume.

It was less easy for his brother Lionel, from his home in Sussex, to accept the speed with which Brian's illness was progressing. They had been close all their lives – only two years apart in age. Although there had been significant disagreements over politics, this was more than outweighed by their shared experiences. They had cared together for their mother after their father died in 1946. She had lived another 34 years, heavily dependent on their weekly visits and telephone calls. Neither Brian nor Lionel had married but both had life-long partners, and both loved the English countryside. One of the reasons that Brian and John had chosen to buy Tanglewood was because it was less than 40 miles from Lionel and his partner at Peasmarsh in Sussex. They regularly got together for weekend lunches and holidays. When Brian was in London Lionel religiously rang him on the dot of 11am every Sunday morning (a ritual Brian tolerated but did not always appreciate). They had mutual friends from the same social circles, many since the 1950s, such as the barrister Milton Grundy, former MP Denzil Freeth and Cecil Gould, Deputy Director of the National Gallery. Brian and Lionel provoked each other as only close siblings can. Yet their family history and its customs, such as the annual Smith family luncheon which meant so much to Lionel (who as elder son had inherited the trust fund and title Lord of the Manor of Wendover), also gave Brian vicarious pleasure. Lionel was outraged that Brian kept his share of the family silver in a saucepan (a common British anti-burglar strategy), but he did acknowledge the loving care that Brian took of family antiques – the Smith's Bank partner's table, and the magnificent semainier chest that he had inherited when Tresco Abbey, one of the Smith family estates, was broken up. Both could be snobbish, Brian despite his avowed socialism, but always with a sense of mischievousness.

After Brian had received the diagnosis he determined to finish as many of his current projects as he could. He established a trust to inherit the bulk of his estate, so that John would receive ongoing financial support – an important move in the time before civil partnerships. He had already had the foresight to put Tanglewood into John's name 12 years earlier.[45] He also wanted to say goodbye to close friends, and to arrange small gifts for his godchildren – the daughters of his oldest friends Charles Schuller and Alistair Sampson. On 3 April Brian invited Elias Mossialos and his secretary Deme Nicolaou Frini to visit him at home for a planning meeting. He asked them to take notes while he smoked and chatted with them and with Pankaj Rawal, one of his research assistants. Mossialos left that afternoon with the impression that Brian was well enough to continue with small pieces of work.

John and Nigel were to go out for a meal that evening – at Brian's insistence – to celebrate Nigel's birthday, and so that Nigel could try again to explain to John how much Brian would need his support in the coming weeks. Brian wanted John to be strong for him and he knew that Nigel could enable this. Maggy Langstone, a friend who looked on Brian as a father figure, came to keep him company but as he was suffering with increasing pain, John and Nigel cancelled their restaurant plans. Brian asked John to telephone their GP for a home visit; however, a locum doctor arrived instead and gave him some morphine. John and Nigel, like Mossialos, could see that Brian was not yet in the final stages of his illness. They believed that he just needed something to make him more comfortable so that he could get through the next few days, and go as planned to Tanglewood at the weekend. There was still so much to be done, and friends to break the news to, including Peter Townsend. After the doctor's visit, John offered to sleep that night in Brian's bedroom, in case he was needed. "Thank you Sweetie" were Brian's last words to his partner of 35 years.

John woke at 3.00am and reached out across the bed. In the darkness of the early morning, he knew that Brian was dead.

On Thursday 11 July, at 6.00pm a commemoration of Brian's life was held in the Grand Committee Room of the House of Commons. The audience and speakers represented the many parts of his long career. He had asked that any memorial service held for him should be non-religious. Appreciations were given by Julian Le Grand, Barbara Castle, Navinchandra Ramgoolam (Prime Minister of Mauritius), Peter Shore and Peter Townsend. John Carrier read 'Hopes and Fears for Art' by William Morris from Albert Sieveking's 1885 book *The Praise of Gardens*. Jane Falkingham read *To bring the dead to life* by Robert Graves. The closing words were given by his brother Lionel.

In addition to specifying in his will that he wished his body to be cremated at Charing in Kent and for his ashes to be scattered at Tanglewood, he had also asked for a party. John and Lionel jointly organised this at Tanglewood on one of the long summer days that followed the formal House of Commons commemoration. It was a real party – exactly as Brian would have organised – at the place he had loved best, where he and John had made a home to share with their families. Over 150 people gathered in the gardens where a large marquee had been erected. There was a magician and dancing to Abba. Passengers in the planes drifting across the blue skies into Gatwick looked down on Tanglewood's meadows, which were a riot of colour – full of Brian's beloved poppies, cornflowers and daisies. This was an English countryside he had seen so often from the air, coming and going on his international travels – a truly global citizen.

Epilogue: Stories, histories and biographies

'Let the story tell itself.' (Brian Abel-Smith to Peter Townsend, 27 September 1976)[1]

I confess, the subject is but dull in itself, to tell the time and places of men's birth, and deaths, their names, with the names and numbers of their books: and therefore this bare skeleton of time, place and person must be fleshed with some pleasant passages. To this intent I have purposely interlaced (not as meat, but as condiment) many delightful stories. (Thomas Fuller, *The worthies of England*, 1662)[2]

'Is this a biography or a history?', the people at Policy Press wanted to know. My reply was that it is both. History and biography are so naturally intertwined it is difficult to write one without the other. As most biographies are singular, focusing on just one life, can we usefully extrapolate from one person's experience to construct a wider history? The biographical intensity of focus on one person is troubling, especially if they are no longer alive. What assurance do we have that they would have agreed to this form of inquisition? The novelist Beryl Bainbridge, when approaching 70, was asked by someone if they could write her biography: 'I was pretty astounded, and wondered why anyone should want to do it, and what the point of it would be. My reaction is, "I'm the only person who knows what it was like, so how can anyone else write it?" So I said no.'[3]

I had a similar feeling when the LSE suggested that I write a biography of Brian Abel-Smith. I have explained in the Acknowledgements how some serendipitous finds during a long day of sampling his archived papers changed my mind. My initial (coping) strategy was to say that I would be writing a history of the development of British and international health and social welfare policy, using Brian Abel-Smith as a prism through which to illuminate this revolutionary half-century. I thus evaded the Bainbridge question by telling myself that I was not writing a biography. This self-deception lasted until my journey through the archive arrived at boxes of personal papers. Brian had kept all letters sent to him from his boarding school days onwards, and his family had kept all of his letters to them, and at some point returned them to him. There were letters from Cambridge friends, increasingly mixed in with semi-public letters and documents about his working life. All were neatly indexed by surname. Did Brian expect someone to write a biography? Perhaps he had intended to write an autobiography. I took reassurance from the fact that he had chosen to deposit these papers at the LSE archives when he retired (although some arrived from his home after his death via his partner John). He had made a decision to put details of his life into the public domain. This helped to overcome my slight queasiness at trying to understand his private life. Further reassurance came from the archive boxes: occasional letters from foreign lovers, sent via his brother Lionel's home to avoid John's attention, which had been tucked into obsolete files. Were these too precious to throw away, kept safe in his university office, but not remembered during the futile, post-diagnosis rush of his last days at the LSE, trying to tie up various projects? Or was this evidence of Brian as historian, consciously retaining this reliable primary source evidence that these liaisons had taken place, vital elements for someone else to be able to develop a more accurate account of 'what it was like' to be Brian Abel-Smith?

I realised that the advantage of giving the biographer the upper hand in this project was that it would allow me a greater degree of freedom in structuring the research project and the book. I have not left out any significant event of Brian's life that was evident from archive or oral history sources. There is, of course, no way of telling whether there were originally more letters (detailing events or relationships) that Brian may have already pruned, but there is enough evidence to be able to discuss how he chose to live his life, and to see how his activities shaped the development of health and social welfare policy in Britain and internationally. A biographical framework has prioritised adjunct histories. I have, for example, written about the development of Fabian socialism and Labour's policy machine, but not about how the Conservatives used think tanks such as the Bow Group to develop their own health and social welfare policies. Yet the histories included here are more than just 'condiments' to Thomas Fuller's biographical 'meat' quoted above. They are integral to understanding Brian Abel-Smith and he is likewise vital to understanding the wider history of health and social welfare.

No biography will ever do full justice to its subject. Brian Abel-Smith, despite leaving indexed personal papers and voluminous copy correspondence from his working life, was essentially a very private man, a consummate compartmentaliser. It was not until he had retired from his academic post at the LSE that he chose to publicly acknowledge his 30-year relationship with John. He was widely sociable, but maintained mutually exclusive sets of academic and private friends. Can anyone say that they knew the 'real' Brian Abel-Smith? John came closest, but even to him there were areas of Brian's life that were difficult to understand.

There were clear and enduring elements to Brian's character, firmly moulded in the English establishment tradition by his family heritage, and reinforced by his education at an elite public school. This gave him a life-long innate ability to position people within a social hierarchy, and he was acutely aware of fine social distinctions. From rare comments to close friends it is apparent that he was sensitive to slight lapses in social etiquette – the woman who wore diamond jewellery in the daytime – but he did not have the overt snobbery associated with some of his class, such as Nancy Mitford or Michael Heseltine. He once said to John, 'I hate people like me'. He had enormous respect for those who fulfilled duties that came with their family position, and for the social honesty of the working classes, but he was less tolerant of what he called 'the barking middle classes'.

Brian's obituary writers – Peter Townsend, Julian Le Grand and Bob Pinker – attempted to explain what had made this upper-class Englishman dedicate his life to improving the lives of those less fortunate. They drew on personal knowledge, and long friendships (Townsend had known Brian since the early 1950s). The consensus view, and one that Brian had himself partly discussed in an LSE lecture in 1995, was that his exposure to the poverty of north London, in the aftermath of the Second World War Blitz, had made him aware of his relative fortune to have been born into a class that did not have to struggle for the bare essentials of life. Colleagues considered him to be a 'radical liberal' with a patrician view of the poor as a class to be helped to achieve their potential, that he could display sympathy but not empathy for their condition. Yet others identified in him a profound and sincere concern for human predicament. This was particularly true for his involvement with developing countries. He had first seen absolute poverty in 1951, when he took part in the British universities debating tour to India, Ceylon and Pakistan. His travel diary and letters home expose a faintly supercilious attitude to these former Imperial subjects: the legacy of his father's tales of military service in India, and his Haileybury education. His later publications, especially those on the poverty of the developing world in the 1970s and its ruthless exploitation by 'us' of the developed world, indicated a genuine sense of responsibility. Alex Preker's observation that people in developing countries 'really loved him' is prescient: it was a mutually supportive relationship.

From early adulthood, Brian was seen by his peers as a sharp mind, eloquent, witty and enthusiastic. He exploited every opportunity to try new experiences. His limitless energy was increasingly channelled into activities that fulfilled his sense of duty, but that also gave him personal fulfilment and pleasure. His political maturity came at Cambridge, and his allegiance to Fabian socialism found practical expression in his commitment to the Labour Party. This allegiance, coupled with his academic research into social justice issues such as poverty, gave him a powerful potential to affect change. By the mid-1950s Brian was secure in his social, political and sexual identity. His nascent political brilliance could have ensured an easy route into a parliamentary career, but he took the astute decision in 1957 that the risks for a gay man in public office were not ones he wished to take when Hugh Dalton offered him the opportunity. Brian's decision not to become an MP saved him from years of 'social work' with constituents and unproductive committee digressions, which he would have found a chore. His experiences had already proved to him that an academic career could be effectively political, and possibly more enduring than a conventional parliamentary one.

Richard Titmuss is central to understanding Brian's life. From 1952, when John Vaizey introduced him to Titmuss's writing, Brian was enthralled. Titmuss articulated the principles of social justice that Brian was beginning to define himself. Their relationship was part paternal/filial loyalty, part intellectual comradeship. It was intensely personal, bringing Brian within the Titmuss family circle in such a way that he felt a duty of care to Richard's wife Kay long after his death in 1973. From Brian's appointment as Assistant Lecturer at the LSE in 1955 they met or telephoned each other nearly daily when they were both working in London, for almost 20 years. Titmuss steered Brian's choice of research projects, and the relationship was strong enough to withstand the inclusion of Peter Townsend in the partnership, the dissolution of the Titmice in the late 1960s, and to prevent Brian's move away from the LSE.

Brian's sense of duty and loyalty to the LSE was rooted in his relationship with Titmuss. It helped during Titmuss's lifetime that

Brian's intellectual development did not veer far from the Titmuss philosophy. He accepted the model of social policy that Titmuss had fashioned, founded on a principle of universal access to state-provided and funded welfare services. Brian was recognised as Titmuss's loyal lieutenant. His elaboration of the Beveridge model developed on a consciously parallel and non-confrontational trajectory to Titmuss's own philosophy of social welfare. Although Brian's undergraduate and postgraduate degrees were in Economics, he increasingly defined himself as an academic of Social Administration. His primary concern was now how to improve health and social welfare, and especially to alleviate the poverty that he saw as the root cause of much social distress. The discipline of Economics in isolation was not capable of providing effective solutions.

Both Titmuss and Brian, and to a lesser extent Peter Townsend, had a great trust in politicians. Their engagement with the Labour Party in the 1950s and 1960s was coloured by a naïve understanding that policy proposals generated from their academic research – on pensions, poverty, social security and healthcare – would have an easy adoption when Labour next returned to government. When that opportunity came in 1964 their ideas initially sank under the weight of the economic crisis, and Labour's internal disputes. By this stage Brian had found satisfaction and impact through alternative channels of influence – the Fabian Society, governorships of hospital management boards and an increasing media profile through his journalism, television and radio work. The experiences of the Child Poverty Action Group from 1965 alerted Brian and other campaigners that a Labour government in Britain was no automatic guarantee of support for the disadvantaged. They learned some hard lessons in the course of trying to translate clear academic evidence of rising poverty into political decisions.

Despite his increasing appreciation of the flaws and frustrations of the British political system, Brian could not resist the invitation in 1968 to become Richard Crossman's special adviser, one of the first such posts created. For two years he was at Crossman's beck and call, completely structuring his life around his part-time duties. To close friends and colleagues it was clear that this experience excited Brian like nothing before. It was a vicarious hold on political power, with none of the mundane political responsibilities. His enthusiasm and desire to fully engage in this hedonistic experiment exposed an element of self-centredness that was not usually visible in his personality. He was prepared to drop major research projects (leaving Townsend to carry on without him on the Rowntree project). He was only able to work at this intense pace because he had the emotional and very practical support of his partner, John, who ensured that their homes (in London and Kent) continued to function smoothly.

The transition from academia to expert policy adviser was relatively easy for Brian. He had a great deal of political nous and an existing network of contacts. He was skilled at translating his academic work, routinely exposed to the 'sharp-fanged critics of the academy', into a language and format useful to politicians. His prodigious energy and the freedom offered by the special adviser role enabled him to function as 'a one-man think tank'. He was a modern Charles Booth with an enormous capacity for work of all types, who did not draw distinctions between his different, parallel roles. He combined academic integrity with political pragmatism, conscious of the ticking clock of the parliamentary session. His return as a special adviser to Barbara Castle when Labour were re-elected in 1974 provided another opportunity to work on policies that he had failed to push through with Crossman between 1968 and 1970. Some of these were achieved, but others still hung in the balance when she was sacked in 1976. His commitment to reforming Britain's welfare state, and personal pleasure from being at the centre of the policy-making process, lay behind his immediate offer to David Ennals to continue as a special adviser. This took precedence over Castle's hurt feelings. When the intellectual satisfaction palled after two years of working with David Ennals, Brian again felt no qualms about moving to work with Peter Shore.

Brian thrived on being needed. This is apparent even in his schooldays, when the headmaster of Haileybury noted that Brian had devoted so much time to his head boy duties that he had not done himself justice in his final exams, and failed to gain a Cambridge scholarship. The death of his father in 1946, when Brian was 20, required him and Lionel to take on a considerable caring role for their mother. They struggled to cope at times with her loneliness and dependency on alcohol, and she did not hide her disappointment that neither of them led conventional married lives, or had given her grandchildren. Brian and Lionel's new relationships in the 1950s appeared to effectively freeze Vivée's life, leaving her marooned in permanent middle age, totally reliant on their support but unable to fully understand or participate in their lives.

Many of the decisions that Brian made in his life have multiple logics. His refusal to consider international academic job offers was partly rooted in his loyalty to the LSE and the need to be on hand for his mother, but also has to be considered within the context of his sexuality. Since 1953 he had constructed in London a supportive and private network of gay friends. Even after the 1967 Act that legalised homosexual acts, there remained a public suspicion of gay men that gave a fragility to their positions in local communities. London's gay scene offered an alternative family. Brian could be 'openly' gay within London's 'closed' gay communities without compromising his public life. His choice of homes, in which he always had male (and sometimes female) lodgers, gave a degree of cover to his relationships.

The creation of his clothing business Just Men illustrates Brian's complexity. It can be seen as a response to his sense of duty to a former partner, Charles Schuller, to give him secure employment: Brian's help was needed and he fulfilled that expectation. It can also be seen as part of his engagement with London's gay scene. Brian deliberately stocked it with clothes that appealed to gay men: it was a legitimate outlet for his personal gay style. But it also played to another deep-seated part of his psyche, the need to be seen as financially successful in relation to his older brother Lionel. Brian was acutely conscious of his family's social position, and their wider wealth. Lionel had inherited a considerable estate, and the title Lord of the Manor of Wendover. He had regularly given Brian large gifts of money through the 1950s, to help with house purchases, cars and holidays that supported Brian's very comfortable lifestyle. By creating Just Men (and his property development company, Lonsdale Road Ltd), Brian had a mechanism through which he could supplement his LSE salary. How (or whether) he reconciled this capitalist entrepreneurship with his socialism is difficult to see.

It is impossible to separate the public and the private, and the British and the international components of Brian's life. His research for the Guillebaud enquiry provided an entrée into the world of international health policy at the WHO and the ILO. This opportunity, and the ways in which he fully exploited it, has to be seen in the context of his earlier fascination with travel – first as part of his National Service with the army in Austria in 1948–49, then through long summer holidays on driving tours of Europe and the Middle East, and the 1951 universities debating tour to India, Ceylon and Pakistan. It was fortunate that his chosen area of academic expertise also allowed him to indulge his love of skiing and foreign travel.

International work, especially in developing countries, satisfied Brian on several levels. Former colonies provided a laboratory in which he could design and test permutations of the Beveridge model of social welfare. Their governments were often more open to radical policy suggestions than the tortuous British systems. His first initiatives in the 1960s – in Tanzania and Mauritius – were imbued with a lingering element of Imperial authority. There was also a sense of frontier culture to these projects – of being there at the creation of new attitudes to social welfare, a very practical, hands-on involvement, of making do with the human and economic resources that their missions uncovered. There was a degree of freedom – from theory, existing systems – and significantly from domestic responsibilities and relationships. These motivations persisted throughout his life. His work in the former Soviet province of Kyrgyzstan in the early 1990s generated the same adrenaline rush as his first trips to Africa – flying in with suitcases full of US dollar notes, high-level diplomacy with government ministers, but always with the same primary concern and compassion for the people who lived in poverty and ill health.

The projects that he undertook for developing countries, through international organisations such as the WHO, ILO and The World Bank, appealed to his sharp, analytical mind and love of problem solving. His methodology, refined over the years, was always to begin by looking at the big picture, working out the sequence of problems and where to begin to solve them. It was exactly the same pragmatism that had guided his advice to British Labour governments. He had an enormous breadth of knowledge across the full spectrum of social welfare, from pensions to social security and healthcare. He did not 'cut and paste' policy ideas from one developing country to another, but combined detailed analysis with an understanding of the views of key stakeholders to produce swift, practical advice. This was novel in the 1960s when development studies were in their infancy, and gained him enormous recognition and respect in international organisations.

Despite his academic home in the LSE's Department of Social Administration, Brian was identified as an economist first and foremost by the organisations and governments that he worked with. He never wrote about how he identified himself academically, perhaps reluctant to engage in the intermittent, and occasionally negative analyses of social administration made by economists such as Tony Culyer.[4] These peaked in the 1980s, at a time when the discipline was experiencing internal change, partly a result of the re-positioning of social sciences expertise within the new British Conservative era. The concept of 'social administration' lacked a clear international profile: there were no academic departments with this name in the US or Europe; the nearest equivalent label – social policy – also had various interpretations.

Brian's reputation as a founding father of health economics was consolidated through his pioneering work on National Health Accounts for the WHO, which remain the basis for the OECD's statistical surveys today. All of his research had a clear practical application. He had little time for theory generating, and chose not to engage with that side of the academic economics community. This perhaps weakened some of his policy work. Had he participated in the Health Economists Study Group, founded by Alan Williams and Tony Culyer at the University of York, he might have acted as a useful bridge between their more theoretical work and that of the rising numbers of economists employed from the 1970s by governments and international organisations. One senses that he did not see the point in devoting energy to discussions that he felt would not be constructive. He disliked confrontation and argument, preferring to quietly ignore criticism directed against his 'theory-lite' work rather than engage in debate.

Increasingly from the 1970s Brian's research interests lay in public service financing rather than pure economics, or Titmuss's brand of social administration. He was widely seen as Titmuss's 'earthly representative', but publications such as *Value for Money in Health Services* indicated a shift away from core principles of universal welfare states and recognised the potential of cost sharing and alternative models of social insurance as ways to achieve effectiveness and efficiency in an era of rising costs and economic crises.[5] He was prepared to explore strategies for cost reduction as long as they did not conflict with his core principles of equity and social justice. He acknowledged the qualified usefulness of markets, choice and privatisation – all terms that would have been an anathema to Titmuss.

Donald McCloskey has said that economists don't prove, they convince.[6] Brian was at the centre of many significant conversations – at expert committees, international workshops and conferences. He was the linchpin between different communities of experts, and a core member of the new network of expert advisers that emerged from the 1970s.[7] To maintain this level of authority he had to ensure that he remained in circulation, intellectually and physically. This became more demanding as the requests for his services grew in the 1980s, especially after the key role Mahler gave him in constructing the economic strategy for Health For All by the Year 2000. He was always moving forward, looking for new opportunities, and claimed he never re-read anything that he had published. He advised his younger LSE colleague, David Piachaud, that he should get up and work from 5.00am if he wanted to be a successful academic. Part of the attraction of policy formation for Brian was the generic process – fast-paced and intellectually satisfying. Yet he worked with a genuine self-effacing modesty, an ability to get on with things without concern for whether he would always get the credit. Like many academics, he was an obsessive character, but as David Donnison recalled, 'He was fun, always fun, there was always a joke'. The tribute to him in *Eurohealth* noted: 'On a personal level he radiated warmth in a way which made it impossible not to notice his presence when he walked into a room'. Engagement with people – friends, colleagues, students – was at the heart of his life. Julian Le Grand summed him up perfectly: 'he was a really delightful human being'.

Brian died 13 months before the return of a Labour government in Britain. He had watched over the previous 17 years as Thatcher's Conservatives slowly dismantled Beveridge's welfare state. They were re-elected three times despite a return to a level of unemployment not seen since the 1930s, which, according to the Chancellor Nigel Lawson, was 'a price well worth paying' for lower inflation.[8] Council housing rents were increased and the best of the stock sold. Pensions were indexed to earnings, not prices. Child benefit was left un-indexed. There were 29 unfavourable changes to the regulations governing unemployment benefit. The 'best twenty years of earnings' clause inserted into the Barbara Castle pensions scheme to reduce the feminisation of poverty was swept away. Supplementary Benefit was rationalised into Income Support with more losers than gainers.[9] David Donnison's carefully designed scheme of legal rights was abandoned and exceptional needs grants became loans.[10] Sixteen- and 17-year-olds were stripped of their right to income support and many of them joined the homeless.

These were the facts Brian selected from the Conservative regime to present in his LSE centenary lecture in July 1995. He acknowledged that the global economic crisis had made government in Britain difficult, but could not condone the disproportionate impact that Conservative policies were having on the poorest people. His assessment of international social welfare was equally bleak: increasing poverty in Europe, and unpayable debts in developing countries. He asked his audience:

> Was all this preventable? Did Keynes get it all wrong? There are now some who argue that what is needed now is Keynesianism on a global scale coupled with an active labour market. The oil price rises dug a deep hole in world demand which Keynesian remedies were needed to fill. But instead governments adopted the failed remedies of the pre-war era.... But the sorrows and concerns of Britain are as nothing compared with the fate of Africa. While OECD countries throw aid at them, at the same time they close away their markets, take their debt repayments and

interest on a scale greater than the aid they give and rival each other in exploiting the vast world market for armaments. There is only one answer to this problem which is debt forgiveness. This would once again enable these countries to buy their drugs and other supplies on the world market. It would also increase Britain's export earnings in its traditional markets. But debt forgiveness now appears to be a reward for political services (eg Egypt). Sadly it is seldom given even in part on the basis of need.[11]

His lecture had the same passionate conviction of his first Fabian essay in 1953. It is a simple message, distilled from years of experience and, to its core, political and historical. It highlights real and relative poverty, and, in common with all of Brian's work, offers a practical solution.

Bibliography of Brian Abel-Smith's publications

Books and major reports

(1956) *The Cost of the National Health Service in England and Wales* (with R.M. Titmuss), Cambridge: Cambridge University Press.

(1960) *A History of the Nursing Profession*, London: Heinemann (reprinted in 1975).

(1961) *Social Policy and Population Growth in Mauritius* (with R.M. Titmuss), London: Methuen.

(1964) *The Hospitals 1800–1943*, London: Heinemann.

(1964) *The Health Services of Tanganyika* (with R.M. Titmuss et al), London: Pitman.

(1964) *British Doctors at Home and Abroad* (with K. Gales), Occasional Papers on Social Administration, No 8, London: Bell.

(1965) *Paying for Health Services*, Public Health Papers, No 17, Geneva: World Health Organization.

(1965) *The Poor and the Poorest* (with P. Townsend), Occasional Papers on Social Administration, No 17, London: Bell.

(1967) *Lawyers and the Courts* (with R.B. Stevens), London: Heinemann.

(1967) *An International Study of Health Expenditure*, Public Health Papers, No 32, Geneva: World Health Organization.

(1968) *In Search of Justice* (with R.B. Stevens), London: Allen Lane.

(1972) *Doctors, Patients and Pathology* (with H. Rose), London: Bell.

(1975) *Legal Problems and the Citizen* (with M. Zander and R. Brooke), London: Heinemann.

(1975) *Accounting for Health. Report of a King's Fund Working Party, et al*, London: King Edward's Hospital Fund.

(1975) *People without Choice*, Report of the 21st Anniversary Conference of the International Planned Parenthood Federation.

(1976) *Report on a National Pension Scheme for Mauritius* (with T. Lynes), Mauritius.

(1976) *Value for Money in Health Services*, London: Heinemann Educational Books.

(1978) *Poverty Development and Health Policy*, Public Health Papers, No 69, Geneva: World Health Organization.

(1978) *National Health Service: The First Thirty Years*, London: HMSO.

(1978) *Pharmaceutical Consumption* (with P. Grandjeat), Commission of the European Communities, Social Policy Series, No 38.

(1979) *The Organisation, Financing and Cost of Health Care in the European Community* (with A. Maynard), Commission of the European Communities, Social Policy Services, No 36.

(1980) *Sharing Health Care Costs* (National Center for Health Services Research, Research Proceedings Series), US Department of Health, Education, and Welfare Publication No 79.

(1982) *Marriage, Parenthood. and Social Policy*, Eleanor Rathbone Memorial Lecture, Liverpool: Liverpool University Press.

(1984) *Cost Containment in Health Care*, Luxembourg: Commission of the European Communities, Luxembourg.

(1984) *Cost containment in health care*, Occasional Papers on Social Administration, No 73, London: Bedford Square Press.

(1984) *Into the Twenty-First Century: The Development of Social Security*, Reporter, Geneva: International Labour Organization.

(1984) *Planning the Finances of the Health Sector* (with E. P. Mach), Geneva: World Health Organization.

(1986) *Future Directions for Social Protection* (with M. Raphael), Athens: M.K. Publishers.

(1987) *The Philosophy of Welfare: Selected Writings of Richard M. Titmuss* (edited with K. Titmuss), London: Allen & Unwin.

(1989) *Recurrent Costs in the Health Sector* (with A. Creese), Geneva: World Health Organization.

(1990) *Health Insurance for Developing Countries* (with A. Ron and G. Tamburi), Geneva: World Health Organization.

(1992) *Cost Containment and New Priorities in Health Care*, Aldershot: Avebury.

(1994) *Cost Containment and Health Care Reform* (with E. Mossialos), Florence: European Institute.

(1994) *Policy Options and Pharmaceutical Research and Development in the European Community* (with E. Mossialos and P. Kanavos), Florence: European Institute.

(1994) *Cost Containment. Pricing and Financing of Pharmaceuticals in the European Community* (with E. Mossialos and C. Ranos, eds), London: LSE Health and Pharmetrica.

(1994) *An Introduction to Health: Policy, Planning and Financing*, London: Longman.

(1994) *Report on the Greek Health Services*, Athens: Pharmetrica.

(1995) *Choices in Health Policy: an Agenda for the European Union*, Aldershot and Luxembourg: Dartmouth Press and Official Publications of the European Communities.

Pamphlets

(1953) *The Reform of Social Security*, London: Fabian Society.

(1955) *New Pensions for the Old* (with P. Townsend), London: Fabian Society.

(1964) *Freedom and the Welfare State*, London: Fabian Society.

(1967) *Labour's Social Plans*, Fabian Tract No 369 (also published in *Socialism and Affluence*, Fabian Society, 1967).

Principal published articles

(1956) 'The Economic Evidence to the Guillebaud Committee', *The Lancet*, 28 January.

(1956) 'Lohngebundene oder Einheitsrenten in Gross Britannien?', *Sozialer Fortschritt*, November/December.

(1957) 'Income Survey', in *The Need for Cross-National Surveys of Old Age*, Copenhagen.

(1957) 'La Indagini sui Reddito', *Tecnica ed Organizzasione*, July/August.

(1957) 'Der Altersrenten in Gross Britannien', *Sozialer Fortschritt*, August/September.

(1957) 'Memorandum on a National Superannuation Scheme' (with R.M. Titmuss and P. Townsend), National Superannuation, Labour Party, May.

(1958) 'Whose Welfare State?', in N. MacKenzie (ed) *Conviction*, London: MacGibbon & Kee.

(1959) 'Social Security', in M. Ginsberg (ed) *Law and Opinion in England in the Twentieth Century*, London: Stevens & Sons.

(1959) 'The Cost of the Support of the Aged in the United Kingdom', in *Aging and Social Health in the United States and Europe*, Ann Arbor, MI: University of Michigan.

(1960) 'Changes in the Use of Institutions in England and Wales between 1911 and 1951' (with R. Pinker), Manchester: Manchester Statistical Society.

(1961) 'Jewkes' Apocrypha', *Medical World*, October.

(1962) 'The Price of Freedom', *Medical World*, January.

(1962) 'Hospital Planning in Great Britain', *Hospital Trustee*, May.

(1962) 'Research Report', *Sociological Review*, November.

(1962) 'Pensions for Dependent Wives', in C. Tibbitts and W. Donahue (eds) *Social and Psychological Aspects of Aging*, New York and London: Columbia University Press.

(1963) 'Paying for the Family Doctor', *Medical Care*, vol I, no I, Jan-March

(1963) *The Stethoscope*, 1 and 15 January, and 1 and 18 February.

(1963) 'Paying for Family Doctor Services', *Medical World*, vol 98, no 2, February.

(1963) 'Beveridge II: Another Viewpoint', *New Society*, 28 February.

(1963) 'Health Expenditure in Seven Countries', *Times Review of Industry and Technology*, March.

(1963) 'Changing Methods of Financing Hospital Care', in *The changing role of the hospital in a changing world*, London: International Hospital Federation.

(1963) 'State Pensions and the Age of Retirement' and 'Recent Developments in Income Security Programs in the United Kingdom', in R.H. Williams, C. Tibbitts and W. Donahue (eds) *Processes of Aging*, Vol II, New York: Atherton Press.

(1964) 'Hospital Planning and the Structure of the Hospital Services', *Medical Care*, vol 2, no I.

(1964) 'The Platt Report', *Nursing Times*, 17 July.

(1964) 'The Voiceless Millions', *New Statesman*, 9 October.

(1965) 'The Price of Mental Health', Proceedings of a Conference of the National Association for Mental Health, London.

(1965) 'The British Labour Government's Plans for Social Security', Papers presented at the Canadian Labour Congress Social Security Conference, Canadian Labour Congress, Ottawa.

(1965) 'The Case That Failed', *The Guardian*, 22 February.

(1965) 'A Prescription for the GP', *The Guardian*, 23 February.

(1966) 'National Insurance and the National Plan', *New Society*, 3 February.

(1966) 'The Economics of Population', *Proceedings of the Royal Society of Medicine*, vol 59, no 7, July.

(1966) 'Low Income Groups in the United Kingdom', in *Low Income Groups and Methods of Dealing with their Problems*, Organisation for Economic Co-operation and Development.

(1966) 'How poverty could be eliminated tomorrow', *Weekend Telegraph*, no 113, 25 November.

(1966) 'Do we care so little about poverty?', *Observer*, 6 November.

(1967) 'A Hospital Commissioner', in B. Robb (ed) *Sans Everything*, London: Thomas Nelson.

(1967) 'Sainsbury and the Drug Industry', *New Statesman*, 6 October.

(1968) 'Child Poverty and Political Action', in *A Personal Service*, Association of Children's Officers.

(1968) 'Health Policies and Investments and Economic Development', in E.M. Kassalow, *The Role of Social Security in Economic Development*, Washington, DC: Department of Health, Education and Welfare.

(1968) 'Paradoxes of the Welfare State', *The Listener*, 30 May.

(1968) 'The Need for Social Planning', in *Social Services for All?*, London: Fabian Society.

(1968) 'What Priority Health?', in M. Prywes and A.M. Davies (eds) *Health Problems in Developing States*, New York: Grune and Stratton (also *Israel Medical Journal*).

(1968) 'Les Aspects Economiques des Services de Santé', *Cahiers de Sociologie et de Démographie Médicales*, Department of Studies and Forecasts, Ministry of Social Affairs, Paris.

(1969) 'Economics and Health Services', *Health Economics*, Copenhagen: World Health Organization.

(1970) 'Major patterns of financing and organisation of medical services that have emerged in other countries', *Medical Care*, vol 3, no I, January–March.

(1970) 'The Problem of Establishing Equivalent Standards of Living for Families of Different Composition' in C. Bagley and P. Townsend (eds) *The Concept of Poverty*, London: Heinemann.

(1970) 'Poor Kids and Rich Kids', *New Statesman*, 6 November.

(1970) 'Major Patterns of Financing and Organisation of Medical Care in Countries other than the United States', in *Social Policy for Health Care*, New York: Academy of Medicine.

(1970) 'Public Expenditure on the Social Services', *Social Trends*, December.

(1971) 'Poverty and the Budget, *New Statesman*, 9 April.

(1971) 'A Hospital Ombudsman', *New Society*, 22 April.

(1971) 'Managing the Health Service', *New Society*, 29 April.

(1971) 'The Politics of Health', *New Society*, 29 July.

(1971) 'Medical Education: Weighing the Costs', in *World Health*, Geneva: World Health Organization, November.

(1972) 'A Hospital Ombudsman', in 'Social Services: A New Society Social Studies Reader', *New Society*.

(1972) 'Ombudsman', *New Society*, 2 March.

(1972) 'Health Priorities in Developing Countries: The Economist's Contribution', *Transactions of the Royal Society of Tropical Medicine and Hygiene*, vol 64, no 4 (also published in *International Journal of Health Services*, February).

(1972) 'The History of Medical Care', in E.W. Martin (ed) *Comparative Development in Social Welfare*, London: Allen & Unwin.

(1972) 'Child Poverty', *FSU Quarterly*, Summer.

(1972) 'Can We Reduce the Cost of Medical Education' (with L. Ekholm, H.E. Klarman and V. Rojo-Fernandez), *WHO Chronicle*, vol 2, no 10, pp 441–50.

(1972) 'Education for Health Service Administration: The Needs of Organisations', in *Education for Health Services Administration*, Ann Arbor, MI: University of Michigan.

(1973) 'Equity and Dependency', *Tax Credit Proposals*, London: Institute for Fiscal Studies.

(1973) 'A Call for Help' (with M. Zander), *New Society*, 8 March.

(1973) 'Major Patterns of Financing and Organization of Medical Care in Countries other than the United States', in L. Corey, S.E. Saltman and M.F. Epstein (eds) *Medicine in a Changing Society*, St Louis, Miss: Mosby.

(1973) 'Social Security and Taxation', in B. Crick and W.A. Robson (eds) *Taxation Policy*, London: Pelican.

(1973) 'Perspectives on Income Inequality and Income Maintenance: Some Dilemmas from British Experiences', in P. Booth (ed) *Social Security Policy for the Seventies*, Ann Arbor, MI: Institute of Labor and Industrial Relations, University of Michigan.

(1973) 'Equity and Dependency', IFS Conference on Proposals for a Tax-Credit System, Institute for Fiscal Studies, Publication No 5, March.

(1973) 'An International Study of Health Expenditure and its Relevance for Health Planning', *Boletim de Conselho Federal de Medicina*, no 2, vol 2, Brazil.

(1973) 'Cost-effectiveness and Cost-benefit in Cholera Control', *WHO Chronicle*, vol 27.

(1974) 'Can We Reduce the Cost of Medical Education' (with L. Ekholm et al), *Development Digest*, vol 12, no 2, April.

(1974) 'Needed Population Policies for Planet Earth', *Canadian Welfare*, vol 50, no 3, May–June.

(1974) 'Economics of Health and Disease', *Encyclopaedia Britannica*.

(1974) 'Value for Money in Health Services', *Social Security Bulletin*, vol 37, no 7, July.

(1974) 'Work and Social Security in a Society in Transition', Keynote Address, Proceedings of the Canadian Conference on Social Welfare, Calgary, June.

(1975) 'The Cost of Medical Care', Ninth CIOMS Round Table Conference on Medical Care and Society, Rio de Janeiro, August, and World Health Organization, Geneva, 1975.

(1975) 'Terveyspal veluj en Kustannukset j a Tuotot', *The Finnish Economic Journal*, LXXI, Nide. 4, Vuosikerta.

(1976) 'Value For Money', Papers presented at the Congress on Health Care Planning, Amsterdam, April, Excerpta Medica.

(1976) 'Introduction', in R.M. Titmuss, *Commitment to welfare*, London: Allen & Unwin.

(1976) 'Introduction', in R.M. Titmuss, *Essays on the welfare state*, London: Allen & Unwin.

(1978) 'Minimum Adequate Levels of Personal Health Care: History and Justification', *Milbank Memorial Fund Quarterly/Health and Society*, vol 56, no 1, Winter.

(1979) 'The Cost of Health Services', *New Society*, 12 July.

(1979) 'Merrison's Medicine for the Health Service', *New Society*, 26 July.

(1980) 'Health Care in a Welfare Oriented Society', WMA Follow-Up Committee on Development and Allocation of Medical Care Resources, Japan Medical Association, Tokyo.

(1980) 'Don't Have a Go at Romantic Fiction if you know Nothing about Sex', *The Times Higher Education Supplement*, 27 June.

(1980) 'Making the Most of Scarce Resources' (with A. Leiserson), World Health Forum, Geneva: World Health Organization, vol 1, nos 1 and 2.

(1979) 'Report of the Seminar', in A. Brandt, B. Horisberger and W.P. von Wartburg (eds) *Cost-Sharing in Health Care*, Proceedings of the International Seminar on Sharing of Health Care Costs, Wolfsberg, Switzerland, 20-23 March, and Springer-Verlag, Berlin, 1980.

(1979) 'Economics and Health Policy: An overview', in A. Griffiths and Z. Bankowski (eds) *Economics and Health Policy*, Proceedings of the XIIIth Round Table Conference, Geneva, November, Council for International Organisations of Medical Sciences and The Sandoz Institute for Health and Socio-Economic Studies, Geneva, 1980.

(1980) 'Address', The 1980 General Assembly Round Table Conference on Regulatory and Economic Aspects of the European Pharmaceutical Industry (European Federation of Pharmaceutical Industries' Association Meeting), Brussels, June.

(1980) 'Health and Economy', Paper presented at the International Symposium 'Health and Economy' organised by the Universitaire Instelling Antwerpen, 17–18 April 1980, and published in *Health and Economy*, Part 2, Van Loghum Slaterus, Antwerpen-Deventer, 1982.

(1981) 'Minimum Adequate Levels of Personal Health Care', in P.R. Lee et al (eds) *The Nation's Health: A Course by Newspaper Readerr*, San Francisco, CA: Boyd & Fraser Publishing Company.

(1981) 'The Cost of Health Services', *New Society Social Studies Reader: Medicine and Health*.

(1981) 'The Role of the Private and Voluntary Sectors in EEC Countries' and 'The United Kingdom Experience with Sharing Health Resources between the Regions', in D.M. Salter (ed) *Health Planning and Resource Allocation*, Wellington, New Zealand.

(1981) 'Minimum Adequate Levels of Personal Health Care: History and Justification', in J.B. McKinlay (ed) *Issues in Health Care Policy*, Milbank Reader, No 3, Cambridge, MA and London: The MIT Press.

(1981) 'Towards a Healthier Population', *New Society*, 15 October.

(1982) 'Economic Commentary', in P. Selby and M. Schechter (eds), *Aging 2000: A Challenge for Society*, published for Sandoz Institute for Health and Socio-Economic Studies by MTP Press Ltd.

(1982) 'Marriage, Parenthood and Social Policy', *Political Quarterly*, vol 53, no 3, July–September.

(1982) 'Income Testing of In-Kind Transfers', in I. Garfinkel (ed) *Income-Tested Transfer Programs: The Case For and Against*, Institute for Research on Poverty Monograph Series, University of Wisconsin, Academic Press.

(1982) 'Planificacion de la salud', in V. Conde et al (eds) *Economia y Salud*, Madrid: Karpos.

(1983) 'Sex Equality and Social Security', in J. Lewis (ed), *Women's Welfare, Women's Rights*, London and Canberra: Croom Helm

(1983) 'Assessing the Balance Sheet', in H. Glennerster (ed) *The Future of the Welfare State: Remaking Social Policy*, London: Heinemann.

(1983) 'Economic Efficiency in Health Care Delivery' and 'Summing-Up', in *Improving Cost Effectiveness in Health Care*, International Social Security Association, Studies and Research Series, No 19, Geneva.

(1983) 'Wirtschaftlichkeit im Gesundheitsweser', *Soziale Sicherheit Wien*, no 11, pp 531-40.

(1983) 'The Attacks on Welfare: a European Viewpoint', *International Journal of Social Economics*, vol 10, no 6/7.

(1983) 'Economic Efficiency in Health Care Delivery', *International Social Security Review*, vol 2, ISSA, Geneva.

(1983) 'Tencencias em Assisteycia Medical!', in C. Barroso Leite (ed) *Un Secure de previcencia Social*, Rio de Janeiro: Zahar, pp 212-22.

(1984) 'Anti-Poverty Policies and the European Community: Powers and possibilities', in J. Brown (ed) *Anti-Poverty Policy in the European Community*, London: Policy Studies Institute.

(1984) 'Improving Cost-Effectiveness in Health Care', *World Health Forum*, vol 5, pp 88-90.

(1984) 'Social Welfare', in B. Pimlott (ed) *Fabian Essays in Socialist Thought*, London: Heinemann, pp 169-84.

(1984) 'Cost Containment in 12 European Countries', *World Health Statistics Quarterly*, Geneva, pp 351-63.

(1984) 'An Overview of Health Care and Financing Studies', in *Financial Planning for Health for all by the year 2000*, SEARO Technical Publications, No 5, WHO New Delhi, pp 9-23.

(1984) 'The Study and Definition of Poverty: Values and Social Aims', in G. Sarpellon (ed) *Understanding Poverty*, Rome: Franco Angeli, Rome, pp 68-86.

(1984) 'Grosbritannien', *Dev Europaische Arneimittelmarkt*, Bonn: Wido, pp 201-12.

(1985) 'Risks in Giving Control to the Providers of Health Care', *World Health Forum*, vol 6, no 1, Geneva, pp 9-11.

(1985) 'The Major Problems of the Welfare State', in S.N. Eisenstadt (ed) *The Welfare State and its Aftermath*, London: Croom Helm, pp 31-43.

(1985) 'Health Care in Europe', in A. Brandt et al, *Eurocare*, Basel: Health Econ, pp 17-24.

(1985) 'Who is the Odd Man Out?', *Milbank Memorial Fund Quarterly, Health and Society*, vol 63, no 1, pp 1-17.

(1985) 'Einflussnahme auf die Entwicklung des Arzneimittelverbrauchs im Rahmen der EG', in von Ferber et al, *Kosten und Effizienz im Gesundheitswesen*, Munich: Oldenbourgh Verlag, pp 251-64.

(1985) 'Present Trends and Future Proposals for the Medical Care and Pension Schemes in the Main Advanced Countries', *Kemporen Social Security Yearbook*, Toyo Keizai Shinposha, Tokyo, pp 13-21.

(1986) 'Funding Health for All: is insurance the answer?', *World Health Forum*, vol 7, no 1, pp 3-11.

(1986) 'Foreword', in G. Rhodes et al, *Primary Health Care in the Inner Cities*, London: Policy Studies Institute.

(1986) 'The World Economic Crisis: Repercussions on Health', *Health Policy and Planning*, vol 1, no 3, pp 202-13.

(1986) 'Foreword', in J. Allsop and A. May, *The Emperor's New Clothes*, London: King's Fund, pp XIII-XV.

(1986) 'What Crisis? Whose Crisis? Which Crisis?', in F. van den Bosch and A. Doncot-Devriendt (eds) *Sociaal en Zeker*, Antwerp: Kluwer-Deventer, pp 243-50.

(1986) 'The World Economic Crisis: Health Manpower Out of Balance', *Health Policy and Planning*, vol 1, no 4, pp 309-16.

(1987) 'The Price of Unbalanced Health Manpower', in Z. Bankowski and T. Fulop (eds) *Health Manpower Out of Balance*, Geneva: CIOMS, pp 49-66, and in Z. Bankowski and A. Mejia (eds) *Health Manpower Out of Balance*, Geneva: CIOMS, pp 110-23.

(1987) 'Health Economics and the World Health Organization', in G. Teeling Smith (ed) *Health Economics: Prospects for the Future*, London: Croom Helm, pp 92-100.

(1987) 'The Market Place for Medical Technology', in F.F.H. Rutten and S.J. Reiser (eds) *The Economics of Medical Technology*, Heidelberg: Springer Verlag.

(1987) 'What Crisis? Whose Crisis? Which Crisis?', *Political Quarterly*, vol 58, no 3, pp 276-82.

(1987) 'Funding Health for All', *Asian News Sheet*, vol XVII, no 4, December, pp 24-32.

(1987) 'Reduire les coûts des soins de santé', in H. Deleeck (ed) *L'avenir de la sécurité en Europe*, Paris: Economica.

(1988) 'Community Financing in Developing Countries: the Potential for the Health Sector', *Health Policy and Planning*, vol 3, no 2, pp 95-108.

(1988) 'Events Leading Up to the Founding of the NHS', *Update*, July, pp 9-13.

(1988) 'A New Regime', *New Society*, 29 April, pp 16-18.

(1988) 'A Decade at the DHSS', *The Health Service Journal*, 30 June, pp 734-5.

(1988) 'The Potential of Community Financing of the Health Sector in Developing Countries' (with A. Dua), Asian Development Bank, *Health Care Financing*, Manila, pp 41-70.

(1988) 'The Rise and Decline of the Early HMOs: Some International Experiences', *Milbank Quarterly*, vol 66, no 4.

(1989) 'Concluding thoughts: an inside view', in M. Bulmer et al (eds) *The Goals of Social Policy*, London: Unwin Hyman, pp 313-16.

(1989) 'Health Economics in Developing Countries', *Journal of Tropical Medicine & Hygiene*, vol 92, pp 229-41.

(1990) 'The first Forty Years', in J. Carrier and I. Kendall (eds) *Socialism and the NHS*, Aldershot: Avebury, pp 11-18.

(1990) 'Sociale Ungleichheit unt Gesundheit', *Sozial Reform*, nos 3/4, March/April, pp 169-78.

(1990) 'The Economics of Health Care', in T.A. Lambo and S.B. Day (eds) *Issues in Contemporary Health*, New York: Plenum, pp 55-71.

(1991) 'Financing Health for All', *World Health Forum*, vol 12, no 2, pp 191-200.

(1992) 'Cost containment and new priorities in the European Community', *Milbank Quarterly*, vol 70, no 3.

(1992) 'Entre 10 publico y 10 privato', *Salud Publica de Mexico*, vol 34, no 4, July-August, pp 467-70.

(1992) 'Health insurance in developing countries: lessons from experience', *Health Policy and Planning*, vol 7, no 3, pp 215-26.

(1992) 'Can the poor afford "free" health services? A case study of Tanzania', *Health Policy and Planning*, vol 7, no 4.

(1992) 'Cost Containment and New Priorities in the European Community', *Milbank Quarterly*, vol 70, no 3, pp 393-416.

(1992) 'Reform of the National Health Service', *Quality Assurance in Health Care*, vol 4, no 4, pp 263-72.

(1992) 'Synthesis', *Technological Innovation and Social Security*, Leuven: European Institute of Social Security, Acco, pp 467-80.

(1992) 'The Beveridge Report: its origins and outcomes', *International Social Security Review*, vol 45, no 1-2.

(1992) 'An overview of sustainable health services', in Save the Children, Denmark, Seminar on Sustainability of Health Services, Red Barnet, Copenhagen.

(1993) 'Age, Work and Social Security: the policy context', in A.B. Atkinson and M. Rein (eds), *Age, Work and Social Security*, New York: St Martin's, pp 255-69.

(1993) 'Financing health services in developing countries: the options', *Nytt Om U-Landshalsovard*, no 2.

(1994) 'The Beveridge Report: Its Origins and Outcomes', in J. Hills et al (eds) *Beveridge and Social Security: an international retrospective*, Oxford: Clarendon Press, pp 10-22.

(1994) 'Tendencias mundiales en el financiamento de la Salud', *Estudios Publicos*, no 55, Winter, pp 171-88.

(1994) 'The Impact of the Single European Market on the Pharmaceutical Sector' (with E. Mossialos and P. Kanavos), in E. Mossialos et al (eds) *Cost Containment: Pricing and Financing of Pharmaceuticals in the European Community*, London: LSE Health and Pharmetrica SA.

(1994) 'Cost containment and health care reform: a study of the European Union', *Health Policy*, vol 28, pp 89-132.

(1994) 'Overview of Health Care Reforms', in OECD, *The Reform of Health Care Systems*, Health Policy Studies No 5, Paris.

(1995) 'Labour and the Tory Health Reforms', *Fabian Review*, vol 107, no 3, June.

(1995) 'Contencion de Costas Y Reforma del Sector Salud en Pais Membros de la OCDE', *Estudios Publicos*, no 58, pp 337-67.

(1995) 'Alter Wein in Neuen Schlauchen', *DOK: politik, praxi Recht*, no 13.

(1995) 'World Trends in Health Care Financing and Delivery', *Congress Monthly*, Taiwan, no 263.

(1995) 'Pharmaceuticals' (with E. Mossialos), in R. Baldwin, *Regulation in Question: The Growing Agenda*.

Endnotes

Chapter 1

1. The General Strike, which took place from 3–13 May 1926, was an attempt by the Trades Union Congress (TUC) to prevent the decline in coal miners' pay and conditions. It caused widespread disruption, and troops were brought in by the government to move coal.

2. *The Times* (1926), 1 November, p 14.

3. JSP, Lionel Abel-Smith Senior, handwritten account of Uncle Philip's trust fund, November 1930.

4. *The Times* (1914), 24 August, p 9, col E.

5. The Irish Free State was relatively recent, having been formed in 1922.

6. *he Times* (1923), 23 August, p 13, col B.

7. Interview with Popsie Chadwick (nee Hamilton), 13 May 2008.

8. Interview with Patrick Nairne, 22 September 2008.

9. HSA, Report for BA-S, 1940.

10. Perhaps the school's traditions were a conscious emulation of older public schools such as Eton (with its top hats) or even Christ's Hospital School, founded in 1553 on a Hertfordshire site not far from Haileybury, where the boys wore long clerical-style black gowns over custard yellow stockings. The status that came from owning an umbrella is redolent of the British civil service's love affair with this badge of hierarchy.

11. C. Attlee (1954) *As It Happened*, London: William Heinemann Ltd, pp 19-25.

12. A. Calder (1969) *The People's War, Britain 1939-45*, London: Cape, p 261.

13. R.M. Titmuss (1950) *Problems of Social Policy*, London: HMSO, pp 335-6.

14. BA-SP 6/8, Lord Calverley (George Muff) to BA-S, 6 July nd (identified as 1946 from reference to BA-S at Trentham). There is no indication of what the 'incident' was.

15. A public school chaplain, the Reverend E.J.H. Nash, established VPS camps in 1930. They were initially held under canvas, until the Second World War, when he arranged to hold them at Clayesmore School during the holidays. The boys worked on local farms during the day, and had morning and evening prayers and talks on Christian life provided by school chaplains, school masters and undergraduates. Women were allowed to attend, but only to cook and clean: they were not allowed to join in any of the activities. The atmosphere was that of a country house party, with recreations such as tennis and music recitals. I am grateful

to the Reverend Prebendary J.T.C. Collins and Pat Starkey for enlightening me on VPS camps.

[16] HSA, Edmonstone House records, summer 1944.

[17] Author correspondence with J.T.C. Collins, 2 February 2009.

[18] HSA, Prefects' meetings minute book, 29 September 1944.

[19] BA-SP 6/1, E.F. Bonhote to BA-S, 31 January 1946.

[20] HSA, Edmonstone House records, winter 1944. The dormitory classroom was near the main dormitory, and where new boys (called 'new governors') were based for the first couple of years, before graduating to the lower houseroom, then upper houseroom, until they achieved the status of being in a study (in groups of 4, 3, 2 or 1, as they became more senior).

[21] Author correspondence with J.T.C. Collins, 22 February 2009.

[22] BA-SP 6/5, LA-S to BA-S, 4 July 1945.

[23] BA-SP 6/5, LA-S to BA-S, 23 July 1945.

[24] BA-SP 6/5, BA-S to LA-S, 16 June 1945.

[25] BA-SP 14/28, BA-S, 'Poverty in Context – A European and Third World Perspective – New Thoughts on Old Themes', 100th anniversary lecture at LSE, July 1995.

[26] E. Hobsbawm (2003) *Interesting Times: a Twentieth-Century Life*, London: Abacus, p 89.

[27] BA-SP 6/1, T. Adams to BA-S, 29 September 1945.

[28] P. Hennessy (2006) *Never Again: Britain 1945–51*, London: Penguin, p 65.

Chapter 2

[1] BA-SP 6/6, BA-S, 'Corps Training', nd.

[2] BA-SP 18/6, *Choin* magazines, 1946.

[3] BA-SP 6/2, BA-S to VA-S, 20 December 1947.

[4] BA-SP 6/4, HA-S to BA-S, 25 February 1947.

[5] A.J. Robertson (1987) *The Bleak Midwinter 1947*, Manchester: Manchester University Press.

[6] Lionel had held a postmastership at Merton College, Oxford, before his call-up in 1944.

[7] BA-SP 6/5, LA-S to BA-S, 6 January 1947.

[8] BA-SP 6/5, LA-S to BA-S, 7 August 1947.

[9] BA-SP 6/3, VA-S to BA-S, 20 July 194?.

[10] Meat rationing continued until 1954, and bread, which had not been rationed during the war, was subject to control between 1946 and 1948 in an effort to help out Germany.

[11] BA-SP 6/1, R. Baker to BA-S, 10 September 1947.

[12] N. Davenport (1974) *Memoirs of a City Radical*, London: Weidenfeld, p 173.

[13] BA-SP 6/6, War Office, BA-S reference for Clare College, Cambridge, 1 November 1948. Sir John Winterton KCB KCMG CBE DL (1898–1987) served as Deputy Commissioner for the Allied Commission for Austria between 1945 and 1949. He sat as the British representative on the Executive Committee that received any

disputes not resolved at the Directorate level. He was accountable to the Allied Council, the supreme governing body in Austria, where the High Commissioners (Commanders-in-Chief) sat.

14 B. Jelavich (1987) *Modern Austria. Empire and Republic, 1815–1986*, Cambridge: Cambridge University Press, pp 254-68.

15 KCLMA GB99, Winterton. Transcript of interview with Professor Peter Sorenson, 1970.

16 BA-SP 6/1, BA-S to VA-S, 23 November 1947.

17 BA-SP 6/5, LA-S to BA-S, November 1947. Henry Abel-Smith was married to Lady May Cambridge, niece of Queen Mary.

18 BA-SP 6/5, LA-S to BA-S, 19 December 1947.

19 BA-SP 6/2, BA-S to VA-S, 4 March 1948.

20 BA-SP 6/1, War Office to BA-S, 26 August 1948.

21 J. Vaizey (1986) *Scenes from Institutional Life and Other Writings*, London: Weidenfeld & Nicholson, p 91.

22 BA-SP 4/1c, E.F. Bonhote to Air Ministry, 10 August 1945.

23 Interview with Jimmy Davis, 26 June 2007.

24 BA-SP 6/4, HA-S to BA-S, 18 January 1949.

25 Interview with Jack Ashley, 25 April 2007.

26 Vaizey (1986), p 93.

27 E. Hobsbawm (2003) *Interesting Times: a Twentieth-Century Life*, London: Abacus, p 105.

28 Vaizey (1986), p 95.

29 Interview with Jack Ashley, 25 April 2007. Edward Greenfield (1928–) went on to become a journalist, initially as lobby correspondent for the *Manchester Guardian*, before becoming the paper's music critic.

30 Interview with Denzil Freeth, 10 June 2008.

31 Interview with Edward Greenfield, 26 November 2010. Hugh Thomas is the historian Lord Thomas of Swynnerton.

32 BA-SP 16/1, 1948 diary.

33 BA-SP 18/1, *The Tatler and Bystander*, 28 November 1951.

34 Interview with Popsie Chadwick, 13 May 2008.

35 BA-SP 6/5, LA-S to BA-S, 1 November 1948. Vivée was beginning to develop a problem with alcohol that required Brian and Lionel to check her into a recovery clinic on several occasions.

36 BA-SP 16/1, 1948 diary.

37 £27,500 in 1949 equates to £679,421 in 2013 values.

38 BA-SP 6/5, LA-S to BA-S, 7 June 1949.

39 Interview with Jimmy Davis, 26 June 2007.

40 *Cambridge Review* (1950), 6 May.

41 Interview with Edward Greenfield, 26 November 2010.

42 *The Middlesex Chronicle* (1950), 14 July. The Labour League of Youth was re-established in 1948 after the Second World War. At its peak in 1951 it had 806

branches. See M. Webb (2007) 'The Rise and Fall of the Labour League of Youth', Unpublished PhD thesis, University of Huddersfield.

[43] BA-SP 6/5, LA-S to BA-S, summer 1950.

[44] BA-SP 6/6, Peter Cropper to BA-S, 19 November 1950.

[45] Interview with Edward Greenfield, 26 November 2010.

[46] P. Hennessy (2006) *Never Again: Britain 1945–51*, London: Penguin, p 202.

[47] H. Dalton (ed B. Pimlott) (1986) *The political diary of Hugh Dalton 1918–40, 1945–60*, London: Cape, pp 508–9, diary entry for 4 March.

[48] BA-SP 6/6, H. Dalton to BA-S, 7 March 1951.

[49] BA-SP 6/6, BA-S to H. Dalton, 4 April 1951.

[50] BA-SP 6/6, H. Dalton to BA-S, 27 April 1951.

[51] BA-SP 6/7, Donald Chapman to BA-S, 29 May 1951.

[52] G. Howe (1994) *Conflict of loyalty*, London: Macmillan.

[53] CUA, Minute book for the Cambridge Union Society, 1950–56, pp 87–142.

[54] BA-SP 6/7, D. Hurd to BA-S, 5 June 1951.

[55] Author conversation with Percy Cradock, 10 February 2009.

[56] BA-SP 6/6, H. Dalton to BA-S, 24 June 1951.

[57] CUA, BOGS 1, 1954–5, Abel-Smith. Correspondence between BA-S and the Board of Research Studies, 6 June 1951.

[58] CUA, BOGS 1, 1954–5, Abel-Smith. Joan Robinson to Board of Studies, 2 May 1951.

[59] CCA, M.P.G. Stoker to B. Reddaway, 2 May 1951.

[60] Robinson also engaged in fruitful collaborations with Michal Kalecki and Richard Kahn, helping to shape her own refinement of neo-classical economic theory, starting not with 'capital as measurement' but from the perspective of institutions and history.

[61] G. Harcourt (2004) 'Robinson, Joan Violet (1903–1983)', *Oxford Dictionary of National Biography*, Oxford: Oxford University Press.

[62] E.A.G. (Austin) Robinson (1897–1993) was a Cambridge economist and appointed Professor in 1950. He took on a wide range of institutional roles outside Cambridge, including temporary appointments as an economic adviser to the Cabinet, the Ministry of Labour and the Board of Trade during the Second World War and post-war period. He was one of the founding fathers of the Overseas Development Institute in 1960, reflecting his service in India and expertise on Africa.

[63] Female interviewees presented quite polarised opinions on Brian's attitude towards women. Some suggested that he disliked women, or at the very least found them difficult to understand and to work with. One commented: 'I do think he struggled to take women seriously. He knew he ought to, but sometimes he couldn't quite make it.' Others highlighted how much he had strongly supported and promoted their careers.

[64] Vaizey (1986), p 101.

[65] BA-SP 6/7, Spelthorne Divisional Labour Party to BA-S, 13 October 1951.

[66] *Cambridge Review* (1951), 21 October.

67 I am grateful to Michael Kaser for telling me about Stephen Potter's popular book and articles in the late 1940s, and his coining of the term 'gamesmanship'. Perhaps these influenced Brian's literary style.

68 *Varsity* (1951), 20 October, 10 November.

69 H. Dalton (ed B. Pimlott) (1986), pp 575–6, diary entry for 14 December 1951.

70 The British Council was formed in 1935 as a non-political body to foster international friendships.

71 BA-SP 6/4, MA-S to BA-S, 17 January 1952.

72 BA-SP 18/13, A.B. Gerrard to BA-S, 20 February 1952.

73 BA-SP 18/12, Diary of debating tour to India, Pakistan and Ceylon.

74 *The Civil and Military Gazette (Karachi)* (1952), 15 February.

75 BA-SP 18/2, Press cuttings book.

76 BA-SP 18/13, Notes on British Council debating tour. The draft article 'Young India' was rejected by the *New Statesman* in May 1952.

77 BA-SP 6/3, BA-S to VA-S and LA-S, 10 February 1952.

78 BA-SP 18/13, Notes on British Council Debating Tour.

79 B. Abel-Smith (1952) 'Goodwill tour', *Overseas*, 37/436, June.

80 BA-S 6/7, Donald Chapman to BA-S 1, May 1952. There is no title or theme indicated in this correspondence.

81 BA-S 6/8, E.A.G. Robinson to BA-S, 5 May 1952.

82 CUA, BOGS 1, 1954–5, Abel-Smith. Joan Robinson to BA-S, 29 April 1952.

83 CUA, BOGS 1, 1954–5, Abel-Smith. BA-S to University, 23 July 1952; Reddaway to Harvey, Board of Research Studies, 26 January 1953: 'In reply to your letter of 9.12.52, Abel-Smith has been rather slow in deciding specifically on the subject which he wanted to tackle, but has worked quite effectively and very fast on particular "sub-topics". He has now decided on his subject + wishes to take the PhD. I consider him suitable as a candidate for that degree + recommend that he be registered accordingly, with effect from 1st October 1951 (one term intermitted).'

84 BA-SP 6/5, LA-S to BA-S, 13 May 1952.

85 BA-SP 6/3, VA-S to BA-S, 3 June 1952.

86 BA-SP 6/3, VA-S to BA-S, 11 March 1952.

87 BA-SP 6/7, B. Lewington to BA-S, 27 August 1952. Shirley Williams later accepted the nomination for the Harwich by-election in 1954.

Chapter 3

1 D. Gelly (1991) 'Blown up, deaded, but not forgotten', *Observer*, 26 May.

2 D. Childs (2006) *Britain since 1945*, London: Routledge, p 47.

3 P. Hennessy (2006) *Never Again: Britain 1945–1951*, London: Penguin, p 2.

4 G. Orwell (1941) *The Lion and the Unicorn: Socialism and the English Genius*, London: Secker & Warburg, pp 15–16.

5 D. Fraser (2003) *The Evolution of the Welfare State* (3rd edn), Basingstoke: Palgrave Macmillan; R. Lowe (2005) *The Welfare State in Britain since 1945* (3rd edn), Basingstoke: Palgrave Macmillan.

[6] C. Barnett (1986) *The Audit of War. The Illusion and Reality of Britain as a Great Nation*, London: Macmillan, p 304.

[7] A. Cairncross (1992) *The British Economy since 1945*, Oxford: Blackwell, pp 5-6.

[8] J. Harris (1994) 'Contract and Citizenship in Social Welfare 1934–48', Conference paper, quoted in H. Glennerster (1995) *British Social Policy since 1945*, Oxford: Blackwell, p 17.

[9] The phrase 'welfare state' is actually Alfred Zimmern's from 1934. Beveridge disliked it, preferring to use the term 'social service state'.

[10] A. Calder (1992) *The People's War*, London: Pimlico, p 526. José Harris also highlights the private side to his character, in which he could be 'generous and sympathetic': J. Harris (1977) *William Beveridge: A Biography*, Oxford: Oxford University Press, pp 1-2.

[11] R. McKenzie (1977) 'My LSE', in J. Abse (ed) *My LSE*, London: Robson Books, p 97.

[12] J. Wheldon (1977) 'My LSE', in J. Abse (ed) *My LSE*, London: Robson Books, p 129.

[13] C. Bermant (1977) 'My LSE', in J. Abse (ed) *My LSE*, London: Robson Books, p 180.

[14] N. Annan (1959) 'The Curious Strength of Positivism in English Social Thought', Hobhouse Memorial Lecture, Oxford: Oxford University Press.

[15] R. Dahrendorf (1995) *LSE: A History of the London School of Economics and Political Science 1895–1995*, Oxford: Oxford University Press, p 380.

[16] T.H. Marshall (1962) 'Reminiscences', in *Link: LSE Department of Social Science and Administration 1912–1962 Jubilee*, London: LSE, p 8.

[17] My thanks to David Donnison for these observations.

[18] A.C. Pigou (1920) *The Economics of Welfare*, London: Macmillan, pp 3-4.

[19] M. Bulmer, J. Lewis and D. Piachaud (eds) (1989) *The Goals of Social Policy*, London: Unwin Hyman; J. Lewis (2003) 'How useful are the social sciences?', *Political Quarterly*, vol 74, no 2, pp 193-201.

[20] R. Mishra (1989) 'The academic tradition in social policy: the Titmuss years', in M. Bulmer, J. Lewis and D. Piachaud (eds) *The Goals of Social Policy*, London: Unwin Hyman, p 68.

[21] M. Bulmer (1991) 'National contexts for the development of social policy research: British and American research on poverty and social welfare compared', in P. Wagner (ed) *Social Sciences and the Modern State: national experiences and theoretical crossroads*, Cambridge: Cambridge University Press, pp 148-67.

[22] H. Glennerster (1989) 'Swimming against the tide: the prospects for social policy', in M. Bulmer, J. Lewis and D. Piachaud (eds) *The Goals of Social Policy*, London: Unwin Hyman, p 125.

[23] M. Bulmer (ed) (1978) 'Introduction', *Social Policy Research*, London: Macmillan, pp 42-3.

[24] D. Donnison (1978) 'Research for policy', in M. Bulmer (ed) *Social Policy Research*, London: Macmillan, pp 54-9.

[25] R.M. Titmuss (1938) *Poverty and Population: A Factual Study of Contemporary Social Waste*, London: Macmillan; R.M. Titmuss (1950) *Problems of social policy*, London: HMSO.

26 A.H. Halsey (2004) 'Titmuss, Richard Morris (1907–1973)', *Dictionary of National Biography*, Oxford: Oxford University Press.

27 M. Gowing (1975) 'Richard Morris Titmuss', *Proceedings of the British Academy*, vol 61, p 411.

28 See especially J. Welshman (2004) 'The Unknown Titmuss', *Journal of Social Policy*, vol 33, pp 225-47.

29 Titmuss (1938), p xxviii.

30 M. Bulmer, J. Lewis and D. Piachaud (eds) (1989) *The Goals of Social Policy*, London: Unwin Hyman, p xiv.

31 K. Banting (1979) *Poverty, Politics and Policy. Britain in the 1960s*, London: Macmillan, p 7.

32 R. Mishra (1989) 'The academic tradition in social policy: the Titmuss years', in M. Bulmer, J. Lewis and D. Piachaud (eds) *The Goals of Social Policy*, London: Unwin Hyman, p 71.

33 M. Gowing (1975) 'Richard Morris Titmuss', *Proceedings of the British Academy*, vol 61, p 428.

34 'An Address given at John Vaizey's Memorial Service by Frank Field', in J. Vaizey, *Scenes from Institutional Life* (London, Weidenfeld and Nicolson, 1986), p 159.

35 BA-SP 6/9, J. Vaizey to BA-S, nd.

36 J. Vaizey (1983) *In Breach of Promise. Gaitskell, MacLeod, Titmuss, Crosland, Boyle. Five Men Who Shaped a Generation*, London: Weidenfeld & Nicholson, p 67.

37 BA-SP 6/9, J. Vaizey to BA-S, 14 August 1952.

38 BA-SP 6/9, J. Vaizey to BA-S, 14 August 1952.

39 BA-SP 6/9, J. Vaizey to BA-S, nd.

40 Now Ann Oakley, the writer and academic sociologist.

41 Vaizey (1983), p 75.

42 Vaizey (1983).

43 Vaizey (1983), p 56.

44 P. Townsend (1952) *Poverty: Ten Years After Beveridge*, London: Political and Economic Planning; B.S. Rowntree and G.R. Lavers (1951) *Poverty and the Welfare State*, London: Longman.

45 B.S. Rowntree (1901) *Poverty, A Study of Town Life*, London: Longman.

46 P. Townsend interviews with P. Thompson, 1997–99. Transcript available from the UK Data Service (http://ukdataservice.ac.uk)

47 Michael Young appointed Titmuss to the chair of the Institute of Community Studies.

48 P. Townsend (1962) *The Last Refuge: a survey of residential institutions and homes for the aged in England and Wales*, London: Routledge & Kegan Paul.

49 P. Townsend interviews with P. Thompson, 1997–99, p 30.

50 P. Townsend interviews with P. Thompson, 1997–99, p 59.

51 P. Townsend interviews with P. Thompson, 1997–99, p 55.

52 D. Donnison (1982) *The Politics of Poverty*, Oxford: Martin Robertson & Co, p 18.

53 K. Jones (1984) *Eileen Younghusband: a biography*, London: Bedford Square Press/ NCVO, pp 58-71.

[54]   M. Gowing (1975) 'Richard Morris Titmuss', *Proceedings of the British Academy*, vol 61, p 412.

[55]   D. Marquand (1988) *The Unprincipled Society: new demands and old politics*, London: Cape, pp 102-7.

[56]   R.M. Titmuss (1950) *Problems of Social Policy*, London: HMSO.

[57]   R.M. Titmuss (1974) 'What is social policy?', in B. Abel-Smith and K. Titmuss (eds) *Social Policy: An Introduction*, London: Allen & Unwin, p 150.

[58]   R.M. Titmuss (1967) 'The relationship between income maintenance and social service benefits – an overview', An introductory paper prepared for the Round Table Meeting on Social Security and Social Services, Leningrad, May, *International Social Security Review*, vol 20, no 1, pp 57-66.

[59]   Fabian Society, 'A History of the Fabian Society' (www.fabian-society.org.uk).

[60]   G.B. Shaw (1892) *The Fabian Society: What it Has Done and How it Has Done It*, London: Fabian Society, p 23.

[61]   R. Mishra (1989) 'The academic tradition in social policy: the Titmuss years', in M. Bulmer, J. Lewis and D. Piachaud (eds) *The Goals of Social Policy*, London: Unwin Hyman, p 65.

[62]   P. Pugh (1894) *Educate, Agitate, Organise. 100 Years of Fabian Socialism*, London: Methuen, p 214.

[63]   Pugh (1894), p 218.

[64]   P. Townsend interviews with P. Thompson, 1997–99, p 174.

[65]   I. Mikardo (1948) *The Second Five Years*, Fabian Society Research Series, London: Fabian Society.

[66]   G.B. Shaw (1889) *Fabian Essays in Socialism*, London: Fabian Society.

[67]   R.H.S. Crossman (ed) (1952) *New Fabian Essays*, London: Fabian Society.

[68]   C.A.R. Crosland (1956) *The Future of Socialism*, London: Cape. This second conference was to be the last held at Buscot Park. The series continued at various Oxford colleges, partly because of the embarrassment caused when Tony Crosland broke a valuable vase at Buscot Park. See also P. Pugh (1894) *Educate, Agitate, Organise: 100 Years of Fabian Socialism*, London: Methuen, p 228.

[69]   E.P. Thompson (1980) *Writing by Candlelight*, London: Merlin Press, p 131.

[70]   B. Rodgers (2000) *Fourth Among Equals*, London: Politico's, p 48.

[71]   R. Plant (1999) 'Democratic Socialism and Equality', in H. Fawcett and R. Lowe (eds) *Welfare Policy in Britain. The Road from 1945*, London: Macmillan, p 94.

[72]   M. Beech and K. Hickson (eds) (2007) *Labour's Thinkers: The intellectual roots of Labour from Tawney to Gordon Brown*, London: Tauris, p 147.

[73]   A. Crosland (2006) *The Future of Socialism* (50th anniversary edn, edited by Dick Leonard), London: Constable, p 103.

[74]   Crosland (2006), p 111.

[75]   K. Jefferys (1997) *Anthony Crosland*, London: Politico's, p 63.

[76]   P. Pugh (1894), p 234.

[77]   M. Summerskill and B. Brivati (1993) *The Group, 1954–1960: A time of hope*, London.

[78]   Interview with Bill Rodgers, 20 May 2010.

[79]   BA-SP 6/4, D.N. Chester to Fabian Society, 20 October 1952.

[80] BA-SP 6/4, Brinley Thomas to J.Vaizey, 6 September 1952. Brinley Thomas (1906–94) was Professor of Economics at University College Cardiff. The other Fabian referee for Brian's pamphlet was D.N. Chester.

[81] BA-SP 6/4, Notes on Brian Abel-Smith's draft pamphlet 'Taxation: A Social Service' by BT, 24 October 1952.

[82] I. Macleod and E. Powell (1952) *The Social Services; Needs and Means*, London: Conservative Political Centre.

[83] BA-SP 3/1, Brinley Thomas comments on BA-S draft, 23 July 1953.

[84] B. Abel-Smith (1953) *The Reform of Social Security*, Fabian Society Research Series No 161, London: Fabian Society, 1 September, p 26; R. Titmuss (1953) 'The Age of Pensions: Superannuation and Social Policy', *The Times*, 30 December.

[85] Abel-Smith (1953).

[86] 'Social Security and unemployment in Lancashire', *PEP Planning*, no 349, p 122.

[87] Abel-Smith (1953), p 1.

[88] Abel-Smith (1953), p 9.

[89] Abel-Smith (1953), p 27.

[90] Abel-Smith (1953), p 37.

[91] B. Wootton (1953) 'The Labour Party and the Social Services', *Political Quarterly*, no 24, p 66.

[92] Abel-Smith (1953), p 40.

[93] *Socialist Commentary* (1955), 10 January.

[94] K. Banting (1979) *Poverty, Politics and Policy*, London: Macmillan, pp 139-40.

[95] H. Heclo (1974) *Modern Social Politics in Britain and Sweden: from relief to income maintenance*, New Haven, CT: Yale University Press, pp 308-9.

[96] A. Seldon (1996) 'Ideas are not enough', in D. Marquand and A. Seldon (eds) *The Ideas That Shaped Post-War Britain*, London: Fontana, p 289.

[97] P. Dunleavy (1989) 'Paradoxes of an ungrounded statism', in F. Castles (ed) *The Comparative History of Public Policy*, Cambridge: Polity Press, p 263.

[98] H. Dalton (1986) *The political diary of Hugh Dalton 1918–40, 1945–60* (edited by B. Pimlott), London: Cape, pp 601-2, diary entry for 11 November 1952. Lady Catherine Walston was the mistress of Graham Greene, and the model for 'Sarah' in his novel *The End of the Affair*.

[99] JSP, BA-S to Margaret Gowing, 13 January 1975.

[100] CUA, BOGS 1 1954–5, Abel-Smith. NIESR to Harvey, Secretary of the Board of Research Studies, Cambridge, 26 March 1953.

[101] Dalton (1986), p 610, diary entry for 28 March 1953.

[102] Dalton (1986), p 629, diary entry for 12 July 1954.

[103] CCA, Harvey to BA-S, 15 June 1953.

[104] L. Dodd (1911) *A National Medical Service*, Fabian Tract No 160, London: Fabian Society.

[105] E. Powell (1962) 'Health and wealth', Lloyd Roberts lecture, *Journal of the Royal Society of Medicine*, vol 55, pp 1-6.

[106] C. Webster (1988) *The Health Services since the War, Vol. I. Problems of Health Care. The National Health Service before 1957*, London: HMSO, p 205.

[107] (1956) *Report of the Committee of Enquiry into the Cost of the National Health Service*, Cmd 9663, London: HMSO.

[108] BA-SP 8/4, I. Stewart to BA-S, 26 August 1955.

[109] CUA, BOGS 1 1954–5, Abel-Smith. BA-S to Harvey, 2 November 1954.

[110] B. Abel-Smith (1955) 'The Cost of the National Health Service (an application in Social Accounting)', Unpublished PhD thesis, University of Cambridge.

[111] CUA, BOGS 1 1954–5, Abel-Smith. Reports of the examiners on the dissertation entitled 'The Cost of the National Health Service' submitted by B. Abel-Smith for the PhD degree.

[112] CUA, BOGS 1 1954–5, Abel-Smith. Notice of Faculty of Economics and Politics Degree Committee, 3 May 1955.

[113] B. Abel-Smith and R.M. Titmuss (1956) *The Cost of the National Health Service in England and Wales*, Cambridge: Cambridge University Press.

[114] TNA DHSS 94501/9/7/2, C. Guillebaud to E. Halliday, 20 January 1955.

[115] TNA DHSS 94501/9/9, I. Macleod to A. Eden, 22 November 1955.

[116] Webster (1988), p 220.

[117] RMTP 1/38, Memo on telephone call to W.A. Sanderson, 28 February 1955.

[118] RMTP 1/38, BA-S to Titmuss, 31 March 1955.

[119] RMTP 1/38, W.A. Sanderson to Titmuss, 24 May 1955.

Chapter 4

[1] E. Hobsbawm (2002) *Interesting Times: A Twentieth-Century Life*, London: Abacus, p 86.

[2] *House Beautiful* (1956), September, pp 43–6.

[3] Interview with Ann Oakley, 23 April 2007. Geraldine Aves (1896–1986) was a civil servant, especially concerned with welfare service provision, and the development of personal social services and social work training. After she retired from the Ministry of Health in 1963 she pioneered the development of the voluntary sector in social welfare. She was appointed DBE in 1977, and Brian was instrumental in gaining this recognition for her work.

[4] P. Dunleavy (1989) 'Paradoxes of an ungrounded statism', in F. Castles (ed) *The Comparative History of Public Policy*, Cambridge: Polity Press, p 263.

[5] B. Rodgers (2000) *Fourth Among Equals*, London: Politico's, p 44.

[6] Rodgers (2000), p 44.

[7] H. Pemberton (2006) 'Politics and Pensions', in H. Pemberton, P. Thane and N. Whiteside (eds) *Britain's Pensions Crisis: History and Policy*, Oxford: Oxford University Press, p 43.

[8] J. Harris (1997) *William Beveridge: A Biography*, Oxford: Oxford University Press, p 409.

[9] Interview with Peter Townsend, 28 April 2009.

[10] B. Abel-Smith (1995) 'Poverty in context – New thoughts on old themes', in H. Sasson and D. Diamond (eds) *LSE on social science: A centenary anthology*, London: LSE Books.

[11] B. Abel-Smith and P. Townsend (1955) *New Pensions for the Old*, Fabian Society Research Series No 171, London: Fabian Society.

12   Ministry of Health (1954) *Report of the Committee on the Economic and Financial Problems of the Provision of Old Age*, Cmd 9333, London: HMSO.

13   BA-SP 14/7, copy of *New Pensions for the Old* pamphlet.

14   B. Abel-Smith (1955) '£500 million for the Rich', *Socialist Commentary*, January.

15   J. Braddock and B. Braddock (1963) *The Braddocks*, London: Macdonald, p 209.

16   M. Beech and K. Hickson (2007) *Labour's Thinkers. The Intellectual Roots of Labour from Tawney to Gordon Brown*, London: Tauris Academic Studies, p 124.

17   D. Marquand (1999) *The Progressive Dilemma*, London: Phoenix.

18   R. Crossman (1965) 'The Affluent Society', in R. Crossman (ed) *Planning for Freedom. Essays in Socialism*, London: Hamilton, p 91. See also K. Theakston (2003) 'Richard Crossman: the Diaries of a Cabinet Minister', *Public Policy and Administration*, vol 18, no 4, p 21.

19   R. Jenkins (1993) *Portraits and Miniatures*, London: Macmillan, p 255.

20   R. Crossman (1972) *The Politics of Pensions*, Eleanor Rathbone Memorial Lectures No 19, Liverpool: Liverpool University Press, p 12. The account he provides of this episode in his published diaries suggests more forethought, and that he had been aware of the pensions debate for some time before the 1955 conference.

21   A. Howard (1990) *Crossman: The Pursuit of Power*, London: Jonathan Cape Ltd, p 210.

22   R. Crossman (1954) 'The End of Beveridge', *New Statesman and Nation*, 11 December, p 772.

23   It has been suggested that Gaitskell made Crossman Chair of the Study Group to distract him from involvement in the current internal fighting in the Labour Party. See P. Baldwin (1990) *The Politics of Social Solidarity: Class Bases of the European Welfare State, 1875–1975*, Cambridge: Cambridge University Press, p 235.

24   R. Titmuss (1956) *The Social Division of Welfare*, The Eleanor Rathbone Memorial Lecture, Liverpool: University of Liverpool. Later reprinted in R. Titmuss (1958) *Essays on the Welfare State*, London: Allen & Unwin.

25   Townsend and Thompson interviews, pp 175-6.

26   K. Theakston (2003) 'Richard Crossman: Diaries of a Cabinet Minister', *Public Policy and Administration*, vol 18, no 4, p 22.

27   H. Heclo (1974) *Modern Social Politics in Britain and Sweden. From Relief to Income Maintenance*, New Haven, CT and London: Yale University Press, p 261.

28   Dennie Oude Nijhuis has suggested that this was immediately rejected by the TUC, who opposed any move to redistribute income to less fortunate workers, thus beginning a long-running battle to gain their support for pensions reform. D. Oude Nijhuis (2009) 'Rethinking the Beveridge Strait-jacket: The Labour Party, the TUC and the Introduction of Superannuation', *Twentieth Century British History*, vol 20, no 3, pp 370-95.

29   Germany introduced a compulsory and universal graduated pension scheme based on earnings in 1957.

30   Baldwin (1990), p 233.

31   LPA, Study Group on Security and Old Age, Minutes, 25 September 1956.

32   BA-SP 5/1, Draft Document on Security and Old Age, Labour Party Study Group on Security and Old Age, RE122, December 1956.

[33] BA-SP 14/8, 'An Industrial Pension Plan'. Correspondence between BA-S and W. Jones and J. Campbell.

[34] LPA, Study Group on Security and Old Age, Minutes, 4 July 1956.

[35] R. Crossman (ed. J. Morgan) (1981) *The Backbench Diaries of Richard Crossman*, London: Hamish Hamilton and Jonathan Cape, p 583.

[36] Crossman (ed. J. Morgan) (1981), p 581.

[37] Titmuss was working with Dean Eugene Rostow at Yale University Law School, where Brian was later to go on secondment in 1962, and also with Eveline Burns at the New York School of Social Work, and in Washington, where he investigated the relationship between industrial pensions and labour mobility.

[38] RMTP 1/12, BA-S to Titmuss, 29 March 1957. This correspondence is interesting for the degree of familiarity it exposes between Brian and the Titmuss family. He signs off his letters 'love to you all'.

[39] BA-SP 3/2, Titmuss to BA-S and P. Townsend, 4 May 1957.

[40] BA-SP 3/2, BA-S to R. Crossman, 4 April 1957.

[41] Labour Party (1957) *National Superannuation: Labour's Policy for Security in Old Age* London. For an analysis of the detailed proposal see B. Ellis (1989) *Pensions in Britain 1955–1975: a history in five acts*, London: HMSO. As a civil servant Bryan Ellis was closely involved with pensions policy.

[42] BA-SP 3/2, BA-S to H.M. Somers, 13 May 1957. Professor Herman (Red) Somers had been a visiting scholar at LSE the previous year.

[43] BA-SP 3/2, M. Stephens to BA-S, 9 May 1957.

[44] BA-SP 5/3, Memo from RMT to BA-S and P. Townsend. The original proposal was made on 24 April 1957, with a plan to begin writing it in 1958. This was re-scheduled to 1959, but the book never materialised.

[45] BA-SP 3/2, W.J. Foster to BA-S, 13 June 1957.

[46] BA-SP 3/2, G. Hutchinson to BA-S, 11 July 1957.

[47] Interview with P. Townsend, 23 January 2007.

[48] P. Hall, H. Land, R. Parker and A. Webb (1975) *Change, Choice and Conflict in Social Policy*, London: Heinemann, pp 109, 119.

[49] Crossman (ed. J. Morgan) (1981), p 580.

[50] Labour Party (1957) *National Superannuation: Labour's Policy for Security in Old Age*, London: Labour Party, p 27.

[51] B. Abel-Smith and P. Townsend (1965) *The Poor and the Poorest*, London: Bell.

[52] *The Times* (1957), 16 October, 18 October, 25 October.

[53] *The Spectator* (1957), 18 October.

[54] Baldwin (1990), p 238.

[55] RMTP 1/12, BA-S to Titmuss, 4 April 1957.

[56] Crossman (ed. J. Morgan) (1981), p 584.

[57] B. Pimlott (1985) *Hugh Dalton*, London: Cape, p 627. See also Bill Rodgers' autobiography (2000) *Fourth Among Equals*, London: Politico's, p 47, for how his political career was nurtured by Dalton with lunches at the Little Acropolis in Charlotte Street.

[58] H. Dalton (1962) *High Tide and After*, London: Muller, p 436.

[59] GP, H. Dalton to H. Gaitskell, 4 October 1957. Sam Watson was Dalton's political agent.

[60] Pimlott (1985), p 627.

[61] M. Summerskill and B. Brivati (1993) *The Group, 1954–1960: A time of hope*, London.

[62] Interview with Peter Townsend, 23 January 2007.

[63] Interview with Sally Sainsbury, 20 February 2007.

[64] Pimlott (1985), p 628.

[65] BBK c/109, Dalton to Beaverbrook, 30 June 1958.

[66] Crossman (1981), p 583. Crossman records Abel-Smith as being '38th in succession to the Throne'.

[67] Interview with David Donnison, 27 November 2008.

[68] Lord Montagu (2001) *Wheels Within Wheels*, London: Wiedenfeld & Nicholson.

[69] G. Gorer (1973) *Sex and marriage in England today*, London, Panther.

[70] T. Driberg (1977) *Ruling Passions*, London: Cape.

[71] M. Houlbrook (2005) *Queer London: Perils and Pleasures in the Sexual Metropolis, 1918–1957*, London: University of Chicago Press.

[72] Author conversations with Ronald Waterhouse and Percy Cradock.

[73] Interview with Roger Lockyer, 26 April 2010.

[74] E.M. Forster also was believed to have had a long relationship with a London policeman.

[75] Interview with Denzil Freeth, 10 June 2007.

[76] Author correspondence with Marina Vaizey, July 2009.

[77] Interview with Shirley Williams, 26 June 2007.

[78] JSP, A.G. Linfield (Chair of the South West Metropolitan Regional Hospital Board) to BA-S, 16 March 1955.

[79] See Chapter 5 for a discussion of Brian's work on health committees.

[80] BA-SP 15/1 folder 2, H. Kissinger to BA-S, 2 October 1957.

[81] N. Mackenzie (ed) (1958) *Conviction*, London: MacGibbon & Kee. The original title for the book was *Disestablishment*. A similar publication, which went to four editions, was *Declaration*, which contained articles from 'angry young men' (and women) including John Osborne, Doris Lessing and Ken Tynan. Bob Pinker had lent Brian his copy, which may have stimulated his choice of style for the *Conviction* essay.

[82] B. Abel-Smith (1958) 'Whose Welfare State?', in N. Mackenzie (ed) *Conviction*, London: MacGibbon & Kee, p 55. (For Townsend and Titmuss's comments on drafts, see BA-SP 14/9.)

[83] Abel-Smith (1958), p 56.

[84] Abel-Smith (1958), pp 63-5.

[85] Abel-Smith (1958), p 67.

[86] Abel-Smith (1958), pp 72-3.

[87] BA-SP 14/8, M.I. Cole to BA-S, 29 November 1958 and 18 December 1958.

[88] BA-SP 14/8, Phyllis Abel-Smith to BA-S, 16 November 1958.

[89] J. Strachey (1958) 'The Lost Evangel', *Observer*, 21 October.

[90] C.A.R. Crosland (1958) 'Leftover Left to Kill', *The Spectator*, 24 October. See also Michael Foot's review in the *New Statesman,* 4 October 1958.

[91] *Observer* (1958), 28 December.

[92] *The Guardian* (1958) 'Nowhere to Go', 29 September.

[93] L. Hannah (1986) *Inventing Retirement: the Development of Occupational Benefits in Britain*, Cambridge: Cambridge University Press, p 56. By 1967 membership of occupational pension schemes had reached 53 per cent of the working population.

[94] Baldwin (1990), p 238.

[95] TNA CAB 129/88, 22 July 1957; C(57)176, 'Pensions', Memorandum by the Prime Minister.

[96] BA-SP 3/5, T. Lynes to BA-S, 8 February 1959.

[97] BA-SP 3/5, Lynes to BA-S, 23 April 1959.

[98] Crossman (1981), pp 683-4.

[99] BA-SP 3/5, BA-S Memo to Crossman, nd.

[100] Iain Macleod, quoted in N. Timmins (1996) *The Five Giants: A Biography of the Welfare State*, London: Fontana Press, p 192.

[101] P. Bridgen (1999) 'Remedy for All Ills: Earnings-Relation and the Politics of Pensions 1950s–1960s', Unpublished paper given at the conference 'Relative decline and relative poverty: signposts to the sixties', at the University of Bristol, 13 May.

[102] BA-SP 3/5, BA-S memo on social security discussions during the last week of June 1959. See also his memo on the meeting with the Institute of Actuaries, 'Dick's attack was very violent …', which details how Brian criticised their pamphlet which provided no facts on the cost of private pensions.

[103] BA-SP 3/5, L. Jeger to H. Gaitskell, 31 October 1958.

[104] R. Crossman (1954) 'The Wykehamist', *New Statesman and Nation*, 18 September, p 328.

[105] T. Dalyell (1989) *Dick Crossman: A Portrait*, London: Weidenfeld & Nicolson, p 16.

[106] D. Healey (1989) *The Time of My Life*, London: Joseph, pp 107-8.

[107] J. Jones (1986) *Union Man*, London: Collins, p 175.

[108] S. Thornton (2009) *Richard Crossman and the Welfare State: Pioneer of Welfare Provision and Labour Politics in Post-War Britain*, London: Tauris Academic Studies, p 86.

[109] D. Marquand (1991) *The Progressive Dilemma*, London: Heinemann, p 143.

[110] 'Less eligibility' meant that working conditions in the Poor Law workhouse had to be worse than the worst job available outside, to deter people from claiming relief.

[111] J. Macnicol (1998) *The Politics of Retirement in Britain, 1878–1948*, Cambridge: Cambridge University Press, p 351.

[112] P. Hall, H. Land, R. Parker and A. Webb (1975) *Change, choice and conflict in social policy*, London: Heinemann, p 410.

[113] Heclo (1974), p 254.

[114] W. Beveridge (1942) *Social Insurance and Allied Services*, Cmnd 6404, London: HMSO, pp 6-7.

[115] BA-SP 3/4, BA-S, 'The Definition of Poverty', Draft manuscript, 17 January 1952.

[116] P. Townsend (1952) *Poverty: Ten Years After Beveridge*, London: Political and Economic Planning.

[117] BA-SP 3/1, NAB official to BA-S, 5 July 1955.

[118] BA-SP 3/1, BA-S correspondence with Miss L. Shaw, Bristol and J. Utting, Cambridge, 1955.

[119] BA-SP 3/1, A.G. Beard to BA-S, 24 January 1956.

[120] BA-SP 3/1, BA-S draft talk to XYZ club, nd.

[121] BA-SP 3/5, R. Titmuss (1958) *Wage Related Contributions and Benefits for Sickness and Unemployment*, 30 November.

[122] BA-SP 5/3, B.P. Rowntree to BA-S, 16 July 1958.

[123] BA-SP 3/5, Titmuss memo, 22 October 1957.

[124] BA-SP 6/5, Townsend memo, 16 April 1958.

[125] BA-SP 3/5, BA-S to Hill, 15 July 1958; Acton Society Trust to BA-S, 6 May 1958. The Acton Society Trust was created in 1948 by the Directors of the Joseph Rowntree Social Service Trust Ltd and named after the Liberal politician Lord Acton (1834–1902). Its mission was 'for the promotion of the study and general knowledge of ethical, economic and social sciences and conditions in the UK and elsewhere on all matters relating to the progress and development of communities and mankind generally'.

[126] BA-SP 3/5, Clough to BA-S, 30 October 1958.

[127] P. Townsend (1959) 'Interview with Widow', *New Statesman*, 3 January; A. Harvey (1958) 'Newington Revisited', *New Statesman*, 13 December.

[128] R. Lowe (1994) 'A Prophet Dishonoured in his own Country? The Rejection of Beveridge in Britain, 1945–1970', in J. Hills, J. Ditch and H. Glennerster (eds) *Beveridge and Social Security*, Oxford: Clarendon Press, p 123.

[129] Treasury memo, 1960. Discussed in G.L. Clark (2003) 'Historical Perspectives and the Politics of Pensions Reform', in G.L. Clark and N. Whiteside (eds) *Pension Security in the 21st Century*, Oxford: Oxford University Press, p 23.

[130] R. Titmuss (1976) 'The Irresponsible Society' in B. Abel-Smith (ed) *Essays on the Welfare State* (3rd edn), London: Allen & Unwin, p 220.

Chapter 5

[1] P. Hennessy (1992) *Never Again: Britain 1945–51*, London: Penguin, p 453.

[2] In 1973 Julian Tudor Hart wrote to Brian to ask him to confirm that he had been present when Bevan made his infamous comment about how he got the medical profession to sign up to the NHS: 'I stuffed their mouths with gold'. Brian replied that Bevan had told him the anecdote over dinner at the House of Commons in the 1950s.

[3] B. Abel-Smith (1956) 'Present and Future Costs of the Health Service. The Economic Evidence to the Guillebaud Committee', *The Lancet*, vol I, 28 January, p 199.

[4] BA-SP 8/3, T. Titmuss to A.G.L. Ives, 18 January 1956.

[5] BA-SP 8/3, B. Cardew to R.M. Titmuss, 30 January 1956.

[6] For more detail on medical politics, see F. Honigsbaum (1979) *The Division in British Medicine*, London: Kegan Paul; D. Fox (1986) *Health Policies, Health Politics: The*

British and American Experience, 1911–1965, Princeton, NJ: Princeton University Press.

[7]   BA-SP 8/7, T.F. Fox to BA-S, 15 February 1956.

[8]   C. Webster (1988) *The Health Services since the War. Volume 1: Problems of Health Care; the National Health Service Before 1957*, London: HMSO, p 230.

[9]   For a full list of its members see the news item in the *British Medical Journal*, 16 March 1957.

[10] RMTP 2/137, RMT memo: Royal Commission on Doctors' Pay, 25 March 1957.

[11] RMTP 2/137, BA-S to RMT. Memo: Evidence to the Royal Commission on Doctors' Pay by B. Abel-Smith on 24 April. See also the Q&A section of the *British Medical Journal* on 23 August 1952, where a GP was told that he could legitimately claim for the maintenance of his front garden as patients had to walk through this to reach his consulting room.

[12] RMTP 2/137, BA-S to RMT. Memo: Evidence to the Royal Commission on Doctors' Pay by B. Abel-Smith on 24 April.

[13] BA-SP 8/2, BA-S to RMT, 6 May 1957.

[14] B. Abel-Smith (1957) 'The Dilemma of the Doctors', *New Statesman and Nation*, 4 May, p 561. I am grateful to Nick Bosanquet for pointing out that the term 'monopoly power' had some echo of the Freidman/Kuznets study of US doctors.

[15] Department of Health and Social Security (1960) *Report of the Royal Commission on Doctors' and Dentists' Remuneration 1957-1960*, Cmnd 939, London: DHSS.

[16] BA-SP 8/2, Report of Symposium held on 27 September 1963.

[17] A. Oakley (2010) 'Appreciation: Jerry [Jeremiah Noah] Morris 1910–2009', *International Journal of Epidemiology*, vol 39, pp 274-6; S. Murphy (1999) 'The Early Days of the MRC Social Medicine Research Unit', *Social History of Medicine*, vol 12, no 3, pp 389-406.

[18] BA-SP 8/3, BA-S to R. Titmuss, 30 April 1956.

[19] BA-SP 8/3, A. Howard to BA-S, 10 August 1957.

[20] Odin Anderson (1914–2003) was a sociologist, who headed the HIF from 1952 until 1962 when it became the Centre for Health Administration Studies at the University of Chicago. See O. Anderson (1991) *The Evolution of Health Services Research. Personal Reflections on Applied Social Science*, San Francisco, CA: Jossey-Bass Publishers.

[21] BA-SP 8/3, BA-S memo to R. Titmuss: 'Notes on Dinner with Odin Anderson', 2 August 1958.

[22] See Chapter 6 for a discussion of this WHO study.

[23] Bob Pinker had joined the Department in October 1956 as a non-graduate student reading for the Certificate in Social Science and Administration. He was on Home Office funding, with the intention of a career in the Probation Service. When Titmuss decided that he had a potential career in academia he persuaded the Home Office to release Pinker from his contract without re-paying the grant, and employed him as a research assistant.

[24] BA-SP 8/3, BA-S to R. Titmuss, 5 October 1960.

[25] BA-SP 8/3, BA-S to O. Anderson, 5 January 1961.

[26] Holly had moved off the HIF project and was now funded by a grant from the National Institute of Mental Health.

27   See Chapter 6 for a discussion of Brian's overseas commitments at this time.

28   B. Abel-Smith (1960) *A History of the Nursing Profession*, London: Heinemann.

29   Z. Cope (1961) 'A History of the Nursing Profession", *British Medical Journal*, vol 2, 28 October, p 1132.

30   J. Vaizey (1960) 'Miss Nightingale's Vision', *Socialist Commentary*, October, p 31.

31   E. W. Martin (1960) 'Persisting Plagues', *Observer*, 25 September.

32   B. Abel-Smith, with the assistance of R. Pinker (1964) *The Hospitals 1800–1948: A Study in Social Administration in England and Wales*, London: Heinemann.

33   B. Abel-Smith (1958) 'Whose Welfare State?', in N. MacKenzie (ed) *Conviction*, London: MacGibbon & Kee. See also Chapter 4, this volume.

34   Interview with Walter Holland, 12 May 2008.

35   BA-SP 8/9, Notes made by Admiral John Godfrey, Chair of Lambeth HMC, 9 May 1950.

36   BA-SP 8/9, Minutes of the Finance Sub-committee of Chelsea HMC, 9 December 1959.

37   Ministry of Health Advisory Council for Management Efficiency (1959) *Improving Efficiency in Hospitals*, London: HMSO.

38   BA-SP 8/9, W.M. Butcher to BA-S, 10 April 1960.

39   BA-SP 8/9, Press cuttings on plans for St Stephen's Hospital, 26 September 1960.

40   BA-SP 8/9, BA-S to J.L. Tunbridge, 30 July 1960.

41   BA-SP 8/9, BA-S memo on visits to St Mary Abbots and the Western Hospitals on 27 June and 12 July 1960.

42   BA-SP 8/9, Letters to BA-S, March 1961.

43   BA-SP 7/1, Proposed programme of work for the working party on the National Health Service. Labour Party 450/October 1958. The Home Policy Committee established the terms of reference on 14 April 1958.

44   BA-SP 7/1, BA-S to A.W. Benn, 7 May 1959.

45   BA-SP 3/4, BA-S, 'The First Ten Years of the National Health Service', Lecture at Northwood conference, 3-7 November 1958.

46   B. Abel-Smith (1958) 'After Ten Years', *New Statesman*, 12 July, pp 37-8.

47   A.D. (Sandy) Robertson (1926–91) went on to work as Executive Director of the Milbank Foundation in New York (1962–69), and then for 20 years for the WHO in the Eastern Mediterranean Region and WHO Geneva.

48   Interview with Walter Holland, 12 May 2008.

49   Archie Cochrane (1908–88) was appointed Professor of Tuberculosis and Chest Diseases at the Welsh National School of Medicine in 1960, and Honorary Director of the Medical Research Council's Epidemiology Unit. On his university retirement in 1969 he was made Director of the Unit.

50   A. Cochrane (1989) *One Man's Medicine*, BMJ Memoir Club Series, London: BMJ, p 208.

51   A. Cochrane, R.G. Carpenter and F. Moore (1959) 'Investigation into the Working of the "Death Benefit" for Coalworkers' Pneumoconiosis', *British Journal of Preventive & Social Medicine*, vol 13, no 3.

52   Interviews with John Sarbutt and Nigel Cox.

53 The Young Fabians had been formed in 1960, as an initiative of Bill Rodgers, then General Secretary, to get more young people into the Society. Members had to be under the age of 30. Interview with Howard and Ann Glennerster, 13 March 2007.

54 Interviews with Robert Stevens, 8 May 2007 and Mike Reddin, 19 February 2007.

55 Interview with David Blewett and Arthur Sheps, 15 June 2010.

56 Abel-Smith, with Pinker (1964).

57 Brian thought that it would be more beneficial for Bob Pinker's career if he were to get his own first author publication from the project, rather than co-authorship of the hospitals book. This was published as R. Pinker (1966) *English Hospital Statistics, 1861-1938*, London: Heinemann. Before they had begun the hospitals project Brian had been invited to give a prestigious lecture to the Manchester Statistical Society on 10 February 1960. The preparation for the lecture provided the opportunity to construct the statistical and conceptual framework for the hospitals project. It was subsequently published as B. Abel-Smith and R. Pinker (1960) *Changes in the use of institutions in England and Wales between 1911 and 1951*, Manchester: Manchester Statistical Society.

58 F. Honigsbaum (1970) *The Struggle for the Ministry of Health, 1914–1919*, London: Bell; F. Honigsbaum (1979) *The Division in British Medicine: a history of the separation of general practice from hospital care, 1911–1968*, London: Kogan Page; G. Ayers (1971) *England's First State Hospitals and the Metropolitan Asylums Board, 1867–1930*, London: Wellcome Institute of the History of Medicine; R. Stevens (1966) *Medical Practice in Modern England: the impact of specialisation and state medicine*, New Haven, CT: Yale University Press.

59 D. Fox (2005) 'Politics matter: re-reading Abel-Smith's history of hospitals', *Journal of Health Services Research and Policy*, vol 10, no 3, pp 187-8.

60 Another book that deserves consideration for tackling this topic is H. Eckstein (1958) *The English Health Service: its origins, structures and achievements*, Cambridge, MA: Harvard University Press.

61 M.R. (1965) 'Review', *New Left Review*, vol I, no 29, Jan/Feb, p 92.

62 A. Daley (1964) 'Hospitals from 1800 to 1948', *British Medical Journal*, 31 October, pp 1124-5.

63 F. Lafitte (1964) '1834 and all that', *New Society*, 12 November, pp 27-8; A. Briggs (1964) 'Workhouse and Hospital', *New Statesman*, 20 November, p 792.

64 R. Hodgkinson (1965) 'Review', *Medical History*, vol 9, no 3, pp 294-6. Henry Sigerist was one of the most eminent medical historians of the period.

65 S.W.F. Holloway (1962) 'Review', *British Journal of Sociology*, vol 16, no 2, June, pp 181-2.

66 BA-SP 1/50, BA-S to K. Tatara, 2 January 1980.

67 B. Abel-Smith (1962) 'Hospital Planning in Great Britain', *Journal of the American Hospital Association*, vol 36, May, pp 30-35; B. Abel-Smith (1962) 'Paying the Family Doctor', *The Stethoscope*, 1 February.

68 Ministry of Health (1962) *A Hospital Plan for England and Wales*, Cmnd 1604, London: HMSO; Ministry of Health (1963) *Health and Welfare: The Development of Community Care*, Cmnd 1973, London: HMSO.

69 B. Abel-Smith (1964) 'Hospital Planning and the Structure of the Hospital Services', *Medical Care*, vol 1, no 1, p 49.

70 Abel-Smith (1964) 'Hospital Planning and the Structure of the Hospital Services', pp 47-51.

71 B. Abel-Smith (1964) 'Major Patterns of Financing and Organisation of Medical Services in Countries other than the US', *Bulletin of the New York Academy of Medicine*, vol 40, no 7, pp 540-59.

72 B. Abel-Smith (1964) 'The Platt Report: Some Implications', *Nursing Times*, 17 July, pp 925-6.

73 B. Abel-Smith and K. Gales (1964) *British Doctors at Home and Abroad*, Welwyn: The Codicote Press for the Social Administration Research Trust. The Nuffield Trust had commissioned this research in response to the publication in 1962 by Dr John Seale of a series of pamphlets and articles that claimed that the NHS had caused doctors to leave Britain. Seale was asked to speak in the US in opposition to President Kennedy's proposals for a move towards a more socialised healthcare system.

74 B. Abel-Smith (1965) 'The Cure that Failed', *The Guardian*, 22 February; B. Abel-Smith (1965) 'A Prescription for the GP', *The Guardian*, 23 February.

75 JSP, M. Brumwell to BA-S, 24 October 1963.

76 BA-SP 7/1, M. Herbison to BA-S, 17 August 1959; BA-S to A.W. Benn, 7 May 1959.

77 Interview with Liz Shore, 23 August 2008.

78 *Radio Times*, 2 May 1963.

79 BA-SP 14/12, Transcript from 'This Nation Tomorrow', pp 15-16.

80 *The Sunday Times* (1963) 'How to make enemies', 12 May.

81 *New Statesman* (1963), 10 May.

82 *Observer* (1963), 12 May.

83 BA-SP 14/12, WM to BA-S.

84 BA-SP 14/1, Correspondence relating to 'This Nation Tomorrow' programme.

85 BA-SP 14/12, BA-S to H. Wheldon, 16 May1963.

86 BA-SP 14/12 Transcript of 'Studying the Social Sciences', BBC, 23 June 1964.

87 *The Times* (1963) 'Marshalling the Facts to Small Purpose', 2 November.

88 B. Abel-Smith (1964) 'The Voiceless Millions', *New Statesman*, 9 October.

89 M. Simms (1964) Letter to the *New Statesman*, 16 October.

90 BA-SP 4/4a, Clark to BA-S, 18 November 1964; *The Guardian* (1965), 6 May.

Chapter 6

1 J.E. Powell (1966) *A New Look at Medicine and Politics*, London: Pitman Medical, p 15.

2 A. Cairncross (1981) 'Academics and Policy makers', in F. Cairncross (ed) *Changing Perceptions of Economic Policy. Essays in Honour of the Seventieth Birthday of Sir Alec Cairncross*, London: Methuen, p 22.

3 G. O'Hara (2007) *From Dreams to Disillusionment, Economic and Social Planning in 1960s Britain*, Basingstoke: Palgrave Macmillan, p 177.

4 TNA MH170/14, Heasman to Winner, 19 August 1963.

5 TNA MH170/14, Aldridge to Adams, 17 March 1964.

6   O'Hara (2007), pp 167-204.

7   G. Forsyth and R.F.L. Logan (1963) *Demand for Medical Care*, Oxford: Nuffield Trust.

8   M.S. Feldstein (1963) 'Economic analysis, operational research and the state', *Oxford Economic Papers*, vol 15, p 28.

9   Powell (1966), p 27.

10   W.J. McNerney (1962 *Hospital and Medical Economics: Population, Services, Costs, Methods and Payments and Controls*, Chicago, IL: Hospital Research and Educational Trust.

11   M. Shain and M.I. Roemer (1959) 'Hospital costs relate to the supply of beds', *Modern Hospital*, vol 92, no 4, pp 71-3. Milton Roemer (1916–2001) had been one of the WHO's first expert advisers, when in 1950 he designed health demonstration areas in El Salvador and Ceylon (now Sri Lanka). He was on the staff at WHO from 1951 to 1953, when he was forced to resign when the US government withdrew approval of his appointment under pressure of McCarthyism. He returned to North America to set up the first social insurance programme in the Canadian province of Saskatchewan, and then held positions at Yale and Cornell Universities before moving to the School of Public Health at the University of California, Los Angeles (UCLA) in 1962. His research encouraged the development of health maintenance organisations (HMOs).

12   R.M. Packard (1997) 'Malaria Dreams: Post-war visions of health and development in the Third World', *Medical Anthropology*, vol 17, pp 279-96.

13   For histories of the WHO see its official publications: WHO (1958) *The First Ten Years of the WHO*, Geneva: WHO; WHO (1968) *The Second Ten Years of the WHO*, Geneva: WHO; WHO (2008) *The Third Ten Years of the WHO*, Geneva: WHO. See also T.M. Brown, M. Cueto and E. Fee (2006) 'The World Health Organisation and the Transition from "International" to "Global" Health', in A. Bashford (ed) *Medicine at the Border*, Basingstoke: Palgrave Macmillan, pp 76-93.

14   BA-SP 11/1, B. Abel-Smith (1957) *The Practical Possibilities of Undertaking a Cross-national Study on the Costs and Financing of Medical Care Services*, A paper prepared at the request of the World Health Organization, 15 April.

15   RMTP 1/12, BA-S to Titmuss, 23 April 1957.

16   World Health Assembly Resolution 5.73, WHO Official Record 42,42.

17   BA-SP 11/1, W. Cohen to BA-S, 16 September 1957.

18   BA-SP 11/1, Draft report with Titmuss annotations.

19   BA-SP 3/6b, Diana to BA-S, 1 May 1958.

20   BA-SP 11/1, WHO/OMC/30, 24 April 1958, 'Medical care in relation to public health: a study on the costs and sources of finance', Prepared by the World Health Organization with the assistance of Brian Abel-Smith and K.J. Mann for submission to an ILO/UN/WHO working party to be held in Geneva, 28-29 July 1958.

21   There is no archive information on how much Brian was paid for his first WHO consultancies, but by 1964 his fee was pro rata US$700 per month, plus maintenance allowance and travel costs.

22   RMTP 2/133. For a history of the Keppel Club, which met monthly, see J. Fry (1991) 'The Keppel Club (1952–1974): lessons from the past for the future', *British Medical Journal*, vol 303, 21 December, pp 1596-8. Its members (never

more than 25 at any one time) included some of the most influential people in British healthcare, including George Godber, John Brotherston, Charles Fletcher, W.P.D. Logan, Jerry Morris, Albertine Winner and Richard Titmuss.

23   BA-SP 11/1, BA-S to JMH, Confidential: Questions of general policy discussed with Czechoslovakian Ministry of Health.

24   B. Abel-Smith (1961) *Changing Method of Financing Hospital Care. Summary and Comment on the 12th International Hospital Congress*, Venice.

25   BA-SP 15/1, Correspondence between Robertson and Roemer, and preliminary programme.

26   MKP, 1961 diary, vol III, entry for 17 August 1961.

27   M.I. Roemer (1962) 'Highlights of Soviet Health Services', *Milbank Memorial Quarterly*, vol 15, no 4, pp 373-406.

28   BA-SP 11/1, D. Coddington to Manuila, 25 July 1962.

29   BA-SP 15/1, BA-S to A. Robertson, 28 June 1962.

30   I. Kramnick and B. Sheerman (1993) *Harold Laski: A Life on the Left*, London: Penguin.

31   D.P. Moynihan (1975) 'The United States in Opposition', *Commentary*, vol 59, March, pp 31-43.

32   P. Strafford (1975) *The Times*, 20 March.

33   The British Survey (1956) *Mauritius*, London: British Society for International Understanding.

34   R. Titmuss and B. Abel-Smith, assisted by T. Lynes (1961) *Social Policies and Population Growth in Mauritius*, London: Methuen, p 234.

35   World Health Organization (1959) *Iron Deficiency Anaemia: Report of a Study Group*, WHO Technical Report Series No 82, Geneva, WHO, p 3.

36   Titmuss and Abel-Smith, assisted by Lynes (1961), p 11.

37   F. Cooper (1997) 'Modernizing Bureaucrats, Backward Africans and the Development Concept', in F. Cooper and R. Packard (eds) *International Development and the Social Sciences*, Berkeley, CA: University of California Press, pp 64-92.

38   TNA CAB 134/155, Prime Minister's minute, 28 January 1957.

39   RMTP 5/648, Perth to R. Scott, 9 January 1959.

40   J. Markoff and V. Montecinos (1993) 'The Ubiquitous Rise of Economists', *Journal of Public Policy*, vol 13, no 1, p 45.

41   BA-SP 3/10a, Titmuss to A. Cochrane, 10 December 1959.

42   RMTP 5/648, BA-S, Notes of talk with Hall, Robertson and Miss Ogilvie, 25 May 1959.

43   RMTP 5/648, Notes of a meeting, 1 August 1959.

44   RMTP 5/648, BA-S to R. Titmuss, 8 August 1959.

45   BA-SP 9/7, Interview with Mr Wilson, 7 August 1959.

46   BA-SP 9/7, Interview with Mr Walter, 7 August 1959.

47   Titmuss and Abel-Smith, assisted by Lynes (1961), p xiii.

48   BA-SP 9/5, R. Titmuss to BA-S, 19 August 1959.

49   BA-SP 9/7, Visit to Père Leval Infirmary, 17 August 1959.

50   BA-SP 9/7, Visit to Jeewanjee Infirmary, Port Louis, 3 August 1959.

[51] BA-SP 9/7, Interview with Dr Stott, Leader of the WHO nutrition survey, 12 August 1959.

[52] Titmuss and Abel-Smith, assisted by Lynes (1961), pp 82-3.

[53] BA-SP 9/7, Notes on the health services from the Teeluck family.

[54] B. Benedict (1960) 'Indians in a Plural Society: A Report on Mauritius', Unpublished manuscript.

[55] Titmuss and Abel-Smith, assisted by Lynes (1961), p 66.

[56] RMTP 5/648, G.J.M. Schilling to R. Titmuss, 8 January 1960.

[57] Interview with Tony Lynes, 23 March 2010.

[58] BA-SP 9/6, BA-S to N. Ringadoo, 25 January 1960.

[59] BA-SP 9/6, BA-S to Zelenka, 11 February 1960.

[60] RMTP 5/648, Talk with Mr Dunnhill (Colonial Office expert on social security and social insurance), 19 February 1960.

[61] BA-SP 9/6, N. Ringadoo to BA-S, 18 September 1959, asking Brian to meet with Meade and sending a suggested new clause for the Terms of Reference. James Meade (1907–95) was one of the leading Keynesian economists of the 20th century. He worked at the League of Nations before joining the Economic Section of the Cabinet Offices of Churchill's wartime Coalition government in 1940, where he and Richard Stone produced Britain's first national accounts, and he drafted the British proposals for the General Agreement on Tariffs and Trade (GATT). He then moved into academia, holding professorial posts at the LSE (1947–57) and Cambridge (1957–67). He jointly shared the Nobel Prize for Economic Sciences with Bertil Ohlin in 1977 for their work on the theory of international trade and international capital movements.

[62] BA-SP 9/9, BA-S to J. Meade, 11 November 1959.

[63] Titmuss and Abel-Smith, assisted by Lynes (1961), p 237.

[64] Titmuss and Abel-Smith, assisted by Lynes (1961), p 234.

[65] R. Hill, J.M. Stycos and K. Black (1959) *The Family and Population Control: A Puerto Rican Experiment in Social Change*, Chapel Hill, NC: University of North Carolina Press.

[66] R.L. Meier (1959) *Modern Science and the Human Fertility Problem*, New York: John Wiley & Sons, pp 53-63.

[67] Titmuss and Abel-Smith, assisted by Lynes (1961), p 187.

[68] J.E. Meade (1961) *The Economic and Social Structure of Mauritius*, London: Methuen.

[69] Titmuss and Abel-Smith, assisted by Lynes (1961), p 229.

[70] Titmuss and Abel-Smith, assisted by Lynes (1961), p 248.

[71] Titmuss and Abel-Smith, assisted by Lynes (1961), p 240.

[72] Titmuss and Abel-Smith, assisted by Lynes (1961), p 184).

[73] BA-SP 9/5, Draft text for pamphlet.

[74] RMTP 5/648, Press comments.

[75] RMTP 5/648, V. Ringadoo to R. Titmuss, 27 April 1960.

[76] BA-SP 9/7, Highly confidential: 'Mauritius – the real dirt', nd, probably BA-S, March 1963.

[77] The International Planned Parenthood Federation (IPPF) had been founded in 1952 in Bombay, with eight founding partners – the Netherlands, Hong Kong,

India, Singapore, Sweden, the UK, the US and West Germany. At that time the only government to actively promote family planning was India; there was no support from international organisations such as the UN. Only Japan, China, Pakistan, Fiji and Korea had followed India's lead by 1962.

[78] BA-SP 9/5, T. Titmuss to A.D.K. Owen, 10 September 1960.

[79] BA-SP 14/7, B. Abel-Smith (1962) 'Population Growth and Public Health in Middle Africa', After dinner speech at the 39th Annual Conference of the Milbank Memorial Fund, Plaza Hotel, New York, 18 September.

[80] BA-SP 9/11, R. Titmuss to H. Villard, 10 December 1962.

[81] BA-SP 9/11, R. Titmuss, Confidential – 'Mauritius population control programme', 17 October 1962.

[82] BA-SP 9/11, R. Titmuss to S. Caine, 6 November 1962.

[83] BA-SP 9/2, Family Planning Campaign memorandum by the Minister of Health and Reform Institutions, 3 January 1963.

[84] BA-SP 9/12, BA-S to B. Duffy, 4 April 1963.

[85] BA-SP 9/11, BA-S to S. Badaoui, 25 February 1963.

[86] BA-SP 9/11, R. Titmuss to BA-S, 14 March 1963.

[87] R. Titmuss (1962) 'Medical Ethics and Social Change in Developing Countries', *The Lancet*, vol 2, 4 August, pp 207-12.

[88] BA-SP 9/12, F. Lafitte to R. Titmuss, 15 March 1963; C. Kiser (1962) *Research in Family Planning*, Princeton, NJ: Princeton University Press.

[89] BA-SP 9/12, BA-S to B. Duffy, 1 May 1963. Le Petit Club Français was a London dining club that Brian and his brother Lionel were members of. They ate there frequently, sometimes a couple of nights a week.

[90] W.M.O. Moore (1964) 'Limiting Families in Mauritius', *New Society*, 30 July.

[91] For a discussion of the impact of the 'Titmuss Mission's' strategy, see Mikko A. Salo (1982) 'Titmuss, Mauritius and the Social Population Policy: a methodological study', *Annales Universitatis Turkuensis*, Sarja-Serie B OSA – Tom 158, Turku University thesis, Finland.

[92] J. Markoff and V. Montecinos (1993) 'The ubiquitous rise of Economists', *Journal of Public Policy*, vol 13, no 1, p 45.

[93] J. Levinson and J. de Onis (1970) *The Alliance That Lost Its Way: A Critical Report on the Alliance for Progress*, Chicago, IL: Quadrangle Books, p 187.

[94] BA-SP 15/1, BA-S to G. Rohrlich, 27 June 1960.

[95] BA-SP 15/1, BA-S to R. Titmuss, 21 June 1961.

[96] B. Abel-Smith (1963) *Paying for Health Services: A Study of the Costs and Sources of Finance in Six Countries*, Geneva: WHO.

[97] Abel-Smith (1963), p 39.

[98] Abel-Smith (1963), p 82.

[99] D.S. Lees (1964) 'Economics of Medicine', *British Medical Journal*, vol 1, 11 July, p 111.

[100] *The Medical Officer* (1963) 'Paying for Health', 27 September.

[101] BA-SP 11/1, Report on a visit by Dr B. Abel-Smith to seven countries, 28 July–28 August 1963.

[102] BA-SP 11/2, BA-S to R.F. Bridgman, 7 October 1963.

[103] BA-SP 11/2, J.S. McKenzie-Pollock to BA-S, 13 September 1964.

[104] BA-SP 13/8, BA-S to J. Griffith, 5 March 1964.

[105] BA-SP 11/1.

[106] B. Abel-Smith (1967) *An international study of health expenditure*, Public Health Papers No 32, Geneva: WHO.

[107] BA-SP 11/1, BA-S to A.L. Bravo, 12 April 1968.

Chapter 7

[1] John Maynard Keynes, quoted in R.M. Titmuss (1938) *Poverty and Population*, London: Macmillan, pp 5-6.

[2] K. Banting (1979) *Poverty, Politics and Policy*, London: Macmillan, p 68.

[3] A. Crosland (1961) 'On Economic Growth', *Encounter*, vol 16, pp 65-6.

[4] G. O'Hara (2007) *From Dreams to Disillusionment: Economic and Social Planning in 1960s Britain*, Basingstoke: Palgrave Macmillan, p 12.

[5] D.N. Winch (1969) *Economics and Policy: a historical study*, London: Hodder & Stoughton, pp 273-4.

[6] R. Ward and T. Doggett (1991) *Keeping Score: the First Fifty Years of the Central Statistical Office*, London: Central Statistical Office, pp 62-3.

[7] In 1957 a steering committee was formed to encourage the use of computers within Whitehall. By 1965 the number of computers being used by central government had increased from 7 to 45. See J. Agar (2003) *The Government Machine: A Revolutionary History of the Computer*, Cambridge, MA: The MIT Press, pp 307, 314-15.

[8] J. Veit-Wilson (1999) 'The National Assistance Board and the "Rediscovery" of Poverty', in H. Fawcett and R. Lowe (eds) *Welfare Policy in Britain: the road from 1945*, London: Macmillan, p 120. Quote taken from an interview with Kenneth Stowe in 1988. Tony Lynes recalled Stowe talking about the 'rotten apple of discretion' in the National Assistance scheme. Author correspondence with Lynes, 16 September 2012.

[9] *The Guardian* (1960), 24 November.

[10] T. Lynes (1962) *National Assistance and National Prosperity*, Welwyn: Codicote Press.

[11] P. Townsend and D. Cole (Wedderburn) (1962) 'Poverty in Britain Today', Paper presented at the Conference of the British Sociological Association, Brighton.

[12] H. Glennerster (1962) *National Assistance: Service or Charity?*, London: Fabian Society.

[13] Veit-Wilson (1999), pp 126-9. There is some evidence that this NAB review was commissioned before the Abel-Smith and Townsend 'Essex' survey on poverty was public knowledge.

[14] Veit-Wilson (1999), pp 142-3. Quote taken from an interview with Kenneth Stowe in 1988.

[15] Robert Windsor Report for NAB, October 1965, vol 2, app 2, para (6)27, quoted in Veit-Wilson (1999), p 139.

[16] TNA BN72/115, Jarrett to M. Herbison (MPNI Minister), 21 October 1965.

[17] Hilary Land recalls that Townsend met Crossman soon after the MPNI review was published. Crossman asked if Townsend was pleased to have been vindicated,

and Townsend replied that he would rather have been proved wrong. Author correspondence with Hilary Land, October 2012.

[18]   Veit-Wilson (1999).

[19]   P. Thompson (1993) 'Labour's "Gannex conscience"? Politics and popular attitudes in the "permissive society"', in R. Cooper, S. Fielding and N. Tiratsoo (eds) *The Wilson Governments 1964–70*, London: Pinter Publishers, pp 136-50.

[20]   A. Sampson (1962) *The Anatomy of Britain*, London: Hodder & Stoughton.

[21]   D. Donnison (2000) 'The Academic Contribution to Social Reform', *Social Policy & Administration*, vol 34, no 1, pp 26-43.

[22]   S. Thornton (2009) *Richard Crossman and the Welfare State: Pioneer of Welfare Provision and Labour Politics in Post-War Britain*, London: Tauris Academic Studies, p 94.

[23]   H. Glennerster (1995) *British Social Policy since 1945*, Oxford: Blackwell, pp 108-9.

[24]   Author correspondence with Tony Lynes, 16 September 2012.

[25]   J.C. Kincaid (1973) *Poverty and Equality in Britain*, Harmondsworth: Penguin, p 126.

[26]   Quoted in N. Thompson (1996) *Political Economy and the Labour Party*, London: UCL Press, p 169.

[27]   Labour Party (1960) *Report of the Labour Party Conference*, London: Labour Party, p 103.

[28]   BA-SP 3/6b, C. Cockburn, Research and interview notes from Sweden 1961; Study Group on Security and Old Age, Minutes, 28 November 1961.

[29]   Labour Party (1963) *New Frontiers for Social Security*, London: Labour Party. See also BA-SP 3/6a for Lynes' correspondence with Crossman, reminding him that he considered it wrong to force employees to accept contracting-out agreements made by employers, but that it might be better to keep quiet about this until after the election, 21 February 1963.

[30]   *The Times* (1963), 2 April.

[31]   Labour Party (1963), p 233.

[32]   D. Cole (Wedderburn) and J.E.G. Utting (1962) *The Economic Circumstances of Old People*, Occasional Papers on Social Administration No 4, Welwyn: Codicote Press. This was the outcome of an extensive study by the Department of Applied Economics at the University of Cambridge, which had begun with pilot surveys in 1958. See also P. Townsend (1957) *The Family Life of Old People*, London: Routledge & Kegan Paul.

[33]   LPA, Study Group on Security and Old Age minutes, 17 July 1962.

[34]   S. Thornton (2009), p 106.

[35]   Labour Party (1963).

[36]   L Jeger, 'Labour and the Poor' *New Statesman*, 31 December 1965.

[37]   Information from Bryan Ellis, 22 April 2013.

[38]   See, for example, Helen Fawcett's theory that all subsequent social policy has been constrained by a 'path dependency' from such critical decisions: H. Fawcett (1996) 'The Beveridge Straitjacket: Policy Formation and the Problem of Poverty in Old Age', *Contemporary British History*, vol 10, no 1, pp 20-42.

[39]   D. Houghton (1967) *Paying for the Social Services*, London: Institute of Economic Affairs, p 12.

[40]   TNA PIN 47/141, 'Matters Relating to the Labour Party', 13 March 1964.

[41] TNA PIN 47/147, Working Group on Pensions, 'The flat-rate and graduated pensions elements', note by the MPNI, 18 August 1964. One of the members of the Official Committee on Social Security was an Oxford economist called Theo (Theodora) Cooper. In some ways she was Brian's counterpart, as she later provided policy advice for the Minister of Social Security, Judith Hart, during her secondment to the Cabinet Office (1965–69).

[42] P. Hall, H. Land, R. Parker and A. Webb (1975) *Change, Choice and Conflict in Social Policy*, London: Heinemann, p 451.

[43] S. Thornton (2006) 'A case of Confusion and Incoherence: Social Security under Wilson, 1964-70', *Contemporary British History*, vol 20, no 3, p 448.

[44] See, for example, O'Hara (2007); A. Blick (2006) 'Harold Wilson, Labour and the Machinery of Government', *Contemporary British History*, vol 20, no 3, pp 343-62; P. Hennessy (2000) *The Prime Minister: the office and its holders since 1945*, London: Allen Lane.

[45] B. Abel-Smith (1962) 'Research Report No 4, Department of Social Administration, London School of Economics and Political Science', *Sociological Review*, vol 10, no 3, pp 329-42. Nancy Seear (1913–97), later Baroness Seear, Leader of the House of Lords, and Leader of the Liberal peers.

[46] Conversation with Adrian Sinfield, 8 October 2012.

[47] BA-SP 3/6b, RMT memo, 'Pensions and Equality', October 1960.

[48] BA-S and Townsend were referred to as 'bogus professors of poverty' in a *Daily Telegraph* article on 1 May 1968 (the article refers to a report by the SBC): 'The Wages of Workshyness', by G.K. Mann.

[49] R.M. Titmuss (1938) *Poverty and Population*, London: Macmillan.

[50] R.M. Titmuss (1962) *Income Distribution and Social Change*, London: Allen & Unwin.

[51] BA-SP 3/4, BA-S, 'The Definition of Poverty', Draft manuscript, 17 January 1952.

[52] P. Townsend (1954) 'Measuring Poverty', *British Journal of Sociology*, vol 5, no 2, pp 130-7.

[53] P. Townsend (1952) *Poverty: Ten Years After Beveridge*, London: Political and Economic Planning.

[54] Glennerster (1995), p 108.

[55] There were significant comparative limitations. The first surveys classified families on the basis of their expenditure, while later ones used income.

[56] BA-SP 3/6b, P. Townsend, *A note on the definition of subsistence*, Minutes of the Labour Study Group on Security and Old Age, RD 49, 29 March 1960. It is interesting that Crosland's book (1962) *The Conservative Enemy: A programme of radical reform for the 1960s*, London: Cape, in which he discusses inequalities of wealth, made no reference to Townsend's work on poverty.

[57] P. Townsend (1962) 'The Meaning of Poverty', *British Journal of Sociology*, vol 18, no 3, pp 210-27.

[58] B. Abel-Smith (1996) 'Poverty in Context – New Thoughts on Old Themes', in H. Sasson and D. Diamond (eds) *LSE on Social Science: A centenary anthology*, London: LSE Books, pp 121-33.

[59] M. Harrington (1962) *The Other America*, New York: Penguin Books. Brian later refuted suggestions that his and Townsend's 1961 project had been a response

to US studies on poverty. See Abel-Smith (1996) 'Poverty in Context – New Thoughts on Old Themes'.

[60] R. Lowe and P. Nicholson (1995) 'The Formation of the Child Poverty Action Group', *Contemporary Record*, vol 9, no 3, p 618.

[61] BA-SP 4/1a, BA-S and P. Townsend, Survey of Poverty, Application to the JRMT, 24 April 1964.

[62] BA-SP 4/1a, BA-S to R. Titmuss, 4 May 1964.

[63] BA-SP 4/1a, BA-S to P. Townsend, 10 September 1964.

[64] BA-SP 4/1a, BA-S, Draft sample interview letter, January 1965.

[65] BA-SP 4/1a, BA-S to E.H. Pierson, Division Officer, London County Council Education Department, 25 September 1964.

[66] BA-SP 4/1a, BA-S to P. Townsend, 18 January 1965.

[67] BA-SP 4/1a, P. Townsend to C. Jarrett, 22 March 1965.

[68] Author correspondence with Hilary Land, October 2012.

[69] BA-SP 4/1c, BA-S to P. Townsend, 1 June 1965.

[70] Abel-Smith (1996) 'Poverty in Context – New Thoughts on Old Themes', pp 121-33.

[71] B. Abel-Smith and P. Townsend (1966) *The Poor and the Poorest: a new analysis of the Ministry of Labour's Family Expenditure Surveys of 1953–54 and 1960*, London: Bell.

[72] Harriet Wilson gives the date as Friday 5 March 1965 in her evidence at the Witness Seminar held on 17 November 1993 at the Institute of Historical Research. See R. Lowe and P. Nicholson (eds) (1995) 'The Formation of the Child Poverty Action Group', *Contemporary Record*, vol 9, no 3, p 617.

[73] Lowe and Nicholson (1995), p 618.

[74] The FSU started in 1940 as Pacifist Service Units (PSU), a national organisation with its headquarters in London, and was made up of conscientious objectors whose principles were informed by a variety of political, religious and philosophical motives. Some were Quakers, but they were in the minority. The PSU became the FSU in 1957, and expanded its social work mission.

[75] BA-SP 4/1a, FSU minutes of meeting, 5 April 1965.

[76] BA-SP 4/2b, CPAG memorandum to D. Houghton, 30 June 1965.

[77] BA-SP 4/1a, BA-S to M. Herbison, 5 April 1965. The Speenhamland system of the pre-1834 Poor Law was a sliding scale means test to allow wage supplements for those in most poverty by the parish authorities. There were already earning disregards in the National Assistance system, most generously for widows and pensioners, but these were abolished for widows for a period in the 1960s. Pensioners' disregards were abolished by Margaret Thatcher's Conservative government.

[78] R. Lowe (1995) 'The Rediscovery of Poverty and the Creation of the Child Poverty Action Group, 1962–68', *Contemporary Record*, vol 9, no 3, pp 602-11.

[79] Abel-Smith and Townsend (1966), p 9. At the Witness Seminar held in 1993 it was noted that *The Poor and the Poorest* did not explicitly justify their 140 per cent poverty line. This was an error that Brian and Townsend subsequently regretted.

[80] Abel-Smith (1996) 'Poverty in Context – New Thoughts on Old Themes', pp 121-33.

[81] BA-SP 4/1c, BA-S to N. Kaldor, 31 January 1966.

[82] *The Times* (1966) 'Sponging on the State', 22 March.

[83] W.C.W. Nixon (1966) 'The Fifth Freedom', *British Medical Journal*, vol 1, 12 February, p 422.

[84] At the Witness Seminar held in 1993 Lynes made an interesting admission: 'I was not and never have been particularly interested in poverty; in fact I always found the title of the group an embarrassment. I did not know what poverty meant, I certainly did not know what child poverty meant, and I could not imagine how you could have child poverty without the whole family being poor. As for defining poverty it seemed to me a totally useless exercise. I was, however, very interested in inequality.' Quoted in Lowe (1995), p 625.

[85] Houghton (1967), p 12.

[86] For a detailed account of the new schemes, see Hall, Land, Parker and Webb (1975).

[87] H. Wilson (1971) *The Labour Government, 1964–70: a personal record*, London: Weidenfeld & Nicholson, p 282.

[88] *Hansard* (1966) House of Commons Debates, vol 725, col 1732.

[89] The NAB's 'wage-stop' policy stipulated that when an unemployed individual's social security benefit exceeded their normal income, the unemployment benefit was cut back accordingly. Its rationale was to make claiming benefits less attractive than employment. It often affected those who were in low-wage jobs and also had large families (for which they would receive National Assistance). The number of 'wage-stop' cases nearly doubled during the winter of 1962–63. It was an indication of increasing poverty. See K. Banting (1979) *Poverty, Politics and Policy. Britain in the 1960s*, London: Macmillan. The unpopular wage-stop policy was eased in 1968 and abolished in 1975. See D. Vincent (1991) *Poor Citizens: The State and the Poor in Twentieth-Century Britain*, London: Longman.

[90] T. Lynes (1967) 'More Money Now!', *Poverty*, vol 5, pp 6–8.

[91] BA-SP 6/3, T. Lynes to BA-S, 21 September 1966. Lynes was then a Temporary Principal at the MPNI, 1965–66.

[92] BA-SP 6/3, D. Nevitt and T. Lynes, Housing Allowances Memorandum, 10 April 1965.

[93] BA-SP 3/4, T. Lynes to L. Jeger, 5 June 1966.

[94] B. Abel-Smith, A. Sinfield and P. Townsend (1966) 'Children hit by wage-stop', Letter to *The Times*, 14 June.

[95] B. Abel-Smith (1966) 'Do we care so little about poverty?', *Observer*, 6 November.

[96] *The Guardian* (1966) 'The Victims of the Welfare State', 18 November.

[97] *The Guardian* (1966), 24 November. All three Titmice lectures along with Crossman's were reprinted by the Fabian Society (1967) *Socialism and Affluence: Four Fabian Essays*, London: Fabian Society, May.

[98] L. Jeger (1966) 'The Politics of Poverty', *The Guardian*, 25 November.

[99] B. Abel-Smith (1966) 'How Poverty Could Be Eliminated Tomorrow', *Telegraph Magazine*, 25 November. Brian received a fee of £120 for this article, which he probably donated to CPAG, judging from their accounts.

[100] A. Watkins (1967) 'Mr Wilson and the long view', *The Spectator*, 21 April.

[101] BA-SP 4/3, BA-S, P. Townsend and T. Lynes to H. Wilson, 12 April 1967.

[102] BA-SP 3/4, Talk to Association of Child Care Officers conference, 14 April 1967. Report in *British Hospital and Social Services Review*, April 1967.

[103] BA-SP 3/4, BA-S, Educational maintenance allowances draft paper.

[104] BA-SP 3/4, BA-S to D. Donnison, 26 May 1966.

[105] BA-SP 3/4, M. Reddin to BA-S, 22 February 1967.

[106] *The Times* (1967) 'Anti-Poverty action group proposed', 15 May.

[107] BA-SP 4/1b, BA-S to Godfrey, 23 December 1966.

[108] BA-SP 4/1b, P. Townsend to P. Herbison, 26 January 1967. This government study had in part been commissioned to disprove the finding of *The Poor and the Poorest*.

[109] BA-SP 4/1c, BA-S to P. Townsend, 3 August 1966.

[110] BA-SP 4/1c, BA-S to T. Simey, 11 July 1966.

[111] BA-SP 4/1c, T. Simey to BA-S, 13 July 1966. It was around this time that signs of Simey's dementia became apparent, which might explain his behaviour.

[112] BA-SP 4/1b, J. Boreham (Chief Statistician at the General Registrar's Office) to BA-S, 2 January 1967.

[113] BA-SP 4/1c, BA-S to H. Land, 21 June 1966.

[114] BA-SP 4/1c, BA-S to P. Townsend, 3 August 1966.

[115] BA-SP 4/4, F. Longman to BA-S and P. Townsend, 23 October 1967.

[116] BA-SP 4/2b, CPAG annual accounts to 21 December 1967. The Poverty Survey money had come from Rowntree's Memorial Trust, and the CPAG donation came from the Charitable Trust.

[117] BA-SP 4/2b, CPAG memo, 3 May 1967.

[118] BA-SP 3/10a, Report by a Committee of Justice (British Section of the International Commission of Jurists). The Committee was set up in parallel with the White Paper *Compensation for Victims of Crimes of Violence* in June 1961 (Cmnd 1406). This had been stimulated by the work of Margery Fry for a state compensation scheme in 1954.

[119] BA-SP 3/10a, BA-S, 'The case against compensation for victims of crimes of violence', nd.

[120] Robert Stevens returned from the US in 1993 to become Master of Pembroke College, Oxford, until his retirement in 2001.

[121] Tanganyika and Zanzibar were joined in 1964 to form Tanzania.

[122] B. Abel-Smith and R. Titmuss (1964) *The Health Services of Tanganyika*, London: Pitman. Chris Wood, from Richard Schilling's Department of Occupational Health at LSHTM was also involved, staying in Tanganyika to set up a four-year medical training course. This was eventually replaced by a formal medical degree programme, which gave a qualification that was recognised internationally, but which also facilitated the emigration of some of the doctors who completed it.

[123] W. Twining (2009) 'Editorial: Special Issue: the work of Robert Stevens', *International Journal of the Legal Profession*, vol 16, no 1, pp 1-3.

[124] B. Abel-Smith and R. Stevens (1967) *Lawyers and the Courts: a sociological study of the English legal system, 1750–1965*, London: Heinemann.

[125] D. Sugarman (2009) 'Beyond ignorance and complacency: Robert Stevens' journey through *Lawyers and the Courts*', *International Journal of the Legal Profession*, vol 16, no 1, pp 7-25.

[126] A. Sampson (1962) *The Anatomy of Britain*, London: Hodder & Stoughton, p 159.

[127] *New Law Journal* (1967), pp 437-8.

[128] Author conversation with Michael Zander, 13 January 2011.

[129] Sugarman (2009), pp 7-25.

[130] B. Abel-Smith and R. Stevens (1968) *In search of justice: Society and the legal system*, London: Lane.

[131] M. Zander (1968) *Lawyers and the Public Interest: a study in restrictive practices*, London: Weidenfeld & Nicholson.

[132] E. Cohn (1969) '*Lawyers and the Public Interest. A Study in Restrictive Practices*, by Michael Zander; *In search of justice*, by Brian Abel-Smith and Robert Stevens', *Modern Law Review*, vol 32, pp 336-41.

[133] L. Blom-Cooper (1968) 'The Indictment of a Profession', *Observer*, 6 December.

[134] BA-SP 14/15, BA-S to C. Clarke, 13 March 1969.

[135] W. Plowden (1969) 'Modernising English Justice', *Book World*, 28 September.

[136] Interview with Lionel Abel-Smith. Lionel invested in the company Just Men (London) Ltd, founded on 11 October 1965.

[137] Charles Schuller (1932–2007) and his wife Dorothy had two daughters to whom Brian was a godfather. Brian set up a company with Schuller called Lonsdale Road Properties Ltd to allow him to help them buy a house. They kept in regular contact, often spending Christmas together.

[138] Interview with Milton Grundy, 26 June 2007.

[139] J. Windsor (1997) 'A dandy has his day', *The Independent*, 29 March.

Chapter 8

[1] P. Thompson (1993) 'Labour's "Gannex conscience"? Politics and popular attitudes in the "permissive" society', in R. Coopey, S. Fielding and N. Tiratsoo (eds) *The Wilson Governments*, London: Pinter, p 143.

[2] R. Crossman (1975) *The Diaries of a Cabinet Minister, Vol 1: Minister of Housing 1964–66*, London: Hamish Hamilton and Jonathan Cape, p 2, diary entry for 22 October 1964.

[3] TNA T227/2589, Earnings-related Pension Scheme, 1968. Discussions with (1) The Lord President's Group of Academic Experts; (2) Confederation of British Industry and the TUC, Letter from Serpell to Houghton, 10 May 1968.

[4] RWP, Crossman, Private office diary, 8 March 1968.

[5] TNA T227/2589, 'Two social security funds?', Note by Professor Brian Abel-Smith, 18 June 1968.

[6] BA-SP 14/14, Radio transcript, BBC Radio 3, 'The Personal View', 18 May 1968.

[7] A. Blick (2004) *People Who Live in the Dark. The history of the special adviser in British politics*, London: Politico's, p 36.

[8] Blick (2004), p 5.

[9] Fabian Society (1964) *The Administrators*, London: Fabian Society.

[10] T. Balogh (1959) 'The Apotheosis of the Dilettante', in H. Thomas (ed) *The Establishment*, London: Anthony Bond, pp 83-126. Balogh was later a member of the Fabian Society's study group that produced *The Administrators: the reform of the civil service* in 1964.

[11] K. Theakston (1992) *The Labour Party and Whitehall*, London: Routledge, p 132.

[12] Blick (2004), p 57.

[13] H. Wilson (1977) *The Governance of Britain*, London: Sphere, pp 202-5.

[14] R. Klein and J. Lewis (1977) 'Advice and Dissent in British Government: the Case of the Special Advisers', *Policy & Politics*, vol 6, pp 1-25.

[15] R. Crossman (1965) 'Scientists in Whitehall', in R. Crossman (ed) *Planning for freedom*, London: Hamish Hamilton, pp 144-5.

[16] R. Crossman (1977) *The Diaries of a Cabinet Minister, Vol 3: Secretary of State for Social Services 1968–70*, London: Hamish Hamilton and Jonathan Cape.

[17] T. Dalyell (1989) *Dick Crossman: A portrait*, London: Weidenfeld & Nicholson; A. Howard (1990) *Crossman. The Pursuit of Power*, London: Jonathan Cape.

[18] S. Thornton (2009) *Richard Crossman and the Welfare State: Pioneer of Welfare Provision and Labour Politics in Post-War Britain*, London: Tauris Academic Studies.

[19] K. Theakston (2003) 'Richard Crossman: The Diaries of a Cabinet Minister', *Public Policy and Administration*, vol 18, no 4, pp 20-40.

[20] J. Markoff and V. Montecinos (1993) 'The Ubiquitous Rise of Economists', *Journal of Public Policy*, vol 13, no 1, pp 37-68.

[21] BA-SP 7/2, BA-S to the Director of LSE, 4 June 1968.

[22] BA-SP 7/2, BA-S to Odgers, 30 May 1968.

[23] JSP, B. McSwiney to BA-S, 2 October 1968.

[24] JSP, J. Prideaux to BA-S, 1 November 1968.

[25] RWP, R. Crossman, Private office diaries, 1968–70.

[26] Interview with R. Wendt, 30 April 2010.

[27] Interview with D. Blewett and A. Sheps, 15 June 2010.

[28] BA-SP 7/2, Revans to BA-S, 17 October 1968. Revans was the driving force behind Wessex splitting away from the South West Metropolitan RHB and establishing its own teaching hospital at Southampton. Prior to that medical education for the region had been provided by St Thomas' Hospital.

[29] See, for example, how Ray Pahl, an adviser to the South East Joint Planning Team, sent Brian draft papers in February 1969 in the hope that he could access more useful statistics on poverty and immigration that would strengthen his policy proposal.

[30] Private information. This was strictly against Whitehall rules, which stipulated that Cabinet papers should not be shown to anyone else.

[31] BA-SP 7/2, Correspondence between BA-S, Schofield, Crossman and Callaghan (Home Secretary), June 1969.

[32] TNA CAB 147/125, 'Social Security: A New Strategy', around September 1968.

[33] Crossman (1977), p 53, diary entry for 8 May 1968.

[34] BA-SP 1/38, BA-S to J. Harris, 27 November 1973.

[35] Department of Health and Social Security (1969) *National Superannuation and Social Insurance*, Cmnd 3883, London: HMSO.

[36] Department of Health and Social Security (1956) *National Superannuation and Social Insurance*, London: HMSO, p 12.

[37] Labour Party Study Group on Security and Old Age, Minutes, 4 July 1956.

[38] H. Heclo (1974) *Modern Social Politics in Britain and Sweden: from relief to income maintenance*, New Haven, CT: Yale University Press, p 278.

[39] P. Bridgen (1999) 'Remedy for All Ills: Earnings-Relation and the Politics of Pensions 1950s-1960s', Unpublished paper given at the 'Relative decline and relative poverty: signposts to the sixties' Conference, University of Bristol, 13 May. This Committee was not even designated a formal Cabinet committee: 'It was not given any precise ministerial direction on its formation and was authorised not to pass its papers to ministers until a proposal had been constructed.' See TNA T227/2216 and 2217.

[40] T. Lynes (1969) *Labour's Pension Plan*, Fabian Tract No 396, London: Fabian Society, p 31.

[41] Quoted in Lynes (1969), p 9.

[42] A. Seldon (1969) *Sunday Telegraph*, 2 February, quoted in Lynes (1969), p 9.

[43] *The Guardian* (1969), 29 January.

[44] Lynes (1969), p 12.

[45] R. Titmuss (1969) 'Superannuation for All: A Broader View', *New Society*, February, pp 315-17.

[46] Crossman (1977), p 176, diary entry for 26 August 1968.

[47] Department of Health and Social Security (1969) *National Superannuation*, Cmnd 4195, London: HMSO.

[48] Interview with David Blewett and Arthur Sheps, 15 June 2010.

[49] R. Crossman (1971) 'The Politics of Pensions', The Eleanor Rathbone Memorial Lecture, Sheffield, 14 May, Liverpool: University of Liverpool Press, p 5.

[50] B. Abel-Smith (1964) *The Hospitals 1800–1948: A Study in Social Administration in England and Wales*, London: Heinemann.

[51] C. McInnes (1966) 'Out of the Way: National Health Lottery', *New Society*, 5 May.

[52] C. Webster (1996) *The Health Services since the War, Volume II*, London: HMSO, p 187. For Robinson's announcement of this committee see *Hansard*, House of Commons Debates, vol 716, cols 8-9, 12 July 1965; vol 733, col 1172, 8 August 1966.

[53] Medical Services Review Committee (1962) *A Review of the Medical Services in Great Britain*, London: Social Assay. This was chaired by Sir Arthur Porritt, and used external consultants to gather data on health service administration and organisation.

[54] Webster (1996), p 328.

[55] Webster (1996), p 213.

[56] *Hansard* (1965) House of Commons Debates, vol 713, col 145, 31 May.

[57] In 1964 Cohen was replaced as Chair by Professor Alastair Macgregor, and some of the functions of the Cohen Committee were transferred to the Dunlop Committee on the Safety of Drugs, which had been formed earlier that year.

[58] (1967) *Report of the Committee of Enquiry into the Relationship of the Pharmaceutical Industry with the National Health Service, 1965–1967*, Cmnd 3410, London: HMSO.

[59] (1967) *Forthcoming Legislation on the Safety, Quality and Description of Drugs and Medicines*, Cmnd 3395, London: HMSO.

[60] Webster (1996), p 217.

61 TNA T 2ss 250/1137/01C, Treasury minutes, 18 September 1967 and 19 September 1967.

62 B. Abel-Smith (1967) 'Sainsbury and the Drug Industry', *New Statesman*, 6 October, pp 426-7.

63 Webster (1996), p 223. One definition for scantlings is the supporting pieces of timber used in buildings. The 1968 Medicines Act established a much narrower Medicines Commission than Sainsbury had envisaged, and made ministers the licensing authority with responsibility for the safety, quality and efficacy of medicines.

64 *Hansard* (1968) House of Commons Debates, vol 767, cols 43-6, 24 June.

65 BA-SP 8/15, BA-S to Sandon, 3 March 1965.

66 BA-SP 8/15, K. Robinson to BA-S, 26 April 1965.

67 BA-SP 8/15, BA-S to Sandon, 1 November 1966.

68 *Hospital Management* (1967) 'Conversation piece: SGH talks to Professor Brian Abel-Smith', May, pp 234-5.

69 The 1959 Mental Health Act, which followed the Royal Commission on Mental Illness (1957), was a commitment to run down long-stay mental hospitals and transfer as many patients as possible to care in the community. It aimed to eliminate distinctions in treatment between physical and mental illness, and between physical and mental handicap by integrating care in district general hospitals with appropriate levels of psychiatric staffing.

70 B. Robb (1967) *Sans Everything: a Case to Answer*, London: Nelson.

71 *Hansard* (1968) House of Commons Debates, vol 768, col 214, 9 July; 'Haste, ignorance and inhumanity', *New Society*, 18 July.

72 Crossman (1977), p 118.

73 Interview with Geoffrey Howe, 20 February 2007.

74 (1969) *Report of the Committee of Inquiry into Allegations of Ill-Treatment of Patients and other Irregularities at the Ely Hospital Cardiff*, Cmnd 3975, London: HMSO.

75 Crossman (1977), p 409.

76 TNA MH 96/2318, Williams Memorandum, Post-Ely Policy Working Party, April 1969; Crossman (1977), p 436, diary entry for 11 April 1969; *Hansard* (1969) House of Commons Debates, vol 780, cols 1808-18, 27 March; vol 782, cols 723-4, 24 April.

77 BA-SP 8/17, E. Skellern to BA-S, 12 July 1969.

78 BA-SP 8/17, E. Skellern to BA-S, 31 May 1969.

79 BA-SP 8/17, Revisions to working party report, 26 June 1970.

80 TNA MH 150/168 PEP (post-Ely policy working party) (69) 62.

81 *The Guardian* (1969) 'New Deal Planned for Subnormal', 20 December.

82 BA-SP 8/17, A.S. Marre to BA-S, 23 July 1970.

83 Department of Health and Social Security (1977) *Proposal for a Health Commissioner in the Reorganised National Health Service*, London: DHSS.

84 Robinson wanted its publication on 5 July, the actual anniversary, but was persuaded to delay it until 23 July to coincide with the publication of the Seebohm report. It thus lost its news opportunity as the Seebohm report was judged more worthy

of attention. The NHS Green Paper, at 10,000 words (23 pages), was less than one fifth the length of Beveridge's 1944 White Paper on the NHS.

[85] Medical Services Review Committee (1962) *A Review of the Medical Services in Great Britain*, London: Social Assay.

[86] Webster (1996), p 327.

[87] Ministry of Health (1967) *First Report on the Organisation of Medical Work in Hospitals*, London: HMSO. It became widely known as 'the Cogwheel report' because of the cover illustration of interlocking cogs.

[88] Webster (1996), p 338.

[89] Crossman (1977), p 456, diary entry for 25 April 1969.

[90] Crossman (1977), p 466, diary entry for 30 April 1969.

[91] Crossman (1977), p 479, diary entry for 7 May 1969.

[92] BA-SP 8/16, J. Morris to BA-S, 24 June 1969.

[93] TNA DH F/P 239/06B PEP (post-Ely policy working party) (69), 10th meeting, 16 July 1969.

[94] (1968) *Report of the Committee on Personal and Allied Social Services*, Cmnd 3703, London: HMSO.

[95] R. Titmuss (1966) Address to the Royal Society of Health, reprinted in *Journal of the Royal Society of Health*.

[96] See Chapter 9 for a discussion of Brian's involvement in the Hunter working party on medical administration, to which he was appointed in April 1970 by Crossman.

[97] In fact, Crossman had initiated the Royal Commission on Local Government without any discussion with Cabinet colleagues, in September 1965, when he was Minister of Local Government. The Royal Commission on Medical Education had been established in June 1965.

[98] TNA DH J/N 179/14C, DHSS minutes, December 1968.

[99] TNA CAB, 16/1 Part III; DH J/N 179/14D, DHSS LP Division minute, October 1969.

[100] Crossman (1977), p 605, diary entry for 4 August 1969.

[101] BA-SP 8/16, BA-S memo to Secretary of State, 'Green Paper – the Central Management of the Service', 15 September 1969.

[102] Crossman (1977), p 752, diary entry for 11 December 1969.

[103] Department of Health and Social Services (1972) *NHS: The Future Structure of the National Health Service*, London: HMSO.

[104] G. Rivett (1998) *From Cradle to Grave. Fifty Years of the National Health Service*, London: The King's Fund, p 264.

[105] Fabian Society (1970) *The National Health Service: Three Views*, London: Fabian Society.

[106] TNA CAB, 16/4 Part I; T, 2SS 21/01P.

[107] Department of Health and Social Services (1972) *National health service reorganisation: England*, London: HMSO.

[108] R. Dahrendorf (1995) *LSE: A History of the London School of Economics and Political Science*, Oxford: Oxford University Press, p 443.

[109] T. Blackstone, K. Gales, R. Hadley and W. Lewis (1970) *Students in Conflict: LSE in 1967*, London: Weidenfeld & Nicholson, pp 163-4.

[110] Dahrendorf (1995), p 455.

[111] C. Crouch (1970) *The Student Revolt*, London: Bodley Head, p 74.

[112] Crouch (1970), p 82.

[113] *Hansard* (1969) House of Commons Debates, vol 776, col 1372, 29 January.

[114] Dahrendorf named the student leaders as David Adelstein, Dick Atkinson, Marshall Bloom, Colin Crouch, Paul Hoch, Chris Middleton, Victor Shoenbach and Peter Watherston. Many of them went on to become respected academics.

[115] Dahrendorf (1995), p 473.

[116] Veit-Wilson saw himself as the most 'expendable' member of the research team, having already encountered difficulties with writing up his research in a style and format that Brian could approve. Interview with John Veit-Wilson, 4 February 2011.

[117] BA-SP 4/4a, F. Longman to P. Townsend, 11 July 1968.

[118] H. Land (1969) *Large Families in London: A Study of 86 Families*, Occasional Papers in Social Administration Series, London: Bell.

[119] A. Sinfield (1968) *The Long-term Unemployed: a comparative survey*, Paris: Organisation for Economic Co-operation and Development.

[120] Interview with Peter Townsend, 28 April 2009.

[121] R. Lowe (1995) 'The Rediscovery of Poverty and the Creation of the Child Poverty Action Group, 1962-68', *Contemporary Record*, vol 9, no 3, p 631, quoting Hilary Land.

[122] Author correspondence with Hilary Land, October 2012.

[123] P. Townsend (1979) *Poverty in the United Kingdom: a survey of household resources and standards of living*, London: Penguin.

[124] BA-SP 1/96, BA-S to P. Townsend, 19 September 1979.

[125] Lowe (1995), p 633, quoting Brian Abel-Smith.

[126] Interview with Peter Townsend, 28 April 2009.

[127] BA-SP 3/8, R.M. Titmuss to BA-S, 18 November 1969, 'on the problem of single men under 45'.

[128] BA-SP 3/8, R.M. Titmuss to P. Townsend, 17 December 1968.

[129] Interview with Peter Townsend, 28 April 2009.

[130] Interview with Peter Townsend, 28 April 2009. Townsend suggested that his decision was partly to protect Brian from any difficulties that his sexuality might have caused if he had gone to the House of Lords. He felt that Brian was 'relieved' by his decision. It does not appear that Lord Longford (Frank Pakenham) actually followed through with his idea to propose them for honours, as there is no record of peerages having been offered and declined.

[131] P. Townsend interviews with P. Thompson, 1997–99. Transcript available from UK Data Service, (http://ukdataservice.ac.uk).

[132] D. Marsden (1969) *Mothers Alone: Poverty and the Fatherless Family*, London: Allen Lane.

[133] Author correspondence with Hilary Land, October 2012.

[134] BA-SP 4/4, R. Titmuss to D. Marsden, 9 May 1969.

[135] BA-SP 4/4, BA-S to L. Waddilove, 7 May 1969.

[136] BA-SP 4/4, L. Waddilove to BA-S, 9 May 1969.

[137] (1974) *The Report of the Royal Commission on One Parent Families – Finer Report*, Cmnd 5629, London: HMSO. Morris Finer (1917–74) was also one of the governors of the LSE from 1969.

[138] BA-SP 4/2a, CPAG Minutes of Appeals Committee, 7 November 1968.

[139] Frank Field was 26 years old when appointed as Director. He had been Deputy Head of General Studies at Hammersmith College, and served as a local councillor for Hounslow.

[140] Author correspondence with Frank Field, 23 October 2012.

[141] Author conversation with Frank Field, 5 October 2012.

[142] Lowe (1995), p 633.

[143] Crossman (1977), p 791, diary entry for 27 January 1970.

[144] F. Field (1982) *Poverty and Politics: the inside story of the Child Poverty Action Group's Campaigns in the 1970s*, London: Heinemann, p 33.

[145] BA-SP 1/96, BA-S to P. Townsend, 19 September 1979.

[146] *Tribune* (1970) 13 February.

[147] *Sunday Times* (1970) 2 March.

[148] Crossman (1977), p 888, diary entry for 16 April 1970.

[149] *The Guardian* (1970) 'Government clashes with poor group', 20 April.

[150] M. Meyer-Kelly and M.D. Kandiah (eds) (2003) *'The Poor Get Poorer Under Labour': The validity and effects of CPAG's campaign in 1970*, London: Institute of Contemporary British History, p 43.

[151] G.K. Mann (1970) 'The Professors of Poverty', *Daily Telegraph*, 17 July.

[152] P. Townsend (ed) (1970) *The Concept of Poverty: working papers on methods of investigation and lifestyles of the poor in different countries*, London: Heinemann; interview with John Veit-Wilson, 4 February 2011.

[153] BA-SP 3/8, D. Piachaud to BA-S, nd.

[154] H. Glennerster (1995) *British Social Policy since 1945*, Oxford: Blackwell, p 121.

[155] P. Hennessy (2000) *The Prime Minister: the Office and its Holders since 1945*, London: Penguin Allen Lane, p 310.

[156] A. Thorpe (1997) *History of the Labour Party*, Basingstoke: Macmillan, p 167.

[157] A. Blick (2006) 'Harold Wilson, Labour and the Machinery of Government', *Contemporary British History*, vol 20, no 3, pp 343-62.

[158] R. Crossman (1972) *The Politics of Pensions*, The Eleanor Rathbone Memorial Lecture, Sheffield, 14 May 1971, Liverpool: University of Liverpool Press, pp 24-6.

[159] Crossman (1977), p 866, diary entry for 19 March 1970.

[160] Crossman (1977), p 921, diary entry for 14 May 1970.

Chapter 9

[1] S. Szreter (2005) *Health is Wealth: Studies in History and Policy*, Rochester, NY: Rochester University Press, p 5.

[2] BA-SP 3/7a, P. Odgers to BA-S, 11 May 1971.

[3] BA-SP 3/7c, J.D. Cooper to BA-S, 29 June 1972.

[4] B. Abel-Smith (1971) 'A Hospital Ombudsman', *New Society*, 22 April, pp 672-4; B. Abel-Smith (1971) 'Managing the Health Service', *New Society*, 29 April, pp 721-2; B. Abel-Smith (1971) 'The Politics of Health', *New Society*, 29 July, pp 190-2.

[5] Abel-Smith (1971) 'The Politics of Health', p 192.

[6] R. Titmuss (1970) *The Gift Relationship: from human blood to social policy*, London: George Allen & Unwin.

[7] BA-SP 3/8, D. Piachaud to BA-S, 30 October 1970; P. Townsend to K. Joseph, 26 October 1970.

[8] BA-SP 3/8, BA-S to D. Piachaud, 5 November 1970.

[9] B. Abel-Smith (1970) 'Poor Kids and Rich Kids', *New Statesman*, 6 November.

[10] BA-SP 3/8, 'Family Income Supplement', 25 August 1970.

[11] See, for example, T. Lynes (1971) 'Milking the Poor', *New Society*, 1 January; D. Barker (1971) 'The Family Income Supplement', *New Society*, 5 August; D. Piachaud (1971) 'Foul Deal for Housing', *New Statesman*, 27 August; F. Field (1971) 'Means Test Madness', *New Statesman*, 1 October.

[12] V. Bottomley (1971) *Families with low income in London*, CPAG Poverty Pamphlet Eight, London: CPAG.

[13] Michael Meacher, Labour MP for Oldham since 1970, had been one of Brian's students at LSE. He had then gone on to lecture at Essex and York in Social Administration, researching elderly people's treatment in mental hospitals.

[14] BA-SP 3/7b, D. Piachaud and BA-S, memos.

[15] BA-SP 3/7b, J. Stackpoole to BA-S, 16 October 1972.

[16] Author correspondence with Bryan Ellis, 22 April 2013.

[17] BA.SP 1/52, BA-S to M. Kaser, 2 May 1973.

[18] BA-SP 3/7c, C. Moser to BA-S, 20 February 1973. Lord Moser had been Professor of Social Statistics at the LSE between 1961 and 1967, when he became Director of the government's Central Statistical Office.

[19] BA-SP 3/7c, 'Distribution of income' Conference, Centre for Environmental Studies, 10 December 1971. Lynes' appointment was as a family casework organiser, because that was the post for which the council had funding available, but he did not actually do this task.

[20] B. Abel-Smith (1971) 'The Department of Social Science and Administration', *LSE: The magazine of the London School of Economics and Political Science*, vol 41, May, pp 3-4.

[21] The Committee had been formed on 22 March 1971. Its members, along with Brian, included Sir Henry Fisher, Miss L. Faithfull, Mr L.F. Neal, Mr S.A. Robinson and Mrs B. Shenfield.

[22] (1973) *Report of the Committee on Abuse of Social Security Benefits*, Cmnd 5228, London: HMSO.

[23] *The Economist* (1971) 'How much nosey-parkering?', 31 March.

[24] D. Piachaud (1973) 'Abuse of Social Security Benefits', *The Times*, 2 April.

[25] C. Webster (1996) *The health services since the War, Vol II*, London: HMSO, pp 448-50.

[26] Department of Health and Social Security (1972) *Report of the Working Party on medical administrators* (Chair R.B. Hunter), London: HMSO; (1968) *The Royal Commission on Medical Education*, Cmnd 3569, London: HMSO.

[27] BA-SP 1/98. Brian's involvement in this work was also possibly due to encouragement from Tony Lynes, who had inherited some shares in the Distillers' group, and was part of a shareholders' campaigning group for a better settlement for the victims.

[28] B. Abel-Smith and M. Zander with R. Brooke (1973) *Legal Problems and the Citizen*, London: Heinemann Educational Books.

[29] Author conversation with Michael Zander, 13 January 2011.

[30] Jones had served as junior British counsel at the Nuremberg trials after the Second World War. He was elected as a Labour MP in 1945, and later served as Lord Chancellor during Labour's 1974–79 government. He was made a life peer in 1974.

[31] (1969) *In Place of Strife: A Policy for Industrial Relations*, Cmnd 3888, London: HMSO.

[32] H. Fawcett (1999) 'Jack Jones, the Social Contract and Social Policy 1970–4', in H. Fawcett and R. Lowe (eds), *Welfare Policy in Britain. The Road from 1945*, London: Macmillan, p 161.

[33] Labour Party (1972) *Annual Conference Report*, London: Labour Party, p 304.

[34] BA-SP 5/3, T. Lynes (1973) 'Should we have a State Pension Fund?', Labour Party Social Policy Sub-committee RD560, January.

[35] 'Economic Policy and the Cost of Living', TUC/Labour Party Liaison Committee Joint Statement, February 1973.

[36] (1972) *Proposals for a Tax Credit System*, Cmnd 5116, London: HMSO.

[37] BA-SP 5/5, Labour Party Working Party on Tax Credits, Minutes, 17 May 1973.

[38] BA-SP 5/5, N. Kaldor to BA-S, nd.

[39] BA-SP 5/5, BA-S to B. Castle, 13 June 1973.

[40] BA-SP 14/7, B. Abel-Smith (1973) 'Equity and Dependency', Paper presented at the Institute for Fiscal Studies Conference on 'Proposals for a tax-credit system', 5 March.

[41] BA-SP 5/2, T. Lynes to BA-S, 24 November 1973.

[42] Department of Health and Social Security (1971) *Strategy for Pensions*, Cmnd 4355, London: HMSO; BA-SP 5/3, BA-S to P. Barry, 13 February 1973.

[43] BA-SP 13/4, B. Abel-Smith (1968) 'Economics and Health Services', Paper delivered at the WHO-EURO Seminar on Health Economics, Moscow, 25 June–5 July.

[44] S. Lee (1997) 'WHO and the developing world: the contest for ideology', in A. Cunningham and B. Andrews (eds) *Western Medicine as Contested Knowledge*, Manchester: Manchester University Press, pp 24–45.

[45] Author conversation and correspondence with Vicente Navarro, July 2013. There is no record in the Brian Abel-Smith archives at the LSE of this trip to Chile. It is possible that, as with his participation in Milton Roemer's working party to the USSR in 1961, he removed politically sensitive material from his files in preparation for future work with the British government, which required his clearance under the Official Secrets Act.

46 BA-SP 13/6 and 11/1, 'Draft report on the Statistical Commission and European Commission for Europe Conference of European Statisticians', Consultation on Health Statistics, WHO Europe Office, Geneva, 11–15 December 1972.

47 BA-S 11/1, B. Abel-Smith (1973) 'Basic Concepts: Macro-Economic Aspects of Health Care', Statistical Commission and Economic Commission for Europe Conference of European Statisticians, Consultation on Health Statistics, Geneva, 2–16 July.

48 B. Abel-Smith, L. Ekholm, H.E. Klarman and V. Rojo-Fernandez (1972) 'Can We Reduce the Cost of Medical Education?', *WHO Chronicle*, vol 26, pp 441-50.

49 B. Abel-Smith (1973) 'Cost effectiveness and cost benefit in cholera control', *WHO Chronicle*, vol 27, pp 407-9.

50 B. Abel-Smith (1974) 'Health and disease, economics of', *Encyclopaedia Britannica* (15th edn), Chicago: Encyclopaedia Britannica, pp 689-93.

51 See, for example, G. Myrdal (1968) *Asian Drama: An Inquiry into the Poverty of Nations*, New York: Twentieth Century Fund and Pantheon Books.

52 M. Finnemore (1997) 'Redefining Development at the World Bank', in F. Cooper and R. Packard (eds) *International Development and the Social Sciences*, Berkeley, CA: University of California Press, p 211.

53 E. Reid (1973) 'McNamara's World Bank', *Foreign Affairs*, vol 51, pp 794-810.

54 R. Ayres (1983) *Banking on the Poor: the World Bank and World Poverty*, Cambridge, MA: Massachusetts Institute of Technology Press.

55 A parallel but separate organisation – the Population Council – was also established in 1952 in the US by John D. Rockefeller III: there is no indication in the Abel-Smith archives that Brian had any contact with this organisation, which also developed and funded family planning services in developing countries.

56 P. Ehrlich (1968) *The Population Bomb*, New York: Balantine Books.

57 M. Mamdani (1972) *The Myth of Population Control*, New York: Monthly Review Press, p 38.

58 B. Abel-Smith (1975) *People without Choice*, London: International Planned Parenthood Federation, p 68.

59 Abel-Smith (1975) *People without Choice*, p 68.

60 M. Gowing (1975) 'Richard Morris Titmuss', *Proceedings of the British Academy*, vol 61, pp 401-28.

61 R.M. Titmuss (1974) *Social Policy: an introduction*, London: George Allen & Unwin Ltd.

62 A. Oakley (1984) *Taking it Like a Woman*, London: Jonathan Cape, p 110.

63 Interview with Liz Shore, 23 August 2008.

64 Interview with Ann Oakley, 23 April 2007, and correspondence.

65 The largest donation to the Titmuss Fund, which resulted in its renaming, came from Marie Meinhardt, a Jewish refugee who had been given employment by Titmuss as a research assistant in the 1940s. When she died in 1986 she left to the Fund her house in Switzerland and a Pisarro painting, in gratitude for Titmuss's help in obtaining British citizenship for herself and her husband.

66 K. Russell (1981) *Changing course: a follow-up study of students taking the certificate and diploma in social administration at the London School of Economics, 1949–1973*, London: LSE.

[67] R. Dahrendorf (1995) *LSE: A History of the London School of Economics and Political Science*, Oxford: Oxford University Press, p 484.

Chapter 10

[1] Quoted in N. Timmins (1996) *The Five Giants: A Biography of the Welfare State*, London: Fontana, p 331.

[2] R. Crossman (1977) *The Diaries of a Cabinet Minister Vol 3: Secretary of State for Social Services 1968–70*, London: Hamish Hamilton and Jonathan Cape, p 921, diary entry for 14 May 1970.

[3] H. Wilson (1976) *The Governance of Britain*, London: Weidenfeld & Nicholson and Michael Joseph, pp 202-5.

[4] A. Thirlwall (1987) *Nicholas Kaldor*, Brighton: Wheatsheaf, pp 250-1.

[5] BA-SP 7/6, T. Lynes to special advisers, 6 January 1975.

[6] P. Hall, H. Land, R. Parker and A. Webb (1975) *Change, Choice and Conflict in Social Policy*, London: Heinemann, p 114.

[7] A. King (1975) 'Overload: Problems of Governing in the 1970s', *Political Studies*, vol 23, pp 284-96; J. Douglas (1976) 'Review article: The Overloaded Crown', *British Journal of Political Science*, vol 6, pp 483-505.

[8] R. Klein and J. Lewis (1977) 'Advice and Dissent in British Government: the Case of the Special Advisers', *Policy & Politics*, vol 6, p 5.

[9] Interview with David Piachaud, 11 June 2008. A. Blick (2004) *People Who Live in the Dark. The history of the special adviser in British politics*, London: Politico's, p 172.

[10] BA-SP 1/13, B. Abel-Smith 'Richard Crossman eulogy', 15 May 1974.

[11] B. Castle, *The Castle Diaries, 1974–76*, London: George Weidenfeld and Nicolson, p 102.

[12] BA-SP 7/2, J. Hunt to BA-S, 2 November 1974.

[13] R.H.S. Crossman (1981) *The Backbench Diaries of Richard Crossman* (ed Janet Morgan), London: Hamilton.

[14] Interview with Milton Grundy, 27 June 2007.

[15] DBASP, BA-S to D. Blewett and A. Sheps, 9 June 1975.

[16] DBASP, BA-S to D. Blewett and A. Sheps, 16 April 1974.

[17] DBASP, BA-S to D. Blewett and A. Sheps, 9 June 1975.

[18] DBASP, BA-S to D. Blewett and A. Sheps, 8 November 1976.

[19] C. Webster (1996) *The Health Services since the War. Vol II*, London: HMSO, p 580.

[20] B. Ellis (1978) 'Pensions: a Touch of Class', *New Window: Official Magazine of the staff of the Department of Health and Social Security*, vol 30, no 12, pp 3-5.

[21] A. Perkins (2002) 'Baroness Castle of Blackburn', *The Guardian*, 4 May.

[22] Castle (1980), p 143, diary entry for 10 July 1974.

[23] Castle (1980), p 38, diary entry for 5 March 1974.

[24] Paul Chapman was told by Brian that he had been offered this DHSS position because he had achieved the best examination results on the LSE Diploma course. He was then in the process of beginning a PhD under Brian's supervision.

[25] Geoff Alltimes was recruited in October 1975 from Lewisham Social Services where he had just been appointed as a team leader. Brian had some difficulty in

persuading the Civil Service Department to pay Alltimes at an appropriate salary. Castle also appointed Dr W.E.J. (Bill) McCarthy, an Oxford academic expert in industrial relations, to undertake a review of the NHS Whitley Council machinery. His report, *Making Whitley Work*, was published in 1977. He was made a life peer in 1975.

[26] Author correspondence with Paul Chapman, 7 January 2013.

[27] Author conversation with Jack Straw, 18 November 2008.

[28] BA-SP 7/6, DHSS Circular HQ 80/75, 1 October 1975.

[29] Lynes felt so uncomfortable with this arrangement that he asked to be transferred to act as adviser to David Donnison, Head of the SBC. Interview with Tony Lynes, 23 March 2010.

[30] Author conversation with Jack Straw, 18 November 2008.

[31] Interview with Patrick Nairne, 22 September 2008.

[32] Interview with David Owen, 13 March 2007.

[33] Castle had also received treatment in a private London hospital in the 1960s, a fact that Norman Warner, her Principal Private Secretary, later had to devise a press strategy to counter.

[34] R.M. Titmuss (1970) *The Gift Relationship: from human blood to social policy*, London: George Allen & Unwin Ltd.

[35] Interview with David Owen, 13 March 2007.

[36] Castle (1980), p 93, diary entry for 26 April 1974.

[37] I. Mikardo (1998) *Back Bencher*, London: Weidenfeld & Nicolson, p 198.

[38] BA-SP 7/11, BA-S to B. Castle, 11 March 1975.

[39] Ruth Lister had been one of Peter Townsend's sociology students at Essex in the late 1960s. She joined the staff of CPAG as a Legal Research Officer in 1971, and was its Director between 1979 and 1987.

[40] BA-SP 7/11, J.W. Stackpoole, Minute, 4 July 1975.

[41] BA-SP 7/11, B. Abel-Smith, RE151: 'The Social Wage: Health, Personal Social Services and Social Security'.

[42] BA-SP 7/11, BA-S to T. Atkinson, 2 June 1975.

[43] BA-SP 7/11, BA-S to T. Atkinson, 2 June 1975.

[44] BA-SP 7/11, BA-S to B. Castle, 28 July 1975.

[45] BA-SP 7/11, BA-S to B. Castle, 31 August 1975.

[46] BA-SP 7/11 BA-S to B. Castle, 8 December 1975.

[47] (1974) *One Parent Families Committee Report. Vols 1 and 2*, Cmnd 5629, London, HMSO. Morris Finer (1917–74) was a lawyer and judge. He chaired a committee for the Society of Labour Lawyers that included three of Brian's associates: Antony Lestor, Geoffrey Bindman and Michael Zander, which produced the report *Justice for All* in 1968. He also served as Vice-Chair of the Board of Governors for the LSE.

[48] P. Townsend (1975) 'Money for a Million Children', *New Statesman*, 27 June.

[49] BA-SP 7/8, BA-S Briefing note, September 1975.

[50] BA-SP 7/11, BA-S to B. Castle, 19 March 1976.

[51] See the discussion later in this chapter.

[52] BA-SP 7/14, BA-S to MS (SS) (Brian O'Malley), 13 February 1976.

[53] BA-SP 7/14, BA-S to B. Castle, 27 February 1976.

[54] Castle (1980), p 668, diary entry for 1 March 1976.

[55] BA-SP 7/14, BA-S to MS (SS) (Brian O'Malley), 3 March 1976.

[56] BA-SP 7/10, Labour Party Working Group on the Pharmaceutical Industry, Minutes, 2 May 1974.

[57] BA-SP 7/10, B. Abel-Smith, Draft RE183 (revised): 'Public Control of the Pharmaceutical Industry', Chapter 5: Sales Promotion.

[58] BA-SP 1/6, BA-S to J. Ashley, 5 November 1976.

[59] BA-SP 7/6, S. Williams to H. Wilson, 6 February 1976.

[60] Webster (1996), p 616.

[61] Castle (1980), p 458, diary entry for 10 July 1975.

[62] Department of Health and Social Security (1976) *Priorities for the Health and Social Services in England: A Consultative Document*, London: HMSO.

[63] Author conversation with Alan Maynard, 7 November 2012.

[64] My thanks to Dan Fox for pointing out that a 'geographical full time' system had been introduced in the US in the 1920s in which institutions allowed doctors to keep a percentage of the fees they brought in (the 'eat what you kill' principle). I am not aware whether the British considered adopting a US-style system as a compromise between private and NHS payments during this dispute.

[65] Interview with Walter Holland, 12 May 2008.

[66] Author conversation with Jack Straw, 18 November 2008.

[67] Webster (1996), p 589.

[68] House of Commons Expenditure Committee (1972) *Fourth Report. Facilities for Private Patients*, London: HMSO.

[69] D. Owen (1991) *Time to Declare*, London: Michael Joseph, p 232.

[70] N. Timmins (1996) *The Five Giants: A Biography of the Welfare State*, London: Fontana, p 334.

[71] Castle (1980), p 209, diary entry for 4 November 1974.

[72] *The Times* (1974), 31 December.

[73] Castle (1980), p 389, diary entry for 12 May 1975.

[74] JSP, B. Castle to BA-S, 13 May 1975.

[75] Department of Health and Social Security (1975) *The Separation of Private Practice from National Health Service Hospitals. A consultative document*, London: HMSO. The Scottish Health Department and the Welsh Office also issued the same document.

[76] Castle (1980), p 389, diary entry for 23 September 1975.

[77] Castle (1980), p 513, diary entry for 7 October 1975.

[78] Castle (1980), p 578, diary entry for 3 December 1975.

[79] *The Times* (1975), 27 November.

[80] Webster (1996), p 941, fn 197.

[81] S. Sheard and L. Donaldson (2005) *The Nation's Doctor. The Role of the Chief Medical Officer, 1855–1998*, Oxford: Radcliffe Medical Press, pp 107-11.

[82] N. Mays and G. Bevan (1987) *Resource Allocation in the Health Service. A review of the methods of the Resource Allocation Working Party*, London: Bedford Square Press, p 7.

83   For an overview of earlier health inequalities debates and more on RAWP see
     J. Welshman (2006) 'Inequalities, regions and hospitals: the Resource Allocation
     Working Party', in M. Gorsky and S. Sheard (eds) *Financing Medicine: the British
     experience since 1750*, Oxford: Routledge, pp 221-41. See also A. Maynard and A.
     Ludbrook (1980) 'Budget allocation in the National Health Service', *Journal of
     Social Policy*, vol 9, pp 289-312.

84   C. Webster (2002) 'Investigating Inequalities in Health before Black', *Contemporary
     British History*, vol 16, no 3, p 91.

85   Author correspondence with Ann Oakley, 17 November 2012

86   J. Morris (1959) 'Health and Social Class', *The Lancet*, vol I, pp 303-5.

87   Committee of Enquiry into the Cost of the National Health Service (1956) *Report*
     (Chair C.W. Guillebaud), London: HMSO, p 104.

88   B. Abel-Smith and P. Townsend (1966) *The Poor and the Poorest: a new analysis of
     the Ministry of Labour's Family Expenditure Surveys of 1953-54 and 1960*, London:
     Bell.

89   *The Lancet* (1967) 'Development Areas in the Hospital Service', vol 1, 3 June, pp
     1201-2.

90   Department of Health and Social Security (1970) *Hospital Revenue Allocations*,
     Paper, RHB Chairmen 3/70, London: DHSS.

91   R. Klein (1983) *The Politics of the National Health Service*, London: Longman, p 82.

92   P.A. West (1973) 'Allocation and equity in the public sector: the hospital revenue
     allocation formula', *Applied Economics*, vol 5, no 3, pp 153-66.

93   Interview with Walter Holland, 12 May 2008.

94   Mays and Bevan (1987), p 12.

95   Department of Health and Social Security (1970) *The Future of the National Health
     Service*, London: HMSO.

96   J. Hurst (1998) 'The impact of health economics on health policy and the impact
     of health policy on health economics 1972-1997', *Health Economics*, vol 7, S47-62.

97   M.S. Feldstein (1965) 'Hospital bed scarcity: an analysis of the economic effects of
     inter-regional differences', *Economica*, vol 32, pp 393-409; M.S. Feldstein (1967)
     Economic Analysis of Health Service Efficiency, Amsterdam: North Holland Publishing
     Company.

98   A. Cartwright (1967) *Patients and their Doctors: a Study of General Practice*, London:
     Routledge & Kegan Paul; A. Cartwright and M. O'Brien (1976) 'Social Class
     Variations in Health Care and in the Nature of General Practitioner Consultations',
     in M. Stacy (ed) *The Sociology of the NHS*, Sociological Review Monograph No
     22, Keele: University of Keele, pp 77-98; M.H. Cooper and A.J. Culyer (1970)
     'An Economic Analysis of Some Aspects of the NHS', in I. Jones (ed) *Health
     Service Financing*, London: BMA, pp 187-250.

99   J. Tudor Hart (1971) 'The inverse care law', *The Lancet*, vol I, pp 406-12.

100 N. Bosanquet (1972) 'Inequalities in Health', in P. Townsend and N. Bosanquet
     (eds) *Labour and Inequality: Sixteen Fabian Essays*, London: Fabian Society, pp
     47-65.

101 J. Noyce, A.J.H. Smith and A.J. Trickey (1974) 'Regional Variations in the Allocation
     of Financial Resources to the Community Health Services', *The Lancet*, vol I, pp
     554-7.

[102] Labour Party (1973) *Opposition Green Paper, Health Care. Report of a Working Party*, London: Labour Party, August.

[103] BA-SP 8/20, Draft speech notes 'Efficiency in Health Services', Helsinki Health Economics Summer Seminar, June 1975.

[104] Department of Health and Social Security (1976) *Sharing Resources for Health in England. Report of the Resource Allocation Working Party*, London: HMSO, p 7.

[105] A.E. Bennett and W.W. Holland (1977) 'Rational planning or muddling through? Resource Allocation in the NHS', *The Lancet*, vol 1, p 464.

[106] Interview with David Owen, 13 March 2007. Author correspondence with Owen, 29 September 2012.

[107] Mays and Bevan (1987); J. Mohan (1998) 'Uneven development, territorial politics and the British health care reforms', *Political Studies*, vol 66, pp 309-27.

[108] N. Bosanquet (1980) 'Health', in N. Bosanquet and P. Townsend (eds) *Labour and Equality A Fabian Study of Labour in Power, 1974–79*, London: Heinemann, p 214.

[109] TNA DH D/M 107/01B, DHSS minute, 15 September 1970.

[110] Department of Health and Social Security (1971) *Better Services for the Mentally Handicapped*, Cmnd 4683, London: HMSO.

[111] P. Townsend (1971) *Sunday Times*, 27 June.

[112] Castle (1980), p 85, diary entry for 23 April 1974.

[113] Webster (1996), pp 399-401.

[114] Department of Health and Social Security (1971) *National Health Service Reorganisation. Consultative Document*, London: HMSO.

[115] B. Abel-Smith (1971) 'A Hospital Ombudsman', *New Society*, 22 April.

[116] Department of Health and Social Security (1973) *Report of the Committee on Hospital Complaints Procedure*, London: HMSO.

[117] (1977) *First Report from the Select Committee on the Parliamentary Commissioner for Administration Session 1977–78. Independent Review of Hospital Complaints in the NHS*, London: HMSO.

[118] Department of Health and Social Security (1975) *Better Services for the Mentally Ill*, Cmnd 6233, London: HMSO.

[119] Webster (1996), p 646.

[120] Department of Health and Social Security (DHSS) (1979) *Report of the Committee of Enquiry into Mental Handicap Nursing and Care*, Cmnd 7468, London: HMSO; DHSS (1979) *Summary of the Jay Report. A Brief Outline of their Report by Members of the Committee of Enquiry into Mental Handicap Nursing and Care*, London: HMSO.

[121] D. Piachaud (1980) 'Social Security', in N. Bosanquet and P. Townsend (eds) *Labour and equality: A Fabian study of Labour in power, 1974–79*, London: Heinemann, p 179.

[122] Castle (1980), p 487, diary entry for 5 August 1975.

[123] For a detailed analysis see B. Ellis (1989) *Pensions in Britain 1955–1975: A history in five acts*, London: HMSO. As a civil servant Bryan Ellis was closely involved with pensions policy.

[124] Labour Party (1974) *Let Us Work Together: Labour's Way out of the Crisis*, February, London: Labour Party.

[125] Author correspondence with Michael Partridge, 25 April 2013.

[126] Department of Health and Social Security (1974) *Better Pensions Fully Protected against Inflation*, Cmnd 5713, London: HMSO.

[127] L. Hannah (1986) *Inventing Retirement: the development of occupational pensions in Britain*, Cambridge: Cambridge University Press, pp 61-3.

[128] G.L. Clark (2003) 'Historical Perspectives and the Politics of Pensions Reform', in G.L. Clark and N. Whiteside (eds) *Pension Security in the 21st Century*, Oxford: Oxford University Press, p 31.

[129] A.W. Benn (1982) *Against the Tide. Diaries 1975–76*, London: Hutchinson, p 375; J. Barnett (1982) *Inside the Treasury*, London: Andre Deutsch, p 83.

[130] Castle (1980), pp 671-2, diary entry for 4 March 1976.

Chapter 11

[1] R. Klein (2001) *The New Politics of the National Health Service*, London: Pearson Education, p 80.

[2] B. Castle (1980) *The Castle Diaries 1974–76*, London: Weidenfeld & Nicolson, p 727, diary entry for 8 April 1976.

[3] Interview with Liz Shore, 23 August 2008.

[4] C. Webster (1996) *The Health Services since the War. Vol II*, London: HMSO, p 627.

[5] *Hansard* (1976) House of Commons Debates, vol 912, col 287, 25 May.

[6] F. Field (1982) *Poverty and Politics: the inside story of the Child Poverty Action Group's Campaigns in the 1970s*, London: Heinemann, p 24.

[7] TBP, unedited diary entry, 20 May 1976.

[8] *New Statesman* (1976), 4 June.

[9] F. Field (1976) 'Killing a Commitment: the Cabinet v. the Children', *New Society*, 17 June.

[10] TNA BA 7/25, Sir Douglas Allen (1976) 'Report of Enquiry into the Child Benefit Leak', unpublished document, June.

[11] BA-SP 4/2a, BA-S to J. Marquand, 31 January 1972.

[12] Field (1982), p 19.

[13] BA-SP 7/6, P. Wood to N. Warner, 12 May 1976.

[14] BA-SP 7/6, R.S. Swift to N. Warner (Parliamentary Private Secretary to Ennals), 15 June 1976.

[15] JSP, P. Nairne to BA-S, 26 April 1977.

[16] BA-SP 7/6, BA-S to M. Lee, 26 April 1977.

[17] Interview with David Owen, 13 March 2007.

[18] JSP, BA-S to B. Castle, 16 March 1977.

[19] Castle (1980).

[20] BA-SP 7/6, BA-S to Ennals, 2 February 1977.

[21] BA-SP 7/6, BA-S to Secretary of State (Ennals), 21 December 1976.

[22] JSP, J. Califano to BA-S, 2 December 1977.

[23] BA-SP 1/12, BA-S to P. Nairne, 6 December 1977.

[24] BA-SP 7/13, BA-S to B. Castle, 22 March 1978.

[25] Department of Health and Social Security (1977) *Priorities for Health and Personal Social Services in England: A Consultative Document*, London: HMSO.

[26] Department of Health and Social Security (1977) *The Way Forward*, London: HMSO.

[27] Members were Barbara Castle, BA-S, Nicholas Bosanquet, Nick Grant, Mike Hartley-Brewer, W. Merritt, Laurie Pavitt MP, Teresa O'Connell, Mrs J. Jones and Renee Short MP. At the first meeting it was agreed to invite Tessa Jowell, Roland Moyle MP, Jennifer Roberts (from LSHTM) and Aubrey Sheiham (a dentist), as well as to identify a suitable community physician (possibly Muir Gray).

[28] BA-SP 7/15, BA-S to Secretary of State (Ennals), 1 October 1976. Castle had proposed replacing Distinction (Merit) Awards with Service Awards, which would not favour London and prestige teaching hospitals.

[29] BA-SP 7/15, W.W. Holland to BA-S, 12 November 1976.

[30] BA-SP 7/15, BA-S to Minister of State (Health) (Roland Moyle), 22 December 1976.

[31] BA-SP 7/15, BA-S, 'Regional Government and the NHS'.

[32] BA-SP 7/15, BA-S to Dr T.E.A. Carr (DHSS), 8 March 1977.

[33] John Redcliffe-Maud, Baron Redcliffe-Maud (1906–82), was a civil servant and diplomat, who had previously chaired the Royal Commission on Local Government that reported in 1969. Quentin Hogg, Lord Hailsham of St Marylebone (1907–2001), was a Conservative politician, who served as Lord High Chancellor from 1979 to 1987 during Margaret Thatcher's government.

[34] BA-SP 13/5, B. Abel-Smith, 'The Report of the Royal Commission on the NHS', Annual Rivers Lecture text.

[35] BA-SP 7/19, Discussion notes from 19 December 1978.

[36] BA-SP 7/19, R. Cunningham to BA-S, 28 December 1978.

[37] (1978) *Report of the Supply Board Working Group*, London: HMSO. This was chaired by Brian Salmon (1917–2001), whose family ran the Lyons catering business. Salmon had also chaired an enquiry in 1963 on senior nursing structures and training. He had previously chaired the Catering Committee at Westminster Hospital in 1949 and was Vice-Chair of its Board of Governors. He was Chair of Camden and Islington Area Health Authority from 1974 to 1977.

[38] TNA T SS 29/24/04J, Treasury minute, 29 June 1978.

[39] Department of Health and Social Security (1976) *Prevention and Health: Everybody's Business. A Reassessment of Public and Personal Health*, Cmnd 7047, London: HMSO.

[40] Webster (1996), p 658.

[41] Department of Health and Social Services (1978) *A Happier Old Age: A discussion document on the elderly in our society*, London: HMSO.

[42] *Hospital and Health Services Review* (1978) Editorial, August.

[43] Webster (1996), p 659.

[44] BA-SP 8/25, L. Shore to BA-S, 8 February 1978.

[45] BA-SP 8/25, A. Yarrow to L. Shore, 27 January 1978.

[46] BA-SP 8/25, A. Winner to BA-S, 15 March 1978.

[47] BA-SP 8/25, J. Hawton to BA-S, 12 March 1978.

[48] BA-SP 8/25, G. Godber to BA-S, 13 March 1978.

[49] B. Abel-Smith (1978) 'Other countries want to copy the service we decry', *Pulse*, 1 July.

[50] *Time* (1978) 'The NHS at 30', 17 July.

51 Webster (1996), p 604.

52 Department of Health and Social Security (1978) *Social Assistance: a Review of the Supplementary Benefits Scheme in Great Britain*, London: HMSO.

53 *Social Trends* (1979), Data from Table 6.26 relating to December 1976.

54 D. Piachaud (1980) 'Social Security', in N. Bosanquet and P. Townsend (eds) *Labour and Equality A Fabian Study of Labour in Power, 1974–79*, London: Heinemann, p 183.

55 BA-SP 1/96, BA-S to P. Townsend, 27 September 1976.

56 For a detailed analysis of the work of the SBC and the Review, see D. Donnison (1982) *The Politics of Poverty*, Oxford: Martin Robertson.

57 Author correspondence with Michael Partridge, 25 April 2013.

58 R. Wilkinson (1976) 'Dear David Ennals ...', *New Society*, 16 December, pp 567-8.

59 V. Berridge (1997) 'The Origin of the Black Report: a Conversation with Richard Wilkinson', *Social Science & Medicine*, vol 44, no 6, pp 120-2.

60 V. Berridge (ed) (1997) 'The Black Report and the Health Divide', Witness Seminar transcript, *Social Science & Medicine*, vol 44, no 6, pp 131-71.

61 Berridge (1997) 'The Black Report and the Health Divide', p 139.

62 Berridge (1997) 'The Black Report and the Health Divide', p 147.

63 P. Jenkin (1980) 'Foreword', in *Report of the Working Group on Inequalities in Health (the Black Report)*, London: DHSS.

64 P. Jenkin (2002) 'Dispelling the Myths of the Black Report: A Memoir', *Contemporary British History*, vol 16, no 3, pp 123-30.

65 Interview with Jerry Morris, 3 November 2008.

66 D.A.K. Black (1982) *Inequalities in health: the Black report by Sir Douglas Black, edited by Peter Townsend and Nick Davidson*, Harmondsworth: Penguin.

67 *The Lancet* (1978) 'The Secretary of State's Special Adviser', vol I, pp 287-8.

68 BA-SP 7/27, BA-S to Secretary of State (Ennals), 2 November 1977.

69 Berridge (1997) 'The Black Report and the Health Divide', p 151. Walter Holland also commented that Brian had become 'very disillusioned with the NHS' by 1978–79. Interview, 12 May 2008.

70 Interview with Liz Shore, 23 August 2008.

71 M. Crick (2004) 'Peter Shore 1924–2001', *Dictionary of National Biography* , Oxford: Oxford University Press.

72 JSP, P. Shore to BA-S, 31 July 1977.

73 BA-SP 7/23, BA-S to Mr Gilbert, 9 March 1979.

74 BA-SP 7/23, 'Conclusions of a joint meeting of members of the Cabinet and National Executive Committee on 14 December 1978 to discuss the Election manifesto'.

75 BA-SP 7/23, BA-S to S of S (Shore), 12 January 1979.

76 BA-SP 7/25, GLC Labour Group (1978) 'Impact of Transfer', 21 September.

77 L. Chapman (1979) *Your Disobedient Servant*, London: Penguin.

78 BA-SP 7/32, BA-S to Secretary of State (Shore), 2 May 1979.

79 BA-SP 7/32, BA-S to Secretary of State (Shore), Briefing for Capital Radio programme interview.

[80] BA-SP 7/6, Roger Darlington, memo to special advisers, 8 February 1978.

[81] BA-SP 7/6, E. Arnott, memo to special advisers, 4 December 1978.

[82] BA-SP 1/47, BA-S to J. Kay, 15 January 1979.

[83] Piachaud (1980), p 173.

Chapter 12

[1] A full list of his publications is included in the Bibliography at the end of this book.

[2] BA-SP 1/19, BA-S to A. Cochrane, 12 September 1973.

[3] BA-SP 1/19, A. Cochrane to BA-S, 17 September 1973.

[4] BA-SP 1/80, correspondence.

[5] BA-SP 1/67, BA-S to I. Merriam, 15 January 1974.

[6] B. Abel-Smith (1974) 'Value for Money in Health Services', *Social Security Bulletin*, July, pp 17-28.

[7] Abel-Smith (1974) 'Value for Money in Health Services', pp 27-8.

[8] B. Abel-Smith (1976) *Value for Money in Health Services: A Comparative Study*, London: Heinemann Educational Books.

[9] BA-SP 1/50, BA-S to A. Hill, 20 January 1975.

[10] A. Cochrane (1972) *Effectiveness and Efficiency*, London: Nuffield Provincial Hospitals Trust.

[11] Abel-Smith (1976) *Value for Money in Health Services*, p 221. He references H. Mahler (1975) 'New possibilities for WHO', *WHO Chronicle*, vol 29, February, p 43.

[12] BA-SP 1/50, A.P. Ruderman to BA-S, 26 May 1976.

[13] BA-SP 1/50, BA-S to A.P. Ruderman, 18 June 1976.

[14] A. Donabedian (1966) 'Evaluating the Quality of Medical Care', *Milbank Quarterly*, vol 44, no 3, pp 166-203; reprinted in *Milbank Quarterly* (2005), vol 83, no 4, pp 691-729.

[15] John Devereaux Thompson (1917–92) was an American nurse and hospital administrator. His concept of DRGs was developed while studying on the hospital administration programme at Yale in 1956 with Bob Fetter in the Administrative Science Department. Together they created an array of hospital statistics applied to surgical procedures to calculate standard lengths of hospital stays and associated costs. He also co-wrote with Grace Goldin (1975) *The Hospital: a social and architectural history*, West Haven, CT: Yale University Press.

[16] BA-SP 1/50, BA-S to A. Hill, 9 May 1978.

[17] I.S. Falk (1978) 'Review of *Value for Money in Health Services: A Comparative Study*', *Medical Care*, vol 16, no 3, pp 263-4.

[18] A. Maynard (1977) 'Review of *Value for Money in Health Services: A Comparative Study*', *Journal of Social Policy*, vol 6, no 3, pp 353-5.

[19] R. Klein (1976) 'Review of *Value for Money in Health Services: A Comparative Study*', *British Medical Journal*, 15 May, p 1217.

[20] K. Boyd (1976) 'Review of *Value for Money in Health Services: A Comparative Study*', *Journal of Medical Ethics*, vol 2, pp 211-12.

[21] Abel-Smith (1976) *Value for Money in Health Services*, pp 136, 182.

[22] BA-SP 9/15, BA-S to B. Castle, 7 March 1975.

[23] BA-SP 9/16, BA-S to V. Ringadoo, 21 April 1975.

[24] Interview with Tony Lynes, 23 March 2010.

[25] Russell Prosser (1915–88) had been educated at the LSE, and held a number of Colonial Office appointments in African countries from 1947 and positions on the UN Social Development Commission. He was Senior Adviser on Social Development in the Overseas Development Administration, 1967–80.

[26] BA-SP 9/17, BA-S to S. Mootoosamy, 18 September 1975.

[27] BA-SP 9/17, BA-S to T. Lynes, 7 November 1975.

[28] BA-SP 9/24, 'A Free General Practitioner National Health Service Report' by Professor B. Abel-Smith'.

[29] BA-SP 5/6, Titmuss Memorial Lecture, 5 April 1978.

[30] The common US term for para-medicals would be 'para-professionals' or 'physician-extenders'. The idea of para-medicals was not Titmuss's. An earlier pioneer was (Neville) Rex Fendall (1917–), Professor of Tropical and Community Health at the Liverpool School of Tropical Medicine, 1971–81. See Fendall's later book (1972) *Auxiliaries in health care: programs in developing countries*, Baltimore, MD: Johns Hopkins University Press.

[31] B. Abel-Smith and A. Leiserson (1978) *Poverty, Development and Health Policy*, Geneva: World Health Organization.

[32] World Health Organization (1977) *Handbook of resolutions and decisions. Volume II*, Geneva: WHO, p 21 (World Health Assembly Resolution 29.74).

[33] BA-SP 12/4, P. Hillary to BA-S, 5 May 1975.

[34] BA-SP 12/4, BA-S to B. O'Malley, 16 May 1975.

[35] BA-SP 12/4, D. White, Memo on the European Social Budget, 26 September 1975.

[36] BA-SP 12/4, BA-S contract, 8 October 1975.

[37] BA-SP 12/4, F.B. Hindmarsh, 'Memo EEC: Matters Affecting DHSS', 5 September 1975.

[38] BA-SP 12/4, BA-S to M. Shanks, 27 October 1975.

[39] BA-SP 12/4, BA-S to M. Shanks, 16 October 1975.

[40] BA-SP 12/4, J.A. Atkinson, memo, 20 October 1975.

[41] BA-SP 12/4, Introductory note on consultation of social protection policies, V/848/75 E.

[42] BA-SP 12/4, F.B. Hindmarsh to J.A. Atkinson, 1 October 1975.

[43] BA-SP 12/4, BA-S to J.A. Atkinson, 27 November 1975.

[44] 'Dynamisation' in this context meant ensuring that benefits were pegged to changes in costs of living, or changes in incomes.

[45] BA-SP 12/5, H. Markman (1978) 'A Model for Making the Retirement Age Flexible', 7 January.

[46] BA-SP 12/7, BA-S to D. Ennals, 22 June 1977.

[47] BA-SP 1/25, Contract with the Commission of the European Communities, 7 November 1977. Brian gave his LSE salary as £9,117 pa and his DHSS special adviser salary as £12,000 pa pro rata.

[48] BA-SP 1/24. In 1978 this cost 620–960 Belgian francs (BF) per night; in 1979 he was paying between 1,040 and 1,460 BF per night.

[49] BA-SP 12/7, E.B. McGinnis to BA-S, 1 November 1977.

[50] BA-SP 12/7, W. Nicol to F. Hindmarsh, 14 September 1978.

[51] BA-SP 1/25, T.E. Chester to BA-S, 27 April 1978.

[52] BA-SP 12/7, B. Abel-Smith (1978) 'A Note on a Community System for Unemployment Insurance (CUI)', 15 February.

[53] BA-SP 12/7, K.E.W. Blunt to BA-S, 14 June 1978.

[54] BA-SP 12/5, BA-S to L.G. Refell, 4 July 1978.

[55] BA-SP 12/8, Commission memo for Commission members, 21 November 1978.

[56] BA-SP 12/8, BA-S to L. Crijns, 22 February 1979.

[57] BA-SP 12/8, BA-S to H. Vredeling, 15 October 1979.

[58] BA-SP 12/8, BA-S to L. Crijns, Note on Pharmaceutical Prices, 26 July 1979.

[59] BA-SP 12/8, BA-S to L. Crijns, Note on Pharmaceutical Prices, 26 July 1979.

[60] BA-SP 12/8, BA-S to L. Crijns, 26 July 1979.

[61] BA-SP 12/8, BA-S (1980) 'The Study of Pharmaceutical Prices', 12 April.

[62] I am grateful to Socrates Litsios for pointing out that in 1985 the Rockefeller Foundation used a similar title for the classic book resulting from one of its Bellagio conferences: see S. Halstead, J. Walsh and K. Warren (eds) (1985) *Good Health at Low Cost*, Bellagio: Rockefeller Foundation.

[63] BA-SP 12/8; European Commission (1979) *Better Health at Lower Cost*, Draft report of the Commission Work Programme on Health, 21 November.

Chapter 13

[1] Mao Zedong, '26 June Directive', reprinted in R. and V. Sidel (1982) *The Health of China*, London: Zed Press, p 4.

[2] World Health Assembly, Resolution 30.43.

[3] S. Litsios (2002) 'The Long and Difficult Road to Alma Ata: A Personal Reflection', *International Journal of Health Services*, vol 32, pp 709-32.

[4] World Health Organization (1978) *Primary Health Care*, Geneva: WHO.

[5] V. Sidel (1972) 'The barefoot doctors of the People's Republic of China', *New England Journal of Medicine*, 15 June, pp 1294-5.

[6] M. Cueto (2004) 'The origins of primary health care and selective primary health care', *American Journal of Public Health*, vol 94, no 11, pp 1864-74.

[7] World Health Organization (1951) Fourth World Health Assembly, WHO Official Records, 35:111. See also S. Amrith (2006) *Decolonizing international health*, Basingstoke: Palgrave Macmillan.

[8] J.H. Bryant (1969) *Health and the Developing World*, Ithaca, NY: Cornell University Press.

[9] Canadian Department of National Health and Welfare (1974) *A New Perspective on the Health of Canadians / Nouvelle perspective de la santé de Canadiens*, Ottawa: Canadian Department of National Health and Welfare.

[10] I. Illich (1975) *Medical Nemesis: the expropriation of health*, London: Calder and Boyars.

[11] World Health Organization (1973) *Organisational Study on Methods of Promoting the Development of Basic Health Services*, Geneva: WHO.

[12] V. Djukanovic and E.P. Mach (eds) (1975) *Alternative Approaches to Meeting Basic Health Needs in Developing Countries: a joint UNICEF/WHO Study*, Geneva: WHO, p 7.

[13] K. Newell (1975) *Health by the People*, Geneva: World Health Organization.

[14] H. Mahler (1975) 'Health for All by the Year 2000', *WHO Chronicle*, vol 29, pp 457-61.

[15] M. Cueto (2004) 'The origins of primary health care and selective primary health care', *American Journal of Public Health*, vol 94, no 11, pp 1864-74.

[16] World Health Organization (1978) *Formulating Strategies for Health for All by the Year 2000: Guiding Principles and essential Issues*, Preliminary document of the Executive Board, A32/8 15 February, Geneva: WHO.

[17] F. Cooper and R. Packard (eds) (1997) *International Development and the Social Sciences*, Berkeley, CA: University of California Press.

[18] W. Rodney (1972) *How Europe Underdeveloped Africa*, London: Bogle-L'Overture.

[19] J. Markoff and V. Montecinos (1993) 'The ubiquitous rise of Economists', *Journal of Public Policy*, vol 13, no 1, p 52.

[20] J.A. Walsh and K.S. Warren (1979) 'Selective Primary Health Care, an Interim Strategy for Disease Control in Developing Countries', *New England Journal of Medicine*, vol 301, pp 967-74. It was reprinted in *Social Science & Medicine* (1980) vol 14c, pp 145-63 as part of an issue devoted to the Bellagio meeting.

[21] Later variants added FFF: food supplementation, female literacy and family planning.

[22] Cueto (2004), p 1869.

[23] See the correspondence in the *New England Journal of Medicine* (1980), vol 302, pp 757-9; S. Rifkin and G. Walt (1986) 'Why Health Improves: Defining the Issues Concerning "Comprehensive Primary Health Care and Selective Primary Health Care"', *Social Science & Medicine*, vol 23, no 6, pp 559-66; and the special issue of *Social Science & Medicine* (1988), vol 26, p 9.

[24] BA-SP 11/4, BA-S notes, nd, attached to draft agenda for RHDAC meeting, 17-18 March 1980.

[25] BA-SP 11/5, WHO Regional Office for Europe, RHDAC, Report on a meeting, Copenhagen, 31 March–2 April 1981, EUR/EXM/81.2.

[26] Author correspondence with Göran Dahlgren, June 2013.

[27] BA-SP 11/6, WHO Regional Committee for Europe, Report on the third meeting of the RHDC, Copenhagen, 18–20 April 1983, EUR/RC33/8/1333D.

[28] Interview with Ted Marmor, 29 June 2007. See also K. Lee and H. Goodman (2002) 'Global policy networks: the propagation of health care financing reform since the 1980s', in K. Lee, K. Buse and S. Fustukian (eds) *Health Policy in a Globalising World*, Cambridge: Cambridge University Press, pp 97-119.

[29] BA-SP 11/8, BA-S to R. Illsley, 5 May 1982.

[30] Keith Joseph, when Secretary of State for Social Services, had suggested in a speech in 1972 that some British families were unable to break out from their experience of inter-generational poverty. It triggered a major research programme. See J. Welshman (2006) *Underclass: A History of the Excluded, 1880–2000*, London: Hambledon Continuum.

[31] A.J. Culyer (1981) *Health and Health Indicators: Proceedings of a European Workshop*; later published as A.J. Culyer (ed) (1983) *Health Indicators: an international study for the European Science Foundation*, Oxford: Robertson.

[32] J. Ahumada et al (1965) *Health Planning: Problems of Concept and Method*, Washington, DC: Pan-American Health Organization.

[33] Author correspondence with Ralph Andreano, 11 January 2013.

[34] A. Enthoven (1978) 'Cutting Cost Without Cutting the Quality of Care', *New England Journal of Medicine*, vol 298, pp 1229-38. Enthoven advised President Carter on managed competition healthcare reform in the US, and was invited to advise the Thatcher government on British NHS reform.

[35] B. Abel-Smith (1980) 'Report on the Seminar', in A. Brandt, B. Horisberger and W.P. von Wartburg (eds) *Cost-Sharing in Health Care*, Berlin: Springer-Verlag.

[36] D. Fox (2011) *The Convergence of Science and Governance*, Berkeley, CA: University of California Press, pp 39-43, 45-8. It was initially called the National Center for Health Services Research and Development. 'Development' was dropped in 1974, the same year that the economist Gerald Rosenthal became its first non-medical Director.

[37] Kerr White (1917–) headed the Johns Hopkins University Division of Hospitals and Medical Care from 1964 to 1976, during which time he led the WHO-sponsored International Collaborative Study of Medical Care Utilisation (WHO/ISMCU). This drew on 48,000 household interviews from 12 countries. His publications with Barbara Starfield demonstrated that where there was adequate primary care, that is, readily available general physicians, hospital utilisation was much less 'no matter what the country', and irrespective of the number of available hospital beds. This contradicted Milton Roemer's law that 'a built bed made is a filled bed'.

[38] B. Abel-Smith and A. Maynard (1979) *The organisation, financing and cost of health care in the European Community*, Social Policy Series No 36, Brussels: Commission of the European Communities. See Chapter 14 for a discussion of this publication.

[39] B. Abel-Smith (1963) *Paying for Health Services: A Study of the Costs and Sources of Finance in Six Countries*, Geneva: WHO; B. Abel-Smith (1967) *An International Study of Health Expenditure*, Public Health Papers No 32, Geneva: WHO.

[40] BA-SP 1/72, J.-P. Poullier to BA-S, 4 November 1982.

[41] BA-SP 1/107, BA-S to E. Mach, 28 October 1981.

[42] BA-SP 1/107, BA-S to E. Mach, 21 April 1982.

[43] B. Abel-Smith and E. Mach (1984) *Planning the Finances of the Health Sector*, Geneva: WHO.

[44] D.A.T. Griffiths and M.H. Mills (1982) *Money for Health. A manual for surveys in developing countries*, Third World Series No 3, Geneva: Sandoz Institute for Health and Socio-Economic Studies and the Republic of Botswana.

[45] *World Health Statistics Quarterly* (1984), vol 37, p 4.

[46] B. Abel-Smith (1983) 'Economic Efficiency in Health Care Delivery', *International Social Security Review*, 2/83, Geneva: ISSA.

[47] Author correspondence with Julio Frenk, 4 March 2013.

[48] BA-SP 1/108, BA-S to M. Sathianathan, 26 October 1984.

[49] B. Abel-Smith (1985) 'Global perspectives on Health Service Financing', *Social Science & Medicine*, vol 21, no 9, pp 957-63.

[50] B. Abel-Smith (1984) 'An overview of health care and financing studies', *Financial Planning for HFA2000*, SEARO Technical Publication No 5, New Delhi: WHO, pp 9-23.

[51] B. Abel-Smith (1987) 'Health Economics and the World Health Organisation', in G. Teeling-Smith (ed) *Health Economics: Prospects for the Future*, London: Croom Helm, p 94.

[52] BA-SP 1/107, H. Hellberg to BA-S, 19 September 1984.

[53] The three-week course at LSE/LSHTM was actually established and run by Anne Mills. Brian had encouraged her to apply for support from WHO Geneva, which she successfully obtained to cover annual courses from 1986 to 1989. Brian delivered several lectures on the course. Author correspondence with Anne Mills, 31 May 2013.

[54] BA-SP 1/107, B. Abel-Smith (1985) *Assignment on Economic Strategy in Support of HFA 2000 1 Jan–31 March 1985*, 21 March.

[55] Abel-Smith (1987) 'Health Economics and the World Health Organisation', p 92.

[56] Abel-Smith (1987) 'Health Economics and the World Health Organisation', p 99.

[57] N. Milio (1981) *Promoting Health through Public Policy*, Philadelphia: F.A. Davis; T. Hancock (1982) 'Beyond Health Care', *The Futurist*, August; T. Hancock (1985) 'Beyond Health Care: from Public Health Policy to Healthy Public Policy', *Canadian Journal of Public Health*, vol 76, supplement 1.

[58] See also Chapter 11 for a discussion of Brian's involvement with the Black Report.

[59] BA-SP 11/6, J. Turner (1984) 'Preparing a path to the year 2000', *Primary Health Care*, February, p 12.

[60] BA-SP 11/7, N. Lee to BA-S, 5 July 1985.

[61] H. Mahler (1982) *Countdown for Health for All, address by Dr H. Mahler in presenting his report for 1980 and 1981 to the Thirty-fifth World Health Assembly*, WHA39/DIV/4, Geneva: WHO.

[62] H. Mahler (1986) *Springboard for action for Health for All, address by Dr H. Mahler in presenting his report for 1984 and 1985 to the Thirty-sixth World Health Assembly*, WHA39/DIV/4, Geneva: WHO.

[63] BA-SP 13/16, B. Abel-Smith (1986) 'Economic Implications of Health Manpower Imbalances', Paper presented at the 20th CIOMS conference, Acapulco, Mexico, 7–12 September. Later published as B. Abel-Smith (1986) 'The World Economic Crisis; Health Manpower out of Balance', *Health Policy and Planning*, vol 1, no 4, pp 309-16.

[64] Ajay Dua was an Indian civil servant who had been a research fellow with Brian at the LSE in 1986. A version of their paper was later published as B. Abel-Smith and A. Dua (1988) 'Community Financing in Developing Countries: the Potential for the Health Sector', *Health Policy and Planning*, vol 3, no 2, pp 95-108.

[65] J.P. Ruger (2005) 'Changing Role of the World Bank in Global Health in Historical Perspective', *American Journal of Public Health*, vol 95, January, pp 60-70; B. de Vries (1996) 'The World Bank as an International Player n Economic Analysis', *History of Political Economy*, vol 28, pp 225-44.

[66] The World Bank (1980) *World Development Report 1980*, Washington, DC: The World Bank.

67 F. Godlee (1994) 'WHO in Retreat; Is it Losing its Influence?', *British Medical Journal*, vol 309, p 1493.

68 K. Newell (1988) 'Selective Primary Health Care: The Counter Revolution', *Social Science & Medicine*, vol 26, p 906. See also M. Cueto (2004) 'The origins of primary health care and selective primary health care', *American Journal of Public Health*, vol 94, no 11, pp 1864-74.

69 P. Lewis (1988) 'Divided World Health Organisation Braces for Leadership Change', *New York Times*, 1 May, p 1.

70 T.M. Brown, M. Cueto and E. Fee (2006) 'The World Health Organisation and the Transition from "International" to "Global" Health', in A. Bashford (ed) *Medicine at the Border*, Basingstoke: Palgrave Macmillan, pp 76-94.

71 G. Walt (1993) 'WHO Under Stress; Implications for Health Policy', *Health Policy*, vol 24, pp 125-44; F. Godlee (1994) 'WHO in Crisis', *British Medical Journal*, vol 309, pp 1424-8.

72 Brown, Cueto and Fee (2006), p 87.

73 J.S. Akin, N. Birdsall and D. de Ferranti (1987) *Financing Health Services in Developing Countries: An Agenda for Reform*, Washington, DC: The World Bank.

74 J.M. Malloy (1989) 'Policy Analysts, Public Policy and Regime Structure in Latin America', *Governance*, vol 2, pp 315-38.

75 D. de Ferranti (1985) *Paying for Health Services in Developing Countries: an Overview*, World Bank Staff Working Papers No 721, Washington, DC: The World Bank.

76 Author conversation with David de Ferranti, 1 August 2013.

77 B. McPake, K. Hanson and A. Mills (1993) 'Community financing of health care in Africa: An evaluation of the Bamako Initiative', *Social Science & Medicine*, vol 36, no 11, pp 1383-95.

78 L. Gilson and D. McIntyre (2005) 'Removing user fees for primary care in Africa: The need for careful action', *British Medical Journal*, vol 331, pp 762-65.

79 P. Gertler and J. van der Gaag (1990) *The Willingness to Pay for Medical Care: Evidence from Two Developing Countries*, Baltimore, MD: Johns Hopkins University Press for The World Bank.

80 P.G.K. Palmer, D.H. Mueller, A. Mills and A. Haines (2004) 'Health financing to promote access in low income settings – How much do we know?', *The Lancet*, vol 364, pp 1365-70.

81 Save the Children (2005) *An Unnecessary Evil? User Fees for Healthcare in Low-Income Countries*, London: Save the Children; C.D. James, K. Hanson, B. McPake, D. Balabanova, D. Gwatkin, L. Hopwood et al (2006) 'To retain or remove user fees? Reflections on the current debate in low-and middle-income countries', *Applied Health Economics and Health Policy*, vol 5, no 3, pp 137-53.

82 R. Knippenberg, F. Traore Nufo, R. Osseni, Y. Boye Camara, A. El Abassi and A. Soucat (2003) *Increasing clients' power to scale up health services for the poor. Background Paper to the World Development Report. The Bamako Initiative in West Africa*, Washington, DC: The World Bank.

83 M. Phillips (1988) 'Health economics research – report of a meeting', *Health Policy and Planning*, vol 3, no 4, pp 316-19.

84 B. Abel-Smith (1989) 'Health Economics in Developing Countries', *Journal of Tropical Medicine and Hygiene*, vol 92, pp 229-41.

85   BA-SP 13/19, B. Abel-Smith (c 1988) 'Priorities for Health Research in the 1990s', Unpublished paper for the Commission on Health Research for Development.

86   E.P. Mach and B. Abel-Smith (1983) *Planning the Finances of the Health Sector*, Geneva: WHO Geneva.

87   Abel-Smith (c 1988).

88   Abel-Smith (c 1988).

89   Akin, Birdsall and de Ferranti (1987).

90   He is referring to R.M. Titmuss, B. Abel-Smith and G. McDonald (1964) *The Health Services of Tanganyika*, London: Pitman.

91   B. Abel-Smith (c 1988).

92   B. Abel-Smith (c 1988).

93   B. Abel-Smith (1985) 'Who is the Odd Man Out? The Experience of Western Europe in Containing the Costs of Health Care', *Milbank Quarterly*, vol 63, no 1, pp 1-17.

94   B. Abel-Smith (1988) 'The Rise and Decline of the Early HMOs: Some International Experiences', *Milbank Quarterly*, vol 66, no 4, pp 694-719.

95   B. Abel-Smith (1991) 'Financing Health for All', *World Health Forum*, vol 12, no 2, pp 191-200.

96   The World Bank (1988) *Kenya: Review of Expenditure Issues and Options in Health Financing*, 8 June, 6963-KE, prepared by Population and Human Resources operations Division, Eastern Africa Department.

97   BA-SP 10/34, A. Bruzelius to BA-S, 29 July 1988.

98   B. Abel-Smith (1989) 'Issues and options in health financing', Discussion paper, Nairobi, January.

99   BA-SP 10/34, BA-S report to SIDA.

100 G. Dahlgren (1994) 'The Political Economy of Health Financing Strategies in Kenya', in L. Chen, A. Kleineman and N. Ware (eds) *Health and Social Change in International Perspective*, Boston, MA: Harvard University Press, p 459.

101 BA-SP 10/34, G. Dahlgren to BA-S, 29 May 1989.

102 *The Nation* (1990), 12 January, quoted in Dahlgren (1994), p 465.

103 G. Dahlgren (1990) 'Strategies for Health Financing in Kenya – the difficult birth of a new policy', *Scandinavian Journal of Medicine*, vol 46, pp 67-81.

104 BA-SP 10/34, E.V.K. Jaycox to G. Dahlgren, 11 June 1990.

105 BA-SP 10/34, G. Dahlgren to E.V.K. Jaycox, 20 June 1990.

106 Dahlgren (1994), p 469.

107 BA-SP 10/34, G. Dahlgren to BA-S, 29 May 1989.

108 BA-SP 13/11, S. Fegan-Wyles to A. Mills, 7 July 1989.

109 Author conversation with David de Ferranti, 1 August 2013.

Chapter 14

1   G. Orwell (1941) *The Lion and the Unicorn: Socialism and the English Genius*, London: Secker & Warburg, pp 11-12.

2   Interview with Robert Stevens, 8 May 2007.

[3] B. Abel-Smith (1980) 'The Welfare State: Breaking the Post-War Consensus', *Political Quarterly*, vol 51, no 1, pp 17-23.

[4] The 'gang of four' were Roy Jenkins, David Owen, Bill Rodgers and Shirley Williams.

[5] Interview with Tony Benn, 24 April 2007.

[6] TBP, unedited diary entry for 17 March 1981.

[7] Interview with Dianne Hayter, 15 September 2008.

[8] Interview with David Lipsey, 13 May 2008.

[9] B. Abel-Smith (1984) 'Social Welfare', in B. Pimlott (ed) *Fabian Essays in Socialist Thought*, London: Heinemann, pp 169-84.

[10] BA-SP 1/73, BA-S to B. Pimlott, 29 September 1983.

[11] (1979) *Royal Commission on the National Health Service. Chairman Sir Alec Merrison, Report*, Cmnd 7615, London: HMSO.

[12] C. Webster (1996) *The Health Services since the War. Vol II*, London: HMSO, p 719.

[13] Webster (1996), p 725.

[14] B. Abel-Smith (1979) 'Merrison's Medicine for the NHS', *New Society*, 26 July, pp 191-2.

[15] B. Abel-Smith (1979) 'Who Should Watch over the NHS?', *New Society*, 16 August, pp 348-9.

[16] BA-SP 1/59, BA-S to J. Pitkin, 14 July 1982.

[17] Other members of Meacher's group were Jean Robinson, Kingsley Williams, Nigel Webb, Chris Ham, Peter Draper, Maurice Dutton, Malcolm Prowle, Sheila Adam, Chris Birt and Barbara Shepherd.

[18] B. Abel-Smith and A. Maynard (1979) *The organisation, financing and cost of health care in the European Community*, Social Policy Series No 36, Brussels: Commission of the European Communities.

[19] Author conversation with Alan Maynard, 7 November 2012.

[20] Abel-Smith and A. Maynard (1979), p 158.

[21] NHS Unlimited (1983) *The Conservatives, the National Health Service and Private Medicine*, Memorandum No 6, April.

[22] Brian also intervened in 1981 on behalf of the unit, following what was judged as an 'unfair' review visit by Chief Scientist Arthur Buller's team, which did not appear to value its training and education role. Brian wrote to the Chief Medical Officer, Sir Henry Yellowlees, to put its case, and a new contract for the unit, with Brian re-appointed as Chair, was signed with the DHSS in 1982.

[23] London Health Planning Consortium (1981) *Primary health care in inner London. Report of a study group* (Chair Donald Acheson), London: DHSS.

[24] BA-SP 8/34, St Thomas' Hospital Medical School, Comments on the report from the London Health Planning Consortium, 'Towards a Balance'.

[25] (1980) *London Medical Education. A New Framework: Report of a working party on medical and dental teaching resources* (Chair Lord Flowers), London: University of London.

[26] London Advisory Group (1981) *Acute Hospital Services in London* (Chair: Sir John Habakkuk), London: DHSS.

[27] BA-SP 1/53, R. Maxwell to BA-S, 1 May 1981.

28 BA-SP 1/52, BA-S to R. Maxwell, 5 October 1983.

29 BA-SP 1/53, BA-S to G. Parston, 17 April 1984.

30 Interview with Howard and Ann Glennerster, 13 March 2007.

31 Interview with Jenny Roberts, 9 December 2008.

32 Interview with Geoffrey and Elspeth Howe, 20 February 2007.

33 In 1992 the title was expanded to 'Health policy, planning and financing', when Lucy Gilson replaced Anne Mills as Course Director.

34 Interview with Anne Mills, 10 December 2008.

35 Interview with Sally Sainsbury, 20 February 2007.

36 Interview with Howard and Ann Glennerster, 13 March 2007.

Chapter 15

1 J. Markoff and V. Montecinos (1993) 'The Ubiquitous Rise of Economists', *Journal of Public Policy*, vol 13, no 1, p 37.

2 B. Abel-Smith (1953) *The Reform of Social Security*, London: Fabian Society Pamphlet; B. Abel-Smith (1992) 'Reform of the National Health Service', *Quality Assurance in Health Care*, vol 4, no 4, pp 263-72.

3 BA-SP 13/6, B. Abel-Smith, *Report on Problems of Health Financing in Asian Countries and their Implications for Donor Agencies*, Overseas Development Administration assignment.

4 BA-SP 13/6, B. Abel-Smith, *Report on Problems of Health Financing in Asian Countries and their Implications for Donor Agencies*, Overseas Development Administration assignment.

5 BA-SP 13/6, B. Abel-Smith, *Report on Problems of Health Financing in Asian Countries and their Implications for Donor Agencies*, Overseas Development Administration assignment.

6 JSP. The party was held on 23 September 1991.

7 Interview with Howard and Ann Glennerster, 13 March 2007. After Brian died, Howard Glennerster had the unpleasant task of telling some of the registered PhD students that their work would never be of sufficient academic quality to achieve the degree.

8 Author correspondence with Alex Preker, 3 May 2013.

9 BA-SP 13/22, B. Abel-Smith (1992) 'The Cost of Health Services', Lecture at the Royal College of Physicians, London, 26 November.

10 European Currency Unit – replaced by the Euro in 1999.

11 B. Abel-Smith (1992) *Cost Containment and New Priorities in Health Care: A Study of the European Community*, Aldershot: Avebury Ashgate Publishing Ltd.

12 B. Abel-Smith (1984) *Cost Containment in Health Care*, Occasional Papers in Social Administration No 73, London: Bedford Square Press.

13 Abel-Smith (1992) *Cost Containment and New Priorities in Health Care*, p viii.

14 Abel-Smith (1992) *Cost Containment and New Priorities in Health Care*, p 112.

15 Abel-Smith (1992) *Cost Containment and New Priorities in Health Care*, p 127.

16 R. M. Titmuss, B. Abel-Smith, G. Macdonald, A. W. Williams and C. H. Wood (1964) *The Health Services of Tanganyika*, London: Pitman.

[17]   BA-SP 10/69, BA-S to C. Griffin, 4 February 1993.

[18]   BA-SP 10/69, Confidential Annex for ODA, National Health Insurance Development: Tanzania 26 January–17 February 1993.

[19]   B. Abel-Smith and P. Rawal (1992) 'Can the poor afford "free" health services? A case study of Tanzania', *Health Policy and Planning*, vol 7, no 4, pp 329-41; B. Abel-Smith and P. Rawal (1994) 'Employer's willingness to pay: the case for compulsory health insurance in Tanzania', *Health Policy and Planning*, vol 9, no 4, pp 409-18.

[20]   B. Abel-Smith (1992) 'Health Insurance in Developing Countries: lessons from experience', *Health Policy and Planning*, vol 7, no 3, pp 215-26.

[21]   Author correspondence with Julian Tudor Hart, 23 May 2008.

[22]   Author correspondence with Julian Tudor Hart, 23 May 2008.

[23]   Author conversation with Jane Falkingham, 26 October 2012.

[24]   B. Abel-Smith (1996) 'Poverty in Context – New Thoughts on Old Themes', in H. Sasson and D. Diamond (eds) *LSE on Social Science: A centenary anthology*, London: LSE Books, pp 121-33.

[25]   D. Donnison (2000) 'The Academic Contribution to Social Reform', *Social Policy & Administration*, vol 34, no 1, p 42.

[26]   B. Abel-Smith (1994) *The Reform of Health Systems: a Review of Seventeen OECD Countries*, Health Policy Studies No 5, Paris: OECD.

[27]   B. Abel-Smith and E. Mossialos (1994) *Cost Containment and Health Care Reform*, London: LSE European Institute.

[28]   LSE Health (1995) *Health Care in Three Southern Member States (Spain, Greece, Italy). A Report Prepared for the European Parliament*, London: LSE Health.

[29]   BA-SP 13/22, B. Abel-Smith (1995) 'The Crisis in Social Policy and the Role of Public Health', Lecture to the School of Public Health, Athens, 1 March.

[30]   See M. Bulmer (1991) 'National contexts for the development of social policy research: British and American research on poverty and social welfare compared', in P. Wagner (ed) *Social Sciences and the Modern State*, Cambridge: Cambridge University Press, pp 148-67.

[31]   Interview with Elias Mossialos, 22 March 2010.

[32]   BA-SP 11/11, Interregional Consultation on Health Insurance Reform, Seoul, Republic of Korea, 3–7 April 1995.

[33]   What is now called the 'Quality Movement' and 'Quality Science' had emerged in the US in the early 1980s, and is associated with the work of William Edwards Deming (1900–93). In the UK assessments of quality in healthcare were studied by Archie Cochrane and his researchers.

[34]   BA-SP 11/11, Interregional Consultation on Health Insurance Reform, Seoul, Republic of Korea, 3–7 April 1995.

[35]   Author conversation with Catriona Waddington, 26 September 2012.

[36]   Cost benefit analysis is a systematic process for comparing the benefits and costs (in monetary terms) of a project or policy. Cost-effectiveness analysis compares the relative costs and outcomes (effects) of two or more possible courses of action, and is often expressed in terms of a ratio where the denominator is a gain in health from a measure (years of life, premature births averted) and the numerator

is the cost associated with the health gain. The most commonly used outcome measure is quality-adjusted life years (QALY).

37   The World Bank (1993) *World Development Report 1993: Investing in Health*, Washington, DC: The World Bank.

38   A.-E. Birn, Y. Pillay and T.H. Holtz (eds) (2009) *Textbook of International Health: Global Health in a Dynamic World* (3rd edn), New York: Oxford University Press, p 559.

39   Global Health Watch (2005) *Global Health Watch 2005–2006: An Alternative World Health Report*, London: Zed Books; A. Costello and D. Woodward (1993) 'The World Bank's World Development Report', *The Lancet*, vol 342, pp 440-1.

40   B. Abel-Smith (1994) *An Introduction to Health: Policy, Planning and Financing*, Harlow: Longman.

41   B. Abel-Smith and H. Glennerster (1993) 'Labour and the Tory Health Reforms', *Fabian Review*, vol 107, no 3, June, pp 1-4.

42   H. Stoate (1995) 'Abel-Smith, Glennerster and the health reforms: a riposte', *Fabian Review*, vol 107, no 4, August, pp 1-4. Stoate had unsuccessfully stood as a Labour candidate in the general elections of 1987 and 1992.

43   BA-SP 8/35, D. Piachaud to 'Brian, Howard and Julian', 8 August 1995.

44   Interview with Elias Mossialos, 22 March 2010.

45   Along with John Sarbutt, the main beneficiaries of Brian's will were CPAG, the Dartmouth Street Trust (Fabian Society) and LSE Health. He left money to friends in Thailand and Zimbabwe, as discussed in this chapter, and Abel-Smith family portraits and silverware to his cousins. His brother Lionel was to be one of the trustees of the fund, and to receive the semainier that had previously belonged to their mother and the circular marble table that had belonged to great uncle Philip. The Smith's Bank partner's table was to be offered to the National Westminster Bank (which had taken over Smith's Bank) with the suggestion that if they wished to acknowledge the gift that a donation be made to CPAG. He appointed the convenor of the LSE Department of Social Policy as his literary executor, with the hope that his books and papers would be taken into the LSE library.

Epilogue

1   BA-SP 1/96, BA-S to P. Townsend, 27 September 1976.

2   T. Fuller (1662) *The worthies of England* (edited and with an introduction by J. Freeman), London: Allen & Unwin, 1952.

3   B. Bainbridge (2004) 'Waiting for the biographer', in M. Bostridge (ed) *Lives for Sale*, London: Continuum.

4   A.J. Culyer (1981) 'Economics, Social Policy and Social Administration: the Interplay between Topics and Disciplines', *Journal of Social Policy*, vol 10, no 3, pp 311-29.

5   B. Abel-Smith (1976) *Value for Money in Health Services*, London: Heinemann Educational Books.

6   D. McCloskey (1986) *The Rhetoric of Economics*, Brighton: Wheatsheaf.

7   See U. Hannerz (1990) 'Cosmopolitans and locals in World Culture', in M. Featherstone (ed) *Global Culture: Nationalism, Globalization and Modernity*, London: Sage Publications.

8   *Hansard* (1991) House of Commons Debates, 16 May, col 413.

9   M. Evans et al (1994) *Designed for the Poor – Poorer by Design*, WSP/105, London: LSE STICERD.

10 R. Cohen and M. Tarpey (1988) *Single Payments: the Disappearing Safety Net*, London: CPAG; M. Evans (1994) *Not Granted? An Assessment of the Change from Single Payments to the Social Fund*, WSP/101, London: LSE STICERD.

11 B. Abel-Smith (1995) 'Poverty in Context – New Thoughts on Old Themes', in H. Sasson and D. Diamond (eds) *LSE on Social Science: a centenary anthology*, London: LSE Books.

Index

Abel-Smith, Brian:

LIFE: family background 2-3, 11-15; birth 11; childhood 16; education 16-24; service at Stepney Boys club 26-8; National Service training 24, 29-38; undergraduate studies at University of Cambridge 38-48; postgraduate studies at University of Cambridge 47-51, 55-57, 86-7; employment at NIESR 84; lectureship at LSE 90; readership at LSE 157; professorship at LSE 201; rejection of peerage 253, 541n; appointments as special adviser to British government ministers 222, 223, 290, 324, 350; appointments as special adviser to EEC 371, 377, 401, appointment as special adviser to Halfdan Mahler 407; directorship of Just Men business 214-6, 224, 262, 287, 432-3, 489, 536n; property speculation 469, 489; retirement from LSE 455-8; death 479-81; memorial service 481; obituaries 485

CHARACTER: 1, 7, 17, 21, 23, 31, 38, 43, 50-1, 54, 80, 92-3, 102-3, 104, 136, 137, 142, 181, 274-5, 292, 449, 454, 486, 480, 485, 486, 491-2; debating skills 22, 41-2, 44, 53-4, 112, 144; lecturing style 195, 446

RELATIONSHIPS: with John Sarbutt x, 3, 119, 134-5, 215, 262, 287-8, 349, 358, 456, 464-5, 469, 470, 478, 479, 480, 481, 484, 485, 488, 565n; with mother 24, 31, 33, 36-7, 56, 135, 136-7, 432, 488; with father 24; death of his father 31; with brother Lionel 17, 24, 32, 36, 42, 137, 432, 479-80, 489; with Susan Hamilton 17, 30, 42; with John Vaizey 70-2, 106; relationship with Hugh Dalton 46-8, 83-4, 102-04; with Richard Titmuss 71-3, 93, 280, 486-7; with Peter Townsend 72-3, 252-3, 257; with Sue Holman 92; with Weston family 104, 136; with Charles Schuller 106, 215, 262, 469, 480; with Laci Tomazi 106, 135; with Richard Crossman 99, 104, 106, 111, 192, 220-1, 224-6, 257-8, 260, 284, 348; with Peter Shore 142, 195, 280, 324-5, 348-54, 433, 481, 488; with Barbara Castle 290-3, 309, 324, 348, 456, 481; with David Ennals 324-5, 328, 331-3, 335, 341, 346, 348; with Djafar Tahar 464; with Sahib Fazilamed 464, 465; with Anusora Ounneharerk 465; with Cheep and Witchian Khemsuk 465; with tenants 136, 287; death of his mother 432; private life 286, 287, 455-6, 469; evidence of personal relationships 465, 484; sexuality 45, 103-6, 136, 488-9

HEALTH: childhood 16; exhaustion, 131; gallstones 136; jaundice 186; bad back 195; illness in India 405; smoking 127, 318, 439; drinking 478; lifestyle 478-9; diagnosis with pancreatic cancer 479; use of private medical insurance 479

HOMES: childhood in Kensington 16-17, 20, 22-4; flat at Vincent Square Mansions 92-3; Elizabeth Street 135-6; Tanglewood (Westwell, Kent) 216-17, 262, 288, 432, 456, 470, 479-80, 481; Westmoreland Place, Lupus Street 288, 349; Bloomfield Terrace 349, 432; Denbigh Street 432, 456, 469; in Thailand 465

POLITICS: socialism 24, 32, 34, 117, 131, 456, 480, 486, 489; Labour
Party 486; roles in the Fabian Society 76, 103, 224, 434; membership
of Cambridge University Labour Club 41-2, 45-6, 47; Clarion Group
campaigning in Spelthorne 44, 50; offer of Harwich Labour nomination
57; participation in 'The Group' 79-80; rejection of safe parliamentary seat
102-04; comments on Barbara Castle's diary publication, 329-31; views
on Richard Crossman's diary publication 286; involvement with Labour's
1979 general election strategy 353-5; views on 1979 election result 433;
participation in Labour Party Social Policy sub-committees and working
parties 96-9, 110-12, 115-16, 191-2, 194-5, 271-2, 293-303, 334-7, 437-9

VIEWS: on population control and development policies 175-6, 278-9,
416-7, 420-3, 453-5, 473, 474, 492-3; on pharmaceutical industry 232-3,
300-02, 383; on the NHS 123, 131-3, 140-1, 244-5, 263, 336-40, 436-7,
460, 477-8; on welfare states and social insurance 143, 453-5, 473-4, 492;
on working with government ministers 348-9; on EEC social policy 380;
on competition and user fees in health services 417, 466-6, 477-8; on
economists and expert advisers 411, 420-1, 455, 492-3; on Citizens Advice
Bureaux 437-8; on 1979 general election 433; on HFA2000 409-10, 413-
14; on World Bank policies 420-3, 426-7, 462-3

WRITINGS: at Haileybury 21, 23; to family 26-7, 31, 33, 35, 36; in the army
31; at Cambridge 50-51; *The Reform of Social Security* 55, 80-3; *The Cost of
the NHS* 86-8; *New Pensions for the Old* 93-4, 95-6; *Whose Welfare State?* 107-
10; 'The Dilemma of the Doctors' 123; *A History of the Nursing Profession*
126-7; *The Hospitals 1800–1948: A Study in Social Administration in England
and Wales* 138-40; *Paying for Health Services: A Study of the Costs and Sources
of Finance in Six Countries* 150-3, 182-4; *Social Policy and Population Growth
in Mauritius* 168-73; *An International Study of Health Expenditure* 184-6; *The
Poor and the Poorest* 201-2; *Lawyers and the Courts* 211-13; *In Search of Justice*
213-14; *Legal Problems and the Citizen* 269-70; relationship with Heinemann
publishers 361-2; *Value for Money in Health Services* 358-65; *Planning the
Finances of the Health Sector* 402-3; *The organisation, financing and cost of health
care in the European Community* 439-40; *Cost Containment and New Priorities
in Health Care* 459-60; *An Introduction to Health: Policy, Planning and Financing*
476; 'Labour and the Tory Health Reforms' 477-8

A

Abel-Smith, Harold 17, 21, 31-2, 37, 39, 45, 48, 215
Abel-Smith, Lionel (brother 1924–2010) x, 16, 17, 22, 24, 30, 31, 32, 35, 36, 38, 42, 43, 45, 51, 56, 93, 106, 108, 134, 135, 136-7, 213, 214-5, 432, 464, 465, 479-80, 481, 484, 488, 489, 508n, 529n, 565n,
Abel-Smith, Lionel (father 1870–1946) 11, 12, 14, 15-16, 22, 24, 31
Abel-Smith, Maud 15, 16, 21, 37, 52, 54, 56
Abel-Smith, Vivée (Genevieve, mother 1898–1988) 11, 15-17, 22, 24, 31-4, 36-7, 42, 52, 56, 94, 135-7, 378, 432, 479, 488, 509n
Acheson, Donald 437, 442, 444
Acton Society Trust 88, 116, 239, 311, 521n
Adams, Edith 166
Adams, Walter 223, 248-51
AEGIS (Aid to the Elderly in Government Institutions) 233-6
Allende, Salvador 274
Alltimes, Geoff 291, 328, 547n
Alma Ata, WHO conference and declaration 390, 392-4, 412, 415, 422
Anderson, Odin 125-6, 522n
Andreano, Ralph 399, 404
Arnott, Elizabeth 298, 355
Ashley, Jack 3, 40, 41, 45, 47, 99, 269, 290, 294, 302
Asvall, Jo 395
Atkinson, Alec 374-5
Atkinson, Tony 294, 295, 296
Attlee, Clement 19, 20, 27, 34, 41, 64, 65, 77, 84
Aves, Geraldine 93, 516n
Azikiwe, Nnamdi 79

B

Bainbridge, Beryl 483
Baker, Richard 34, 39
Ball, Robert (Bob) 99, 359, 363
Balogh, Thomas 177, 220, 536n
Bamako initiative 419
Bambridge, Tony 42, 105
Banda, Hastings 79
Banting, Keith 69, 83, 187

barefoot doctors 274, 390
Barnett, Corelli 63
Beaverbrook, Lord (Max Aitken) 104
Belgravia Leaseholders Association 352
Benedict, Burton 166, 177
Benn, Tony 79, 107, 131, 142, 195, 289, 321, 326, 330, 433, 434
Benson, Sheila 110, 126, 209
Berrill, Kenneth 40
Bevan, Aneurin 85, 95, 120, 138, 240, 305, 337, 521n
Beveridge Report (*Social Insurance and Allied Services*, 1942) 63, 64, 79, 82, 85, 96, 114, 117, 172, 193
Beveridge, William 7, 29, 62, 65, 75, 93-4, 97, 114, 138, 196, 226, 240, 492, 512n
biography 483-4
Bindman, Geoffrey 547n
Birdsall, Nancy 418
birth control (population control, family planning) 145, 162, 169-75, 176, 177, 178-9, 203, 275-9, 439, 476, 528-9n
Black Report on Inequalities in Health 344-8
Black, Douglas 305, 346, 348, 440
Blanpain, Jan 400
Blewett, David 137, 225, 228, 287, 288, 469
British Medical Association (BMA) 303, 436
Bonar Law Trust 33
Bonhote, E.F. 19, 23, 27, 39
Bosanquet, Nicholas 264, 295, 297, 300-01, 312, 314, 333, 522n
Boston University School of Public Health 468
Boyd Carpenter, John 101, 111, 320
Braddock, Bessie 41, 95
Bravo, Leonardo 186
Brenner, Harvey 399
Bridgman, R.F. 184
British Council 51-55, 56, 511n
Brooke, Rosalind 212, 269
Bryant, John 391
Bulmer, Martin 67

C

Cabinet Papers – confidentiality 224, 226, 537n; leak 325-8

Cadbury, Caroline 197
Caine, Sydney 157, 161, 177, 248, 249
Califano, Joseph 332
Callaghan, James 193, 201, 256, 321, 324, 326, 328, 330, 347, 349, 352, 353, 354, 433
Cambridge Union 41, 44, 47-8
Cambridge, University of – Labour Club 45-7, 83; post-war student life 38-43; Economics tutors 40-1; gay networks at 105-6
Candau, Marcolino 149
Cardew, Bruce 121, 131
Carrier, John 447, 456, 481
Carrington, Peter 13
Castle, Barbara: political career 289-90, 321; appointment as Secretary of State for Social Services 284; and her special advisers 284, 290-91, 303, 355, 366-7, 372, 547n; as chair of Labour Party Social Policy Sub-Committee 294-5, 333; policy on private medicine in NHS hospitals 292, 305-08; on NHS reorganisation, budgets and disputes 303-05, 309-10, 552n; pay, pensions and tax policies 247, 271-2, 297-8, 319-21; mental health and disability policies 315, 317-8; dismissal by Jim Callaghan 321, 324-5; relationship with BA-S 292-3, 309, 324, 348, 456, 481; on child benefit 325-8; publication of her diaries 329-31; use of private medicine 547n
Ceylon – see Sri Lanka
Chapman, Donald 47, 55, 79, 80
Chapman, Paul 290-1, 376, 546n
Chapman, Leslie 353
Charge of the Light Brigade 216
Charing Cross Hospital 307
Charity Organisation Society 66
Chester, D.N. 55, 80
Chester, T.E. 88, 380
Child Benefit (see also family allowances) 296-7, 299, 325-8, 354, 381, 384, 492
Child Poverty Action Group (CPAG) 1, 200-204, 207, 210, 224, 226, 252, 255-8, 263-4, 294, 325-7, 534n, 547n, 565n

Chile 150, 152, 182, 274, 277, 332, 471, 544n
Chisholm, Brock 149
cholera 275, 468
Churchill, Winston 24-5, 27, 63, 77
Citizens' Advice Bureaux 5, 235, 302, 437-8
Clare College, Cambridge 19, 24, 39, 51
Cochrane, Archie 134, 162, 177, 210, 288, 358-9, 360, 361, 362, 401, 466, 523n, 564n
Cockburn, Christine 69, 192
Cohen, Henry 231, 538n
Cohen, Wilbur 151, 157, 226, 280, 364
Cole, Dorothy 189, 192
Cole, G.D.H. 64, 226
Cole, Margaret 109
Collins, John T.C. 22, 24, 39
Colombia 331, 403, 408, 409, 471
Colonial Office 6, 159, 160, 161, 162-3, 168, 178, 367
Commission on Health Research for Development 419-23
community financing of health services 417, 474
comparative analysis 6, 86, 89, 153, 179, 181-6, 361, 375, 400, 401-02, 424, 439, 458, 459, 461, 471, 472
Conservative government 189, 264, 413-4, 436, 440, 492-3
Conviction 107-9, 519n
Coopers & Lybrand 475
Cornford, James 354
cost benefit analysis 273, 411, 564n
cost containment 6, 403, 404, 409, 452, 459-60, 466, 471
Costa Rica 152, 408, 409, 423, 473
Council for International Organisations of the Medical Sciences (CIOMS) 401, 416
Cowling, David 350, 351, 353
Cox, Nigel 469, 479-80
Cradock, Percy 48, 105
Crosland, Tony (Anthony) 51, 77-79, 103, 104, 107, 109, 111-12, 188, 191, 240-41, 514n, 532n

Crossman, Richard (Dick): political
career 79, 95-6, 112-3, 193, 236,
258, 259-60; role in pensions
policy development 95-6, 97,
98-102, 112, 220-1, 226, 228-9,
517n, 530-1n; on social insurance
policies 111-12, 113, 191, 206,
255; appointment as Secretary
of State for Social Services 220;
reform of the NHS 239-46, 267-8,
327; allocation of NHS resources
(the Crossman Formula) 311-12;
creation of the Hospital Advisory
Service 315-6; relationship with
the medical profession 246-7;
the Ely Hospital scandal 236-8;
relationship with BA-S 5, 99,
104, 106, 111, 192, 220-1, 224-6,
257-8, 260, 284, 348; views on
the Civil Service 220, 223; on
leaking documents 227; setting
up Royal Commission on Local
Government 540n; personal life
236; post-government activities
259-60; diaries 191, 286-7, 329,
330; death 286
Culyer, Tony (Anthony) 312, 399,
453, 490, 491
cycle of deprivation 262, 399
Czechoslovakia 152-3, 182

D

Dahlgren, Göran 397, 425, 427-9
Dahrendorf, Ralph 66, 248, 251, 372,
377, 407, 469, 541n
Dalton, Hugh 34, 46-9, 51, 65, 70,
83-4, 102-4, 486, 518n
Dalyell, Tam 112
Dartmouth Street Trust – see Fabian
Society
David, Alvin 99
Davies, Gavyn 356
Davis, Jimmy 43
de Ferranti, David 403, 408, 418, 429
Democracy in the NHS 303
Dennison, Stanley 40

Department of Health and Social
Security (DHSS) 17, 134, 188,
223, 225-6, 232, 237, 238, 240,
242, 244-7, 254, 263, 265, 268,
284, 291-2, 295-6, 297, 298-300,
304-5, 307-8, 313-5, 317, 321,
324-5, 327, 328-9, 332, 333, 334,
337, 339, 340, 342, 343, 344, 345,
347, 348-9, 354, 369, 372-4, 375-
6, 377, 378, 379, 381, 442, 444,
446, 456
Department of the Environment 324,
348-53, 444
devaluation 230, 256, 407
development economics 156, 160-1,
175-6, 184-5, 275-6, 365-7, 391-5,
398-401, 418-23, 428-9, 464, 510n
development theories 275-6
Deverell, Colville 276
Diagnosis-Related Group
methodology (DRG) 364, 476,
554n
disabilities, car policy 318
Disablement Income Group 441
Dobb, Maurice 40, 87
Dobson, Frank 438-9, 440
Donabedian, Avedis 364
Donnison, David 4, 73, 79, 104, 195,
207, 208, 253, 281, 298, 345, 468,
469, 491, 492, 512n
DRG – see Diagnosis-Related Group
methodology
Driberg, Tom 20, 104, 105, 145
Dua, Ajay 417, 559-60n
Duffy, Benedict 177

E

East India Company 18
ECAFE (Economic Commission for
Asia and the Far East) 55
economist expert advisers 49-50, 112,
148, 149, 162, 180, 185, 188, 220,
223, 259, 261, 273, 275-6, 312,
365, 393, 399-400, 404, 411, 418,
421, 425, 429, 457, 466, 476, 491,
528n
EEC 300, 353, 355, 371-85, 398, 400,
433, 437
Ellis, Bryan 265, 288, 295, 298, 376,
518n
Ely Hospital, Cardiff 234-9

Ennals, David: political career 257-8, 324, 348-9; appointment as Secretary of State for Social Services 324; handling of DHSS policy 325, 328, 334, 338, 340-1, 343, 436; Black enquiry into Inequalities in Health 346; relationship with BA-S 328, 331-3, 335, 341, 346, 348
Enthoven, Alain 6, 400, 462, 558n
European Economic Community – see EEC
expert adviser 4, 6, 147, 169, 177, 259, 389, 398, 451, 491, 526n

F

Fabian Society 47, 55, 64, 70, 76-7, 79, 83, 93, 94, 95, 101, 103, 134, 210, 222, 224, 335, 349, 434-5
Faculty of Community Medicine 359
Falk, I.S. 364
Falkingham, Jane 467-8, 481
family allowances (see also child benefit) 63, 108, 145, 196, 201-2, 207, 210, 256, 258-9, 264, 272, 319, 325
Family Expenditure Survey 196-7, 200, 298
Family Income Supplement 264, 272, 296
family planning – see birth control
Faringdon, Gavin 77
Farris, Dianne 125, 127
Fazilamed, Sahib 464, 465
Feldstein, Martin 148, 312
Fendall, Rex (Neville) 369, 555n
Field, Frank 70, 255-7, 264, 294, 326-7, 354, 542n
Financial Master Plan 402-3, 406, 408-9, 464
Finer committee on one parent families 255, 297, 547n
Fisher committee on the abuse of social security benefits 267, 543n
Fisher, Alan 298, 308
Fitzroy, Hugh (Duke of Grafton) 30
Flowers report on London medical education 441, 443
Flynn, Pádraig 472
Ford Foundation 157, 176-7, 179, 223, 269, 391, 420

Foreign and Commonwealth Office (FCO) 324, 325, 332, 381, 429
Forget, Guy 174
Fox, Daniel 138, 548n
Fraser, Derek 63
free school meals 208, 296
Freeth, Denzil 47, 106, 134, 280, 479
Frenk, Julio 405, 448

G

gay clubs 136
Gaitskell, Hugh 79, 80, 95, 97, 98, 100, 102, 103, 104, 111, 112, 191, 517n
general election 3; (1945) 26, 27; (1950) 44, 62; (1959) 112, 113, 191; (1964) 191; (1970) 229, 258, 289; (1974) 288-9; (1979) 352, 433
Geneva 42, 70, 135, 149-50, 157
Glaser, Bill 154
Glass, David 68, 177
Glennerster, Ann 457
Glennerster, Howard 67, 189, 191, 227, 446, 477-8, 563n
Godber, George 184, 225, 229, 237, 239, 240, 241, 243, 246, 247, 342, 343, 445, 527n
Goodman, Arnold 298, 310
Gray, Muir 295, 335, 552n
Greece 45, 405, 424, 471-2
Greenfield, Edward 41, 42, 44, 46, 509n
Greve, John 375
Griffin, Charles 462
Griffiths, Adrian 403, 411
Guillebaud report on the cost of the NHS 84-6, 87, 89
Guillebaud, Claude 40, 85, 87

H

Habakkuk, John 443
Haileybury College 15, 17-24, 27, 39, 84, 146, 488, 507n
Haileybury Guild Boys Club, Stepney 19, 26-7
Halsey, A. H. 65, 75, 208
Hamilton, Popsie 17
Hamilton, Susan 17, 30, 42
Hamilton-King, Ann and Roger 464
Harris, José 64, 226, 512n
Hart, Judith 226, 271, 532n

Hart, Julian Tudor 312, 438, 466-7, 521n
Hartley-Brewer, Mike 325, 349, 552n
Harvey, Audrey 116, 201, 235
Hawton, John 120, 121, 343
Hayek, von Friedrich 65
Hayter, Dianne 434, 435
Healey, Denis 107, 113, 284, 299, 304-5
Health Advisory Service (formerly Hospital Advisory Service) 263, 315, 316
health economics 148-9, 185, 273-5, 305, 315, 332, 358-60, 361, 363, 395, 398-411, 420-22, 441, 446, 448, 475, 490; training courses in 305, 404, 405, 408, 409, 448
Health Economists' Study Group (University of York) 312, 491
Health for All by the Year 2000 (HFA2000) 390, 392, 398-400, 406-7: initial proposal 393-4; WHO-EURO Regional Health Development Advisory Council 395-8; British government response to 413-14, 445; economic strategy 398-11, 407-11, 424; health promotion linked to HFA2000 411-12; targets and assessments of 412-17, 420, 459-60
health inequalities 306-07, 310-14, 334, 344-8, 413, 532n, 549n
Health Information Foundation (HIF) 125-7, 138
health insurance (see also private health insurance) 63, 122, 149, 305-7, 338, 400, 405, 406, 408, 411, 421-3, 425-9, 439, 451-5, 461-4, 468, 473-4, 475, 479
Health Maintenance Organisations (HMOs) 423, 424, 452, 460, 526n
health manpower 273, 404, 416
Health Planning and Financing – Joint LSHTM/LSE MSc 7, 447-8, 458, 563n
health promotion 318, 411-12
health statistics 185, 275, 401, 403
Healthy Cities 412
Heclo, Hugh 83, 97
Hellberg, Håkan 403, 408
Hennessy, Peter 27, 46, 62, 119, 259

Herbison, Peggy 97, 131, 192, 193, 201, 203, 204-05
Hobsbawm, Eric 26, 40, 91
Holland, Walter 133-4, 199, 209, 306, 312, 335, 440, 442, 458, 471, 478, 553n
Holly, Norman 126, 522n
Holman, Sue 92
Holmes, Gillian 429, 467
Honigsbaum, Frank 124, 125, 126, 138
Hopkin, W.A.B. 84, 89
Hordle House Preparatory School 17
hospital planning 140-1, 185, 229
Houghton, Douglas 82, 191, 192-3, 194, 201, 220, 229
Houlbrook, Matt 105
House Beautiful x, 92
housing policy 88, 192, 205-06, 207, 294, 319, 339, 351-3, 375, 438, 469-70, 492
Howe, Elspeth 217, 447
Howe, Geoffrey 47, 212, 214, 217, 236, 237, 302, 456
Hsiao, William 453
Hunt, John 286
Hunter committee on NHS management 267-9
Hurd, Douglas 47, 48, 51

I

Illsley, Raymond 398
Imperial Service College, Windsor 20
inequalities (see also health inequalities) 4, 6, 49, 67, 69, 78, 94, 208, 271, 320
Income Guarantee 189, 192-3, 194, 201, 204-05
INDEVELOP 475
India 11, 14, 15, 51-3, 54, 152, 157, 176, 274, 276, 277, 362, 405, 406, 417, 485, 510n, 529n
Indonesia 405, 408, 409, 448, 452-4, 461, 463-4, 473, 474
Institute of Community Studies 69, 72, 513n
Institute of Hospital Almoners 89
International Journal of Health Services 274

International Labour Organisation (ILO) 114, 149, 150, 151, 157, 168, 180-81, 185, 273, 277, 358, 359, 366, 367, 379, 417, 452, 454, 455, 463, 464, 465-6, 489

international organisations 276, 358, 393, 401, 418, 420, 424, 440, 452, 457, 491

International Planned Parenthood Federation 174, 276-9, 529n

International Social Security Association (ISSA) 152, 185, 397, 405

Invalid Care Allowance 318

Israel 29, 151, 152, 154, 182, 405

Ives, A.G.L. 121

Ivory Coast 184

J

Jacques, Peter 295, 298-300, 308-09, 334

Jay, Douglas 41, 97, 116

Jay, Peggy 317

Jaycox, Edward 428

Jeger, Lena 112, 193, 205, 206

Jenkin, Patrick 47, 347-8

Jenkins, Roy 79, 95, 244, 562n

Jones, Jack 113, 270-1, 272, 376, 544n

Jones, Frederick Elwyn 270

Joseph Rowntree Memorial Trust (JRMT) 198, 224, 243, 251, 254-5

Joseph Rowntree Social Service Trust – funding for government research assistants 284, 521n

Joseph, Keith 100, 238, 246, 255, 262, 263, 264, 267, 268, 272, 292, 315, 316, 317, 318, 319, 320, 399, 558n

Just Men 214-6, 224, 262, 287, 432-3, 489, 536n

Justice Committee on Compensation for the Victims of Crime and Violence 210-11

K

Kaldor, Nicholas 84, 87, 188, 202, 220-1, 271-2, 285

Kanavos, Panos 472

Kaprio, Leo 185, 395

Kaser, Michael 154-6, 265, 511n

Kaufman, Gerald 79

Kaunda, Kenneth 79

Kennedy, Edward 332, 364

Kensington High School for Girls 16

Kenya 157, 184, 408, 424-9, 453, 454

Kenyatta, Jomo 157

Keppel Club 153, 527n

Keynes, John Maynard 40, 49, 65, 116, 187, 188, 492, 528n

Khemsuk, Cheep 465

Khemsuk, Wichian 465

Kiev, Ukraine 155-6

Kindersley Pay Review Body for Doctors and Dentists 123, 247

King's Fund 121, 124-5, 129, 130, 347, 443-6, 476

Kissinger, Henry 107

Klein, Rudolf 323, 365

Kuwait 184

Kyrgyzstan 466-8, 490

L

Labour Party 3, 11, 26-7, 44, 49, 62, 63, 64-5, 69, 72, 75, 76-80, 83, 93, 96, 100, 101, 113, 126, 145, 190-94, 196, 205, 206, 207, 221, 227, 230, 240, 256, 258-9, 285, 288-9, 302-03, 306-7, 312, 314, 317, 318-19, 325, 330-1, 334-5, 337, 341, 350, 351, 352-6, 433-9, 487, 517n; Clarion groups 44; *Signposts for the Sixties* manifesto 145; working party on the NHS 131, 142; Research Department 222; Home Policy sub-committee working party on pharmaceutical industry 300-02; legal aid Working Group 270; Legal Action Group 270; relations with trade union movement 270, 356; *In Place of Strife* White Paper 270; National Executive Committee (NEC) policy committees 270, 293-300; 332, 350; Social Policy sub-committee 256, 271-1, 332, 333, 334; Study Group on Security and Old Age 96-7, 99, 110-12, 115-17, 191-4, 197; Labour League of Youth 509n; Society of Labour Lawyers 547n; creation of the Policy Unit 285

Lambeth Group Hospital Management Committee 107, 120, 128

Land, Hilary 198, 199, 206, 208, 209, 252, 531n
Laski, Harold 26, 64, 65, 75, 157
Le Grand, Julian 2, 478, 481, 485, 492
Lees, Dennis 183, 185
Leigh, Vivien 92
Leonard, Dick 79
Lewis, Arthur 276
Lewis, Jane 67
Lipsey, David 285, 355, 435
Lister, Ruth 264, 294, 295, 296, 297, 345, 547n
Lockyer, Roger 105, 106, 134, 329
Logan, W.P.D. 185, 527n
London – 1960s fashion scene 5, 215-6, 287, 432
London – health services 442-6; Acheson review of primary health care 442, 444
London County Council Family Units 116
London Health Planning Consortium 442-3
London School of Economics and Political Science (LSE) 1, 26, 64-6, 68, 145, 157-8, 163, 177, 192, 196, 203, 207, 210, 212, 248, 265, 280, 284, 327, 332, 445, 446-7, 456-7, 458, 484, 486, 492, 565n: courses, Department of Social Administration 4, 66-7, 68-9, 73-4, 115, 125, 133, 195, 266-7, 281, 449; Diploma in Social Administration 74, 266; Diploma in Social Work Studies 266; student sit-ins and boycotts 248-51; Degree in Social Administration 266; Diploma in Housing 470-1
LSE Health 458-9, 471, 472, 565n
London School of Hygiene and Tropical Medicine (LSHTM) 133, 153, 226, 241, 273, 327, 346, 405, 408, 420, 429, 447-8, 457, 475, 535, 559n; MSc in Health Policy, Planning and Financing 7, 447-8; MSc in Social Medicine 266-7
long-stay hospitals for the mentally ill 234-9, 259, 317, 539n
Lowe, Rodney 63
Lynes, Sally 368-9

Lynes, Tony 110-11, 112, 125, 161, 162, 163-73, 177, 189, 191, 192, 201, 203-4, 205, 207, 210, 227, 228, 255, 256, 264, 265, 267, 271, 272, 276, 285, 290, 291-2, 294, 295, 297, 318, 326, 328, 333, 345, 366, 367-9, 375 , 530n, 531n, 534n 543n, 544n, 547n

M

MacDonald, Alistair 52-3, 54
MacDonald, Ramsay 64
Mott MacDonald Ltd 475
Mach, Edward 402-3, 408, 411
MacKenzie, Norman 107, 123
Macmillan, Donald 48-9
Macmillan, Harold 68, 109, 110, 113, 160
Mahler, Halfdan 363, 364, 392-3, 394, 399, 403, 407-09, 410, 411, 414-6, 417
Makover, Henry 154
Manley, Roy 52, 54
Manley, Michael 157
Mann, Bruce Douglas 434
Mann, Kalman 151, 153
Mannheim, Karl 65
Mansfield, Peter 42, 134
Marquand, David 256
Marquand, Hilary 97, 115, 116
Marquand, Judith 327
Marsden, Dennis 199, 209, 254
Marshall, Alfred 40
Marshall, T.H. 66, 68
Maude, John 87, 202
Maudsley Hospital and Institute of Psychiatry 229, 233, 237
Mauritius 157-180, 276, 280, 365-71, 474-5, 481
Maxwell, Robert 365, 443-4, 445
Maynard, Alan 365, 382, 401, 439-40, 476
Mboya, Tom 79
McKenzie-Pollock J.S. 184-5
Macleod, Iain 80-1, 88, 93, 111, 258, 264
McNamara, Robert 276, 394
McSwiney, Brian 133, 224, 442
Meacher, Michael 264, 272, 294, 297, 414, 438, 543n, 562n
Meade, James 49, 168, 169, 170, 188, 528n

Medical officers of health 243, 267–8
Medical Practitioners Union (MPU) 121, 131
mental illness and handicap 238, 314–18, 539n
Merriam, Ida 99, 157, 186, 273, 359, 364
Merrison, Alec 304, 334, 436–7
Mikardo, Ian 77, 79, 294
Milbank Memorial Fund 157, 175, 459
Mills, Anne 405, 408, 429, 447–8, 559n, 563n
Mills, Michael 403, 409, 411
Ministry of Health – Organisation and Methods Unit 148
Ministry of Social Security – The Circumstances of Large Families poverty survey 208
Monk, Mary 154
Moore, O'Connor 177, 179
Moore, Richard 133, 137, 157
Mootoosamy, Sandrasegaram 368
Morris, Alf 290, 291, 294, 299, 330
Morris, Jerry 68, 124, 177, 241–2, 243, 268, 311, 346–7, 438, 527n
Moser, Claus 265, 543
Mossialos, Elias 458–9, 471–2, 478, 480
Moyle, Roland 336, 382, 552n
Muff, George (Lord Calverley) 20–1
Myrdal, Gunnar 84, 275–6

N

Nabarro, David 429, 475
Nairne, Patrick 17, 292, 329, 332, 377
Nakajima, Hiroshi 417–18
National Accounts 182–3, 185, 275, 528n
National Assistance 113–14, 115, 189, 190, 192, 195, 197, 203, 204–05, 530n, 533n, 534n
National Assistance Board (NAB) 81, 88, 114, 116
National Center for Health Services Research 400–1, 558n
National Communities Resource Centre (Trafford Hall) 469–71
national health accounting 401, 439
national health services 154, 172, 369, 424, 458, 471

National Health Service, British (NHS) (*see also* Guillebaud Report on Cost of the NHS, London health services) anniversaries 131–2, 236, 340–4; Advisory Committee on the long term development of 229–30; Best Buy projects 343; budgets (including RAWP) 230, 304–05, 310–14, 333–4, 356; charges 85, 86, 210, 230, 241, 304; Community Health Councils 263, 316, 438; complaints procedures 235, 315–7, 334, 336, 438; costs 84–8, 122, 124, 301–2, 439; creation of 63, 521n; *Democracy in the NHS* 303; Development of 229–30; Health Services Board 325; history of 125–6, 138–40, 172; Hospital (Health) Advisory Service 237–8, 263, 315–6; hospital ombudsman 235, 237, 263, 315–6, 358; hospital closures 340, 424, 440; Joint Consultants' Committee 239, 336; management 239, 267–9; Main Costing Scheme 148; morale of staff 121–2, 246–7, 304, 308, 438; *NHS Unlimited* 440–1; pay beds policy, 305–10, 325, 440; pay disputes 247, 304, 309–10, 342; pharmaceuticals 230–3, 300–2; *Planning for Health and Personal Social Services in England* 305, 333–4; private medicine in 123, 292–3, 307–10, 325, 440, 441, 548n; reform of 141–2, 234, 438, 439, 452, 459–60, 471, 477–8, 558n; regional management of 127–33, 225; re-organisation 239–46, 263, 292, 303–04, 327, 334–40, 540n; Royal Commission on 304, 334–40, 436–7; threats to 440–1
National Institute of Economic and Social Research (NIESR) 84, 88, 89
National Insurance 96, 98, 102, 110–13, 114, 117, 193, 195, 201, 230, 296, 319, 334, 345, 425, 463, 477
National Superannuation 94, 96, 98, 99–102, 111, 113, 116, 172, 190–4, 227–8, 271, 320
Navarro, Vicente 274, 544n

Negative Income Tax 193, 201, 265, 272, 297, 298
Nevitt, Della 205, 266
Newell, Ken 390, 392, 399, 445
Nicolaou, Demi 468, 480
Nigeria 453, 455, 471
Non-Contributory Invalidity Pension 318
Nuffield Foundation 72, 89-90
Nuffield Trust 142, 148, 152, 525n
Nyere, Julius 79, 211

O

O'Malley, Brian 272, 290, 294, 298-9, 320, 321, 325, 372
Oakley, Ann (Titmuss) 280, 311, 513n
OECD (Organisation for Economic Co-operation and Development) 40, 379, 400, 401, 457, 471, 490, 492
Office of Health Economics 363, 441
Ogino rhythm method (birth control) 177, 178
Olivier, Lawrence 92
OPEC oil crisis – impact on government budgets 304, 312, 321
Orwell, George 63, 431
Ounneharerk, Anusora (Toi) 465
Outer Circle Policy Unit 354
Overseas Development Administration (ODA) 429, 452, 453, 454, 461, 462, 468, 475, 555n
Owen, David 256, 290, 292, 293, 295, 300, 302, 303, 307, 308-09, 313, 314, 316, 317, 318, 321, 325, 330, 442
Oxford University Extension Lectures 88
Oxfordshire and Buckinghamshire Light Infantry 30, 31, 33

P

PAHO 184-5, 186, 274, 409
Pakistan 51, 53-4, 184, 276, 408, 416, 476, 529n
Parry, John 39
Parry, Terry 299
Partridge, Michael 320, 345
Pater, John 343
Peacock, Alan 86, 99, 312
peerages 64, 67, 253, 541n

Pensions (*see also* national superannuation) 81, 89, 93-102, 110-13, 114, 116-17, 143, 180, 194, 220-21, 226, 228-9, 270-3, 296, 299-300, 303, 318-21, 333, 366-9, 375, 376, 381, 492, 517n, 518n, 538n
Peterson, J.S. 151
pharmaceuticals 300-2, 332, 343, 419, 472; cost to the NHS 230-1; definition of 183; Voluntary Price Regulation Scheme 230, 301; Sainsbury committee 231-3; Cohen committee on prescribing statistics 231, 538n
Philp, Fred 201, 202, 255
Piachaud, David 67, 258, 262, 263-4, 265, 267, 271, 272, 285, 295, 298, 327, 345, 356, 437, 478, 491
Pigou, Arthur 67
Pilkington, Harry 122, 246-7
Pimlott, Ben 103, 435
Pinker, Bob 115, 125, 126, 138, 216, 485, 519n, 522n, 524n
Political and Economic Planning (PEP) 72, 81, 94, 139
Political Quarterly 281, 354, 433
Popper, Karl 65
population control – *see* family planning
Poullier, Jean-Pierre 401, 457
poverty (*see also* Child Poverty Action Group) 1, 2, 4, 7, 19, 26, 49, 69, 93, 94, 98, 113-14, 116, 117, 143, 159, 165, 172, 175, 180, 187, 190, 192, 193, 196, 201, 203, 203, 204, 205, 206, 226, 256, 257, 258, 264, 275-7, 297, 319, 326, 344, 354, 358, 370-1, 375, 393, 398-9, 413, 425, 426, 427, 468, 485-6, 487, 492, 493, 532n, 533n, 534n, 537n, 557n; definitions of 72, 78, 101, 114-5, 196-8, 257; JRMT survey 198-200, 207-10, 251-5, 344-5
Powell, Enoch 80, 85, 93, 141, 147, 148, 229, 231, 239
Power, Anne 469-70
Preker, Alex 457, 486
Prideaux, John 133, 224

primary health care 444; selective
primary health care 394, 413, 415;
comprehensive primary health
care 417
Prime, Audrey 295, 299, 302, 308, 334
Prims, André 379, 400
Priority Estates Project 469
private health insurance 305-6, 426,
479
Public Schools Committee 145

R

Ramgoolam, Seewoosagur 158, 160,
163, 164, 173, 174, 177, 178, 180,
366, 368, 369, 370
Ramgoolam, Navinchandra 481
Rathbone, Eleanor 68
Rawal, Pankaj 461, 462-3, 480
RAWP (NHS Resource Allocation
Working Party) 310-14, 334, 339,
356, 442, 549n
Rayner, Derek 309
Reddaway, Brian 40, 48-9, 56, 87
Reddin, Mike 110, 207, 208, 264, 279
retirement age 298, 320, 376
Revans, John 225, 243, 537n
Rice, Dorothy 273, 361, 476
Ringadoo, Nades (Veerasamy) 366,
367, 368, 369, 158, 163, 167, 168,
173, 174, 180
Robb, Barbara 235, 315, 340
Robbins, Lionel 65
Roberts, Jenny 273, 447, 552n
Roberts, John 474-5
Robertson, Denis 40, 87
Robertson, Sandy 133, 137, 152, 154,
155, 157, 175
Robinson, Austin 50, 55, 84, 87, 510n
Robinson, Joan 40, 48-9, 51, 56, 65,
188, 510n
Robinson, Kenneth 206, 222, 229-31,
233, 234, 235-6, 240, 241, 242,
539-40n
Rockefeller Foundation 149, 174,
175, 212, 366, 394, 447, 545n,
556n
Rodgers, Bill 78, 79-80, 93, 103,
518n, 524n, 562n
Roemer, Milton 149, 151, 154, 155-6,
526n, 558n
Rogers, Philip 292, 307, 372
Rogers, Richard 470

Rohrlich, George 181, 359
Romero, Hernan 150-1
Ron, Aviva 464, 465
Roosevelt, Eleanor 54
Rothschild, Nathan 13
Rowntree, Joseph 65, 66
Rowntree, Joseph Rowntree
Memorial Trust 198, 209, 210, 251,
254
Rowntree, Joseph Rowntree Social
Service Trust 284, 521n
Rowntree, Joseph Rowntree Reform
Trust 354
Rowntree, Philip 115
Rowntree, Seebohm 72
Royal Commission on Doctors' and
Dentists' Remuneration (1960)
122-3, 522n
Royal Commission on the
Distribution of Income and
Wealth 375
Royal Commission on Local
Government (1969) 243, 540n,
552n
Royal Commission on Medical
Education (1968) 243, 268-9
Royal Commission on Mental Illness
(1957) 315, 539n
Royal Commission on the NHS
(1979) 304, 334-40, 436-9
Royal Commission on the Poor Laws
(1909) 63, 113
Ruderman, Peter 185, 363
Russell, Kit 69, 74, 281

S

Sanderson, W.A. 89-90
Sandier, Simone 400
Sarbutt, John x, 3, 119, 134-5, 215,
262, 287-8, 349, 358, 456, 464-5,
469, 470, 478, 479, 480, 481, 484,
485, 488, 565n
Schuller, Charles 106, 178, 215-6, 262,
432-3, 469, 480, 489, 536n
Seear, Nancy 145, 195, 353, 532n
Seebohm, Frederick 243
Seebohm committee on the future of
personal social services 242-3, 246,
539-40n
Seldon, Anthony 83, 228
Senegal 184
Serota, Bea 241, 242, 243

SERPS (State Earnings-Related Pension) – *see* pensions

Sexual Offences Act (1967) 105

Shaw, George Bernard 64, 76, 77

Sheps, Arthur 137, 225, 228, 287, 288, 469

Shore, Liz (Elizabeth) 142, 195, 245, 280, 324-5, 342, 347, 349

Shore, Peter 142, 145, 195, 222, 280, 324-5, 348-54, 433, 481, 488

Shore, Piers 142, 349

Silver, George 273, 364

Simey, Tom 202, 208-09, 535n

Sinfield, Adrian 145, 195, 205, 252, 354

Skellern, Eileen 237-8

Smith, Albert (grandfather 1841–1914) 13-14

Smith family 12-15

Smith, Ann Fortune 30

Smith, Cyril 346

Smith, John (1923–2007) 13

Smith's Bank 12-3, 480, 565n

smoking policies 143, 296, 318, 385, 446

Social Administration, LSE department of – *see* LSE; discipline of 68-9, 140, 145, 230, 266, 487, 490

Social Democratic Party (SDP) 434, 435

social insurance 63, 114, 151, 160, 161, 165, 171, 192, 227, 346, 364, 367, 376, 452-3, 465, 473-4, 491, 526n

social justice 4, 5, 64, 76, 187, 210, 319, 353, 381, 486, 491

Social Science Research Council 191, 263

social welfare 67, 75, 80, 93-4, 96, 110, 162, 167, 180, 188, 189, 191, 194, 205, 211, 222, 226, 235, 273, 281, 295, 356, 358, 359, 364, 366, 367, 370, 373, 418, 429, 435, 437, 451, 452, 457, 467, 474-5, 490, 492-3

Somers, Red (Herman) 99, 157, 518n

South West Metropolitan Regional Hospital Board 87, 107, 120, 128, 312, 537n

Southern Rhodesia 184

special adviser 4, 221-2, 252, 271, 284-5, 287, 290-2, 302-3, 306, 325, 327, 328, 332, 348, 349, 350, 352, 353, 354-5, 372, 377-9, 407-8, 435, 442, 487, 488, 555n

Spelthorne 44, 50

Sri Lanka (Ceylon) 29, 51, 54, 152, 153, 182, 390, 403, 405, 526n

St John Stevas, Norman 42, 47, 353

St Thomas' Hospital 107, 120, 125, 133, 140, 233, 306, 314, 340, 441, 443

St Thomas' Medical School, 199, 441, 537n

Stackpoole, John 264, 265, 295

Stevens, Robert 211-12, 213, 432, 535n

Stevens, Rosemary 138, 211

Stowe, Kenneth 188-9, 377, 530n

Straw, Jack 5, 290-1, 292, 294, 295, 299, 306, 308, 324-5, 330, 331, 345, 350, 352, 355

subsistence (*see also* poverty, definitions of) 82, 88, 94, 98, 101, 109, 115, 189, 197, 206, 532n

Summerskill, Edith 96, 97, 116

Supplementary Benefits Commission 204-05, 210, 253, 254, 267, 345-6, 553n

Supplementary Benefits Scheme 204-05, 259, 344

Sweden 64, 97, 152, 153, 182, 185, 192, 276, 339, 397, 399, 408, 425, 471, 473, 529n

Swedish International Development Agency (SIDA) 425-9

T

Tahar, Djafar 464

Tanganyika – *see* Tanzania

Tanzania 126, 175, 184, 211, 275, 368, 370, 394, 423, 429, 461-3, 467, 535n

Tata, Ratan 66

Tatara, Kozo 140

Taverne, Dick 79, 103, 145

Tawney, R.H. 4, 64, 68, 435

Taylor, Carl 390, 417

Terris, Milton 154

Thailand 7, 423, 453, 456, 461, 465, 470, 473, 474, 478, 565n thalidomide – panel of Financial Advisers for thalidomide victims 5, 231, 269

Thatcher, Margaret 245, 264, 289, 290, 354, 393, 413-4, 433, 440, 453, 459-60, 492, 533n

Theakston, Kevin 223

Thomas, Brinley 55, 80-1, 515n

Thomas, Hugh 42, 509n

Thompson, John Devereaux 6, 364, 476, 554n

Titmice, the 4, , 6, 73, 95, 98, 102, 111, 113, 115, 175, 188, 189, 196, 197, 205, 206, 251-3, 260, 287, 344, 486, 534n

Titmuss Memorial Fund 280, 545n

Titmuss, Ann – see Oakley, Ann

Titmuss, Kay 68, 71, 93, 111, 192, 216, 253, 279-80, 370, 456, 486

Titmuss, Richard, 3-4, 20, 68-72, 73, 74-5, 76, 80, 81, 84, 87, 89-90, 93, 95, 96-9, 100, 101, 102, 107, 110, 111, 115-17, 121-2, 123, 124, 125-6, 131, 133, 136, 145, 150, 151, 158, 161-75, 176-7, 178-81, 188-9, 192, 194-5, 196, 198, 200, 204, 209, 211, 216, 220, 227, 228, 242, 243, 251, 253-4, 258, 260, 262, 263, 265, 266, 274, 279-80, 281, 293, 311, 345, 365, 370, 447, 458, 486-7, 491, 518n, 522n, 527n, 545n

Tomazi, Laci 106, 135

Townsend, Peter 2, 72-3, 74, 76, 94-5, 96-102, 103-4, 107-8, 111, 115-17, 130, 134, 145, 188, 189-90, 192, 195, 196-209, 216, 224, 237, 251-8, 260, 263-4, 271, 279, 295, 297, 298, 315, 326, 333, 344, 346-8, 398, 437, 480, 481, 485, 486, 487, 530-1n, 532n, 533n, 541n, 547n

Townsend, Ruth 104, 111, 195, 216

Trades Union Congress (TUC) 45, 100, 192, 208, 230-1, 270-1, 293, 297-300, 302, 308-09, 319, 320, 328-9, 337, 349, 355, 356, 376, 414, 507n, 517n

Trafford Hall – see National Communities Resource Centre

Transport and General Workers Union 98, 113, 270

Tregenza, W.A. 18, 22, 24

Trentham Park 31

TUC – see Trades Union Congress

Turner, Jill 348, 413

U

United Nations 54, 149, 367, 397

USA (see also PAHO) 34, 54, 149, 154, 185, 197, 201, 205, 332, 391, 406, 420-1, 423-4, 454, 458, 462-3, 472, 475, 526n

USAID 277, 397, 408-09, 421, 425-7, 429, 453, 454

user fees (see also health service financing) 418-9, 423, 436, 429-30, 448, 466, 468

USSR (former Soviet Union) 40, 149, 154-6, 273, 362, 390, 391, 403, 467, 544n

Utting, G.E.G. 190, 192

V

Vaizey, John 40, 45, 48, 50, 70-2, 80, 92, 106, 127, 486

Value for Money 336, 359-60, 361, 474

van Langendonk, Jef 400

Varsity and Public Schools camps (VPS) 21, 22, 507n

VE (Victory in Europe) Day 25-6

Veit-Wilson, John 198-9, 201, 251, 258, 541n

Vienna, Austria 34-8

Villard, Henry 176-7

Vredeling, Henk 350, 377-9, 381-4

W

wage stop, the 143, 145, 201, 205-6, 120, 380, 534n

Wallas, Graham 64

Walsh, Robert (grandfather) 15

Walston, Catherine 83-4, 515n

Walter, Harold 164, 178, 180, 366

Warner, Norman 309, 324, 547n

Waterhouse, Ronald 79, 105

Webb, Beatrice 63, 64, 65, 66, 89, 99, 109, 113, 458, 469

Webb, Sidney 64, 65, 66, 77, 113

Webster, Charles 230, 231, 233, 268, 288, 304, 311, 325, 341, 343, 436

Wells, H.G. 64

Wendover, Buckinghamshire 13–16, 31, 32, 42, 56, 137, 214, 480, 489
Wendt, Robin 224–5
Wessex Regional Hospital Board 225, 237, 243, 537n
Wheeler, Mark 471
White, Kerr 401, 558n
White, Tom 333
Whitehead, Margaret 348
Wilkinson, Richard 346
Williams, Alan 273, 334, 491
Williams, Shirley 79, 103, 107, 207, 208, 281, 289, 303, 330, 434, 562
Wilson, Harold 1, 4, 29, 79, 97, 98, 112, 142, 190, 191, 193, 194, 202, 207, 221–2, 230, 237, 247, 253, 257, 258, 259, 284–5, 288–9, 290, 294, 302–04, 308, 310, 318, 321, 324, 325–6, 330, 334, 350, 355
Wilson, Harriet 199, 200–02
Winner, Albertine 342, 527n
Winterton, John 34–8, 46, 508n
Wolfenden Report (1957) 105
Woolf, Virginia 64
Wootton, Barbara 82, 202
Workers Educational Association 71, 88, 101
World Bank 7, 40, 180, 273, 276, 277, 358, 390, 394, 403, 408, 410, 417–19, 420–1, 422–3, 425–30, 440, 452–5, 457, 462–4, 467, 476, 490
World Health Assembly 184, 371, 390, 392, 393, 410, 412, 415, 417, 420, 429
World Health Organisation (WHO) 147, 149–54, 156, 160, 165, 180–6, 273, 274–5, 277, 331–2, 358, 363, 370–1, 390–420, 424, 452, 453, 455, 459, 464, 471, 473, 474–5, 490, 523n, 526n, 558n, 559n
Worthington, Shirley 92, 135

X

XYZ Club 103, 115

Y

Yale University 157, 181, 210, 211, 364, 476, 518n, 526n, 554n
Yellowlees, Henry 307, 310, 324, 335, 336–7, 562n

York, University of, MA in Health Economics 305
Young, Michael 69, 72, 76, 127, 513n
Younghusband, Eileen 69, 73–4, 202

Z

Zander, Michael 210, 213, 223, 269, 270, 281, 547n
Zimbabwe 408, 409, 423, 464, 565n
Zöllner, Herbert 395, 397, 399, 403, 404